CHILD
DEVELOPMENT
RESEARCH
AND
SOCIAL POLICY

Volume One

Editorial Board

CHILD DEVELOPMENT RESEARCH AND SOCIAL POLICY

Volume One

Edited by Harold W. Stevenson and Alberta E. Siegel

*Prepared under the auspices of the
Society for Research in Child Development*

The University of Chicago Press
Chicago and London

The University of Chicago Press, Chicago 60637
The University of Chicago Press, Ltd., London
© 1984 by The University of Chicago
All rights reserved. Published 1984
Printed in the United States of America
Library of Congress Catalog Card Number: 84-50197
ISBN 0-226-77396-5
ISBN 0-226-77397-3 (pbk.)

With respect and affection,
the editors dedicate this volume
to our professor at Stanford University,
who was a founding member of SRCD and
a pioneer in child development research and social policy,
Lois Meek Stolz

Contents

Introduction

THE SOCIETY for Research in Child Development has just passed its half century. Founded in 1933, the Society is composed of scholars from several disciplines who share an interest in research about children. Though in the past the SRCD has drawn most of its members from the United States and Canada, it is now increasingly international in its scope.

At the time the SRCD was founded, there was a need for vehicles of scholarly communication among individuals in its field. These individuals were scattered at universities around the continent, and articles about child development appeared in a broad array of professional journals. Even though the number of active investigators was not large, the lack of opportunity for communication made it difficult to keep up with the field.

The Society quickly met these needs, not only by holding biennial meetings at which the results of research were reported and discussed, but also by sponsoring scholarly publications. The SRCD's journal *Child Development* is the world leader in its field. Also preeminent are the Society's *Monographs*, a repository for major research endeavors. For the past half century, the *Abstracts and Bibliography* have provided a convenient and well-organized overview of research in this interdisciplinary field. All these have been published continuously over the past half century, and all are vigorous today. Members of the society have been served also by the SRCD *Newsletter*, which not only provides an archival record of SRCD business affairs but also is a vehicle for exchange of views and information about current issues, meetings, and publications.

Scholars can communicate with each other through these publications. What about communication to other audiences?

In the early decades of this century, parents were viewed as an important audience for the rapidly expanding body of information about the development of children. Research workers used diverse outlets to inform parents of their findings. Articles appeared in scholarly journals and also in publications that parents would be likely to read. *Parents* magazine is a prime example; it had official ties to the institutes of child development founded by the Laura Spelman Rockefeller Memorial in the 1920s, and it had a large readership. Hall, Gesell, and Watson were among the researchers who spoke and wrote directly for parents in the early decades of our century (Borstelmann, 1983; Schlossman, 1976). Over the years, magazine and newspaper columns have been written by specialists in child development research, and occasional books for parents have been written by research scholars.

As research knowledge burgeoned during the past several decades, the gap between parents and research workers seemed to grow wider. Generalists among us seem rarer. Even a lifetime program of research may strike an audience of parents as being highly specialized and of very limited scope. Many researchers do not have the gift of communicating their findings to lay audiences. As a consequence, the vital task of communicating with parents about research increasingly has been assumed by practitioners, especially pediatricians and teachers but also social workers and psychiatrists. Quite appropriately, parents typically turn to members of the professions rather than to scientists for advice about their children (Stolz, 1967).

In response to this situation, special efforts have been made by the SRCD to bring research findings about children to the attention of professional practitioners whose daily work is with children. Communication of research findings to parents and others in the lay public came to be seen as a three-step process. The first step is for the research worker to report to colleagues in research, through an archival journal and at scholarly meetings. The second step is for the distillate of the contents of scholarly journals to be communicated by research workers to practitioners. The third is for the practitioner to communicate with the public, including especially parents, combining research findings with clinical experience and professional judgment.

The *Reviews of Child Development Research*, launched by the SRCD in 1964, are a notable example of how the second step is taken. That series now consists of six volumes; a seventh is in preparation. Hoffman and Hoffman (1964), the editors of the first volume, suggested that the major purpose of their effort was "to disseminate the advances in scientific knowledge about children among practitioners in such areas as pediatrics, social work, clinical psychology, nursery and elementary education, and child psychiatry."

Another vehicle for this second step is the classroom. Members of the SRCD often hold academic appointments in schools of education, home economics, medicine, nursing, and social work. Classroom teaching about research findings in child development is often directed to students in the professional schools—future doctors, teachers, and social workers.

Taking that second step of synthesizing research knowledge is also the task of our textbooks. Through them, both beginning and advanced students gain an appreciation of the research that has been done concerning child development, the many different questions there are to ask, and the many different approaches that have been tried. The student learns not only what is known but also what remains to be learned.

This three-step system of communication has worked well. The number of active research workers in child development is not large (SRCD membership is under 4,000 persons), but public awareness of research in child development is widespread. Our members have been effective in communicating an awareness of child development research among practitioners, and through them the awareness has reached the clientele they serve.

Other audiences remain unreached. A new vehicle of communication now seems needed for SRCD, a vehicle which reaches beyond the readership of our archival publications and also beyond the wider readership of our *Reviews* volumes.

One relatively new audience for research findings consists of science writers. When the public reads about research findings in newspapers and magazines, it is reading the work of a science writer. When the public watches television shows about research findings, it is seeing those findings through the eyes of a science journalist.

Other audiences have emerged because of the avalanche of social change which has engulfed the world of the child since World War II. Members of the television industry are but one example of a group of consumers of the results of child development research which has emerged in recent decades.

Social change in the United States and Canada has forced all of us to recognize facts that were evident also to the founders of the SRCD in the desperate days of the early 1930s. The growth and development of a child depend on forces outside the family, outside the school, and beyond the confines of the hospital and clinic.

Whether or not a child will have any chance to benefit from the knowledge possessed by a pediatrician depends on the workings of the health care system. Access to that system is influenced by decisions of legislatures, courts, government officials, hospital administrators, and insurance companies. While recognizing the continuing need for health practitioners to be educated about research, we also need to recognize that access to the services of these practitioners is facilitated or impeded by legislators, judges, elected officials, and clinic managers. The well-being of the nation's mentally ill children depends on decisions in the courthouse as well as in the hospital. Nor is it sufficient to inform early childhood educators about the findings of research in child development. That information is required as well by those who legislate programs of early childhood education, those who make court judgments about the availability of such programs, and those who reach financial decisions about their support.

The Committee on Child Development and Social Policy of the SRCD is an effort to confront these realities. Elsewhere we have sketched the origins of this Committee and surveyed the range of its accomplishments since it was established in 1977 on the recommendation of a four-person Study Group on which we served along with T. Berry Brazelton and Harriet L. Rheingold (Siegel & Stevenson, 1984). The Committee was active in arranging for SRCD's sponsorship of this volume; two of the Committee's chairmen are the editors, and a third chairman (Luis Laosa) is not only a member of this volume's Editorial Board but also the author of a key chapter.

We see the need for an authoritative publication by respected specialists which will be accessible to a wide audience. We envision that the readers of this volume will include attorneys, judges, faculty members in law schools, journalists, and faculty members in schools of public administration, as well as government servants and public administrators. We hope the volume will gain a wide readership among school people, including school board members as well as school administrators and teachers. We want to reach the clinical practitioners who are the intended readers also of the *Reviews*: the pediatricians, psychiatrists, nursery school teachers, clinical psychologists, and social workers. And we welcome our colleagues in research and teaching to the audience for this volume. But we have asked our authors to speak to a broader audience than those colleagues and to omit discussion of aspects of their topics which might hold most interest for them alone. We have asked our authors to use technical terms sparingly, to avoid detailed critiques of research methods, and to abjure extensive consideration of the links between research and theory. We have asked them to supply only selected references, providing a list of sources which is authoritative rather than comprehensive.

Objectivity and freedom from bias are the principal assets that scientists bring to the public policy arena, along with their extensive specialized knowledge and experience. We have asked the scholarly reviewers of each chapter to assure us that the chapter is free of bias or partisanship. In our role as scientists, our task is not to advocate for the needs of children, but to provide information and evaluations that will be helpful to advocates.

This is a first volume. We expect there will be more. Unless our knowledge about children can begin to exert a stronger influence on the development of policies that influence the lives of children, we are vulnerable to the charge that we are not meeting our full social responsibility. Society provides funds for reseach in child development with the expectation that the lives of children and their families will be improved through that research. This can occur through application of research findings to everyday problems and to the policies that influence and guide these applications.

Planning this volume involved many persons and numerous steps. We relied heavily on our Editorial Board for assistance in selecting the topics for the chapters. We relied on the authorities who wrote the chapters and their colleagues who reviewed them for us. We rejected the idea of adopting a single theme for the volume in favor of a plan that would highlight areas of research related to important contemporary social problems. We have tried to avoid areas that have already received extensive attention or for which there is little debate about the policies that should be adopted. For some of our topics there is an extensive research literature; for others the literature is smaller. In all cases, however, we believe the conceptualization of the problems and issues of interest to policymakers is clear and sufficiently well developed to merit their attention. We hope this volume will be a further step toward insuring that policy formation relies on data and analysis rather than solely on argument and belief.

HAROLD W. STEVENSON
University of Michigan

ALBERTA E. SIEGEL
Stanford University

REFERENCES

Borstelmann, L. J. Children before psychology: Ideas about children from antiquity to the late 1800s. In Paul H. Mussen (Ed.), *Handbook of Child Psychology.* 4th ed. Vol. 1. New York: Wiley, 1983.

Hoffman, M. L., & Hoffman, L. W. (Eds.). *Review of Child Development Research.* Vol. 1. New York: Russell Sage, 1964.

Schlossman, S. L. Before home start: Notes toward a history of parent education in America, 1897–1929. *Harvard Educational Review,* 1976, **46,** 436–467.

Siegel, A. E., & Stevenson, H. W. SRCD's Committee on Child Development and Social Policy. In A. Smuts & J. W. Hagen (Eds.), History of research in child development: In celebration of the fiftieth anniversary of SRCD. *Monographs of the Society for Research in Child Development,* in preparation, 1984.

Stolz, L. M. *Influences on Parent Behavior.* Stanford, Calif.: Stanford University Press, 1967.

Social Policies toward Children of Diverse Ethnic, Racial, and Language Groups in the United States

LUIS M. LAOSA
Educational Testing Service

The 1960s saw the beginning of a new era in the history of U.S. public policies directed toward children. Although in many ways similar to earlier eras, the new one was marked by unique characteristics. Among them was its focus on the development and education of children of poor families in general and of certain ethnic, racial, and language groups in particular, especially Black, Hispanic, and American Indian children. In earlier eras children in these groups had been of marginal concern at best, while other groups of children were the focus of attention.

In this sense there is remarkable historical continuity in Anglo-American social-welfare policies toward children: in every era over the past 400 or more years, certain groups of children have been identified as being "at risk" and hence of social concern and responsibility (Bremner, 1970, 1971, 1974; Grotberg, 1976; Steiner, 1976; White, 1973). These groups consist of the physically handicapped and those with serious diseases; the emotionally disturbed; the mentally retarded; orphans; children whose mothers or fathers are permanently or temporarily absent; and illegitimate, destitute, indigent, neglected, abused, and antisocial or delinquent children. Only very recently have the children belonging to specified ethnic, racial, and language groups been added as major "risk" categories and thus become a major focus of social concern and public responsibility.

The source of the social concern about all the groups listed above is the alleged inability of the family (when it exists) to cope with the problems implied by membership in the group, or the public danger that follows from leaving these problems untreated. This social concern does not mean that American society has always accepted full responsibility for children in these risk categories. It has not always provided care, treatment, or rehabilitation, nor has it always sought to prevent their misfortunes. Since colonial times, however, it has at least shown concern for certain categories of children (Bremner, 1970, 1971, 1974; Grotberg, 1976; White, 1973). My principal purpose in this chapter is to trace major trends in the evolution of those aspects of social policies toward children that bear directly on issues of ethnic, racial, and language diversity in our society. I also seek to examine the public attitudes, the intellectual assumptions, and the sociodemographic trends that have accompanied these policy developments. In addition, I wish to pay some attention to the roles that the social and behavioral sciences have played with regard to policies bearing on these issues.

EARLY SOCIAL POLICIES TOWARD CHILDREN OF DIVERSE ETHNIC, RACIAL, AND LANGUAGE GROUPS

Whatever little public policy concern about Black, Hispanic, and American Indian children there had been prior to the mid-1950s stood in sharp contrast to the social policies directed toward the children descended from European immigrants. Indeed, social policies directed toward some ethnic, racial, and language groups served to isolate them from, rather than to include them in, the mainstream of American social, educational, economic, and political life. Let us now examine the early history of U.S. social policies toward Black, Hispanic, and American Indian children and compare these policies with those directed toward the children of European immigrants.

EARLY SOCIAL POLICIES TOWARD BLACK CHILDREN

Among the earliest public policies toward children in North America were those directed against the education of slaves. As Bremner (1970) points out in his monumental documentary history, the education of slaves raised serious questions for their owners. If slaves assembled to learn to read and write, would not rebellion be encouraged? If they gained even a small amount of learning, would not enhanced self-esteem lead them to scorn field and domestic labor? The answers given to these questions tended to curtail the opportunities for slaves to acquire education. As the number of slaves in the southern colonies increased, restrictions on the opportunities for slave children to develop fully as individuals were made more severe; these restrictions were designed to maintain White power. Although religious organizations continued to sponsor schools for slaves, the trend in the southern colonies was directed against any kind of slave education (see Bremner, 1970; Bullock, 1967; Du Bois, 1979; Ogbu, 1978).

The education of slaves was first prohibited by statute in 1740, in

South Carolina. A wave of fear swept that colony after a band of slaves had risen in rebellion, killed some Whites, and set out for refuge in Spanish Florida before they were rounded up by the militia. To prevent a recurrence the assembly adopted severe measures, including a law making it a crime to teach slaves to write. The same law, but with a lesser penalty, was enacted in Georgia in 1770. In South Carolina, following another rebellion scare in 1800, meetings of slaves "for the purpose of mental instruction in a confined or secret place" were outlawed (7 S.C. Stat. 440 [1800], reprinted in Bremner, 1970, pp. 338–339). For the time being, other slave states did not pass such laws, and even in South Carolina and Georgia they were not ordinarily enforced. Conscientious masters and mistresses, missionaries, free Blacks, and other patrons of slaves taught many to read and write, and the provision of elementary education for slaves was not uncommon. Nevertheless, as Bremner (1970) concludes after documenting the chronology of these events, the laws of 1740 and 1800 suggested a willingness to keep slave children in utter ignorance if that was deemed necessary for the security of Whites.

The education of Blacks came under closer restriction after the slave revolt led by Nat Turner in 1831. Although lasting only 48 hours, this revolt cost Black and White lives and engendered a great deal of fear because Nat Turner had been a model slave, deeply religious and obedient (Billingsley, 1968). One southern state after another, fearing assemblies of slaves and their communication with each other and with free Blacks, outlawed their elementary instruction. For example, the Virginia assembly enacted legislation that read as follows:

> All meetings of free negroes or mulattoes, at any school-house, church, meeting-house or other place for teaching them reading or writing, . . . under whatsoever pretext, shall be deemed and considered as an unlawful assembly. . . .
>
> . . . If any white person or persons assemble with free negroes or mulattoes . . . for the purpose of instructing [them] to read or write, such person or persons shall, on conviction thereof, be fined . . . and moreover may be imprisoned at the discretion of a jury. . . .
>
> . . . If any white person, for pay or compensation, shall assemble with any slaves for the purpose of teaching, and shall teach any slave to read or write, such person, or any white person or persons contracting with such teacher so to act, who shall offend as aforesaid, shall, for each offence, be fined at the discretion of a jury. [*Acts Passed at the General Assembly of the Commonwealth of Virginia*, 1831, pp. 107–108, reprinted in Bremner, 1970, pp. 513–514]

Most of these laws remained in force until the Civil War, although their harshness was somewhat lessened to the point of allowing free Blacks to receive instruction under the auspices of trusted Whites acceptable to the legislature or local authorities. Because enforcement of the law was weak, occasional slave owners acquiesced in the instruction of their slaves and even participated in it themselves. Thus, in Bremner's words (1970, p. 437), "the literate slave was not, then, unknown in the old South, but he [or she] was a rarity."

The exclusionary policies were directed not only toward slaves; free Blacks were affected as well. The situation of free Black children was substantially the same in North and South; in neither section was there equality before the law. Discriminatory legislation in civil rights, access to courts, occupations, property, and schools could be found in every southern state and nearly all those in the North (Bremner, 1970). Segregated schools were the rule. Only in remote areas and small towns with few Black inhabitants was it common for Black and White children to attend school together. In some towns and states separate schools for Black children were maintained by law. Schools were often financed in a discriminatory fashion. No efforts were made to assure that the separate schools should be equal in length of the school term, teachers' pay, or expenditures on equipment. Not only were Black children excluded and isolated; they generally also were given inferior treatment, almost uniformly receiving less attention and care than their White counterparts[1] (Bremner, 1970).

These exclusionary and discriminatory policies in education reflected general public attitudes and actions toward non-Whites. History suggests that, from the beginning, American Whites rejected the proposition that free Blacks were entitled to the same treatment as other free persons. Such attitudes help to explain how Africans slipped almost unnoticed from a status of indentured servitude to one of permanent slavery before the middle of the seventeenth century. In 1642, a Virginia magistrate, for the offense of running away, sentenced two White indentured servants to an additional year of service and a Black indentured servant to labor for the remainder of his life (Franklin, 1981). In short order, slavery would be legalized. The slave status was unique to Blacks; no other race in the United States was comparably treated.

In 1790 Congress enacted a law limiting naturalization to White

---

[1]Only in Massachusetts was legal action successful in changing this situation. In Boston, segregated primary schools for Blacks were maintained by the school committee. In the 1849 case of Sarah C. Roberts v. City of Boston, a Black father sued in behalf of his daughter for admittance into a nearby all-White school. Although the state supreme court upheld the school committee's racial discrimination among pupils, the state legislature, responsive to opinion in the rural areas outside Boston, reversed the court's decision in 1855. This was the only pre–Civil War legislative victory that Black parents and children in the North could claim in their struggle for equal rights (Bremner, 1970).

aliens. Two years later it restricted enlistment in the militia to able-bodied White men, thus declaring to the 5,000 Blacks who had fought in the War for Independence that their services were no longer required. When the federal government was moved to the new capitol at Washington in 1801, Congress passed laws for the operation of that government that excluded free Blacks from participating in its affairs. In the following year Congress passed a law, signed by President Thomas Jefferson, specifically excluding Blacks from carrying the U.S. mail (Franklin, 1976, 1981). During early colonial times, the right to vote had been available to free Black men who met the property and other qualifications; soon Blacks were disfranchised, however, as one state after another passed laws expressly confining the right to vote to White men (see Du Bois, 1979).

Very significant but exceedingly short-lived changes in public policies toward Black children occurred as a result of the emancipation of slaves and from attempts to reconstruct state governments in the South immediately following the Civil War. In 1865 Congress passed a bill creating the Bureau of Refugees, Freedmen, and Abandoned Lands to assist recently freed slaves and White war refugees. The activities of the "Freedmen's Bureau" went, however, far beyond providing temporary relief for the poor. It was, according to some scholars (e.g., Billingsley & Giovannoni, 1972, p. 42), "for its day, and for a long time to come, a model of comprehensive social welfare planning." It was also the first federal agency to exercise direct control over education (Bremner, 1970). The bureau operated under chaotic conditions (see Bennett, 1964; Du Bois, 1979), and its activities were substantially over by 1870. It accomplished, however, many worthwhile results, including the establishment of hospitals, orphan homes, schools, and colleges. Many of the present historically Black colleges like Howard, Fisk, and Atlanta Universities—which have produced a large proportion of the most distinguished Black scholars and professionals—were founded or substantially aided in their earliest days by the Freedmen's Bureau. Other major policy developments of the Reconstruction Era included the Fourteenth Amendment (1868) to the U.S. Constitution, which conferred citizenship on Blacks; the Fifteenth (1870), which guaranteed their right to vote; and the passage of a major civil rights bill (1875), which represented further evidence of the extent of federal efforts to improve the conditions of this racial group. Blacks now enjoyed and exercised specific civil rights, including the right to hold public office. Also significant among the policy developments of the Reconstruction Era was the emergence of public education throughout the South. The Reconstruction constitutions of the states provided for the establishment of free, universal public education for Whites and Blacks. Indeed, during the decade following the end of the Civil War, the education of the two races was maintained on a more or less equal basis, although controversies over racially mixed schools were never entirely resolved (Carnoy, 1974; Du Bois, 1979; Ogbu, 1978).

Thus from 1865 to 1877 Blacks experienced a brief and partial release from certain of their most onerous conditions. But this progress elicited strong and bitter opposition. Reactions against the new policies came swiftly. By 1877 control of the legislatures in the southern states had passed from the alliance among carpetbaggers (northern-born Whites), scalawags (White southerners), and Blacks to the conservative Democratic leaders (Bennett, 1964; Du Bois, 1979; Ogbu, 1978). In 1883 the U.S. Supreme Court declared the 1875 civil rights bill unconstitutional. The majority of Blacks, who lived in southern states, found themselves disempowered through denial of the ballot (Bennett, 1964; Jones, 1981; Woodward, 1966). In 1896 the Court, in the case of *Plessy* v. *Ferguson*, institutionalized the racially separate and unequal conditions that were legally imposed until the middle of the twentieth century.

Legal slavery ended formally on January 31, 1865, with the passage of the Thirteenth Amendment to the Constitution. But racial inequality had been so well established during slavery that it became the universal model in the years following Reconstruction (Du Bois, 1979; Woodward, 1966). Indeed, by the last quarter of the nineteenth century, the United States had established a policy that denied to persons of African descent the opportunity to become assimilated.

EARLY SOCIAL POLICIES TOWARD HISPANIC CHILDREN[2]

Although in many significant respects the historical circumstances of Hispanics in the United States are quite different from those of Blacks, in some respects both groups have certain experiences in common—specifically, a history of exclusion and isolation from the U.S. social, economic, and educational mainstream. Such experiences are relevant to an understanding of their position in U.S. society today.

Only recently has the general public become aware that Hispanic Americans form a sizable and permanent part of the U.S. population. Significantly, school textbooks have tended to ignore them (Grebler, Moore, & Guzman, 1970; U.S. Commission on Civil Rights, 1972). So many Americans, having a limited knowledge of their country's history, are only dimly aware that parts of the Southwest were colonized early by

---

[2]The terms *Hispanic American* and *Hispanic* are used in this chapter to refer to a broad category of persons that includes Mexican Americans (Chicanos), Cuban Americans, Puerto Ricans, and other persons of South American, Central American, or other Spanish-speaking origin in the United States. The terms *Chicano* and *Mexican American* are used interchangeably in this chapter.

people of Hispanic-Mexican origin. Those who do know about it are inclined to shrug it off as a quaint accident of history without consequence. Because Hispanic Americans have never suffered outright slavery, their problems have never weighed on the national conscience as have those of the Blacks or even the American Indians.

Like the American Indians, the Hispanic Americans "were here first," a fact that has led some writers (e.g., de la Garza, Kruszewski, & Arciniega, 1973) to refer to these two groups as "the territorial minorities." Indeed, no one who has come to know the Southwest—Texas, California, New Mexico, Arizona, Colorado—can fail to have been intrigued with the Spanish-language place names that tell so much of its history. Its geography seems stamped throughout with ethnic claims and counterclaims. Five themes in particular emerge: the American Indian and the Spanish European past, the Mexican American and the Anglo American present, and a revival of the mixed Indian and Spanish past.

Under the terms of the 1848 Treaty of Guadalupe Hidalgo, which ended the war between the United States and Mexico, Mexico ceded to the United States a vast territory, including Arizona, California, Nevada, New Mexico, Utah, and one-half of Colorado, and also approved the prior annexation of Texas. The lands that Mexico ceded to the United States represented one-half of the territory that Mexico possessed in 1821. All citizens of Mexico residing within the ceded domain were to become citizens of the United States if they failed to leave the territory within 1 year after ratification of the treaty. Only a few thousand Mexican nationals relocated; the rest became U.S. citizens by default. The great majority of these people were mestizos, persons of mixed Spanish and Indian ancestry. The remainder were Indians who had never been vanquished by the Spanish but were citizens under Mexican rule and also came under U.S. sovereignty with the ratification of the treaty. The treaty provided specific guarantees of the property and political rights of all the inhabitants of the ceded lands and attempted to safeguard their cultural autonomy; that is, they were given the right to retain their language, religion, and culture. No provisions were made, however, for the integration of these peoples as a group, as a society. "With the signing of the Treaty of Guadalupe Hidalgo," observed Rodolfo Alvarez (1973, p. 924), "the Mexican American people were created *as a people*: Mexican by birth, language and culture; United States citizens by the might of arms." After the incorporation of the Southwest into the United States, the new citizens who had been acquired by military conquest began to experience exclusion, isolation, ethnic and racial prejudice, and social and economic subordination (Alvarez, 1973; Camarillo, 1979; Estrada, García, Macías, & Maldonado, 1981; McLemore, 1973; McWilliams, 1968; Meier & Rivera, 1972).

Immigration, both legal and illegal, contributed substantially to the Mexican American population in the United States. The newly created United States–Mexico border was open to unrestricted immigration until the creation of the Border Patrol in 1924. Even then, however, large parts of the 2,000-mile border were unguarded, making it difficult to assess the accuracy of all immigration figures. Immigration was stimulated by economic and political conditions in Mexico and by the rapidly growing demand for labor during the development of the southwestern United States (Ríos-Bustamante, 1981; Estrada et al., 1981).

Many Mexican Americans were discouraged from political participation by such measures as the imposition of voting requirements based on educational and literacy testing, the use of poll taxes, the gerrymandering of voting districts to minimize minority representation, the intimidation of potential voters, and the threat of deportation. Another measure that discouraged many Mexican Americans from voting was the use of English-language voting requirements (California State Advisory Committee to the United States Commission on Civil Rights, 1971; Camarillo, 1979).

At the turn of the century, the social policies toward Chicano (Mexican American) children in the Southwest were in many respects not very different from those directed toward Black children in the North. As the Chicano population in the Southwest began its rapid increase during the first years of this century, the dominant, non-Hispanic White society was generally unconcerned about the schooling of "Mexicans." Educators seemed to share the community's apparent view of Chicanos as outsiders who were never expected to participate fully in American life. Attitudes appeared tinged with racial and ethnic prejudice; the literature emphasized the inadequacies of the child of Mexican descent. "Mexicans" were said to be capable only of manual labor; in fact, some non-Hispanic Whites appeared to be afraid that education would make Chicanos useless even for farm work (Carter, 1970). Some considered the typically low test scores of Chicano children as evidence of innate intellectual inferiority, which in turn was thought to justify school segregation. As Carter and Segura (1979, p. 16) characterize the evolution of the relationships between Chicanos and non-Hispanic Whites in the Southwest, "A *patrón* and *peón* society was fostered, supported, and perpetuated. . . . Too much education for the docile workers might destroy the delicate social equilibrium necessary to maintain these economic systems. The school reflected and perpetuated local society." (See also McLemore, 1973.)

Segregation of Chicanos in the five southwestern states has been practiced not only in the schools of the region but in other aspects of life as well. In Texas there developed a tri-ethnic school system with segregated facilities for Chicano, Black, and non-Hispanic White students. Separate "Mexican schools" were maintained on the grounds that the separation was beneficial to Chicano children. As reasons for segregation, school officials stressed the children's language handicap and need to learn English; their need to be "Americanized" before mixing with non-Hispanic Whites; and their slowness in school, which would hinder the progress of non-Hispanic White students. Other reasons for separation were the reputed irregular attendance of Chicano children, their different social habits, and their poor health. It was argued that separate schools gave Chicano children the opportunity to overcome these deficiencies, isolated from the non-Hispanic White children's competitiveness and thus protected from feelings of inferiority. Segregation further protected them from the non-Hispanic White practice of hazing and other discriminatory practices reported to be prevalent before the 1950s (Carter, 1970; Carter & Segura, 1979; Cruz, 1973; U.S. Commission on Civil Rights, 1971, 1972).

These ostensibly altruistic reasons stand, however, in apparent contradiction to several observed practices: (*a*) the placement of all Spanish-surnamed children in segregated schools, even though some were fluent in English; (*b*) the tendency of these "Mexican schools" to have vastly inferior physical facilities; (*c*) the lax enforcement of attendance laws in those schools; and (*d*) the tendency to discourage many Chicano children from pursuing advanced schooling (Carter & Segura, 1979; Cruz, 1973). Moreover, an impartial observer might have suggested that segregating Chicano children could effectively limit their opportunities to acquire the language and sociocultural characteristics of the dominant group and could increase the likelihood that they would remain an isolated and excluded, nay subordinate, ethnic group.

Policies regarding children's use of language in school and language policies in general were additional factors that contributed to the social exclusion and isolation of Hispanics in the United States. It hardly need be said that the ability to communicate is essential to attaining an education, to conducting affairs of state and commerce, and generally to exercising the rights of citizenship. When Mexico, by the aforementioned 1848 treaty, ceded the territory that is now the southwestern part of the United States, the dominant language in the territory was Spanish. As the population in this area subsequently changed, English became the language of government and education. Nevertheless, Spanish continued to be the language used by the Hispanic population. Although a great many Hispanic children did not—and to this day do not (U.S. Bureau of the Census, 1982a)—speak English as well as their non-Hispanic counterparts, many educators in the Southwest forbade the use of the child's native language in the classroom.

In essence, they have compelled children to learn a new language and at the same time to learn course content in that new language—something that any adult would find unusually challenging.

School policies prohibiting Spanish have been documented by data from a large-scale survey of school districts conducted by the U.S. Commission on Civil Rights (1972). As recently as a decade ago, the "no-Spanish" rule was enforced by various alleged forms of punishment ranging from fines (such as five cents every time the child was caught using Spanish) to violation slips used to place children in detention halls. Although no school officials admitted to administering physical punishment for speaking Spanish, allegations of its use were made to the commission at its 1968 hearing in San Antonio.

The unique historical circumstances of Chicanos, combined with the exclusionary and discriminatory policies toward them, may explain, at least in part, why as a group Chicanos have not followed the historical pattern of acculturation and assimilation characteristic of many other major ethnic groups. The historical reasons for the presence of Chicanos in the United States are, except for the American Indians, entirely different from those of other major ethnic groups. Peoples migrating from Europe are assumed to have come to North America not only for economic reasons but also—perhaps chiefly—to escape political or religious oppression and to benefit from the liberties promised by the North American democratic ideology. This assumption implies another strong motivation, namely, that immigrants desired to adopt Anglo American values, customs, and manners (Ramírez & Castañeda, 1974). In contrast, persons of Mexican descent residing in the Southwest had cultural, linguistic, and familial ties with Mexico that remained strong in spite of the Treaty of Guadalupe Hidalgo. Cultural and linguistic ties remain strong to this day by virtue of continuous immigration from Mexico, geographical proximity, and communication and transportation technology. Moreover, Mexicans have been perceived as a racially non-White group and, as such, have been systematically and rigidly prohibited from full entry into, and participation in, mainstream (i.e., White) U.S. society (Arce, 1981; Camarillo, 1979; Ramírez & Castañeda, 1974). Such exclusion and discrimination in the economic, political, social, and education sectors of U.S. life are additional barriers to fuller and more equitable participation of Chicano children and their parents in U.S. society.

EARLY SOCIAL POLICIES TOWARD AMERICAN INDIAN CHILDREN

During the eighteenth century, contact between Whites and American Indians, including their children, was primarily through trade and warfare. Education occasioned few contacts between Indian children and Whites during this period, although some missionary organizations, such as Spanish Catholic padres and the Society for the Propagation of the Gospel, continued their efforts to seek contact with Indians and to bring Indian youth into schools and convert them to Christianity (Bremner, 1970). The U.S. federal government first assisted in the education of Indian children after the War of 1812. Having brought the Indians under greater control, the government turned from a military approach to what was called a "civilization policy": the Indians would now be transformed into White Americans, or at least a manageable facsimile. The task of "civilizing" the Indians was not the government's alone, however. The government cooperated with private agencies, subsidizing missionary agencies as the primary means of educating Indian children (Bremner, 1970; Dorris, 1981).

The kind of schooling and community that would be effective for Indian children was difficult to determine. Most of the teachers tried to combine the ordinary kinds of elementary instruction with lessons in piety. This seldom produced more than a veneer of education that was stripped away as soon as the Indian child returned to the tribe. Once the failure of conventional education was recognized, those concerned began to seek alternatives. They hit upon combining a measure of conventional education with instruction in manual trades. Another possibility was the boarding school in which children were removed from the influence of parents and tribal ways in the hope that they would adopt the outlook of Whites. This movement was to be implemented in the late nineteenth century (Bremner, 1970).

All in all, Indians in the nineteenth century, even those who early converted to Christianity and sought to adopt "the White man's ways," were only occasionally allowed in public or private schools. Increasingly herded onto reservations, managed at best by well-meaning if paternalistic overseers, they were systematically denied access to education or other levers of social and economic power.

EARLY SOCIAL POLICIES TOWARD CHILDREN OF EUROPEAN IMMIGRANTS

The inferior status that children of the poor in all ethnic and racial groups experienced was somewhat alleviated as the spread of compulsory schooling opened opportunities for upward mobility. Having come early, Germans, Scandinavians, and other northern Europeans had the easiest time entering the English-dominated mainstream of eighteenth- and nineteenth-century North America and gaining increasing political, economic, and social power with the attendant benefits. They were not about to yield these hard-won prizes to successive waves of the Irish, Italians, southern and eastern Europeans, Jews, and other ethnic latecomers in the late nineteenth and early twentieth centuries (Collins, 1981). In 1908 the U.S. Senate Immigration Commission compiled data on the ethnic origin of school children in 37 major cities. Fifty-eight percent of all students had fathers born abroad—New York led with 72%; Chicago, 67%; Boston, 64%; Cleveland, 60%; and San Francisco, 58%—almost all of whom were White (Tyack, 1974).

In the scramble up the educational ladder these recent immigrants began only slightly above Blacks, Hispanics, and American Indians. However, in contrast to the pervasive efforts to keep the latter three groups outside the mainstream, the educational policy toward White immigrant children was one of aggressive and heavy-handed assimilation. Although this orientation toward White children of the foreign-born did nothing to lessen their shame or their invidious treatment, it was to lead to very different consequences in later years for their second and third generations (Collins, 1981; Tyack, 1974).

INTELLIGENCE TESTING AND EARLY SOCIAL POLICIES TOWARD ETHNIC, RACIAL, AND LANGUAGE MINORITY CHILDREN

The history of U.S. social policies toward children is closely intertwined with the history of mental testing. Children of poor families and children whose primary home language was not English were observed to score generally lower on standardized ability tests than did the children of White, middle-class, English-speaking families. Some influential psychologists and educators interpreted this difference as proof of innate racial and ethnic group differences in intelligence and as further proof of the racial and cultural superiority of persons of northern European ancestry. The work of these social and behavioral scientists contributed significantly to the formulation and perpetuation of ethnically and racially discriminatory policies.

The first intelligence test was developed by the French psychologist Alfred Binet in 1905. Appointed by the French minister of public instruction to study the problem of mental retardation among schoolchildren in Paris, Binet published with his colleague, T. Simon, the first scale for yielding an overall index of intelligence. Binet also formulated the concept of mental age, which permitted the mental development of children to be compared and, on the basis of statistical distribution, average ("normal") and atypical ("abnormal") children to be identified. Henry H. Goddard, the research director at the Vineland Training School for Feeble-minded Boys and Girls in New Jersey, brought the Binet-Simon scale to the United

States, translating it into English in 1908 (Hunt, 1961). Of the various intelligence tests developed in the United States during the early part of the century, including a number of revisions, translations, and adaptations of the 1905 and 1908 Binet-Simon scales, the one with the widest accept-ance was the Stanford version of the Binet-Simon Scale, published in 1916 by Lewis M. Terman. This version supplanted earlier translations and revisions, and with it intelligence testing became firmly established in U.S. schools and psychological clinics (Du Bois, 1970).

The Stanford-Binet Scale, in Terman's view, was particularly useful in the diagnosis of "high-grade" or "border-line" deficiency, that is, IQs in the 70–80 range. That level of intelligence, he observed,

> is very, very common among Spanish-Indian and Mexican families of the Southwest and also among negroes. Their dullness seems to be racial, or at least inherent in the family stocks from which they come. The fact that one meets this type with such extraordinary frequency among Indians, Mexicans, and negroes suggests quite forcibly that the whole question of racial differ-ences in mental traits will have to be taken up anew and by experimental methods. The writer predicts that when this is done there will be discovered enormously significant racial differences in general intelligence, differences which cannot be wiped out by any scheme of mental culture.
>
> Children of this group should be segregated in special classes and be given instruction which is concrete and practical. They cannot master abstrac-tions, but they can often be made efficient workers. . . . There is no possibil-ity at present of convincing society that they should not be allowed to repro-duce, although from a eugenic point of view they constitute a grave problem because of their unusually prolific breeding. [Terman, 1919, pp. 91–92]

In contrast to Binet, who did not contend that intelligence was fixed—rather, he believed that intellectual attainment could be modified by environmental factors—Goddard and other pioneers of mental testing in the United States believed in the utmost importance of hereditary in-fluence on intelligence. They not only preached the doctrine of fixed intelligence but also provided leadership for a eugenics movement, which advocated improving hereditary traits by selective human mating (Gould, 1981; Hunt, 1961). Binet disagreed with the American pioneers. Indeed, he protested the "brutal pessimism" of "some recent philosophers" who had given their "moral support" to the idea that "the intelligence of an individual is a fixed quantity, a quantity which one cannot augment" (Binet, 1913, cited in Kamin, 1974, p. 5).

Nevertheless, according to the pioneers of the testing movement in the United States, the intelligence test could be used to detect the geneti-cally inferior, whose reproduction was a menace to the future of the state.

The promise of the Stanford-Binet test was made explicit in Terman's opening chapter: "It is safe to predict that in the near future intelligence tests will bring tens of thousands of these high-grade defectives under the surveillance and protection of society. This will ultimately result in curtailing the reproduction of feeble-mindedness and in the elimination of an enormous amount of crime, pauperism, and industrial inefficiency. It is hardly necessary to emphasize that the high-grade cases, of the type now so frequently overlooked, are precisely the ones whose guardianship it is most important for the State to assume" (Terman, 1919, pp. 6–7).

Thus the "findings" of the new science of mental testing were used to document the intellectual inferiority of certain ethnic and racial groups and to "demonstrate" the genetic origins of this inferiority. These findings also were used to rationalize the passage of a racist immigration law and to justify such exclusionary school practices as the assignment of large proportions of Black and Hispanic children to classes for the mentally retarded and to inferior educational "tracks" or courses of study.

As we have seen, at the turn of the century the new immigration from southern and eastern Europe began to assume massive proportions. The English, Scandinavian, and German stock that had predominated earlier was now becoming outnumbered by a wave of Italian, Polish, Russian, and Jewish immigrants. The popular press and the literary magazines of the period were filled with articles "questioning the assimilability of the new and exotic breeds" (Kamin, 1974, p. 16). There arose a public clamor for some form of "quality control" over the flow of immigrants. Here was an opportunity for the new science of mental testing not only to meet a public need but also to contribute to the formulation of public policy.

In 1912 Henry Goddard was invited by the U.S. Public Health Service to the immigrant receiving station at Ellis Island, in New York harbor, "to observe conditions and offer any suggestions as to what might be done to secure a more thorough examination of immigrants for the purpose of detecting mental defectives" (Goddard, 1917, p. 243). There he administered the Binet-Simon scale and supplementary performance tests to representatives of what he called "the great mass of 'average immigrants'" (p. 244). The results were sure to produce grave concern in the minds of thoughtful citizens. The data showed that 83% of the Jews, 80% of the Hungarians, 79% of the Italians, and 87% of the Russians were "feeble-minded" (Goddard, 1917, p. 252). The "surprising results," Goddard wrote, "must be accepted or rejected. If accepted they furnish important considerations for future action both scientific and social as well as legislative" (p. 261). Goddard was able to report also that "the number of aliens deported because of feeble-mindedness . . . increased approximately 350 per cent in 1913 and 570 per cent in 1914. . . . This was due to the untiring efforts of the physicians who were inspired by the belief that mental tests could be used for the detection of feeble-minded aliens. . . . If the American public wishes feeble-minded aliens excluded, it must demand that Congress provide the necessary facilities at the port of entry" (1917, p. 271).[3]

World War I occasioned the first large-scale use of intelligence tests in the United States. A committee of the American Psychological Association formulated the U.S. Army Alpha and Beta Tests of Intelligence. The data from the army testing program provided the first massive demonstration that Blacks scored lower than Whites on IQ tests. However, of greater concern immediately after the war were the results for the draftees who had reported that they were foreign-born (Kamin, 1974). Published in 1921 by the National Academy of Sciences, the results indicated that "the range of differences between countries is a very wide one. . . . In general, the Scandinavian and English speaking countries stand high in the list, while the Slavic and Latin countries stand low" (cited in Kamin, 1974, p. 19). These scientific data, according to Kamin (1974, pp. 19, 26) "speedily became 'generally known in Congress,' with the considerable assistance of the scientists of the Eugenics Research Association. . . . The mental testers brought the facts not only to Congress but also to the thoughtful reading public. Their relevancy to immigration policy was made entirely explicit." A House of Representatives Committee on Immigration and Naturalization was told that

---

[3]In fairness, it should be pointed out, as Kamin (1982) recently has done, that Goddard did not use his scientific data to argue unqualifiedly against immigration: "Assuming for the sake of argument that the percentages and mental levels . . . are approximately correct, what is to be done about it? Shall we say that . . . we want no feeble-minded persons in the country, at least no more than we can produce ourselves? . . . Let us look at the matter broadly. . . . A very large percentage of these immigrants . . . do a great deal of work that no one else will do. . . . It is perfectly true that there is an immense amount of drudgery to be done, an immense amount of work for which we do not wish to pay enough to secure more intelligent workers. It is a very big social and economic problem" (Goddard, 1917, p. 269). Also in fairness to Goddard it should be emphasized that, as Dorfman (1982) observes, he did not conclude that the high percentage of feeblemindedness was evidence of a hereditary defect in the immigrants. Goddard (1917) wrote in his summary, "Assuming that they are morons, we have two practical questions: first, is it hereditary defect or; second, apparent defect due to deprivation? If the latter, as seems likely, little fear may be felt for the children" (p. 243). Moreover, Gould (1981) reminds us that, as Binet had done earlier, by 1928 Goddard was arguing that most "morons," if not all, could be educated and trained to lead useful lives in society: "I have no difficulty in concluding that when we get an education that is entirely right there will be no morons who cannot manage themselves and their affairs and compete in the struggle for existence. If we could hope to add to this a social order that would literally give every man a chance, I should be perfectly sure of the result" (Goddard, 1928, pp. 223–224, cited in Gould, 1981, p. 172). Terman, too, modified his position; by 1937 he was cautioning his readers about the difficulties involved in determining, on the basis of average group differences, the relative contributions of genetic and environmental factors (Gould, 1981).

> the country at large has been greatly impressed by the results of the Army
> intelligence tests. . . . With the shift in the tide of immigration . . . to
> southern and eastern Europe, there has gone a decrease in intelligence test
> scores. . . . The experts . . . believe that . . . the tests give as accurate a
> measure of intelligence as possible. . . . The questions . . . were selected
> with a view to measuring innate ability. . . . Had mental tests been in
> operation . . . over 6,000,000 aliens now living in this country . . . would
> never have been admitted. . . . Aliens should be required to attain a passing
> score of, say, the median in the Alpha test. [*Hearings before the Committee on
> Immigration and Naturalization, House of Representatives,* 1924, cited in
> Kamin, 1974, pp. 24–25]

The Johnson-Lodge Immigration Act of 1924 was enacted after the
conclusion of the congressional hearings in which the research work of the
mental testers figured prominently. Establishing national-origin quotas as
a permanent part of immigration policy, the law was designed to exclude
from this country the peoples of southern and eastern Europe—the peoples who, according to the interpretations of the intelligence test data,
were "biologically inferior" (Kamin, 1974; National Research Council,
1982a).

When the Johnson-Lodge Immigration Act of 1924 was enacted, the
intellectual inferiority of the "new immigrants" had, as Kamin observes,
"already been amply documented." To demonstrate conclusively its genetic origin, Nathaniel D. Hirsch, a National Research Council Fellow in
Psychology at Harvard University, administered intelligence tests to the
U.S.-born children of various immigrant groups. The children "were to
provide a clear test of the genetic hypothesis. They had attended American
schools, they spoke the English language, but they carried their parents'
genes" (Kamin, 1974, p. 27). The results of his research, published in the
Genetic Psychology Monographs, indicated that for almost all groups the
children of immigrants were intellectually inferior. In discussing the policy
implications of his data, Hirsch applauded the Immigration Act of 1924.
Moreover, he warned in his scientific treatise that

> that part of the law which has to do with the non-quota immigrants should be
> modified. . . . All mental testing upon children of Spanish-Mexican descent
> has shown that the average intelligence of this group is even lower than the
> average intelligence of the Portuguese and Negro children . . . in this study.
> Yet Mexicans are flowing into the country. . . .
>   Our immigration from Canada . . . we are getting . . . the less intelligent
> of working-class people. . . . The increase in the number of French Canadians
> is alarming. Whole New England villages and towns are filled with them. The
> average intelligence of the French Canadian group in our data approaches the
> level of the average Negro intelligence. [Hirsch, 1926, cited in Kamin, 1974,
> p. 28]

Following the creation and adoption of the U.S. Army Alpha Test for the psychological assessment of recruits during World War I—the first large-scale use of mental testing in the United States—schools, colleges, and other organizations during the early 1920s also found standardized testing useful and convenient. The early advocates of IQ tests in school administration urged that they be employed to segregate students by ability, to aid in vocational guidance, to detect unusually able or retarded students, and to diagnose learning problems (National Research Council, 1982a; Tyack, 1974).

A principal function of standardized tests has been to classify school children into homogeneous groups according to ability. Homogeneous ability grouping, when applied to a total school system, is called "tracking" in the United States. Students are classified according to level of achievement or native potential, usually assessed by means of standardized tests. Homogeneous ability grouping by means of standardized testing has become an integral part of the educational system in the United States as well as in other countries (Bryson & Bentley, 1980; Samuda, 1975), and it was embraced as the basic method of curricular organization. In 1926, a U.S. Bureau of Education survey discovered that 37 out of 40 cities with populations of 100,000 or more reported that they used ability grouping in some or all elementary grades and a slightly smaller percentage used it in junior and senior high schools. Indeed, the testing movement was transforming administrative practice in urban schools (Tyack, 1974). By 1929, more than 5 million tests were being administered annually (Houts, 1975). In 1932, three-fourths of 150 large cities reported using intelligence tests in assigning pupils (Tyack, 1974, p. 208). Standardized testing became so widespread in the United States that it is a rare individual, especially among children and youth, who has not taken a standardized mental ability test—a test that probably has played a significant role in determining his or her place in society (Brim, Glass, Neulinger, Firestone, & Lerner, 1969; Holtzman, 1971; Laosa, 1977b; National Research Council, 1982a).

It is a well-documented fact that children of lower-socioeconomic-status families and of Black, Hispanic, and similarly placed ethnic and racial groups tend to obtain lower average scores on many tests of intellectual ability and achievement than do children of middle-class, non-Hispanic White families (Coleman, Campbell, Hobson, McPartland, Mood, Weinfeld, & York, 1966; National Research Council, 1982a; Shuey, 1966). Since standardized test scores became the basis for assigning children to ability groups, the classes for slow learners and mentally retarded students have been found to contain grossly large proportions of Black and Hispanic children (Bryson & Bentley, 1980; Finn, 1982). Critics of standardized testing and of organizing classes by ability groups point to the effects of these practices in maintaining and supporting ethnic and racial cleavages (De Avila, 1973; Guthrie, 1976; Laosa, 1973, 1977b; Oakland & Laosa, 1977; Olmedo, 1981; Samuda, 1975). Paradoxically, although at its inception ability grouping was heralded as the means of achieving educational opportunity for the mass of citizens in a democratic society, it has come to be seen as retarding ethnic and racial integration and as relegating the poor and certain ethnic and racial groups to an inferior education.

It is in the sphere of mental measurement that behavioral scientists have taken the greatest pains to establish their scientific status; it is also in this sphere that they have had their greatest impact on social policies. Ironically, it is also in this sphere that their scientific credibility has been most persistently challenged and their impact on social policies most fiercely contested. Later in this chapter I return to this topic to examine recent developments in policies influencing the educational and psychological assessment of children of ethnic and language minorities.

EARLY SOCIAL POLICIES: SUMMARY AND CONCLUSIONS

Present-day ethnic and racial inequalities are deeply rooted in earlier periods of history. Indeed, many aspects of the present-day inequalities in the United States can be understood only in the light of the historic castelike structures that have evolved out of the earliest interrelationships between European settlers and their descendants and other ethnic and racial groups. Americans of northern European ancestry seemed persuaded not only that they were capable of building a social order and a civilization superior in every respect to anything that existed in the New World, but also that they themselves were superior to their contemporaries. In this attitude they appeared to find justification for appropriating the lands they desired and for subjugating and isolating first the aboriginal populations and subsequently others not of northern European descent (Dorris, 1981; Franklin, 1981). Although at first the waves of immigration to the United States from southern and eastern Europe were resisted, effective policies were soon established to integrate these new immigrants and their children. In contrast, certain ethnic and racial groups remained the target of exclusionary policies. By the last quarter of the nineteenth century, the United States had established policies that socially, politically, educationally, and economically isolated and excluded Blacks, Hispanics, and American Indians and that limited and often denied them the opportunity to become integrated. Thus, families and children in these groups have inherited long-standing inequalities in education, income, housing, political participation, and availability of options.

During the earlier periods in the history of such social policies, government in general only indirectly affected most aspects of children's lives; they were most affected by unofficial, less formal institutions of society. In education, government largely maintained legal and sociocultural distinctions between the treatment of the children of certain ethnic and racial groups and the children of the White middle class. Indeed, the school appears to be the institution where the influence of social policies on children was most direct. Where it was possible for Black children to go to school at all, laws were passed to keep them in segregated schools. Hispanic children in the Southwest, just as Blacks did, attended separate and generally inferior schools. Very few Indian children were given any kind of instruction. Moreover, grossly large proportions of Black, Hispanic, and American Indian children were labeled as mentally retarded and relegated to inferior educational "tracks" (Bremner, 1970; Carter & Segura, 1979; U.S. Commission on Civil Rights, 1971).

The obstacles put in the way of schooling for non-White and Hispanic children and their exclusion from the superior schooling available to non-Hispanic White children—a common theme in every period of U.S. history—seem to account, at least in part, for the occupational inequalities affecting certain non-White and Hispanic groups today (Featherman & Hauser, 1978; Laosa, 1982a). Andrew Billingsley (1968), in his classic analysis of the history, structure, aspirations, and problems of Black families in the United States, identified three characteristics of formal schooling that make it "a major key to the understanding of Negro family and community life" (p. 79); the same conclusion seems to apply to other excluded ethnic and racial groups as well, namely, Hispanics and American Indians. First, schooling is a reliable index of, and a potent means of gaining, social mobility and economic stability in our society. The prolonged, sustained absence of systematic training and schooling depresses a group's position in the social structure, just as the availability of education even "in small and scattered doses" can be a powerful source of achievement. Second, schooling is a major tool that "enables families to meet the responsibilities placed on them by society" (p. 79). Third, schooling is a key medium for the interaction of family and society. Considering that the Emancipation Proclamation and the enactment of the Fourteenth and Fifteenth Amendments to the Constitution in the aftermath of the Civil War had failed to bring about equal access to schooling, it is ironic that, as David B. Tyack has documented in his history of urban education, "during the nineteenth century no group in the United States had a greater faith in the equalizing power of schooling or a clearer understanding of the democratic promise of public education than did black Americans" (1974, p. 110).

Ethnic and Racial Diversity and Inequality in Contemporary U.S. Society

The complexity and diversity of America's ancestral makeup are illustrated in data from the 1980 census, which show that more than 83% of the U.S. population today identifies with at least one specific ethnic group and 52% with a single ethnic group. (The remaining 17% of the population included about 6% who reported "American" or "United States" and 10% who did not report any ancestry.) This was the first decennial census to collect ancestry data on persons regardless of the number of generations removed from their country of origin. Exceptions include such ethnic/racial categories as American Indian, Black, Spanish-origin (Hispanic), and certain Asian-origin groups, on which information was collected in previous censuses. Providing no prelisted categories to the questionnaire respondents, the 1980 census identified more than 100 ethnic groups in the United States (U.S. Bureau of the Census, 1983). Table 1 presents 1980 census totals for major U.S. ethnic and racial groups.

Although the population of the United States contains a large number

TABLE 1
U.S. POPULATION BY RACE AND ETHNIC ORIGIN, 1980

Ethnic Origin or Race	Number (in thousands)	Percentage of Total U.S. Population
American Indian	1,418[a]	.63
Asian	3,501[b]	1.55
Black	26,488	11.69
Dutch	1,405	.62
English	23,749	10.48
French	3,062[c]	1.35
German	17,943	7.92
Hispanic	14,606	6.45
Irish	10,337	4.56
Italian	6,883	3.04
Norwegian	1,261	.56
Polish	3,806	1.68
Russian	1,380	.61
Scottish	1,173	.52
Swedish	1,288	.57
Other	108,205	47.77

SOURCES.—Figures on American Indians, Asians, Blacks, and Hispanics from U.S. Bureau of the Census, 1981b, Table 1; 1983, Table 3a.
[a]Includes Eskimos and Aleuts.
[b]Includes Pacific Islanders.
[c]Excludes French Basque.

of distinguishable ethnic groups of diverse sizes, social policy issues related to children and families are usually presented in terms of "minority-group problems" with regard to only certain groups, usually Blacks, Hispanics, and American Indians. Given their history of exclusion and isolation, this pattern should perhaps not come as a surprise. The great majority of the ethnic groups are not considered to be in need of intervention. Indeed, in discussions about social policy, ethnicity is considered to be an issue for only some groups. Why?

To answer this question, we need only compare ethnic groups on the basis of certain characteristics. We shall then realize that there is a high probability of association between membership in a given ethnic group and standing on measures of such objective variables as income, schooling, and unemployment—and, of course, their concomitants, poverty versus relative affluence, and social prestige versus social stigma.

Tables 2 through 6 present the income, occupational, and schooling characteristics of several of the major U.S. ethnic and racial groups. These

TABLE 2

INCOME CHARACTERISTICS OF SELECTED U.S. ETHNIC AND RACIAL GROUPS, 1969[a]

Group	Per Capita Income of Persons ($)	Median Family Income ($)	Percentage of Families with Incomes below Poverty Level
American Indian	1,573	5,832	33.3
Black	1,800	6,063	29.9
Chinese	3,122	10,610	10.3
Filipino	2,790	9,318	11.5
Hispanic[b]	2,000	7,348	21.2
Japanese	3,602	12,515	6.4
White	3,314	9,961	8.6
Total U.S. population	3,139	9,590	10.7

SOURCES.—U.S. Bureau of the Census, 1972, 1973a, 1973c, 1973d, 1973f.
[a]1969 is the year for which annual income was reported in the 1970 census.
[b]Hispanics may be of any race.

TABLE 3

MEDIAN FAMILY INCOME OF FOUR U.S. EUROPEAN-ORIGIN GROUPS, 1968 AND 1970

Group	1968 ($)	1970 ($)
German Americans	8,607	10,402
Irish Americans	8,127	9,964
Italian Americans	8,808	11,089
Polish Americans	8,849	11,619

SOURCE.—U.S. Bureau of the Census, cited in Sowell, 1978.

TABLE 4

SCHOOLING CHARACTERISTICS OF SELECTED U.S. ETHNIC AND RACIAL GROUPS, 1970[a]

Group	Median School Years Completed	Percentage of High School Graduates	Percentage with 4 or More Years of College
American Indian	9.8	33.3	3.8
Black	9.8	31.4	4.4
Chinese	12.4	57.8	25.6
Filipino	12.2	54.7	22.5
Hawaiian	12.1	53.2	5.6
Hispanic[b]	9.1	32.1	4.5
Japanese	12.5	68.8	15.9
Korean	12.9	71.1	36.2
White	12.1	57.1	11.3
Total U.S. population	12.1	52.4	10.7

SOURCES.—U.S. Bureau of the Census, 1973a, 1973b, 1973c, 1973d, 1973f.

[a]Persons 25 years old and over. Data on Hawaiians and Koreans are included here but not in Table 2 because family income data on these two groups were not available from the examined sources.

[b]Hispanics may be of any race.

figures are obtained from the 1970 U.S. decennial census and are subject to all the limitations of this source of data; nevertheless, they are the best available source of national sociodemographic data for cross-group comparisons. At the time of this writing, such figures from the 1980 decennial census have not yet been published. However, in a later section of this chapter I present sociodemographic data based on very recent national surveys comparing the total White population with two of the largest disadvantaged groups, Blacks and Hispanics; those data show a pattern of inequality discouragingly similar to the 1970 pattern.

Some ethnic groups are not directly identifiable from the 1970 census categories, nor would its "nativity and parentage" data cover them, because these groups immigrated so long ago that many or most living in 1970 had native-born parents (Sowell, 1978). However, special surveys were conducted by the U.S. Bureau of the Census in 1968 and 1970. Because these surveys do not cover 1969, the year for which income is reported in the 1970 census, Table 2 shows the incomes of several groups for the year 1969, and Table 3, the incomes of several European ancestry groups for 1968 and 1970.

Although there is a tendency to think of "minorities" as poorer and less educated than the general U.S. population, the data in Tables 2 through 6 clearly show that some ethnic and racial groups are above the national average in income, years of schooling, and occupational status, and

TABLE 5

OCCUPATIONAL STATUS OF EMPLOYED U.S. MALES 25–34 YEARS OLD BY ETHNIC AND RACIAL GROUP, 1970 (%)

Major Occupation Group	American Indian	Black	Hispanic[a]	Chinese	Japanese	Filipino	Total U.S. Population[b]
Professional, technical, and kindred workers	12.5	8.1	9.1	48.8	35.4	35.2	19.9
Managers and administrators, except farm	4.0	3.1	5.5	7.5	10.9	3.8	9.8
Sales workers	2.2	2.5	4.2	3.4	6.6	2.7	6.7
Clerical and kindred workers	6.2	8.9	8.0	7.9	9.4	12.8	7.2
Craftsmen, foremen, and kindred workers	23.6	16.2	21.4	6.7	18.9	13.7	21.9
Operatives, including transport	26.7	33.0	29.2	6.9	7.8	13.3	20.4
Laborers, except farm	11.0	13.3	8.6	1.8	4.3	5.1	5.2
Farmers and farm managers	1.1	.4	.4	.2	.8	.1	1.6
Farm laborers and foremen	4.3	2.5	3.8	.1	.9	3.5	1.2
Service workers, except private household	8.3	11.7	9.8	16.6	4.7	9.8	5.9
Private household workers	.1	.2	.0	.1	.2	.0	.0
Male employed	100	100	100	100	100	100	100

SOURCES.—U.S. Bureau of the Census, 1973a, Table 7; 1973c, Tables 7, 22, 37; 1973d, Table 7; 1973e, Table 40; 1973f, Table 8.
[a]Hispanics may be of any race.
[b]All employed U.S. males 25–34 years old.

TABLE 6

Occupational Status of Employed U.S. Females 25–34 Years Old by Ethnic and Racial Group, 1970 (%)

Major Occupation Group	American Indian	Black	Hispanic[a]	Chinese	Japanese	Filipino	Total U.S. Population[b]
Professional, technical, and kindred workers	12.9	14.4	10.1	37.3	29.8	44.0	21.6
Managers and administrators, except farm	2.1	1.2	1.7	2.6	2.8	1.3	2.7
Sales workers	3.3	2.5	4.2	2.6	3.4	2.5	4.9
Clerical and kindred workers	27.1	24.6	30.3	30.8	39.2	28.5	35.4
Craftsmen, foremen, and kindred workers	2.4	1.6	2.4	.9	1.1	.8	1.7
Operatives, including transport	20.2	19.8	28.0	15.1	6.8	7.8	15.0
Laborers, except farm	1.3	1.5	1.2	.5	.3	.4	.9
Farmers and farm managers	.3	.1	.0	.0	.2	.2	.1
Farm laborers and foremen	1.8	1.0	1.7	.2	.6	.8	.6
Service workers, except private household	24.3	24.0	16.9	8.7	14.1	12.1	14.6
Private household workers	4.1	9.4	3.4	1.3	1.6	1.5	2.4
Female employed	100	100	100	100	100	100	100

Sources.—U.S. Bureau of the Census, 1973a, Table 7; 1973c, Tables 7, 22, 37; 1973d, Table 7; 1973e, Table 40; 1973f, Table 8.

[a]Hispanics may be of any race.

[b]All employed U.S. females 25–34 years old.

some are below it. Several striking contrasts emerge from an examination of these figures.

Focusing first on the higher end of the economic and educational distributions, we see that the Asian American groups are at or very near the top. On all three economic indices displayed in Table 2, Japanese Americans show a clear advantage over all the other ethnic and racial groups, including White Americans. The other two Asian American groups represented, Chinese and Filipino, although not surpassing the economic attainment of White Americans, are close to it and certainly surpass those of the other groups in Table 2. It is also worth noting that, as a comparison of Tables 2 and 3 shows, the incomes of the European-origin groups are not above those of the Chinese and Japanese.

On all three indices of schooling attainment shown in Table 4, four of the five Asian American groups (Chinese, Filipino, Japanese, Korean) show an advantage over all other groups in these tables, including White Americans. The remaining Asian American group, the Hawaiian, shows a level of schooling that, although not superior, is close to that of the White American population.

What factors might explain the superior schooling attainment of Asian Americans? The Coleman survey provides some relevant data concerning the educational aspirations of "Oriental Americans": "The Oriental Americans show by far the highest aspirations toward college of any group in the entire sample, 64 percent reporting wanting to finish college or go beyond." Asian Americans are further reported to plan to have a professional occupation higher in status than the overall average of all groups (Coleman et al., 1966, pp. 279–280). Perhaps equally relevant is that portion of the Coleman report that centers on the child's sense of control of the environment: "It is clear that the average child from each of these minority groups feels a considerably lower sense of control of his environment than does the average white child. It appears that the sense of control is lowest among Puerto Ricans, and among Negroes lowest for those outside metropolitan areas, and that except for the whites it is highest for the Oriental Americans" (Coleman et al., 1966, p. 289).

Although more research evidence certainly is needed before we can conclusively identify causal factors, it appears clear that their high educational aspirations and schooling achievement set Asian American children and families apart from the educational world of many other ethnic and racial groups. Perhaps it is because Asian American parents in general consider education one of the most important symbols of success and a channel of upward social mobility (Huang, 1976; Kitano & Kikumura, 1976; see also Vernon, 1982) that this group has come to occupy its relatively high economic position, as we saw in Table 2.

Asian Americans—both men and women—also surpass other ethnic and racial groups in occupational status, as Tables 5 and 6 show. In 1970 the proportion of employed Asian Americans between 25 and 34 years of age who held professional, technical, and kindred occupations was about twice as large as that of the total employed U.S. population and about four times as large as those of employed American Indians, Blacks, and Hispanics of the same age.

Asian Americans also surpass other groups in the health status of children, a factor related to family economic status. One indicator of health status is the infant mortality rate, the number of deaths for infants under 1 year of age per 1,000 live births. The infant mortality rate is much lower for Asian Americans than it is for other racial groups in the United States; indeed, for Chinese Americans and Japanese Americans in 1977 it was about half that for Whites and about one-fourth that for Blacks (Administration for Children, Youth, and Families, 1980, p. 133).

The generally superior educational and economic achievement of Asian Americans is especially worth noting in light of the fact that these ethnic groups are visibly, persistently, and genetically different from the general population—and, moreover, in light of the fact that, like most other non-White groups in the United States, they have suffered substantial prejudice and discrimination.

Between the late nineteenth century and World War II, Asian Americans were subjected to virulent racial prejudice. Their status in the western states, especially California, was barely better than that of Blacks. However, after World War II their position drastically improved (Vernon, 1982). Japanese Americans were especially successful in schooling attainment and entry into the middle class, but the Chinese, too, began to disperse from their traditional ghettos and be increasingly accepted. The proportion of Chinese Americans in professional, technical, and kindred occupations has been increasing over the past 40 years. Among Chinese Americans in 1940, only 2.4% of employed males and 7.6% of employed females were in the professions, compared with over 30% and over 20%, respectively, in 1970 (U.S. census figures cited by Huang, 1976). Successive waves of Korean, Filipino, and, most recently, Indochinese immigrants all show signs of fairly rapid acculturation to and fairly easy acceptance by the White population. Rates of intermarriage are quite high not only between most Asian American groups but also with Whites (Huang, 1976; Kitano & Kikumura, 1976; van den Berghe, 1981). Indeed, there is now a strikingly high proportion of dating and marriage outside the given group. For example, for the Japanese, historically a "closed group" in which intermarriage was controlled by both ethnic community preferences and antimiscegenation laws, there now are out-marriage rates of approximately 50% in areas such as San Francisco, Fresno, Los Angeles, and Honolulu (Kitano & Kikumura, 1976; Massey, 1981).

An important group, Jewish Americans, is not included in the government's data base because of constitutional limitations on religious inquiries by the Bureau of the Census. A private survey by the National Jewish Population Study (NJPS) found a median family income of $19,259 among Jewish Americans in 1969 (cited in Sowell, 1978), a figure almost twice as high as that reported by the U.S. census for all Whites. Even though the exact NJPS figure may be questioned (the survey nonresponse rate was about one-third on this question), the general position of the Jews as first in income among U.S. ethnic groups agrees with the findings of other surveys (Glazer & Moynihan, 1970; Sowell, 1978), including a very recent one sponsored by the American Jewish Committee (see Cohen, 1982).

Jews have been in America since the colonial period, although they arrived in large numbers relatively recently. The Sephardic, German, and eastern European Jews differ for a variety of historical, cultural, and economic reasons. Those immigrating from eastern Europe, though the last to arrive, make up by far the largest number of U.S. Jews; their mass migration began in the 1880s and continued at a high level until the passage of the restrictive immigration laws in 1924. The massive flow began chiefly because of the pogroms—organized acts of violence and terror against Jews—by the Imperial Russian Government in 1881 (Dawidowicz, 1981; Farber, Mindel, & Lazerwitz, 1976). Until the time of Hitler, the largest concentration of Jews lived in Europe. Now approximately 44% of the world's Jews, or about 6 million, live in the United States (Schmelz & DellaPergola, 1981). Historically this ethnic group, more than any other, has suffered discrimination, oppression, and persecution. Nevertheless, Jews have tended to maintain their ethnic identity and, in contrast to other ethnic groups in the United States, have come to occupy perhaps the highest educational and economic position. Nathan Glazer and Daniel P. Moynihan estimate that in the United States the college-educated proportion is "perhaps three times as large among Jews as in the rest of the population" (1970, p. 156). Indeed, a comparison of the data from the NJPS survey with those reported in the 1970 U.S. census for the total White population documents the sharp educational differences. Just over half (51.6%) of the Jewish Americans, but only 22% of all Whites, had some college education. The greatest difference characterized those with some graduate studies: 18% of the Jewish Americans compared with 5% of all Whites. At the other extreme, only 16% of the Jewish Americans had less than 12 years of schooling, compared with 46% of all Whites (Goldstein, 1980). These statistics agree with those of very recent surveys (see Cohen, 1982). Clearly, Jewish Americans are characterized by distinctively high levels of educational achievement, and this holds for both men and women. Chief among the values transmitted by Jewish parents to children is that of learning. The emphasis on getting a college education, observe Glazer and Moynihan, "touches almost every Jewish schoolchild. The pressure is so great that what to do about those who are not able to manage college intellectually has become a serious social and emotional problem for them and their families" (1970, p. 156). Reflecting their high levels of education, Jewish Americans are, like Asian Americans, disproportionately represented in the upper ranks of the occupational structure (see Goldstein, 1980).

Thus, both Asian American and Jewish American families tend to place an exceptionally high value on their children's schooling attainment; indeed, they stand clearly apart from other ethnic groups in this dimension of childhood socialization. Might this characteristic partly explain the astonishingly rapid and unparalleled movement of these two ethnic groups from their earlier excluded, inferior status to their present occupationally and economically superior standing?

Additional research is needed to determine why, in spite of their initially excluded, subordinate, and oppressed positions in American society, certain ethnic groups, but not others, have come to occupy superior educational and economic standings. Of particular value to the field of child development and social policy would be comparative research designed to identify the variables contributing to the superior achievement of ethnic groups that historically have suffered from prejudice and discrimination. Also of value would be research conducted to identify the characteristics and special circumstances of those few children who, although belonging to the ethnic groups at the bottom of the social order, nevertheless come to surpass the educational and economic attainments of the average individual in the more privileged groups.

ETHNIC GROUPS AT THE BOTTOM

At the bottom of the socioeconomic scale are three broad ethnic and racial groups: American Indians, Blacks, and Hispanics. Not only do these groups have the lowest average incomes and the least schooling, but they also have the highest proportions of families with incomes below the official poverty level, as a survey of Tables 2 through 6 makes evident.

At the very bottom of the socioeconomic ladder are the American Indians. At least one-third of all American Indian children and families live in extreme poverty. The unemployment rate among American Indians in the labor force in 1970 was well over twice that of White Americans—and this held true for both men and women (U.S. Bureau of the Census, 1972, 1973a).

For American Indians the median family income was less than two-thirds (59%) that of White families, and the per capita income was less than half that of Whites (see Table 2). Indeed, fully one-third of all American Indian families had incomes below the poverty level; an overwhelming proportion of these (81%) were families with children (U.S. Bureau of the Census, 1973a).

In contrast to the U.S. population as a whole, American Indians are underrepresented in the white-collar occupations (clerical and kindred workers; sales workers; managers and administrators, except farm; professional, technical, and kindred workers) and overrepresented in the lower-status occupations. Indeed, in the United States in 1970, of all employed American Indians between 25 and 34 years old, only 25% of the men and 45% of the women were in white-collar occupations, compared with 44% of all employed men and 65% of all employed women of the same age in the U.S. population (see Tables 5 and 6).

A relatively high proportion of American Indian families are female-headed, a proportion that in 1970 was twice as high as that for White families. In 32% of such American Indian families there were children under 6 years old, and in 66% there were children under 18 years old. As in any ethnic group, female-headed American Indian families face especially difficult economic circumstances; they constituted nearly one-third (31%) of all American Indian families below the poverty level and, indeed, had a median income less than one-third (32%) that of all White families (U.S. Bureau of the Census, 1972, 1973a).

Schooling attainment is generally low among American Indians, as Table 4 shows: for those 25 years old and over, the median school years completed was only 9.8, compared with 12.1 for Whites; only 33.3% were high school graduates, and a negligible percentage (3.8%) had 4 or more years of college, compared with respective percentages of 57.1 and 11.3 for Whites. Eight percent of American Indians 25 years of age and older had not completed even 1 year of schooling, compared with only 1% of the White population of the same age (U.S. Bureau of the Census, 1972, 1973a).

Both linguistically and culturally, American Indians are enormously diverse. The 1970 census identified 13 major Indian mother tongues and over 800 different tribes. This enormous diversity presents extremely difficult challenges to policymakers and service providers. Consider, for example, the difficulties involved in developing culturally and linguistically appropriate curriculum materials and assessment techniques for early-childhood education programs. Because these diverse populations represent relatively small markets, commercial companies are seldom willing or able to invest resources in developing the needed products and services.

Although the infant mortality rate among American Indians has declined markedly over the past several decades, in 1977 it was still higher than that of the general U.S. population (Administration for Children, Youth, and Families, 1980). The health and housing conditions on the reservations are generally poor; a large proportion of the housing is below minimum standard (Price, 1976). In 1970, 28% of the total Indian population was living on reservations, although the figure varies greatly across tribes; for some tribes, such as the Pueblo, it was higher than 60% (U.S. Bureau of the Census, 1973a).

In sum, for a very large proportion of American Indian families with children, the quality of life, measured by such major social indicators as employment, income, housing, schooling, and health standards, looks quite inferior to that of the U.S. population as a whole.

Not very far behind the American Indians on measures of socioeconomic disadvantage is the Black population. Its unemployment rate in 1970 was well over 50% higher than that of White Americans—respective unemployment rates for men and women in the civilian labor force were 76% and 62% higher for Blacks than they were for Whites (U.S. Bureau of the Census, 1972, Table 77).

Among Blacks in 1969 the median family income was just under two-thirds (61%) that of White families, and the per capita income was only about half (54%) that of Whites. Nearly one-third (29.9%) of all Black families had incomes below the poverty level; in a staggeringly high proportion of those families (79.5%) there were children (U.S. Bureau of the Census, 1972, 1973d).

Schooling attainment is also low among Blacks (see Table 4). For those 25 years of age and older, the median school years completed was only 9.8; only 31.4% were high school graduates, and only 4.4% had 4 or more years of college.

Black Americans were even more underrepresented than American Indians in white-collar occupations (see Tables 5 and 6). Of all employed Blacks between 25 and 34 years old, only 23% of the men and 43% of the women were in white-collar occupations in 1970, compared with 44% of all employed men and 65% of all employed women of the same age in the U.S. population.

The infant mortality rate among Black Americans is about double that of Whites (Administration for Children, Youth, and Families, 1980, p.

133). Moreover, Black infants are two-and-one-half times more likely than White infants to be of very low birth weight (1,500 grams or less) (Kleinman, 1981).

Sharing the low end of the socioeconomic spectrum with American Indians and Blacks are the Hispanic Americans. Their unemployment rate has been higher than that of the total White population, by 51% for men and 69% for women. The median family income of Hispanics was only three-fourths (74%) that of all Whites (see Table 2). However, given how these two groups differ in family size, the income disparity becomes more evident when one considers the per capita income: for Hispanics it was only three-fifths that of all Whites. Over one-fifth of all Hispanic families had incomes below the poverty level, and in an overwhelmingly high proportion of those families (82.7%) there were children (U.S. Bureau of the Census, 1972, 1973f).

Schooling attainment is also very low among Hispanic Americans (see Table 4). For those 25 years of age and over, the median school years completed were only 9.1; only 32.1% were high school graduates, and only 4.5% had 4 or more years of college. Over 7% of all Hispanic Americans in this age group had not completed even 1 year of school (U.S. Bureau of the Census, 1973f).

Hispanic Americans are also underrepresented in the higher-status occupations (see Tables 5 and 6). Of all the employed Hispanics between 25 and 34 years old, only 27% of the men and 46% of the women were in white-collar occupations in 1970; each percentage is about 20 points lower than those of the total U.S. population.

ETHNIC AND RACIAL DIVERSITY AND INEQUALITY:
SUMMARY AND CONCLUSIONS

When drawing inferences from sociodemographic data such as those examined in the preceding sections, it is important to keep in mind that considerable variability usually exists *within* each ethnic category. For example, within the Hispanic American population there are several distinct ethnic groups, including the Cuban American, Mexican American, and Puerto Rican. Although such groups have many cultural, sociolinguistic, and demographic characteristics in common, they also differ in others (Laosa, 1975). In some respects, each group presents a unique pattern of needs that must be examined in detail when one designs, implements, or evaluates policies aimed at meeting the needs of children and families. However, beyond such gross classifications as White and Black or White and non-White, accurate and up-to-date statistics more finely descriptive of ethnic group membership are often difficult or impossible to find.

Indeed, one is often frustrated by the many empirical, conceptual, and methodological gaps and flaws in the data available on ethnic groups.

It is ironic that in 1980 the largest identifiable ethnic group in the United States was that of Blacks (see Table 1). Indeed, Blacks constitute roughly 12% of the U.S. population, compared with roughly 6% of Hispanic ancestry, 8% of German, 10% of English, 4% of Irish, and 3% of Italian. Other groups, including American Indians and Asian Americans, constitute only a tiny proportion of the total U.S. population. Of course, if we consider broad racial categories rather than ethnic origin, then obviously the overwhelming majority of the U.S. population is White, and other racial groups are clearly in the minority. With regard to ethnicity, however, clearly the pluralistic mosaic is more descriptive of American social reality than is a simplistic ethnic majority-minority dichotomy.

Thus, although in a numerical sense we cannot speak meaningfully of ethnic *minorities* in the United States, if we consider the sharing of society's resources we certainly can speak realistically of ethnic group *inequality*. Certain ethnic groups are disproportionately represented at the bottom of the socioeconomic status scale. I examine later in the chapter the discouraging fact that the inequalities are there today as they were in 1970, when the data examined in the preceding sections were collected.

The implications that these ethnic inequalities hold for social policies toward children should be clear: in this society socioeconomic status and ethnic group membership are highly significant in determining the environmental circumstances in which children grow and develop. These implications were at the heart of the public policy initiatives that emerged in the United States in the 1960s.

PRECURSORS TO THE POLICY INITIATIVES OF THE 1960s

By the time of World War II, the public investment in the assimilation of children of European immigrants was widely accepted as being in the public interest (White, 1973). It was not until the 1960s, however, that any vigorous action was taken to include Blacks, Hispanics, and Indians in the vision of a unified U.S. culture. What led to the unprecedented social concerns and public policies that emerged then toward children of these ethnic, racial, and language groups? It was the convergence of several historically significant social, political, economic, and intellectual trends, which we now examine.

CIVIL RIGHTS MOVEMENT

Doubtless of major significance among the inextricably intertwined influences leading to the policy initiatives of the early 1960s were the social and political struggles of the civil rights movement. The Supreme Court's decision, in 1954, in the landmark case of *Brown* v. *Board of Education of Topeka, Kansas*, had a tremendous impact on the movement to achieve racial and ethnic equality. In ruling that "in the field of education the doctrine of 'separate but equal' has no place," the Court reversed an earlier decision, *Plessy* v. *Ferguson*, of 1896, which rested on the principle that there could be "separate-but-equal" treatment of people. From 1896 to 1954 northern and southern state policies and practices had confirmed the prediction made by Justice Harlan in his dissenting opinion in *Plessy*; he had argued that the decision would place "in a condition of legal inferiority a large body of American citizens" (*Plessy* v. *Ferguson* 1896, cited in Jones, 1981). The *Brown* decision encouraged civil rights groups to initiate further legal action, political pressure, and civil protests to challenge the separate-but-equal doctrine in other fields.

The major civil rights victories came in the courtroom, but there was also a major legislative victory. In 1957 Congress passed the first civil rights act since Reconstruction. Intended to counter resistance to full voter participation, the act created the U.S. Commission on Civil Rights and the Civil Rights Division of the Department of Justice. It also vested the Department of Justice with authority to sue on behalf of persons denied the right to vote (President's Commission for a National Agenda for the Eighties, 1980).

Civil rights leaders and supporters—of all races—moved the fight for racial equality and justice from the courts to the buses, to the lunch counters, to the streets; they marched, sat in, and even went to jail in the quest for equality. A notable example was the event that took place on August 28, 1963, when some 200,000 Americans of all races converged on the nation's capital in what was perhaps the largest demonstration in the history of the United States. They gathered on the grounds of the Lincoln Memorial to present a "living petition" for equality. Among the several persons who presented the cause that they espoused, it was Martin Luther King, Jr., who spoke most eloquently to the point of the American dream of equality. He had a dream, he said, that one day the "sons of former slaves and the sons of former slaveowners will be able to sit down together at the table of brotherhood" and that "little black boys and black girls will be able to join hands with little white boys and white girls as sisters and brothers." Public sensibilities were stirred by televised newscasts of these events and by other media explorations of the problems, concerns, and goals of groups that were excluded from the democratic ideal of full participation in society.

At the other end of the spectrum there were those seen to be part of a "backlash," those, for example, demanding that Supreme Court Chief Justice Earl Warren, during whose tenure the Court was deciding in favor of civil rights, be impeached. However, those who sought to restore the status quo ante generally received little encouragement. The reactions were generally more positive than negative; White Americans, on the whole, supported the dismantling of legal barriers that perpetuated discrimination and were indignant about the violence perpetrated by extremists against Blacks and their White supporters (Jones, 1981).

Under the leadership of presidents John F. Kennedy and Lyndon B. Johnson, the executive branch of government took a position in the vanguard of the struggle to end racial discrimination. One of the ideas born of the civil rights movement was that the government was obligated to help disadvantaged groups in order to compensate for inequalities in social and economic conditions.

ACUTE AWARENESS OF POVERTY

Parallel to the growth of the civil rights movement there was a sudden awareness that in the United States many persons lived in extreme poverty amid the growing affluence of the majority. The country in effect had suddenly awakened to the realization that poverty was indeed widespread, and that the consequences of the existence of this "other America" that Michael Harrington (1962) so very poignantly described were threatening the nation's economic, nay moral, well-being. Among the intellectual precursors of the public focus on poverty were Harrington's book, *The Other America*, and Dwight Macdonald's article in the *New Yorker* reviewing Harrington and other, more technical works on poverty (for discussions of these influences see, for example, Levine, 1970; Moynihan, 1969a; Sundquist, 1968). These writings dramatized the impact and the extent of poverty.

According to James L. Sundquist (1968, pp. 111–112, 113), who has done a detailed study of the origins of the War on Poverty, "until 1964 the word poverty did not appear as a heading in the index of either the *Congressional Record* or the *Public Papers of the Presidents. . . .* By the spring of 1963 [President Kennedy, according to Arthur M. Schlesinger, Jr.], "was reaching the conclusion that tax reduction required a comprehensive structural counterpart, taking the form, not of piecemeal programs, but of a broad war against poverty itself. Here perhaps was the unifying theme which would pull a host of social programs together and rally the nation behind a generous cause."

It appears, however, that the set of programs in which Kennedy was interested were those attacking the social problems that prevented equality of opportunity. Membership in certain racial and ethnic groups, for example, was almost synonymous with poverty or near-poverty and with its consequences for the poor and their children. Indeed, it seems to have been as much the obstacles to equal opportunity as the existence of very low incomes that impelled first President Kennedy and then President Johnson and their advisers. As an illustration of their ambivalence in this regard, Robert A. Levine (1970), who served as assistant director for Research, Plans, Programs, and Evaluation of the Office of Economic Opportunity, points to the fact that their War on *Poverty* began with an Economic *Opportunity* Act.

Indeed, a major point in Levine's (1970, p. 33) historical review of events surrounding the emergence of the War on Poverty is to suggest strongly that "neither the conscious nor the subconscious" impetus to the War on Poverty was solely low-income misery, but the concentration of this misery in groups within which the individual's opportunity to rise was very limited. The stress on group poverty and unequal opportunity distinguished the program from earlier efforts. During the days of the Great Depression and the New Deal, poverty was so widespread a problem that poor people were indistinguishable from the majority by race or other characteristics. The New Deal ethos called for improving the economy so that the vast majority of people could make it on their own; for using Social Security so that those who lost their economic self-sufficiency because of age, accident, or economic fluctuation could continue the standard of living to which they were accustomed; and for assisting or supporting the presumed random remainder with Public Assistance. It was not until the 1960s, when it was discovered that this remainder was not random at all but concentrated very highly in groups characterized by unequal opportunity, that poverty as a specific, separable problem became a concern in the United States (Levine, 1970).

A TIME OF AFFLUENCE AND OPTIMISM

Although there certainly was poverty concentrated in certain groups, the 1960s was for the country as a whole a time of relative affluence. The active fiscal policy of the Kennedy administration had, by the end of 1963, begun to create the climate of prosperity necessary for the success of antipoverty programs. The big fiscal boost to the economy came only after the president's assassination, with the passage of the Kennedy-proposed tax reduction; but by late 1963 the movement was well under way toward unemployment rates of less than 4% that supported the War on Poverty after its first year. It was an era of very rapid growth. Indeed, for its first year of operation, while it was still almost nonexistent as an organization, the Office of Economic Opportunity had been appropriated by Congress a budget of $750 million to be spent in half a year (Levine, 1970).

It was an era of high spirit and excitement, as all things looked possible. It attracted to the policymaking process some of the brightest social thinkers in the country—"the best and the brightest," as Pulitzer Prize winner David Halberstam (1972) would refer to them in his highly engaging chronicle of people and events of the era. "It was a glittering time," Halberstam wrote, "They literally swept into office, ready, moving, generating their style, their confidence—they were going to get America moving again" (p. 50). Bettye M. Caldwell (1974, p. 491) described the great excitement and the unbounded optimism of many researchers and professionals in the field of child development: "No one who was not a part of it could possibly appreciate the excitement of that spring and summer of 1965. Impassioned rhetoric flowed like foam at a beerfest in Munich. We were going to accomplish miracles for the children of America. After all, miracles were needed."

Indeed, out of the affluence seemed to grow both an enormous optimism and great intellectual excitement—both centered on the policymaking process as a means of solving social inequalities. As director of the Office of Economic Opportunity, established in 1964, Sargent Shriver attracted many brilliant and deeply concerned intellectuals. Many of them were interested primarily in solving the problems of unequal opportunity and of group poverty, and particularly the problems of urban minorities and Blacks, including their political powerlessness.

INTERETHNIC COOPERATION

Times of affluence and optimism carry with them both a lessening of competition among ethnic groups and an emphasis on leisure and social reform. In the 1960s, despite the continual undercurrent of protest and youthful political energy unleashed, the cultural emphasis—in the media, in the Democratic administrations, in the expressed concerns of youth— was on personal and social improvement: the expansion of consciousness, the development of self, the discovery of vehicles for personal and spiritual fulfillment (see, e.g., Rothchild & Wolf, 1976). There was widespread dissatisfaction with the status quo, and many sought change. At the same time, as resources became more plentiful there seemed to be enough for everyone. The abundance of resources somewhat obviated the competition that often pits ethnic groups against one another during times of scarcity. The social altruism of the time found partial expression in a proliferation of social policies and government programs on behalf of disadvantaged and minority children and families.

ETHNIC REVITALIZATION MOVEMENTS

In the 1960s, perhaps in response to the inequality and institutionalized discrimination that certain ethnic groups were experiencing, ethnic
revitalization movements emerged. These movements deepened the
groups' expressions of ethnic consciousness and their sense of integrity and
pride and gave new vigor to their quests for equality. Many intellectuals
began to question—and even dismiss as a myth—the once popular concept
of the United States as a melting pot, at least insofar as it was applied to the
descendants of what Michael Novak (1972) called the "unmeltable
ethnics." By one device or another, American Indians, Blacks, and Hispanics—among many others—began to draw attention to themselves, seeking
to "revise" traditional histories and offering new strategies for political and
social action. Indeed, many in this country began to rethink the character
of U.S. society, insisting that the earlier histories were too Euro-centered;
the concepts of ethnic diversity and cultural pluralism became popular.
Ethnic pluralism was seen as not only real and alive but also as consistent
with U.S. democratic ideals.

However, pluralism and toleration were very slow coming in the area
of racial and ethnic relations, where often majority-minority lines could be
drawn; indeed, as Thomas Sowell (1978, p. 233) has observed, pluralism
and toleration were not "ideals from which Americans started, but necessi-
ties to which they were driven." Nazism and its abhorrent consequences
had brought racism and ethnic discrimination in general into disrepute in
the postwar United States and set the stage for a series of changes in public
opinion and government policy. In the early 1960s, racial and ethnic
inequalities and their effects on children had become a major national
issue, and federal intervention to end these inequalities became a major
element of public policy.

PERSONAL CIRCUMSTANCES OF POLITICAL LEADERS

The unique personal circumstances of key movers of the period also
contributed to the unprecedented social concerns and public policies
toward poor and ethnic minority children. As Edward Zigler and Karen
Anderson (1979) remind us in their review of the intellectual and political
climate surrounding the emergence of Head Start, both President Johnson
and Sargent Shriver, his chief strategist and field commander in the War on
Poverty, had personal interests in the issues surrounding education and
the disadvantaged. Johnson had begun his career as a schoolteacher in
rural Texas (see Miller, 1980). Shriver had served 5 years as the president

of the Board of Education in Chicago, where he saw firsthand the problems of a large inner-city school system; he had also served as director of the Peace Corps, a program intended to bring the knowledge of the economically successful to the aid of the poor. His wife, Eunice Kennedy Shriver, was an active member of the President's Task Force on Mental Retardation; she and other members of the Kennedy family had an intense personal interest in problems of mental retardation because of their experiences with a mentally retarded family member. Just as many others, Shriver and Johnson were amazed and encouraged by claims that "severe degrees of social and cultural deprivation" in poor children had apparently been reversed by educational-intervention experiments. The intention of employing this sort of intervention on a national scale led Shriver to consult child development scholars about proposed social policy. The actual design of Head Start was assigned to a committee of child development experts.

CHILD DEVELOPMENT RESEARCH

In the 1950s and 1960s there was a revival of scientific interest in the role of environmental stimulation in human development. During the 1940s and 1950s a number of studies of both animals and humans supported the conclusion that restricted patterns of living such as those found in severely impoverished areas could lead to deficiencies in human development. This rediscovery of the idea that the development of human behavior is strongly influenced by environmental factors cast serious doubts on the prevailing hereditary and maturationist view that the pattern of intellectual development is predetermined. J. McVicker Hunt's (1961) book, *Intelligence and Experience*, was particularly influential in stimulating a turnabout in thinking by presenting a research base for the proposition that intelligence is not fixed at birth but may be altered by conditions of environment. Also highly influential during the 1960s in directing public attention to child development in general and to children of economically disadvantaged families in particular was Benjamin S. Bloom's (1964) *Stability and Change in Human Characteristics*. Bloom analyzed several major longitudinal studies and concluded that the years between conception and age 4 are critical in the development of intelligence: "In terms of intelligence measured at age 17, about 50% of the development takes place between conception and age 4, about 30% between ages 4 and 8, and about 20% between ages 8 and 17" (p. 88). Moreover, Bloom proposed that the effects of environment on intellectual development appear to be greatest in the early, most rapid, periods of development. Influenced by this interpretation, environmentalists saw the preschool years as the critical period during which to enrich the environment and affect intellectual growth;

they implied that nonintervention was tantamount to opportunities lost. The introduction of these ideas had the effect of redirecting public concern from child welfare and day care to child development (Harman, 1978). Moreover, researchers consistently argued that early-childhood experiences in poor families were closely linked to mental retardation. The theoretical work and the empirical research were accompanied by the design and development of educational-intervention efforts for disadvantaged children, who became the target of proliferating early-childhood curriculum programs, Head Start, and other publicly funded projects intended to enhance their development. Skeptics who would point out the fallacies in Bloom's interpretation of the data (for a review see Wohlwill, 1980) and those who would argue for a return to the interpretation that intellectual development is determined largely by heredity (e.g., Jensen, 1969) were not to be in the spotlight until late in the 1960s.

GROWTH OF PUBLIC CONCERN ABOUT CHILDREN

There had been no systematic investigation of child life until the 1880s, when G. Stanley Hall, the pioneer in child psychology (Kessen, 1965), developed the child-study movement (Boring, 1950). Although the methodology and data of Hall's studies were of questionable value, the conception of normative study did take hold of educators' and psychologists' imaginations and influenced the directions of later developmental research (Sears, 1975). The most direct line of Hall's influence was to Arnold Gesell (Ross, 1972). In 1911, at Gesell's suggestion, Yale University gave him a room and equipment for a newly organized Yale Clinic for Child Development, the precursor of the child development institutes that were created in the 1920s (see Senn, 1975).

The turn of the century also saw what was perhaps the first period of great, nationwide concern about the welfare of children and the adequacy of public institutions for children in the United States; the first decennial White House Conference on Children was held in 1909. Behind these concerns were new attitudes toward children, reflected in a change in their status in society. As Grotberg (1976) has summarized these trends, this change essentially was "from children's subordinate and incidental position in the family to one of greater equity and with individual needs and rights" (p. 405). A review of Philippe Ariès's (1962) detailed historical researches suggests that a similar if not identical shift in attitudes and behavior toward children was taking place elsewhere in the world, specifically in western Europe. Early in this century the child came to be seen as exploited and mistreated by the harsh industrial society; nineteenth-century Romantic views of children had combined with the progressive, twentieth-century ideas to create an intense interest in protecting children, particularly children of poor families who tended to be economically exploited. Child welfare consequently became an important concept. Also behind these concerns was the assumption by the government that it had a responsibility for protecting all children, particularly those at risk.

The federal establishment of the National Institute of Mental Health (NIMH) in 1946 had been motivated partly by concerns to prevent abnormal development and enhance normal psychological development and behavioral adjustment. But the first explicit federal reference to *child* and *development* was the National Institute of Child Health and Human Development (NICHD), established in 1963. As part of the National Institutes of Health, the NICHD was to conduct research and training in maternal and child health and in human development. Although the approach to human development was largely biomedical, it soon involved psychological aspects, particularly with respect to child development (Grotberg, 1976). Child development issues were directly addressed also by the Economic Opportunity Act of 1964, which established the Comprehensive Child Development Program, more commonly known as Head Start, and by the formation of the Office of Child Development in 1969, which inherited Head Start and portions of the Children's Bureau (see Steiner, 1976). These events showed that although protective care, health, and education continued to be the recognized focus of expanded efforts, the new nationally recognized goal was to enhance the development of the total child (Grotberg, 1976).

Thus in the 1960s the great public concern about children was accompanied by an unprecedented expansion in government support of social service programs and social and behavioral science research in general and addressed to child development in particular. Many of the service programs and much of the research centered on the problems of ethnic minorities, especially of economically disadvantaged Black children and families. As the fiscal resources made available for social reform were increasing, so were the sources of information by which such reforms might be guided. Whereas in 1956 social science research received a mere $4 million in federal funds, by 1966 this figure had risen to $44 million (Moynihan, 1969a, p. 31). At such rates of expenditure, it is to be expected that there would be some increase in knowledge, and almost certainly during this period there was. Moreover, it was an era in which the policymakers and the program designers actively sought these sources of information.

In assessing the impact of child development research on policy making, it is probably realistic to conclude, however, as Gilbert Y. Steiner (1976, p. 26) does, that neither Hunt's *Intelligence and Experience* nor

Bloom's *Stability and Change in Human Characteristics*—nor, I would add, any other report of child development research—"directly triggered public policy activity. Whatever their importance for later efforts to effect social policy change, the short-run importance of these works was in the coincidence of their timing with the political needs and purposes of the Kennedy and Johnson presidencies."

Nevertheless, it seems equally realistic to qualify this conclusion by recognizing that the child development policies and programs of that era would never have emerged if researchers had not accumulated the body of scientific theory and data on child development produced over the previous decades. Indeed, when Shriver and his associates at OEO sought to develop a more comprehensive program that would show the quick, dramatic results necessary for continued political support, they broadened community-action efforts to include preschool children among the groups served; they would not have thought of doing so had it not been for the claims—now more generally and soberly seen as exaggerated—proffered on the basis of the serious scientific work of child development researchers.

GROWTH OF KNOWLEDGE

The expansion of support for child development research and the revival of interest in the sociocultural determinants of human development were not isolated events in the history of scientific knowledge. They were part of an extraordinary growth of knowledge in general and of the social and behavioral sciences in particular. There was, for example, the "econometric revolution": "The same quantified knowledge of the economy which was making economic theory increasingly operational," Daniel P. Moynihan wrote of this period, "was also pointing up social problems that persisted despite the onset of persistent prosperity" (1969a, p. 29). Moynihan identifies an irony behind this growth in knowledge. The U.S. business community, during the first half of the twentieth century when it was "fiercely opposed to the idea of economic or social planning," nonetheless supported, even pressed for, "the development of a national statistical system that largely as a result of this support became perhaps the best in the world" (p. 30). This in turn made certain types of planning and regulation feasible and in a measure inevitable. Indeed, social critics sometimes point, not altogether inaccurately, to the indispensable role of the statisticians in modern societies, who seem never to do anything about problems until they learn to measure them. A sharp historical contrast that Moynihan (1969a, pp. 30–31) brings to our attention highlights the dazzling rapidity of the change taking place in the availability of social science research data:

If one recalls that the nation went through the entire depression of the 1930s without ever really knowing what the unemployment rate was (the statistic was then gathered once each ten years by the Census Bureau), one gains a feeling for the great expansion of knowledge in this and related fields in the quarter century that followed. By the 1960s, the monthly employment data had become a vital, sensitive, and increasingly reliable source of information about American society, and that information increasingly insisted that although the majority of Americans were prosperous indeed, a significant minority were not.

The period following World War II was thus an era of expansion in financial support for social and behavioral science research. As it would be reasonable to expect of any field of inquiry, the success of social and behavioral scientists in answering their own and society's questions has, in some measure at least, reflected investment in the field. However, assessing the relative success of the various disciplines requires keeping in mind that the social and behavioral sciences have received only a small fraction compared with the resource allocation that the physical sciences have received.

RISING EDUCATIONAL ASPIRATIONS

Both reflecting and shaping the growth of knowledge were an expansion of the field of education and, for the general population, a rise in schooling attainment and educational expectations. Indeed, one of the most prominent demographic changes in U.S. society in this century is reflected in its educational statistics. As measured by the years of formal schooling completed by successive birth cohorts in this century, Americans in the 1960s were more highly educated than ever before, as data from a national survey, shown in Table 7, attest. For the oldest cohort in the sample—male civilians born between 1907 and 1911—mean education was 9.87 years, with a standard deviation (SD) of 3.74. For the youngest cohort—those born between 1947 and 1951—mean education was 12.81 years, with SD 2.38. Between these first and last birth cohorts, average education rose 3 years, an amount nearly equivalent to the SD of the oldest cohort. At the same time that the means rose, the spreads of the respective distributions around these means decreased; these decreases, whether measured by the SD or the coefficient of variation (SD/mean), have been in the range of one-half to one-third across the educational experiences of the cohorts represented in the sample (Featherman & Hauser, 1978). In sum, there has been a steady increase in the schooling level of the population; at the same time, the population has become more homogeneous in its schooling attainment.

TABLE 7
DISTRIBUTION OF COMPLETED SCHOOLING FOR COHORTS AGED 21–65:
U.S. MALE CIVILIAN NONINSTITUTIONAL POPULATION IN MARCH 1973, BY YEAR OF BIRTH

	1907–1911	1912–1916	1917–1921	1922–1926	1927–1931	1932–1936	1937–1941	1942–1946	1947–1951
Mean years of school completed	9.87	10.55	11.03	11.46	11.72	12.02	12.40	12.76	12.81
Standard deviation	3.74	3.50	3.42	3.38	3.39	3.31	3.01	2.76	2.38
Coefficient of variation	.374	.332	.310	.295	.289	.275	.243	.216	.186

SOURCE.—Featherman & Hauser, 1978, Table 5.5

Events in the nation's foreign affairs contributed significantly to increased pursuit of education and to the rise in the educational expectations of the citizenry. Mobilization for World War II was the occasion for large-scale intelligence-testing programs by the armed forces; during the war there was a significant increase in the birthrate, the so-called baby boom; near the war's end the GI Bill was passed; and the rivalries of the Cold War spurred the race for technological superiority.

The GI Bill had broadened the educational horizons of all socioeconomic groups by enabling former servicemen to obtain college-level training. Within 12 years of its passage in 1944, 8 million veterans had studied in colleges and universities, vocational schools, and other training programs. The aftermath of the baby boom was an unprecedented growth of the nation's school-age population, which increased the demands for educational personnel, products, and services. Academic competition, triggered by the Cold War with the Soviet Union and particularly by the Soviet launching of the Sputnik satellite, gained impetus as U.S. military and political leadership sought to hedge against the grim experience of two world wars when armed-forces intelligence tests revealed vast numbers of U.S. citizens to be intellectually deficient for either military or civilian tasks (Collins, 1981).

Also contributing to the need for a more highly educated work force was the increasing complexity of the means of production. The business world and the general public became more aware of the personnel demands of an increasingly complex technology as automation, computerization, synthetics, the mass media, mass marketing, and the mushrooming service industry transformed the economy (Collins, 1981).

Education was seen also as a necessary step toward reducing unemployment among disadvantaged ethnic and racial minorities and the poor. The unemployment rate in 1964 of persons with some college education was roughly half that of those who had not finished high school (Collins, 1981).

At every school level, Black, Hispanic, and American Indian children failed to keep up with the quicker pace of postwar schooling. By the 1960s a large measure of public attention was already focused on education, which had come to be seen as a means of improving the social conditions of these and similarly placed ethnic and racial minorities.

A SENSE OF URGENCY AND THE BIRTH OF A NEW ERA:
1960–1980

Accompanying the social, political, economic, and intellectual developments and secular trends that converged in the early 1960s was a prevailing sense of poignant urgency. Although preoccupied with other issues—not the least of which was the war in Vietnam—the country seemed to feel that questions of racial and ethnic equality could not be set aside for another time. From this sense of urgency emanated a national resolve to find effective solutions to social issues. Answers to questions of racial and ethnic inequality found expression in a seemingly endless stream of court decisions, public demonstrations, legislation, and a proliferation of government programs. All of this activity took place in a society that was massively divided; more informed and more concerned than ever before about the lives of its children, not only those of the disadvantaged but also the increasingly alienated youth of the more privileged families; troubled about its legacy to its children; and groping toward greater racial and ethnic equality.

The result was a new era in the history of U.S. public policies toward children. Among the unique aspects of this era, which spanned the period roughly between 1965 and 1980, were its focus on overcoming poverty and on achieving equal social, educational, and economic opportunity—enabling all children, irrespective of ethnic or racial background or family socioeconomic status, to succeed in school and later life as their innate ability allowed. The principal stimulating force was the federal government. Indeed, to an unprecedented degree in U.S. history, federal action dominated policy initiatives for children—chiefly in the form of federal programs that focused on the development and education primarily of children of poor families, with particular attention to those of ethnic and racial groups disproportionately represented among the poor.

The upsurge in federal spending for children's programs reached unprecedented proportions during the 1960s and early 1970s. For example, from 1965 to 1979 federal expenditures for 16 programs for young children grew from under $400 million to over $11 billion. These programs (some of which did not exist in 1965) include Head Start, Title I of the Elementary and Secondary Education Act, Follow Through, emergency school aid, aid for mothers with dependent preschool children, a work incentive program, a maternal and child health program, a child nutrition program, handicapped and bilingual education, child welfare, child health research, research and demonstration in child development, child abuse treatment and prevention, and special day care. Moreover, if Title XX social services and Title XIX Medicaid are included (both of which provide extensive services to young children), these programs add $22 billion (Collins, 1981). The U.S. public's willingness to spend for educational and other children's programs seemed to peak in the mid-1970s.

In the sections that follow I review and analyze several major policy developments of the 1960–1980 era. My focus is on policies addressed to the development and education of low-income and ethnic, racial, and language minority children. I have selected only some of the principal federal initiatives; there are others that I do not discuss here because they were short-lived or modest in scope or were primarily designed to serve functions other than the reduction of ethnic and racial inequalities through the development and education of children. For example, I do not discuss here redistributive policies and public assistance programs designed to augment the incomes of needy families by means of cash transfer payments or by such nonpecuniary transfers as food stamps, medical services, housing, and child-care subsidies (e.g., Aid for Families with Dependent Children and Medicaid). I also do not discuss here policies concerning the provision of educational and other services to migrant children or to children of undocumented citizenship, efforts of the courts or of the U.S. Department of Justice to improve the racial integration of schools, recent judicial action requesting that schools recognize Black English as a formal dialect, or the emerging policy initiatives that address inequalities in financing elementary and secondary education. I do, however, discuss the actions of professional associations and of judicial and legislative bodies taken to influence policies and practices regarding the use of ability tests for classifying ethnic, racial, and language minority children in schools.

The centerpieces of the federal compensatory programs for children that became part of the War on Poverty were Head Start and Title I of the Elementary and Secondary Education Act. Before analyzing the intellectual assumptions and theoretical views underlying the policy initiatives that resulted in these programs, let us briefly review the programs themselves.

HEAD START

Project Head Start was launched in 1965 as part of the massive community-action program legislated by the Economic Opportunity Act passed in August 1964. The act legislated several antipoverty programs, and a new federal agency, the Office of Economic Opportunity, was created to manage three of them: the Job Corps, a residential training program for young men and women between the ages of 16 and 21, to provide education and training for employment; the Community Action Program, a set of comprehensive and locally initiated and planned programs to aid communities in planning and administering their own assistance programs for the poor; and the Volunteers in Service of America, the domestic analogue of the Peace Corps. As mentioned earlier, Head Start was invented 6 months after enactment of the act, as Sargent Shriver, director of the Office of Economic Opportunity, and his associates refined the concept of community action in hopes of developing both a more comprehensive program and one that would show quick results. To this end, they introduced the idea of directing community action efforts to a variety of groups, including preschool children. Several individuals, including many who played key roles in developing the policies and programs of the War on Poverty, have written their personal accounts of the events surrounding the creation of Head Start (see, e.g., Levine, 1970; Moynihan, 1969a; Steiner, 1976; Sundquist, 1968; Zigler & Valentine, 1979; the last cited is the most detailed of all the historical accounts).

Shriver put the actual design of Head Start into the hands of a committee of child development experts headed by Robert Cooke, the pediatrician-in-chief at Johns Hopkins Hospital (Zigler & Anderson, 1979). This committee made its final recommendations for Head Start in a memorandum from Cooke to Shriver on February 19, 1965 (Cooke, 1965/1972), in which it was argued that "there is considerable evidence that the early years of childhood are the most critical point in the poverty cycle. . . . Within recent years there has been experimentation and research designed to improve opportunities for the child of poverty." The planners cautioned, however, that "while much of this work is not yet complete there is adequate evidence to support the view that special programs can be devised for these four and five year olds which will improve both the child's opportunities and achievements" (Cooke, 1965/1972). The planners emphasized that they intended Head Start to be a comprehensive program "*involving activities generally associated with the fields of health, social services, and education*" (Cooke, 1965/1972; emphasis in the original). A comprehensive preschool program for children was unknown before Head Start. The attempt to reach the whole child was based on the recognition that the family, rather than the school, is the ultimate source of the child's values and behavior.

Even more revolutionary was the idea that poor and ethnic and racial minority parents should participate in preschool intervention programs, both on administrative policy committees and in the classroom. The idea was very much in accord, however, with the community-action philosophy of the designers of the War on Poverty programs (see Levine, 1970; Moynihan, 1969a). This philosophy of "maximum feasible participation" saw the poor and ethnic and racial minority families not as passive recipients of services but as active participants and decision makers. Indeed, with the Economic Opportunity Act, Congress had instructed the Office of Economic Opportunity to rely on community involvement. Although insistence on community involvement was not a completely new concept in U.S. federal policy toward children—it had been part of the federally funded early-education and day-care centers administered by the Works Project Administration and by the Federal Works Administration during the Great Depression and World War II (see Ross, 1979)—for the first time, in 1964, community involvement meant "the maximum feasible participation of residents of the areas and members of the groups served" (U.S. Congress, 1964, cited in Ross, 1979, p. 38). The emphasis on local initiative no doubt results in varied perceptions and interpretations of the goal and objectives of Head Start and in varied emphases in their implementation (Laosa, 1982b; Royster, Larson, Ferb, Fosburg, Nauta, Nelson, & Takata, 1978; White, 1973).

Although begun as a summer program, Head Start quickly expanded to year-round operation. By 1980, 15 years after its inception, Head Start had served over 7.5 million economically disadvantaged children and their families at a cost of $6.5 billion. Head Start continues to serve over 375,000 children a year in over 1,000 communities nationwide; the Head Start budget for 1980 was $735 million (Calhoun & Collins, 1981; *Head Start in the 1980s*, 1980; U.S. Bureau of the Census, 1982e).

What is the ethnic and racial composition of the population served by Head Start? The results of a national survey of Head Start programs answer this question (Royster et al., 1978). Slightly over half the children in Head Start were Black (55.3%), about one-quarter were White, 15.3% were Hispanic, and 10% were of other ethnic groups. Thus, the percentages of Black and Hispanic children in Head Start are twice as high as their respective proportions in the U.S. poverty-level population; conversely, the percentage of White children was approximately half their proportion in the poverty population. The results of the survey illustrate that public policies toward children over the past 2 decades have indeed defined the needs of the nation's children and families by poverty status, focusing attention on the children and families of the ethnic and racial groups that are overrepresented among the poor.

It is worth noting, however, that the ethnic composition of the Head Start staff did not match the ethnic composition of the children served. Non-Hispanic Whites were overrepresented among supervisory staff, teachers, and aides. In contrast, Blacks were underrepresented among the supervisory staff; and Hispanics, Asians, and American Indians were underrepresented in all three staff categories (Royster et al., 1978). A similar mismatch between the ethnic composition of the staff and that of the children served has been observed in Title I programs of the Elementary and Secondary Education Act, where, among teachers, non-Hispanic Whites were overrepresented and Blacks, Hispanics, and American Indians were underrepresented (National Institute of Education, 1976). Given such underrepresentation of some ethnic and racial groups among the staff, one cannot help but wonder about the extent to which the concept of "maximum feasible participation" has been implemented.

ELEMENTARY AND SECONDARY EDUCATION ACT

Capitalizing on the success of the 1964 Civil Rights and Economic Opportunity acts, President Johnson sent his historic Elementary and Secondary Education Bill to the Congress in January 1965. Following its speedy enactment, Johnson, with typical fervor, underscored the significance of the new legislation with such statements as, "I think Congress has passed the most significant education bill in the history of the Congress. We have made a new commitment to quality and to equality in the education of our young people" (cited in Hughes & Hughes, 1972, p. 13).

Indeed, the Elementary and Secondary Education Act of 1965 represented the largest single commitment to improving the education of children from poverty backgrounds. By establishing a program providing compensatory educational expenditures for children from low-income families nationwide, it broke the long tradition of opposition to federal educational support. The massive size of the program is indicated by the fact that its principal component, Title I, received over $12 billion in appropriations over the first decade, beginning with about $960 million in 1966 and rising to approximately $1.8 billion in 1973 (Levin, 1977).

And Title I indeed was of particular relevance to children of poor and minority families; it emerged as the educational component of the opportunity strategy. Under it, funds were allocated to the states according to their numbers of children from low-income families. Both states and local educational agencies were given a great deal of discretion in how the funds were spent. Title I guidelines did require, however, that the funds be used to supplement support that would normally be spent on disadvantaged children and that spending plans be approved by Title I advisory committees that were representative of the local communities served (Levin, 1977). The most common spending strategies were those reducing class size and providing more remedial teachers and other specialized personnel, such as psychologists, counselors, and curriculum consultants; also common were teacher training and the use of new curricula for disadvantaged children. But as Levin (1977) points out, the diversity of local programs makes any generalization about Title I programs impossible. Many descriptions can be found of particular approaches to compensatory education that were adopted under the Title I rubric (see, e.g., Beck & Saxe, 1965; Gordon & Wilkerson, 1966; National Institute of Education, 1976; Passow, 1972).

Although Title I projects typically stated a number of educational objectives, the most common one was to raise the academic performance of disadvantaged students in cognitive subjects. Accordingly, the largest portions of Title I budgets were allocated to academic instruction in reading, mathematics, and similar subjects. Health and nutritional services were also eligible for support under Title I; however, only about 5% of the funds were thus allocated (Wargo et al., 1972, cited in Levin, 1977; see also National Institute of Education, 1976). The heavy emphasis on cognitive learning was, as Levin (1977, p. 135) observes, apparently a response to the concern with relatively low scholastic achievement among pupils from low-income backgrounds and the tacit assumption that improvements in cognitive skills would significantly improve the "life chances" of the youngsters.

Other portions of the Elementary and Secondary Education Act also had implications for low-income children, although not to the degree that Title I did. Title II of the act provided library resources, textbooks, and other instructional materials for schools; the allocations would be made on the basis of relative need of children and teachers. Title III created supplementary educational centers and services, such as teacher-training television networks. Title IV was designed to support educational research and training with some attention to the needs of disadvantaged youth. In 1968 the act was amended to provide special funds for bilingual education under Title VII. Because many children who speak a language other than English in the home are also from low-income backgrounds, bilingual education could also be considered an antipoverty program. (Bilingual education and other, related policies are examined in greater detail later in this chapter.) Another amendment of the Elementary and Secondary Education Act was Title VIII, which provided assistance to schools to reduce student dropout in low-income, high-dropout areas (Levin, 1977).

Although the Elementary and Secondary Education Act of 1965 was the major piece of legislation providing compensatory services for disadvantaged children, a number of other programs for students from poverty backgrounds were initiated or expanded during the decade, including Upward Bound, the School Lunch Program, the Emergency School Aid Act, the Vocational Education Act, the National Teacher Corps, the Neighborhood Youth Corps, and the Job Corps. In addition, legislation such as the Higher Education Act, the Adult Education Act, and the Manpower Development Training Act, and several programs of the Economic Opportunity Act other than those already mentioned, provided training and educational opportunities for adults (for a description of these programs see, e.g., Levin, 1977).

Let us now examine the intellectual assumptions and theoretical premises guiding the policy initiatives behind the programs we have just reviewed.

PREMISES OF THE NEW ERA OF POLICIES

Each policy initiative undertaken in the United States on behalf of children has reflected prevalent views regarding (*a*) the nature of childhood itself, (*b*) society's function of encouraging what are considered appropriate modes of child rearing, and (*c*) the causes of the problems that the policy seeks to solve. The policies and programs initiated on behalf of children as part of the War on Poverty were predicated largely on great hopes that education, especially early education, would somehow break the "cycle of poverty" by "striking at its roots." The interlocking assumptions supporting these hopes can be found in a staff memorandum of President Kennedy's Council of Economic Advisors. Indeed, the Kennedy administration had laid the groundwork for the children's policies of the Great Society by initiating the first, tentative efforts of the federal government to involve itself with the question of the life-style of the lower-class person. The council's staff memorandum, prepared only weeks before President Kennedy's assassination in 1963, spelled out the anticipated strategy. The memorandum, cited by Moynihan (1969b, p. 9) in a paper sardonically titled "The Professors and the Poor," read in part:

The Poverty Cycle

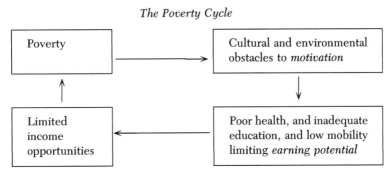

The sources of poverty are not listed in chronological sequence. The vicious cycle, in which poverty breeds poverty, occurs through time, and transmits its effects from one generation to another. There is no beginning to the cycle, no end. There is, therefore, no one "right" place to break into it: increasing opportunities may help little if health, educational attainments and motivation are unsuitable; making more education available may bear little fruit unless additional employment opportunities exist; altering adverse environmental factors may not be feasible or effective unless access to education and ultimately job opportunities is enhanced.

Programs to attack each of the three principal stages in the poverty cycle may be directed at one or more of three levels: (1) *prevent* the problem from developing, (2) *rehabilitate* the person who has been hurt, and (3) *ameliorate* the difficulties of persons for whom prevention or rehabilitation are not feasible. Each type of "treatment" is associated generally with a separate stage in the life cycle. Prevention of poverty calls for attention principally to youngsters (and to their parents, insofar as parents' attitudes and values affect the children). Rehabilitation of those missed by preventive efforts, or for whom these efforts were ineffective, seems best designed for adults in their productive work years. Amelioration of poverty seems called for in the case of the aged, the physically and mentally disabled, and those for whom prevention and rehabilitation are ineffective.

This theme, proposed by members of the Kennedy administration, was attractive to the New Deal, populistic style of the new president, Lyndon B. Johnson, who, in the aftermath of the Kennedy assassination, directed that planning of the poverty program receive administrative priority (Levine, 1970; Moynihan, 1969b). The survivors of Kennedy's thousand days threw themselves into this effort. In his State of the Union Message of 1964, Johnson set the dominant theme of his domestic policies: "This administration today, here and now, declares unconditional war on poverty in America."

The designers of its philosophy and enabling legislation had to determine the best means of attaining this stated goal. Two strategies offered themselves (Hughes & Hughes, 1972). One was to deal with the consequences, or symptoms, of the simple lack of money through a massive, straightforward, across-the-board welfare program. It was argued, however, that welfare programs alone had never produced any marked incentive, or opportunities, for their beneficiaries to move up the socioeconomic ladder. Thus, the other strategy—and a new one of the times—was to deal with the root causes of poverty: the lack of self-realization or, more specifically, the lack of opportunity for self-realization because of discrimination and deprivation. This strategy addressed more than the economic aspect alone. Within the latter strategy—chosen by Sargent Shriver and his codesigners in 1964 as the means to overcome poverty and unequal opportunity—education, through the opportunities it could provide, was perceived as the principal vehicle by which the poor could achieve self-realization (Hughes & Hughes, 1972; Levine, 1970). Education and training, and particularly early-childhood education, became the principal strategy for "striking at the roots of poverty."

EARLY-CHILDHOOD INTERVENTION AND COMPENSATORY EDUCATION

The assumptions underlying the domestic policies of Johnson's Great Society programs can be articulated graphically, in slightly more detail than the staff memorandum of Kennedy's Council of Economic Advisors, as Gallagher, Haskins, and Farran (1979) have done—see Figure 1. Each arrow represents an assumed causal relationship between variables. The principal preventive strategy, often referred to as "striking at the roots of poverty," was to break the "cycle of poverty" that perpetuates low income by educational intervention during early childhood. Educational programs aimed at young children were to compensate for a deprivation or paucity of childhood experiences because of a deficient home environment (Deutsch, 1967; Riessman, 1962). The preschool programs would give adequate skills at school entry, which in turn would lead to successful school performance and perhaps even college attendance, which in turn would lead to better jobs and more income.

Traditionally, in the United States, schools have been viewed as an avenue of social mobility for children of poor and immigrant families. Compensatory education was intended to make that avenue more accessible to those who had been excluded from using it successfully. Because,

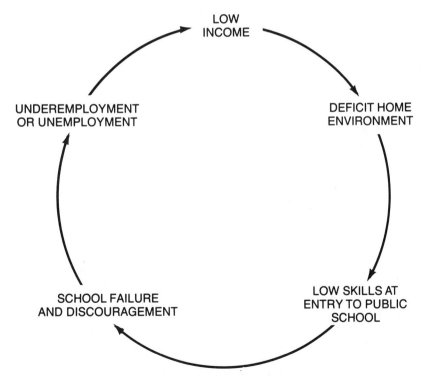

FIG. 1.—Assumed cycle underlying the policies and programs on behalf of children during the past 2 decades. (Adapted from Gallagher et al., 1979.)

contrary to the traditional expectations, there were inequalities in the extent to which different ethnic, racial, and socioeconomic groups benefited from schooling in later grades, early-childhood education was provided as compensation, social parity being seen as the ultimate aim. The expectations of the success of early-childhood education programs—where educational programs at later stages had been failing—were based on changing views of learning and developmental theories; it was believed that efforts aimed at educating younger children might have greater long-range consequences than comparable efforts with older children (Spodek & Walberg, 1977).

The early years, especially those in the lives of children of the poor and of certain ethnic and racial groups, were clearly spotlighted as the new frontier in education. Early-childhood intervention was seen as having an unlimited potential not only for breaking the cycle of poverty, but also as a possibility for forging revolutionary changes in the entire educational system (Akers, 1972). Child psychologists, early-childhood educators, and pediatricians were ready and eager to respond to the challenges presented by the political leaders of the emerging era—perhaps too eager, indeed, given that the demand for professional knowledge and scientific expertise often greatly exceeded the available supply. "Placed in the uncomfortable role of experts without expertise," wrote Harvard psychologist Sheldon H. White at the time, "we are all in the business of trying to supply educated guesses about the nature of children's cognitive development" (1968, p. 204). For many of the questions there were simply no answers that could be derived unequivocally from the available scientific evidence. Indeed, the newly launched programs created new needs for understanding individual development.

The provision of unprecedented federal funds facilitated the "pioneering" movement in early-childhood education. As we have seen, in addition to those moneys available for Project Head Start, even greater funds for compensatory programs came from a variety of titles of the Elementary and Secondary Education Act. (For a listing of federal programs for research on and services for young children see White, 1973, vol. 3, app. IIIb.) Throughout the country, research-and-development centers were established as funds for such activities flowed in a seemingly endless stream into universities and other organizations, some of them created specifically to meet the new demand for research, program design, and evaluation. The child development research community was fully embarked on the task of finding out more about the nature of the learning process, what ethnic and racial minority children knew, what they needed to know, how they could learn what White middle-class children knew, and the optimum time for learning it.

Thus, compensatory education, conceived and launched in the 1960s, was an attempt to remedy the poor academic achievement of low-income and ethnic and racial minority children, to enable them to rise from their parents' social class. Compensatory education was based on the premise that there was some deficiency in these children, their families, and their cultures that had to be corrected (Laosa, 1977d). Preschools (through, e.g., Head Start) and schools (through, e.g., the Elementary and Secondary Education Act Title I programs and Follow Through) were designated as the agents of change responsible for exposing these children to a set of experiences that their "culturally deprived" families were unable to provide. The minority child would participate in school activities designed to foster the development of intellectual skills and attitudes that enabled the typical child from a middle-class family to attain academic success. According to this reasoning, once the poor and ethnic and racial minorities were skilled and educated, they could achieve middle-class economic and social status and thus break out of the "cycle of poverty" (Laosa, 1983). Various models for preschool and primary education were developed and implemented, each with different emphases and based on different theoretical frameworks. (For examples of some specific programs see Maccoby & Zellner, 1970.)

Despite their variety, compensatory programs may be classified, as Getzels (1968) does, into three broad categories. In one, the predominant assumption, explicit or implicit, is that the observed deficiencies of the "culturally deprived" child are more superficial than fundamental—the differences are in quantity rather than in kind—and the preschool experiences that are needed are *supplementary*; from this point of view, if a nursery or preschool activity is good for the middle-class child, it is also good (if perhaps at some simpler level) for the lower-class child. In the second, the assumption is that the significant deficiencies reside in unfamiliarity with school-related objects and activities—say, pencils, books, the use of crayons, following directions—and the preschool experiences the "culturally deprived" child needs are predominantly *academic-preparatory*. In the third, the assumption is that because of powerful environmental effects, the "culturally deprived" child becomes fundamentally different in self-concept, language, values, and perceptual process; from this point of view neither the supplementary nor the preparatory activities in themselves are sufficient: what is required are specialized programs that will *counteract* the deleterious (pathological) environmental effects (Getzels, 1968). Compensatory education programs generally have in common a premise that the child is suffering from a deficit or social or cultural pathology that should be remedied through professional intervention. Later in this chapter I examine these premises and resulting intervention approaches in greater detail and discuss alternative viewpoints that challenge them.

FAMILY INTERVENTION

In the 1970s parent education came to replace compensatory education as the popular strategy for social and economic reform (Schlossman, 1978). National statistics were showing alarming rates of divorce, child neglect, teenage drug and alcohol abuse, runaway children, teenage pregnancy, and other symptoms of family disorder. A spate of reports by social scientists, study groups, and commissions on the state of the American family began appearing (e.g., Family Impact Seminar, 1977; Keniston & Carnegie Council on Children, 1977; Lasch, 1977; National Research Council, 1976; Vaughan & Brazelton, 1976). From various quarters could be heard calls for the formulation of a national policy dedicated to reverse these trends and to shore up family life (Steiner, 1981). Family dysfunction became a public policy issue, in part because increasing numbers of White middle-class families began to realize that problems hitherto attributed to conditions surrounding poor and non-White families were confronting them. A general unease about family stability began to pervade U.S. society, and government increasingly was called on to intervene on behalf of the "troubled" and "endangered" family.

President Richard Nixon, in his 1969 welfare-reform message to Congress, described his new family assistance plan as rejecting "a policy that undermines family life." Besides increasing the will to work, the plan would result in "the survival of more marriages, the greater stability of families" (cited in Steiner, 1981, p. 200). Although Nixon's family assistance plan lost, a coalition of civil rights and women's groups advanced a child development program as a new initiative in family policy. The bill—Senator Walter F. Mondale's Comprehensive Child Development Act of 1971—passed the Congress but was vetoed by President Nixon, who couched his action as a defense of "family-centered" child rearing over the bill's "communal approaches" (Mondale, 1973; Steiner, 1981).

Earlier, during the Johnson administration, Daniel P. Moynihan, then assistant secretary of labor for policy planning and research, had prepared a report that proclaimed the Black family to be "in the deepest trouble" and referred to its weakness as a "tangle of pathology" (U.S. Department of Labor, 1965, pp. 4, 30). In a speech delivered at Howard University—a speech drafted by Moynihan and Richard N. Goodwin—President Johnson adopted Moynihan's position about the central importance of family stability:

The family is the cornerstone of our society. More than any other force it shapes the attitudes, the hopes, the ambitions, and the values of the child. When the family collapses it is the children that are usually damaged. When it happens on a massive scale the community itself is crippled.

So, unless we work to strengthen the family, to create conditions under which most parents will stay together—all the rest: schools and playgrounds, public assistance and private concern, will never be enough to cut completely the circle of despair and deprivation. [Lyndon B. Johnson, 1965, cited in Rainwater & Yancey, 1967, p. 130]

These suggestions that strengthening the family is a precondition for the success of related social policies, propounded within the context of a civil rights initiative, were interpreted by some Black activists and some Black intellectuals as implying a collective abnormality among Black families (Hall & Freedle, 1975; Hill, 1972; McAdoo, 1981). Indeed, the social policy proposals in the Moynihan report, entitled *The Negro Family: The Case for National Action*, were based on the conclusion that the Black community was characterized by broken families, illegitimacy, matriarchy, economic dependency, failure to pass armed-forces entrance tests, delinquency, and crime. The report attributed these problems to a supposedly broken and unstable Black family. Moynihan, having found a "tangle of pathology," called for policies to cure the pathological Black family. Black groups denied that the Black family was pathological and called for equal opportunity and job creation as their policy priorities and for research that would focus on the strengths of Black families. However, following the trend set by the Moynihan report, policymakers and social and behavioral scientists—the vast majority of whom were non-Hispanic White—generally emphasized a perspective that viewed Black and other non-White families as not only deficient (e.g., Riessman, 1962) but frequently also socially pathological.

Interest in family policy escalated in the mid-1970s when Jimmy Carter, first as presidential nominee and then as president, expressed concern about a perceived erosion and weakening of families. "There can be no more urgent priority for the next administration," Carter said 3 months before his election, "than to see that every decision our government makes is designed to honor and support and strengthen the American family. . . . We need a government that thinks about the American family and cares about the American family and makes its every decision with the intent of strengthening the family." Two months later, Carter's approach seemed no less aggressive: "I believe that government ought to do everything it can to strengthen the American family because weak families mean more government" (cited in Steiner, 1981, p. 14). He appointed A. Sidney

Johnson III, director of the Family Impact Seminar and former staff director of Mondale's Senate Subcommittee on Children and Youth, as a special adviser to help him develop a "pro-family policy." Moreover, the new president asserted in his inaugural address that strengthening the family would be an important administration goal. Apparently stimulated by the positive reaction to the family issue that he raised during his campaign, President Carter early in his administration gave families formal recognition as a national and government concern. When the Department of Health, Education, and Welfare was reorganized, the Office of Child Development was renamed the Administration for Children, Youth, and Families (ACYF). About 2 years later, an Office for Families was created within ACYF to focus attention on the impact that federal policies and programs have on families and to examine selected policies to determine how they help or hurt families (Steiner, 1981, pp. 211–212). The interest in family issues culminated in the first White House Conference on Families; in fact, three White House Conferences on Families were held in 1980 in Baltimore, Minneapolis, and Los Angeles.

President Carter, on receiving the White House Conference report, expressed his "determination" that its recommendations "will lead to real improvements in policies and programs to strengthen and support the American family as an institution" (White House Conference on Families, 1980a, p. 4). Among the issues raised at the conference were concerns related to ethnic and racial diversity and equality of opportunity. In his "Message from the Chair," Jim Guy Tucker, the conference chair, stated, "We've learned that our families are enormously diverse—regionally, racially, ethnically and structurally. Discrimination and poverty intensify the pressures facing families, but all families are finding it more difficult to cope with contemporary challenges" (White House Conference on Families, 1980a, p. 9). At the conference various ethnic and racial groups were represented. Although on many issues there was consensus across ethnic and racial lines, there was diversity in how different groups ordered their priorities and in how they viewed the recommendations. Let us examine the recommendations given by the Black, Hispanic, American Indian, and Asian American delegates, published in the Conference Summary Report (White House Conference on Families, 1980a).

Black delegates.—As a group Black delegates gave strong, consistent support to recommendations addressing major economic issues. At Baltimore, for example, 11 of the top 12 proposals they approved reflected the intense concern within the Black community for improvement in the national economy. Full employment and more-sensitive personnel policies ranked highest among the 11 proposals. Similarly, 10 of the top 20 recommendations approved by Black delegates in Minneapolis called attention to the economic pressures felt by many Black families. In Los Angeles, full employment was ranked second, and equal pay for comparable work, fair employment practices, and support for the proposed Equal Rights Amendment to the Constitution were also among the top 10. Black delegates also gave high priority to recommendations dealing with substance abuse, comprehensive health care, family violence, handicapped persons, housing discrimination, and social services. Minority reports submitted by Black delegates stressed overcoming racism in government research practices and concerns about media programming.

Hispanic delegates.—The top priority recommendations of Hispanic delegates at all three conferences stressed the need for sensitive support services: bilingual and bicultural education, family support services, services for the elderly and the disabled, and family violence prevention. In Los Angeles, two specific Hispanic concerns were parental involvement in educational policy and recognition of ethnic and cultural diversity. The need to combat substance abuse ranked in the top five proposals adopted by the Hispanic delegates at the Baltimore and Minneapolis conferences. Hispanic minority reports submitted at each of the three conferences called for bilingual and bicultural education, better housing, and sensitivity to Hispanics in social services. They also stressed greater sensitivity in health services, employment of Hispanics, and support for the extended family.

American Indian delegates.—Among American Indians, recognition of cultural and ethnic diversity and provision for parental involvement in educational policy were strongly supported in Los Angeles; recommendations on substance abuse, family support services, foster-care reform, multicultural education, and family violence ranked very high in Baltimore; opposition to abortion, concern with the media, increased parental involvement in education and health programs, and support for disabled persons were high among the recommendations in Minneapolis. In Los Angeles, American Indian delegates gave strongest support to family impact analysis, family courts, and family-oriented personnel policies. Minority reports submitted on American Indian issues included concerns over tribal rights, funding of the Indian Child Welfare Act, and penalties for those who threaten Indian lands.

Asian American delegates.—Among the Asian American delegates, those at the Los Angeles and Minneapolis conferences emphasized economic issues, among them full employment, family-oriented personnel policies, employment discrimination, and the inequities of the marriage and inheritance taxes; those in Baltimore supported the education recommendations, such as funding and multiethnic, multicultural education. They also strongly supported recommendations regarding child-care needs and the special needs of the handicapped and their families. In general, minority reports submitted by Asian delegates included recommendations for multicultural and multilingual services and education, equal employment, affirmative action, and special programs for the elderly and immigrants.

Concerns about issues of ethnic and racial diversity also emerged at the National Research Forum on Family Issues. This forum, which brought together family researchers and scholars, was one of the activities organized to form the basis for discussion at the White House Conference on Families. In the forum panel on racial and ethnic diversity, for example, Juan Ramos, director of Special Mental Health Programs at the National Institute of Mental Health, voiced concern about the lack of racial and ethnic content in the curriculum taught to the "mental health core—psychiatrists, psychologists, social workers and psychiatric nurses—who too often know little or nothing about the culture and values of their patients and clients. Yet the assumption is made that they're skilled, expert and trained. This is nonsense, yet we continue to believe this is the right way" (White House Conference on Families, 1980a, p. 71). Another example was the forum panel on the impact of public and private institutional policies on families, in which I discussed the empirical and theoretical bases of parent-education programs aimed at ethnic and racial minority families (White House Conference on Families, 1980b, p. 5).

COMPENSATORY EDUCATION, PARENT EDUCATION,
CITIZEN PARTICIPATION

Thus, in the 1970s the focus of compensatory intervention programs had broadened to include the family as well as the child; family intervention in general, and parent education in particular, became major social policy issues (Chilman, 1973; Goodson & Hess, 1975; Harman & Brim, 1980; Laosa, 1983; Powell, 1982; Schlossman, 1976). This change was consistent not only with national concern about the welfare of families but also with research evidence suggesting that the effects of early-childhood interventions are strengthened when parents are involved (Bronfenbrenner, 1974). Parent involvement in education was motivated by yet another factor, one consistent with the community-action approach of the 1960s antipoverty programs: a desire to transform parents into agents of social change among disadvantaged segments of society (Knitzer, 1972; Moore & McKinley, 1972).

Parent-education policies are those that lead to interventions designed to give parents new competencies and new knowledge to guide their relationships with their children. They typically specify desirable parental behavior that, if acquired, supports the children's increased cognitive and social development. Thus, such interventions generally share similar goals of invoking the implicit standards of parental behavior considered most likely to produce well-adjusted, intelligent, and academically successful children.

Parent education, like compensatory education, was an attempt to remedy the poor academic achievement of low-income and minority children and thus enable them to move up from their parents' social class. How, then, do compensatory education and parent education differ? Compensatory education was child centered: the schools were to be the agents of change to compensate for the continuing "cultural deprivation" of the home. In parent education, by contrast, parents became the agents of change: poor and ethnic minority parents were to be taught childrearing techniques thought to produce children with the intellectual skills and attitudes necessary for successful academic competition with their middle-class peers. Although statements to the contrary are now fashionable among parent educators, a careful comparison of the two approaches yields profound similarities. Historically, both approaches are deeply rooted in the same conceptual foundation and the same research base. To lay these bare, let us now probe deeper into the alleged causes of the ethnic and racial inequalities that the children's policies of the 1960–1980 era sought to eliminate.

THE SOCIAL AND BEHAVIORAL SCIENCE BASES OF THE POLICIES

To wage a successful campaign against poverty and ethnic and racial inequality, it was necessary first to explain why poverty existed: hence, as we have seen, the theory of the poverty cycle, in which insufficient and inadequate schooling was seen as perhaps the most important causal link. It was assumed that poverty stemmed from lack of formal education or of the skills prerequisite to successful employment and upward occupational mobility. Thus, the strategy for eliminating income inequalities among ethnic and racial groups was to provide more and better education to the groups at the bottom. However, this rationale also required an explanation of why Blacks, Hispanics, and similarly placed ethnic and racial groups tended to be less educated and to have lower average academic performance than non-Hispanic Whites (Ogbu, 1978). Of the several explanations advanced, based to a large extent on the work of social and behavioral scientists, a few formed the conceptual basis of the policies and programs aimed at improving the academic performance of ethnic and racial minority children.

There is a long evolution of the ideologies and value orientations underlying these explanations. Indeed, throughout history, not only social and behavioral scientists but also social critics and reformers have advanced various points of view to explain the lower social position of disadvantaged groups and, more recently, the persistent presence of ethnic and racial inequalities in schooling and occupational attainment in the United States. The definitions of the problem and the explanations of the causes are varied, but they can be classified into five broad perspectives, or paradigms: (1) cultural deficit or pathology, (2) genetic inheritance, (3) institutional deficiency, (4) structural characteristics, and (5) developmental, socioculturally relativistic. Let us examine each in turn.

According to the *cultural-deficit or -pathology paradigm*, inequalities are caused by inherent flaws in the individual members, families, or cultures of the groups at the bottom of the socioeconomic order. Although the defect may be seen as deriving totally from environmental forces, it still is located within the subject. The solutions that flow from this paradigm involve attempts to change or rehabilitate these individuals, their families, or cultures. If any extrafamilial institutional modifications are thought necessary, they are seen only as a means to correct the diagnosed deficiencies or pathologies in the individual, family, or culture.

According to the *genetic-inheritance paradigm*, ethnic and racial inequalities in school achievement and occupational attainment are caused by hereditary differences in intellectual ability; members of certain ethnic and racial groups are thought to have an inferior genetic capacity for intellectual performance and thus to be less educable and incapable of playing societal roles similar to those occupied by members of the genetically superior races.

According to a third perspective, to which I refer for easy reference as the *institutional deficiency paradigm*, the causes of the problem lie in the extrafamilial societal institutions (e.g., the school, the business firm) in which the members of some ethnic and racial groups fail to achieve on par with members of the more successful groups. Something is alleged to be wrong with how these institutions are organized and run. Although the problem may be seen to result from differences or incompatibilities between the familial culture and that of the extrafamilial institution, the differences are not defined as deficiencies in the individual, family, or culture. Change is sought to make the extrafamilial institution more compatible with the sociocultural characteristics of the child and family. Thus, the solutions that flow from this paradigm call for reforms in the organization and operation of the extrafamilial institutions, such as changes in the school curriculum.

According to the *structural characteristics paradigm*, the causes of ethnic and racial inequalities are structural characteristics of the society. The society as a whole is seen to be rigidly organized into castelike groupings that historically exclude some ethnic and racial groups from social, political, and economic opportunities available to other groups. The solutions that stem from this paradigm call for a comprehensive national policy to eliminate the castelike barriers that keep certain ethnic and racial groups from full participation in all aspects of the society.

Most theories that have been advanced to explain ethnic and racial socioeconomic inequalities and that underlie proposals for children's policies aimed at reducing or eliminating such inequalities can be classified as belonging to one of the four paradigms described above. In addition, a few conceptualizations—most of them recent—represent attempts to synthesize aspects of two or more of these paradigms; among these evolving conceptualizations is the developmental, socioculturally relativistic paradigm.

According to the *developmental, socioculturally relativistic paradigm*, the development of social competence involves functional adaptations to the environment. Insofar as environments differ in the kinds of functional adaptations they require, a child's being successful in two different environments—say, the home and the school—depends on the degree of similarity between the two environments. This paradigm rejects the view that some social or cultural groups are superior to others. It calls for understanding behavior from the varied perspectives of the different groups. From it come proposals for developing biculturism and bilingualism, that is, the ability to function competently in different environments, and proposals for communication and mutual adaptation between the home and extrafamilial institutions (Laosa, 1979, 1982a).

Let us now review the major theories within each paradigm most frequently advanced by social and behavioral scientists to explain the lower social position in general and the school failure in particular of Blacks, Hispanics, and similarly placed ethnic and racial groups.

THE CULTURAL-DEFICIT OR -PATHOLOGY PARADIGM

It is beyond the scope of this chapter to trace the long philosophical evolution of the modern view that the social position of disadvantaged groups is attributable to mental or behavioral defects from which these groups suffer. The contemporary American manifestation of this paradigm has its immediate roots in the intellectual history of the past 30 years

(Valentine, 1968), and is prefigured in *The Negro Family in the United States* (1939) and other works by Black sociologist E. Franklin Frazier. Indeed, many of the writings within this paradigm published during the past 30 years are based on studies of low-income Black Americans. Chief among Frazier's contributions is the theme of disorganization in the life of the urban Black poor. Frazier described existence among the modern urban Black poor as a chaos infected with social pathologies brought about by the disintegration of Black folk culture under the impact of urbanization. Consider, for example, Frazier's description of family socialization:

> As the result of family disorganization a large proportion of Negro children and youth have not undergone the socialization which only the family can provide. The disorganized families have failed to provide for their emotional needs and have not provided the discipline and habits which are necessary for personality development. Because the disorganized family has failed in its function as a socializing agency, it has handicapped the children in their relations to the institutions in the community. Moreover, family disorganization has been partially responsible for a large amount of juvenile delinquency and adult crime among Negroes. [Frazier, 1950, pp. 276–277]

Anthropologist Charles A. Valentine, a stern critic of Frazier's ideas, has written: "In the end, the only cultural validity Frazier grants to modern Negro Americans is, as he puts it, 'taking on the [middle-class] folkways and mores of the white race' " (1968, p. 20).

Within the cultural-deficit or -pathology paradigm we find several theoretical variants. One, with direct roots in Frazier's work, holds that the family structures or cultures of certain groups are pathological and produce children with deviant personality characteristics. For example, Moynihan in his widely controversial report, *The Negro Family: The Case for National Action* (U.S. Department of Labor, 1965), saw generations of slavery and injustice as having brought about "deepseated structural distortions in the life of the Negro American" (p. 47); a "tangle of pathology" characterized the Black community, a pathology "capable of perpetuating itself without assistance from the white world" (p. 47). He believed that "at the heart of the deterioration of the fabric of Negro society is the deterioration of the Negro family" (p. 5). Indeed, the basis of the "tangle of pathology" was to be found in the Black family, which, "once or twice removed, . . . will be found to be the principal source of most of the aberrant, inadequate, or antisocial behavior that did not establish, but now serves to perpetuate the cycle of poverty and deprivation" (p. 30). Moynihan argued that the treatment of Blacks in U.S. society had created conditions in the Black community that made it all but impossible for the great majority of Blacks to take advantage of the new opportunities created by the government's antidiscriminatory actions, such as the Supreme Court decision in *Brown v. Board of Education*, the Civil Rights Act, and the Economic Opportunity Act.

A cultural-deficit or -pathology orientation can be found also in the writings of child development researchers. A large number of research studies of maternal behavior have been conducted over the past 20 years, largely in order to seek an explanation for the statistics documenting the poor school performance of many ethnic and racial minority children, especially Blacks (for a review see Laosa, 1981). The major impetus behind these researches can be found, however, in the policy initiatives that sought to remedy the situation reflected by these statistics. Most of these studies were conducted within the cultural-deficit or -pathology paradigm, as is exemplified by the inference made by Kamii and Radin (1967, pp. 308–309) from their data on maternal behavior in low-income Black families: "The influence techniques used by disadvantaged mothers may in part account for the lack of inner controls observed in school among lower-class children. . . . The lower-class Negro child, whose socioemotional needs are not met and who does not develop an emotional dependence on his mother, is known, in general, to fail to behave in accordance with society's norms."

A pathology approach is found also in much of the literature on Hispanic children and families. Indeed, throughout the history of the social and behavioral sciences in the United States, discussions of socialization in Hispanic families generally occur within a comparative model of European-descent and middle-class values, and often, a social pathology model. Much of the literature on Chicano families has relied on only a very few dimensions, which became the variables for explaining Chicano socialization and child development. Two such dimensions have been the stereotypical constructs "machismo" and "passivity." Hence, a rash of generalizations has placed "*the* Mexican-American family" in a perspective of cultural pathology.

A theoretical variant within the cultural-deficit or -pathology paradigm is the assumption that a subculture, the "culture of poverty," exists among the poor everywhere. This subculture, it is argued, is self-perpetuating and self-defeating, producing in its members a sense of resignation or fatalism and an inability to put off the satisfaction of immediate desires in order to plan for the future. These characteristics are viewed as leading to low educational motivation and, in turn, to inadequate preparation for an occupation—factors that perpetuate unemployment and poverty. For example, Oscar Lewis, who is generally regarded as the originator of this concept, has offered the following characterization (1966, p. 21): "[The culture of poverty] is both an adaptation and a reaction of the poor to their marginal position. . . . Once [it] has come into existence it tends to perpetuate itself. By the time slum children are six or seven they have usually absorbed the basic attitudes and values of their subculture. Thereafter they are psychologically unready to take full advantage of changing conditions or improving opportunities that may develop in their lifetime."

However, the theoretical variant of the cultural deficit or pathology paradigm that has had the most influence on social policies toward children over the past 2 decades is based on the concept of "cultural deprivation" (Riessman, 1962). Most proponents of this concept point not to the school or to society but to the child, family, or culture as the principal explanation of the school failure. There are two versions of the cultural-deprivation theory. One holds that children of the traditionally excluded ethnic and racial groups fail in public schools because of retarded cognitive, linguistic, social, or personality development; the other holds that such children fail in school because they grow up in cultures that are different from and inferior to the European-descent "mainstream" middle-class culture on which public education is based. The cultural deprivation theory was expounded in Basil Bernstein's earlier writings (1961). Indeed, much of the research that shaped the conceptual basis for policy and programs in both compensatory education and parent education drew heavily from Bernstein's theoretical formulations.

In contrast to those who sought a biological explanation of social class and ethnic group differences in school performance, Bernstein sought environmental explanations (see Ginsburg, 1972). He proposed that middle- and lower-class parents employ different child-rearing techniques, which result in different patterns of language and thought. In Bernstein's (1961) view, middle-class life is oriented toward the values of order, rationality, stability, planning for long-range goals, and the control of emotion. The child in a middle-class home is encouraged to verbalize emotions, to control them, and to try to understand them rationally. Middle-class parents tend to impose discipline by verbal means rather than physical punishment, to explain why an act was an infraction and why it must be disciplined, and to explore the child's motivation. This style of interaction is viewed as fostering the development of a language that is complex and can carry subtle shades of meaning. Through exposure to this kind of language—which Bernstein called an "elaborated code"—and to these child-rearing practices, the middle-class child is thought to develop superior abilities to reason abstractly and to engage in complex, subtle intellectual activity.

In contrast, Bernstein viewed lower-class socialization and its results as almost the opposite. He theorized that lower-class parents do not present the child with an ordered, planned, and rational system of living; moreover, they administer discipline arbitrarily, and their expression is emotional, direct, and often volatile. Their language he considered to be ill-suited for the expression of subtle shades of meaning or the elaboration of thought. Consequently, in Bernstein's view, the lower-class child is not faced with the problem of comprehending complex chains of reasoning involving relations and abstract categories. Thus, the lower-class child is thought to acquire a language that is considered to be in many respects deficient—a language that, being a poor vehicle for thought, limits the generality and abstraction of thought, resulting in a "low level of conceptualization, an orientation to a low order of causality, a disinterest in processes, a preference to be aroused by, and respond to, that which is immediately given; . . . this partly conditions the intensity and extent of curiosity. . . . There will be a tendency to accept and respond to an authority that inheres in the form of the social relationships, rather than in reasoned or logical principles" (Bernstein, 1961, pp. 302–303). These alleged characteristics have been presumed to inhibit the lower-class child's ability to learn from the environment.

Many child development scientists whose research-and-development work involved low-income and minority populations found Bernstein's views highly persuasive and were influenced by them. Thus, for example, Hess and Shipman (1968, p. 103) concluded from their observations of maternal teaching behavior in Black families of varied socioeconomic levels, "The cognitive environment of the culturally disadvantaged child is one in which behavior is controlled by imperatives rather than by attention to the individual characteristics of a specific situation, and one in which behavior is neither mediated by verbal cues which offer opportunities for using language as a tool for labeling, ordering, and manipulating stimuli in the environment, nor mediated by teaching that relates events to one another and the present to the future. The meaning of deprivation would thus seem to be a deprivation of meaning in the early cognitive relationships between mother and child." Similarly, Bee, Van Egeren, Streissguth, Nyman, and Leckie (1969, pp. 733–734) interpreted their data on maternal teaching behavior thus: "Our findings, as those of Hess and Shipman, provide evidence of an impoverished language environment and ineffectual teaching strategies experienced by the lower-class child. Such a child may learn a good deal about what *not* to do, or at least about global rules of conduct, but he may not be well equipped with the language tools or learning sets required for a systematic approach to the analysis of problems. He has not, judging from our results, been encouraged to learn general techniques of problem solving, and he has not been exposed to the highly differentiated language structure that is most suitable for verbally mediated analysis of the environment."

The researchers reviewed above, and others with similar views, intended that their work should have humane and progressive results in public understanding, policymaking, and community programs. Thus, for example, after concluding from their data that the learning styles and information-processing strategies acquired through interaction with the mother may limit the child's potential mental growth, Hess and Shipman called for new programs to "*resocialize* or *reeducate* the child toward more effective cognitive strategies" (1968, p. 103). Other investigators recommended that programs be designed to effect permanent changes in the perceived cause of the lower-class and ethnic and racial minority child's lack of success in school: the behavior of poor and ethnic and racial minority mothers (fathers were assumed to be absent). For example, Kamii and Radin concluded from their data that "compensatory education must include an attempt to alter the socialization practices of disadvantaged mothers" (1967, p. 309).

Although certainly well intended, the work of these and other social and behavioral science researchers was seen by some, especially by members of the minority groups that were studied, as reinforcing popular misconceptions and stereotypes on the basis of rather limited research. Not only the researchers' interpretations of the data but also the designs of their studies—including their selection of variables—were cast within the cultural-deficit or -pathology paradigm, then a popular conceptual framework for research and program design in child development and education. (For a review and critique of this research see Laosa, 1981.)

Today, a growing minority of scholars question the adequacy of the assumptions underlying this paradigm and the concepts, theories, and methods that emanate from it. Such critics have considered much of the research on and program design for ethnic and racial minority and low-income populations to have a European-derived, middle-class bias that prejudices our understanding of those groups. Because those who employ a premise of cultural deficit or pathology, or any other aggressively ethnocentric framework, are predisposed to identify order with conformity to the norms of their own group, they will be unable to find another kind of social organization or cultural pattern in their observations of other ethnic and racial groups (Baratz & Baratz, 1970; Hill, 1972; Laosa, 1981; Nobles, 1978).

Policies and practices based on the cultural-deficit or -pathology paradigm are seen by some as tacit attempts to melt away sociocultural diversity by imposing one group's standard of parental behavior on others. The "melting pot" view of U.S. society expressed the expectation that all subcultures would become amalgamated into a new, superior culture. Critics of this view argue that such an outcome might not be healthy for certain groups (Laosa, 1974b), because amalgamation, if directed by a dominant class or group, would cause the influence of subcultures to dwindle, making one group's culture preponderant. Critics note that almost all of the data have been collected in studies designed and executed by European-descent, middle-class researchers. The importance of this criticism is that not only the interpretation of results and the consequent policy recommendations but also the policy and research questions posed are likely to be influenced by the cultural value orientations of the investigator.

THE GENETIC-INHERITANCE PARADIGM

The genetic-inheritance paradigm comprises a set of theories that explains presumed defects in the mentality or behavior of disadvantaged racial or ethnic groups or social classes by postulating hereditary differences in intellectual ability. This view is based in part on the plethora of studies demonstrating ethnic and racial differences in measured intellectual performance. On reviewing more than 500 studies that had used 81 different tests of intellectual ability covering a period of 50 years, Shuey (1966) concluded that Blacks average about 1 standard deviation (that is, 15 IQ points) below Whites on tests of intellectual or academic aptitude. Other studies have shown that other groups (e.g., low-income Puerto Ricans and Chicanos) also score below average.

Throughout history, much theorizing about individual and group differences has centered on whether heredity or environment is the greater determinant of ability. Both sides in the controversy have supported their positions with collections of evidence. This controversy again became salient among research scientists during the 1960s and emerged in bitter public debates regarding social policies toward children. In 1966 James Coleman and others published the first analysis of data from the Equality of Educational Opportunity Survey (Coleman et al., 1966). The analysis suggested that the differences in intellectual and academic performance between Blacks and non-Hispanic Whites were caused more by differences in home environments than by differences in school environments—that the schools did not make much difference in the intellectual or academic performance of children. If the cause of the differences was not in the school, where else could it be? Some highly publicized papers (Herrnstein, 1971; Jensen, 1969) suggested the possibility that heredity and genetic makeup, rather than psychosocial environmental factors, were preponderant determinants of the observed differences in the average scores of children from non-Hispanic White and minority group backgrounds.

Much of the renewed interest in the nature-versus-nurture controversy originated with an article by Arthur Jensen of the University of California, Berkeley, in the winter 1969 issue of *Harvard Educational Review.* In "How Much Can We Boost IQ and Scholastic Achievement?" Jensen reviewed past research and discussed the relative influences of genetic inheritance and environment on IQ. His conclusions were generally interpreted to be that observed differences in mental-test performance are largely genetic in origin and that comparatively little can be done to reduce them through practicable educational and social reforms. A bitter controversy in professional journals and the mass media immediately followed the publication of Jensen's article. Princeton University professor Leon J. Kamin, in his book, *The Science and Politics of IQ* (1974, pp. 1–2), concisely summarized the bitter criticisms directed at the social and political consequences of standardized IQ testing:

> The I.Q. test in America, and the way in which we think about it, has been fostered by men committed to a particular social view. That view includes the belief that those on the bottom are genetically inferior victims of their own immutable defects. The consequence has been that the I.Q. test has served as an instrument of oppression against the poor—dressed in the trappings of science, rather than politics. The message of science is heard respectfully, particularly when the tidings it carries are soothing to the public conscience. There are few more soothing messages than those historically delivered by the I.Q. testers. The poor, the foreign-born, and racial minorities were shown to be stupid. They were shown to have been born that way. The underprivileged are today demonstrated to be ineducable, a message as soothing to the public purse as to the public conscience.

The matter of test bias became of central concern in the controversy. Many critics saw the genetic paradigm as indefensible in the light of strong allegations that there are sociocultural and linguistic biases inherent in many standardized tests that unfairly penalize persons from other than middle-class, White, English-speaking backgrounds. During the past decade, these allegations have formed the bases of a series of actions by the judicial, legislative, and executive branches of government and by professional associations and test-producing organizations. These actions, which I review later in this chapter, have exerted a profound influence on policies governing the psychological and educational measurement of ethnic, racial, and language minority children.

THE INSTITUTIONAL DEFICIENCY PARADIGM

Making up the institutional deficiency paradigm is a set of theories that explain the socioeconomic standing of disadvantaged ethnic and racial groups by blaming the schools. Although the idea that schools might contribute to the failure of some children is certainly not new, this explanation has gained increased attention from social scientists and reformers over the past 20 years (e.g., Baratz & Baratz, 1970; Cárdenas & Cárdenas, 1973; Laosa, 1977c; Leacock, 1969; Rist, 1970; Rosenthal & Jacobson, 1968; U.S. Commission on Civil Rights, 1971). Many critics have questioned the effectiveness of the traditional classroom arrangement.

Among the theoretical variants of the institutional deficiency paradigm is the Cárdenas-Cárdenas theory of incompatibilities, a conceptual framework for responding to the educational needs of Mexican American children (B. Cárdenas & J. A. Cárdenas, 1973; J. A. Cárdenas & B. Cárdenas, 1977; Cárdenas & Zamora, 1980). This theory attributes the school failure of Black, Mexican American, and economically disadvantaged children to "incompatibilities between the characteristics of minority children and the characteristics of a typical instructional program." Cárdenas and Cárdenas forcefully contend that "an instructional program developed for a white, Anglo Saxon, English-speaking middle class school population cannot be and is not adequate for a non-white, non-Anglo Saxon, non-English-speaking, or non-middle class population" (1977, p. 1). They group the incompatibilities into five categories—poverty, culture, language, mobility, and social perceptions. They exhort each school to develop a comprehensive educational plan to eliminate the incompatibilities by reforms in educational philosophy, school policy, curriculum, cocurricular activities, student services, staffing, community involvement, and evaluation. Such reforms would "change the instructional program to fit the child" (p. 11). Thus, proposed reforms that have flowed from the institutional deficiency paradigm include replacing the traditional school or classroom with alternative schools, open schools, performance-contract systems, bilingual or bidialectical instruction, multicultural education, and other alternative forms of education.

THE STRUCTURAL CHARACTERISTICS PARADIGM

To explain the lower average school achievement of children of socioeconomically disadvantaged ethnic and racial groups, theories that compose the structural characteristics paradigm emphasize the relationship between schooling and social structure. Such theories derive from

evidence that within the present structure of U.S. society, members of the
historically disadvantaged ethnic and racial groups who have nevertheless
acquired the requisite schooling traditionally have been denied equal
access to the more desirable social and occupational roles in society; thus,
they have not been permitted to advance to higher positions in life on the
basis of their education and abilities. From this evidential basis it is argued
that the poorer average school performance of these children is not itself
the central problem but an expression of a more fundamental one. In this
view the principal causes of these children's academic retardation are
threefold. First, because of the inferior social and economic status of
certain ethnic and racial groups, the schools give their children an inferior
education; second, the social structure incorporates castelike barriers prohibiting members of "outcaste" groups, such as Blacks and Hispanics, from
translating their academic skills into desirable jobs, income, and other
benefits available to the more privileged groups; third, as a result of both of
these conditions, children and parents in the excluded groups develop
attitudes and skills that are different from those of the more privileged
groups (i.e., the non-Hispanic White middle class). These "alternative"
attitudes and skills fostered in the family socialization of children in the
outcaste groups are functional and adaptive to their ascribed status as
outcastes but dysfunctional and maladaptive to achieving success as defined by the more privileged, dominant groups. This chain of causes
becomes a vicious cycle that keeps the outcaste groups in their inferior
position. Proponents of this paradigm include Richard H. de Lone (1979)
and John U. Ogbu (1974, 1978, 1981).

Proposals that stem from this paradigm call for the elimination of
castelike barriers as the only lasting solution to the problem of academic
retardation among ethnic and racial minority children. The predicted
outcome would be that Blacks, Hispanics, and similarly placed groups
could achieve the same desirable social, occupational, and economic positions as non-Hispanic Whites for their training and ability. For their part,
members of what were hitherto outcaste groups "would respond to their
new opportunities by persevering in their schoolwork and by developing
behavior patterns compatible with high academic achievement" (Ogbu,
1978, p. 360); as they found their scholastic efforts better rewarded by the
school (i.e., by a better and more equitable education) and by society (i.e,
by more equitable occupational and economic returns for schooling), they
would find schooling itself more rewarding. Such rewards and their prospects would lead to higher academic motivation and hence performance.
Policies that seek to change only school practices or family life, however
necessary, are seen as only auxiliary to the elimination of castelike barriers;

by themselves such policies could not eliminate the ethnic and racial inequalities in children's educational development.

THE DEVELOPMENTAL, SOCIOCULTURALLY RELATIVISTIC PARADIGM

A fifth paradigm combines aspects of two or more of the foregoing paradigms, recognizing that they identify potentially influential factors in children's development but that they may nevertheless be insufficient to explain children's development of social competence and the socioeconomic inequalities and other differences among ethnic groups. Such a paradigm I have proposed (Laosa, 1979): *the developmental, socioculturally relativistic paradigm.*

Briefly, according to this paradigm (Laosa, 1979), social competence involves functional adaptations to more than one environment. Insofar as different environments may demand different functional adaptations, a child's success in two different environments, for example, home and school, may depend on how much the characteristic demands of the two environments overlap.

According to this paradigm no societies or subcultures are superior to others. Thus, behavior must be understood in its own terms, in the context of the institutions, values, and systems of meaning of its particular culture. From this paradigm also would emanate proposals that children be exposed to experiences designed to develop biculturism (see Laosa, 1977a). Bicultural development requires nurturant and educationally appropriate exposure to two different cultural environments. Such exposure would result in the acquisition of two parallel sets of competencies, a set for each environment, and the ability to perform the "right" (successful) kinds of behavior in each environment.

Another reform that can emanate from the developmental, socioculturally relativistic paradigm is my recent proposal (Laosa, 1982a) calling for the home and the school to engage in a process of *mutual* adaptation to eliminate the incompatibilities between these two environments and to produce *articulated continuity* between them. The results of a series of recent studies that I have been conducting suggest that effective change must be a two-way, or dialectical, process that involves both the school and the home; the data point to some ways in which both the home and the school can contribute to an articulated continuity between them (Laosa, 1982a).

In sum, the retarded educational and economic development of Black, Hispanic, and similarly placed groups has been explained by means of five broad conceptual frameworks or paradigms: (1) the cultural-deficit or

-pathology paradigm, (2) the genetic-inheritance paradigm, (3) the institutional deficiency paradigm, (4) the structural characteristics paradigm, and (5) the developmental, socioculturally relativistic paradigm. Each paradigm offers a different perception of the nature and the causes of ethnic inequalities and therefore a different perspective on strategies for social change and for policy formulation. Historically, U.S. policies toward children in socioeconomically disadvantaged ethnic and racial groups have been based for the most part on assumptions and premises derived from the first two paradigms and have made very little use of proposals that logically flow from the other three paradigms.

In the sections that follow I examine two additional sets of policy initiatives with profound implications for the development of minority children: those regarding the provision of educational services for children whose home language is not English, and those regarding the psychological and educational assessment and classification of ethnic, racial, and language minority children. Like the policy initiatives of the early 1960s that I reviewed in the preceding sections, the more recent policy developments that I discuss in the sections that follow were aimed at increasing equality of opportunity for ethnic and racial minority children.

BILINGUAL EDUCATION

In many significant respects, language is an inherent aspect of ethnicity, and the U.S. population has always contained language minority groups. Indeed, today a large proportion of U.S. citizens have a home language other than English. In 1976, approximately 28 million persons (or one person in eight), including about 5 million school-age children (one in 10) had mother tongues other than English or lived in households in which languages other than English were spoken (National Center for Education Statistics, 1978). About two-thirds of all these persons and more than four-fifths of the school-age children were born in this country. A more recent survey, conducted by the U.S. Bureau of the Census in November 1979, indicated that among persons 14 years old and over, 32 million reported that a language other than English was spoken in their childhood homes (U.S. Bureau of the Census, 1982a). By far the most numerous U.S. language minority group consists of Spanish speakers; in 1976 they numbered 10.6 million, making up more than a third of all the language minority persons and 60% of the language minority school-age children (National Center for Education Statistics, 1978). Other language minority groups with substantial numbers are speakers of Italian, German, and various Asian languages.

Because a person may never have learned to speak his or her mother tongue (i.e., the language spoken at home when the person was a child), or may no longer speak a language spoken as a child, mother tongue might not be an accurate measure of the population's current language ability or usage. Thus, we also must examine the statistics on current language usage. These data, in a special report of the U.S. Bureau of the Census (1982a), indicate that 18 million persons aged 5 and over were reported as currently speaking a language other than English at home. (There may well have been additional speakers of languages other than English who only used the language someplace other than home; moreover, doubtless many who were able to speak a language other than English did not do so at home.) The numbers and percentages of persons speaking a language other than English at home are shown in Table 8, separately by language.

Spanish is, again, by far the most frequently spoken language other than English. Approximately one-half of those who speak a language other than English at home speak Spanish. Among children of elementary-school age, 1.8 million speak Spanish at home. The Spanish-speaking children constitute two-thirds of all children of this age who speak a language other than English and about 6% of all elementary-school-aged children.

TABLE 8

PERSONS 5 YEARS OLD AND OVER SPEAKING A LANGUAGE
OTHER THAN ENGLISH AT HOME IN THE UNITED STATES, BY LANGUAGE: 1979[a]

	Number of Persons (in Thousands)	Percent
Total persons in the U.S.	200,812	. . .
Persons speaking language other than English	17,985	100.0
Chinese	514	2.9
French	987	5.5
German	1,261	7.0
Greek	365	2.0
Italian	1,354	7.5
Japanese	265	1.5
Korean	191	1.1
Philippine languages	419	2.3
Polish	731	4.1
Portuguese	245	1.4
Spanish	8,768	48.8
Yiddish	234	1.3
Other languages[b]	2,651	14.7
Not reported	6,508	. . .

SOURCE.—U.S. Bureau of the Census, 1982a, Tables 5 and 6.
[a]Civilian noninstitutional population.
[b]No language included as "other" was spoken by 200,000 persons or more.

Language minority groups also differ dramatically in intragroup age distributions. For example, of those persons (5 years old and over) who speak Spanish at home, 79% are younger than 45 years of age. In contrast, of those who speak Yiddish at home, over 50% are older than 64 years of age (U.S. Bureau of the Census, 1982a).

Of special interest are the self-report data on the *ability* to speak English. Of the 18 million persons 5 years old and over who spoke a language other than English at home in 1979, 3.9 million (22%) were reported as not speaking English at all or speaking it "not well." Age differences among language groups are also evident in these data; that is, the proportion of those whose ability to speak English was limited or nil varied by age within languages. For example, of persons under 65 with limited or no ability to speak English, a clear majority spoke Spanish; in contrast, of those aged 65 and over, only 40% spoke Spanish. Differences among language groups in the relation between age and ability to speak English may reflect differences in the periods and levels of migration and in the extent of their exposure to the use of English (U.S. Bureau of the Census, 1982a).

Prior to the nineteenth century, non-English and bilingual instruction were not uncommon in many parts of North America. For example, during the 1770s there were German-speaking schools in Pennsylvania, Maryland, Virginia, and the Carolinas. In these schools, "instruction . . . was given in German, often to the exclusion of English" (Leibowitz, 1971, p. 6; see also Kloss, 1977). At the time that California became a state, 18% of all education in the state is estimated to have been private and Catholic; in these schools were mainly pupils of Spanish descent, who were taught in the Spanish language under the direction of the padres (Leibowitz, 1971). As late as 1884, a law was passed in New Mexico that recognized the public Spanish-language elementary schools: "Each of the voting precincts of a county shall be and constitute a school district . . . in which shall be taught orthography, reading, writing, arithmetic, . . . in either English or Spanish or both, as the directors may determine" (cited in Kloss, 1977, p. 134).

The nineteenth-century U.S. public school movement discouraged the preservation of languages other than English. Many state statutes were enacted that expressly forbade instruction in any language other than English. For example, in 1870 California passed a law requiring that "all schools shall be taught in the English language" (Cal. Stat., ch. 556, § 55 [1870], cited in Leibowitz, 1980, p. 4), as did New Mexico in 1891; in the latter state the law reflected a broader struggle over land that was developing between the non-Hispanic White settlers and the Mexican Americans (Leibowitz, 1980). In 1879 the off-reservation boarding schools were established, separating Indian children from their parents and imposing a ban on Indian language, customs, and dress (Leibowitz, 1980). These restrictive policies in education had parallels in other policies limiting the political, social, and economic rights of language minorities. English literacy requirements as a condition of voting and holding office, passed in over three-fourths of the states, limited access to the political arena; and statutes requiring English-language tests as a condition for entry into various occupations restricted social and economic access to the U.S. mainstream (Leibowitz, 1980).

There were, however, some non-English-speaking public schools during this period. Notable among these were the German-speaking schools. In response to the demands of German settlers, the Ohio legislature passed a law allowing German to be used as the language of instruction in the public schools in those districts where a large German population resided; in 1840 German-English public schools were introduced in Ohio (Kloss, 1977; Leibowitz, 1980). In general, however, the national policy of assimilation meant the repudiation of the native culture and language that the children of immigrants brought to U.S. schools. Moreover, with World War I came anti-German as well as general antiforeign sentiments and an end to national permissiveness regarding schooling in languages other than English. Laws were passed nationwide permitting only English as the language of instruction in U.S. public schools; in 1971 35 states still had English-only instruction laws (Leibowitz, 1971; Santiago, 1978).

In the 1960s there was a growing recognition that language minority children needed some manner of special assistance if they were to have an equal opportunity to succeed in school (U.S. Commission on Civil Rights, 1975). Where efforts were made to provide such assistance, they usually took the form of supplemental English language development, commonly known as the "English as a Second Language" (ESL) approach. For example, in its spring 1969 survey of education in the five southwestern states of Arizona, California, Colorado, New Mexico, and Texas, the U.S. Commission on Civil Rights (1972) found that although approximately 50% of Mexican American school children in the Southwest needed some form of language assistance, only 5.5% were enrolled in ESL programs, and even fewer (2.7%) were in bilingual education programs.

As we saw earlier, by 1960 the civil rights movement, gaining strength after World War II, was at flood tide. The federal executive and legislative branches had come out strongly for civil rights and focused on the deprivation suffered by ethnic minority groups. In addition to civil rights legislation, the 1964 Economic Opportunity Act and the 1965 Elementary and Secondary Education Act had focused on the poor and made education a matter of national policy and priority for all disadvantaged youth. With the wave of ethnic consciousness that accompanied the civil rights movement and social changes in the sixties, Spanish-speaking parents no longer felt constrained to remain mute or to soften their desire that the Spanish language be given a more meaningful role in their children's education (Leibowitz, 1980).

Although the history of public concern about language diversity in the United States extends back to colonial times (see Kloss, 1977), prior to 1968 the federal law was, with a few limited exceptions, silent on the special needs of limited- or non-English speakers. An important exception was the Migration and Refugee Assistance Act of 1962, which allocated funds for programs in the schools of Dade County (Miami), Florida. These programs were to help recently arrived Cuban refugees become proficient in English so that they could attend regular classes and follow the normal curriculum (González, 1982; Schneider, 1976). The success of these bilingual education programs soon attracted national attention. Josué M. González (1975, p. 10)—later appointed by President Jimmy Carter to head the U.S. Department of Education's Office of Bilingual Education and Minority Language Affairs—described the far-reaching influence of these programs on the federal role in policies toward language minority children:

> The Dade County experience was a clear indication that bilingual schooling was a viable concept. . . . The bilingual schools in Miami . . . became unofficial demonstration centers for the nation. Advocates [of bilingual education] from other Spanish-speaking areas made pilgrimages to Miami. . . . Observing instruction, they reviewed curriculum materials, and interviewed staff members. Then, they returned to their monolingual ambience and sought to persuade their respective institutions to move along similar paths.
>
> By 1967 when the U.S. Senate Subcommittee on Bilingual Education called for hearings on the question of a federal subsidy for bilingual education, an impressive array of documents and educational and civic leaders were on hand to present a convincing case: bilingual schooling could improve the Spanish-speaking child's chances of success in school but federal funding was necessary for the development of pilot programs to guarantee the development of adequate materials, personnel, and instructional techniques.

In 1968 the federal government for the first time, by its passage of the Bilingual Education Act (Title VII of the Elementary and Secondary Education Act), suggested the permissibility, even the desirability, of instruction in the native language. A 1967 Senate bill introduced by Senator Ralph Yarborough of Texas had directed itself to the Spanish-speaking only. In the House of Representatives at about the same time a number of similar bills advocating bilingual education were introduced, most notably by Representatives Augustus Hawkins and Edward Roybal of California and Jerome Sheuer of New York. The Hawkins-Roybal bill broadened the Yarborough bill to include assistance to the French-speaking as well, and the Scheuer bill authorized bilingual instruction for all children whose native tongues were not English (Leibowitz, 1980). The final 1968 law reflected the broader approach; its declaration of policy expressed the concerned recognition of Congress that children from homes in which the dominant language is not English have special needs:

DECLARATION OF POLICY

Sec. 702. In recognition of the special educational needs of the large numbers of children of limited English-speaking ability in the United States, Congress hereby declares it to be the policy of the United States to provide financial assistance to local educational agencies to develop and carry out new and imaginative elementary and secondary school programs designed to meet these special educational needs. For the purposes of this title, "children of limited English-speaking ability" means children who come from environments where the dominant language is other than English. [P.L. No. 90-247, Title VII, § 702, 20 U.S.C.A. 880b, 81 Stat. 816 (1968)]

Between 1969 and 1973, $117.9 million was expended under the 1968 Bilingual Education Act. Most of these funds went to support bilingual programs in elementary schools; 12% of the total was used for special bilingual education projects, including bilingual children's television programs, curriculum centers, and a dissemination center (U.S. Commission on Civil Rights, 1975, p. 171).

The 1968 Bilingual Education Act emphasized a set of poverty criteria whereby to be eligible children had to be of low-income families. The poverty criteria, according to the U.S. Commission on Civil Rights, prevented the act "from meeting the needs of large numbers of language minority children" (1975, p. 172). However, the act granted the U.S. Commissioner of Education some discretion in applying the poverty criteria. The commissioner was charged with giving "highest priority to States and areas within States having the greatest need for programs . . . [taking] into consideration the number of children of limited English-speaking ability" and approving those grant applications "designed to meet the special educational needs of children of limited English-speaking ability in schools having a high concentration of such children from families (A) with incomes below $3,000 per year, or (B) receiving payments from a program of aid to families with dependent children" (P.L. No. 90-247, Title VII, § 702, 20 U.S.C.A. 880b-2, 81 Stat. 817 [1968]).

Subsequent amendments to the 1968 Bilingual Eduation Act softened the low-income requirements. The 1974 amendment no longer required that the children be of low-income families (P.L. No. 93-380, 88 Stat. 503

[1974]). The 1978 amendment mandates the commissioner "to the extent feasible [to] allocate funds appropriated in proportion to the geographical distribution of children of limited English proficiency throughout the Nation with due regard for the relative ability of particular local educational agencies to carry out such programs and the relative numbers of persons from low income families sought to be benefited by such programs" (P.L. No. 95-561, 92 Stat. 2270 [1978]).

The passage of the 1968 Bilingual Education Act was a major legislative breakthrough influencing public policies toward language minority children. Among its many significant results, three are of particular relevance to the topic at hand. First, the act demonstrated the political feasibility of changing policies toward language minorities, thereby raising serious questions about the English-only laws of many states. Second, the act was a step toward the formal recognition of national-origin minorities as constituencies that may seek differentiated policies on grounds other than those of race and racism or segregation versus integration. Third, the act began the process of institutionalizing the concept that *equality of educational opportunity* is not synonymous with *identical education* (González, 1975).

Legislative action on bilingual education has also been taken in the states. Three years after passage of the 1968 national Bilingual Education Act, the state of Massachusetts enacted its Transitional Bilingual Education Act, which stated in its declaration of policy that "pursuant to the policy of the commonwealth to insure equal educational opportunity to every child, and in recognition of the educational needs of children of limited English-speaking ability, it is the purpose of this act to provide for the establishment of transitional bilingual education programs in the public schools, and to provide supplemental financial assistance to help local school districts to meet the extra costs of such programs" (Mass. Ann. Laws, ch. 71A, § 1, 40 [1971]). With this statement, Massachusetts launched mandatory bilingual education. Similar laws in other states followed (see U.S. Commission on Civil Rights, 1975). These laws required instruction in the native language and culture of children with limited English-speaking ability to equalize their educational opportunities. The 1973 Texas law, for example, emphasized not only the child's native language but also native culture, making the following provisions for program content and method of instruction:

> The bilingual education program established by a school district shall be a full-time program of instruction (1) in all subjects required by law or by the school district, which shall be given in the native language of the children of limited English-speaking ability who are enrolled in the program, and in the English language; (2) in the comprehension, speaking, reading, and writing of

the native language of the children of limited English-speaking ability who are enrolled in the program, and in the comprehension, speaking, reading, and writing of the English language; and (3) in the history and culture associated with the native language of the children of limited English-speaking ability who are enrolled in the program, and in the history and culture of the United States. [Tex. Code Ann., Educ. Code 21.454, 25–26 (1973)]

The first expression of executive policy in the area of equal educational opportunity for language minority children came in May 25, 1970, when J. Stanley Pottinger, then director of the U.S. Office for Civil Rights, issued a memorandum to "School Districts with More Than Five Percent National Origin–Minority Group Children" on the subject of "Identification of Discrimination and Denial of Services on the Basis of National Origin" (35 Fed. Reg. 11595–11596 [1970]). This memorandum clarified policies of the U.S. Department of Health, Education, and Welfare "on issues concerning the responsibility of school districts to provide equal educational opportunity to national origin–minority group children deficient in English language skills." The memorandum listed "some of the major areas of concern that relate to compliance with Title VI" of the Civil Rights Act of 1964:

> (1) Where inability to speak and understand the English language excludes national origin–minority group children from effective participation in the educational program offered by a school district, the district must take affirmative steps to rectify the language deficiency in order to open its instructional program to these students.
> (2) School districts must not assign national origin–minority group students to classes for the mentally retarded on the basis of criteria which essentially measure or evaluate English language skills; nor may school districts deny national origin–minority group children access to college preparatory courses on a basis directly related to the failure of the school system to inculcate English language skills.

The memorandum, which was to provide a critical underpinning in the 1974 U.S. Supreme Court decision in *Lau* v. *Nichols* (see Oakland & Laosa, 1977; Teitelbaum & Hiller, 1977), indicated that failure of federally funded school districts to comply with these provisions would be considered a violation of Title VI of the 1964 Civil Rights Act.[4]

Another major influence on policies toward language minority chil-

---

[4]Title VI, § 601 of the 1964 Civil Rights Act states, "No person in the United States shall, on the ground of race, color, or national origin, be excluded from participation in, be denied the benefits of, or be subjected to discrimination under any program or activity receiving Federal financial assistance" (78 Stat. 252 [1964]; 42 U.S.C. 2000d [1965]).

dren has been the judiciary. The most important judicial action to date regarding the equality of opportunity for such children is the Supreme Court decision in *Lau* v. *Nichols*. In 1971 the District Court of the Northern District of San Francisco found that a large number of children of Chinese ancestry in the San Francisco Unified School District spoke little or no English and could not, therefore, comprehend the language of instruction. Most of these children received no instruction or special help in English, and the rest received only part-time supplemental courses in English. The non-English-speaking students filed a class-action suit against the school district, seeking relief against the unequal educational opportunities that allegedly violated their legal rights guaranteed under the Fourteenth Amendment of the U.S. Constitution, the California Constitution, the 1964 Civil Rights Act, and provisions of the California Education Code. The plaintiffs, Chinese American children, requested that the school district provide special English classes with bilingual teachers for all non-English-speaking children. The defendants, the officials of the school district, admitted that the failure to teach the English-deficient children bilingually meant poor performance in schools and that placements of students in special English classes were made arbitrarily in the absence of reliable testing procedures to ascertain language proficiency. The defendants contended that the provision of special classes for non-English-speaking children was not a matter of "right and duty" but a gratuitous effort by the school district contingent on availability of money and personnel. The District Court and the U.S. Court of Appeals for the Ninth Circuit agreed with the defendants. The courts ruled that as long as these children received the same education made available under the same terms and conditions to the other tens of thousands of children in San Francisco, the educational program was adequate. The courts denied relief to the plaintiffs, stating that there was no evidence to substantiate a violation of the Equal Protection Clause of the Fourteenth Amendment or of Title VI of the 1964 Civil Rights Act (Applewhite, 1979; *Lau* v. *Nichols*, 414 U.S. [1974]; Santiago, 1978).

In 1973 the Supreme Court heard arguments and in January 1974 ruled unanimously in favor of the plaintiffs, reversing the lower-court ruling. The Court observed that offering the same services to *all* children cannot be construed to mean that *each* child was receiving educational benefits equitably. The Court ruled that "the failure of the San Francisco school system to provide English language instruction to . . . students of Chinese ancestry who do not speak English, or to provide them with other adequate instructional procedures, denies them a meaningful opportunity to participate in the public educational program" (*Lau* v. *Nichols*, 414 U.S. 563 [1974]). The Court found that this failure of the school system violated

section 601 of the 1964 Civil Rights Act (see text n. 4) "and the implementing regulations of the Department of Health, Education, and
Welfare" (p. 563). (The implementing regulations to which the Court refers
are those set forth in the aforementioned "May 25 Memorandum" of the
U.S. Office for Civil Rights.)

In dismissing the lower courts' equal-access argument, the Supreme
Court found that use of the same textbooks, classrooms, and teachers can
constitute a denial of meaningful opportunity to participate if the language
barrier is not considered (p. 566): ". . . there is no equality of treatment
merely by providing students with the same facilities, textbooks, teachers,
and curriculum; for students who do not understand English are effectively
foreclosed from any meaningful education. . . . Imposition of a requirement that, before a child can effectively participate in the educational
program, he must already have acquired [basic English] skills is to make a
mockery of public education."

Prior to the 1970s the judicial branch had little or no impact on public
policies toward language minority children; such policies were untouched
by the 1954 U.S. Supreme Court in *Brown* v. *Board of Education* (and
indeed by the 1964 Civil Rights Act as well). But the U.S. Supreme Court
in *Lau* v. *Nichols* and subsequent court cases have had a significant
influence on such policies, broadening the principles of equal opportunity
in education to encompass the constitutional and statutory rights of children of limited English-speaking ability. Other landmark cases bearing on
the provision of equal educational opportunities for language minority
children include *Keys* v. *School District No. 1, Denver, Colorado* (1973);
Serna v. *Portales Municipal Schools, New Mexico* (1974); *Aspira of New
York* v. *Board of Education of the City of New York* (1974); *Rios* v. *Reed,
New York* (1978); *U.S.* v. *State of Texas* (1981); *Castaneda* v. *Pickard, Texas*
(1981) (for reviews and discussions of these court cases see Applewhite,
1979; González, 1982; Leibowitz, 1982; Santiago, 1978; Teitelbaum &
Hiller, 1977).

Many advocates of bilingual education, although valuing the legislative, judicial, and executive developments in policies toward language
minority children of the past decade as very positive, consider one element
of them to be negative—specifically, that the policies are based on a
remedial or compensatory model of minority group education. Indeed,
most current policies call for using the native language only temporarily, to
help remediate or compensate for child-rearing practices and experiences
that are considered inadequate in preparing the child for learning in a
"regular" (English-only) instructional program. Thus, the use of, say,
Spanish with Chicano children may be seen "as an *unfortunate necessity*
rather than an opportunity for enrichment" (González, 1975, p. 11). The

ultimate aim of such policies is to move children out of bilingual instruction into English-only instruction. Some (e.g., González, 1975) see such *transitional* approaches to bilingual education as yet another attempt to melt away sociocultural diversity by imposing the language and culture of one group over all groups. Those who object to transitional approaches to bilingual education advocate instead policies that encourage the *maintenance* and development of the child's native language while he or she acquires English-language skills.

RECENT POLICIES IN PSYCHOLOGICAL AND EDUCATIONAL TESTING OF MINORITY CHILDREN: 1960–1980

As we saw earlier, the testing movement enjoyed wide public acceptance from World War I until about 1955 but has since become increasingly controversial. Advocates of standardized testing consider it the best available means of impartial selection by ability, arguing that it can reveal undiscovered talent and that it also contributes to increased efficiency and accountability. The criticisms have been directed in part at the basic logic of measuring human abilities and in part at the effects of measurement practices on our society. The principal criticism is that standardized tests are allegedly biased against persons from certain cultural and socioeconomic groups—that most tests reflect largely non-Hispanic White, English-speaking, middle-class experiences and values and not the experiences and linguistic, cognitive, and motivational styles and values of many children of Black, Hispanic, and other ethnic groups. Critics also note that assessments are sometimes conducted incompetently, by persons ignorant of the children's culture and language and thus unable to elicit a level of performance that accurately reflects the child's competence. Critics further allege that testing practices foster diminished expectations that have the damaging effects of a self-fulfilling prophecy, ensuring subsequent low-level achievement for persons who score low on tests. Thus, some spokespersons for the interests of Blacks, Hispanics, and similarly placed ethnic, racial, and language groups have attacked standardized tests as artificial barriers to educational, social, and economic opportunity.

Much of the controversy has centered on the use of standardized psychological and educational tests to assign students to ability groups. It is specifically alleged that such practices have serious social consequences because they discriminate against children of certain ethnic and racial backgrounds and further exclude them from the superior educational opportunities generally available to the children of the more privileged groups. Allegations of discrimination were triggered by the discovery that children of certain ethnic, language, and racial groups are overrepresented in classes for the mentally retarded and underrepresented in other categories designated for special educational services, such as the physically handicapped and the gifted.

In part as a response to the public controversy over the social consequences of standardized testing, actions have been taken in the last 2 decades that, directly or indirectly, are profoundly influencing policies regarding the psychological and educational assessment of ethnic, racial, and language minority children. Four major sources of influence on policies regarding the use of nondiscriminatory assessment procedures for classifying minority children in schools are the professional associations, the test-producing organizations, the judiciary, and legislative bodies. Compared with that of either the professional associations or the test-producing organizations, a much stronger influence has been exerted through legislative and judicial action. Let us now consider some of the most important policy developments emanating from these four sources of influence over the past 2 decades.

Policies affecting the psychological and educational assessment of children are influenced directly and indirectly by legislation at the local, state, and national levels. By powers claimed through the Tenth Amendment of the U.S. Constitution, the legal control of education generally resides at the state level. However, the states generally have transferred much of this control to local school districts. Thus, districts often are granted broad discretionary authority over local practices, although the policies within each district must conform generally to policies established at the state and federal levels (Oakland & Laosa, 1977). The federal government historically had exercised relatively little direct authority over psychological and educational assessment practices in schools until the 1960–1980 era, during which its influence became increasingly direct.

Constitutional and statutory provisions guarantee the right not to be discriminated against for unjustifiable reasons (such as race or ethnicity). Several such guarantees and their implementing regulations have had significant direct or indirect impact on assessment policies. Among them are the Fourteenth Amendment of the U.S. Constitution and the 1964 Civil Rights Act, often cited in court cases of alleged discriminatory assessment practices.

The executive branch of government has exercised influence over assessment practices by issuing regulatory standards and by monitoring such practices to insure compliance with the regulations and the law. A noteworthy example of federal regulations are those issued by the U.S. Office for Civil Rights to carry out provisions of Title VI of the Civil Rights Act of 1964: the Title VI Regulation (published as Pt. 80, Title 45 of the

Code of Federal Regulations) prohibits recipients of federal financial assistance from discriminatory action because of race, color, or national origin. Another example of federal attempts to prevent discriminatory practices in schools is the OCR "May 25 Memorandum," mentioned earlier. This memorandum is of historical significance in part because of its specific reference to the assessment and classification of national origin–minority group children. As one means of discharging its responsibility, the Office for Civil Rights sent a memorandum to school districts with more than 5% such children (35 Fed. Reg. 11595–11596 [1970]). This memorandum clarified policies of the U.S. Department of Health, Education, and Welfare on the responsibility of school districts to provide equal educational opportunity to minority group children. It indicated that "school districts must not assign national origin–minority group students to classes for the mentally retarded on the basis of criteria which essentially measure or evaluate English language skills." A subsequent Office for Civil Rights memorandum to state and local education agencies charged that

> in many local educational agencies a substantially higher percentage of minority children have been assigned to special education classes for the mentally retarded than the minority student population of the district would normally indicate.
>
> [The Office for Civil Rights] reviews of many local educational agencies lead us to believe that in many instances the racial and ethnic isolation of minority children in such classes which has occurred has in turn resulted from a failure by local educational agencies to utilize non-discriminatory evaluation and assignment standards and procedures with respect to minority group children.

This memorandum is also of historical significance because it proposes a comprehensive set of guidelines for psychological assessment practices in schools and contains a set of minimum procedures for evaluating and assigning racial and ethnic and language minority children to classes for the mentally retarded (the two memoranda are reprinted in Oakland & Laosa, 1977).

Another federal law with significant implications for the assessment and classification of ethnic and language minority children is the Education for All Handicapped Children Act of 1975 (P.L. No. 94-142, 20 U.S.C., regulations at 45 C.F.R.). Hailed as the most significant piece of educational legislation in the history of the United States, this law has as a major purpose to ensure that all handicapped children are provided free and appropriate educational opportunities that meet their unique needs; it also requires that assessment and classification procedures ensure that the legal rights of the children and their parents be protected. Several features of the law directly address assessment: "Testing and evaluation materials and procedures . . . must be selected and administered so as not to be racially or culturally discriminatory"; assessment should be conducted "in the child's native language."

Advocates of nondiscriminatory assessment policies have been active not only at the federal level but also at the state and local levels. For example, in 1973 the Texas legislature, responding to Mexican American parents and others seeking reforms in the assessment and educational classification of ethnic minority children, passed Senate Bill 464 requiring the administration of intelligence tests in the child's primary home language as a prerequisite to being placed in a special-education class (Oakland & Laosa, 1977).

The judiciary has been another avenue by which advocates of nondiscriminatory assessment policies have exerted their influence. Over the past decade, various court cases have challenged the testing practices used to place ethnic, racial, and language minority children in ability groups. In such cases, on the basis of U.S. and state constitutional and statutory guarantees and regulations (such as those derived from the 1964 Civil Rights Act, the 1973 Rehabilitation Act, the 1975 Education for All Handicapped Children Act, and various state laws), plaintiffs have usually charged one or more of the following violations (see Oakland & Laosa, 1977). (1) Assessment practices are discriminatory because children are not tested in their dominant language or dialect. (2) Tests are culturally biased because they primarily reflect White middle-class values and abilities rather than those of other ethnic backgrounds. (3) Tests are used in a discriminatory way, as is documented by the overrepresentation of minority group children in special-education classes and lower-ability groups. (4) Test administrators are professionally incompetent or are not fully sensitive to the sometimes subtle effects of cultural and language diversity in the testing situation. (5) Children are placed in lower-ability groups or special classes on the basis of little information (such as achievement and intelligence test data alone). (6) Parents have not been allowed adequate participation in the decision making that affects their children.

A landmark case in the small but growing body of judicial decisions significantly affecting policies regarding assessment of minority group children is *Diana* v. *California State Board of Education* (No. C-70 37 R.F.P. [1970]), filed in the U.S. District Court of Northern California. The plaintiffs, nine Mexican American children from predominantly Spanish-speaking homes, claimed they were placed in classes for the educable mentally retarded (EMR) on the basis of inappropriate measures—IQ scores derived from the Stanford-Binet and Wechsler Intelligence Scale for Children. The children had been tested in English, and their scores fell within the range calling for placement in classes for the mentally retarded. But when they were retested by a bilingual psychologist and permitted to answer in either English or Spanish, their scores increased 15 points on the average. The tests used for placement were challenged as violating the Fourteenth Amendment and Title VI of the 1964 Civil Rights Act (Hollander, 1982; Ross, De Young, & Cohen, 1971).

An out-of-court settlement was negotiated that required the following practices to be adopted in the future. (1) Children whose home language is not English should be tested in both their primary language and English. (2) Such children should be given only tests or sections of tests that do not depend on vocabulary, general information, or other unfair verbal questions. (3) Each school district should submit to the state in time for the next school year a summary of retesting and reevaluation of all language minority students already in classes for the mentally retarded and a plan listing special supplemental individual training to be provided to help each child return to the regular class. (4) Psychologists in the state of California were to develop and standardize an IQ test appropriate for Mexican American and other language minority children in the state (Goldberg, 1971; Hollander, 1982; Oakland & Laosa, 1977; Ross et al., 1971).

The *Diana* case exerted a pivotal influence on state and federal policies. Very shortly after its settlement in February 1970, the California legislature acted specifically to prevent excessive reliance on IQ test scores for EMR placements. It passed legislation requiring that test scores be substantiated by other techniques, such as a complete evaluation of the child's developmental history, academic achievement, and family and cultural background (Burrello, De Young, & Lang, n.d.; Hollander, 1982; Oakland & Laosa, 1977). Also in 1970, as we saw earlier, the U.S. Office for Civil Rights issued its "May 25 Memorandum."

Larry P. v. *Riles* proved to be another landmark case. Filed in the U.S. District Court of Northern California in 1971 on behalf of several Black elementary school children, the suit alleged they had been wrongly placed and retained in EMR classes (National Research Council, 1982a; Oakland & Laosa, 1977). The plaintiffs supported their claim that they were not in fact retarded by affidavits that, when psychologists from the Bay Area Association of Black Psychologists gave them the same tests as those used by the school, they scored significantly above the cutoff score required for such placement. The Black psychologists, it was argued, were able to establish rapport with the children, to reword the test items to suit the children's cultural background, and to count as correct certain answers that, though not correct according to the manual, were intelligent responses in light of the children's background (Hollander, 1982).

The plaintiffs charged that the placement procedure violated the Civil

Rights Act of 1871 and the right to equal protection set forth in the California constitution and the Fourteenth Amendment of the U.S. Constitution. They argued that their placement in EMR classes had been wrongful because the testing procedures failed to recognize their unfamiliarity with White middle-class culture and ignored their different language aptitudes and experiences. They further charged that because of this improper placement they had been stigmatized and given a life sentence of illiteracy and public dependency (Friedman, 1973; Oakland & Laosa, 1977). The plaintiffs sought to shift the burden of proof so that the school officials would have to justify the use of IQ tests. The basis for their complaints was statistical evidence showing disproportionate numbers of ethnic and racial minority children in EMR classes (Hollander, 1982).

The court agreed with the plaintiffs that there was racial imbalance in EMR classes: "The fact of racial imbalance is demonstrated by plaintiffs' undisputed statistics, which indicate that while blacks constitute 28.5 percent of all students in the San Francisco United School District, 66 percent of all students in San Francisco's EMR program are black. Statewide, the disproportion is similar. Blacks comprise 9.1 percent of all school children in California, but 27.5 percent of all school children in EMR classes. Certainly these statistics indicate that there is a significant disproportion of blacks in EMR classes in San Francisco and in California (343 F. Supp. 1311 [1972], cited in Hollander, 1982, p. 205). Moreover, the court was not persuaded by the evidence produced by the defendants to justify the use of IQ tests as a means of classifying ethnic minority children: "Defendants do not seem to dispute the evidence amassed by plaintiffs to demonstrate that the IQ tests in fact are culturally biased. Indeed, defendants have stated that they are merely awaiting the development of what they expect will be a minimally biased test" (343 F. Supp. 1313 [1972], cited in Hollander, 1982, pp. 206–207).

During these hearings in 1972 the court also mandated a moratorium on the use of the Revised Wechsler Intelligence Scale for Children (WISC-R) and the Stanford-Binet in the placement of minority-group children in EMR and learning-disabled special-education programs until a full trial could be heard. Given the court's mandate, the California State Board of Education broadened the moratorium on the use of these two tests to include *all* children being considered for placement in such programs. As a result, fewer children were placed in these programs, and other tests and techniques were used to ascertain children's intellectual abilities (Oakland & Laosa, 1977).

The plaintiffs in *Larry P*. v. *Riles* also requested that the schools be required to hire minority group psychologists and consultants so that "psychological assessment of black school children be conducted and interpreted by persons adequately prepared to consider the cultural background of the child, preferably by a person of similar ethnic background as the child" (343 F. Supp. 1314 [1972], cited in Hollander, 1982, p. 208). The court supported this concept, at least indirectly: ordering that the yearly reevaluations of Black children in EMR classes be conducted by means that do not deprive them of the equal protection of the law, the court indicated that the hiring of minority group psychologists and consultants might help the defendants comply (Hollander, 1982).

Not until 1977, 6 years after it was filed, did the full trial on the merits of *Larry P. v. Riles* begin. Two years later, in October 1979, Chief Justice Peckham of the U.S. District Court in San Francisco signed the opinion in this gargantuan case. Regarding the charge that cultural bias is the cause of the disparity in the IQ scores of Black and White children, he held that the evidence indicated that IQ tests could not give a simple number corresponding to an innate trait called intelligence. Moreover, because the tests had been standardized on White middle-class children, their validity for measuring Black children's skills and potential could not be assumed (Hollander, 1982).

Regarding intent, Judge Peckham held that the plaintiffs had proved the defendants' discriminatory intent. He enjoined the defendants "from utilizing, permitting the use of, or approving the use of any standardized tests . . . for the identification of black E.M.R. children or their placement into E.M.R. classes, without first securing approval by this court" (cited in Bersoff, 1981, p. 1048). Requests for such approval should include evidence that the tests were not discriminatory. The defendants also were ordered to eliminate disproportionate placement of Black children in EMR classes. Finally, the court found that on the basis of relevant evidence, the plaintiffs were not retarded (Bersoff, 1981; Hollander, 1982).

Only 9 months later, a quite opposite decision was rendered in *Parents in Action on Special Education (PASE) v. Hannon* (1980), another major case of alleged racial bias. The allegation was that two Black Chicago schoolchildren had been placed erroneously in EMR classes by the use of IQ tests. The children's parents joined in a class-action suit against the Chicago school system, alleging that the error in placement resulted from cultural bias in the standardized intelligence tests. Unlike Judge Peckham, Judge Grady, presiding in *PASE v. Hannon*, refused to bar use of such tests, even though they were part of a classification process that placed a disproportionate number of Black children in EMR classes. Judge Grady held that "the WISC, WISC-R and Stanford-Binet tests, when used in conjunction with the statutorily mandated '[other criteria] for determining an appropriate educational program for a child' [under P.L. No. 94-142] . . . do not discriminate against black children" (cited in Bersoff, 1981, p.

1048). The resolution of this judicial conflict awaits decision in appellate tribunals and, perhaps, final petition to the Supreme Court.

As Bersoff points out, these cases should not be viewed as being against testing or special education, although they certainly affect policies regarding the use of assessment procedures for the educational classification of children. Like much litigation over employment policies, they are racial and ethnic discrimination cases. They flow from *Brown* v. *Board of Education*, once again adjudicating the claim of ethnic, racial, and language minority children to an integrated and equal education. They are the most recent challenges to policies and practices that are perceived as attempts to continue, in more subtle forms, the racial and ethnic separation, isolation, and inequality that for too long has been a sad tradition in U.S. social policies toward children.

Although having a much weaker impact than judicial and legislative action, professional associations and test-producing organizations have had some influence on policies of assessment and classification of minority children. Professional associations have done so through their participation in professional training programs, certification, and licensing boards, and through research and publication activities. One of the first attempts by a professional association to provide leadership in clarifying issues regarding assessment of minority group children was made by the Society for the Psychological Study of Social Issues, Division 9 of the American Psychological Association. In 1964 the society published a monograph that emphasized the importance of using "tests with minority children in ways that will enable these children to attain the full promise that America owes to all of its children" (Deutsch, Fishman, Kogan, North, & Whiteman, 1964, p. 129); it introduced issues important in the selection, use, and interpretation of psychological tests with ethnic and racial minority group children and indicated the need to be sensitive to whether the tests differentiate reliably, have predictive validity, and are interpreted adequately when given to such children.

Not until the early and mid-1970s did other professional organizations present positions on the testing of minority group children (for a review see Oakland & Laosa, 1977). The positions ranged from calls for a national moratorium on standardized testing (National Education Association, 1973), to pointing out the need to distinguish between issues that should be settled by litigation and legislation and those that should be settled by professional associations (Association for Measurement and Evaluation in Guidance, American Personnel and Guidance Association, & National Council on Measurement in Education, 1972), to setting forth specific guidelines and ethical standards for test developers and users (American Psychological Association, 1972; American Psychological Association,

American Educational Research Association, & National Council on Measurement in Education, 1974).[5]

The National Education Association and five other major professional educational associations, in the first isssue of a new National Council on Measurement in Education periodical, state their points of view regarding the uses of tests in schools (*Educational Measurement: Issues and Practices*, 1982). While recognizing the usefulness of tests in educational practice, these associations identify what they consider to be their undesirable and improper uses as well as their desirable and appropriate uses.

In addition to those of major professional associations, the activities of two ethnic minority professional organizations—the Association of Black Psychologists and a Chicano group, the Association of Psychologists for La Raza—have played important roles by raising critical issues with their parent association, the American Psychological Association (see Bernal, 1975; Jackson, 1975; Williams, 1972). The National Association for the Advancement of Colored People, although not a professional organization, has also considered issues relevant to testing Blacks—particularly the negative impact of testing (see Gallagher, 1976).

Although policies regarding the psychological and educational assessment of minority children have been little influenced by professional associations, it can be argued that such policies have been substantially influenced by ethnic and racial minority psychologists and educators, despite their small numbers. Ronald W. Henderson and Richard R. Valencia (in press) identify three ways in which minority professionals were influential: (1) in the late 1960s they exposed the gross overrepresentation of minority children in EMR classes; (2) they engaged other members of the professional associations in debates that, although often polemic and hostile, helped to identify more clearly the issues; and (3) they provided their expertise in litigation and legislation. As Bernal (1975) points out, it would behoove the majority psychologists to work with minority psychologists in joint enterprises that might improve assessment in general.

Other sources of influence on policies affecting assessment practices are the organizations that produce tests and the institutions that use them. It is useful to distinguish, as Novick (1982) does, the three participants in the ability-testing process: the institution, using the test for some decision-making purpose; the test producer, who develops and markets or administers and scores the tests; and the test taker, who takes the test by choice,

[5]The Committee to Develop Joint Technical Standards for Educational and Psychological Testing, chaired by Prof. Melvin Novick of the University of Iowa, has been established and is charged with the task of revising the *1974 Standards for Educational and Psychological Tests*. The committee is sponsored by the American Educational Research Association, the American Psychological Association, and the National Council on Measurement in Education.

direction, or necessity. Although historically the test-using institutions have had the most influence over ability-testing policies and practices, the test-producing organizations also exert great influence on the testing process. However, the common perception that test-producing organizations set educational (or employment) policy is inaccurate. The test-producing organizations, because of their technical expertise, have influence through exhortation. But, like many of the major professional associations of psychologists and educators, they have been reluctant to use such influence (Novick, 1982; Oakland & Laosa, 1977). The test-producing organizations have, however, contributed to the evolution of guidelines and standards of practice. For example, the Board of Trustees of Educational Testing Service, a major testing organization, adopted in 1981 a set of standards, policies, and procedural guidelines designed to insure that ETS products and services meet certain demonstrable criteria; these standards also establish the responsibility of the testing organization to discourage or eliminate test misuse (Educational Testing Service, 1979, 1981, 1983; see also Novick, 1982).

EPILOGUE

In every era of U.S. history since colonial times, the nature of social policies toward children has been such that the children of some ethnic, racial, and language groups have been systematically isolated and excluded from preparation for full participation in the responsibilities and rewards of full citizenship. Simultaneously, a different, parallel set of policies toward children has aggressively sought and effectively obtained the integration and full participation of members of other ethnic, racial, and language groups. The 1960s saw a dramatic change in U.S. social policies toward children—the emergence of a series of policies aimed at redressing the effects of the earlier exclusion and discrimination. Among the unique aspects of these policies was their emphasis on the development and education of poor children, and particularly those of certain minority groups, as a means of achieving ethnic and racial equality in this society. Strong leadership in these new policy initiatives came from the federal government. Many view the time from 1960 to 1980 as an era when this nation made long-overdue strides toward the formulation and implementation of policies aimed at improving the chances of children to achieve their full potential, regardless of racial, ethnic, language, or socioeconomic background.

Yet that era has come to an end. In the 1980s a new one has begun— one characterized by strong resistance by government in general and by the federal government in particular to providing either the leadership or the resources necessary to build on, or even to sustain, the policy developments of the past 2 decades. In contrast to the social, economic, intellectual, and political trends that converged in the 1960s and gave impetus to that era of reform, the sociopolitical and economic climate of this nation in the early 1980s is such that policy initiatives aimed at erasing ethnic and racial inequalities are not likely to receive strong government support, at least in the immediate future.

Thus, the central contradiction of this great nation—a contradiction that Gunnar Myrdal (1944) identified in *An American Dilemma* nearly 40 years ago—still exists today: the gap between the creed of equality and the persistent ethnic and racial inequalities of our social system. This point is well illustrated by a comparison of the sociodemographic data of over a decade ago (Tables 2 and 4) with those collected recently (Tables 9, 10, 11, and 12). There have been modest increases in the schooling attainment of Blacks and Hispanics, but the differences between them and non-Hispanic Whites in both schooling attainment and income are still today quite vast.

Socioeconomic status has great relevance to social policies toward children because it determines highly significant aspects of the environmental circumstances in which children grow and develop. Indeed, the dimensions most commonly used to assess the quality of a child's environment have been related to socioeconomic status (for reviews see Caldwell, 1978; Deutsch, 1973; Hess, 1970; Laosa, 1981). These dimensions have been of immense historical and practical importance in understanding human development, because, as a plethora of scientific studies indicates, the likelihood that a child will be able to maximize his or her potential, as generally defined in U.S. society, is largely determined by the family's socioeconomic status. Given, then, the strong correlation that we have observed between socioeconomic status and ethnic, racial, and language

TABLE 9

Income Characteristics of Families for Three
U.S. Ethnic and Racial Groups, 1980

Group	Median Family Income ($)	Mean Income per Family Member ($)	Percentage of Families with Income Below Poverty Level
Black	12,674	4,321	28.9
Hispanic[a]	14,717	4,549	23.2
White	21,904	7,787	8.0

Sources.—U.S. Bureau of the Census, 1981a, 1982b.
[a]Hispanics may be of any race.

group membership, there is an urgent need for social policies on behalf of children and families that directly address issues of ethnic, racial, and language group inequalities. But as historical and sociodemographic trends reviewed in this chapter further suggest, such policies, to be effective, must be formulated and implemented as part of a comprehensive set of national policies aimed at all sectors of the society and at all age groups and designed to eliminate the structural, castelike barriers that perpetuate the exclusion and isolation of certain groups from full participation in the responsibilities and rewards of citizenship.

If present demographic trends are extrapolated into the future, ethnic groups differ substantially in their likely rates of population growth and

TABLE 10

MEDIAN INCOME (in Current Dollars) OF HOUSEHOLDS FOR
THREE U.S. ETHNIC AND RACIAL GROUPS, 1972–1980

Year	Black	Hispanic[a]	White
1980	10,764	13,651	18,684
1979	10,216	13,423	17,333
1978	9,411	11,803	15,660
1977	8,422	10,647	14,272
1976	7,902	9,569	13,289
1975	7,408	8,865	12,340
1974	6,964	8,906	11,710
1973	6,485	8,144	11,017
1972	5,938	7,677	10,173

SOURCE.—U.S. Bureau of the Census, 1982b.

NOTE.—The average number of persons per household in 1980 was 2.98 for Blacks, 3.47 for Hispanics, and 2.68 for Whites. A household consists of all persons occupying a housing unit, including related family members and unrelated persons, if any, who share the unit. (In contrast, a family is a group of two or more persons related by blood, marriage, or adoption and residing together.)

[a]Hispanics may be of any race.

TABLE 11

SCHOOLING CHARACTERISTICS OF THREE
U.S. ETHNIC AND RACIAL GROUPS, 1979[a]

Group	Median School Years Completed	Percentage High School Graduates	Percentage with 4 or More Years of College
Black	11.9	49.4	7.9
Hispanic[b]	10.3	42.0	6.7
White	12.5	69.7	17.2

SOURCE.—U.S. Bureau of the Census, 1980a.

[a]Persons 25 years old and over.

[b]Hispanics may be of any race.

TABLE 12
PERCENTAGE OF U.S. POPULATION 25 YEARS OLD AND OVER WITH
FEWER THAN 5 YEARS OF SCHOOL AND WITH 4 OR MORE YEARS OF HIGH SCHOOL
FOR THREE ETHNIC AND RACIAL GROUPS, 1970–1980

Schooling Level and Ethnic and Racial Group	YEAR		
	1970	1975	1980
Fewer than 5 years of school:			
All ethnic and racial groups[a]	5.5	4.2	3.4
Black	14.6	12.3	9.2
Hispanic[b]	19.5	18.5	15.4
White	4.5	3.3	2.6
Four or more years of high school:			
All ethnic and racial groups[a]	52.3	62.5	68.6
Black	31.4	42.5	51.2
Hispanic[b]	32.1	37.9	45.3
White	54.5	64.6	70.5

SOURCE.—U.S. Bureau of the Census, 1981d, Table 230.
[a]Includes groups not shown separately.
[b]Hispanics may be of any race.

need of services for children. Ironically, the ethnic groups on the lower rungs of the socioeconomic ladder are growing at a much faster rate than are the more privileged groups. The rate is particularly accelerated for Chicanos. Indeed, if the Hispanic population continues to grow at its present rate, it is estimated that during this decade Hispanics will become the largest ethnic group in this country (see Table 13). Children in the ethnic groups at the bottom of the socioeconomic ladder represent a substantial and increasingly large proportion of the total population of children in the United States. The combined numbers of Black and Hispanic children under 15 years of age in the United States in 1980 reached over 12 million: 7,604,272 Black and 4,680,767 Hispanic (U.S. Bureau of the Census, 1982c). The proportion of children in the United States who are Hispanic, Black, and American Indian is becoming increasingly large in relation to the proportion of children who are non-Hispanic White.

There is an urgent need to collect accurate, up-to-date data on the conditions and characteristics of children and families in the various ethnic groups—while, of course, protecting the individual's right of privacy. Adequate data are essential for policy planning and evaluation. Inaccurate or incomplete data can distort or mask the needs of diverse children and families and mislead policymakers regarding the impact of policies and programs. Whereas the research information readily available on non-Hispanic White and Black children and families is rapidly expanding, very

TABLE 13

POPULATION INCREASE, 1970 TO 1980:

BLACK, HISPANIC, INDIAN, AND WHITE AMERICANS

(Numbers in Thousands)

Group	1970	1980	Percent Change[a]
American Indian[b]	827	1,418	+71.46
Black	22,581	26,489	+17.31
Hispanic (total):[c]	9,073	14,609	+61.02
Chicano	4,532	8,740	+92.85
Puerto Rican	1,429	2,014	+40.94
Cuban American	545	803	+47.34
Central, South American, or other Hispanic origin	2,567	3,051	+18.86
White	177,749	188,341	+ 5.96

SOURCES.—U.S. Department of Commerce, 1981; U.S. Bureau of the Census, 1973f, 1981b, 1982d.

[a]Calculated as (A − B) ÷ B × 100, where A = population in 1980 and B = population in 1970. It should be noted that the larger 1980 counts are partly the result of improved census procedures.

[b]Includes Eskimos and Aleuts.

[c]Hispanics may be of any race.

little information can be found on the Hispanic and other ethnic populations. For example, there are few published studies that focus on Hispanic children and families, and what there is consists largely of anecdotal and stereotypic treatises or case studies, often criticized for their inadequate portrayals of families (Arciniega, Casaus, & Castillo, 1982; Mirandé, 1977; Montiel, 1970; Romano, 1973). Government-gathered statistics are frequently analyzed and displayed separately for Whites and Blacks; however, such data are seldom presented separately for other ethnic groups. Unless differences and similarities between and within ethnic groups are known and documented, tailoring policies to specific needs will be impossible. For example, even within the Hispanic American population there exists considerable social, demographic, cultural, and linguistic diversity among such varied ethnic groups as the Mexican American, the Cuban American, and the Puerto Rican (Laosa, 1975). Consider, for example, that the median age of the Hispanic American population as a whole is 22 years, substantially lower than that of persons not of Hispanic origin (30 years). However, when these data are analyzed separately by the various Hispanic ethnic groups, it can be seen that the median age of Mexican Americans (Chicanos) is 21 and of Puerto Ricans is 20, whereas that of Cuban Americans is 33 years (U.S. Bureau of the Census, 1981c). Clearly, such a difference in age structure suggests corresponding differences in the needs of these ethnic groups. Nevertheless, such breakdowns by ethnic group are seldom available. Moreover, even when the data are available, one is often frustrated by their many conceptual and methodological problems.

To find examples of egregious omissions in the use of ethnic group data for policy recommendations one need only turn to the major reports of the committees on child development of the National Research Council (1976, 1981). These are reports of studies carried out by the National Academy of Sciences and designed to proffer recommendations on national policies for children and families and on the conduct of research on children's services. The reports present extensive data and analyses on the status of Black and White children and families—information on which the committees base their recommendations for national policies—but the reports are virtually silent about the unique needs of Hispanic children and families. From a perspective that views accurate information as an essential element in the responsible formulation of social policies, this is indeed an egregious omission.

Let us hope that this nation continues its quest for effective solutions to ethnic and racial inequalities, and that this new era of public policies does not signal, as many fear, a return to situations similar to those of the pre-1960s eras. As we have seen, for some ethnic, racial, and language groups, social policies during those eras (either implicitly or explicitly) served to isolate them from, rather than to include them in, the mainstream of U.S. social, educational, economic, and political life.

REFERENCES

Administration of Children, Youth, and Families, U.S. Department of Health and Human Services. *The status of children, youth, and families 1979* (DHHS Publication No. OHDS 80-30274). Washington, D.C.: Government Printing Office, 1980.

Akers, M. E. Prologue: The why of early childhood education. In I. J. Gordon (Ed.), *Early childhood education.* Seventy-first Yearbook of the National Society for the Study of Education, Part 2. Chicago: University of Chicago Press, 1972.

Alvarez, R. The psycho-historical and socioeconomic development of the Chicano community in the United States. *Social Science Quarterly*, 1973, **53** (4), 920–942.

American Psychological Association. *Ethical standards of psychologists.* Washington, D.C.: American Psychological Association, 1972.

American Psychological Association, American Educational Research Association, & National Council on Measurement in Education. *Standards for educational and psychological tests.* Washington, D.C.: American Psychological Association, 1974.

Applewhite, S. R. The legal dialect of bilingual education. In R. V. Padilla (Ed.), *Ethnoperspectives in bilingual education research.* (Vol. 1): *Bilingual education and public policy in the United States.* Ypsilanti, Mich.: Eastern Michigan University, Department of Foreign Languages and Bilingual Studies, 1979.

Arce, C. H. A reconsideration of Chicano culture and identity. *Daedalus*, 1981, Spring, 177–191.

Arciniega, M., Casaus, L., & Castillo, M. *Parenting models and Mexican Americans: A process analysis.* Albuquerque, N.M.: Pajarito, 1982.

Ariès, P. *Centuries of childhood: A social history of family life* (R. Baldick, Trans.). New York: Knopf, 1962.

Association for Measurement and Evaluation in Guidance, American Personnel and Guidance Association, & National Council for Measurement in Education. The responsible use of tests: A position paper of AMEG, APGA, and NCME. *Measurement and evaluation in Guidance,* 1972, **5**, 385–388.

Baratz, S. S., & Baratz, J. C. Early childhood intervention: The social science base of institutional racism. *Harvard Educational Review,* 1970, **40**(1), 29–50.

Bean, F. D., & Frisbie, W. P. (Eds.). *The demography of racial and ethnic groups.* New York: Academic Press, 1978.

Beck, J. M., & Saxe, R. W. (Eds.). *Teaching the culturally disadvantaged pupil.* Springfield, Ill.: Thomas, 1965.

Bee, H. L., Van Egeren, L. F., Streissguth, A. P., Nyman, B. A., & Leckie, M. S. Social class differences in maternal teaching strategies and speech patterns. *Developmental Psychology,* 1969, **1**, 726–734.

Bennett, L., Jr. *Before the Mayflower: A history of the Negro in America 1619–1964* (Rev. ed.). New York: Penguin, 1964.

Bernal, E. M., Jr. A response to "Educational uses of tests with disadvantaged subjects." *American Psychologist,* 1975, **30**, 93–95.

Bernstein, B. Social class and linguistic development: A theory of social learning. In A. H. Halsey, J. Floud, & C. A. Anderson (Eds.), *Education, economy, and society.* New York: Free Press, 1961.

Bersoff, D. N. Testing and the law. *American Psychologist,* 1981, **36**, 1047–1056.

Billingsley, A. *Black families in white America.* Englewood Cliffs, N.J.: Prentice-Hall, 1968.

Billingsley, A., & Giovannoni, J. M. *Children of the storm: Black children and American child welfare.* New York: Harcourt Brace Jovanovich, 1972.

Bloom, B. S. *Stability and change in human characteristics.* New York: Wiley, 1964.

Boring, E. G. *A history of experimental psychology.* New York: Appleton-Century-Crofts, 1950.

Bremner, R. H. (Ed.). *Children and youth in America: A documentary history.* Vol. 1: *1600–1865.* Cambridge, Mass.: Harvard University Press, 1970.

Bremner, R. H. (Ed.). *Children and youth in America: A documentary history.* Vol. 2: *1866–1932.* Cambridge, Mass.: Harvard University Press, 1971.

Bremner, R. H. (Ed.). *Children and youth in America: A documentary history.* Vol. 3: *1933–1973.* Cambridge, Mass.: Harvard University Press, 1974.

Brim, O. G., Jr., Glass, D. C., Neulinger, J., Firestone, I. J., & Lerner, S. C. *American beliefs and attitudes about intelligence.* New York: Russell Sage Foundation, 1969.

Bronfenbrenner, U. *Is early intervention effective? A report on longitudinal evaluations of preschool programs* (Vol. 2). (DHEW Publication No. OHD 76–30025). Washington, D.C.: Office of Child Development, Department of Health, Education, and Welfare, 1974.

Bryson, J. E., & Bentley, C. P. *Ability grouping of public school students: Legal aspects of classification and tracking methods.* Charlottesville, Va.: Michie, 1980.

Bullock, H. A. *A history of Negro education in the South: From 1619 to the present.* Cambridge, Mass.: Harvard University Press, 1967.

Burrello, L., De Young, H., & Lang, D. *Special education and litigation: Implications for professional and educational practice.* Ann Arbor: Institute for the Study of Mental Retardation and Related Disabilities, University of Michigan, n.d.

Caldwell, B. M. A decade of early intervention programs: What we have learned. *American Journal of Orthopsychiatry*, 1974, **44**(4), 491–496.

Caldwell, B. M. *Home observation for measurement of the environment*. Little Rock: Child Development Research Unit, University of Arkansas, 1978.

Calhoun, J. A., & Collins, R. C. From one decade to another: A positive view of early childhood programs. *Theory into Practice*, 1981, **20**(2), 135–140.

California State Advisory Committee to the United States Commission on Civil Rights. *Political participation of Mexican Americans in California*. Washington, D.C.: Government Printing Office, 1971.

Camarillo, A. *Chicanos in a changing society: From Mexican pueblos to American barrios in Santa Barbara and southern California, 1848–1930*. Cambridge, Mass.: Harvard University Press, 1979.

Cárdenas, B., & Cárdenas, J. A. Chicano, bright-eyed, bilingual, brown, and beautiful. *Today's Education*, 1973, **62**, 49–51.

Cárdenas, J. A., & Cárdenas, B. *The theory of incompatibilities: A conceptual framework for responding to the educational needs of Mexican American children*. San Antonio, Tex.: Intercultural Development Research Association, 1977.

Cárdenas, J. A., & Zamora, G. The early education of minority children. In M. D. Fantini & R. Cárdenas (Eds.), *Parenting in a multicultural society*. New York: Longman, 1980.

Carnoy, M. *Education as cultural imperialism*. New York: McKay, 1974.

Carter, T. P. *Mexican Americans in school: A history of educational neglect*. New York: College Entrance Examination Board, 1970.

Carter, T. P., & Segura, R. D. *Mexican Americans in school: A decade of change*. New York: College Entrance Examination Board, 1979.

Chilman, C. S. Programs for disadvantaged parents. In B. M. Caldwell & H. N. Ricciuti (Eds.), *Review of child development research* (Vol. 3). Chicago: University of Chicago Press, 1973.

Cohen, S. M. The 1981–1982 National Survey of American Jews. In M. Himmelfarb & D. Singer (Eds.), *American Jewish Year Book 1983* (Vol. 83). New York and Philadelphia: American Jewish Committee and Jewish Publication Society of America, 1982.

Coleman, J. S., Campbell, E. Q., Hobson, C. J., McPartland, J., Mood, A. M., Weinfeld, F. D., & York, R. L. *Equality of educational opportunity*. Washington, D.C.: Government Printing Office, 1966.

Collins, R. C. *Children and society: Child development and public policy*. Unpublished doctoral dissertation, Princeton University, 1981.

Cooke, R. *Improving the opportunities and achievements of the children of the poor*. (Recommendations for a Head Start Program, by panel of experts chaired by R. Cooke, February 19, 1965.) Washington, D.C.: Department of Health, Education, and Welfare, Office of Child Development, 1965/1972.

Cruz, J., Jr. *Political influence and educational change: A selected case study*. Unpublished doctoral dissertation, University of Wisconsin, 1973.

Dawidowicz, L. S. A century of Jewish history, 1881–1981: The view from America. In M. Himmelfarb, D. Singer, and M. Fine (Eds.), *American Jewish Year Book 1982* (Vol. 82). New York and Philadelphia: American Jewish Committee and Jewish Publication Society of America, 1981.

De Avila, E. A. I.Q. and the minority child. *Journal of the Association of Mexican American Educators*, 1973, **1**(1), 34–38.

de la Garza, R. O., Kruszewski, Z. A., & Arciniega, T. A. (Eds.). *Chicanos and Native Americans: The territorial minorities*. Englewood Cliffs, N.J.: Prentice-Hall, 1973.

de Lone, R. H. *Small futures: Children, inequality, and the limits of liberal reform.* New York: Harcourt Brace Jovanovich, 1979.

Deutsch, C. P. Social class and child development. In B. M. Caldwell & H. N. Ricciuti (Eds.), *Review of child development research* (Vol. 3). Chicago: University of Chicago Press, 1973.

Deutsch. M. (Ed.) *The disadvantaged child.* New York: Basic, 1967.

Deutsch, M., Fishman, J., Kogan, L., North, R., & Whiteman, M. Guidelines for testing minority group children. *Journal of Social Issues,* 1964, **20**, 127–145.

Dorfman, D. D. Henry Goddard and the feeble-mindedness of Jews, Hungarians, Italians, and Russians. *American Psychologist,* 1982, **37**, 96–97. (Comment)

Dorris, M. A. The grass still grows, the rivers still flow: Contemporary Native Americans. *Daedalus,* 1981, Spring, 43–69.

Du Bois, P. H. *A history of psychological testing.* Boston: Allyn & Bacon, 1970.

Du Bois, W. E. B. *Black Reconstruction in America.* New York: Atheneum, 1979. (Originally published, 1935)

Educational Measurement: Issues and Practice, 1982, **1**(1), 17–19.

Educational Testing Service. *Principles, policies, and procedural guidelines regarding ETS products and services.* Princeton, N.J.: Educational Testing Service, 1979.

Educational Testing Service. *ETS Standards for quality and fairness* (1981 ed.). Princeton, N.J.: Educational Testing Service, 1981.

Educational Testing Service. *ETS Standards for quality and fairness* (1983 ed.). Princeton, N.J.: Educational Testing Service, 1983.

Estrada, L. F., García, F.C., Macías, R. F., & Maldonado, L. Chicanos in the United States: A history of exploitation and resistance. *Daedalus,* 1981, Spring, 103–131.

Family Impact Seminar. *Family Impact Seminar: An introduction.* Washington, D.C.: Institute for Educational Leadership, George Washington University, 1977.

Farber, B., Mindel, C. H., & Lazerwitz, B. The Jewish American family. In C. H. Mindel & R. W. Habenstein (Eds.), *Ethnic families in America: Patterns and variations.* New York: Elsevier, 1976.

Featherman, D. L., & Hauser, R. M. *Opportunity and change.* New York: Academic Press, 1978.

Finn, J. D. Patterns in special education placement as revealed by the OCR surveys. In National Research Council, *Placing children in special education: A strategy for equity.* Washington, D.C.: National Academy Press, 1982.

Franklin, J. H. *Racial equality in America.* Chicago: University of Chicago Press, 1976.

Franklin, J. H. The land of room enough. *Daedalus,* 1981, Spring, 1–12.

Frazier, E. F. *The Negro family in the United States.* Chicago: University of Chicago Press, 1939.

Frazier, E. F. Problems and needs of Negro children and youth resulting from family disorganization. *Journal of Negro Education,* 1950, Summer, 269–277.

Friedman, P. *Mental retardation and the law: A report on status of current court cases.* Washington, D.C.: Department of Health, Education, and Welfare, Office of Mental Retardation Coordination, 1973.

Gallagher, B. G. (Ed.). *NAACP report on minority testing.* New York: National Association for the Advancement of Colored People Special Contribution Fund, 1976.

Gallagher, J. J., Haskins, R., & Farran, D. C. Poverty and public policy for children. In T. B. Brazelton & V. C. Vaughan III (Eds.), *The family: Setting priorities.* New York: Science & Medicine, 1979.

Getzels, J. W. Preschool education. In J. L. Frost (Ed.), *Early childhood education rediscovered: Readings.* New York: Holt, Rinehart & Winston, 1968.

Ginsburg, H. *The myth of the deprived child: Poor children's intellect and education.* Englewood Cliffs, N.J.: Prentice-Hall, 1972.

Glazer, N., & Moynihan, D. P. *Beyond the melting pot: The Negroes, Puerto Ricans, Jews, Italians, and Irish of New York City* (2d ed.). Cambridge, Mass.: MIT Press, 1970.

Goddard, H. H. Mental tests and the immigrant. *Journal of Delinquency,* 1917, **2**(5), 243–277.

Goddard, H. H. Feeblemindedness: A question of definition. *Journal of Psycho-Asthenics,* 1928, **33**, 219–227.

Goldberg, I. Human rights for the mentally retarded in the school system. *Mental Retardation,* 1971, **9**, 3–7.

Goldstein, S. Jews in the United States: Perspectives from demography. In M. Himmelfarb, D. Singer, & M. Fine (Eds.), *American Jewish Year Book 1981* (Vol. **81**). New York and Philadelphia: American Jewish Committee and Jewish Publication Society of America, 1980.

González, J. M. Coming of age in bilingual/bicultural education: A historical perspective. *Inequality in Education,* 1975, February, 5–17.

González, J. M. *Hispanics, bilingual education and desegregation: A review of major issues and policy directions.* Mimeographed. U.S. Commission on Civil Rights, Washington, D.C. 1982.

Goodson, B. D., & Hess, R. D. *Parents as teachers of young children: An evaluative review of some contemporary concepts and programs.* Stanford, Calif.: Stanford University, 1975. (ERIC Document Reproduction Service No. ED 136 967)

Gordon, E. W., & Wilkerson, D. A. *Compensatory education for the disadvantaged: Programs and practices, preschool through college.* New York: College Entrance Examination Board, 1966.

Gould, S. J. *The mismeasure of man.* New York: Norton, 1981.

Grebler, L., Moore, J. W., & Guzman, R. C. *The Mexican-American people: The nation's second largest minority.* New York: Free Press, 1970.

Grotberg, E. H. (Ed.). *200 years of children* (DHEW Publication No. OHD 77-30103). Washington, D.C.: Government Printing Office, 1976.

Guthrie, R. V. *Even the rat was white: A historical view of psychology.* New York: Harper & Row, 1976.

Halberstam, D. *The best and the brightest.* New York: Fawcett Crest, 1972.

Hall, W. S., & Freedle, R. O. *Culture and language: The black American experience.* New York: Wiley, 1975.

Harman, D. *Early childhood: A new look at policymaking.* New York: Aspen Institute for Humanistic Studies, 1978.

Harman, D., & Brim, O. G., Jr. *Learning to be parents: Principles, programs, and methods.* Beverly Hills, Calif.: Sage, 1980.

Harrington, M. *The other America: Poverty in the United States.* New York: Macmillan, 1962.

Head Start in the 1980s: Review and recommendations—a report requested by the President of the United States (DHHS Publication No. OHDS 81-31164). Washington, D.C.: Government Printing Office, 1980.

Henderson, R. W., & Valencia, R. R. Nondiscriminatory school psychological services: Beyond nonbiased assessment. In J. R. Bergan (Ed.), *School psychology in contemporary society.* Columbus, Ohio: Merrill, in press.

Herrnstein, R. I.Q. *Atlantic Monthly,* 1971, **228**(3), 43–64.

Hess, R. D. Social class and ethnic influences on socialization. In P. H. Mussen (Ed.), *Carmichael's manual of child psychology* (Vol. **2**). New York: Wiley, 1970.

Hess, R. D., & Shipman, V. C. Maternal influences upon early learning: The cognitive environments of urban pre-school children. In R. D. Hess & R. M. Bear (Eds.), *Early education: Current theory, research, and action*. Chicago: Aldine, 1968.

Hill, R. B. *The strengths of Black families*. New York: Emerson Hall, 1972.

Hollander, P. Legal context of educational testing. In National Research Council, Committee on Ability Testing, *Ability testing: Uses, consequences, and controversies* (Pt. 2). Washington, D.C.: National Academy Press, 1982.

Holtzman, W. H. The changing world of mental measurement and its social significance. *American Psychologist*, 1971, **26**, 546–553.

Houts, P. L. Standardized testing in America. *National Elementary Principal*, 1975, **54**(6), 2–3.

Huang, L. J. The Chinese American family. In C. H. Mindel & R. W. Habenstein (Eds.), *Ethnic families in America: Patterns and variations*. New York: Elsevier, 1976.

Hughes, J. F., & Hughes, A. O. *Equal education: A new national strategy*. Bloomington: Indiana University Press, 1972.

Hunt, J. McV. *Intelligence and experience*. New York: Ronald, 1961.

Jackson, G. D. On the report of the ad hoc committee on educational uses of tests with disadvantaged students. *American Psychologist*, 1975, **30**, 88–93.

Jensen, A. R. How much can we boost IQ and scholastic achievement? *Harvard Educational Review*, 1969, **39**, 1–123.

Jones, F. C. External crosscurrents and internal diversity: An assessment of black progress, 1960–1980. *Daedalus*, 1981, Spring, 71–101.

Kamii, C. K., & Radin, N. L. Class differences in the socialization practices of Negro mothers. *Journal of Marriage and the Family*, 1967, **29**, 302–310.

Kamin, L. J. *The science and politics of I.Q.* New York: Wiley, 1974.

Kamin, L. J. Mental testing and immigration. *American Psychologist*, 1982, **37**, 97–98. (Comment)

Keniston, K., & Carnegie Council on Children. *All our children: The American family under pressure*. New York: Harcourt Brace Jovanovich, 1977.

Kessen, W. *The child*. New York: Wiley, 1965.

Kitano, H. H. L., & Kikumura, A. The Japanese American family. In C. H. Mindel & R. W. Habenstein (Eds.), *Ethnic families in America: Patterns and variations*. New York: Elsevier, 1976.

Kleinman, J. C. Trends and variations in birth weight. In U.S. Department of Health and Human Services, *Health, United States, 1981* (DHHS Publication No. PHS 82-1232). Washington, D.C.: Government Printing Office, 1981.

Kloss, H. *The American bilingual tradition*. Rowley, Mass.: Newbury, 1977.

Knitzer, J. Parental involvement: The elixir of change. In D. N. McFadden (Ed.), *Early childhood development programs and services: Planning for action*. Washington, D.C.: National Association for the Education of Young Children, 1972.

Laosa, L. M. Reform in educational and psychological assessment: Cultural and linguistic issues. *Journal of the Association of Mexican American Educators*, 1973 **1**(1), 19–24.

Laosa, L. M. Child care and the culturally different child. *Child Care Quarterly*, 1974, **3**(4), 214–224. (a)

Laosa, L. M. Toward a research model of multicultural competency-based teacher education. In W. A. Hunter (Ed.), *Multicultural education through competency-based teacher education*. Washington, D.C.: American Association of Colleges for Teacher Education, 1974. (b)

Laosa, L. M. Bilingualism in three United States Hispanic groups: Contextual use of language by children and adults in their families. *Journal of Educational Psychology*, 1975, **67**(5), 617–627.

Laosa, L. M. Cognitive styles and learning strategies research: Some of the areas in which psychology can contribute to personalized instruction in multicultural education. *Journal of Teacher Education*, 1977, **28**(3), 26–30. (a)

Laosa, L. M. Nonbiased assessment of children's abilities: Historical antecedents and current issues. In T. Oakland (Ed.), *Psychological and educational assessment of minority children.* New York: Brunner/Mazel, 1977. (b)

Laosa, L. M. Socialization, education, and continuity: The importance of the sociocultural context. *Young Children*, 1977, **32**(5), 21–27. (c)

Laosa, L. M. Social competence in childhood: Toward a developmental, socioculturally relativistic paradigm. In M. W. Kent & J. E. Rolf (Eds.), *Primary prevention of psychopathology.* (Vol. 3): *Social competence in children.* Hanover, N.H.: University Press of New England, 1979.

Laosa, L. M. Maternal behavior: Sociocultural diversity in modes of family interaction. In R. W. Henderson (Ed.), *Parent-child interaction: Theory, research, and prospects.* New York: Academic Press, 1981.

Laosa, L. M. School, occupation, culture, and family: The impact of parental schooling on the parent-child relationship. *Journal of Educational Psychology*, 1982, **74**(6), 791–827. (a)

Laosa, L. M. The sociocultural context of evaluation. In B. Spodek (Ed.), *Handbook of research in early education.* New York: Free Press, 1982. (b)

Laosa, L. M. Parent education, cultural pluralism, and public policy: The uncertain connection. In R. Haskins & D. Adams (Eds.), *Parent education and public policy.* Norwood, N.J.: Ablex, 1983.

Lasch, C. *Haven in a heartless world: The family besieged.* New York: Basic, 1977.

Leacock, E. *Teaching and learning in city schools: A comparative study.* New York: Basic, 1969.

Leibowitz, A. H. *Educational policy and political acceptance: The imposition of English as the language of instruction in American schools.* Washington, D.C.: ERIC Clearinghouse for Linguistics, 1971. (ERIC Document Reproduction Service No. ED 047 321)

Leibowitz, A. H. *The Bilingual Education Act: A legislative analysis.* Rosslyn, Va.: InterAmerica Research Associates, National Clearinghouse for Bilingual Education, 1980.

Leibowitz, A. H. *Federal recognition of the rights of minority language groups.* Rosslyn, Va.: InterAmerica Research Associates, National Clearinghouse for Bilingual Education, 1982.

Levin, H. M. A decade of policy developments in improving education and training for low-income populations. In R. H. Haveman (Ed.), *A decade of federal antipoverty programs: Achievements, failures, and lessons.* New York: Academic Press, 1977.

Levine, R. A. *The poor ye need not have with you: Lessons from the War on Poverty.* Cambridge, Mass.: MIT Press, 1970.

Lewis, O. The culture of poverty. *Scientific American*, 1966, **215** (October), 19–25.

Maccoby, E. E., & Zellner, M. *Experiments in primary education: Aspects of Project Follow-Through.* New York: Harcourt Brace Jovanovich, 1970.

Macdonald, D. Our invisible poor. *New Yorker*, January 19, 1963, 82.

Massey, D. S. Dimensions of the new immigration to the United States and the prospects for assimilation. In R. H. Turner & J. F. Short, Jr. (Eds.), *Annual review of sociology* (Vol. 7). Palo Alto, Calif.: Annual Reviews, 1981.

McAdoo, H. P. (Ed.). *Black families.* Beverly Hills, Calif.: Sage, 1981.

McLemore, S. D. The origins of Mexican American subordination in Texas. *Social Science Quarterly*, 1973, **53**(4), 656–670.

McWilliams, C. *North from Mexico: The Spanish-speaking people of the United States.* New York: Greenwood, 1968. (Originally published, 1949.)

Meier, M. S., & Rivera, F. *The Chicanos: A history of Mexican Americans.* New York: Hill & Wang, 1972.

Miller, M. *Lyndon: An oral biography.* New York: Ballantine, 1980.

Mirandé, A. The Chicano family: A reanalysis of conflicting views. *Journal of Marriage and the Family,* 1977, **39,** 747–756.

Mondale, W. F. A statement by Senator Walter F. Mondale. *Harvard Educational Review,* 1973, **43**(4), 483–486.

Montiel, M. The social science myth of the Mexican American family. *El Grito,* 1970, 3(4), 56–63.

Moore, E. K., & McKinley, M. K. Parent involvement/control in child development programs. In D. N. McFadden (Ed.), *Early childhood development programs and services: Planning for action.* Washington, D.C.: National Association for the Education of Young Children, 1972.

Moynihan, D. P. *Maximum feasible misunderstanding: Community action in the War on Poverty.* New York: Free Press, 1969. (a)

Moynihan, D. P. The professors and the poor. In D. P. Moynihan (Ed.), *On understanding poverty: Perspectives from the social sciences.* New York: Basic, 1969. (b)

Myrdal, G. *An American dilemma: The Negro problem and modern democracy.* New York: Harper, 1944.

National Center for Education Statistics. Geographic distribution, nativity, and age distribution of language minorities in the United States: Spring 1976. *Bulletin* (78B-5). Washington, D.C. Department of Health, Education, and Welfare, Education Division, August 22, 1978.

National Education Association. *Task force and other reports.* Presented to the fifty-second Representative Assembly of the National Education Association, July 3–6, 1973. Washington, D.C.: National Education Association, 1973.

National Institute of Education. *Evaluating compensatory education: An interim report on the NIE compensatory education study.* Washington, D.C.: Government Printing Office, 1976.

National Research Council. *Toward a national policy for children and families.* Advisory Committee on Child Development. Washington, D.C.: National Academy of Sciences, 1976.

National Research Council. *Services for children: An agenda for research.* Committee on Child Development Research and Public Policy. Washington, D.C.: National Academy Press, 1981.

National Research Council. *Ability testing: Uses, consequences, and controversies* (2 vols.). Committee on Ability Testing. Washington, D.C.: National Academy Press, 1982. (a)

National Research Council. *Placing children in special education: A strategy for equity.* Panel on Selection and Placement of Students in Programs for the Mentally Retarded, Committee on Child Development Research and Public Policy. Washington, D.C.: National Academy Press, 1982. (b)

Nobles, W. W. Toward an empirical and theoretical framework for defining black families. *Journal of Marriage and the Family,* 1978, **40**(4), 679–688.

Novak, M. *The rise of the unmeltable ethnics: Politics and culture in the seventies.* New York: Macmillan, 1972.

Novick, M. Ability testing: Federal guidelines and professional standards. In National Research Council, Committee on Ability Testing. *Ability Testing: Uses, consequences, and controversies* (Pt. 2). Washington, D.C.: National Academy Press, 1982.

Oakland, T., & Laosa, L. M. Professional, legislative, and judicial influences on psychoeducational assessment practices in schools. In T. Oakland (Ed.), *Psychological and educational assessment of minority children.* New York: Brunner/Mazel, 1977.

Ogbu, J. U. *The next generation: An ethnography of education in an urban neighborhood.* New York: Academic Press, 1974.

Ogbu, J. U. *Minority education and caste: The American system in cross-cultural perspective.* New York: Academic Press, 1978.

Ogbu, J. U. Origins of human competence: A cultural-ecological perspective. *Child Development*, 1981, **52**, 413–429.

Olmedo, E. L. Testing linguistic minorities. *American Psychologist*, 1981, **36**, 1078–1085.

Passow, H. A. *Opening opportunities for disadvantaged learners.* New York: Teachers College Press, 1972.

Powell, D. R. From child to parent: Changing conceptions of early childhood intervention. *Annals of the American Academy of Political and Social Science*, 1982, **461**(May), 135–144.

President's Commission for a National Agenda for the Eighties. *Government and the advancement of social justice: Health, welfare, education, and civil rights in the eighties.* Report of the Panel on Government and the Advancement of Social Justice. Washington, D.C.: Government Printing Office, 1980.

Price, J. A. North American Indian families. In C. H. Mindel & R. W. Habenstein (Eds.), *Ethnic families in America: Patterns and variations.* New York: Elsevier, 1976.

Rainwater, L., & Yancey, W. L. *The Moynihan report and the politics of controversy.* Cambridge, Mass.: MIT Press, 1967.

Ramírez, M., III, & Castañeda, A. *Cultural democracy, bicognitive development, and education.* New York: Academic Press, 1974.

Riessman, F. *The culturally deprived child.* New York: Harper, 1962.

Ríos-Bustamante, A. (Ed.). *Mexican immigrant workers in the U.S.* Los Angeles: Chicano Studies Research Center, University of California, 1981.

Rist, R. D. Student social class and teacher expectations: The self-fulfilling prophecy in ghetto education. *Harvard Educational Review*, 1970, **10**, 411–451.

Romano, O. I. V. The anthropology and sociology of the Mexican Americans: The distortion of Mexican American history. In O. I. V. Romano (Ed.), *Voices: Readings from El Grito, a journal of contemporary Mexican American thought.* Berkeley, Calif.: Quinto Sol, 1973.

Rosenthal, R., & Jacobson, L. *Pygmalion in the classroom.* New York: Holt, Rinehart & Winston, 1968.

Ross, C. J. Early skirmishes with poverty: The historical roots of Head Start. In E. Zigler & J. Valentine (Eds.), *Project Head Start: A legacy of the War on Poverty.* New York: Free Press, 1979.

Ross, D. G. *Stanley Hall: The psychologist as prophet.* Chicago: University of Chicago Press, 1972.

Ross, S. L., De Young, H. G., & Cohen, J. S. Confrontation: Special education placement and the law. *Exceptional Children*, 1971, **38**, 5–12.

Rothchild, J., & Wolf, S. B. *The children of the counterculture.* Garden City, N.Y.: Doubleday, 1976.

Royster, E. C., Larson, J. C., Ferb, T., Fosburg, S., Nauta, M., Nelson, B., & Takata, G. *A national survey of Head Start graduates and their peers* (Report No. AAI-77-54). Cambridge, Mass.: Abt, 1978.

Samuda, R. J. *Psychological testing of American minorities: Issues and consequences.* New York: Dodd, Mead, 1975.

Santiago, I. S. *A community's struggle for equal educational opportunity: Aspira v. Board of Education.* Princeton, N.J.: Educational Testing Service, Office for Minority Education, 1978.

Schlossman, S. Before Home Start: Notes toward a history of parent education in America, 1897–1929. *Harvard Educational Review*, 1976, **46**(3), 436–467.

Schlossman, S. The parent education game: The politics of child psychology in the 1970s. *Teachers College Record*, 1978, 79(4), 788–808.

Schmelz, U. O., & DellaPergola, S. World Jewish population. In M. Himmelfarb, D. Singer, & M. Fine (Eds.), *American Jewish Year Book 1982* (Vol. 82). New York and Philadelphia: American Jewish Committee and Jewish Publication Society of America, 1981.

Schneider, S. G. *Revolution, reaction or reform: The 1974 Bilingual Education Act.* New York: Las Americas, 1976.

Sears, R. R. Your ancients revisited: A history of child development. In E. M. Hetherington (Ed.), *Review of child development research* (Vol. 5). Chicago: University of Chicago Press, 1975.

Senn, M. J. E. Insights on the child development movement in the United States. *Monographs of the Society for Research in Child Development*, 1975, 40(3–4, Serial No. 161).

Shuey, A. M. *The testing of Negro intelligence* (2d ed.). New York: Social Science Press, 1966.

Sowell, T. Ethnicity in a changing America. *Daedalus*, 1978, Winter, 213–237.

Spodek, B., & Walberg, H. J. Introduction: From a time of plenty. In B. Spodek & H. J. Walberg (Eds.), *Early childhood education: Issues and insights.* Berkeley, Calif.: McCutchan, 1977.

Steiner, G. Y. *The children's cause.* Washington, D.C.: Brookings Institution, 1976.

Steiner, G. Y. *The futility of family policy.* Washington, D.C.: Brookings Institution, 1981.

Sundquist, J. L. *Politics and policy: The Eisenhower, Kennedy, and Johnson years.* Washington, D.C.: Brookings Institution, 1968.

Teitelbaum, H., & Hiller, R. J. Bilingual education: The legal mandate. *Harvard Educational Review*, 1977, 47(2), 138–170.

Terman, L. M. *The measurement of intelligence.* London: Harrap, 1919.

Tyack, D. B. *The one best system: A history of American urban education.* Cambridge, Mass.: Harvard University Press, 1974.

U.S. Bureau of the Census. *1970 census of population: General social and economic characteristics, United States summary* (Final Report PC(1)-C1). Washington, D.C.: Government Printing Office, 1972.

U.S. Bureau of the Census. *1970 census of population: American Indians* (Subject Reports, Final Report PC(2)-1F). Washington, D.C.: Government Printing Office, 1973. (a)

U.S. Bureau of the Census. *1970 census of population: Educational attainment* (Subject Reports, Final Report PC(2)-5B). Washington, D.C.: Government Printing Office, 1973. (b)

U.S. Bureau of the Census. *1970 census of population: Japanese, Chinese, and Filipinos in the United States* (Subject Reports, Final Report PC(2)-1G). Washington, D.C.: Government Printing Office, 1973. (c)

U.S. Bureau of the Census. *1970 census of population: Negro population* (Subject Reports, Final Report PC(2)-1B). Washington, D.C.: Government Printing Office, 1973. (d)

U.S. Bureau of the Census. *1970 census of population: Occupational characteristics* (Subject Reports, Final Report PC(2)-7A). Washington, D.C.: Government Printing Office, 1973. (e)

U.S. Bureau of the Census. *1970 census of population: Persons of Spanish origin* (Subject Reports, Final Report PC(2)-1C). Washington, D.C.: Government Printing Office, 1973. (f)

U.S. Bureau of the Census. *Educational attainment in the United States: March 1979 and 1978* (Current Population Reports, Series P-20, No. 356). Washington, D.C.: Government Printing Office, 1980.

U.S. Bureau of the Census. *Money income and poverty status of families and persons in the United States* (Current Population Reports, Series P-60, No. 127). Washington, D.C.: Government Printing Office, 1981. (a)

U.S. Bureau of the Census. *1980 census of population: Age, sex, race, and Spanish origin of the population by regions, divisions, and states: 1980* (Supplementary Reports, PC80-S1-1). Washington, D.C.: Government Printing Office, 1981. (b)

U.S. Bureau of the Census. *Persons of Spanish origin in the United States: March 1980 (advance report)* (Current Population Reports, Series P-20, No. 361). Washington, D.C.: Government Printing Office, 1981. (c)

U.S. Bureau of the Census. *Statistical abstract of the United States: 1981.* Washington, D.C.: Government Printing Office, 1981. (d)

U.S. Bureau of the Census. *Ancestry and language in the United States: November 1979* (Current Population Reports, Series P-23, No. 116). Washington, D.C.: Government Printing Office, 1982. (a)

U.S. Bureau of the Census. *Money income of households, families, and persons in the United States: 1980* (Current Population Reports, Series P-60, No. 132). Washington, D.C.: Government Printing Office, 1982. (b)

U.S. Bureau of the Census. *1980 census of population and housing: Provisional estimates of social, economic, and housing characteristics: States and selected standard metropolitan statistical areas* (Supplementary Report, PHC80-S1-1). Washington, D.C.: Government Printing Office, 1982. (c)

U.S. Bureau of the Census. *1980 census of population: Persons of Spanish origin by state: 1980* (Supplementary Report PC80-S1-7). Washington, D.C.: Government Printing Office, 1982. (d)

U.S. Bureau of the Census. *Statistical abstract of the United States: 1982–83.* Washington, D.C.: Government Printing Office, 1982. (e)

U.S. Bureau of the Census. *1980 census of population: Ancestry of the population by state: 1980* (Supplementary Report PC80-S1-10). Washington, D.C.: Government Printing Office, 1983.

U.S. Commission on Civil Rights. *Ethnic isolation of Mexican Americans in the public schools of the Southwest.* Report I of the Mexican American Education Study. Washington, D.C.: Government Printing Office, 1971.

U.S. Commission on Civil Rights. *The excluded student: Educational practices affecting Mexican Americans in the Southwest.* Report III of the Mexican American Education Study. Washington, D.C.: Government Printing Office, 1972.

U.S. Commission on Civil Rights. *A better chance to learn: Bilingual bicultural education.* Washington, D.C.: Government Printing Office, 1975.

U.S. Department of Commerce. *News,* CB 81-32, February 23, 1981.

U.S. Department of Labor, Office of Policy Planning and Research. *The Negro family: The case for national action.* Washington, D.C.: Government Printing Office, 1965.

Valentine, C. A. *Culture and poverty: Critique and counter-proposals.* Chicago: University of Chicago Press, 1968.

van den Berghe, P. L. *The ethnic phenomenon.* New York: Elsevier, 1981.

Vaughan, V. C., III, & Brazelton, T. B. (Eds.). *The family: Can it be saved?* Chicago: Yearbook Medical Publishers, 1976.

Vernon, P. E. *The abilities and achievements of Orientals in North America.* New York: Academic Press, 1982.

White, S. H. Some educated guesses about cognitive development in the pre-school years. In R. D. Hess and R. M. Bear (Eds.), *Early education: Current theory, research, and action.* Chicago: Aldine, 1968.

White, S. H. *Federal programs for young children: Review and recommendations* (4 vols.). Washington, D.C.: Government Printing Office, 1973.

White House Conference on Families. *Listening to America's families: Action for the 80's. A summary of the report to the President, Congress and families of the Nation.* Washington, D.C.: White House Conference on Families, 1980. (a)

White House Conference on Families. *National Research Forum on Family Issues: Program.* Washington, D.C.: White House Conference on Families, 1980. (b)

Williams, R. Abuses and misuse in testing black children. In R. Jones (Ed.), *Black psychology.* New York: Harper & Row, 1972.

Wohlwill, J. F. Cognitive development in childhood. In O. G. Brim, Jr., & J. Kagan (Eds.), *Constancy and change in human development.* Cambridge, Mass.: Harvard University Press, 1980.

Woodward, C. V. *The strange career of Jim Crow* (2d rev. ed.). Oxford: Oxford University Press, 1966.

Zigler, E., & Anderson, K. An idea whose time had come: The intellectual and political climate. In E. Zigler & J. Valentine (Eds.), *Project Head Start: A legacy of the War on Poverty.* New York: Free Press, 1979.

Zigler, E., & Valentine, J. (Eds.). *Project Head Start: A legacy of the War on Poverty.* New York: Free Press, 1979.

Child Health Policy

JOHN A. BUTLER
Harvard Medical School

BARBARA STARFIELD
Johns Hopkins School of Hygiene and Public Health

SUZANNE STENMARK
Harvard School of Public Health

The term "child health policy" is something of a misnomer. Most decisions affecting child health are embedded in larger policy realms, many of which are not principally concerned with children; and some policies that are not ostensibly health related have major consequences for child health. Both factors make it difficult in a chapter such as this to avoid full-scale analysis of a very broad range of legislative, judicial, and administrative activities, as well as of many activities in the private sector. It is also difficult to decide which research literatures are the ones with greatest policy significance.

We embark on a review of recent developments in child health policy with an awareness of these complexities, and our discussion is by no means exhaustive. This chapter is divided into major sections. We begin with a summary of vital statistics from recent decades and data on the epidemiology of childhood disorders, focusing especially on trends in childhood mortality, morbidity, the "new morbidity," and disability. These descriptive data are important as background information. Then we examine the research evidence on four major topics: the determinants of child health and illness; the effects of illness on the development of children; patterns of access to health care in childhood and consequences of insufficient access; and the acquisition in childhood of health-related concepts, beliefs, attitudes, and behavior. The literature on each of these topics supports certain inferences of potential significance for policymakers.

The third section describes the decision-making context of national child health policy, and then we briefly analyze several controversial issues. These issues are by no means the only ones that continue to confront members of Congress, federal agency personnel, and other

policymakers, but they are among the most important in dollar consequences and in the value conflict they embody. They include: how further
to improve pregnancy outcomes; how to respond to the problem of teen
pregnancy; how to reduce the incidence of death and disability associated
with motor vehicles; whether to strengthen the role of schools and preschools as sites of case finding and care; and how to define the public
responsibility for the health care of chronically ill and handicapped children. The significance of each issue will have been made clear by information presented in earlier sections of the chapter.

The final section is devoted to discussion of research and data needs in
support of child health policy, with particular attention to the need for
better indicators of child wellness and functioning, improved policy-
oriented epidemiology and outcome measurement to assess program impact, more research on the efficacy of psychosocial components of pediatric
care, and policy research and training combining the insights of health
professionals and others in the field of child development. These areas
deserve concentrated effort in the years to come.

HEALTH STATUS AND THE EPIDEMIOLOGY OF CHILDHOOD DISORDERS

If we are to understand the development of policies related to children's
health, it helps to begin by reviewing relevant vital statistics and
epidemiologic data from various national surveys. In the past 3 years, a
number of reports and articles have offered detailed interpretive analyses
of U.S. data on mortality, morbidity, and chronic disability in infancy and
childhood (Egbuonu & Starfield, 1982; Lash, Sigal, & Dudzinski, 1980;
Select Panel for the Promotion of Child Health, 1981a, 1981b; Starfield &
Pless, 1980; U.S. Surgeon General, 1979; Zill, 1983). These analyses have
been based on annual or periodic data from the National Health Interview
Survey (HIS), the National Health and Nutrition Examination Survey
(HANES), and the National Vital Statistics Series, supplemented by addi-
tional federal and state survey data and information from the National
Survey of Children, conducted in 1976 by the Foundation for Child
Development (FCD) (Zill, 1983).

Four major themes are consistent in all of these sources and underlie
much of what we will discuss throughout the chapter: (1) the remarkable
decline over the past century in child mortality, or rates of death, and
morbidity, or incidence of certain types of illness, with infectious diseases
becoming far less frequent as a cause and accidents and violence becoming
more so; (2) the reduced but still notable differences in mortality and

morbidity among children according to socioeconomic status (SES), race, ethnicity, geographic region, residential area, and sex; (3) the new profile of childhood morbidity in the United States, in which behavioral, social, emotional, family, and school-related problems have become a larger component; and (4) the continuing presence of serious chronic disability and handicap among a small number of children, for some of whom medical technology, by improving prognosis, has placed new demands on the children themselves, their families, and the service system.

MORTALITY

At present, infant and childhood mortality is the lowest it has ever been in our country. By 1979 only 13 U.S. infants died per 1,000 live births, approximately half as many as in 1960 or one-eighth as many as during the first 2 decades of the century (Fig. 1). For older children, too, death rates have dropped substantially. In 1930, 5.6 children per 1,000 died between ages 1 and 4 years; by 1969, this figure was 0.8, and by 1978,

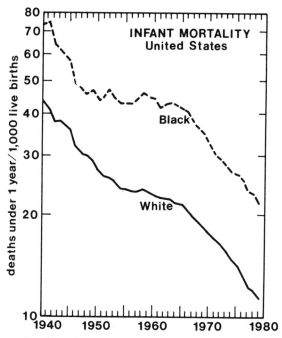

FIG. 1.—Infant mortality rates by race: United States, 1940–1979. Deaths under 1 year per 1,000 live births. Source.—Select Panel for the Promotion of Child Health, 1981.

0.7. Average death rates among 5- to 14-year-olds, always lower than for other age groups, had dropped by 1978 to one-third of the 1940 rate (0.3 as compared with 1.0 per 1,000). Only among adolescents are the figures discouraging, with death rates actually increasing since 1960 and remaining higher than for other youngsters. The chance of dying escalates from ages 12 to 24—for example, in 1976, death rates were 0.4 per 1,000 among 12- to 15-year-olds, 0.9 per 1,000 for 16- to 17-year-olds, and 1.3 per 1,000 for 18- to 24-year-olds.

Underlying these changes in mortality are changes in the causes of death. Improvements in living conditions over the century, accompanied by significant improvements in public health and health care, have resulted in the decline of infectious disease as a major risk factor. Reductions in infant mortality, as a case in point, may be attributed to improvements in living environments, maternal health, nutrition, and prenatal care; to the decline in births to women at high risk because of age or parity (number of previous births); to technical improvements in medical care and regionalization of perinatal services; and to the legalization of therapeutic abortions.

But as some risks have diminished, others have taken on a new salience (Fig. 2a). Accidents, and violence in particular, have become the leading cause of death for children, accounting in 1978 for 42% of deaths

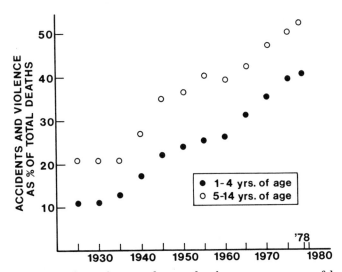

FIG. 2a.—Death rate from accidents and violence as percentage of death rate from all causes (deaths/100,000 resident population) by age. Source.—Select Panel for the Promotion of Child Health, 1981.

among 1- to 4-year olds, 51% among 5- to 14-year-olds, and approximately two-thirds of all deaths among 15- to 18-year-olds. Auto accidents account for fully one-quarter of all deaths among children and youths under 18, and a far greater proportion of teenage deaths, especially among males (Fig. 2*b*). Drownings and fires account for another 11%. As a result of these trends, childhood accidents have received increasing attention from pediatricians and public health professionals in recent years (Berger, 1981). In general, the increased salience of accidents as a cause of death does not reflect an absolute increase in accident rates but, rather, a smaller reduction in this than other causes of mortality. One major exception is among 15- to 24-year-olds, however, for whom accident, homicide, and suicide rates actually have risen in the past 10 years. Accidents, homicide, and suicide now account for three-quarters of all deaths in this age group, although they accounted for only half in 1950.

Rates and causes of mortality differ by socioeconomic group, residential area, race, and sex. Comparisons by socioeconomic level and residential area (urban, suburban, rural) show persisting differences in infant, child, and adolescent death rates (Mare, 1982), even though average rates are not as divergent as they once were for the affluent compared with the poor and the suburban compared with rural and central city dwellers.

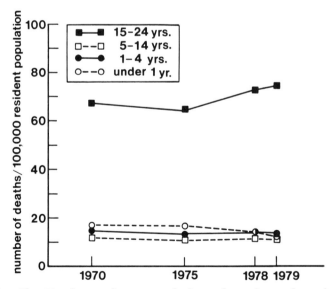

FIG. 2*b*.—Death rates for motor vehicle accidents, homicide, and suicide, according to age: United States, selected years 1970–1980. (Data are based on the national vital registration system.) Source.—National Center for Health Statistics, 1983.

Infant mortality rates have been declining faster for black Americans than for whites but are still almost twice as high for blacks. Death rates are half again as high for nonwhite children between ages 1 and 4 years, and a third again as high between ages 5 and 14. Minority-group teenagers are less likely to be killed in auto accidents but more likely to die from homicide—which is the leading cause of death among nonwhite 15- to 24-year-olds, accounting for 30% of deaths.

Differences in mortality according to sex also are pronounced, increasing as children grow older. Boys are more at risk throughout childhood for fatal disease and especially for death caused by accidents, poisoning, and violence. In 1976 boys under age 6 were almost twice as likely to die from these causes as girls; among teenagers, males were three times as likely to have a fatal accident, largely because of differences in automobile use (Kovar & Meny, 1981).

MORBIDITY

Paralleling the decline in childhood mortality are major reductions in infant and child morbidity from infectious disease. Advances in immunization combined with the development of antibiotics and other medications have greatly curtailed the extent and seriousness of childhood illness.

Parent and teacher reports now suggest that the vast majority of American children—94% or more—are in "excellent" or "good" health. Only 3.4% of children in the 1976 FCD survey were reported by their parents as being in "fair" or "poor" health, and less than 6% were reported by their teachers as being in these categories. The parent estimate (3.4%) represents a slight but statistically significant improvement over survey results on identical questions in the 1963–1965 Health Examination Survey (Zill, 1983).

Children between 7 and 11 years old have the fewest health problems of any age group. On average, they go to the doctor only about three times each year. However, because physician visits are not evenly distributed across the child population, most children go far more seldom than the average would suggest; in any year, over half of those aged 7–11 see a doctor only once or not at all.

Even during the preschool years, when children tend to get sick often, only infrequently do they experience prolonged limitation of activity or major secondary disability. Children lose more days of school, have more days of restricted activity, and spend more time in bed for respiratory illnesses than for other acute-care conditions. Respiratory problems alone account for over 60% of all missed school days, over half of all visits to office-based physicians, and a fifth of child days spent in short-stay hospitals (Kovar & Meny, 1981). In the decade 1972–1981 there was a modest decline, however, in the average number of days of restricted activity and the average number of school days lost as a result of respiratory problems.

Injuries from accidents represent a major component of child morbidity. More than half occur in or near the home or school. In the FCD Survey, 20% of children reported having experienced a bad accidental injury at some point in their lives; 3% had experienced such an accident within the last year; and 4% reported more than one such episode (Zill, 1983).

Socioeconomic status–related differences in the prevalence of acute illnesses among children do not show up strongly in national interview surveys, but specific serious conditions such as rheumatic fever, hemophilus influenza meningitis, gastroenteritis, and parasitic disease are much more commonly found among low-SES youngsters. Even when race is controlled for, SES remains a strong predictor of the prevalence of such typical health problems as iron deficiency anemia, lead poisoning, and recurrent infections. Low-SES parents in the National Health Interview Survey also report a greater percentage of children in "fair" or "poor" health than do middle- or upper-income parents. In 1976, 9% of children in families with incomes below $5,000 were reported in fair or poor health as compared with 2% of children from families with incomes above $15,000.

Low-SES children also have more restricted-activity days, miss more school, and are more often confined to bed. Average duration of each hospitalization of low-SES children is roughly twice that of affluent children, and average total hospital days—calculated from both admission rates and length of stay—is four times as great (Egbuonu & Starfield, 1982).

Dental caries, dental disease, and tooth loss remain major problems in the United States; they are far more prevalent than other types of childhood morbidity and often result in permanent disability. The American Dental Association reports that by the time a child reaches age 17, an average of eight or nine permanent teeth have decayed and have either been filled or are missing. Periodontal disease affects 65% of high school students. But decay usually begins much earlier; even 5-year-olds have an average of 2.2 decayed, carious, or filled teeth. Among children ages 6–11, 55% have one or more decayed, missing, or filled teeth, and a third have two or more such teeth (Kovar & Meny, 1981). Average numbers of carious teeth do not differ significantly by family income or parent education, but family income is strongly associated with whether teeth receive dental care and caries are filled. Among white adolescents, four-fifths with decayed teeth have been treated, but only half that many have been treated among the poor—and one in five among black adolescents. Failure to receive timely care often results in permanent tooth loss.

THE "NEW MORBIDITY"

As mortality and morbidity from infectious disease have decreased over recent decades, more attention has been given to behavioral, social, and school-related problems, which have been termed the "new morbidity." As Haggerty, Roghmann, and Pless (1975) observe: "The current major health problems of children, as seen by the community, are those that would have barely been mentioned a generation ago. Learning difficulties and school problems, behavior disturbances, allergies, speech difficulties, visual problems and the problems of adolescents in coping and adjusting are today the most common concerns about children." Behavioral and social difficulties are themselves a form of health risk, for they contribute to mortality and the likelihood of physical illness. In many instances, they also are risk factors for long-term disease, disability, or lack of productivity (Hamburg, 1982).

Although prevalence estimates for behavioral and social problems are less precise than those for medical problems, current research suggests that new morbidity problems affect a significant proportion of the population under 18. After reviewing diagnostic data from seven different sizable primary care facilities, Starfield, Gross, Wood, Pantell, Allen, Gordon, Moffatt, Drachman, and Katz (1980) report that at least 5% and as many as 15% of children seen in 1 year had one or more psychosocial problems. Recent research in other pediatric practice settings yields comparable estimates (Goldberg, Regier, McInerny, Pless, & Roghmann, 1979; Gortmaker, Walker, & Weitzman, 1979; Jacobson, Goldberg, Burns, Hoeper, Hankin, & Hewitt, 1980). These same studies all show that prevalence varies markedly by the child's age, sex, SES, and family status (i.e., number of parents living in the home).

Starfield et al. (1980) also demonstrate that prevalence estimates for psychosocial disability vary among practice settings—more so, for instance, than diagnoses of psychosomatic illness (Table 1). The investigators hypothesize that this variation results from one or more of four differences: in diagnostic nomenclature, in the relationship between practitioners and patients, in reimbursement for providing services, and in practitioners' recognition of psychosocial problems. Their research further indicates that fewer visits are initiated explicitly for psychosocial reasons that would be predicted from prevalence estimates based on diagnosis. This discrepancy could be interpreted to suggest that there is an unmet need or "pent-up

TABLE 1

PERCENTAGE OF CHILDREN WITH PSYCHOSOCIAL AND PSYCHOSOMATIC DIAGNOSES IN 1977[a] FOR SELECTED MEDICAL CARE FACILITIES AND SERVICES

FACILITY AND SERVICE

| | Multispecialty Group | | | | Pediatric Service | Family Practice | |
| | Harvard Community Health Plan | | Columbia Medical Plan | | Johns Hopkins Children and Youth Project | Medical University of South Carolina | Medical College of Virginia[b] |
	Pediatrics	Internal Medicine	Pediatrics	Internal Medicine			
Psychosocial diagnoses:							
Children	15.5	13.6	5.4	1.1	15.0	14.2	5.7
Visits	6.4	7.6	2.0	.6	6.9	7.1	3.6
Psychosomatic diagnoses:							
Children	9.6	8.5	9.5	6.4	10.8	10.8	6.2
Visits	4.4	4.4	4.0	2.7	4.7	4.9	4.2

SOURCE.—Starfield et al., 1980.

[a] Values are percentages with diagnoses in 1 year.

[b] Medical College of Virginia has four separate clinical units.

demand" or might simply mean that parents regard health care professionals as a resource only for some types of psychosocial care.

Is the "new morbidity" really new? Certainly some forms of behavior have become major health threats only fairly recently, as the automobile and the handgun have become widely accessible to young people. But it is plausible to assume that other concerns, such as reading problems and hyperactivity in the classroom, have become the object of pediatric practice mainly because pediatricians now have more time to address them and the society does a better job of documenting them. Hence, the new concern about behavioral and social morbidity among children reflects not only possible increases in its prevalence but also larger social and economic trends in the society.

Can anything be said, then, about trends in the underlying distribution of psychosocial problems? Zill and Peterson (1982) shed some light on this issue in summarizing available social indicators from various national surveys, including their own, that measured children's attitudes. There is no evidence suggesting a massive increase in child behavioral or mental health problems during the past 2 decades. On the other hand, it seems clear that stress in childhood has increased as family disruption has become more prevalent, and such stress may be an important precursor of new behavioral problems.

Violence among children, especially suicide and homicide, is one disturbing indicator that suggests the need for increased attention to psychosocial concerns. As Eisenberg (1980) reports, among 15- to 24-year-olds suicide and homicide by firearms doubled between 1966 and 1975. In that age group, suicide has become the third leading cause of death among males and the fourth among females. In the past 2 decades, male suicide rates more than tripled for both the 10- to 14-year-old and the 15- to 19-year-old age groups. Fear of violence also is reported by children themselves as a major concern (Zill, 1983).

CHRONIC DISABILITY AND HANDICAP

There continues to be a limited and particularly unfortunate group of American children who are afflicted with serious chronic illness or physical handicaps. Their needs for health care are qualitatively different from and more intensive than the routine preventive and acute care required by others. Chronically ill and handicapped children need normal primary care but also may require costly surgical interventions, recurrent hospitalization, long-term care, and special counseling and psychological support services for the child and other family members (Breslau, 1982; Hobbs, Perrin, & Ireys, 1983; Ireys, 1981).

Just as the decline of serious infectious disease has changed the profile of acute care for children, so has it changed the distribution of serious childhood disabilities. Poliomyelitis, which only 30 years ago was a major preoccupation of pediatrics and had devastating consequences in death and secondary disability among children, is no longer a problem in this country. Numerous other illnesses are now preventable or have controllable health consequences. Particularly dramatic has been the recent progress in metabolic screening, surgical intervention, chemotherapy, and other forms of secondary and tertiary prevention; these have greatly improved life chances and prognosis for children with illnesses that only a generation ago would have proved fatal at an early age. One indirect consequence has been an increased number of older children and teenagers with chronic or terminal illnesses such as spina bifida, cystic fibrosis, juvenile diabetes, and cancer, who now require health maintenance and recurrent medical care as well as specialized psychological care.

Serious impairments fall into several broad categories according to the demands they place on the health care system. Major medical problems, including arthritis, cancer, cerebral palsy, diabetes, epilepsy, paralysis, cystic fibrosis, and cardiac and neurologic disabilities, affect no more than 2% of the child population at any time but may require prolonged and costly health care. Some medical problems, such as asthma, hay fever, and other allergic manifestations, are less serious but also constitute a troublesome element of chronic disability in children; these conditions often necessitate extensive health supervision, even though hospitalization is not likely. The remaining major categories of chronic childhood disability are handicapping sensory and speech impairments and handicapping mental retardation and mental illness; the latter two contribute an additional 2%–5% to overall prevalence estimates, depending on how broadly severe mental retardation and mental illness are defined. Although these forms of disability do not themselves often require a high level of medical care, they may accompany major medical impairments.

Though the percentage varies by condition, overall no more than one-quarter of those children with major medical problems have functional limitations severe enough to restrict their ability to play or to attend school (Butler, Budetti, McManus, Stenmark, & Newachek, 1984). However, data on limitations of activity among children remain important in policy discussions because functional restrictions are strongly correlated with actual use of medical services—and hence, cost. In 1979, the 3.9% of children who had limitations of activity accounted for 18.8% of all child hospital discharges and 30.2% of child hospital days.

Over the past 15 years, there has been a steady increase in reported prevalence of children with limitations of activity (Table 2). In a recent

TABLE 2
TRENDS IN NUMBER AND PERCENTAGE OF CHILDREN WITH LIMITATIONS OF ACTIVITY, 1957–1979

	1967	1968	1969	1970	1971	1972	1973	1974	1975	1976	1977	1978	1979
Percentage with limitation of activity (LA)	2.1	2.1	2.6	2.7	2.9	3.0	3.4	3.7	3.7	3.7	3.4[a]	3.9	3.9
Percentage unable to carry on major activity (LA1) and limited amount or kind of major activity (LA2)[b]	1.1	1.2	1.2	1.3	1.5	1.6	1.9	1.9	1.9	1.9	1.8	2.0	2.1
N (in thousands) with LA	1,418	1,427	1,760	1,820	1,942	1,921	2,149	2,305	2,283	2,267	2,012	2,309	2,291
N (in thousands) with LA1 and LA2	712	825	810	873	972	1,037	1,191	1,199	1,165	1,179	1,104	1,178	1,232

SOURCE.—Butler et al., 1984.

[a] NCHS attributes this fluctuation between 1976 and 1978 to temporary changes in survey procedure (ser. 10, no. 126).

[b] Persons limited in (LA2) or unable (LA1) to perform their major activity: This category includes those unable to carry on the usual activity for their age-sex group (e.g., working or going to school) and those restricted in the amount or kind of usual activity for their age-sex group.

analysis, Gortmaker (1983) points out that incidence at birth of various disabling conditions has been fairly stable over this interval and argues that increased prevalence probably can be attributed largely to improved cohort survivorship. Serious chronic conditions and handicaps are generally more prevalent among poor than nonpoor children; and as Figure 3 shows, consequent limitations of activity also vary considerably by family SES. Low-SES children are much more likely to be unable to attend regular school because of a chronic condition or to be limited in their ability to do so (Egbuonu & Starfield, 1982; Starfield, 1982).

DETERMINANTS OF HEALTH

In addition to descriptive data on trends in health status, a second and more complex order of information is relevant to child health policy. It is provided by research on statistical associations and causal relationships among several major sets of variables, including: antecedents of child

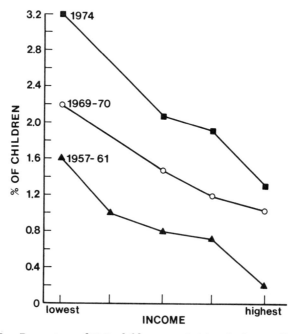

FIG. 3.—Percentage of U.S. children ages 0–16 with chronic illness limiting their major activity. Income categories were made comparable by adjusting the categories in the original data for changes in the Consumer Price Index with 1960 as the base. Source.—Starfield, 1982.

health (the child's genetic endowment, prenatal and perinatal events, and family socioeconomic background); elements of the child's physical and social environment contributing to health or illness; the child's pattern of health service use; child and family concepts, beliefs, and behavior relevant to health care; and short- and long-term health outcomes. Not enough is yet known to unify our understanding of how all these elements interrelate, but research on various specific combinations of factors supports certain generalizations with potential policy implications.

This section reviews the evidence on four topics in particular: the determinants of health status in childhood, the effects of illness on child development, the determinants of health service use among children, and the acquisition in childhood of health-rated beliefs and behavior. We briefly discuss the research literature on each of these topics.

DETERMINANTS OF CHILD HEALTH STATUS

Health status is the result of interactions among biological, social, and environmental factors. How much do we know about the relative importance of these factors as determinants?

Genetic Factors

In recent years there have been considerable advances in understanding of the relative contribution of genetic factors, prenatal and perinatal events, and family background to the status of children's health. Certain uncommon but serious forms of health impairment are known to have genetic components, including mental retardation resulting from Down's syndrome, some chronic illnesses such as cystic fibrosis, and some types of serious mental illness such as schizophrenia (Edgerton, 1979; Kety, 1976; Milunsky, 1975). Although genes can have a direct role in limiting a child's mental ability and life chances from birth, genetic contributions to disease often are more complex and interactive. For example, genes may play a role in predisposing some children to obesity, high blood cholesterol, and other conditions that in turn can become risk factors later in life (U.S. Surgeon General, 1979). For some conditions, such as juvenile-onset diabetes, a latent genetic predisposition may exist that requires very special environmental circumstances to be triggered.

Much less is known about genetic predispositions to learning disabilities, emotional balance, and other forms of the "new morbidity." Evidence from family histories can be marshaled to support the hypothesis that certain forms of learning problems may be genetically influenced (Lewitter, DeFries, & Elston, 1980; Pennington, Bender, Puck, Saltenblatt, &

Robinson, 1982; Smith, Kimberling, Pennington, & Lubs, 1983), but genetic contributions to most forms of psychosocial morbidity are assumed to be small (Levine & Palfrey, 1982).

Prenatal and Perinatal Factors

A second major cluster of determinants of child health is composed of prenatal and perinatal factors. Prenatal factors known to increase the infant's risk of impaired health and development include maternal viral illness, diabetes, and other illnesses; chronic illness such as maternal undernutrition; alcohol, tobacco, and drug abuse; number of previous births; maternal age of under 15 or over 35, and inappropriate prenatal and delivery care (Palfrey, 1982; Select Panel for the Promotion of Child Health, 1981a). Low birth weight, in particular low birth weight for gestational age, has proved to be among the stronger predictors of immediate and long-term developmental risk (Friedman & Sigman, 1981; Hemminki & Starfield, 1979; McCormick, Shapiro, & Starfield, 1980). However, all such research suffers from the limitation that it cannot fully separate the contributions of pregnancy outcome from subsequent influences in the child's environment. The postnatal period also presents a series of hazards, such as asphyxia, hypoxia, traumatic delivery, hypoglycemia, bacterial infections (especially meningitis), and central nervous system bleeding. Extreme events of this kind clearly can be related to irreversible health impairment, but they are far less common than they once were because of advances in access to services and the technology employed in delivery and neonatal care.

Evidence from both prospective and retrospective studies suggests that infants who have suffered serious complications during gestation, labor, delivery, or the neonatal period are at risk for significant neurological, mental, and behavioral problems in later childhood. But such studies have shown little predictive value for milder neonatal complications (Bee, Barnard, Eyres, Gray, Hammond, Spietz, Snyder, & Clark, 1982; Cohen, Parmalee, Sigman, & Beckwith, 1981; Parmalee, Beckwith, Cohen, & Sigman, 1980). Most children with medical problems in the neonatal period do not show developmental delays or other long-term consequences. Retrospective analysis does indicate, however, that many adolescents with learning disabilities and behavior disorders often had earlier biological and temperamental markers as correlates, including perinatal stress, low birth weight, congenital anomalies, or low levels of activity as infants (Starfield & Pless, 1980).

The Role of Family Background and Environment

For most children, including those with mild medical problems at birth, family background and the environment play a far more consequential role than do biomedical factors in determining developmental and health outcomes. Family SES, in particular, is the single best predictor of child health status and developmental functioning in cohort studies, even after numerous other variables have been adjusted for (Morse, Hyde, Newberger, & Reed, 1977; Schaefer, 1979). Three major longitudinal studies, one British and two conducted in the United States, lend support to this generalization (Browman, Nichols, & Kennedy, 1975; Davie, Butler, & Goldstein, 1972; Werner, Brennan, & French, 1971). All these investigations found that various severe impairments, such as cerebral palsy, serious mental retardation, and major sensory handicaps, could be identified rather well at birth or predicted by birth events, but that more moderate developmental dysfunction, school failure, and behavioral disturbances were more strongly predicted by family SES.

The Kauai study (Werner, Brennan, & French, 1971) also produced evidence of an interaction between perinatal factors and the child's environment. By age 10, of those who had been at perinatal risk, middle-class children were comparable to their peers in number and severity of developmental problems, whereas low-SES children had a higher number of such problems than either middle-class or low-SES peers. Parmalee et al. (1980) speculate that children at medical risk who are reared in high-SES families experience a form of environmental compensation. By contrast, low-SES children at risk appear to be especially susceptible to what has been called developmental attrition or cumulative failure (Eisenberg, 1977).

Although these data do not immediately suggest precise recommendations for policy, they do support two generalizations. First, advances in genetic counseling, genetic screening, and medical technology surrounding birth will continue to be very important in reducing the incidence of a limited number of serious biologically defined problems in children. Second, however, these interventions cannot be expected to significantly reduce the many disparities in health status and levels of developmental functioning among different groups in the child population. In concert with birth-related medical care, strategies that address family background and the environmental determinants of health and functioning will continue to be required.

Effects of Medical Care

What can be said about the role of medical care as a determinant of health outcomes in later childhood and adolescence? Certainly, many forms of preventive care and medical therapy are of demonstrated efficacy and, when administered properly, can make a significant difference in child health (Canadian Task Force on the Periodic Health Examination, 1979; Harvard Child Health Project Task Force, Vol. 2, 1977; Select Panel for the Promotion of Child Health, 1981a). The data are particularly clear for immunizations, good nutrition, various forms of early childhood screening (especially for vision and hearing defects, lead poisoning, and iron-deficiency anemia), preventive dental care, and the treatment of common bacterial infections by antibiotics. There is much room for improvement in the delivery of these and other effective services.

Nonetheless, analyses of large sets of data generally confirm the view that use of medical services throughout childhood, although one factor in determining health status, is not as powerful as a family SES and home environment in shaping health outcomes (Gortmaker, 1981; Grossman, 1981; Haggerty et al., 1975). Frequency of physician visits, and of well-child visits, in particular, is especially hard to link with better health outcomes. For example, in an analysis of data from the 1963–1965 Health Interview Survey, Grossman, Coote, Edwards, Shatkotko, & Chermichovsky (1980) found strong evidence that some preventive interventions and public health measures (e.g., preventive dental care and fluoridation) are effective, but they could not find a clear relationship between the number of child physician visits and several measures of the status of health at middle childhood. This analysis suffered from the limitation that health was measured according to only a few indicators, including measures of iron-deficiency anemia, obesity, and hypertension, and parent perceptions of their child's general health. But similar results have been reported elsewhere and have occasioned reconsideration of the content of pediatric well-child care (Casey, Sharp, & Loda, 1979).

Effects of Family Income and Mother's Education

Are some elements of family SES and the home environment more important than others in predicting health? If the effect of various factors in family background and the environment could be separated and their relative contribution assessed, those with the largest contribution might merit highest priority as objects of public policy.

One topic of discussion in the recent literature on health services has been the relative importance of family income and mother's education as explanatory variables. Ample documentation can be found that family is a strong predictor of both health status and appropriate use of health services even after race, ethnicity, family composition, and other background variables are adjusted for (Dutton, 1978, 1981; Egbuonu & Starfield, 1982). But parent education, usually the mother's, is also a major explanatory variable. Mother's education usually accounts for some variance in status of child health and use of health services that is not explained by income (Franks & Bisseau, 1980; Kirscht, Becker, & Eveland, 1976; Schaefer & Hughes, 1976). Mother's education is also better than income as a predictor of certain health-related behaviors, such as seeking prenatal care (Zill, 1983).

Differences among data sets, outcome measures, and analytic methods may explain why some researchers find income more salient and others find maternal education. Dutton (1981), for example, reanalyzed 1972 health status and use data for low-income, mainly black children attending various facilities for providing health care in Washington, D.C.; she argues for the greater importance of income as a predictor. She finds a U-shaped relationship between health status and family income when families are grouped in three categories: the Medicaid-eligible poor, the near-poor, and the affluent. Dutton argues that, without this type of analysis, income effects are masked.

By contrast, Grossman et al. (1980), in their analysis of a limited number of health status variables in the 1963–1965 National Health Examination Survey, find few differences by income in health status at middle childhood and find mother's education a better predictor. They offer the interpretation that income differences typically reported in health care research hide the multidimensional nature of child health. Traditional forms of morbidity are higher for the poor, but prevalence rates of parent-reported allergy, high blood pressure, and other disorders are not. It is important to recognize that the Grossman et al. findings antedate the Medicaid program, which greatly increased low-income families' use of health services and reporting of illness.

On the basis of their work, Grossman et al. (1980) make the provocative argument that child health would be little affected by changing the income differential among families and sizably affected by changing maternal education levels. In their judgment, policy recommendations such as those made by the Carnegie Council on Children (Keniston, 1977) or the National Research Council (1976), which propose that a national incomes policy is the best single way to affect child health, are incorrect. Unfortunately, effects on child health were not a major focus of the recent national income-maintenance demonstrations; hence policy inferences on this issue still must be based largely on survey data.

Whatever its effect, maternal education probably operates indirectly, because we know that well-educated women do not spend more time than other women explicitly teaching their children about health (Mechanic, 1980). We also know that some types of intervention to educate mothers and fathers about various facts of parenting and child health care have developmental benefits, though modest ones, for children (Harman & Brim, 1980).

EFFECTS OF ILLNESS ON CHILD DEVELOPMENT

Just as it is important for policymakers to understand the deteminants of child health, so is it important to assess the consequences of child illness. How serious are these? What realms of functioning do they affect? Do they tend to persist?

It is generally recognized that poor physical health in childhood can be a risk to cognitive development. Health problems can limit or distort the child's biological growth, prevent school attendance, limit attention, and otherwise constrain the child's ability to process information or act. Birch and Gussow (1970) document many of the health risks to intellectual development, although they also acknowledge that there is not much understanding of the mechanisms by which poor health contributes to poor intellectual performance or of how poor health and low SES interact to contribute to developmental deficits.

The effects of serious malnutrition on intellectual development have been studied extensively, but because severe protein and calorie malnutrition among children almost vanished from the United States in the 1970s, the extreme effects discussed in comparative research and research from developing countries generally are not applicable. The Ten-State Nutrition Study and the Health and Nutrition Examination Survey indicate that in recent years average nutrient intakes of infants and young children in all income groups have been well above the recommended daily allowance. Rates of physical growth also have been similar for all income groups (Popkin, Akin, Kaufman, & MacDonald, 1981).

More significant are persisting iron deficiencies and nutritional imbalances among a sizable number of pregnant women and youngsters. These are known to contribute to risks at birth, attention problems in school, and increased likelihood of infection (Dwyer, 1981). Obesity is also a problem among a significant number of American children and often leads to problems of function and low self-concept in the short term and greater risk of heart disease and other forms of morbidity in adulthood. The implications of these findings for nutrition policy are discussed in another chapter of this volume. Some now believe that malnutrition could again become a problem in the United States if present federal cutbacks in the various major food supplement programs continue (Amidei, 1982).

Edwards and Grossman (1977) have shown that certain health conditions make a statistically significant contribution to explaining variation in school achievement and IQ, when family background and home environment variables are held constant. Low birth weight, poor hearing, uncorrected or poor vision, and school absences because of illness are among the major correlates of below average achievement and IQ. Effects on school achievement were found even when IQ was held constant.

Two well-documented causes of short-term child learning deficits are low-level lead poisoning (Needleman, Gunroe, Leviton, Reed, Peresie, Maher, & Barnett, 1979) and hearing loss from untreated otitis media (Brody, 1978; Paradise & Rogers, 1980; Thibodeau & Berwick, 1980; Zinkus, Gottlieb, & Shapiro, 1978). Clearly, these conditions are amenable to screening and medical care.

Both the cognitive development and social development of children can be very substantially affected by long-term illness or handicap (Ireys, 1981; Pless & Pinkerton, 1975; Weitzman, 1981). Children with chronic impairments are at far higher risk than other children for psychological, sibling-related, social, and family financial problems. And children with both a chronic disorder and a low level of family functioning are at greater risk of psychological maladjustment than those with just one of these problems (Starfield & Pless, 1980). A Rochester, New York, study comparing 124 school-aged chronically ill children with a group of healthy peers (Wolfe, 1981) has further shown that health status is associated with school achievement both directly and, indirectly, through the effects of absenteeism on achievement. This study also reveals that some forms of chronic illness are much more likely than others to affect school performance.

Measures of self-concept, level of aspiration, and locus of control generally reveal greater problems among chronically ill and handicapped children than others, although we can hope that recent policies of deinstitutionalization and mainstreaming, and the changes of attitude in the larger society that they reflect, may no longer make low self-esteem and limited sense of competency inevitable (Gliedman & Roth, 1980). But long-term employment prospects for the chronically impaired remain far worse than for other children, even those with more "socially acceptable" disorders such as orthopedic impairments (Pless & Pinkerton, 1975). Of the 15 million disabled persons in the United States between 16 and 24 years of age, more than half are either unemployed or out of the labor force—meaning neither employed nor seeking employment (Hammerman & Markowski, 1981).

There remains, of course, the question of why some children seemingly at risk of negative developmental outcomes because of physical illness or handicap nonetheless do not succumb and turn out to lead relatively normal or successful lives. The issue of vulnerability has recently been discussed by Rutter (1980) and by Werner and Smith (1982). Rutter concludes that, although no simple generalizations can be derived from the research literature about predictors of child resiliency, single sources of stress seem easier to resist than multiple sources; and child personality, temperament, sex, and family circumstances interact to create a unique vector of risk for each child.

Stability and Change in Illness

Obviously, much chronic illness in childhood persists into later life. But for the larger population, what can be said about stability and change in patterns of illness between childhood and adulthood? In their review of longitudinal evidence on stability and change, Starfield and Pless (1980) conclude that many common conditions do display patterns of consistency over childhood, but prospective predictions for individual children are not strong enough to be of policy significance. Few specific factors that predispose persons to the persistence of such illnesses as respiratory problems, asthma, hay fever, hypertension, and urinary tract infections have been identified, and such factors may be social rather than biological.

Psychosocial problems, in particular, can change rapidly in type, severity, and phenotypic expression with age. An example of this phenomenon is found in data from the Brookline Early Education Project, a longitudinal study in a single Massachusetts community following a sample of children from birth to school entry (Levine, Palfrey, Lamb, Weisberg, & Bryk, 1977). This research reveals a high rate of emerging developmental concerns at the kindergarten checkpoint even among a group of children who had been closely monitored over the preschool years (Palfrey, Levine, & Pierson, 1982). Thus, even across one point of transition, from before to after kindergarten, patterns of continuity and change in child health and behavior are complex.

Evidence bearing on the stability of health-related behavior is too inconclusive to provide a sound basis for theories of health education. Mechanic (1964, 1979, 1980) surveyed a sample of 350 Wisconsin children and their parents in 1961 and performed a follow-up study of the children 16 years later. Data were collected on 10 types of adult health and illness behavior, including such factors as seat-belt use, smoking, exercise, drinking, and risk taking, and their precursors in childhood. These behaviors showed only modest intercorrelation in adulthood and according to self-report had low continuity over 16 years, throwing into question whether a stable risk-related behavior profile or personality could ever be described. Moreover, each behavior apparently had unique determinants, suggesting that it may not be feasible to base an educational intervention on some latent trait or disposition affecting all health-related behavior. Onset of health-related behaviors also differed by category of risk, implying that the timing of interventions might have to be different to prevent each one.

DETERMINANTS OF APPROPRIATE USE OF HEALTH CARE

What contributes to appropriate patterns of health service use for children, and for which children do these patterns give cause for concern? From the family's perspective, appropriateness of use is determined by adequate access to services combined with adequate knowledge regarding health and the health care system (Aday & Andersen, 1981). Barriers to appropriate use may be financial, relating to the cost of care to the family, or nonfinancial, including constraints imposed by inconveniences of time or distance, cultural or psychological factors, and poor information regarding services.

From the provider's perspective, appropriate care means care of high quality—timely, efficacious, and with sufficient continuity and breadth of concern for the patient. Quality has proven much harder to measure than most other aspects of care, but various indicators and proxy measures are generally accepted (Starfield, 1982). A very substantial literature has developed over the past 20 years on both use and quality of services.

Correlates of Health Service Use

A recent comprehensive review of research by the National Center for Health Services Research (Maurana, Eichhorn, & Lonnquist, 1981) divides the correlates of health service use into three categories: predisposing factors (family or individual characteristics other than family SES), enabling factors (access considerations, including family SES), and characteristics of the delivery system. Outcome measures typically used in the reported studies were physician visits, visit rates adjusted for need, interval since previous contact with a physician, hospital admissions and discharges, and length of hospital stay.

Many of the studies reviewed show a set of factors predisposing to differences in use among children; these factors included age, sex, parent marital status, family size and composition, living arrangements, birth order, race and ethnicity, attitudes toward health, knowledge of health care resources, family stress and support, perceived barriers to care, and previous use. Enabling factors predicting differences in use included parent education, income, occupational status, method of financing (e.g., type and extent of insurance coverage), availability of services in region and residential area, proximity (in distance and time) to source of care, and whether the child had a regular source of care. Salient characteristics of the delivery system included type of provider, health care resources available, physician specialty, and characteristics of appointments. Many of these same predisposing and enabling factors and delivery system characteristics also have been significant predictors of use in the major national surveys, including the Health Examination Survey, the Health and Nutrition Examination Survey, and the Health Interview Survey (Colle & Grossman, 1978).

Although most correlates of use are the same for adults as children, not all are. Among predisposing characteristics, for example, family size seems to have a significant, if poorly understood, effect on use for children but not for adults. Even after adjusting for family income, children in larger families tend to use fewer services than their needs would suggest (Andersen & Kasper, 1973). Family size is inversely related to the likelihood of seeing a physician and to mean number of physician visits, especially for low-income rural or inner-city children and those 13–17 years of age.

Such evidence is hardly surprising in light of the amount of time it requires for most parents to take care of sick children in the course of the year and the obstacles to committing this time. Home nursing of sick children and escorting children to sources of formal medical care are time-consuming activities. Both activities are significant nonmarket contributions to the household economy, usually performed by mothers and adult daughters (Carpenter, 1980). One interpretation of the family size data is that the extra time required for care of the additional children in larger families simply cannot be found by either low- or middle-income mothers, most of whom must work during the hours when primary medical care is most accessible.

Effects of Medicaid and Other Public Programs

Over the past 2 decades Medicaid and other public programs such as the federally initiated Comprehensive Health Centers have greatly reduced income-related inequities in access to physicians and hospitals (Butler & Scotch, 1978; Rogers, Blendon, & Moloney, 1982; Starfield, 1982) (Fig. 4). Prior to passage of Medicaid in 1965, the relationship between income and use of services was approximately linear: The lower a family's income, the fewer services used. Aday, Andersen, and Fleming (1980) report that in 1963, prior to enactment of Medicaid, only 52% of

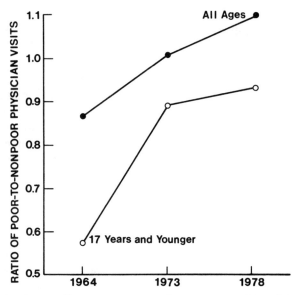

Fig. 4.—Ratios of poor-to-nonpoor physician visits, United States, 1964, 1973, 1978, adjusted for chronic illness and age adjusted by the direct method to the 1970 civilian noninstitutionalized population. Source.—Health U.S., 1980.

children aged 1–5 and 41% of those aged 6–17 in low-income families saw a physician in the previous year, compared to 87% and 70%, respectively, in the high-income group. By the early 1970s, rates among poor children eligible for Medicaid were roughly comparable to those for affluent children. In 1976, 87% of the children in the United States aged 1–5 saw a physician, ranging from 97% of those in high-income families to 78% of those in low-income families (Aday et al., 1980). Only near-poor children continued to have acute problems of financial access throughout the decade (Gortmaker, 1981).

Despite the effects of Medicaid on access, considerable evidence suggests that, when rates of use are adjusted for health need and for quality of care, equity for poor children still has not been attained. After age and health status have been adjusted for, the poor still have fewer visits and receive less preventive care (Kleinman, Gold, & Makuc, 1981; Newacheck, Butler, Harper, Piontkowski, & Franks, 1980; Wolfe, 1980). In particular, inner-city and rural children receive less preventive care, use fewer medical and dental services, keep fewer appointments, and follow through on fewer referrals than other children. It also remains to be seen whether gains in access to health care will be maintained in the next several years, when reductions in Medicaid eligibility and benefits and less aggressive implementation of the Early and Periodic Screening, Diagnosis, and Treatment Program (EPSDT) seem inevitable (Rosenbaum & Weitz, 1983). The EPSDT program is discussed by Meisels elsewhere in this volume.

Evidence on the effects of persisting financial barriers is particularly significant at a time when the federal government is considering a requirement of nominal family co-payment under Medicaid. Many states already have requested waivers under the existing Medicaid law to institute this provision. Evidence on cost sharing suggests that preventive care for children, which is relatively inexpensive, is especially sensitive to price (Davidson, Connelly, Blim, Strain, & Taylor, 1980). Hence, even nominal family co-payment for poor children's preventive services under public programs may not be advisable, even if such a policy for other age groups is. By contrast, findings from the RAND National Health Insurance Study (Newhouse, Manning, Morris, Orr, Duan, Keeler, Leibowitz, Marquis, Marquis, Phelps, & Brook, 1981) suggest that children's hospital admissions may not respond significantly to variations in parent cost sharing. Demand for hospital care is inelastic for children, although it is not for adults. The policy implications of these data are not clear, especially because we know that when implementation of Medicaid increased hospitalization coverage, poor children's use of hospital services greatly increased, consistent with their unmet needs. Moreover, the RAND study findings pertain to a cross section of the population and not to families with marginal financial resources. Also, the study placed a specified ceiling on financial liability for all participating families.

Data on rates of use among poor and affluent children tend to obscure the fact that the sources and patterns of care for these groups differ sharply. Child health care is offered at a wide range of sites, more than one of which may be used by a single family. Affluent children are more likely to use office-based pediatricians than are poor children, especially those in inner cities and rural areas, who frequently use hospital outpatient departments, neighborhood health centers, and general practitioners as sources of care (Butler & Baxter, 1977; Colle & Grossman, 1978; Gortmaker, 1981; Wolfe, 1980). Although pediatricians and general and family practitioners offer almost three-quarters of all office-based care for children, many low-income inner-city parents continue to use specialty clinics and emergency rooms at urban hospitals as their regular source of child health care (Palfrey, Levy, & Gilbert, 1980). Almost one-half of a recent sample of Boston children living in close proximity to five neighborhood health centers were found to be seeking primary care in hospitals or using multiple sites of care (Levy, Bonanno, Schwartz, & Sanofsky, 1979). Medicaid families generally do not overuse hospitals and their emergency rooms by seeking care when need is not evident, but inner-city families do continue to prefer hospitals as sites because of their proximity and the fact that they are open at all hours (Weitzman, Moomaw, & Messenger, 1980).

However effective the Medicaid program, it seems certain that there will also continue to be a need for targeted categorical programs to support care for children in certain hard-to-reach groups such as Native Americans, migrant workers, those living in remote rural areas, and refugees.

Quality of Care

Quality of care is known to be affected both by the individual physician's characteristics and by the structure of the practice (Dutton, 1978; Dutton & Silber, 1980; Starfield, 1982). In general, low-SES children experience an unfortunate pattern. When sick, they take longer to enter the health care system, and once there, they have greater use of nonelective procedures and hospitalizations than do higher-SES children (Dutton, 1981). Low-SES families also react to financial barriers by reducing preventive care such as prenatal services and well-child visits (Slesinger, Tessler, & Mechanic, 1976). Delays in coming for care may in turn reduce the recognition of illness in poor children and perhaps result in higher disability later. Several studies have shown that delivery of routine preventive care in particular is more common in pediatricians' offices and prepaid group practices than in other forms of organization, and the prescription of medication is more likely in hospital outpatient departments and emergency rooms (Dutton, 1979).

Discussions of quality in health services have often favored continuity and comprehensiveness of care as desirable in any primary care setting (Select Panel for the Promotion of Child Health, 1981a). However, what is meant by these concepts remains somewhat murky and has seldom been measured well (Davidson & Perloff, 1980; Rogers & Curtis, 1980). Various face-valid indicators of continuity suggest that, on this criterion, more affluent children receive better care. Pediatricians may be less immediately accessible than general practitioners and family physicians because they tend to require appointments (Fishbane & Starfield, 1981) and have longer waiting times for those appointments (Weiner, 1981), but they probably provide more continuity of care over time than do other types of providers, especially for young children. Comprehensiveness can mean many different things, but one defining criterion is that a provider offers ready access to a wide range of health and health-related services. Organized settings, including group practice arrangements and community health centers, may do a better job on this count than many solo practitioners. Coordination of health-related social and nutritional services for the poor is a particular problem for providers in inner cities, where unplanned visits are common and existing information about children can be overlooked or misunderstood by primary care practitioners unfamiliar with the child (Starfield, Simborg, Horn, & Yourtee, 1976).

One aspect of quality is parental compliance with a physician's instructions concerning the child. Overall, it is estimated that 50% of all pediatric patients fail to comply with prescribed therapies—a figure similar to that for adults (Litt & Cuskey, 1980). Thus, many children fail to receive the full benefits of treatment (Sackett & Haynes, 1976).

Regular Source of Care

In numerous studies, the family's ability to identify a regular source of care is a strong correlate of appropriate use and quality. Children whose parents report having such a source are more likely to receive needed preventive care (Wan & Gray, 1978), to keep appointments, to not overuse or underuse services (Aday & Andersen, 1981), to use medications sparingly and appropriately (Roghmann, 1981), and to come for follow-up visits after treatment (Dutton, 1981). Many more low-income children lack a regular source of care than affluent children (Butler & Scotch, 1978; Gortmaker, 1981). Lave, Lave, Leinhardt, & Magin, (1979) studied low-income and predominantly black families in East Palo Alto, California, and found that the strongest predictors of whether a child had a regular care source were length of residence in the community, family income, the child's health status, and the child's age.

Although the concept of the regular care source seems quite robust in large-scale survey analysis as a predictor of appropriate use, three caveats are warranted. First, the regular source may itself have certain deficiencies in continuity of care and yet prevent the use of other sites of care (Starfield, Bice, Schach, Rabin, & White, 1973). Second, Medicaid may inadvertently be creating regular care sources for some inner-city children that are not of high quality; in low-income areas sometimes the only providers are so-called Medicaid mills, that cater exclusively to a Medicaid-eligible clientele, relying on economies of scale and high volume of billable procedures to make a profit despite low fee schedules (Kronenfield, 1978). Third, there is considerable turnover from year to year in those with a regular source, in part because of family migration, as shown by Lave et al. (1979), but also within stable populations. Finally, the regular source of care for a given family frequently can change. The Brookline Early education Project noted, for example, that although almost all participant preschoolers reported a regular source, lists of these sources needed to be updated at 6-month intervals (Levine & Palfrey, 1982).

Personal Characteristics of Parents

Because parents mediate the health care of their children, their personal characteristics must also be examined as predictors of appropriate child use. Two determinants have received attention in health services research: parental stress and parental knowledge and attitudes regarding health and the health care system. Psychological distress in some parents has some effect—although not a strong one—on deciding to seek care for children (Tessler & Mechanic, 1978). Roghmann and Haggerty (1975) reported that, for a random sample of families in Rochester, New York, with children under age 18, family stress did increase use of medical services, especially when a child was sick. Only certain kinds of medical contact were found to be stress sensitive, however, notably telephone calls and visits to emergency and outpatient departments.

Parental knowledge or attitude may affect the decision to seek care for a child or, as we shall see in the next section, may influence the child's own health benefits and behavior. Maternal knowledge of disease and the medical care system proves to be a rather strong predictor of use (Geersten, Klauber, Rindflesh, Kane, & Gray, 1975), although no study has reported the independent or partial effect of this variable by controlling for mother's level of education. Research by Bass and Cohen (1982) suggests that in as many as one-third of parent-initiated sick child visits, the parent may entertain unverbalized fears that something much more serious is wrong with the child than the stated reason for seeking care. Levy (1980) also reports that one major correlate of inappropriate use may be the parents' fear of the child's "vulnerability." In her study of reasons for medical care visits in a large urban practice setting, she found numerous visits motivated by parents' fears that a child was uniquely threatened by illness, even though often there was no clinical basis for fear. She draws a policy conclusion that corresponds to common sense: One good way to reduce inappropriate use is to allay parental concerns.

CHILDREN'S ACQUISITION OF HEALTH-RELATED CONCEPTS, BELIEFS, ATTITUDES, AND BEHAVIOR

Children's use of health services is usually mediated by parents, especially before adolescence. But as they grow older, children are increasingly able to comprehend their own health, the appropriate use of services, and the relation between behavior and health. Autonomous activity becomes an increasingly significant determinant of health status, and awareness of the consequences of health-related behavior grows.

The research literature on children's acquisition of health-related concepts, beliefs, attitudes, and behavior is limited and does not yet extend our knowledge much beyond what can be inferred from more general developmental research regarding concept attainment, personality, cognition, and behavior. Those studies that do exist have been reviewed recently by Lewis and Lewis (1980) and Green and Johnson (1982). The most interesting and methodologically adequate among them tend to fall into three categories: survey research based on social-learning theory; small-scale studies of stage-sequential concept attainment; and child-rearing research on the relation between parental beliefs and behavior and the child's.

Social-Learning Research

Since the late 1950s social-learning theory has been the dominant paradigm for research on health beliefs, attitudes, and behavior; a number of models have been proposed and fairly extensive research conducted to test them (Roghmann, 1975). Cummings, Becker, and Maile (1980) offer a comprehensive review of these models, including their own Health Belief Model, which has been used to explore interrelationships between a wide range of attitudinal and self-reported behavioral factors. Research based on the Health Belief Model has focused only occasionally on children, and the model is generally not well suited to analysis of developmental change because items are the same for all age groups. But certain valuable data have been collected. It is known, for instance, that differences in perceived vulnerability to illness emerge in the elementary school years and tend to remain fairly stable through age 16 (Gochman, 1971).

Data reported by Radius, Dillman, Becker, Rosenstock, and Horvath (1980) have interesting implications for policy because they illuminate the shaky connection between health knowledge and health behavior. The researchers interviewed a sample of Michigan children and youth 6–17 years old from various socioeconomic backgrounds. All youngsters in the sample found health a meaningful concept and a concern and could discriminate among various illnesses or health risks according to their own perceived personal vulnerability to the conditions. But accuracy of health knowledge and beliefs did not correlate highly with avoidance of risk behaviors. In particular, only about half the 12- to 18-year-olds said they worried at all about health, and only one-third acknowledged personal accountability for any health-related outcomes. A substudy of teenage drinkers revealed higher, not lower, concern in this group for personal health, suggesting perhaps that concern may be a marker of generalized anxiety or low self-esteem rather than an influence on behavior.

Stage-sequential Cognitive Research

The second category of research focuses on stage-sequential development in children's concepts of health and illness. Among the most interesting studies are two that apply Piagetian theory to relate children's knowledge of the causes of disease to their attainment of concepts. Bibace and Walsh (1980) provide evidence for the validity of six developmentally ordered categories of children's explanation of illness, ascending in complexity according to Piagetian stages of cognitive development and causal understanding. Perrin and Gerrity (1981) provide very similar evidence from research on kindergarten, fourth grade, and eighth grade children. Kindergartners typically understand the causes of illness as magical or as the consequence of their own transgressions, and fourth-graders believe that disease is caused by germs whose very presence will make the child sick. Not until eighth grade at the earliest can the multiple causes of health and illness be understood in their full complexity. Both studies suggest that the child's understanding of illness develops somewhat later than understanding of physical causality, perhaps being more synchronized with moral development. Kister and Patterson (1980) also find Piagetian concepts of immanent justice useful in describing children's conceptions of the causes of illness.

This line of investigation has great potential relevance for policymakers. What cannot be understood by the child certainly cannot be a basis of children's education or legal responsibility. Weithorn and Campbell (1982), for example, recently conducted a study in which they employed Piagetian hypothetical dilemmas to measure developmental differences in competency to make informed health care treatment decisions, according to four legal standards. Subjects were 9, 14, 18, and 21 years old. The investigators report that 14-year-olds performed as well as older subjects, but that 9-year-olds were less competent in their ability to reason about and understand the treatment information provided in the dilemmas. Even 9-year-olds appear able to participate in some aspects of health care decision making.

Implications of developmental differences in children's understanding also are being explored for physicians' training and practice (Brewster, 1982; Lewis & Lewis, 1980). Findings from pilot studies suggest that doctors overestimate the sophistication of young children and underestimate that of older children (Perrin, 1981).

Parental Influence

Few studies have focused explicitly on how and to what degree parents influence their children's health-related knowledge, attitudes, and behavior. The extant studies confirm what is found elsewhere in research on child rearing and socialization: Parents are only one among many and diverse influences on the child; parental influence tends to diminish as the child grows older; and knowledge and behavior are transmitted from one generation to the next by mechanisms that are more subtle, complex, and difficult to document than we might expect.

The most careful research to date does not, in fact, explore those mechanisms of transmission but instead simply measures the congruence or incongruence between parents and children in health-related attitudes and behaviors and use of services. In the light of the developmental findings just discussed, it is not surprising that parents and their children differ in their beliefs and understanding. Robertson, Rossiter, and Gleason (1979), for example, found that elementary school children manifest more anxiety than their parents about illness, worry more about getting sick, and believe more in the efficacy of medicine. In a study of 6- to 13-year-olds and their mothers, Campbell (1975) reported that health history and age interacted to predict the child's concept of illness, but no pairwise pattern could be found linking mother's and child's concepts. Older children's health concepts generally resembled their mothers', but apparently as a function of age alone.

Longitudinal findings from Mechanic's 16-year follow-up study (1964, 1979, 1980) also fail to show a strong relationship between the beliefs of parents and their children. Those with fewer symptoms of illness as young adults remembered their parents as having been concerned with self-care and as favoring health maintenance; but when data collected 16 years earlier on parent and family background factors—such as maternal interest in health, health promotion and modeling in the family, and parental self-esteem—were assessed prospectively, they were not associated significantly with their children's subsequent health behaviors, such as smoking, drinking, and engaging in little exercise. Sixteen years later, the child's own education level was a stronger predictor of these variables.

Mechanic's study does lend some support to the view that children who are "stoics" in childhood—according to such variables as reluctance to go to a physician, to be absent from school, relinquish responsibilities when ill, and to discuss symptoms—will be stoics later as well. However, this pattern could not be linked simply or conclusively to learning from parents.

New approaches to the study of cultural transmission that adopt models from population biology further suggest that there is only a weak relationship between health-related behaviors of parents and children (Cavalli-Sforza, Feldman, Chen, & Dornbusch, 1982). In the future, such research may enable a better understanding of which behaviors parents are more likely to influence and which ones less. Only one study (Pratt, 1973) has suggested that traditional child-rearing variables may be significant predictors. This research found that persons whose parents had granted them autonomy in childhood reported better health care practices later in life than did those whose parents had been authoritarian.

Research on health care use by children and their parents provides somewhat stronger circumstantial evidence of parental effects. In particular, studies of child-initiated use of school health services show that: (1) 5- to 12-year-olds have already developed distinctive patterns of health care use (Lewis, Lewis, Lorimer, & Palmer, 1977); (2) these patterns vary according to the child's characteristics and family background, and show clear differences according to sex as early as the first grade (Nader & Brink, 1981); and (3) there is a suggestive relationship between high-use children and high-use parents (De La Sota, Lewis, & Lewis, 1980). Reflecting on this evidence and the data from his own study, Mechanic (1980) hypothesizes that generalized patterns of illness behavior do exist; in large measure they are learned but evolve through complex interaction among such factors as parent attentiveness to the child's symptoms, patterns of health service use and school absenteeism, and broader social reinforcement. Clearly, the wider social context of extended family, peer group, child-care setting, school, and neighborhood play a very important role in socializing the child in behavior relating to health service use as well as in understanding and attitudes (Mullen, 1981). These influences may take on a new saliency as more mothers join the work force and parents spend less time each day with their children (Medrich & Rubin, 1979).

NATIONAL POLICY CONTEXT AND ISSUES

Only a few basic approaches to improving child health are available to national policymakers. Four will be described. First, policymakers may attempt to change family SES, reasoning that child health will be improved by the effects of income maintenance, housing subsidies, education supports, job programs, and other interventions that are not aimed directly at improving health. Public support may be general, as in the case of income support through Aid to Families with Dependent Children (AFDC), or may be more immediately health related, as in the case of food stamps. Various mechanisms to improve the purchasing power of American parents clearly have helped establish the preconditions for better child health, although current evidence is stronger for investments such as nutrition subsidies than for support of family income per se.

A second major approach is environmental protection: reducing environmental risks to health through regulation; subsidies to states, communities, and corporations; or direct federal public safety measures or public works. In addition to childhood accidents of all kinds, three types of environmental risk for children have been of recent policy concern: chemical and radiation risks to the fetus and the newborn, especially risks from toxic wastes, pesticides, lead, and other pollutants, and from X-rays; risks posed by drugs and foods, especially nonprescription drugs and substances presenting special risk for pregnant women; and the persisting public health problem in some areas of unhealthful water supplies and inadequate sanitation (Select Panel for the Promotion of Child Health, 1981a).

Risks in the physical environment apply to the entire population but may prove especially consequential for children, who are more vulnerable physiologically, have lower tolerance for certain substances, and by virtue of age differences may undergo longer periods of exposure than older persons. Regulatory policy concerning environmental risk has been controversial in recent years, some perceiving it as placing excessive public prohibitions on freedom of choice and competition, others seeing it as insufficiently protecting public health. Much evidence suggests that many kinds of injury and health problems can be more economically and efficiently reduced by changing environments than by trying to change behavior (Robertson, 1981a).

The third major policy approach is to provide health services, either directly or by subsidizing health care through third-party reimbursements. All of the major federal health care programs, including Medicaid and EPSDT, Title V, Family Planning, the Supplemental Food Program for Women, Infants and Children (WIC), Childhood Immunizations, and the Adolescent Pregnancy Program, contribute to health care either directly or indirectly. Public support for health services may lead to improved health status or may at least assure that children of all socioeconomic backgrounds have an equal opportunity to benefit from care. Although these programs are the components of national child health policy most visible to the public, it is clear from the evidence reviewed earlier that this avenue of policy is only one means to improve health—and not necessarily the most consequential. On the other hand, the positive effects of this form of policy intervention have repeatedly been demonstrated (Foltz, 1981; Freeman,

Kiecolt, & Allen, 1982; Kotch & Whiteman, 1982; Lefkowitz & Andrulis, 1981).

Finally, there is health education, broadly defined to include all the various methods the public has at its disposal to persuade children and their parents to act in healthier ways. Because behavior relevant to health is integral to overall life-style, the impact of this policy approach has generally proved harder to demonstrate than the other three, although most would agree that behavior change would be a powerful outcome (Green, 1981). Decision makers hoping to improve health behavior must begin by acknowledging the enormous diversity among children in age, stage of development, profile of developmental risk, family background, types of socializing influences, and chances for learning. Consequently, health education policies and programs for children have been directed through parents and the family, the community, the schools, the media, or the workplace (Mullen, 1981). Effective intervention has usually involved the simultaneous use of more than one of these avenues (McAlister, 1981; McAlister & Gordon, 1980). Health education often has proved no less controversial in public policy debate than have regulatory measures, because it may be perceived as an unwarranted intrusion on the right of individual choice and the responsibility of parents and children themselves. Adding to the complexity is the fact that degree of implicit public control over health-related behavior is not the same for all members of society or for children and adults. In particular, the life circumstances of high-SES families make it much easier for them to adopt healthy habits than for low-SES families (Eisenberg & Parron, 1979).

A member of Congress, program manager, administrator, or voter seldom has the opportunity to ask whether, in the effort to improve child health, it would be better to improve family SES, alter or constrain activity in the physical environment, increase access to health services, or offer more comprehensive health education to more people. Each approach has its advocates, and our present understanding of their comparative advantages is partial at best. Judgments about how to devote policy attention "at the margin" or invest the marginal dollar for children require knowing not only which addresses the most significant health determinants but also which one is embodied in programs and policy interventions known to work. Even the most pressing problems cannot be solved without effective means; and many of the consequences of policy implementation over the past decade have reminded us that the best-intended policy or program may be ineffective or have consequences far from what were anticipated (Pressman & Wildavsky, 1973; Stokey & Zeckhauser, 1978).

PREVENTION AND ITS LIMITS

Prevention is a concern that cuts across the four major approaches to policy—income support, environmental protection, health services, and health education—and contributes to the rationale for each. Broad, bipartisan support for prevention has grown over the past decade, gaining impetus from the U.S. Surgeon General's 1979 report, *Healthy People*, in which the case was made that most of the major health gains of the past century have come from improvements in sanitation, housing, nutrition, immunization, contraception, and health habits.

The theme of prevention has at times created strange bedfellows (Eisenberg, 1981). Liberals argue on humanitarian grounds for doing all that is possible to avert child disability. Conservatives argue on grounds of social investment that prevention in childhood is the only way to avert certain types of major health care cost later in life. The case for prevention, on grounds both of humanitarian concern and of social investment, is especially strong for immunizations, prenatal care, nutritional care, hearing and vision screening, and other interventions in childhood (Canadian Task Force on the Periodic Health Examination, 1979; Hiatt, 1982; Morris, 1982).

COST-BENEFIT ANALYSIS OF PREVENTION

In discussions of prevention, immunizations serve as a cost-benefit paradigm of sorts. For example, one study by the National Centers for Disease Control showed that $180 million spent on measles vaccinations between 1966 and 1974 saved $1.3 billion in anticipated medical care and long-term care by reducing incidences of secondary disabilities such as deafness and retardation (Witte & Axnick, 1975). In the realm of social and behavioral interventions, as well, a growing literature shows that prevention may be the most cost-effective strategy against various forms of pathological behavior. For instance, various investigators (Cohn, 1980; Helfer & Kempe, 1976; Newberger, Hampton, Kassler, Daniel, White, & Newberger, 1981) maintain that it may prove far more inexpensive and effective to use paraprofessional home visitors to work with parents identified in the maternity hospital as being at risk for child abuse than to rehabilitate parents and children once abuse is discovered.

In the coming decade, more evidence will be needed to document the effectiveness of prevention. Evaluation of preventive efforts by cost-benefit analysis can be complicated and inconclusive because of the numerous assumptions such analysis requires (Layde, von Allmen, & Oakley, 1979; Scheffler & Paringer, 1980; U.S. Office of Technology Assessment,

1980). Moreover, there is a danger in overselling what can be achieved by preventive care before truly effective interventions have been developed (Rutter, 1982; Shadish, 1980).

SOME CAVEATS ABOUT PREVENTION

It is important for policymakers to remember that many of the factors known to contribute to illness in childhood and in later life are essentially beyond the reach of public policy, especially within the bounds imposed by values and politics. Most important decisions regarding primary prevention are political, not medical. Whether we prohibit use of firearms, create disincentives to the use of tobacco products and alcohol, or impose a lower speed limit are choices directed more by economics and concern for civil liberties than concern for health (Eisenberg & Parron, 1979).

Most examples of effective prevention have three features in common: a clear and acceptable point of policy intervention, method of intervention, and means of measuring effects. Particularly clear recent illustrations include improved immunization of schoolchildren (Robbins, Brandling-Bennett, & Hinman, 1981), child-proof packaging for nonprescription drugs (Clarke & Walton, 1979; McIntire, Angle, Sathees, and Lee, 1977), and installation of bars on apartment house windows to keep young children from accidentally falling out (Spiegel & Lindamen, 1977).

By contrast, other environmental or behavioral problems have more than one cause or contributing factor and therefore have no single decisive point of policy intervention or any clear evaluation criteria. Lead contamination of drinking water, the air, and paint is an example of a pervasive problem that is difficult to solve without major expense, even though blood lead levels offer a reasonably clear marker for the problem (Cherry, 1981). A recent survey by the National Center for Health Statistics states that 4% of American preschool children have excessive levels of lead in their blood, and that levels of lead are higher in black children than white children regardless of family income (Mahaffey, Annest, Roberts, & Murphy, 1982). Obesity is another problem for which no satisfactory therapy or educational intervention exists yet (Coates & Thoresen, 1978). The difficulty of addressing certain serious hazards cautions one not to overgeneralize from the immunization paradigm.

Environmental and behavioral risks must be reassessed continually as new information comes to light, and determinations must be made about degree of risk as that relates to appropriate policy response. In some instances, the response is quite clear if funds are available, as when it was discovered that far more asbestos was present in Vermont schools than had previously been identified (Novick, Rice, Freedman, & Lillson, 1981). But ambiguous evidence or evidence without knowledge of associated risk presents a real problem for policymakers. There remains serious debate, for instance, about the biomedical danger of a childhood diet high in cholesterol; as new information has come to light, various expert groups have made conflicting recommendations (National Research Council, 1980; U.S. Surgeon General, 1979). Some very successful primary prevention strategies also may have unintended consequences. The success of rubella vaccination campaigns over the past decade has dramatically changed the age-specific attack rate of this disease. One consequence has been that more youngsters than ever before are reaching adolescence still unexposed, increasing the risk that teenagers who become pregnant will contract rubella, with serious consequences to the fetus (Krugman, 1979).

Screening, which is discussed at greater length in another chapter of this volume, is also known to be effective only under well-defined circumstances (Dershewitz & Williamson, 1977; Frankenburg, 1973). Studies of screening often make several points: (1) If prevalence of a condition is too high or too low, screening may not be cost effective (Berwick, Cretin, & Keeler, 1981). (2) Effective screening requires a clear marker or threshold to trigger diagnosis and possible treatment (Levine & Palfrey, 1982). (3) Screening does no good if instruments are not sufficiently sensitive or specific and produce significant numbers of false positives or negatives (Eisenberg, 1981). (4) The psychological cost of labeling children incorrectly must be weighed, especially in developmental assessment (Children's Defense Fund, 1977). (5) Screening is pointless unless an effective therapy is accessible (Bernick, 1977). (6) One consequence of new screening and treatment procedures may be the creation of new medical risks, as in the case of successful screening and therapy for PKU, which have led to a new generation of women with PKU living to biological maturity, resulting in new hazards for their fetuses during pregnancy (Levy, 1982).

Finally, many factors determine the appropriate timing and duration of preventive efforts. For example, it is often argued that social investment should be as early as possible in the life cycle, to preclude the onset of serious problems. Although this view has obvious merit in some domains, such as screening for metabolic disorders, it cannot be assumed that for every problem or risk there is a critical early period after which intervention is unsuccessful (Brim & Kagan, 1980; Rutter, 1980; Starfield & Pless, 1980). These caveats notwithstanding, the repertoire of techniques for prevention available to policymakers is impressive indeed and may prove to be the best means of further combating childhood illness and the precursors of adult disease.

SELECTED POLICY ISSUES

So far we have examined what is known about the causes of mortality and morbidity, the nature of various influences on health status, and general approaches to questions of policy. We now turn to a discussion of five specific issues that illustrate the complexity of policy formation in child health. Each poses a major dilemma or lesson for decision makers.

IMPROVEMENT OF PREGNANCY OUTCOMES:
HIGH TECHNOLOGY OR PRIMARY HEALTH CARE?

In the early 1960s, data indicating that infant mortality rates in the United States were higher than those in various other industrialized countries galvanized national concern. Since that time, infant mortality has steadily declined. The determinants of this decline are several, and new national health policies are only partly responsible for them (Shapiro, 1981). But among those policies that have contributed to the trend, probably the most dramatic are those that, through expanded regional care networks, vastly improved access to the high medical technology surrounding delivery and neonatal care. It is a fair generalization that we are now doing a much better job than 20 years ago in providing high-technology medical care in the maternity hospital for low-SES women, those in rural areas, and others at particular risk during pregnancy.

It is also true, however, that there has been no equally dramatic improvement in the provision, in the home or community, of prenatal care and primary health services before and after birth for women at risk and their infants. One indicator of this fact is that, although U.S. infant mortality adjusted for birth weight is now among the lowest in the world, the incidence of low birth weight is itself still relatively high (Lee, Paneth, Gartner, Pearlman, & Gruss, 1980) and continues to be the main correlate of infant mortality.

Low birth weight results from premature birth or from intrauterine growth retardation (IUGR) or both. Greater risk of developmental disability and morbidity is generally associated with low birth weight in survivors (Gortmaker, 1979; McCormick et al., 1980) and is especially associated with intrauterine growth retardation (Starfield, Shapiro, McCormick, & Bross, 1982). Women of low SES and those who live in adverse physical and social environments are at particularly high risk of having low-birth-weight infants (Eisner, Pratt, Kexter, Chabot, & Sayal, 1978), especially infants with intrauterine growth retardation (Placek, 1977).

Although we do not know the extent to which declines in infant mortality are a result of better survival of prematurely born infants or of growth-retarded infants or both, much of the technology of prenatal care concerns the inhibition of labor and intensive care of the immature new-born. Therefore it seems likely that technology has exerted its effect primarily by reducing mortality among premature rather than growth-retarded infants. Reductions in neonatal mortality and morbidity of growth-retarded infants are likely to require significant advances in areas other than the purely technological (Hemminki & Starfield, 1979), as will further reductions in postneonatal mortality (deaths occurring between 1 month and 1 year after birth). Social programs initiated in the 1960s helped to reduce the discrepancy in postneonatal mortality between upper and lower socioeconomic classes (Davis & Schoen, 1978), but rates of decline in postneonatal mortality (in contrast to neonatal mortality) stabilized when these programs were cut back.

Further declines in neonatal and postneonatal mortality are likely to require that public policy develop along lines that have been controversial. For one, decline in infant mortality has been strongly associated with the availability of legal abortion (Grossman & Jacobowitz, 1981). Also, the cost of saving infants of very low birth weight is high; hospital expenditures for neonatal care are a very large cost component of children's medical care (Budetti, McManus, Barrand, & Heinen, 1980), and, if an infant is born with a disability, high costs can extend over a lifetime. Infants saved at marginally low birth weight may not influence the overall prevalence of neurological impairments (Shapiro, McCormick, Starfield, Bross, & Crow-ley, 1980), but absolute numbers of disabled youngsters surely will in-crease as more infants of very low birth weight are saved. Moreover, not all investigators agree that the prevalence of handicap will be reduced. Paneth, Kiely, Stein, and Susser (1981) argue that in the next decade the prevalence of cerebral palsy is likely to increase by 10% and that of retardation by 5%. Budetti et al. (1980) conclude that it is cost effective to treat babies weighing 1,000–1,500 grams but perhaps not those weighing 1,000 grams or less. Hard decisions will be required to balance the lifetime cost of caring for the severely handicapped infants who are saved against the benefit derived from saving potentially normal individuals who would have died without neonatal intensive care.

Although investment in hospital care may have reached a point of diminishing returns, it could prove difficult to generate the national will to allocate more resources and attention to other interventions such as family planning, abortion counseling, and prenatal care. Gains in these areas, and in postnatal care, will not be technological but political and social. Would it make sense for policy to focus on primary health care and counseling preceding and following birth rather than concentrate on birth-related medical technology?

Clearly, family planning, prenatal care, and access to primary care services in the first year of life can affect low birth weight and other pregnancy-related risk factors (Quick, Greenlick, & Roghmann, 1981; Select Panel for the Promotion of Child Health, 1981a; Sinclair, Torrance, Boyle, Horwood, Saigal, & Sackett, 1981). Such care offers a major opportunity to educate prospective parents and to combat various well-known hazards to fetal development, including undernutrition and nutritional imbalance; alcohol, tobacco, and drug abuse; and pregnancy-related accidents (Richmond & Janis, 1980). However, even the sizable policy commitments of the 1960s and 1970s failed to bring all those at risk into appropriate patterns of care. In 1977 one-quarter of all women received no prenatal care in the first trimester of their pregnancies (U.S. Surgeon General, 1979). In New York City, 22% received either no care at all or care only in their last trimester (Shorey, 1980). An even smaller percentage of women in the principal risk groups (low income, black, and teenagers) received adequate prenatal care.

Various forms of health-related care after birth in the maternity hospital and follow-up with families during infancy also can have positive benefits. Social factors amenable to intervention include parents' emotional reaction to prematurity, their psychological needs during the—often long—neonatal hospital stays, the quality of parent-child interaction, and various health-related, developmental, and familial risks after hospital discharge (Bricker, 1982; Crnic, Greenberg, Rogozin, Robinson, & Basham, 1983; Parmalee et al., 1980; Simeonsson, Cooper, & Scheiner, 1982). Although evidence that the first days of life are a sensitive period for parent-infant bonding remains inconclusive (Klaus & Kennell, 1983; Rutter, 1980), it is clear that the perinatal period is a particularly good time for providing anticipatory guidance to parents, especially parents of a firstborn (Brazelton, 1976). Examples of such guidance include familiarizing mothers with their infant's capacity to interact (Brazelton, 1975), teaching mothers about health-related practices such as breast-feeding (Winikoff & Baer, 1980), and helping fathers understand the full importance of their role with the infant (Yogman, 1980). Some also have argued that this is a good time to identify parents likely to have special problems accepting an infant. Evidence from pilot studies and demonstrations suggests that the preventive benefits of working with new parents determined to be at risk in the setting of the maternity hospital may be considerable (Brazelton, 1976; Kempe, 1976). However, large-scale data that might further inform policymakers have not yet been collected.

After discharge, risks of "pediatric social morbidity" and dysfunctional parent-child interaction become important (Morse et al., 1977; Newberger et al., 1981; Newberger & Marx, 1982). Follow-up and additional intervention with the family during the first year of life can be of three types: pediatric counseling, usually in the office; home visits or developmental outreach by a public health nurse, social worker, or paraprofessional; and infant-stimulation programs of various kinds. Pediatricians can help improve mother-child interaction, but the long-term effectiveness of special pediatric counseling on health status remains to be demonstrated (Casey & Whitt, 1980). Risk of poor development (except for manifest congenital or birth-related problems) is difficult to predict in infancy and may not become obvious until several years have elapsed.

Home visiting is a cornerstone of infant care in some other countries, but the findings of U.S. studies remain difficult to interpret. After reviewing many intervention studies that differ in the form of intervention, evaluation methods, and measures of outcome, Haggerty (1980) concludes that on balance the evidence shows home visiting and developmental outreach to be valuable. What is not clear is whether the weight of the evidence merits a national policy commitment. For a member of Congress or assistant secretary of the Department of Health and Human Services, the issue is a difficult one. Visiting-nurse programs have traditionally been part of public health practice in this country, with apparently good results, and nations such as Sweden attribute much of their success in reducing infant mortality to these types of efforts. But the evidence may not be persuasive without the accumulation of a strong data base in this country and a strong national commitment to child health (Mahoney, 1980).

For infant stimulation programs, too—another candidate for public investment—it is difficult to make a compelling case from the existing data. The National Center for Clinical Infant Programs (1979) has described preliminary findings from 24 demonstration programs for children aged 3 years and under. From evaluations, it has been concluded that these projects can achieve short-term effects on children's psychological development and parent education; but because it is difficult to predict which children are at risk for long-term problems, it is difficult to target efforts. There is also little agreement on the means of assessing emotional impairment, and there are few follow-up data from which to assess the long-term effects of programs. Very few of the programs are broad enough to be reasonably expected to have major or enduring effects. The same can also be said for stimulation programs for disabled infants (Denhoff, 1981). None of this array of inconclusive data gives the policymaker clear direction.

Lack of clear answers need not preclude policy commitments. The challenge is to assure that those participating in policy formulation are aware of the basis for choice and that decisions are made as wisely as possible under conditions of uncertainty. But this much is clear: Continued improvement of pregnancy outcomes will depend on many forms of social investment, not investment in medical technology alone.

ADOLESCENT PREGNANCY: WHAT IS THE POLICY ISSUE, AND CAN IT BE ADDRESSED BY CATEGORICAL PROGRAMS?[1]

Sometimes national data are a trigger for policy concern. One example is information on pregnancy among adolescents, which for the past 15 years has supplied the impetus for numerous local, state, and federal program activities. Yet even today, after more than a decade of policy focus on teenage pregnancy, major differences of opinion can be found regarding the scope of the problem and the types of intervention most likely to prove effective in addressing it. This is at least partly because pregnancy in women under 20 is associated with not one but four significant phenomena: (1) increased sexual activity outside of marriage; (2) increased health risks during pregnancy; (3) the issue of abortion; and (4) the potentially negative consequences of adolescent child rearing both to the infant and to the adolescent herself. The salience of any one of these phenomena and whether it should be the one to receive most policy attention are a matter for political as well as scientific judgment.

Many would regard the dramatic increase of sexual activity among teenagers as morally and psychologically damaging, particularly if onset is early. In the United States between 1971 and 1979, the percentage of 17-year-old women who reported having had sexual intercourse at least once increased from 27% to 41%; the percentage of 15-year-olds rose from 14% to 18%. By 1979, 50% of unmarried women aged 15–19 residing in U.S. metropolitan areas had premarital sexual experience, and among 15-year-olds alone, 15% had such experience (Zelnick & Kantner, 1980). Data such as these motivated the 1981 federal adolescent pregnancy legislation. As it was originally proposed, one purpose of this legislation was to promote abstinence. Congress broadened the scope of the bill before its passage so that the Adolescent Family Life Demonstration Projects Act (Title XX of the Public Health Service Act) authorizes funds for programs which provide services to pregnant and parenting adolescents. The program received initial strong support from conservative members of Congress who, morally opposed to premarital sex and abortion, generally believed that the problem of adolescent pregnancy is better avoided by discouraging intercourse—thus the nickname "teenage chastity bill"—

[1]The authors are grateful to Dr. Lorraine V. Klerman, of Brandeis University, for her assistance in preparing this section.

than by encouraging contraceptive use. Despite skepticism about the feasibility of primary prevention (Jekel, 1976), many others of varying political persuasions share this view to some degree, arguing that early intercourse is psychologically unwise for adolescents even when it does not result in conception (Eisenberg, 1981; Hamburg, 1980; Select Panel for the Promotion of Child Health, 1981a).

The second phenomenon related to teenage pregnancy is the health risk to the mother and fetus during pregnancy and at delivery. Clinical evidence suggests that childbearing risks for adolescents older than 15 are not as great as had once been thought, if adequate prenatal care is provided (Baldwin, 1981; Naeye, 1981; Rothenberg & Varga, 1981). This is a big "if," however, because teenagers are less likely to seek prenatal care than women in the more traditional childbearing years. For those 15 and younger, the risks associated with maternal immaturity may be particularly important. These risks include an increased likelihood of maternal or fetal undernutrition, low birth weight, and complications of delivery (Blum & Goldhagen, 1981; Eisenberg, 1981). In 1980, infants live-born to girls younger than 15 totaled 10,169, and those to 15-year-olds totaled 28,178. Among those younger than 15, there was an 8.3% decline in live births between 1979 and 1980, continuing an encouraging recent trend toward fewer births in this age group (National Center for Health Statistics, 1982) (Fig. 5).

Federal authorities currently are attempting to institute a regulation which would prohibit federally supported family planning clinics from providing contraceptives to minors without prior parental consent (the so-called squeal law). It remains uncertain what effect this policy would have on adolescent pregnancy rates, but many public health officials believe that the regulation would discourage significant numbers of adolescents from seeking family planning services; hence pregnancy rates would increase.

A third aspect of the problem is abortion. High abortion rates have been a controversial but very significant determinant of recent declines in adolescent birthrates, especially among those under 15 (Cates, 1982). Of approximately 1.3 million abortions performed in the United States in 1977, one-third were to women under 21 (U.S. Department of Health and Human Services, 1982). Among those under 15 who conceive, there continue to be many more abortions than live births, especially for whites (Kreipe, Roghmann, & McAnarny, 1981). In the late 1970s total abortions declined, for this age group, to a reported 12,754 in 1978, although abortion rates did not.

Federal financial support for legal abortion services has been an important factor in providing access for low-income populations. The Hyde

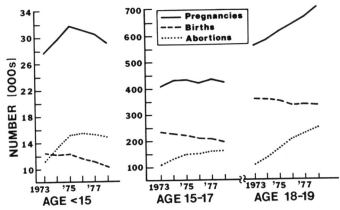

FIG. 5.—Number of births per 1,000 females in various age groups; United States, 1961–1974. Reprinted with permission from *Teenage Pregnancy: The Problem That Hasn't Gone Away*, published by The Alan Guttmacher Institute, New York, 1981.

Amendment and similar state laws forbidding federal Medicaid reimbursement for abortion are expected to reduce abortion rates among teenagers as well as other groups. Similarly, preliminary evidence suggests that stricter state laws concerning parental consent for abortion have resulted in reduced abortion rates (Cartoof & Klerman, 1982). Whether such outcomes are applauded or condemned depends wholly on one's values.

The fourth aspect of the problem is the psychological, social, and economic risks to mother and child once the infant arrives. For those who believe that such risks are the central issue, adolescent pregnancy is not exclusively a health problem (Klerman, 1981a). Teenagers who conceive tend to be already at risk economically, being disproportionately from low-SES and minority-group backgrounds (Kovar & Meny, 1981). Risk factors for the mother have been documented in various studies that confirm higher than normal rates of single parenthood, marital instability, failure to complete school, difficulties in regulating family size, and limited prospective lifetime earnings (Card & Wise, 1978; Furstenburg, 1976; Moore & Waite, 1977; Ooms, 1981; Trussell, 1976). Risks for the child include abuse and neglect, developmental delay, and somewhat lower IQ and school performance than children of older women (Baldwin & Cain, 1980; Bolton, Laner, & Kane, 1980; Hardy, Welcher, Stanley, & Dallas, 1978; Kinard & Klerman, 1980).

To the extent that policymakers focus on the socioeconomic and psychological problems of adolescent parenthood, policy considerations extend well beyond the provision of health services. Adolescent pregnancy and parenthood must be addressed by providing special access to jobs, enabling pregnant girls and new mothers to stay in school, specialized parent counseling, and other postnatal interventions that might last a number of years. Some such programs now exist (Field, Widmayer, Greenberg, Stoller, 1982; Klerman, 1981a), but they are few and their continued funding is usually uncertain.

Many who oppose abortion encourage adoption as an alternative to adolescent parenthood. Most young unmarried women now elect to keep their babies, and many report when pregnant that they want the child (Freeman, Rickels, Huggins, Mudd, Garcia, & Dickens, 1980; Ryan & Sweeney, 1980). Those who are at higher risk of adverse pregnancy outcomes because of lower SES also are less likely to terminate pregnancy or give up their child. A pregnancy can be unplanned yet desired once it has occurred; hence parent desires can be hard to assess (Kreipe et al., 1981).

The factors contributing to a teenager's desire to keep her child are psychologically complex, admitting of various interpretations. On the one hand, it can be argued that teenagers are in no position to anticipate the consequences of their decisions to keep their children. On the other hand, nothing could be harsher than to urge separation of mother and child when adequate nurturance is possible. Present federal policy, through various health and human service programs, encourages unwed teenage mothers to give their children up for adoption. The consequences of this policy are not yet known.

The four aspects of the issue of adolescent pregnancy provide another example of uncertainties regarding policy commitment "at the margin": How should additional dollars be spent, or where should cutbacks come? Federal authorities have generally considered adolescent pregnancy to be a problem with various facets and worthy of national policy attention. But policy response has been limited, in part perhaps because adolescent pregnancy affects fewer citizens than many other problems and does not involve a concentrated bloc of voters.

Under the Carter administration's adolescent-pregnancy initiative, several policy steps were taken: Family planning programs were encouraged to serve adolescents; demonstration programs in family life education were funded; legislation was developed authorizing categorical grants for programs aimed at assisiting pregnant adolescents; and the Office of Adolescent Pregnancy Programs was created to coordinate federal programs. The current administration is withdrawing support from family life education programs and family planning efforts. The Office of Adolescent Pregnancy Programs continues with its small categorical program with greater emphasis on abstinence, adoption, and family involvement. The struggle for Congressional appropriations continues.

Although the Reagan administration's modest and patchwork approach may be politically wise because it satisfies many factors—especially abortion foes—it may also prove ineffective because no single program will receive sufficient assured funding for long enough to have an impact. Also, the focus on adolescent pregnancy, rather than on the full range of adolescent health problems using a comprehensive service model, may prove unwise. As Steiner (1981) observes, an "adolescent parenthood policy is not an adolescent pregnancy policy."

AUTOMOBILE ACCIDENTS: THE TRADE BETWEEN PERSONAL SAFETY AND FREEDOM OF CHOICE

Accidents are now the major cause of death among children and youths of all ages, and automobile accidents alone account for one-quarter of all fatalities among those under 18. The toll in injury and lifelong disability is equally serious. Effective policies to reduce automobile-related mortality and injury would be a major step toward improvement of child health—perhaps the single most important step that could be taken in the United States today (Paulson, 1981).

As a policy problem, automobile accident prevention has two aspects: Younger children die or are injured only as passengers or pedestrians, whereas many teenagers have serious accidents as drivers. Passenger death and injury are most frequent during infancy and the preschool years (Agran, 1981; Barker, 1979), then again in adolescence; pedestrian deaths are most frequent among younger children old enough to play outside the home in the neighborhood and school.

The combined frequency of driver and passenger deaths among teenagers is the largest single component of the problem. A recent study by the Insurance Institute for Highway Safety (1981) shows that teenagers suffer motor-vehicle-related fatalities at more than twice the expected rate: Although 8% of the population is between 16 and 19, 17% of all fatal accidents occur in this age group. Teenage drivers also cause more passenger and pedestrian deaths than any other age group. Adolescent males show a death rate half again as high as females (Fig. 6).

The dilemma facing policymakers is that all of the most effective strategies for reducing auto accidents, in whatever age group, involve significant infringements on the free market for auto producers or freedom of choice among drivers, or both. For very young children, the evidence suggests that improved safety engineering and automatic restraint systems such as air bags would dramatically reduce passenger fatalities (Robertson, 1981a, 1981b). But 10 years of attempts by the National Highway Traffic Safety Commission to regulate the safety features of automobiles still have

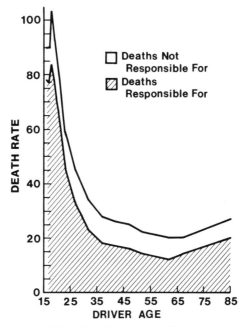

Fig. 6.—Deaths per 100,000 male license holders, 1978. Source.—Williams & Karpf, 1982.

not resulted in politically feasible solutions. The auto industry continues to perceive changes as excessively costly, and many citizens see them as an undesirable intrusion on the traditional freedom to travel without restraints. The alternative has been voluntary seatbelt use and encouragement of parents to use infant car seats for very young children. These interventions, too, are of known efficacy when used correctly, but getting parents and children to use them has proved to be a real problem (Hoadley, Macrina, & Peterson, 1981; McDonald, 1979; Pless, 1978; Widome, 1979).

In general, public policies requiring use of seatbelts and other car restraints for children have proved somewhat more effective than attempts to persuade parents to comply voluntarily. Forty-six states and the District of Columbia now have laws requiring the use of restraint systems for young children. Two studies have been conducted in Tennessee, the first state to pass such a law, to see whether it has made any difference in parental compliance. The original Tennessee law had an unfortunate loophole permitting parents to carry an infant on the lap as an alternative to a car seat. Early reports comparing driver behavior in Tennessee and two adjoining states before and immediately after passage of the law were quite pessimistic. Seatbelt use among child passengers had gone up modestly in

Tennessee (from 8% to 16%), but this could not necessarily be attributed to the new law because use had also risen from 11% to 15% in Kentucky, which had no statute. Moreover, the proportion of infants carried in the arms of parents in Tennessee had increased from 23% to 28% (Williams, 1979). A follow-up 2½ years later was more positive, however, suggesting that 29% of Tennessee children were traveling properly restrained, while only 14% of the sample from Lexington and Louisville, Kentucky, were (Williams & Wells, 1981a). Another child restraint law in Rhode Island has also increased proper car seat use and decreased unrestrained front seat travel (Williams & Wells, 1981b).

International evidence lends further support to these observations. In Quebec, for example, the compulsory seat belt law, although not aimed at children, has had an indirect positive effect on their safety. During their 6-year study, Stulginskas and Pless (1981) found that there was a significant correlation between driver use of restraints and their use by child passengers.

The American Academy of Pediatrics has placed high priority on educating parents about car seat use and on the use of car seats beginning with the infant's return from the maternity hospital (Christopherson & Sullivan, 1982). However, one study (Reisinger & Williams, 1978) suggests that educational initiatives by office-based pediatricians may not be particularly effective in isolation from other activities that reinforce them. Parents of newborns were randomly assigned to three treatment groups: One was given car seats and instructed by the pediatric care team in their use, the second was instructed but not given seats, and the third, a control group, received only literature on the availability of car restraints. Parent use of the seats was measured by observing arrivals by car for subsequent well-child visits. Use by the first group differed only modestly from use by the others, even at a first return visit. In no group were the seats used for a high proportion of children. Such data tend to support the view that only involuntary interventions will be truly effective.

The same trade-off between individual freedoms and public safety seems to be true for accident prevention among teenage drivers, with starker policy choices to consider. Voluntary use of seatbelts among teenagers is the lowest for any age group, reflecting the difficulties of teaching adolescents about risk (Green, 1979). The only nationwide policies that appreciably affected teenage accident rates in the 1970s were the imposition of the 55-MPH speed limit, which somewhat reduced the death rate for this age group as for other groups, and the indirect policy of not further subsidizing gasoline prices, which reduced average miles per teen driver (Zill, 1983). Otherwise, the death toll has been largely unabated.

At the state level, two types of policy clearly would be effective, and are gaining serious consideration even though they remain controversial: Raise the minimum licensing age from 16 to 18, and raise the drinking age from 18 to 21. Somewhat less restrictive alternatives to the first option include allowing only essential driving for 16- and 17-year-olds to and from work, placing a driving curfew on teenagers, or making licensing conditional on the agreement to use seatbelts. The potential problems of enforcing these options are self-evident. More promising and politically feasible have been laws raising minimum drinking ages. In the early 1970s more than half the states lowered their drinking ages, but between 1976 and 1980 14 states reversed this trend; as a result fatal accidents among teenagers at night (when half of all fatal crashes involving adolescents occur) were reduced an average of 28%. Recent data also show that stricter laws regarding licensing of motorcycle riders and requiring helmet use helped reduce death rates (Robertson, 1981b).

One especially provocative finding was made in Connecticut, where, because of funding cutbacks, driver education programs were dropped from high school curricula in some communities in 1976. The result was a substantial drop in teenage driving fatalities. In this natural experiment, teenage accident rates dropped by half in communities where driver training was eliminated and did not change at all in communities where it was kept (Robertson, 1980; Robertson & Zador, 1978). The investigators conclude that any educational benefits of high school driver education are outweighed by the harmful effects of promoting early licensing. Green (1980) disagrees, arguing that this analysis does not fully estimate the likely effects of such programs on driving behavior after age 18. But the weight of the evidence again suggests that a policy that tends to limit individual freedom to drive may be the most effective one. How, then, should policymakers balance the competing social goals of public safety and access to the automobile, which remains a major instrumentality of American economic life and a symbol of freedom of movement in our society?

SCHOOL HEALTH: SHOULD SCHOOLS AND PRESCHOOLS BE STRENGTHENED
AS SITES OF CASE FINDING AND CARE?

There is a strong prima facie case to be made for using schools and preschools as a locus of health care and health education. The nation has approximately 16,000 public school districts where over 95% of all 5- to 15-year-olds and 90% of 16- and 17-year-olds can readily be found during at least 9 months of the year (Masnick & Bane, 1980). A smaller proportion of children are enrolled in preschool and day-care programs, but such programs are rapidly proliferating as more women have joined the labor force. Now over 25% of all children under 5 can be found in a licensed facility or

Head Start program for at least some part of each weekday (U.S. Bureau of Labor Statistics, 1978).

Tax support of school nurses and school physicians is a major and largely overlooked form of public subsidy for child health services. Over a billion dollars drawn mainly from local and state tax revenues are spent annually for school health programs; there are approximately 30,000 full-time school nurses, and approximately one in six pediatricians has at least some involvement in schools (Grant, 1980). Why not simply use schools and preschools as the institutional base for assuring that all children receive needed health services or at least have their needs assessed and referrals made?

The pros and cons of this line of reasoning are numerous, and no national consensus has emerged (Select Panel for the Promotion of Child Health, 1981a). Those who would increase the responsibility of schools and preschools in health care delivery argue that there is a good cost-effectiveness rationale for performing screening and primary prevention, including health education, in a site where most of the target group is already assembled (Nader, Gilman, & Bee, 1980). Schools may also have unique importance in care of the chronically ill and follow-up of acute infection and trauma (Brink & Nader, 1981) and may have unique advantages as a site for Medicaid/EPSDT services (Adams, 1980). Health services in preschool and Head Start programs as well as the early grades of school have proven generally effective in improving immunization rates, identifying vision and hearing problems, offering medical and dental examinations, discovering and alleviating nutritional deficiencies, and increasing parent awareness of health issues (North, 1979; Robbins et al., 1981). As more parents work, the amount of time they have to supervise their children's health and health-related behavior has declined, making schools and preschools proportionally more responsible for health supervision (Masnick & Bane, 1980; Medrich & Rubin, 1979). Basic dental care also can be provided cost effectively in the schools, although this has been done on a much broader scale in other countries, such as New Zealand (Dunning & Dunning, 1978).

It can further be argued that there are economies of effort in linking health services with health education and broader health promotion, and that this may best be done in schools and preschools (Green & Iverson, 1982; Iverson, 1981). Almost all districts offer health education programs, although few are comprehensive (Benton, 1979). Development of these programs could lead to significant improvement of health-related behavior among children and youth. Psychosocial and learning problems, which physicians are being asked to deal with as part of the "new morbidity," are perhaps also best understood and treated in the school setting, where many of them originate or are diagnosed. In addition, recurrent school absence remains a good indicator of psychosocial and health risk, perhaps enabling the more efficient targeting of family services if schools are used as a point of first contact (Weitzman, Klerman, Lamb, Menary, & Alper, 1982).

Finally, it might be most efficient to strengthen the role of the schools in orchestrating services for handicapped children. Most children with disabilities are now found in the schools as a result of the Education for All Handicapped Children Act (P.L. 94-142). Public schools are now obligated to offer or otherwise pay for various health and health-related services deemed prerequisite to a full and appropriate education. To date the schools have identified approximately 4 million chronically disabled children, of whom 169,000 (4.2%) need special medical services. An additional 355,000 (8.8%) require such related services as occupational or physical therapy, audiology, and counseling (U.S. Office of Special Education, 1980). These children will continue to require specialized health care.

Despite these arguments, some would still question the wisdom of requiring the schools to deliver more health care services. The traditional role of school health has been circumscribed, both by state laws limiting what can be done medically in this setting and by dollar commitments, which are far lower per child than comprehensive primary care would cost. Comprehensive care might cost less per child in schools than in physicians' offices (Porter, 1981; Posen-Robbins School Health Corporation, 1980), but such costs are still substantially higher than traditional school health expenditures. Primary care programs and typical school health programs emphasize different priorities—those of the latter being school safety, injury prevention and treatment, routine and sometimes cursory physical examinations, and checking of immunization records. With the exception of Head Start programs, preschools and day-care centers have not done well at providing even these routine aspects of care (Aronsen & Aiken, 1980; Chang, Zuckerman, & Wallace, 1978). Health services may also be the first to be cut in schools and preschools during periods of fiscal hardship.

Like health departments, schools and preschools have an inherent political problem in trying to provide personal health services beyond minimal preventive care and referrals. This is because they may be perceived as competing with private, office-based physicians. The evidence on enlarged health department and school activities during the 1960s and 1970s does not suggest that such competition need be a problem in every community (Miller & Moos, 1981; Miller, Moos, Kotch, Brown, & Brainard, 1980), but in communities with significant numbers of office-based practitioners relative to numbers of children, resistance remains likely.

Physicians sometimes point out that using the schools as the site of screening makes follow-up and continuous care problematic, especially if health personnel are employees of the school rather than of a health department clinic or a continuing-care provider (Porter, 1979; Porter, Liebel, Gilbert, & Fellows, 1976). There is the risk of creating a dual system of care, with school services substantially separate from other health services, fragmenting the service system. Schools and preschools are usually closed at night and on weekends, further complicating service access. In addition, many health and mental health–related problems, especially among adolescents, raise concerns about confidentiality and consent, that may not be best handled in educational settings.

A final argument against increased expenditures for school health education is that, although it may have great potential, so far it has shown very modest measurable results except in certain demonstration programs (Kolbe & Iverson, 1981). Moreover, to the extent that increased success in health education requires increased per pupil expenditure, it is not likely to be forthcoming, for schools are more likely to invest additional funds in the teaching of basic cognitive skills and knowledge.

Views such as these for and against school-based health services can never be adequately resolved except in the context of particular communities or child populations and their needs. It is clear that a variety of innovative school programs have worked well, such as the Cambridge, Massachusetts, system of comprehensive school-based primary care units (Porter, 1979), the Galveston, Texas, system of school-based care (Brink & Nader, 1981), and, of course, Head Start health programs (North, 1979). It is equally clear, however, that these and other successful programs have evolved as the unique interaction of local conditions, individual entrepreneurship, and cooperation from the medical sector. It is hard to know which program elements may prove widely replicable.

One attempt to address the replication issue is the recent four-state demonstration project in school-based use of specially trained nurse practitioners initiated by the Robert Wood Johnson Foundation (De Angelis, 1981). Employment of the new personnel is being assessed under differing school circumstances to evaluate impact on children's use of services, patterns of referral, and assistance to parents. The economic feasibility of the model is also being assessed. Another national project is being sponsored jointly by the U.S. Office of Special Education and Health Care Financing Administration to demonstrate innovative implementation of EPSDT and P.L. 94-142 in the schools. Various attempts to develop nationally acceptable school health-education curricula also are underway (Green, 1981; Lewis & Lewis, 1980; Mullen, 1981).

Is a unified national school health policy feasible? In a system of educational governance such as ours, where federal influence on the schools is surprisingly small, the answer may be no. Federal dollars contribute less than 10% of total per pupil expenditures; states and localities pay the remainder in roughly equal proportions. Federal influence on policy may inevitably be commensurate in scale with its role in financing services. Even under the Education for All Handicapped Children Act, the federal government pays only 12% of marginal per pupil expenditure for special education (Osman & Evans, 1980).

On the other hand, for children in some subgroups, notably low-income inner-city children, the combined federal contribution to school and health services is much larger. Various major federal programs for children—including Head Start, Title XX Childcare, EPSDT, Crippled Children's Services under Title V, the Developmental Disabilities Program, mental health programs, and programs for the handicapped—all have school-related components or involve the schools in service delivery. Moreover, P.L. 94-142, despite its modest federal financial support, has had a major impact on local school programs in a relatively brief span of time. As a composite, these programs' elements may constitute a de facto or implicit national policy that has never been clearly articulated.

Whether or not we have a recognized national school health policy, analysis of the impact of federal programs on school- and preschool-based health services will deserve much policy-related research in the years to come.

FINANCIAL SUPPORT FOR HEALTH CARE OF CHRONICALLY ILL CHILDREN: WHAT IS THE PUBLIC RESPONSIBILITY?

Youngsters with serious chronic illness make up a very small proportion of the child population but require disproportionately high health care expenditures. Corrective surgery, medical care, and other health-related services can be very costly and sometimes can be necessary from birth (Budetti, Butler, & McManus, 1982). Children with prolonged or degenerative illness also can anticipate frequent high-cost care throughout an indefinite life span, conforming to what is now understood as the typical profile of high-cost illness in the United States (Zook, Moore, & Zeckhauser, 1981). Catastrophic illness is less likely to affect children than persons in other age groups; nevertheless, aggregate expenditures for the care of seriously ill children have been rising faster over the past decade than expenditures for adults and the aged, largely as a result of improved medical knowledge and technology (Trapnell & McFadden, 1977).

Children with severe limitations of activity totaled 1.2 million in 1979 (U.S. Health Interview Survey, 1979). Those with chronic functional limitations are estimated to account for approximately one-third of all child hospital days (Butler et al., 1984); excluding those in permanent institutional care and long-term residents of acute-care hospitals (principally psychiatric hospitals), children with limitations of activity stay on average twice as long as counterparts without limitations; those with serious functional impairments averaged 4.1 days per year in the hospital. Functionally impaired children also, on average, visited physicians twice as often as other children during the year.

How much does this care cost? What is known about direct health care expenditures for children with disabilities does not take into account consequent indirect ("opportunity") costs to society and the family, including reduced labor-force participation, productivity, and life expectancy. Total direct expenditures for physician visits and hospitalizations for those with activity limitations were in excess of $1.7 billion in 1980 (Butler et al., 1984). Average annual hospital costs for children with functional limitations were $511, compared to only $66 for children without them. In ambulatory care, expenditure was not so heavily skewed toward those with limitations; but even here they occasioned 10% of all expenditures (Table 3).

Who paid for all this care? It is difficult to answer accurately because no national household interview data exist which could show how cost is apportioned from private and public insurance sources, direct private contributions (e.g., from disease-specific philanthropies), research sources, and family out-of-pocket payments. But we do know certain relevant facts. First, according to estimates based on the health care financing model of the Department of Health and Human Services (Bonhag, 1981), 10.3% of all children with functional limitations have no insurance whatsoever; the proportion is even higher for low-income children—19.5%. Not all uninsured children may require high levels of medical care; but whatever they do receive is paid for by out-of-pocket payments and private contributions. Second, because eligibility requirements vary widely among the states, Medicaid covers only about 60% of children with functional disabilities whose families are below federal poverty standards—such coverage ranges from 20% to more than 95% (McManus & Davidson, 1982). Third, private group and individual insurance covers about 60% of all disabled children—a significant proportion, though not as high as the 75% covered in the general child population (Fig. 7).

Often those just above poverty cannot participate in the more gener-

TABLE 3

TOTAL PER CHILD EXPENDITURES FOR PHYSICIAN VISITS AND HOSPITALIZATION
OF CHILDREN WITH AND WITHOUT ACTIVITY LIMITATIONS, 1980[a]

	All Children	No Limitation of Activity	With Limitation of Activity	With Severe Limitation of Activity
Physician visits, (average charge per contact with physician = $25.10): Total expenditures (m = millions)	$6,053 m	$5,509 m	$554 m	$407 m
Per child expenditure	$120.46	$98.44	$237.59	$330.00
Hospitalization (average charge per inpatient day for children = $183.20):[b] Total expenditures (m = millions)	$2,868 m	$2,698 m	$1,170 m	$935 m
Per child expenditure	$66.39	$48.21	$510.51	$758.36

SOURCE.—Butler et al., 1983.

[a]Estimates based on 1979 use data from the U.S. Health Interview Survey.

[b]Average charge based on 1977 cost estimates adjusted according to the medical care component of the Consumer Price Index for hospital room and board. For 1977 base rates, see Cooper et al., 1980.

ous group insurance plans, which are linked to place of employment. The worst cases may involve parents who are working but in a place of employment that does not have coverage under a group plan or are self-employed with family income above the Medicaid cutoff but too low to enable payment of high premiums for individual or family coverage. If such parents have a child requiring extensive medical services, the financial consequences can be very serious. Even those who are insured may not be safe from high family expenditures. Benefits under different insurance plans vary greatly, but all tend to limit reimbursement to medical care narrowly defined, with inadequate incentives for preventive care and often no reimbursement for custodial care, primary health care, and health-related services such as transportation, counseling, respite care, prosthetic devices, and other hidden costs.

Depth of coverage under Medicaid varies by state; some states are much more generous in paying for optional services than others. In 1980, nearly all programs provided prescription drugs and intermediate care

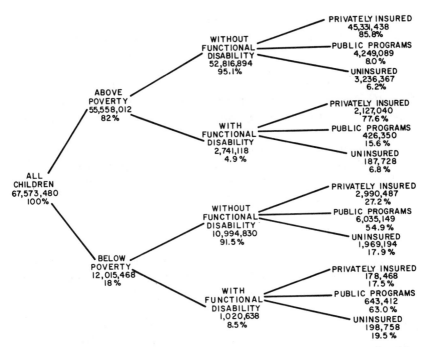

FIG. 7.—Insurance coverage for children 0–18 from private and public sources, by poverty status and limitations of activity, 1979. Source.—Butler et al., 1984.

facilities for severely mentally retarded youngsters, but a significant number (15 states) did not provide glasses; inpatient psychiatric care (17 states); physical therapy (18 states); services for speech, learning, and language disorders (22 states); occupational therapy (26 states); and dental services (20 states) (Intergovernmental Health Policy Project, 1981).

The Crippled Children's Program (CCS) under Title V is the other major public source of care, supporting clinics and outpatient and inpatient services for approximately a million children each year. States define eligibility and benefits under CCS for themselves, and programs vary greatly in the conditions they treat; average per capita expenditure for the children treated was approximately $259. Total federal budget allocations in 1979 were only $86 million.

Data collected at five major chronic-condition centers—the University of Florida Kidney Center, the University of California, San Francisco (UCSF) Renal Center, the National Jewish Hospital Asthma Center, the UCSF Pediatric Malignancy Center, and the University of Oregon Spina

Bifida Center—demonstrate that a number of sources may contribute to total payment, and that Medicaid, Medicare (for renal disease only), and the CCS program jointly play a major role. In each center, four to six payment sources contribute to total treatment expenditures, with out-of-pocket payment continuing to be a major factor. Families pay anywhere from 1%–2% of total costs at the five centers, not including additional expenses for outpatient care, medical equipment, and transportation (Table 4).

Even this partial profile of expenditure reveals a number of apparent inequities, including the burden of out-of-pocket expenditure for families of disabled children; the fact that this burden varies by disease entity, family income level, and state of residence; the differing patterns of care for those eligible and ineligible for private group insurance; and the generally inadequate coverage of services that are not strictly medical.

What is the role of public policy in addressing these problems? In the coming decade, care for the chronically ill will be an area in which the appropriate role of private and public health financing will be renegotiated. Current and contemplated cutbacks in Title V, Medicaid, and other public programs (Budetti et al., 1982), combined with the rising cost of care and insurance coverage, are likely to have one or all of three adverse consequences: to reduce eligibility and scope of services; to redistribute the balance of expenditure from public to private sources; and to increase the cross subsidies that already support a significant component of care for chronically ill children. Should special policy steps be taken to mitigate these outcomes and preclude further financial risks for disabled children and their families?

RESEARCH AND DATA NEEDS

The role of research in policy formation is not simple or direct. In a certain sense, everything that biomedical and social science tells us about children and families is relevant to policy formation, but in another sense this information seldom relates in any direct way to policy decisions (Lynn, 1978; National Research Council, 1978; Pless & Pekeles, 1981; Senn, 1975; Weiss, 1978). What can be said, therefore, about the kinds of research and data most needed to inform policymakers in the coming decade? Is all research equally valuable, or should priority be given to some types over others?

In our judgment, three broad categories of behavioral and social research, if pursued jointly by health care researchers and developmental psychologists, would be especially relevant to national child health policy.

TABLE 4
PERCENTAGE OF CASES COVERED BY VARIOUS SOURCES AT SELECTED CHRONIC DISEASE CENTERS

		SPECIFIC CENTERS				
SOURCE OF PAYMENT	University of Florida Comprehensive Children's Kidney Failure Center	University of California, San Francisco Renal Center — Dialysis	University of California, San Francisco Renal Center — Nondialysis	National Jewish Hospital/National Asthma Center	University of California, San Francisco Pediatric Malignancies (radiation oncology)	University of Oregon Spina Bifida
Private insurance	14.5	{ 1.2	35.3	71	51.6	22.6
Self-pay	4.5	...	...	7	1.3	26.9
Medicaid (or Medi-Cal)	10.5	29.5	18.4	16	15.6	{ 7.2
Medicare	42.4	26.5	14.7	...	2.6	...
Medicare with Medi-Cal	...	21.2	16.7	...	...	...
CCS	11.9	21.6	14.9	...	8.8	21.7
Charity/Research	...	...	...	6	...	20.1
Kaiser/Champus/Unknown	4.9	...	...	...	19.6	1.4
Other	11.2	...	...	...	...	...

SOURCE.—Butler et al., 1984.

We believe priority should be given to: (1) the improvement of health status indicators and the social and behavioral "epidemiology" of childhood; (2) combined pediatric and developmental research on efficacy of treatment for psychosocial components of health care; and (3) better applied research on those aspects of knowledge in child and family development that primary care physicians are most in need of learning as an integral part of their training and residency. Our emphasis on these three areas is anticipated by the discussion throughout the chapter. We focus on social and behavioral research topics mindful that, if the current federal bias against funding behavioral and social inquiry is a presage, those who in the future wish to develop these lines of investigation may not find it easy to do so with public support.

HEALTH STATUS INDICATORS

It is ironic that discussion of child health usually begins by describing child death, illness, and disability. National data collection systems, especially the vital statistics series (Health Interview Survey and Health and Nutrition Examination Survey) define health in these terms because the epidemiological information and data on service use and expenditure routinely collected under the various national surveys are based on traditional medical and public health models of disease. They fail to provide an adequate profile of health among children and shed no light on variability in normal activity or on those behavioral and social elements of life that may predispose to or prevent subsequent organic, functional, or social problems (Antonovsky, 1979).

There is a need for new types of health indicators and for different ways of obtaining them, commensurate with increasing recognition of the interaction among physical, behavioral, and social determinants of health (Rogers et al., 1981). More emphasis must be placed on obtaining information that relates to the child as an individual rather than as a sum of separate diseases or conditions. Also, systems for classifying clusters of problems rather than individual diagnoses are required in order to determine the full impact of various health risks on children, their families, their communities, and society as a whole, and to determine their effects on health later in childhood and adulthood.

A recent inquiry by the Social Science Research Council (Watts & Hernandez, 1982) concludes that the collection of social indicators should be expanded for children and made routine. Four broad categories of data are required, relating to functional health status, health care, health-related behavior, and environmental influences. Significantly departing from past practice, the National Health Interview Survey greatly expanded data collection on health-related behavioral and social factors in its 1981 Child Health Supplement (Kovar, 1982). Although this supplement was administered only once, some of its items may endure as part of HIS data collection. The supplement was developed partly on the basis of information from the Foundation for Child Development (FCD) surveys of children, which are documenting the behavioral and emotional well-being of youngsters in the United States (Zill, 1983).

Zill, Sigal, and Brim (1982) have surveyed recent advances in the development of childhood social indicators, including those for health. They distinguished between two elements: Social indicators are general phenomena not specifically related to problems addressed by the health or social system, whereas needs assessment addresses those problems for which there is currently a policy intervention. Child health policy must, by definition, focus on both. Needs assessment identifies subgroups of the population who may not be receiving appropriate attention, and indicators can provide information regarding issues requiring research and development of new types of interventions. New systems of data collection are certainly required as new paradigms of illness are recognized, but existing systems also could be better exploited to provide data for use in making policy (Zill & Mount, 1981).

An indirect consequence of improved health indicator technology is the new opportunity it creates to develop innovative outcome measures for health-related intervention programs. Once norms have been established for health indicators, changes in the indicators may afford important new measurements of program impact. Levine and Palfrey (1982) have summarized some of the limitations of current outcome measurement based on changing morbidity alone. Improved health indicators also increase the feasibility of monitoring the health effects of larger policy developments, such as the recent cutbacks in various federal and state health programs. The recent RAND National Health Insurance Study measured the components of children's health status in terms broader than illness alone by also including mental and social components (Eisen, Donald, Ware, & Brook, 1980; Eisen, Ware, Donald, & Brook, 1979). There is, of course, no necessary correlation between a high score on health indicators and reduced use of services (Wilson, 1981).

The following areas need particular attention:

1. *Development of measures of health status that include more than standard diseases.*—Although research on the development of such measures is still in its infancy, progress has been made in conceptualizing the issues. At the very least, specifications of health should include consideration of expected life span, current state of activity, and disability; the extent of comfort and satisfaction with health status; physiological and psycho-

logical problems; the achievements of individuals as compared with their peers; and resilience in the face of threats to health. Of particularly high priority are phenomena that relate specifically to children and derive from their own experience rather than from the world as perceived by adults. Methodologic research on measures of child health status should be based on, but not limited to, the pioneering effort of the National Center for Health Statistics, which has for many years employed selected measures of functioning in its surveys of the population.

2. *Population-based approaches.*—The distribution of health problems cannot be understood only through studies conducted in medical institutions. Knowledge about the causes of illness and how they develop also requires studies conducted where the problems arise—which almost always is the community in which children live. Similarly, the effects of care cannot be understood unless we measure how therapy is carried out by ordinary people under everyday living conditions. Much more attention also needs to be devoted to linking data on ill health and dysfunction to data obtained from defined geographic areas with known sociodemographic characteristics. Linkages of data tapes from health surveys to data from homogeneously grouped census tracts would greatly help us to understand the distribution of ill health, its correlates, and its response to medical and social intervention.

3. *Data collection and evaluation making possible a longitudinal view of the development of illness and its response to intervention.*—As more individuals survive, with a variety of types of handicap, only longitudinal evidence can provide certain important types of information required to assess the impact of ill health, its prognosis, and its response to various interventions.

EFFICACY OF PEDIATRIC CARE FOR BEHAVIORAL AND SOCIAL PROBLEMS

As noted throughout this chapter, pediatricians have increasingly been called upon to deal with a wide range of psychological, social, and family-related problems and to serve as counselors as well as medical specialists. Greater pediatric involvement with the schools is a good example of this trend (Levine, 1982). Other examples include increased physician involvement in the prevention of mental illness and problems of adjustment among children with minor neurological dysfunctions (Denhoff, 1976); more time spent on boundary areas of practice such as juvenile detention and out-of-home placement (Hein, Cohen, Litt, Schonberg, Meyer, Marks, & Sheehy, 1980; Schor, 1982); the design and management of self-help and educational programs for chronically ill children (Staudenmayer, Harris, & Selner, 1981); and rapid development of the field of adolescent medicine as a pediatric specialization (Silber, 1980).

Despite the recent attention given to psychological and social components of pediatric care and their clear relevance to child health outcomes, much confusion still exists about how to categorize psychosocial problems, how they relate to normal child development, and what pediatrics can realistically do to prevent such problems or mitigate their consequences. The relevant behavioral domain is large and its relationship to health outcomes inadequately understood, so that the entire topic can become confused. Included under psychosocial issues are psychological problems with an organic or genetic basis, psychosomatic problems, various types of mild or moderate developmental disability, problems which manifest themselves in or are defined by certain institutions such as the school, and immediate and long-term behaviors predisposing to high risk. The potential involvement in education, early detection, and treatment by health care providers is vast and needs to be better delineated.

One area of high priority for research concerns the identification of children who are at greatest risk for delayed or dysfunctional development. Evidence that neither utilization of services nor morbidity is distributed randomly in the population, even in early childhood (Starfield, Katz, Gabriel, Livingston, Benson, Hankin, Horn, & Steinwachs, 1983), speaks to the needs to explore the reasons why morbidity of one type predisposes to other types, especially with regard to the overlap among developmental, psychosocial, and somatic problems.

Studies of psychosocial morbidity and developmental pathology require the development of classifications that are better suited to the task than is the case at present. Burns, Burke, and Regier (1982) have described several new systems for classifying morbidity, including ones that are multiaxial and allow for the coding of different types of coexisting problems. In childhood, where there are large variations in "normality" rather than definite "abnormality," systems that allow for the coding of problems rather than diagnoses (U.S. Department of Health, Education, and Welfare, 1979) are particularly suitable for studies of the range and interrelationships of types of morbidity.

Other examples of needed research include investigations that: (1) describe natural variations in normal health-related behaviors and how these contrast with deviancy; (2) increase knowledge of how children acquire health concepts and the ability to anticipate the consequences of health-related actions; (3) increase understanding of the needs—cognitive, emotional, and social—and potential of chronically ill and handicapped children in the family, peer group, and school; (4) contribute to a coherent theory of health education in childhood; and (5) enhance our understanding of psychosomatic disorders of all kinds and child predisposition to heavy or inappropriate use of services. All of these topics are relevant to policy.

Also needed are evaluative activities to determine whether there are any measurable benefits of various types of physician involvement, such as anticipatory guidance, school program participation, and other activities to influence children's and parents' health-related attitudes and habits. The impact of preventive care in particular is often poorly understood and remains low on the national agenda of behavioral and social research. A surprisingly high percentage of all topics listed as priorities at a recent national conference on needed maternal and child health research were in the category of preventive care, including studies on the impact of smoking, alcohol, and drug abuse prevention, investigations of how to prevent the "new morbidity," studies to evaluate the effectiveness of new policies and laws designed to prevent accidents, and studies in child self-care (Klerman, 1982).

TRAINING OF PEDIATRICIANS AND HEALTH PROFESSIONALS IN
PSYCHOSOCIAL AND DEVELOPMENTAL ASPECTS OF CARE

Although no rigorous study has been performed of behavioral and social science curricula in medical schools, these curricula are generally thought to be insufficient and too seldom taught by nonphysicians. In general, methods to evaluate psychosocial components of care during training also remain inadequate, and pediatric clerkships still focus too little on these aspects of primary care. As a result, pediatricians often still rely only on clinical judgment, not more precise techniques, for assessment of developmental disabilities (Shonkoff, Deworkin, Leviton, & Levine, 1979). For the 1980s, pediatric training in psychology, especially normal developmental psychology, is a major challenge (American Academy of Pediatrics, 1982; Faust, Ulissi, & Thurber, 1980; Tuma, 1980).

The disciplines of child development and pediatrics have tended to address policy issues in parallel and in isolation from one another, despite obvious overlapping concerns. Except in research on infants, where a promising pattern of collaboration has evolved, there are few good examples of substantially shared research and teaching between these disciplines. There also are few institutional structures by which developmentalists can contribute routinely to medical education; likewise, most students in child development are poorly exposed to medical topics or topics in the delivery of health care. This is a problem caused by organizational and professional boundaries and the constraints of time for training rather than the disdain of one profession for the other. Exceptions to this pattern can be found, of course, in a number of universities whose medical schools and developmental psychology faculties have evolved a wider range of joint teaching and research activities in behavioral pediatrics (Richmond & Janis, 1983).

We believe that in addressing policy topics there is an especially strong rationale for collaborative research and training. The intersecting concerns of behavioral pediatrics and child development should be further mapped, and a shared agenda of teaching and research should be elaborated for the future.

REFERENCES

Adams, R. M. EPSDT—Can schools save the faltering giant? *Journal of School Health*, 1980, **50**, 484.

Aday, L. A., & Andersen, R. M. *Equity of access: An overview.* Paper prepared for President's Commission for the Study of Ethical Problems in Medicine and Biomedical Behavioral Research, Center for Health Administration Studies, University of Chicago, 1981.

Aday, L. A., Andersen, R. M., & Fleming, G. V. *Health care in the United States: Equitable for whom?* Beverly Hills, Calif.: Loge, 1980.

Agran, P. F. Motor vehicle occupant injuries in non-crash events. *Pediatrics*, 1981, **67**, 838–840.

American Academy of Pediatrics. Pediatrics and the psychosocial aspects of child and family health. *Pediatrics*, 1982, **70**, 126–127.

Amidei, N. Testimony before the Sub-committee on Oversight of the Committee on Ways and Means and the Sub-committee on Health and Environment of the Committee on Energy and Commerce. House of Representatives joint hearing on impact of Budget Cuts on Children, 97th Cong., 2d sess., March 3, 1982, Committee Print, WMCP, 97–30.

Andersen, R. M., & Kasper, J. D. The structural influence of family size on children's use of physician services. *Journal of Family Studies*, 1973, **6**, 116–130.

Antonovsky, A. *Health, stress, and coping.* San Francisco: Jossey-Bass, 1979.

Aronson, S., & Aiken, L. S. Compliance of child care programs with health and safety standards: Impact of program evaluation and advocacy training. *Pediatrics*, 1980, **65**, 318–325.

Baldwin, W. Adolescent pregnancy and childbearing—An overview. *Seminars in Perinatology*, 1981, **5**(1), 1–8.

Baldwin, W., Cain, V. S. The children of teenage parents. *Family Planning Perspectives*, January/February 1980, **12**, 34–43.

Barker, S. P. Motor vehicle occupant deaths in young children. *Pediatrics*, 1979, **64**, 860–861.

Bass, L. W., & Cohen, R. L. Ostensible versus actual reasons for seeking pediatric attention: Another look at the parental ticket of admission. *Pediatrics*, 1982, **70**, 870–874.

Bee, H. L., Barnard, K. E., Eyres, S. J., Gray, C. A., Hammond, M. A., Spietz, A. L., Snyder, C., & Clark, B. Prediction of IQ and language skill from perinatal status, child performance, family characteristics, and mother-infant interaction. *Child Development,* 1982, **53**, 1134–1156.

Benton, R. D. (Ed.). *Final report of task force on comprehensive school health education.* Des Moines, Iowa: Department of Public Instruction, 1979.

Berger, L. R. Childhood injuries: Recognition and prevention. *Current Problems in Pediatrics,* 1981, vol. **12**(1).

Bernick, K. Screening for hearing impairments. In Report of the Harvard Child Health Project, *Children's medical care needs and treatments* (Vol. 2). Cambridge, Mass.: Ballinger, 1977.

Berwick, D. M., Cretin, S., & Keeler, E. Cholesterol, children and heart disease: An analysis of alternatives. *Pediatrics,* 1981, **68**, 721–730.

Bibace, R., & Walsh, M. E. Development of children's concepts of illness. *Pediatrics,* 1980, **66**, 912–917.

Birch, H. G. & Gussow, J. D. *Disadvantaged children: Health, nutrition and school failure.* New York: Harcourt Brace Jovanovich, 1970.

Blum, R. W., & Goldhagen, J. Teenage pregnancy in perspective. *Clinical Pediatrics,* 1981, **20**, 335–340.

Bolton, F. G., Jr., Laner, R. H., & Kane, J. P. Child maltreatment risk among adolescent mothers: A study of reported cases. *American Journal of Orthopsychiatry,* 1980, **50**(3), 489–504.

Bonhag, R. L. *A description of the health financing model: A tool for cost estimation.* Washington, D.C.: Department of Health and Human Services, Office of the Assistant Secretary for Planning and Evaluation, February 1981.

Brazelton, T. B. Anticipatory guidance. *Pediatric Clinics of North America,* 1975, **22**, 533–544.

Brazelton, T. B. Early parent-infant reciprocity. In V. C. Vaughan & T. B. Brazelton (Eds.), *The family—Can it be saved?* Chicago: Year Book Medical, 1976.

Breslau, N. Continuity reexamined: Differential impact on satisfaction with medical care for disabled and normal children. *Medical Care,* April 1982, **20**, 347–360.

Brewster, A. B. Chronically ill hospitalized children's concept of their illness. *Pediatrics,* 1982, **69**, 355–362.

Bricker, D. *Infant monitoring, evaluation and intervention project,* Unpublished research report, University of Oregon, Center on Human Development, April 1982.

Brim, O. G., Jr., & Kagan, J. (Eds.). *Constancy and change in human development.* Cambridge, Mass.: Harvard University Press, 1980.

Brink, S. G., & Nader, P. R. Utilization of school and primary health care resources for common health problems of school children. *Pediatrics,* 1981, **68**, 700–704.

Brody, J. E. Middle ear disease is linked to learning. *New York Times,* December 26, 1978.

Browman, S. H., Nichols, P. L., & Kennedy, W. A. *Preschool IQ: Prenatal and developmental correlates.* New York: Wiley, 1975.

Budetti, P., Butler, J. A., & McManus, P. Federal health program reforms: Implications for child health care. *Milbank Memorial Fund Quarterly/Health and Society,* 1982, **60**(1), 155–181.

Budetti, P., McManus, P., Barrand, N., & Heinen, L. A. *The costs and effectiveness of neonatal intensive care.* (U.S. Office of Technology Assessment, Library of Congress No. 80-600161.) Washington, D.C.: Government Printing Office, 1980.

Burns, B., Burke, J., & Regier, D. Considerations related to a child-oriented psychosocial classification for primary health care. In M. Lipton, Jr., W. Gulbinot, & J. Kupka (Eds.), *Psychosocial factors affecting health.* New York: Praeger, 1982.

Butler, J. A., & Baxter, E. Current structure of the health care delivery system for children.

In Report of the Harvard Child Health Project Task Force, *Developing a better health care system for children* (Vol. 3). Cambridge, Mass.: Ballinger, 1977.

Butler, J. A., Budetti, P., McManus, P., Stenmark, S., & Newacheck, P. Health care expenditures for children with chronic disabilities. In N. Hobbs, H. T. Ireys, & J. Perrin (Eds.), *Public policies affecting chronically ill children and their families. A project of the Institute for Public Policy Studies, Vanderbilt University.* San Francisco: Jossey-Bass, 1984.

Butler, J. A., & Scotch, R. S. Medicaid and children: Some recent lessons and reasonable next steps. *Public Policy,* 1978, **26**, 3–27.

Campbell, J. D. Illness is a point of view: The development of children's concepts of illness. *Child Development,* 1975, **46**, 92–100.

Canadian Task Force on the Periodic Health Examination. The periodic health examination. *Canadian Medical Association Journal,* 1979, **121**, 3–45.

Card, J. J., & Wise, L. L. Teenage mothers and teenage fathers: The impact of early childbearing in the parent's personal and professional lives. *Family Planning Perspectives,* July/August, 1978, **10**, 199–205.

Cartoof, V. G., & Klerman, L. V. Massachusetts' parental consent law: A preliminary study of the law's effects. *Massachusetts Journal of Community Health,* Spring/Summer, 1982, vol. **1**(4), 14–19.

Carpenter, E. S. Children's health care and the changing role of women. *Medical Care,* 1980, **18**, 1208–1218.

Casey, P., Sharp, M., & Loda, F. Child health supervision for children under two years of age: A review of its content and effectiveness. *Journal of Pediatrics,* 1979, **95**, 1–9.

Casey, P. H., & Whitt, J. K. Effect of the pediatrician on the mother-infant relationship. *Pediatrics,* 1980, **65**, 815–820.

Cates, W., Jr. Legal abortion: The public health record. *Science,* 1982, **215**, 1586–1590.

Cavalli-Sforza, L. L., Feldman, M. W., Chen, K. H., & Dornbusch, S. M. Theory and observation in cultural transmission. *Science,* 1982, **218**, 19–27.

Chang, A., Zuckerman, S., & Wallace, H. M. Health service needs of children in daycare centers. *American Journal of Public Health,* 1978, **68**, 373–377.

Cherry, F. F. *Childhood lead poisoning prevention and control: A public health approach to an environmental disease.* New Orleans: Maternal and Child Health Section, Office of Health Services and Environmental Quality, Department of Health and Human Resources, December 1981.

Children's Defense Fund. *EPSDT: Does it spell health care for poor children?* Washington, D.C.: Children's Defense Fund, 1977.

Christopherson, E. R., & Sullivan, M. A. Increasing the protection of newborn infants in cars. *Pediatrics,* 1982, **70**, 21–25.

Clarke, A., & Walton, W. W. Effect of safety packaging on aspirin ingestions by children. *Pediatrics,* 1979, **63**, 687–693.

Coates, T. J., & Thoresen, C. E. Treating obesity in children and adolescents: A review. *American Journal of Public Health,* 1978, **68**, 143–151.

Cohen, S. E., Parmalee, A. H., Sigman, M., & Beckwith, L. *Neonatal risk factors in preterm infants.* Unpublished manuscript, University of California, Los Angeles, School of Medicine, Department of Pediatrics, 1981.

Cohn, A. H. The pediatrician's role in the treatment of child abuse: Implications from a national evaluation study. *Pediatrics,* 1980, **65**, 358–361.

Colle, A. D., & Grossman, M. *Determinants of pediatric care utilization* (NBER Working Paper 240). New York: National Bureau of Economic Research, April 1978.

Crnic, K. A., Greenberg, M. T., Rogozin, A. S., Robinson, N. M., & Basham, R. B. Effects of stress and social support on mothers and premature and full-term infants. *Child Development*, 1983, **54**, 209–217.

Cummings, K. M., Becker, M. H., & Maile, M. C. Bringing the models together: An empirical approach to combining variables used to explain health actions. *Journal of Behavioral Medicine*, 1980, **3**, 123–145.

Davidson, S. M., Connelly, J. P., Blim, R. D., Strain, J. E., & Taylor, H. D. Consumer cost sharing as a means to reduce health care costs. *Pediatrics*, 1980, **65**, 168–169.

Davidson, S. M., & Perloff, J. *Continuous care: The concept and research issues* (Working Draft). Northwestern University, Center for Health Services and Policy Research, March 1, 1980.

Davie, R., Butler, N., & Goldstein, H. *From birth to seven: The second report of the National Child Development Study*. London: Longman, 1972.

Davis, K., & Schoen, C. *Health and the war on poverty: A ten-year appraisal*. Washington, D.C.: Brookings Institution, 1978.

De Angelis, C. The Robert Wood Johnson Foundation National School Health Program. *Clinical Pediatrics*, 1981, **20**, 344–348.

De La Sota, A., Lewis, M. A., & Lewis, C. E. *Actions for health*. Reading, Mass.: Addison-Wesley, 1980.

Denhoff, E. Learning disabilities: An office approach. *Pediatrics*, 1976, **58**(3), 409–411.

Denhoff, E. Current status of infant stimulation or enrichment programs for children with developmental disabilities. *Pediatrics*, 1981, **67**, 32–37.

Dershewitz, R. A., & Williamson, J. W. Prevention of childhood household injuries: A controlled clinical trial. *American Journal of Public Health*, 1977, **67**, 1148–1153.

Dunning, J. M. & Dunning, N. An international look at school-based children's dental services. *American Journal of Public Health*, 1978, **68**, 664–668.

Dutton, D. B. Explaining the low use of health services by the poor: Costs, attitudes, or delivery systems? *American Sociological Review*, 1978, **43**, 348–368.

Dutton, D. B. Patterns of ambulatory health care in five different delivery systems. *Medical Care*, 1979, **17**, 221–243.

Dutton, D. B. Children's health care: The myth of equal access. In the Report of the Select Panel for the Promotion of Child Health, *Better health for our children: A national strategy* (Vol. 4). (DHHS, PHS, Publication No. 79-55071.) Washingon, D.C.: Government Printing Office, 1981.

Dutton, D. B., & Silber, R. S. Children's health outcomes in six different ambulatory care delivery systems. *Medical Care*, 1980, **18**, 693–714.

Dwyer, J. Nutrition education and information. In the Report of the Select Panel for the Promotion of Child Health, *Better health for our children: A national strategy* (Vol. 4). (DHHS, PHS, Publication No. 79-55071.) Washington, D.C.: Government Printing Office, 1981.

Edgerton, R. B. *Mental retardation*. Cambridge, Mass.: Harvard University Press, 1979.

Edwards, L. N., & Grossman, M. *The relationship between children's health and intellectual development* (NBER Reprint 80). New York: National Bureau of Economic Research, 1977.

Egbuonu, L., & Starfield, B. Child health and social status. *Pediatrics*, 1982, **69**, 550–557.

Eisen, M., Donald, C. A., Ware, J. E., Jr., & Brook, R. H. *Conceptualization and measurement of health for children in the health insurance study*. Santa Monica, Calif.: RAND, May 1980.

Eisen, M., Ware, J. E., Jr., Donald, C. A., & Brook, R. H. Measuring components of children's health status. *Medical Care*, 1979, **17**, 902–921.

Eisenberg, L. Controversial issues in health care for children. In Harvard Child Health Project, *Children's medical care needs and treatment* (Vol. 2). Cambridge, Mass.: Ballinger, 1977.

Eisenberg, L. Adolescent suicide: On taking arms against a sea of troubles. *Pediatrics*, 1980, **66**, 315–320.

Eisenberg, L. Social context of child development. *Pediatrics*, 1981, **68**, 705–712.

Eisenberg, L., & Parron, D. Strategies for the prevention of mental disorders. In E. O. Nightingale (Ed.), *Background papers for healthy people: The Surgeon General's report on health promotion and disease prevention.* (Department of Health, Education, and Welfare, PHS, Publication No. 79-55071A.) Washington, D.C.: Government Printing Office, 1979.

Eisner, V., Pratt, M. W., Hexter, A., Chabot, M. J., & Sayal, N. Improvement in infant and perinatal mortality in the United States, 1965–1973: Priorities for intervention. *American Journal of Public Health*, 1978, **68**, 359–366.

Faust, D. S., Ulissi, S. M., & Thurber, S. Postdoctoral training opportunities in pediatric psychology: A review. *Journal of Pediatric Psychology*, 1980, **5**, 277–286.

Field, T., Widmayer, S., Greenberg, R., & Stoller, S. Effects of parent training on teenaged mothers and their infants. *Pediatrics*, 1982, **69**, 703–707.

Fishbane, M., & Starfield, B. Child health care in the United States: A comparison of pediatricians and general practitioners. *New England Journal of Medicine*, 1981, **305**, 552–556.

Foltz, A. M. The organization and financing of child health services: Options for policy. In The Report of the Select Panel for the Promotion of Child Health, *Better health for our children: A national strategy* (Vol. 4). (DHHS, PHS, Publication No. 79-55071.) Washington, D.C.: Government Printing Office, 1981.

Frankenburg, W. K. Pediatric screening. *Advances in Pediatrics*, 1973, **20**, 149–175.

Franks, P., & Bisseau, V. Educational status and health. *Journal of Family Practice*, 1980, **10**, 1029–1034.

Freeman, E. W., Rickels, K., Huggins, G. R., Mudd, E. H., Garcia, C.-R., & Dickens, H. O. Adolescent contraceptive use: Comparisons of male and female attitudes and information. *American Journal of Public Health*, 1980, **70**, 790–797.

Freeman, H. E., Kiecolt, K. J., & Allen, H. M., II. Community health centers: An initiative of enduring utility. *Milbank Memorial Fund Quarterly/Health and Society*, 1982, **60**, 245–267.

Friedman, S. L., & Sigman, M. (Eds.). *Preterm birth and psychological development.* New York: Academic Press, 1981.

Furstenberg, F. F., Jr. *Unplanned parenthood—The social consequences of teenage childbearing.* New York: Free Press, 1976.

Geertsen, R., Klauber, M. R., Rindflesh, M., Kane, R. L., & Gray, R. A re-examination of Suchman's views on social factors in health care utilization. *Journal of Health and Social Behavior*, 1975, **16**, 226–237.

Gliedman, J., & Roth, W. *The unexpected minority: Handicapped children in America.* New York: Harcourt Brace Jovanovich, 1980.

Gochman, D. Some correlates of children's health beliefs and potential health behavior. *Journal of Health and Social Behavior*, 1971, **12**, 148–154.

Goldberg, I. D., Regier, D. A., McInerny, T. K., Pless, I. B., & Roghmann, K. J. The role of the pediatrician in the delivery of mental health services to children. *Pediatrics*, 1979, **63**, 898–909.

Gortmaker, S. L. The effect of prenatal care upon the health of the newborn. *American Journal of Public Health*, 1979, **69**(7), 653–657.

Gortmaker, S. L. Medicaid and the health care of children in poverty and near poverty. *Medical Care*, 1981, **19**, 567–581.

Gortmaker, S. L. Chronic childhood diseases: Demographic considerations for public policy. In N. Hobbs, H. T. Ireys, & J. Perrin (Eds.), *Public policies affecting chronically ill children and their families*. San Francisco: Jossey-Bass, 1983.

Gortmaker, S. L., Walker, D. K., & Weitzman, M. *Chronic illness and psychosocial problems among children: Prevalence and patterns of service utilization.* Paper presented at annual meeting of the American Public Health Association, New York, November 1979.

Grant, C. 1980. A management alert—How schools are delivering ambulatory care. *Journal of Ambulatory Care Management*, 1980, 3(2), 53–69.

Green, L. W. National policy in the promotion of health. *International Journal of Health Education*, 1979, **22**, 161–168.

Green, L. W. To educate or not to educate: Is that the question? *American Journal of Public Health*, 1980, **70**, 625–626.

Green, L. W. Lessons from the past, plans for the future. *Health Education Quarterly*, 1981, 8, 105–117.

Green, L. W., & Iverson, D. C. School health education. In L. Breslow, J. E. Fielding, & L. Lave (Eds.), *Annual Review of Public Health*, 1982, 3, 321–338.

Green, L. W., & Johnson, K. W. Health education and health promotion. In E. Mechanic (Ed.), *Handbook of health, health care and health professions*. New York: Wiley, 1982.

Grossman, M. *Determinants of children's health* (Research Summary Series). Washington, D.C.: National Center for Health Services Research, 1981.

Grossman, M., Coote, D., Edwards, L. N., Shakotko, R. A., & Chermichovsky, D. *Determinants of children's health*. New York: National Bureau of Economic Research, February 1980.

Grossman, M., Edwards, L. N., & Shakotko, R. A. *Effects of children's health on their intellectual development*. New York: National Bureau of Economic Research, April 1980.

Grossman, M., & Jacobowitz, S. Variations in infant mortality rates among counties of the United States: The roles of public policies and programs. *Demography*, 1981, **18**, 695–773.

Haggerty, R. J. Damn the simplicities. *Pediatrics*, 1980, **66**, 323–324.

Haggerty, R. J., Roghmann, K. J., & Pless, I. B. (Eds.), *Child health and the community*. New York: Wiley, 1975.

Hamburg, B. A. Teenagers as parents: Developmental issues in school-age pregnancy. In E. F. Purcell (Ed.), *Psychopathology of children and youth: A cross cultural perspective: Report of a conference*. New York: Josiah Macy, Jr., Foundation, 1980.

Hamburg, D. A. Health and behavior. *Science*, 1982, **217**, 399.

Hammerman, S., & Markowski, S. *The economics of disability: International perspectives*. New York: Rehabilitation International, 1981.

Hardy, J. B., Welcher, D. W., Stanley, J., & Dallas, J. R. Long-range outcome of adolescent pregnancy. *Clinical Obstetrics and Gynecology*, 1978, 21(4), 1215–1232.

Harman, D., and Brim, O. G., Jr. *Learning to be parents: Principles, programs and methods*. Beverly Hills, Calif.: Sage, 1980.

Harvard Child Health Project Task Force. *Children's medical care needs and treatments.* (Vol. **2**). Cambridge, Mass.: Ballinger, 1977.

Hein, K., Cohen, M. I., Litt, I. F., Schonberg, S. K., Meyer, M. R., Marks, A., & Sheehy, A. J. Juvenile detention: Another boundary issue for physicians. *Pediatrics*, 1980, 66(2), 239–245.

Helfer, R. E., & Kempe, C. H. *Child abuse and neglect*. Cambridge, Mass.: Ballinger, 1976.

Hemminki, E., & Starfield, B. Prevention of low birth weight and pre-term birth. *Milbank Memorial Fund Quarterly/Health and Society*, 1979, **56**, 339–361.

Hiatt, H. H. The physician and national security. *New England Journal of Medicine*, 1982, **307**, 1142–1145.

Hoadly, M. R., Macrina, D. M., & Peterson, F. L. Child safety programs: Implications affecting use of child restraints. *Journal of School Health*, 1981, **51**, 352–355.

Hobbs, N., Perrin, J. M., & Ireys, H. T. Summary of findings and recommendations: Public policies affecting chronically ill children and their families. Nashville: Center for the Study of Families and Children, Vanderbilt University Institute for Public Policy Studies, 1983.

Insurance Institute for Highway Safety. Teens and autos: A deadly combination. *Insurance Institute for Highway Safety Status Report*, 1981, **16**, 14.

Intergovernmental Health Policy Project. *Recent or proposed changes in state Medicaid programs: A fifty state survey*. Washington, D.C.: National Health Policy Forum, 1981.

Ireys, H. T. Health care for chronically disabled children and their families. In the Report of the Select Panel for the Promotion of Child Health. *Better health for our children: A national strategy* (Vol. 4). (DHHS, PHS, Publication No. 79-55071.) Washington, D.C.: Government Printing Office, 1981.

Iverson, D. C. (Ed.). Promoting health through the schools: A challenge for the 80s. *Health Education Quarterly*, Spring 1981, Vol. 8 (Special Issue).

Jacobson, A. M., Goldberg, I. D., Burns, B. J., Hoeper, E. W., Hankin, J. R., & Hewitt, K. Diagnosed mental disorder in children and use of health services in four organized health care settings. *American Journal of Psychiatry*, 1980, **137**, 559–565.

Jekel, J. F. *Primary or secondary prevention of adolescent pregnancies?* Paper presented at the annual American Public Health Association meeting, Miami Beach, October 1976.

Kempe, C. H. Approaches to preventing child abuse: The health visitors concept. *American Journal of Diseases of Children*, 1976, **130**, 532–536.

Keniston, K. The Carnegie Council on Children. *All our children: The American family under pressure*. New York: Harcourt Brace Jovanovich, 1977.

Kety, S. Studies designed to disentangle genetic and environmental variables in schizophrenia. *American Journal of Psychiatry*, 1976, **133**, 1134–1137.

Kinard, E. M., & Klerman, L. V. Early parenting and child abuse: Are they related? *American Journal of Orthopsychiatry*, 1980, **50**, 481–488.

Kirscht, J. P., Becker, M. H., Eveland, J. P. Psychological and social factors as predictors of medical behavior. *Medical Care*, 1976, **14**, 422–431.

Kister, M. C. & Patterson, C. J. Children's conceptions of the causes of illness: Understanding of contagion and use of immanent justice. *Child Development*, 1980, **51**, 839–846.

Klaus, M. H. & Kennell, J. H. *Bonding: The beginnings of parent to infant attachment*. St. Louis: Mosby, 1983.

Kleinman, J. C., Gold, M., & Makuc, D. Use of ambulatory medical care by the poor: Another look at equity. *Medical Care*, 1981, **19**, 1011–1029.

Klerman, L. V. 1981. *Adolescent development: Its impact on sexuality and parenting*. Paper delivered at a conference on Adolescent Sexuality—A Multidisciplinary Approach. Waltham, Mass.: Brandeis University, 1981.(a)

Klerman, L. V. The maternal and child health and crippled children's services section of the Social Security Act: Problems and opportunities. In the Report of the Select Panel for the Promotion of Child Health, *Better health for our children: A national strategy* (Vol. 4). (DHHS, PHS, Publication No. 79-55071.) Washington, D.C.: Government Printing Office, 1981.(b)

Klerman, L. V. Programs for pregnant adolescents and young parents: Their development and assessment. In K. G. Scott, and E. G. Robertson (Eds.), *Teenage parents and their offspring*. New York: Grune & Stratton, 1981.(c)

Klerman, L. V. *Research priorities in maternal and child health: Report of a conference*. Washington, D.C.: Office of Maternal and Child Health, DHHS, 1982.

Kolbe, L. J., & Iverson, D. C. *Integrating school and community efforts to promote health: Strategies, policies, and methods*. Paper presented at the International Seminar on School Health Education, Southampton, England, 1981.

Kotch, J. B., & Whiteman, D. Effect of a WIC program on children's clinic activity in a local health department. *Medical Care*, 1982, **20**, 691–698.

Kovar, M. G. Health status of U.S. children and use of medical care. *Public Health Reports*, 1982, **97**, 3–15.

Kovar, M. G. & Meny, D. J. A statistical profile. In the Report of the Select Panel for the Promotion of Child Health, *Better health for our children: A national strategy* (Vol. 3). (DHHS, PHS, Publication No. 79-55071.) Washington, D.C.: Government Printing Office, 1981.

Kriepe, R. E., Roghmann, K. J., & McAnarny, E. R. Early adolescent childbearing: A changing morbidity? *Journal of Adolescent Health Care*, 1981, **2**(2), 127–131.

Kronenfeld, J. J. The Medicaid program and a regular source of care. *American Journal of Public Health*, 1978, **68**, 771–773.

Krugman, S. Rubella immunizations: Progress, problem and potential solutions. *American Journal of Public Health*, 1979, **69**, 217–218.

Lash, T. W., Sigal, H., & Dudzinski, D. *State of the child: New York City-II*. New York: Foundation for Child Development, 1980.

Lave, J. R., Lave, L. B., Leinhardt, S., & Nagin, D. Characteristics of individuals who identify a regular source of medical care. *American Journal of Public Health*, 1979, **69**, 261–267.

Layde, P. M., von Allmen, S. D., Oakley, G. P. Maternal serum alpha-fetoprotein screening: A cost-benefit analysis. *American Journal of Public Health*, 1979, **69**, 566–573.

Lee, K.-S., Paneth, N., Gartner, L. M., Pearlman, M. A., & Gruss, L. Neonatal mortality: An analysis of the recent improvement in the United States. *American Journal of Public Health*, 1980, **70**, 15–21.

Lefkowitz, B., & Andrulis, D. The organization of primary health and health-related preventive, psychosocial and support services for children and pregnant women. In the Report of the Select Panel for the Promotion of Child Health, *Better health for our children: A national strategy* (Vol. 4). (DHHS, PHS, Publication No. 79-55071.) Washington, D.C.: Government Printing Office, 1981.

Levine, M. D. The child with school problems: An analysis of physician participation. *Exceptional Children*, 1982, **48**, 296–304.

Levine, M. D., & Palfrey, J. S. The health impact of early childhood programs: Perspectives from the Brookline Early Education Project. In J. R. Travers & R. J. Light (Eds.), *Learning from experience: Evaluating early childhood demonstration programs*. Washington, D.C.: National Academy of Sciences, 1982.

Levine, M. D., Palfrey, J. S., Lamb, G. A., Weisberg, H. I., & Bryk, A. S. Infants in a public school system: The indicators of early health and educational need. *Pediatrics*, 1977, **60**, 579–587.

Levy, H. PKU: A threat to the second generation. *Harvard Medical Area Focus*, February 11, 1982, pp. 4–5; 12.

Levy, J. C. 1980. Vulnerable children: Parents' perspectives and the use of medical care. *Pediatrics*, 1980, **65**, 956–963.

Levy, J. C., Bonanno, R. A., Schwartz, C. G., & Sanofsky, P. A. Primary care: Patterns of use of pediatric medical facilities. *Medical Care*, 1979, **17**, 881–893.

Lewis, C. E., & Lewis, M. A. *The determinants of children's health-related beliefs and behaviors: Preparing tomorrow's consumers today.* Unpublished paper, University of California, Los Angeles, Department of Medicine, November 1980.

Lewis, C. E., Lewis, M. A., Lorimer, A., & Palmer, B. B. Child-initiated care: The use of school nursing services by children in an "adult-free" system. *Pediatrics,* 1977, **60,** 499–507.

Lewitter, F. I., DeFries, J. C., & Elston, R. C. Genetic models of reading disability. *Behavior Genetics,* 1980, **10,** 9–30.

Litt, I. F., & Cuskey, W. R. Compliance with medical regimens during adolescence. *Pediatric Clinics of North America,* 1980, **27,** 3–14.

Lynn, L. E. (Ed.). *National Research Council Study project on social research and development: Knowledge and policy: The uncertain connection* (Vol. 5). Washington, D.C.: National Academy of Sciences, 1978.

Mahaffey, K. R., Annest, J. L., Roberts, J., & Murphy, R. S. National estimates of blood lead levels: United States, 1976–1980: Association with selected demographic and socioeconomic factors. *New England Journal of Medicine,* 1982, **307,** 573–579.

Mahoney, M. E. Children's health care needs lack broad-based constituency. *Hospital Progress,* 1980, **61,** 56–59.

Mare, R. D. Socioeconomic effects on child mortality in the United States. *American Journal of Public Health,* 1982, **72,** 539–547.

Masnick, G., & Bane, M. J. *The nation's families: 1960–1990.* Cambridge, Mass.: Joint Center for Urban Studies of M.I.T. and Harvard University, 1980.

Maurana, C. A., Eichhorn, R. L., & Lonnquist, L. E. *The use of health services: Indices and correlates: A research bibliography, 1981.* Washington, D.C.: National Center for Health Services Research, November 1981.

McAlister, A. L. Social and environmental influences on health behavior. *Health Education Quarterly,* 1981, **8,** 25–31.

McAlister, A. L., & Gordon, N. Prevention during early adolescence. In W. Bukoski (Ed.), *Prevention evaluation.* Washington, D.C.: National Institute on Drug Abuse, 1980.

McCormick, M. C., Shapiro, S., & Starfield, B. H. Rehospitalization in the first year of life for high-risk survivors. *Pediatrics,* 1980, **66,** 991–999.

McDonald, Q. H. Children's car seat restraints: When top-tether straps are ignored, are these restraints safe? *Pediatrics,* 1979, **64,** 848–855.

McIntire, M. S., Angle, C. R., Sathees, K., & Lee, P. Safety packaging—What does the public think? *American Journal of Public Health,* 1977, **67,** 169–170.

McManus, M. A., & Davidson, S. M. *Medicaid and children: A policy analysis.* Paper commissioned by the American Academy of Pediatrics, Division of Pediatric Practice, Committee on Child Health Financing. Evanston, Ill.: American Academy of Pediatrics, November 1982.

Mechanic, D. The influence of mothers on their children's health attitudes and behavior. *Pediatrics,* 1964, **33,** 444–453.

Mechanic, D. The stability of health and illness behavior. *American Journal of Public Health,* 1979, **69,** 1142–1145.

Mechanic, D. Education, parental interest, and health perceptions and behavior. *Inquiry,* 1980, **17,** 331–338.

Mechanic, D. Some dilemmas in health care policy. *Milbank Memorial Fund Quarterly/Health and Society,* 1981, **59,** 16–43.

Medrich, E., & Rubin, V. *After-school services in a time of lower expectations* (Children's Time Study, School of Law, Boalt Hall). Berkeley: University of California, 1979.

Miller, C. A., & Moos, M. K. *Local health departments: Fifteen case studies.* Baltimore: American Public Health Association, 1981.

Miller, C. A., Moos, M. K., Kotch, J. B., Brown, M. L., & Brainard, M. P. *Role and new initiatives of local health departments in delivery of personal health services.* Paper presented at National Symposium on Role of State and Local Governments in Relation to Personal Health Services. Chapel Hill, N.C.: University of North Carolina School of Public Health, 1980.

Milunsky, A. *Prevention of genetic disease and mental retardation.* Philadelphia: Saunders, 1975.

Moore, K., & Waite, L. Early childbearing and educational attainment. *Family Planning Perspectives,* 1977, **9**, 220–225.

Morris, J. N. Epidemiology and prevention. *Milbank Memorial Fund Quarterly/Health and Society,* 1982, **60**, 1–16.

Morse, A. E., Hyde, J. N., Newberger, E. H., & Reed, R. B. Environmental correlates of pediatric social illness: Preventive implications of an advocacy approach. *American Journal of Public Health,* 1977, **67**, 612–615.

Mullen, P. D. Behavioral aspects of maternal and child health: National influences and educational intervention. In the Report of the Select Panel for the Promotion of Child Health, *Better health for our children: A national strategy* (Vol. 4). (DHHS, PHS, Publication No. 79-55071.) Washington, D.C.: Government Printing Office, 1981.

Nader, P. R., & Brink, S. G. Does visiting the school health room teach appropriate or inappropriate use of health services? *American Journal of Public Health,* 1981, **71**, 416–419.

Nader, P. R., Gilman, S., & Bee, D. E. Factors influencing access to primary care via school health services. *Pediatrics,* 1980, **65**, 585–591.

Naeye, R. L. Teenaged and pre-teenaged pregnancies: Consequences of the fetal-maternal competition for nutrients. *Pediatrics,* 1981, **67**, 146–150.

National Center for Clinical Infant Programs. *Clinical infant intervention research programs.* Washington, D.C.: Mental Health Study Center, National Institute of Mental Health, 1979.

National Center for Health Statistics. *Monthly vital statistics report,* 1982, vol. **31**.

National Research Council. *Toward a national policy for children and families.* Washington, D.C.: National Academy of Sciences, 1976.

National Research Council. *Study project on social research and development: The federal investment in knowledge of social problems* (Vol. 1): *Study project report.* Washington, D.C.: National Academy of Sciences, 1978.

National Research Council. Food and Nutrition Board. *Towards healthful diet.* Washington, D.C.: National Academy of Sciences, 1980.

Needleman, H. L., Gunnoe, C., Leviton, A., Reed, R., Peresie, H., Maher, C., & Barrett, P. Deficits in psychologic and classroom performance of children with elevated dentine lead levels. *New England Journal of Medicine,* 1979, **300**, 689–695.

Newacheck, P. W., Butler, L. H., Harper, A. K., Piontkowski, D. L., & Franks, P. E. Income and illness. *Medical Care,* 1980. **18**, 1165–1176.

Newberger, C. M., Hampton, R. L., Kessler, D., Daniel, J., White, K., & Newberger, E. H. *Child abuse and childhood accidents: A comparative analysis.* Unpublished manuscript, Boston, Children's Hospital Medical Center, 1981.

Newberger, E. H., & Marx, T. J. Ecologic reformulation of pediatric social illness. Paper presented at the annual meeting of the Society for Pediatric Research, Washington, D.C., 1982.

Newhouse, J. P., Manning, W. G., Morris, C. N., Orr, L. L., Duan, N., Keeler, E. B., Leibowitz, A., Marquis, K. H., Marquis, M. S., Phelps, C. E., & Brook, R. H. Some interim results from a controlled trial of cost sharing in health insurance. *New England Journal of Medicine,* 1981, **305**, 1501–1507.

North, A. F., Jr. Health services in Head Start. In E. Zigler & J. Valentine (Eds.), *Project Head Start: A legacy of the war on poverty.* New York: Free Press, 1979.

Novick, L. F., Rice, C., Freedman, M. A., & Lillson, D. Asbestos in Vermont schools: Findings of a state-wide on-site investigation. *American Journal of Public Health*, 1981, **71**, 744–746.

Ooms, T. (Ed.). *Teenage pregnancy in a family context: Implications for policy.* Philadelphia: Temple University Press, 1981.

Osman, D., & Evans, A. Education of the handicapped issue brief number 1B78040. Washington, D.C.: Library of Congress, Congressional Research Service, January 1980.

Palfrey, J. S. 1982. *Intrinsic risk factors and their stability over time.* Paper presented at Symposium on Middle Childhood: Developmental Variation and Dysfunction between Six and Fourteen Years. New Orleans, 1982.

Palfrey, J. S., Levine, M. D., & Pierson, D. E. *Antecedents of middle childhood performance: A study of preschool service needs.* Unpublished manuscript, Brookline Early Education Project, October 1982.

Palfrey, J. S., Levy, J. C., & Gilbert, K. L. Use of primary care facilities by patients attending specialty clinics. *Pediatrics*, 1980, **65**, 567–572.

Paneth, N., Kiely, J. L., Stein, Z., & Susser, M. Cerebral palsy and newborn care: Estimated prevalence rates of cerebral palsy under differing rates of mortality and impairment of low-birth weight infants. *Developmental Medicine and Child Neurology*, 1981, **23**, 801–807.

Paradise, J. L., & Rogers, K. D. Ubiquitous otitis media: A child health problem of uncertain dimensions. *American Journal of Public Health*, 1980, **70**, 577–578.

Parmalee, A. H., Jr., Beckwith, L., Cohen, S. E., & Sigman, M. *Early intervention: Experience with preterm infants.* Unpublished manuscript, University of California at Los Angeles, School of Medicine, Department of Pediatrics, 1980.

Paulson, J. A. The case for mandatory seat restraint laws. *Clinical Pediatrics*, 1981, **20**, 285–291.

Pennington, B. F., Bender, B., Puck, M., Salbenblatt, J., & Robinson, A. Learning disabilities in children with sex chromosome anomalies. *Child Development*, 1982, **53**, 1182–1192.

Perrin, E. C. *Who knows what kids know?* Paper read at Ambulatory Pediatrics Association Meeting, Vanderbilt University School of Medicine, 1981.

Perrin, E. C., & Gerrity, P. S. There's a demon in your belly: Children's understanding of illness. *Pediatrics*, 1981, **67**, 841–849.

Placek, P. Maternal and infant health factors associated with low infant birth weight: Findings from the 1972 National Natality Survey. In D. Reed & F. Stanley (Eds.), *The epidemiology of prematurity.* Baltimore: Urban & Schwarzenberg, 1977.

Pless, I. B. Accident prevention and health education: Back to the drawing board? *Pediatrics*, 1978, **62**, 431–434.

Pless, I. B., & Pekeles, G. Applications of health care research to child health services: A problematic relationship. *Israel Journal of Medical Sciences*, 1981, **17**, 192–200.

Pless, I. B. & Pinkerton, P. *Chronic childhood disorder: Promoting patterns of adjustment.* Chicago: Year Book Medical Publishers, 1975.

Popkin, B. M., Akin, J., Kaufman, M., & MacDonald, M. Nutritional program options for maternal and child health: A summary. In the Report of the Select Panel for the Promotion of Child Health, *Better health for our children: A national strategy* (Vol. 4). (DHHS, PHS, Publication No. 79–55071). Washington, D.C.: Government Printing Office, 1981.

Porter, P. J. The Cambridge experience. *Robert Wood Johnson Foundation Newsletter*, 1979, **1**, 15–17.

Porter, P. J. Realistic outcomes of school health service programs. *Health Education Quarterly*, 1981, **8**, 81–87.

Porter, P. J., Liebel, R. L., Gilbert, G. K., & Fellows, J. A. Municipal child health services: A ten-year reorganization. *Pediatrics*, 1976, **58**, 704–712.

Posen-Robbins School Health Corporation. *National school health program evaluation: Progress report: September 1977 through May 1979.* Chicago: Posen-Robbins School Health Corp., 1980.

Pratt, L. Child rearing methods and children's health behaviors. *Journal of Health and Social Behavior*, 1973, **14**, 61–69.

Pressman, J. L., & Wildavsky, A. B. *Implementation.* Berkeley and Los Angeles: University of California Press, 1973.

Quick, J. D., Greenlick, M. R. & Roghmann, K. Prenatal care and pregnancy outcome in an HMO and general population: A multivariate cohort analysis. *American Journal of Public Health*, 1981, **71**, 381–390.

Radius, S. M., Dillman, T. E., Becker, M. H., Rosenstock, I. M., & Horvath, W. J. Adolescent perspectives on health and illness. *Adolescence*, 1980, **15**, 375–384.

Reisinger, K. S., & Williams, A. F. Evaluation of programs designed to increase the protection of infants in cars. *Pediatrics*, 1978, **62**, 280–287.

Richmond, J. B., & Janis, J. M. A perspective on primary prevention in the earliest years. *Children Today*, 1980, **9**, 2–8.

Richmond, J. B., & Janis, J. M. Ripeness is all: The coming of age of behavioral pediatrics. In M. D. Levine (Ed.), *Developmental behavioral pediatrics.* Philadelphia: Saunders, 1983.

Robbins, K. B., Brandling-Bennett, D., & Hinman, A. R. Low measles incidence: Association with enforcement of school immunization laws. *American Journal of Public Health*, 1981, **71**, 270–274.

Robertson, L. S. Crash involvement of teenaged drivers when driver education is eliminated from high school. *American Journal of Public Health*, 1980, **70**, 599–603.

Robertson, L. S. Environmental hazards to children: Assessment and options for amelioration. In the Report of the Select Panel for the Promotion of Child Health, *Better health for our children: A national strategy* (Vol. 4). (DHHS, PHS, Publication No. 79–55071.) Washington, D.C.: Government Printing Office, 1981. (a)

Robertson, L. S. Patterns of teenaged driver involvement in fatal motor vehicle crashes: Implications for policy choice. *Journal of Health Politics, Policy and Law*, 1981, **6**, 303–314. (b)

Robertson, L. S., & Zador, P. L. Driver education and fatal crash involvement of teenaged drivers. *American Journal of Public Health*, 1978, **68**, 959–965.

Robertson, T. S., Rossiter, J. R., & Gleason, T. C. Children's receptivity to proprietary medicine advertising. *Journal of Consumer Research*, 1979, **6**, 247–255.

Rogers, D. C., Blendon, R. J., & Hearn, R. P. Some observations on pediatrics: Its past, present and future. *Pediatrics*, *1981*, **67**, 776–784.

Rogers, D. C., Blendon, R.J., & Moloney, T. W. Who needs medicaid? *New England Journal of Medicine*, 1982, **307**, 13–18.

Rogers, J., & Curtis, P. The concept and measurement of continuity in primary care. *American Journal of Public Health*, 1980, **70**, 122–127.

Roghmann, K. J. Available models. In R. J. Haggerty, K. J. Roghmann, & I. B. Pless, (Eds.), *Child health and the community.* New York: Wiley, 1975.

Roghmann, K. J. The health of preschool children. In L. B. Klerman (Ed.), *Research priorities in maternal and child health. Report of a conference.* Washington, D.C.: Office for Maternal and Child Health, PHS, DHHS, 1981.

Roghmann, K. J., & Haggerty, R. J. The stress model for illness behavior. In R. J. Haggerty, K. J. Roghmann, & I. B. Pless (Eds.), *Child health and the community.* New York: Wiley, 1975.

Rosenbaum, S., & Weitz, J. *Children and federal health care cuts.* Washington, D.C.: Children's Defense Fund, 1983.

Rothenberg, P. B., & Varga, P. E. The relationship between age of mother and child health and development. *American Journal of Public Health, 1981,* **71**, 810–817.

Rutter, M. Maternal deprivation, 1972–1978: New findings, new concepts, new approaches. In S. Chess & A. Thomas (Eds.), *Annual progress in child psychiatry and child development.* New York: Brunner/Mazel, 1980.

Rutter, M. Prevention of children's psychosocial disorders: Myth and substance. *Pediatrics,* 1982, **70**, 883–894.

Ryan, G. M., & Sweeney, P. J. Attitudes of adolescents toward pregnancy and contraception. *American Journal of Obstetrics and Gynecology,* 1980, **137**, 358–366.

Sackett, D. L., & Haynes, R. B. *Compliance with therapeutic regimens.* Baltimore: Johns Hopkins University Press, 1976.

Schaefer, E. S. Professional paradigms in child and family health programs. *American Journal of Public Health,* 1979, **69**, 849–850.

Schaefer, E. J., & Hughes, J. R. Socioeconomic factors and maternal and child health care. *Medical Care,* 1976, **14**, 535–543.

Scheffler, R. M., & Paringer, L. A review of the economic evidence on prevention. *Medical Care,* **18**, 473–484.

Schor, E. L. The foster care system and health status of foster children. *Pediatrics,* 1982, **69**, 521–527.

Select Panel for the Promotion of Child Health. *Better health for our children: A national strategy.* (Vol. 1): *Major findings and recommendations.* Washington, D.C.: Government Printing Office, 1981. (a)

Select Panel for the Promotion of Child Health. *Better health for our children: A national strategy.* (Vol. 2): *Analysis and recommendations for selected federal programs.* Washington, D.C.: Government Printing Office, 1981. (b)

Select Panel for the Promotion of Child Health. *Better health for our children: A national strategy.* (Vol. 3): *A statistical profile.* Washington, D.C.: Government Printing Office, 1981. (c)

Senn, M. 1975. *Insights on the child development movement in the United States.* Monographs of the Society for Research in Child Development, 1975, **40**(3–4, Serial No. 161).

Shadish, W. R. *Effectiveness of preventive child health care* (Working Draft). Northwestern University, March 1, 1980.

Shapiro, S. New reductions in infant mortality: The challenge of low birth weight. *American Journal of Public Health,* 1981, **71**, 363–364.

Shapiro, S., McCormick, M., Starfield, B., Bross, D., & Crowley, B. Changes in infant morbidity associated with decreases in infant mortality. Unpublished paper presented at American Public Health Association, Detroit, October 21, 1980.

Shonkoff, J. P., Deworkin, P. H., Leviton, A., & Levine, M. D. Primary care approaches to developmental disabilities. *Pediatrics,* 1979, **64**, 506–514.

Shorey, C. E. *Testimony presented on behalf of March of Dimes Birth Defects Foundation.* Select Panel for the Promotion of Child Health. Washington, D.C., February 1, 1980.

Silber, T. J. Adolescent medicine: The development of a new speciality. *Adolescence,* 1980, **15**, 495–500.

Simeonsson, R. J., Cooper, D. H., & Scheiner, A. P. A review and analysis of the effectiveness of early intervention programs. *Pediatrics,* 1982, **69**, 635–641.

Sinclair, J. C., Torrance, G. W., Boyle, M. H., Horwood, S. P., Saigal, S., & Sackett, D. L. Evaluation of a neonatal-intensive-care program. *New England Journal of Medicine*, 1981, **305**, 489–494.

Slesinger, D. P., Tessler, R. C., & Mechanic, D. The effects of social characteristics on the utilization of preventive medical services in contrasting health care programs. *Medical Care*, 1976, **14**, 392–404.

Smith, S.D., Kimberling, W. J., Pennington, B. F., & Lubs, H. A. Specific reading disability: Identification of an inherited form through linkage analysis. *Science*, 1983, **219**, 1345–1347.

Spiegel, C. N., & Lindamen, F. C. Children can't fly: A program to prevent childhood morbidity and mortality from window falls. *American Journal of Public Health*, 1977, **67**, 1143–1147.

Starfield, B. Stability and change: Another view. *American Journal of Public Health*, 1981, **71**, 301–302.

Starfield, B. Family income, ill health, and medical care of U.S. children. *Journal of Public Health Policy*, 1982, **3**, 244–259.

Starfield, B., Bice, T., Schach, E., Rabin, D., & White, K. L. How "regular" is the "regular source of medical care"? *Pediatrics*, 1973, **51**, 822–832.

Starfield, B., Gross, E., Wood, M., Pantell, R., Allen, C., Gordon, I. B., Moffat, P., Drachman, R., & Katz, H. Psychosocial and psychosomatic diagnosis in primary care of children. *Pediatrics*, 1980, **66**, 159–167.

Starfield, B., Katz, H., Gabriel, A., Livingston, G., Benson, P., Hankin, J., Horn, S., Steinwachs, D. *Morbidity in childhood: A longitudinal view*. Manuscript submitted for publication, 1983.

Starfield, B., & Pless, I. B. Physical health. In O. G. Brim, Jr., & J. Kagan (Eds.), *Constancy and change in human development*. Cambridge, Mass.: Harvard University Press, 1980.

Starfield B., Shapiro, S., McCormick, M., & Bross, D. Mortality and morbidity in infants with intrauterine growth retardation. *Journal of Pediatrics*, 1982, **101**, 978–983.

Starfield, B., Simborg, D. W., Horn, S. D., & Yourtee, S. A. Continuity and coordination in primary care: Their achievement and utility. *Medical Care*, 1976, **14**, 625–636.

Staudenmayer, H., Harris, P. S., & Selner, J. C. Evaluation of self-help education—Exercise program for asthmatic children and their parents: Six-month follow-up. *Journal of Asthma Research*, 1981, **18**, 1–5.

Steiner, G. Y. *The futility of family policy*. Washington, D.C.: Brookings Institute, 1981.

Stokey, E., & Zeckhauser, R. *A primer for policy analysis*. New York: Norton, 1978.

Stulginskas, J. V. & Pless, I. B. Six consecutive years of observed seat restraint use. *Papers accepted at Ninth International Meeting of the Epidemiological Association*. Edinburgh, August 22–28, 1981. (Abstract)

Tessler, R., and Mechanic, D. Psychological distress and perceived health status. *Journal of Health and Social Behavior*, 1978, **19**, 254–262.

Thibodeau, L. A., & Berwick, D. M. Variation in rates of diagnosis of acute otitis media. *Journal of Medical Education*, 1980, **55**, 1021–1026.

Trapnell, G., & McFadden, F. *The rising cost of catastrophic illness*. Falls Church, Va.: Actuarial Research Corp., December 1977.

Trussell, T. J. Economic consequences of teenage child bearing. *Family Planning Perspectives*, 1976, **8**, 184–190.

Tuma, J. M. Training in pediatric psychology: A concern of the 1980s. *Journal of Pediatric Psychology*, 1980, **5**, 229–243.

U.S. Bureau of Labor Statistics. *Children of working mothers, March 1977*. Washington, D.C.: Special Labor Force Report 217, 1978.

U.S. Department of Health, Education, and Welfare, *Public Health Service: A reason for visit classification for ambulatory care.* (DHEW Publication No. [PHS] 79–1352). Hyattsville, Md.: National Center for Health Statistics, 1979.

U.S. Department of Health and Human Services. Childbearing and abortion patterns among teenagers—United States. *Mortality and Morbidity Weekly Report* (HHS Publication No. CDC 81–8017). Washington, D.C.: December 18, 1982, **30**(49), 611–620.

U.S. Health Interview Survey. *Current estimates from the Health Interview Survey, 1978* (Series 10, No. 130). Hyattsville, Md.: National Center for Health Statistics, 1979.

U.S. Office of Special Education. *The implementation of Public Law 94-142: The Education for All Handicapped Children Act.* Second Annual Report to Congress. Washington, D.C.: Department of Education, 1980.

U.S. Office of Technology Assessment. *The implementation of cost-effectiveness analysis of medical technology.* Washington, D.C.: Office of Technology Assessment, Congress of the United States, August 1980.

U.S. Surgeon General. *Healthy people: The Surgeon General's report on health promotion and disease prevention.* (DHEW, PHS, Publication No. 79–55071.) Washington, D.C.: Government Printing Office, 1979.

Wan, T. T. H., & Gray, L. C. Differential access to preventive services for young children in low-income urban areas. *Journal of Health and Social Behavior,* 1978, **19**, 312–324.

Watts, H. W., & Hernandez, D. J. *Child and family indicators: A report with recommendations.* Washington, D.C.: Social Science Research Council, Center for Coordination of Research on Social Indicators, 1982.

Weiner, J. *The Baltimore City primary care study: An analysis of office-based primary care.* Unpublished doctoral dissertation, Johns Hopkins University School of Hygiene and Public Health, 1981.

Weiss, C. Improving the linkage between social research and public policy. In L. E. Lynn, Jr. (Ed.), *Knowledge and policy: The uncertain connection.* Washington, D.C.: National Academy of Sciences, 1978.

Weithorn, L. A., & Campbell, S. B. The competency of children and adolescents to make informed treatment decisions. *Child Development,* 1982, **53**, 1589–1598.

Weitzman, M. 1981. *Medical services for children with chronic illness.* Unpublished manuscript, Boston University School of Medicine.

Weitzman, M., Klerman, L. V., Lamb, G., Menary, J., & Alpert, J. J. School absence: A problem for the pediatrician. *Pediatrics,* 1982, **69**, 739–746.

Weitzman, M., Moomaw, M. S., & Messenger, K. P. An after-hours pediatric walk-in clinic for an entire urban community: Utilization and effectiveness of follow-up care. *Pediatrics,* 1980, **65**, 964–970.

Werner, E. E., Brennan, J. M., & French, F. E. *The children of Kauai: A longitudinal study from the perinatal period to age ten.* Honolulu: University of Hawaii Press, 1971.

Werner, E. E., & Smith, R. J. *Vulnerable but invincible: Study of resilient children.* New York: McGraw-Hill, 1982.

Widome, M. D. Vehicle occupant safety: The pediatrician's responsibility. *Pediatrics,* 1979, **64**, 966–967.

Williams, A. F. Evaluation of the Tennessee child restraint law. *American Journal of Public Health,* 1979, **69**, 455–458.

Williams, A. F., & Karpf, R. S. *Teenaged drivers and fatal crash responsibility: Preliminary report.* Washington, D.C.: Insurance Institute for Highway Safety, 1982.

Williams, A. F., & Wells, J. K. The Tennessee child restraint law in its third year. *American Journal of Public Health,* 1981, **71**, 163–165. (a)

Williams, A. F., & Wells, J. K. Evaluation of the Rhode Island child restraint law. *American Journal of Public Health*, 1981, **71**, 742–743.

Wilson, R. W. Do health indicators indicate health? *American Journal of Public Health*, 1981, **71**, 461–463.

Winikoff, B., & Baer, E. C. The obstetrician's opportunity: Translating "breast is best" from theory to practice. *American Journal of Obstetrics and Gynecology*, 1980, **138**, 105–117.

Witte, J. J., & Axnick, N. W. The benefits from ten years of measles immunizations in the United States. *Public Health Reports*, vol. 90, May–June 1975.

Wolfe, B. L. Children's utilization of medical care. *Medical Care*, 1980, **18**, 1196–1207.

Wolfe, B. L. *School outcomes of chronically ill children and their siblings: A multivariate approach.* Stanford, Calif.: Stanford University Institute for Research on Educational Finance and Governance, June 1981.

Yogman, M. W. Development of the father-infant relationship. In H. Fitzgerald, B. Lester, & M. W. Yogman (Eds.), *Theory and research in behavioral pediatrics* (Vol. 1). New York: Plenum, 1980.

Zelnick, M., & Kantner, J. F. Sexual activity, contraceptive use and pregnancy among metropolitan-area teenagers: 1971–1979. *Family Planning Perspectives*, September/October 1980, **12**, 230–237.

Zill, N. *Happy, healthy and insecure.* Garden City, N.Y.: Doubleday Anchor, 1983.

Zill, N., & Mount, R. National information needs in maternal and child health. In the Report of the Select Panel for the Promotion of Child Health, *Better health for our children: A national strategy* (Vol. 4). (DHHS, PHS Publication No. 79–55071.) Washington, D.C.: Government Printing Office, 1981.

Zill, N., & Peterson, J. L. *Trends in behavior and emotional well-being of U.S. children (findings from a national survey).* Paper prepared for annual meeting of the American Association for the Advancement of Science, Washington, D.C., 1982.

Zill, N., Sigal, H., & Brim, O. G., Jr. 1982. Development of childhood social indicators. In E. Zigler, S. L. Kogan, & E. Klugman (Eds.), *America's unfinished business: Child and family policy.* New York: Cambridge University Press.

Zinkus, P. W., Gottlieb, M. I., Shapiro, M. Developmental and psychoeducational sequelae of chronic otitis media. *American Journal of Diseases of Children*, 1978, **132**, 1100–1104.

Zook, C., Moore, F., & Zeckhauser, R. "Catastrophic" health insurance: A misguided prescription? *Public Interest*, Winter, 1981, vol. **62**.

Divorce, Children, and Social Policy

ROBERT E. EMERY, E. MAVIS HETHERINGTON, AND
LISABETH F. DILALLA
University of Virginia

The increase in the divorce rate in the last 20 years has been dramatic. In 1960, fewer than 10 out of every 1,000 marriages annually ended in divorce, but the figure more than doubled by 1980 (Cherlin, 1981). Given this rapid increase, it has been projected that 38 percent of the first marriages of young women who married in the late 1970s will end in divorce (Glick & Norton, 1978). Of those people who do divorce, three out of four women and five out of six men will remarry, half within 3 years following divorce. However, these remarriages may be even more likely to end in divorce than are first marriages (Cherlin, 1981).

There was a time when couples stayed married "for the children's sake," but this is not true of today's couples (Cherlin, 1977). Between 1950 and 1965 the proportion of divorces involving children rose from 44 to 60 percent, and today approximately 60 percent of all divorces continue to involve children (Bane, 1979; Bumpass & Rindfuss, 1978). In 1970 there were 2.3 million children living with a mother who was divorced. By 1982 that figure had risen by 122 percent to 5.1 million (Select Committee on Children, Youth, and Families [SCCYF], 1983). It is estimated that between now and the end of the twentieth century, 33 percent of this generation of children will experience a parental divorce before they are 18 years old (Glick, 1979).

Some social critics have noted the increase in divorce and offered such warnings as "the family, in its old sense, is disappearing from our land, and not only our free institutions are threatened, but the very existence of our society is endangered" (cited in Cherlin, 1981, p. 3). This particular warning, offered in 1859, seems to have been misguided, and some have suggested that today's social critics may be equally off the mark (Cherlin, 1981; Helm, 1981). The two-parent, nondivorced family is still the most

Preparation of this chapter was supported in part by a grant to Robert E. Emery from the William T. Grant Foundation, and by a grant to E. Mavis Hetherington from the John D. and Catherine T. MacArthur Foundation.

frequently found family form, and in 1982, 63 percent of American families were headed by the children's two biological parents (SCCYF, 1983). Moreover, advocates for various ethnic groups particularly have objected to the gloomy picture that is often painted of divorce. Among black families, twice as many children are separated from a parent because of divorce or spousal separation as are in white families, and in 1982, only 42.4 percent of black children lived with two biological, adoptive, or step-parents, in contrast to 80.8 percent of the children of whites (SCCYF, 1983). Therefore, calling the divorced or single-parent family unhealthy is tantamount to saying that the black family is pathogenic. In objection to such an implicit conclusion, it has been argued that low-income black families have developed stable extended-kin networks that provide a healthy alternative family environment (Cherlin, 1981; Peters & McAdoo, 1983). Finally, still others who have objected to the view that divorce is inevitably pathogenic argue that divorce may in fact have positive consequences for parents and children: It offers an opportunity for escape from unhappy relationships and provides a greater diversity of options in family forms for people of all cultural backgrounds (Bane, 1976).

Although it is clear that divorce does not inevitably result in enduring adverse outcomes for children, the divorce process often does entail a series of stressful life events for most family members. Further, some families appear to have great difficulty in coping with the events that surround the process of marital dissolution and require professional assistance as a result. Finally, whether divorce provides the opportunity for personal growth and escape from unfulfilling relationships or is the beginning of a destructive life transition, for parents and for children it is an increasingly common event in contemporary American life. For these reasons, it is important that research findings be used in shaping future social policy in order that the unique needs of divorcing and divorced families can be met.

METHODOLOGICAL CONCERNS IN RESEARCH ON
CHILDREN AND DIVORCE

Given the wide diversity of social opinion, research findings delineating the consequences of divorce for children and for families need to be examined carefully. For years professionals and the public have been warned about the pathological effects of disrupted bonds of attachment (Bowlby, 1951) and broken homes (Glueck & Glueck, 1950), and some therapists have issued unequivocal warnings that whenever there is a problem child, there is a problem family (Framo, 1975). At the other extreme, the assertion that divorce creates psychological difficulties for children is dismissed as merely another political tactic used to discourage marital dissolution (Haldem, 1981).

When the psychological literature on children and divorce is examined, therefore, it must constantly be kept in mind that social and political views affect both lay and professional opinion regarding the effects of divorce on children. Indeed, public views may partially determine *whether* divorce is detrimental to children. For example, one study found that teachers tend to hold negative expectations in regard to the emotional adjustment of the children from divorced families (Santrock & Tracey, 1978). Such negative expectancies may be particularly important to guard against because they can become self-fulfilling prophecies (Emery, 1982).

Biased expectations are but one of many potential methodological problems complicating the conduct and interpretation of research on how divorce affects children. Because several recent reviews focus on the methodological problems of interpreting divorce research (Atkeson, Forehand, & Rickard, 1982; Emery, 1982; Levitin, 1979), only a few of the most salient difficulties are presented here.

Measurement, whether biased or not, is a particular problem in research on this topic. Much of the research on divorce makes use of unstandardized interviews or paper-and-pencil measures that do not have demonstrated reliability or validity. Furthermore, the content of the measurements has often been restricted: Congruent with the expectations that divorce must create psychological problems for children, researchers have focused on assessing pathological domains of children's functioning. Assessment of weaknesses—aggression, disruptions in sex role development, and intellectual deficits—has been common; almost completely overlooked is assessment of the potential impact of divorce on developing strengths such as increased prosocial behavior, independence, sensitivity to the feelings of others, or the ability to cope well with stress.

The measurement of family factors that are expected to predict children's adjustment has been even more problematic. Although most researchers no longer commit the error of studying "father absence" (lumping together absences due to divorce, death, and out-of-wedlock births), undue attention continues to be paid to the effects on children of family *structure* rather than family *process*. Emerging research suggests that structural distinctions in family forms (such as "intact" vs. "broken") may bear less important relations to children's adjustment than do process dimensions (Hess & Camara, 1979; Hetherington, Cox, & Cox, 1982). That is, such factors as child-rearing styles, family conflict, and the quality of parent-child emotional bonds appear to be important predictors of children's psychological adjustment in both married and divorced families.

Researchers who fail to assess such critical dimensions of family functioning can inappropriately attribute problems in children's adjustment to divorce per se rather than to family processes that commonly accompany family dissolution. If the deleterious and beneficial outcomes of divorce for parents and children are to be understood, it will be through more careful examination of these mediating altered experiences and shifts in patterns of family interaction.

When it is recognized that the appropriate focus for divorce research is family process rather than family structure, it becomes apparent that divorce researchers too often have overlooked salient mediating variables; among the most salient are individual differences, cultural diversity in the meaning of a divorce, the availability of intrafamilial and extrafamilial social supports, the variety of postdivorce legal and physical custody arrangements, the effect of cumulative stressors, and the family's process of adaptive accommodation to changes over time.

Children of different ages, sex, and temperaments are likely to cope with divorce in ways that lead to different outcomes, but the influence of divorce on children too often has been assumed to be uniform. Divorce also holds different meanings, occurs with differing frequency, and likely leads to different consequences for the members of diverse subcultures in the United States, yet many researchers have failed to report on the demographic characteristics of their samples, let alone control for these variables in statistical analyses. Some divorced parents continue to support each other's child-rearing efforts following the marital dissolution, others do little to aid one another, and still others actively subvert their former spouses' parenting efforts; some divorced parents have kinship or other extrafamilial social support readily available, others become more socially isolated than they ever have been. Still, the potential buffering effects of social support are considered infrequently in divorce research. Likewise, researchers have very rarely considered the influence of postdivorce living arrangements on children. There are virtually no systematic studies contrasting such arrangements as joint versus sole custody arrangements, custody by the mother versus custody by the father, or the consequences of various visitation practices. The influence of cumulative stressors, particularly those associated with remarriage and other commonly occurring post-divorce familial changes, remains unclear. Finally, it is disheartening to realize that many researchers apparently have not considered that the passage of time influences family adaptation to a divorce. Many studies of families following a divorce make no mention of how long it has been since the divorce took place. Given that adverse sequelae affect most families in the short run but only a minority in the long run, the failure to consider the moderating influence of the passage of time is a most unfortunate omission.

Given the litany of methodological problems in past research, some may be tempted to declare the literature uninterpretable and begin the pursuit of knowledge anew. It is extremely unlikely, however, that any single study could satisfy all of the methodological rigors demanded by divorce research. Moreover, there appears to be a convergence of evidence among the findings of research projects that otherwise differ in their methodological sophistication and flaws. Therefore, rather than being nihilistic, it seems prudent to glean the consistent findings from the growing body of research on children's divorce adjustment.

Drawing conclusions from the convergent research and clinical evidence, however, requires caution: Even if the research literature were perfectly adequate, some basic limitations on the process of extrapolating from research findings to making public policy recommendations must be recognized. In general, psychological research is more likely to permit conclusions about groups than individuals; it often, for practical and ethical reasons, has not directly tested specific policy initiatives; and there often is a reliance on competing theories, each of which can be called into question on conceptual grounds (Thompson, 1983). The policymaker may be most concerned with the individual, a specific new program or policy, or facts rather than theory; yet there is inherent difficulty in drawing upon research in a manner that will lead to unquestionable conclusions for the implementation of social policy.

That the translation is an imperfect one does not mean that no interpretation should be offered, however. Rather, the recognition of the difficulties in drawing inferences for social policy from psychological research means that caution is appropriate. In this chapter we present an overview of the implications of social science research on the divorced family as related to various social, legal, economic, and mental health policy initiatives. Given the broad scope of the topic and our limited space, we suggest general directions for policy change, rather than providing great detail on any specific initiative. Furthermore, the present conceptualization of divorce as a process requires not only that the outcome—social, legal, or economic—of social policy programs be discussed, but that the processes that underlie and accompany the effort to achieve a given outcome be considered as well.

Processes are more difficult to identify and quantify than are outcomes, however. Thus, the processes involved in a social intervention such as a custody hearing, for example, have not been as clearly articulated by researchers or policymakers as has the outcome of this event. Therefore, in the following discussions of the family system and in subsequent sections on divorce and the legal, economic, and social and mental health systems, data pertaining to outcomes are examined before the processes thought to produce them are discussed. We hope to thus provide a context in which the series of events that lead to a given outcome can be better understood.

CHILDREN'S SOCIAL, EMOTIONAL, AND COGNITIVE OUTCOMES FOLLOWING DIVORCE

Researchers have focused particular attention on the effects of divorce on children's cognitive development and achievement and on their social and emotional adjustment. In the area of social and emotional development, an emphasis on sex typing, moral development, and self-control is found. Such emphasis is a legacy of conceptualizing divorce and one-parent families in terms of father absence. Because both psychoanalytic and social-learning theories suggest that fathers play a central role in the sex typing and moral development of sons, the preponderance of studies focus on the effects of father absence on boys and not on girls. Only recently have investigators broadened their concern to include children of both sexes. In the following discussion, an attempt is made to focus on recent divorce research, but in discussing topics where more recent research is sparse, we critically examine aspects of the "father absence" research.

SOCIAL AND EMOTIONAL DEVELOPMENT

Mental health referrals.—There is little doubt that children from divorced families are proportionally overrepresented in the outpatient psychiatric and psychological treatment populations. Several studies of clinics in various geographic regions in the United States have revealed that between two and four times as many children from divorced households are brought for treatment as would be expected from the prevalence of divorce in the general population (Kalter, 1977; Kalter & Rembar, 1981; Tuckman & Regan, 1966). Furthermore, these referrals do not appear to be made simply as a reaction to the immediate crisis precipitated in a family at the time of divorce: According to the findings of one investigation, treatment referrals are made an average of 5 years following the divorce (Kalter & Rembar, 1981). Thus, the children of divorce appear to be at increased risk for general long-term emotional difficulties, at least as indexed by outpatient clinic referrals.

Probably the best estimate of the increased risk for postdivorce childhood psychological problems comes from the one study that was conducted on a nationally representative sample. Zill (1978, 1983), in a stratified probability sample of 1,747 U.S. households, found that 14 percent of the children in divorced homes were described by their parents as needing psychological help in the past year, and 13 percent of the children in the sample had actually seen a psychologist or psychiatrist at some point. Comparable figures for children in two-parent families were 6 percent identified as needing help and 5½ percent said to have been in treatment. However, one must interpret any figures on treatment referral cautiously, because, as noted earlier, both current parental report and their prior treatment referrals may well have been influenced by the divorced parents' expectations that their children would experience psychological problems as a consequence of the divorce. Nevertheless, because of the exemplary sampling, Zill's (1978, 1983) identified increase in the risk for general psychological problems among the children of divorce remains the best current general estimate. Although these data suggest that divorce may be associated with a doubling or tripling of the rate of perceived psychological problems among children, it is important to keep in mind that the data also indicate that over 85 percent of American children are seen by their parents as coping with divorce sufficiently well so as not to need psychological help.

Presenting problems.—If children from divorced families are referred to mental health professionals for treatment more frequently than other children, what are the presenting problems? Research would suggest that by far the most common referral problems are conduct disorders, aggression, impulsivity, and apparent disruption in moral development (Emery & O'Leary, 1982; McDermott, 1968, 1970; Porter & O'Leary, 1980; Rutter, 1971; Tuckman & Regan, 1966; Zill, 1983). In a study of a nonclinic sample, Hetherington, Cox, and Cox (1978) found that, as a group, children whose parents were divorced were more disobedient, aggressive, whining, demanding, unaffectionate, and lacking in self-control than were children from intact marriages. According to studies of clinic populations, it is problems of this nature that most commonly lead parents to seek professional help.

It should be noted that conduct disorders in children from widowed families are less frequently found or are not significantly different from those in two-parent households (Felner, Stohlberg, & Cowen, 1975; Tuckman & Reagan, 1966; Zill, 1983). Therefore, the high rate of problems of self-control, aggression, and moral development is not a simple effect of loss of an attachment figure or absence of a father. Although disruptions in attachment bonds and multiple stressors following divorce may indirectly contribute to conduct problems by increasing frustration and anger, more direct causal factors seem to include family conflict (Emery , 1982) and the lack of consistent, firm, authoritative parental control following divorce (Hetherington et al., 1982; Santrock & Warshak, 1979).

Although the relation between divorce and increased levels of aggressive, noncompliant behavior among children is quite clear, research relating divorce to an increase in more "neurotic" problems—anxiety, withdrawal, and depression—has been equivocal (Emery, 1982), leading some to conclude that such a relation does not exist (Rutter, 1971). A number of clinicians, however, have reported observing internalized problems, particularly depression, among children of divorce (Gardner, 1978; McDermott, 1968, 1970; Wallerstein & Kelly, 1980). A closer examination of the research on children's social and emotional outcomes following divorce, particularly an examination of sex differences, helps to explain this discrepancy.

Sex differences in social and emotional development.—A number of researchers have documented that more obvious and lasting difficulties in response to divorce are found among boys than girls (Cadoret & Cain, 1980; Guidubaldi, Perry, & Cleminshaw, 1983; Hess & Camara, 1979; Hetherington et al., 1978; McDermott, 1968; Wallerstein & Kelly, 1980; Zill, 1983). It is also well known that boys respond to stress in general with a higher level of aggression than do girls (Rutter, 1970). Because children are more commonly referred to clinic settings for externalizing, aggressive disruptions than for internalized problems, aggressive boys may be overrepresented in the clinic samples used in studies of children of divorce. Girls may find a parental divorce as stressful as do boys, but may respond with more internalized problems that are less likely to bring them to the attention of mental health professionals. If this were so, one would expect to find an association between marital problems and increased anxiety and withdrawal among girls in nonclinic samples, and this indeed seems to be the case (Block, Block, & Morrison, 1981; Guidubaldi et al., 1983; Hess & Camara, 1979; Whitehead, 1979; Zill, 1983).

If there is a sex difference in children's social and emotional responses to divorce, what may be the processes underlying it? It has been argued that boys may be more predisposed to aggression either biologically or because of greater acceptance of assertiveness in traditional male sex roles. Hence, male children may be in greater need of firm discipline in order to develop and internalize standards of self control. Boys and girls are more obedient to fathers than to mothers in both divorced and intact families, whereas children, particularly boys, are less obedient to divorced mothers (Hetherington et al., 1982). Thus, the erratic discipline that often takes place during a divorce may have more deleterious effects for boys than girls. In addition, because most children of divorce live in the custody of the mother, problems of identification and parental control may most frequently affect boys, who are living with the opposite-sex parent (Santrock & Warshak, 1979). However, there are other important reasons why conduct problems may be more common among boys than girls. Boys are usually disciplined more by *both* parents than are girls, so they may be exposed to more inconsistency and may more often become the target of a parental power struggle than girls (Emery, 1982). Moreover, boys are more often exposed directly to interparental conflict during and following divorce (Hetherington et al., 1982). Finally, boys receive less support from parents, peers, and teachers than do girls, and thus must cope more independently with the stressors associated with divorce.

In interpreting the seemingly more subtle impact of divorce on girls, one study of a nonclinic sample of children in intact families suggests a particularly interesting manifestation of their internalization. In this longitudinal investigation, a measure of parental disagreement over child rearing, which was predictive of eventual marital dissolution, was also predictive of a lower level of aggression in girls' behavior in school and higher levels of anxiety in this setting (Block et al., 1981). This finding, together with those reviewed above, has been interpreted as suggesting that girls, in contrast to boys, may react to divorce by internalizing their emotional upset, a response that may increase their prosocial behavior (Emery, 1982). Such a speculation is congruent with some clinical observations on girls' increased parental role behavior at home following divorce (Weiss, 1975), as well as with some recent research on the school functioning of children from divorced households (Guidubaldi et al., 1983). As is discussed later, however, the reliability of these findings remains at issue, as does the question of whether such increases in girls' prosocial behavior mask underlying resentment, anxiety, or depression.

Age differences in social and emotional development.—In addition to the child's sex, the child's age at the time of divorce would be expected to be an important moderator of the child's social and emotional adjustment. Surprisingly, however, differences in outcome related to children's age have not been well researched, and the results of studies investigating age effects have been inconsistent. Rather than stating that divorce is more difficult for children of different ages, it is more accurate to say that the quality of the adjustment varies with the developmental status of the children, their competencies and resources, and the developmental tasks that they confront.

Wallerstein and Kelly (1974, 1975, 1980; Kelly & Wallerstein, 1975, 1976), who conducted the most frequently cited study in regard to age differences in children's divorce adjustment, reported finding subtly different outcomes among children of different ages. Unfortunately, given their small samples at different ages and a heavy reliance on clinical impressions, such differences cannot be viewed as reliable without replication. Although researchers have generally been slow to further investigate the sensitive developmental hypotheses put forth by these researchers, there is converging evidence to support some of Wallerstein and Kelly's (1980) observations. It appears, for example, that adolescents may be somewhat better able than young children to cope with a parental divorce (Kurdek & Berg, 1983; Kurdek, Blisk, & Siesky, 1981; Kurdek & Siesky, 1980; Zill, 1983). However, even these findings are tentative, and the influence of a child's age interacts with a host of additional factors.

Too often researchers have committed two critically important omissions in studies of age influences: They have failed to distinguish the effects of the child's age at the time of the divorce from the effects of age at the time of the research study, and they have not considered length of time since the divorce took place. Obviously, such oversights can lead to incorrect conclusions. Evidence indicates that although for some children social and emotional problems may persist over time, the long-term consequences of divorce are less dramatic than the short-term outcomes (Hetherington et al., 1982; Wallerstein & Kelly, 1980; Zill, 1983). That is, although most children experience short-term social and emotional difficulties as a result of a parental divorce, a minority continue to have such problems 2 years later (Hetherington et al., 1982). Thus, age at the time of the divorce is the appropriate focus for investigations of the influence of children's developmental status on their divorce adjustment, and short-term adaptations must be distinguished from long-term outcomes.

In summary, divorce can lead to a diversity of psychosocial outcomes among children. For most children, the long-term outcome appears to be eventual adjustment to their new family situations. Among those children who do have continuing social and emotional difficulties, increased aggression appears to be the most common problem, especially among boys. On the other hand, girls who react adversely to divorce appear to be more likely to show evidence of depression, anxiety, or perhaps exaggerated prosocial, "parental" behavior.

Sex-typed behavior and attitude.—In the 1950s and 1960s much of the concern about the consequences of divorce for children was directed toward potential disruptions in the development of the child's sex role behavior. For boys in particular, it was hypothesized that the absence of a male model with whom the boy could identify would lead to "abnormal" sex role attitudes and behavior. It was feared that boys would be "feminized" in the mother-dominated environment of the single-parent family. One particularly problematic reaction that some boys were expected to show as an overcompensation for their "feminized" behavior was increased aggression and sexuality (Miller, 1958). Thus, one prominent early explanation of the link between divorce and aggressive, delinquent behavior in boys was the "feminine-aggressive" hypothesis.

Although it may appear that the 1970s and 1980s have witnessed a dramatic shift in the American public's view of what types of behaviors are sex role appropriate, many children and parents' sex role concepts remain predominantly stereotyped (Feldman, Biringen, & Nash, 1981; Stericker & Kurdek, in press). The impact of the women's movement on the public's view of appropriate sex role behavior may be smaller than expected. Nevertheless, the current social climate and focus on androgyny appear to have led to a reduction in psychologists' interests in traditional aspects of sex-typing among the children of divorce. Thus, there is little recent research to rely upon in drawing conclusions. Still, one cannot ignore two themes that consistently have appeared in the literature. First, some researchers have found that young boys from father-absent families engage in more activities that are traditionally considered to be feminine than do boys from father-present homes (e.g., Biller, 1969; Biller & Bahm, 1971; Santrock, 1972); the same pattern has been noted in households where divorce was the reason for father absence (Hetherington, Cox, & Cox, 1978). Second, girls whose parents divorced have been found to manifest precocious sexual concerns and sexual activity in comparision to girls whose fathers have died or whose parents are still married (Hetherington, 1972; Wallerstein & Kelly, 1980).

This latter finding may be more significant than the first. Clinicians have noted that children from divorced households have more concerns with sexuality at an earlier age, and demographic data indicate that people from divorced households tend to marry at a younger age (Pope & Mueller, 1976). Because those who marry before the age of 20 are twice as likely to eventually divorce as young adults who marry during their twenties (Glick & Norton, 1978), it is intriguing to speculate that early concerns about, preoccupation with, and involvement in heterosexual relationships at least partially explain the finding that people from divorced households are somewhat more likely to eventually get divorced themselves (Pope & Mueller, 1976).

As for the research on the more feminine behavior among boys from divorced families, it appears to be a considerable conceptual leap to use this finding to explain the increased aggression also found in this group. Preferences for certain types of toys and playmates may not be strongly indicative of future sex-typed self-concepts or behavior (Herzog & Sudia, 1973), and investigators who have directly tested it have failed to support the feminine-aggressive hypothesis (McCord, McCord, & Thurber, 1962).

Still, data indicate that among young boys in mother-headed homes from which the father became absent before the boy was 5 years of age, their behavior, interests, and human figure drawings are more similar to those of girls than of boys in two-parent homes. However, this difference in sex-typed behavior usually disappears as boys grow older and are influenced by their peer group. For younger boys, although continued contact with the noncustodial father or other males following divorce plays an important role in their sex-typing, the custodial mother's attitudes and behavior become increasingly important. In two-parent households, the father is most salient in the sex role development of boys and girls. However, in mother-custody homes, several factors are associated with masculine sex-typing in sons: low anxiety in the divorced mothers; their encouragement of independent, exploratory, and risk-taking behaviors; reinforcement for activities traditionally viewed as masculine; and lack of denigration of the father by the mother (Hetherington et al., 1982). Feminized behavior is not an inevitable concomitant of separation and loss of the father.

What about children in mother-absent households? One investigation that compared father-custody and mother-custody homes found that girls in father-custody families were rated as being less feminine and more independent and demanding, whereas boys were found to be more sociable and mature (Santrock & Warshak, 1979). However, simply very little is known about the sex-typing of children in single-parent, father-headed families.

In summary, cultural views about appropriate sex role behavior have not changed as much as might be expected. Sex-typed behavior still is expected in many settings, and at least some evidence suggests that children of divorced and nondivorced parents differ in their sex role behavior. Perhaps the most important area for future research on sex-typed behavior is in investigating what link there may be between a parental divorce and later peer, sexual, and marital relationships.

INTELLECTUAL FUNCTIONING AND ACHIEVEMENT

The intellectual functioning and achievement of children from single-parent and father-absent homes has been of nearly as much concern as the children's social and emotional development. It has been argued that children in father-absent homes can be expected to show cognitive deficits. These predicted deficits are attributed to such diverse factors as the failure to have a male with whom to identify (Carlsmith, 1964), the interference with cognitive functioning caused by anxiety over the stressful home situation (Maccoby & Rau, 1962), or the decreased parental attention and contact found in one-parent homes (Shinn, 1978). In addition, it has recently been proposed and demonstrated that household disorganization, inconsistency, and poor control in divorced families may lead to high distractability and short attention spans in children, which in turn may result in poor performance on problems requiring sustained attention (Hetherington et al., 1982).

Few question that in most studies of one-parent homes, children are found to perform more poorly on a variety of measures of cognitive functioning (for detailed reviews, see Herzog & Sudia, 1973; Hetherington, Camara, & Featherman, 1981; Shinn, 1978). Still, some have objected that, however well established these group differences are, attributing the difference to the absence of one parent is mistaken. One concern is raised most frequently: Is the discrepancy in academic potential and performance found between children from one- and two-parent families a function of socioeconomic differences rather than family structure (Herzog & Sudia, 1973)? This is a legitimate question, because children from families of lower socioeconomic status do perform more poorly on traditional measures of cognitive skill, they are more likely to come from single-parent households, and divorce often results in economic decline (Cherlin, 1981; Jencks, 1972).

Although socioeconomic status must not be overlooked, it does not appear to fully explain the intellectual differences found between children in one- and two-parent families. The complex and often variable economic standing of the one-parent family makes the measurement and control for socioeconomic factors difficult (Hetherington, Cox, & Cox, 1982). Nevertheless, several investigators have found that academic differences between children in one- and two-parent families are lessened but still persist even when the effects of social class are taken into account (Ferri, 1976; Guidubaldi et al., 1983; Lambert & Hart, 1976; Zill, 1983).

One must consider whether the reason for the one-parent status differentially influences the child's academic outcome, yet the vast majority of studies to date have not done so. The few studies that have taken the reason for one-parent status into account (Ferri, 1976; Gregory, 1965; Guidubaldi et al., 1983; Santrock, 1972; Zill, 1983) have generally found children from divorced households to perform more poorly than children who have a parent absent for some other reason. Children in this latter group, in turn, perform more poorly than children from two-parent families. Thus, although the academic problems may be attributable in part to the absence of the father's input, they may derive as well from unique family interactions created by divorce.

A closer examination of how children in divorced, single-parent, and two-parent families differ academically suggests some hypotheses about the cause of the differences. In general, compared to children of two-parent families, children of one-parent families obtain significantly lower scores on standardized measures of intellectual capacity and academic achievement, but the absolute magnitude of the difference is quite small (Hetherington, Cox, & Cox, 1982). In contrast, when indexed by such measures as teacher ratings, grade-point averages, attendance, and number of years of schooling completed, the differences between the two groups of children are considerably larger (Hetherington, Cox, & Cox, 1982; Zill, 1983). Thus, the differences stand out more readily in teachers' perceptions of academic competence than on standardized measures. Therefore, any explanation of the poorer academic standing of children whose parents divorce would do well to focus more on explaining differences in academic performance rather than intellectual capacity. It may be, for example, that the more disruptive classroom behavior found among the children of divorce (Guidubaldi et al., 1983; Zill, 1983) both directly interferes with their classroom work and alters teachers' expectations of success. Simultaneously, there may be more demands that the child from a single-parent home actively participate in household routines, leaving less time, energy, and interest for schoolwork and related intellectual activities.

Age and sex differences.—As with research on the social and emotional adjustment of children of divorce, it is surprising how infrequently the child's age has been examined as a moderator of the relation between family structure and academic functioning. Some evidence suggests that academic difficulties following divorce are delayed or cumulative and therefore are more pronounced among late-school-age children and adolescents than among preschool or early-school-age children (Hess, Shipman, Brophy, & Bear, 1968; Hess, Shipman, Brophy, Bear, & Adelberger, 1969; Rees & Palmer, 1970). However, it may that disruptive classroom behavior, not lower intellectual aptitude, is found more commonly among older children from single-parent households (Hetherington, Cox, & Cox, 1982).

While age differences in the effects of divorce on children's academic performance are not especially clear, notable sex differences have emerged. As in social and emotional adjustment, boys from divorced households show greater academic deficits than do girls (Guidubaldi et al., 1983; Zill, 1983). In fact, whereas boys from single-parent families have lower quantitative scores on standardized tests than do boys from two-parent families, some girls from mother-headed one-parent homes have higher verbal scores than their two-parent family counterparts (Hetherington, Camara, & Featherman, 1981). This pattern of sex differences is difficult to explain by applying traditional theories to the adjustment of children from one-parent families, because these theories have focused on the lowered rather than enhanced academic functioning of all children in single-parent households. The superior female performance presents a particular difficulty for theories of anxiety interference or decreased parental attention. However, given sex differences in available models and in discipline issues in mother-headed families, identification and behavioral control theories can more readily assimilate the finding. The improved performance among girls also is consistent with the different psychosocial compensations, discussed earlier, that boys and girls typically use in dealing with stress. A family-systems perspective on the compensatory hypothesis and on other family processes that are linked to children's psychosocial and cognitive outcomes following divorce is discussed in greater detail below.

DIVORCE AND THE FAMILY SYSTEM

Children's and parents' experience of divorce and adjustment to family disruption and reorganization will vary according to the number and types of stressors they encounter, the resources of the family and the children in coping with stress, their perceptions or evaluations of the situation, and their developmental life-style (Hetherington & Camara, 1984; Kurdek, 1981). Furthermore, different stressors and resources are more likely to be involved at different stages in the divorce process. Because important alterations in family functioning may occur before, during, and after a divorce, discussed below are the different family processes that begin within the stages of: (1) the distressed marriage, (2) the separation and the divorce, (3) life in the single-parent family, and (4) remarriage and the blended family.

THE DISTRESSED MARRIAGE

Conflict and uncertainty.—All children from divorced families are also children who have lived in unhappy two-parent homes for varying periods of time. The decision to divorce is rarely made suddenly, especially when children are involved. Most couples have considered divorcing for some time, and as many as 42 percent may have separated and reconciled before eventually seeking a divorce (Kitson & Raschke, 1981). From the first questioning of the marriage to the decision to divorce, parents are involved in a prolonged period of weighing the strengths and weaknesses of the marriage against the uncertainties of single life; they consider possible outcomes for themselves and the children, and seek rationales and practical supports for making the difficult transition. For children, this can be a time of uncertainty, ambiguity, and feeling left out. Their parents may be preoccupied, depressed, or irritable, and the children frequently are caught in the middle of intense family conflict.

Children can suffer particularly damaging consequences from expo- sure to conflict in the intact but discordant family, following the parental separation, during the legal proceedings, and throughout postdivorce family life. In fact, several investigators have found that children from happy single-parent homes are better adjusted in general than are children from discordant two-parent families (Gibson, 1969; Hetherington et al., 1978; McCord et al., 1962; Nye, 1957; Power, Ash, Schoenberg, & Sorey, 1974), and data from one longitudinal study suggested that many of the problems found among children from broken homes begin well before the parents separate (Lambert, Essen, & Head, 1977). Moreover, although children in high-conflict divorced families have more personality and behavior problems (Hetherington et al., 1982), they show a pattern of adverse reactions sufficiently similar to those of children from discordant two-parent homes to suggest that the two family types share many common stressors that have a similar impact on children (Emery, 1982).

Involvement in interparental conflict would therefore seem to pose a particularly salient dilemma for children from intact but discordant, di- vorcing, and divorced families. One must appreciate the tremendous cognitive dissonance that conflict between two highly valued parents cre- ates for children—dissonance for which there often is no simple resolution. The child is confronted with the complicated loyalty conflict of deciding how it is possible to love both a mother and a father who do not love each other, and may appear to hate each other.

Family-systems theory.—The family-systems perspective advocated by numerous family therapists (Gurman & Kniskern, 1981) provides a useful, although speculative, conceptual model for understanding how children can attempt to resolve the cognitive dissonance described above. According to this model, children's behavior in large part is determined by the structural, functional, and transactional nature of family relationships, and therefore changes in the patterns of any family relationships necessar- ily result in changes in the children's behavior. Family-systems theorists suggest that conflict between the two parents not only creates cognitive dissonance for the individual child but also has the more general effect of upsetting the homeostatic balance in the relationships among all family members. Acrimony in the marriage forces children to alter their rela- tionships with their parents and among themselves in an attempt to dimin- ish the threat posed by the parental conflict and to restore the family to a state of relative equilibrium (Minuchin, 1974). Several different ways in which children may respond in order to maintain homeostatis have been proposed, and children's various homeostatic maneuvers may well explain some of the large individual differences among children's adaptation to discord and divorce.

One of the most commonly discussed homeostatic maneuvers of children in a high-conflict family is to alter their own behavior in such a dramatic way so as to detour parental concern away from their own disagreements and onto the "disturbed" child (Minuchin, 1974). Exactly how children alter their behavior to refocus parental attention may depend on a number of factors, such as cultural background, the age and sex of the child, and the perception of what is sex role appropriate. The variety of possibilities may explain some of the sex differences in children's outcomes discussed earlier. Consistent with sex role expectations, boys might become aggressive, noncompliant, or do poorly in school, whereas girls may withdraw, become anxious, or exhibit extremely prosocial behavior (Emery, 1982).

Rather than deflecting parental concern through detouring, some children, particularly older ones, may attempt to directly intervene in the family conflict in an attempt to mediate a resolution. Alternatively, children may resolve the dissonance created by loyalty conflicts by taking sides with one parent against the other. Finally, some children may withdraw from the conflict altogether and as a result feel helpless, fearful, and depressed (Minuchin, Baker, Rosman, Liebman, Milman, & Todd, 1975).

The child's developmental status may influence the choice of these homeostatic maneuvers. Young children are less able than older ones to accurately appraise the situation and their own role in the family conflicts. Given their egocentrism and limited cognitive and social skills, young children can be more likely to blame themselves for problems between parents (Tessman, 1978; Wallerstein & Kelly, 1974, 1975), and given their limited means for directly diffusing the situation, they may succeed most in distracting the parents from their problems by notably changing their behavior. A young child who is unsuccessful in detouring parental concern may become withdrawn and confused as a consequence.

Older children, on the other hand, because they better understand the family situation, may be more likely to attempt to mediate the conflict, to side with one parent against the other, or to disengage from the family. Following divorce, adolescents are better able to understand the reasons for their parents' relationship problems, to resolve loyalty conflicts, or to accept such conflicts as out of their realm of responsibility (Wallerstein & Kelly, 1974, 1975). They also have the option to seek support elsewhere if the home situation is particularly painful. Older children spend much more time in other social settings—the neighborhood, the school, the church, and, for some adolescents, at work. Thus, they have more opportunities to find support systems outside the home that may mitigate the deleterious effects of the discordant home.

This latter point is particularly important. For the young child, the stress and turmoil in the family are inescapable; disruptions between parent and child may undermine the only important relationships in a child's life. Thus, it is not surprising that young children are partially "buffered" from the effects of conflict in a two-parent family if they maintain particularly good relations with one parent (Rutter, 1971). The same result is found in divorce if the child maintains a good relationship with the custodial parent (Hess & Camara, 1979; Hetherington et al., 1978).

Inconsistent discipline and modeling.—Parental conflict not only can create loyalty conflicts that can lead children to engage in potentially maladaptive behaviors that nevertheless can serve the function of returning the family system to a state of homeostatis, it can have at least two other negative consequences for them: (1) discipline practices may become inconsistent, and (2) rancorous and hurtful outbursts may take place in front of the children, thus providing them with inappropriate models for handling conflict.

Researchers have repeatedly noted that inconsistent discipline is associated with increased incidence of conduct problems and aggression in children (Becker, 1964; Becker, Peterson, Luria, Shoemaker, & Quay, 1962; Patterson, 1977), and two important longitudinal studies have suggested that inconsistent discipline in two-parent families is predictive both of subsequent conduct problems among children and of eventual marital dissolution. Block et al. (1981) found that a measure of disagreement over child rearing predicted increased levels of aggression among boys and increased anxiety among girls several years after the measure was obtained. The index of disagreement over child rearing was also predictive of eventual dissolution of the marriage. Recently published data from the well-known New York Longitudinal Study replicate and extend these findings (Chess, Thomas, Korn, Mittelman, & Cohen, 1983). Conflict between parents of 3-year-olds, particularly disagreements over issues of discipline, was found to be predictive of poorer adjustment among the children during their early adult life. It is important to note that, when the effects of conflict were taken into account, parental separation or divorce was *not* related to the child's level of adjustment as a young adult. Thus, inconsistent discipline appears to be one characteristic of the discordant intact family that often precedes divorce and may lead to increased aggression and adjustment problems for children. Moreover, disharmony may lead not only to inconsistency between parents as discipline becomes a topic of dispute, but also it may increase the inconsistency of each parent as he or she becomes preoccupied with marital rather than parental concerns.

Finally, conflict between parents in intact or divorced families provides the child with aggressive models that may be directly imitated. Evidence of the possible contribution of modeling to problems of aggression in children comes from research on the type, length, and timing of interparental conflict (Emery, 1982). Conflict that is relatively contained and not openly hostile appears to create fewer difficulties for children than does openly expressed acrimony (Hetherington et al., 1982; Porter & O'Leary, 1980; Rutter, Yule, Quinton, Rowlands, Yule, & Berger, 1974). Moreover, the severity of children's conduct problems is more strongly related to their perceptions of the degree of discord between their parents than to their parents' view of the marriage (Emery & O'Leary, 1982). Not surprisingly, conflict that is of shorter duration seems to have a less damaging effect on the child than does longer-lasting hostility (Rutter, 1980). Finally, proximal conflict is more strongly related to children's adjustment problems than is temporally distal conflict (Hetherington et al., 1982; Wallerstein & Kelly, 1980).

In summary, how parents in the intact but discordant family deal with their feelings of anger may have consequences in terms of creating loyalty conflicts in their children, influencing the degree to which the parents become inconsistent in their discipline, and providing their children with inappropriately aggressive models.

THE SEPARATION AND LEGAL DIVORCE

Eventually the dissatisfaction with the marriage becomes so great that one parent, most commonly the father, leaves the family home. For some parents and children the decision to separate brings relief and may reduce family conflict and tension, but for other families separation can increase hostility as jealousies, suspicions, and acrimony intensify (Hetherington et al., 1982; Wallerstein & Kelly, 1980; Westman, Cline, Swift, & Kramer, 1970) and spouses feel insecure and ambivalent about their decision to separate (Weiss, 1975). When conflict continues after the separation, children seem to have the most difficult time adjusting to a parental divorce (Anthony, 1974; Hetherington, Cox, & Cox, 1976; Jacobson, 1978; Kelly & Wallerstein, 1976; Westman et al., 1970). However, additional stressors may be encountered at this time.

Whether the parental separation relieves or exacerbates family tensions, it entails at least one further potentially difficult transition for the child. The child has far fewer opportunities to interact with the parent who has left the home, and in some cases the loss of contact is almost total. The parent who leaves may choose to dissolve not only the role of spouse but the parental role as well (Furstenberg, 1982). Thus, the period of separation and divorce is often characterized by uncertainty, change, acrimony, and loss for the child. Most children, even those in conflict-ridden families, do not want their parents to divorce and initially view the divorce as an unreasonable, undesirable, and painful transition to an unknown future in a one-parent household. Because the father becomes the noncustodial parent in 90 percent of divorces, and because the father can be a particularly important socializing agent for sons, it is not surprising that boys appear to have a more difficult time handling the parental separation (Santrock & Warshak, 1979).

Separation from an attachment figure.—Researchers have repeatedly documented how separation from a parent adversely affects a child, regardless of the reason for separation (Bowlby, 1973). A well-documented reaction to prolonged separations is an "acute distress syndrome": a three-stage process in which children experience acute upset, then apathy or depression, and finally loss of interest in the parent (Bowlby, 1973) or adaptation to the new situation (Rutter, 1981). This three-stage process is most clearly delineated when a young child (6 years or younger) is separated from a parent to whom he or she is closely attached. Consistent with this, the loss of a parent following divorce results in the most intense adverse reactions among children who had a close relationship to that parent before the divorce (Hetherington et al., 1982; Wallerstein & Kelly, 1980).

A similar, although less clearly defined, process may also occur among older children. Thus, the experience of separation from an attachment figure likely explains some of the emotional distress such as ambivalence, anger, fearfulness, inhibition, habit disturbances, and neediness that children experience during the period immediately following their parents' separation (Fulton, 1978; Hess & Camara, 1979; Hetherington et al., 1978; Kelly & Wallerstein, 1976; Wallerstein & Kelly, 1974, 1975, 1976, 1980). Moreover, the child's emotional upset at being separated from an attachment figure is likely to be prolonged in a divorce, because the terms of the separation and the pattern of future visitation may not be clear-cut, and the child's expectations about contact with the absent parent may therefore be distorted. In one investigation, for example, 42 percent of a sample of divorced people had separated and reconciled at least once prior to their divorce, thus fueling children's fantasies of reconciliation and uncertainties about the future (Kitson & Raschke, 1981). Erratic and unpredictable patterns of contact with the nonresident parent following a permanent separation can further confuse children and prevent them from progressing through the stages of adjustment to separation. The child's adaptation to the loss may be delayed as a result.

Contributions of fathers.—Although attachment research sheds light particularly on the young child's short-term responses to separation, reduced contact with the father may have more far-reaching effects on children of all ages. Although their importance has all too often been overlooked, fathers make unique direct and indirect contributions to family functioning (Lamb, 1981). In the traditional nuclear family, the father has indirect influence on the children through his support of their mother. In addition to financial assistance, the importance of the father's provision of respites from household and child-rearing tasks, and his support, encouragement, and appreciation of his wife's performance as a mother, influence her effectiveness as a parent. In two-parent families, high mother-child involvement and competent, affectionate mother-infant relationships have been found when fathers are supportive of mothers (Lewis, Feiring, & Weinraub, 1981; Pedersen, Anderson, & Cain, 1977). Similarly, the supportive involvement of the father with the custodial mother and children has been found to be of considerable benefit for preschool children and their divorced mothers (Hetherington et al., 1978).

The father also directly provides emotional support for children and shapes their behavior through the type of role model, discipline, and skills training he provides. In both divorced and nuclear families, children are more likely to obey fathers than mothers (Hetherington et al., 1978), a factor that may be related to the increased aggression found among children who live in the custody of their divorced mothers. Even children who adjust well to a divorce have fewer opportunities to interact with a father who may have a range of interests and skills that are different from the mother's (Pedersen, Rubenstein, & Yarrow, 1979).

Most children from divorced families wish to maintain a relationship with their father, and preschool children may entertain fantasies of reconciliation for several years after the separation (Hetherington et al., 1978; Tessman, 1978; Wallerstein & Kelly, 1975). Maintaining the relationship with the father can be very beneficial. Unless the father is quite poorly adjusted or there is continued intense child-involved conflict between parents, contact with the father is associated with better adjustment, especially in boys (Hess & Camara, 1979; Hetherington et al., 1978; Wallerstein & Kelly, 1980; Westman et al., 1970).

Divorce proceedings.—At some time before or after the marital separation, the legal divorce proceedings are begun. Because the legal divorce is such an important formal intervention with divorcing families in American society, and because the legal history of family dissolution is long and complex, the topic is discussed in detail later. For now, it is sufficient to note what research clearly shows: contact with the legal system often exacerbates divorcing parents' problems (Spanier & Anderson, 1979). Furthermore, legal proceedings pose potentially difficult stressors for children because they often increase parental conflict, raise uncertainties about future contact with both parents, and challenge the child's fantasies about reconciliation (Wallerstein & Kelly, 1980). Finally, children can be further stressed by direct involvement in legal action—for example, by being asked by a judge to publicly state with which parent they would prefer to reside. Unfortunately, there is virtually no social science research on the specific, direct effects of legal procedures on children. Thus, the idea that the legal divorce often entails a particularly trying set of events is a speculative, though reasonable, suggestion.

LIFE IN THE SINGLE-PARENT FAMILY

Most social science research concerning divorce has been conducted on families who have already divorced. Thus, the research on family members' experience and adjustment in the divorced, single-parent household is much more detailed than is evidence on the period prior to the divorce. There are numerous redefinitions of roles and realignments of relationships as the original nuclear family becomes the postdivorce family residing in separate households. Some of the common challenges encountered by the postdivorce family are: (1) economic problems as expenses are increased by the need to maintain two residences; (2) task overload as the custodial parent not only negotiates the increased responsibilities of single parenthood but also encounters new occupational, social, and emotional demands; (3) a sense of isolation, lack of support, and uncertainty about the future that is experienced by both custodial and noncustodial parents as well as by the children; and (4) an attempt to assimilate additional members into the family system as relatives become involved in assisting the postdivorce family, or as the divorced parents find new partners. Although one or more of these factors may affect a particular family member most directly, the impact extends to all family members because of their mutual dependency. Given the breadth of research on divorced families and the present focus on family processes, discussion in the following section is limited primarily to one important aspect of living in the divorced household—namely, changes in parent-child relationships. In subsequent sections, other social and economic characteristics of these households are discussed.

Custodial mothers, noncustodial fathers.—The following discussion of parent-child relationships concentrates most on custodial mother-child and noncustodial father-child relationships. This apparent imbalance reflects both the amount of available research and the fact that most divorced, single-parent families are headed by women. Although it may appear that the proportion of single-parent father-headed families is growing dramatically, this is not the case. Although the number of families headed by a single father has increased dramatically in the last 10 years, the proportion has not changed because the number of families headed by a single mother has also increased markedly (SCCYF, 1983). In 1982, 20.0 percent of all families in the United States were headed by a single mother, and 1.9 percent by a single father (SCCYF, 1983). Although it may be asked whether this nine-to-one ratio accurately reflects the presumed recent increase in fathers' requests for custody, some data suggest that this proportion may remain fairly stable. In 1968, when California law contained an explicit maternal preference statute, mothers were awarded sole custody 88 percent of the time. In 1977, 4 years after a sex-neutral law was enacted, California mothers continued to receive custody in nearly 90 percent of divorces (Weitzman, 1981). Furthermore, these figures cannot be attributed solely to judicial bias. One study found that fathers who sought custody obtained it 63 percent of the time, and even in cases that were fully contested before a judge, the father won custody one-third of the time (Weitzman & Dixon, 1979). If fathers frequently are awarded custody when they request it, but mothers nevertheless receive custody most of the time, it follows that relatively few fathers request custody. Perhaps more fathers than mothers consider it socially acceptable not to seek custody and also recognize the difficulties of being a single parent, or perhaps fathers see little hope of winning a custody battle except when the mother is viewed as being potentially unfit. In any case, the mother-headed family continues to be the predominant result of divorce involving children, and there is no compelling evidence that this situation is changing; thus the present focus on custodial mothers and noncustodial fathers.

Many children in single-parent households experience the problems of continued involvement in interparental conflict and limited contact with the noncustodial parent. Researchers have shed light on a variety of additional important changes in parent-child relationships that take place after the divorce, as parents and children engage in a series of transactions that eventually lead to a redefinition of family roles and the rules for relating in the new family. Thus, the process of divorce does not end with a legal document, as families continually attempt to reestablish a new equilibrium in the single-parent household. In most families, this new homeostasis occurs within 2–3 years after the divorce, and is accompanied by a notable reduction in problems, unhappiness, and dissatisfaction by parents and children (Hetherington et al., 1982; Wallerstein & Kelly, 1980; Weiss, 1975).

Mother-child relationships.—Although the experiences of families vary widely following divorce, there is a group of common stressors that are encountered by most single-parent, divorced families. One is a disruption of parent-child relationships associated with task overload as the custodial parent attempts to learn to manage not only the children but also house-hold, economic, and social responsibilities. Custodial mothers experience more difficulty in their parental role than do nondivorced mothers (Fur-stenberg, Spanier, & Rothschild, 1982; Hetherington et al., 1982; Zill, 1983), and custodial mothers of young children tend to use more restrictive and negative sanctions, be more inconsistent with their discipline, and demonstrate less affection toward their children (Burgess, 1978; Colletta, 1979; Hetherington et al., 1982; Kriesberg, 1970; Phelps, 1969). Disrup-tions in child rearing following divorce are so common and dramatic that some have referred to this as a period of "diminished parenting" (Waller-stein & Kelly, 1980).

The parents are not solely responsible for the change in parent-child relationships, however. Children's apprehensions and needs for reassur-ance can lead them to make excessive demands of their parents. Hence, it is not just an overburdened and distressed divorced mother who affects her children. Confused, irascible, noncompliant, and demanding children can further burden their mother. As evidence of this, it has been noted that divorced mothers who have three or more children or very young or male children show more signs of depression than mothers with fewer, older, or female children (Price-Bonham & Balswick, 1980). Longitudinal studies have shown that acting out, resistant behavior in children leads to in-creased anxiety and depression and decreased self-esteem and feelings of internal control in custodial mothers but not in noncustodial fathers. The custodial mother who confronts the day-to-day problems of living with a disturbed child is affected more deleteriously than is the removed non-custodial father (Hetherington et al., 1982).

Divorced mother-son relationships can be particularly troublesome, because they often evolve into escalating cycles of coercive behavior (Hetherington et al., 1982; Patterson, 1977; Patterson & Reid, 1970). As has been noted, boys have a more difficult time coping with the divorce transition, and their disruptive behavior often brings no firm disciplinary response from a mother who feels particularly incompetent and guilty about how to best handle her son now that his father is absent. Because of her indecisiveness and guilt, she capitulates to her unhappy, noncompliant son's unreasonable demands and hence further escalates her feelings of helplessness and low self-esteem.

Problems in parent-child relationships may be more common in one-parent families of middle rather than lower socioeconomic status (Colletta, 1979) and for mothers of younger than older children (Wallerstein & Kelly, 1980; Weiss, 1975). Older children, especially eldest girls, may not only be less of a burden on their mothers, but may, in fact, be integral helpers as they assume more parental responsibility in the family and participate in family decision making (Fulton, 1979; Kurdek & Siesky, 1979; Weiss, 1979a; Zill, 1983). Children's help with routine household and child-care tasks may have benefits beyond being of considerable assistance to the single parent, as some children learn to be more self-sufficient at an earlier age (Weiss, 1979a). However, the push toward what Weiss has called "growing up faster" can also have the opposite effect and be associated with feelings of resentment and helplessness, and early withdrawal from the family (Kelly, 1978; Wallerstein & Kelly, 1980).

Father-child relationships.—What about the children's contact with the other parent? Children's relationships with noncustodial parents, typically their father, can be extremely important. When the father is not available, both the constructive and destructive behaviors of a divorced mother are funneled more directly to the child, and the quality of the mother-child relationship is reflected more in the adjustment of the child than it is in a nuclear family (Hetherington, Cox, & Cox, 1978, 1982). Moreover, in the divorced family the noncustodial parent is unable to buffer the adverse effects of a destructive relationship between the custodial parent and child. Given that the study of buffering in one-parent households has been done only on mother-custody families, it might be argued that the buffering effect could be due to either the sex or the custodial status of the parent. However, in nuclear families an exceptionally good relationship with either the mother or the father is equally effective as a buffer, so it seems that the effect is attributable to the relative unavailability of the noncustodial parent. Thus, for a variety of reasons, children's contact and relationship with the noncustodial father can be beneficial to them.

Noncustodial parents of either sex experience fewer stresses in day-to-day child rearing but feel more dissatisfied, rootless, deficient, and powerless, and, most important, they feel left out of family affairs and cut off from their relations with the children. Noncustodial fathers may feel that they are losing their children and that their financial or emotional support is unappreciated (Hetherington et al., 1976). This may explain why immediately following the divorce many fathers actually spend more time with their children, and it also may account for the fact that this contact usually diminishes rapidly (Furstenberg et al., 1982; Hetherington et al., 1982). While with their children, many noncustodial fathers are more indulgent, permissive, and less emotionally available than they were prior to the divorce; ironically, they also have less difficulty controlling their children than do divorced mothers (Hetherington et al., 1982). However, this experience is neither universal nor predictable. In general, little continuity is found between the quality of the predivorce and postdivorce father-child relationship, a finding with potentially important implications

214 Emery, Hetherington, and DiLalla

for custody decisions. Some fathers who had been intensely involved cannot tolerate part-time parenting and the "hassles" of visitation and become disengaged; other previously distant fathers become committed and actively involved following a divorce (Gersick, 1979; Hetherington et al., 1982; Wallerstein & Kelly, 1980).

Very little is known about the experience of fathers as custodial parents. Available data suggest that they are not necessarily younger and more radical than noncustodial fathers but, in fact, may be slightly older and more conservative (Gersick, 1979), with some higher education and a profession or managerial position (Chang & Deinard, 1982). Furthermore, in one investigation, custodial and noncustodial fathers were not found to differ in their involvement in predivorce child rearing (Gersick, 1979). Interestingly, less emotional stress is reported by fathers who want child custody (Mendes, 1976).

Although custodial fathers encounter many similar problems to mothers, such as task overload, social isolation, and the challenge of rearing a family alone, their solutions to these problems may differ. For many fathers the postdivorce period is the first time they must manage their household on their own (Hetherington et al., 1976). Many divorced men come from households in which their wives had stayed at home and had been in charge of such routines as meal preparation, housework, and child care. Such fathers may feel overwhelmed when suddenly there is no one to manage the daily household routines. As might be expected, one study of custodial fathers found that they adjusted to the new demands of household tasks by delegating much of the responsibility to their children and thus sharing the new load of work (Gasser & Taylor, 1976). This obviously makes the issue of whether "growing up faster" has positive or negative consequences particularly salient to father-custody households.

Custodial fathers report fewer problems than do custodial mothers in controlling their children in general, but they report having more problems with their daughters (Santrock & Warshak, 1979), and they have more concerns about sexuality and sex education with adolescent girls. Although no clear information is available, the age of the child would seem to be an important factor influencing the relationships of sons and daughters who are living with either their mothers or their fathers.

Healthy parent-child relationships.—Problems in children's adjustment in the divorced, single-parent family are least likely to occur when parent-child relationships are warm, predictable, secure, and conflict-free. Emotional disturbance in children is minimized if discipline is authoritative and consistent, if there is warm and clear communication between the parents and children, and if the custodial parent is happy and well-adjusted (Hess & Camara, 1979; Hetherington, Cox, & Cox, 1982; Jacobson, 1978;

Wallerstein & Kelly, 1980). In addition, the continued relationship between the divorced parents plays a significant role in helping children to cope successfully. Low conflict and absence of mutual denigration, high support and agreement on child rearing and discipline, and frequent contact with the noncustodial parent, if that parent is not extremely deviant or destructive, are associated with positive adjustment in children (Hess & Camara, 1979; Hetherington et al., 1982; Nelson, 1981; Wallerstein & Kelly, 1980).

A final aspect of healthy parent-child relationships in mother-custody and father-custody divorced families needs to be mentioned, although initial findings are tentative and based on very small samples. Some evidence does suggest that children who are in the custody of their same-sex parent may adjust better to family life in the divorced home (Santrock & Warshak, 1979). However, this potentially important finding needs to be replicated before it can be viewed as reliable.

REMARRIAGE AND THE BLENDED FAMILY

The remarriage of divorced adults may present new challenges for all family members and may affect each family member according to how he or she perceives the marriage. Although research on remarriage and family reconstitution is still in its early stages, several patterns that deserve further investigation are beginning to emerge.

Families are reconstituted in a variety of ways. Children may live in the same household with the remarried parent and new spouse, or may have a visiting relationship with them. In some instances, two different sets of children are brought together into a "blended" family living in a single home. Whatever the arrangement, when a remarriage occurs, children become members of both the first marriage nuclear family and the remarried family.

Probably the most common reconstituted family form is the remarriage of a childless or noncustodial father to a custodial mother. The stepfather's involvement with his stepchildren tends toward extremes: Either he is disengaged and inattentive, thus offering the mother little support in child rearing, or he tries to become actively involved in child rearing, sometimes to the point of being restrictive in dealing with his stepchildren, especially stepsons. However, when the mother welcomes her new husband's involvement, and he is willing to support her in her parenting role rather than trying to take over completely, children in stepparent families, particularly boys, function better than those in divorced, single-parent families or conflict-ridden nondivorced families (Hetherington et al., 1982; Zill, 1983). Such a positive effect is not immediate (Zill, 1983). Stern (1978) has suggested that stepfathers may take up to 2 years to establish a friendly relationship with their stepchildren and become equal to their wives in the disciplinary role.

To reach successful integration of allegiances to various family roles, individuals must be able to acknowledge the affection that exists among family members regardless of living arrangements (Ranson, Schlesinger, & Derdeyn, 1979; Walker & Messinger, 1979). The difficulty or ease in establishing new relationships among members of the reconstituted family depends on their willingness to relinquish or alter the roles and boundaries of the former nuclear family (Walker & Messinger, 1979).

Adolescents, particularly those in the custody of the remarried parent, appear to have particular difficulty establishing new roles and alliances (Bernard, 1972; Hetherington et al., 1982). Children aged 9–15 are less likely to accept even a good stepparent than are younger or older children. Another particular problem can be blended families, where both sets of children reside in the same household. Parents in blended families report higher rates of marital conflict, inconsistency in discipline, and differences between how each parent treats his or her own children and how he or she treats the stepchildren (Hetherington et al., 1982).

There is some evidence to suggest that noncustodial fathers become markedly less involved with their original family after they remarry (Furstenberg, Spanier, & Rothschild, 1980; Hetherington et al., 1982). The change may be particularly dramatic if the former spouse remains single. Decreased contact between remarried fathers and children is most notable with daughters. Divorced fathers visit sons more often and for longer periods of time following divorce, and they are more likely to continue their contact with sons than daughters following remarriage (Hetherington et al., 1982). As noted earlier, a divorced father's continued involvement with the child, even after remarriage, can lead to positive outcomes for the child; but, unfortunately, the remarriage of either parent can diminish this involvement.

SUMMARY OF DIVORCE AND THE FAMILY SYSTEM

It is evident from the preceding review that separation and divorce initiate a complex series of challenges and stresses in the lives of parents and children. The characteristics and resources of the family members, the number and type of stresses encountered, and the support available will jointly lead to positive or deleterious outcomes of divorce. Many children may be exposed to high levels of parental conflict before, during, and after the divorce. Involvement in parental hostilities can pose particularly difficult dilemmas for children as they encounter cognitive dissonance, loyalty conflicts, inconsistent discipline, and aggressive models. Parental disagreements seem to pose fewer problems for children when parents do not express their conflict openly, when they are able to eventually resolve or accept their differences, when the child has a particularly good relationship with one parent, and when the parents can at least agree on how to handle the children. Moreover, if the escape from family disharmony through divorce is followed by life in a stable one-parent family, the effects can be salutary for both parents and children.

Loss of contact with the noncustodial parent entails a twofold adaptation for the children involved. In the short term, an acute distress syndrome can be expected, one that the uncertain terms of the marital separation may prolong, thereby delaying the child's adaptation. In the longer term, children have fewer opportunities to interact with a parent who may have been able to offer the children emotional support, to teach the child unique skills, serve as a healthy model to imitate, and buffer problems between the child and the custodial parent. On the positive side, if parental conflict is contained and if the noncustodial parent is well adjusted, frequent and consistent contact with the noncustodial parent appears to have a beneficial effect on child development.

A number of potentially detrimental changes in family relationships can occur among single-parent, divorced families. Affectional exchanges often diminish, and discipline can become less effective and more inconsistent. Parents and children often find one another's emotional difficulties mutually aversive. Some children are forced by necessity to take over parental responsibilities, a change that may cause the child either to grow or to become resentful. However, if the initial problems of separation, loss, conflict, change, and uncertainty are not compounded by subsequent stressors, most parents and children can cope with the divorce transition within 2–3 years. Adaptation to the single-parent family is considerably less difficult when the custodial parent is well adjusted, when the divorced parents are mutually supportive, and when the child is provided with a secure, stable environment. Still, additional stressors such as multiple changes in the environment, task overload, social isolation, emotional instability, and remarriage can upset the balance of relationships among postdivorce family members.

Having reviewed the family's experience with the divorce process and the transition to single-parent family life, the legal divorce is examined next. Because the public plays a role in marital dissolution through its shaping of the legal divorce process, this is an area where important changes in social policy can be implemented. Legal proceedings, the one intervention that all divorcing families undergo, provide a unique opportunity for social policymakers to address some of the family's needs.

DIVORCE AND THE LEGAL SYSTEM

For many people, the only time that they directly interact with the court system is when they obtain a divorce. Unfortunately, this experience often leads the divorced family to develop a negative view of the legal system. Gersick (1979) found that 23 of a sample of 40 fathers had major complaints about their attorneys, such as feeling that they were incompetent or that they favored the wife. In another investigation, 55 percent of 205 survey respondents reported that, as a result of their divorce, they were dissatisfied with the entire legal system, including the laws, judges, and lawyers (Spanier & Anderson, 1979).

It can be argued, however, that divorce law and formal courtroom procedures have little relevance to most divorcing families, because no more than 10 percent of all divorces involve a formal court hearing (Bodenheimer, 1977). The greatest percentage of divorce settlements are negotiated out of court by the divorcing parents and their attorneys, and although the court has the power to reject such negotiated settlements, it rarely does so in practice (Mnookin & Kornhauser, 1979). However, as many as one-third of all divorces involving children are followed by subsequent litigation (Foster & Freed, 1973–1974), and the number of litigated cases may be increasing (Bodenheimer, 1977). Furthermore, it must be recognized that litigation is an ever-present backdrop for out-of-court negotiation. If, then, attorney-negotiated settlements are conducted in "the shadow of the law" (Mnookin & Kornhauser, 1979), they are greatly influenced by the laws that guide judicial decision making and by the litigation process itself.

Of the three principal domains of divorce law most relevant to children—custody, visitation, and support—custody decisions are probably of foremost importance. Full understanding of current child custody law requires some history of how custody decisions have been made.

HISTORICAL REVIEW OF CUSTODY DECISIONS FOLLOWING DIVORCE

The history of judicial custody decisions must be considered within the context of the grounds under which divorces have traditionally been granted. This is necessary for two reasons. First, for a considerable period of time the grounds for divorce determined judicial custody decisions; the party found to be at fault was generally denied custody—particularly in the case of adultery, as the adulterous party was judged morally unfit to rear children (Weitzman, 1981a). Second, although most current statutes do not designate that fault should be considered in making custody decisions "in the child's best interests," they give judges wide discretion (Mnookin,

1975). Such discretionary decisions are very likely to be affected by such contextual factors as fault or behavior that once constituted the grounds for finding fault. In fact, judicial custody decisions appear to be influenced by traditional "moral" fault principles, although there is little evidence that such "immoral" behavior necessarily affects child rearing and thereby compromises the child's best interests (Weitzman, 1981a).

Historical grounds for divorce.—Until the sixteenth century, divorce in Europe was a religious rather than a civil matter and could be granted on only three grounds: adultery, cruelty, or heresy (Scanzoni, 1979). Following the Reformation, marriage and divorce gradually came under civil control. In the American colonies, the government controlled marriage and divorce from the outset in the Puritan settlements of the North, whereas religious control was the rule, albeit temporarily, in the South (Halem, 1981).

As marriage and divorce came under civil rather than religious control, two important changes took place. First, the grounds for divorce were broadened somewhat to include, in addition to adultery and cruelty, such related grounds as habitual drunkenness and desertion. These general grounds for divorce, in fact, remained quite constant throughout American history; important revisions have been made only recently (Halem, 1981).

The second, more dramatic change was that, unlike the church, the state for the first time permitted divorced people to remarry. However, the state was far from encouraging couples to freely enter into and dissolve marriages. Laws governing divorce were strict, discouraging divorce by making the process difficult (Halem, 1981; Mnookin, 1975; Weitzman, 1981a). The judiciary began to interpret the narrowly defined legal statutes somewhat more flexibly only in the middle of the this century, as legal professionals were forced to accommodate the increasing numbers of couples seeking divorce (Halem, 1981). However, statutes requiring the finding of fault as the only grounds for divorce were kept in place, and the high "exit costs" served to dissuade many couples from seeking divorce.

The state's continuing investment in preserving marriages is exemplified most dramatically by the attempts of various courts to promote reconciliation among couples filing for divorce (Halem, 1981). Especially popular during the 1950s, couples filing for divorce in certain jurisdictions were required to first enter into counseling with the goal of reconciling marital differences and thereby preserving the family. Most interventions proved unsuccessful, however, and gradually the goal of reconciliation has been dropped by most courts (Gurman & Kniskern, 1978).

The introduction of California's "no-fault" divorce law on January 1, 1970, which was rapidly followed by adoption of similar laws in 48 of the 50 state legislatures (Freed & Foster, 1981), dramatically changed the process of granting a divorce. Their adoption having accompanied the marked rise in the incidence of divorce, no-fault divorces are now the most common legal grounds for marital dissolution. Thus, a major historical factor in judicial child custody decisions—the finding of fault—has been removed from most divorce proceedings. However, as mentioned above, vestiges of this historical precedent remain and continue to play an important role in the exercise of judicial discretion. For example, findings as to whether a parent is "unfit" are often based on grounds similar to those used in determining fault: habitual drunkenness, adultery, and gross immorality (Podell, Peck, & First, 1972). The extent to which such factors play a role in current judicial decision making is a topic needing social science research.

Criteria for making custody decisions.—Whereas fault thus appears to have had both a direct and an indirect historical influence on judicial custody decisions, other criteria have been used as legal guidelines at different times in history. Unlike recent custom, the custom for the greater part of history was to give the father rather the mother preference in custody decisions. Roman law gave fathers total control over their children, and this authority was vested in men with little change throughout the Middle Ages (Derdeyn, 1976). A man's children, like his wife, were his property to supervise as he saw fit. By the nineteenth century, however, the man's power over his children and wife was diminished, no longer absolute, although judicial decisions clearly acknowledged his superior right in custody disputes. For example, in 1860 a New Hampshire judge noted, "It is a well-settled doctrine of the common law that the father is entitled to the custody of his minor children, as against the mother and everybody else" (*State v. Richardson*, 1860, p. 273). In addition, some determinations of fault—adultery, for example—were more readily judged as suitable grounds for divorce when the wife rather than the husband was at fault (Halem, 1981).

The nineteenth century, nevertheless, was a time when the ground-work was laid supporting the presumption that mothers had superior right to custody. In 1817, the poet Percy Bysshe Shelley lost custody of his children despite the widely acknowledged belief in the father's superior right. Shelley was found immoral because of his atheistic beliefs (Group for Advancement of Psychiatry, 1981). An 1840 custody decision further weakened the concept of paternal superiority by acknowledging the father's right to custody "with the exception of very tender infancy" (*Ahrenfeldt v. Ahrenfeldt*, 1840). The "tender-years" doctrine rapidly grew in popularity during the second half of the nineteenth century, although its application was primarily to give mothers superior rights to custody of young children (Derdeyn, 1976). By the 1920s, mothers' and fathers' legal rights to custody were about equally balanced by the competing principles of the fathers' vested rights and maternal preference based on the tender-years presumption (Brown, 1926).

It was in the 1920s that a third legal doctrine in regard to custody crystallized: the best interests of the child. This doctrine had, in fact, been noted since the early 1800s (*Commonwealth of Pennsylvania* v. *Addicks and Wife*, 1813), but received little attention during most of the nineteenth century. In 1925, Judge Cardozo's historic opinion in *Finlay* v. *Finlay* stated that the judge "does not proceed upon the theory that the petitioner, whether father or mother, has a cause for action against the other or indeed against anyone. He acts as *parens patriae* to do what is best for the interests of the child" (*Finlay* v. *Finlay*, 1925, p. 626). This case established a precedent that eventually led to the courts' taking on the difficult task of seeking the custody decision that would be in the child's best interest.

Throughout the first half of the twentieth century, however, maternal custody, based on the tender-years presumption, was increasingly viewed as best serving the child's interest. Gradually the interpretation of what constituted the tender years was extended from infancy up until adolescence (Weiss, 1979b). The eventual result was that by 1970 the laws of several states explicitly gave preference to mothers over fathers regardless of the child's age (Trenkner, 1976).

In the 1970s, however, the presumption of maternal superiority was questioned. The changing social climate—in particular, the elevation of women's status—as well as legal questions of legal protection under the law both led to the current explicit legal presumption that mothers and fathers have equal rights to custody (Weitzman, 1981a). Whether they do in practice can be called into question, however. Most states have custody laws that, without giving preference to the mother, give judges wide discretion on the basis of the indeterminant "best-interests" standard (Mnookin, 1975). It is not unlikely that the exercise of this discretion conforms in part to the recent historical preference for mothers. How judges are to exercise their almost complete discretion is, in fact, a dilemma for them and for all parties involved in divorce.

CURRENT ISSUES IN CUSTODY DECISIONS

Sole custody.—A major consequence of the evolution of child custody law is that, with the decline of the historical determinants of fault, paternal preference, and the tender-years doctrine, most current statutes exhort judges to make decisions in the child's best interests without providing guidelines as to how this determination is to be made (Mnookin, 1975). Further, case precedent offers scant help, because each case is to be decided on its unique merits. Proponents of current law applaud the judiciary's wide powers of discretion, arguing that judges need the flexibility to decide individual cases; opponents argue that ambiguity opens the door for judicial bias. Both sides agree, however, that judges are confronted with a most difficult decision in trying to predict what will, in the future, be in the child's best interests (Mnookin, 1975).

Mnookin (1975) has argued that the indeterminate standards require judges to use scanty information to make an impossible prediction—for which, moreover, there are no agreed-upon criteria for assessing the outcome. Perhaps because the decision is so difficult and the criteria to guide it are so ambiguous, a variety of judicial aides have been enlisted to provide input into the process. These consultants may include the child, attorneys for the child, and mental health professionals.

A few state statutes require that a child's preference be considered in making a custody determination if the child has the "mental capacity" or is of a certain age, typically 12 or 14; and two states, Georgia and Texas, make the preference of a 14-year-old child mandatory (Siegel & Hurley, 1977). According to most statutes and to case history, however, courts can overrule a child's stated preference, the chief reasons being concerns as to whether a child has the "mental capacity" to identify his or her best interests, the possible ill effects of forcing children to choose between their parents, and the potential for parents to use coercion to influence that choice. For these reasons the child's preference is treated as but one piece of evidence to be solicited and considered in a custody hearing (Group for Advancement of Psychiatry, 1981).

Even attorneys appointed by the court to represent the child's interest have been found to make recommendations to the court that are contrary to the child's expressed preference (Landsman & Minow, 1978). *Guardians ad litem*, as these lawyers are often called, typically function as the child's advocate or as an independent fact finder, rather than acting as a third legal adversary (Landsman & Minow, 1978). In one study, attorneys who served as *guardians ad litem* reported that they judged their position to be an important one that allowed them to obtain unique information relevant to custody decisions; they also believed that judges relied heavily on their input in court (Landsman & Minow, 1978). Some argue, however, that *guardians ad litem* should function as a third adversary, and assert that lawyers are failing their clients when they serve as fact finders or mediators. Others have supported the fact finder/advocate approach but questioned whether attorneys are the best trained professionals to serve this role. It is suggested instead that a mental health professional would better perform the intermediary function, since the role is one of helper rather than of legal adversary (Solow & Adams, 1977).

Mental health professionals have been involved in custody decisions for some time, but usually they perform quite a different service from that of *guardians ad litem*. Mental health professionals typically have served as a witness for one or the other parent and have been asked to provide expert testimony on what is or is not in the child's best interests; judges or children's attorneys also occasionally ask for independent psychological evaluations (Group for Advancement of Psychiatry, 1981). But the role of the mental health professional in conducting custody evaluations remains controversial, for two main reasons: First, if they represent only one parent, their testimony may be biased and may be contradicted by other experts and therefore discounted by the judge. Second, although better trained in interview techniques and psychological theories, they have not demonstrated that they can reliably predict the future best interests of the child any better than a judge can (Group for Advancement of Psychiatry, 1981; Mnookin, 1975). Mental health professionals can avoid the first problem by refusing to perform an evaluation for one side or the other and serving only as a friend of the court (Gardner, 1982). The second problem can be resolved only through systematic research and application of its findings, although even if research could tell us what custody decisions would lead to what outcomes, there would still be debate over which of a range of outcomes is "better" (Mnookin, 1975).

Some mental health professionals have offered guidelines for predicting what will be in the child's best interest (e.g., Goldstein, Freud, & Solnit, 1973). However, such predictions have necessarily been based on theoretical rather than empirical rationales, relevant research being scarce and difficult to conduct. Further, much of the theory and research that has been drawn upon has been based on general studies of parent-child relations, attachment, separation, and loss, and has been only tangentially relevant to divorce. Indeed, it may have very limited application to children of divorce because, as was discussed earlier, divorce involves a unique set of processes that distinguish it from other forms of parental loss.

Although an accumulating body of studies on divorce allows for more directly applicable recommendations to be made, most of these suggestions must be viewed tentatively, for reasons discussed earlier. Nevertheless, one conclusion seems clear: the potential for increased family conflict is one consequence of the indeterminant statutes that give judges wide discretion in deciding upon the child's best interests. As long as the opposing parties—the parents—are uncertain about the outcome of a custody battle, they are more likely to engage in a prolonged custody fight (Mnookin, 1975). As noted earlier, conflict between divorcing parents poses a major dilemma for the children involved, and there can be little doubt that parental conflict is exacerbated by threats of litigation during out-of-court negotiation or in-court testimony about why one's former spouse is an unfit parent. Furthermore, a divisive process in which there are winners and losers may well diminish the "loser's" commitment to the family and result in less parental contact and involvement. Thus, any reduction in indeterminacy has the potential to better serve the child's best interests by reducing litigation and thereby eliminating one source of conflict (not to mention reducing court costs and attorney's fees and relieving judges of making the difficult decisions required in contested custody cases).

Are there ways to alter custody statutes so as to reduce indeterminacy? Previous alternatives—deciding against the spouse found at fault, automatically preferring the father or mother, or making the child's preference determinative—have been found to be problematic. Furthermore, most of the guidelines proposed by social scientists to reduce indeterminacy are controversial, and some are based on debatable rationales (Clingempeel & Reppucci, 1982). Given the current state of knowledge, even those suggestions that draw some support from empirical research, such as giving preference to the same-sex parent, seem premature (Santrock & Warshak, 1979). Others have suggested replacing the best-interests standard with a determination of custody based on who has been "the primary caretaker parent" (Neely, 1981). Under such a rule, the judge would award custody to the parent who was most involved in child rearing, a comparatively unambiguous determination. Increased paternal involvement in parenting notwithstanding, such a guideline would most often favor women. In addition, as was noted earlier, one cannot predict a father's postdivorce relationship with his children from his predivorce involvement, and it is future rather than past behavior that is most important to the long-term well-being of the child. Therefore, none of these options for reducing indeterminacy appears completely satisfactory, and the search for new options must move forward.

As to the present role of the child, the child's attorney, and mental health professionals in influencing judicial custody decisions, each of these individuals is subject to a unique set of biases, as is the judge. Investigation of each party's biases and of how the different parties influence each other is an area ripe for important, if difficult, research. At present, given the current ambiguous and perhaps impossible decision-making criteria, solicitation of input from these multiple sources might be viewed as merely a method of diffusing responsibility for the custody decisions. However, such diffusion of responsibility might well have a positive consequence: individual biases of different sources may cancel each other out and mitigate extreme views leading to a more balanced decision. Parents might also be more likely to view the final custody decision as being more just when many people have had input into the decision. If they therefore more readily accept the court's opinion, that may speed the adjustment to postdivorce life. Still, parents who bring their custody dispute before the court have lost control over a decision that they potentially could have made themselves, and considerable emotional and financial costs are exacted in the process. The effects of this process on families are examined later, but first a new custody proposal merits attention.

Joint custody.—Recently, joint custody, wherein both parents are given equal legal rights and responsibilities for their children, has been strongly advocated (Abarbanel, 1979; Roman & Haddad, 1978; Weiss, 1979b) and just as strongly opposed (Cox & Cease, 1978; Roman & Haddad, 1978). Proponents of the option argue that joint custody is to the child's benefit because it increases contact between each parent and the child and because it gives each parent respite from the stress involved in single parenting (Clingempeel & Reppucci, 1982). As noted earlier, recent research on divorced families has documented that having good relations with both parents is related to a child's healthier adjustment following divorce. In addition, if divorced parents agree and if both are involved in child rearing and decisions about children, the noncustodial father serves as an extremely effective support for custodial mothers (Hetherington et al., 1982). Task overload is a common complaint of single parents (Brandwein, Brown, & Fox, 1974; Hetherington et al., 1978), and joint custody could help free parents from the sole responsibility of caring for the children.

These arguments assume a reasonably cooperative relationship between parents, which often is not the case. Because joint custody necessitates increased contact and cooperation between spouses whose acrimony often persists long after the legal divorce (Hetherington et al., 1979; Wallerstein & Kelly, 1980), it can lead to an increase of conflict in some families. In addition, joint custody may result in children alternating more frequently among parents, residences, schools, and sets of friends, and some evidence suggests that such frequent changes may be difficult for children to assimilate (Alexander, 1977; Clarke-Stewart, 1977; Hodges, Wechsler, & Ballentine, 1979; Jenkins, 1977).

Moreover, the term joint custody has plural meanings, because it encompasses a variety of different practical solutions. In some cases, the child resides in one home with one parent and sees the other parent according to some fixed visitation schedule. This is very much as is done in many sole custody cases, with the difference that the nonresidential parent maintains the legal right of equal parental authority and is presumably more involved in decisions affecting the children. Such a joint custody arrangement can be a useful "face-saving" arrangement, differing from sole custody only in name but allowing parents to avoid a certain amount of acrimony and perhaps increasing the commitment of the nonresident parent. Other, less traditional arrangements are also subsumed under the joint-custody option: for example, keeping the child in the same home but having each parent move in and out after a set time, having the child alternate between parental homes each year, splitting child care daily so that each parent cares for the child for some portion of the day, and many more. Thus, joint custody can mean many different things in terms of the actual experience of the child. However, each option shares the similarity that, in presuming more parental involvement with the children, it necessitates more contact and cooperation between parents than does single-parent custody.

In summary, it would appear that each opposing position in the argument about joint custody has merit. Joint custody seems to be a reasonable and probably beneficial option in cases where neither parent insists on sole custody, where interparental conflict is low, and where the practicalities of everyday living will be minimally disrupted in the child's life. Thus, joint custody seems to be a good option for parents who agree that this is what they want. But in other circumstances, joint custody may only increase difficulties. One research project found, for example, that joint custody was not successful when there was little agreement between parents or when one parent insisted on sole custody (Folberg & Graham, 1979). It should also be noted that studies of families in which parents have successfully elected joint custody may be irrelevant to the issues involved in mandatory joint custody. Parents who opt for joint custody may already be more child oriented and less acrimonious than those who choose sole custody or who contest the custody decision. Thus, those litigated cases in which a judge is forced to make a difficult custody decision may be exactly the ones for whom joint custody will not work (Derdeyn & Scott, 1983). It would seem that parents who are sufficiently acrimonious to bring a custody dispute to litigation are very unlikely to be sufficiently cooperative to implement joint custody as a solution. Thus, joint custody does not appear to be the solution to the indeterminacy confronting judges who hear custody disputes.

VISITATION

The issues raised in regard to joint custody apply equally to visitation in cases where a single parent is awarded custody. That is, frequent visitation can potentially be beneficial to children, both directly by increasing contact between the children and the noncustodial parent, and indirectly by providing respite to the custodial parent. Unfortunately, it appears that some noncustodial parents "don't die. They just fade away" (Grollman, 1969). In many families, the frequency of visitation by the noncustodial parent has been found to decrease rapidly during the interval following divorce (Hetherington et al., 1982), with an especially steep decline following remarriage (Furstenberg, 1982).

One controversy unique to visitation is the suggestion that the custodial parent should have complete control over the child, including the right to deny visitation (Goldstein et al., 1973). The rationale for this assertion is based in part on the assumption that children have but one "psychological parent." But this assumption has been contradicted by research that finds that any one child can be attached to several adults (Lamb, 1977). Furthermore, vesting such decision-making power in the hands of custodial parents might reduce their motivation to resolve conflict and to facilitate relations with the other parent. It is also quite possible that such a radical visitation arrangement sometimes would lead the other parent to resort to such extreme measures as continued litigation, harassment, or even child snatching.

A second controversy is the degree to which the custodial parent should use denial of visitation as a tactic to reduce the other parent's noncompliance. Specifically, can visitation be denied to a parent who, though able to, fails to pay support? Visitation cannot legally be so denied in most cases, nor can support be denied to a parent who prevents visitation (Mnookin & Kornhauser, 1979). Practically, however, many divorced parents probably use these contingencies. Mnookin and Kornhauser (1979) argue that this informal contingency should be acknowledged and given legal sanction. Not only would explicit legal sanction seem to fit the common moral assumption that visitation and child-support payments be linked, they argue, but it might also make denial of visitation a more effective tactic and less a source of acrimony than when used with no legal backing. Further, withholding visitation would certainly be a faster and more economical means of remedy than renewed litigation.

A third and final controversy concerns the visitation rights of grandparents and other people who have been closely involved with a child whose parents divorce. There has been an increasing legal trend to grant visitation to interested third parties who can demonstrate a significant involvement with the children, and it is likely that this trend will continue. This visitation issue presents few problems when the grandparents maintain a link to the divorced family through their own child. However, when that link is missing—when a father or mother has lost contact with his or her children because of lack of interest, a change in circumstances, or death—the grandparents' rights to visitation can become a very controversial intergenerational issue. In general, it appears that most courts have interpreted it as being in "the child's best interests" to maintain contact with grandparents, although there is no empirical research on this topic. Thus, given the legal trend toward giving grandparents and other involved parties visitation rights, and given the commonly felt tension between parents and grandparents about how best to raise children, the area is ripe for investigation.

CHILD SUPPORT

Usually, the noncustodial parent is ordered to pay some form of child support. Although gender-neutral laws may state that "the spouse with the greater financial resources" provides support to the other spouse, the effect is almost always that fathers are ordered to pay child support to custodial mothers, whose economic hardships following divorce are likely to be greater (Espenshade, 1979). In 1981, for example, the median income for female-headed families was $8,653, whereas it was $25,636 for two-parent families (SCCYF, 1983). One study indicated that children who stayed with their mothers following divorce experienced a 13.8 percent drop in real income, whereas those who stayed with fathers experienced a 49.4 percent increase in income (Duncon & Morgan, 1976).

As is discussed shortly, many factors contribute to the economic insecurity of the divorced single-parent family, but several child-support issues are related to the poverty found in many households following divorce. The first issue is the level of support that is ordered by the court. Theoretically, the amount of support awarded is one that provides an income sufficient to insure adequate provision for a child's needs (Clark, 1968). In practice, however, the award is more often determined by set schedules that are devised in various jurisdictions (Weitzman, 1981a). According to these schedules, the percentage of the father's net income that is ordered for support usually depends on his income level, the mother's income, and the number of children. However, that percentage rarely climbs over 50 percent, because judges are concerned about eliminating "a man's incentive to earn" (Walzer, 1968). In fact, discussion of the 50 percent figure is misleading, since in practice the percentage is much lower on average, and whereas even 10 or 20 percent of the noncustodial parent's income may be a substantial sum of money, it is considerably less than what was available in most families for child support before the divorce (Weitzman, 1981b). Studies of California samples have found that court-ordered support payments are set at levels equaling less than half what is needed to raise a child in a low-income family (Weitzman, 1981b; Weitzman & Dixon, 1979). The Select Committee on Children, Youth, and

Families (1983) of the U.S. House of Representatives recently revealed that the average annual support provided by fathers who do make payments is $2,000. Further, most support agreements do not include provisions to change payment levels to reflect inflation or increases in the wage earner's salary. Only 10 percent of the California samples had such provisions (Weitzman & Dixon, 1979). Given our recent high levels of inflation and the fact that divorces involving children are most common among young wage earners whose salaries are likely to increase, both factors—size of payments and provision for increase—are critical factors for inclusion.

Unfortunately, these important points may be moot, since in most cases support is not paid as ordered. Although estimates from different studies vary, it appears that in at least one-quarter of all cases not one single support payment is ever made, and that in less than half of all cases is strict compliance with court orders found (Espenshade, 1979; Weitzman, 1981a, 1981b). The recent House of Representatives Committee's report cited above was even more pessimistic, suggesting that support is paid in only one-third of all cases. Although only 14.4 percent of all families were female headed in 1977, they accounted for 49.1 percent of the families below the poverty line (U.S. Bureau of the Census, 1978). Thus, 34 percent of divorced mothers receive public assistance (Bradbury, Dansinger, Smolensky, & Smolensky, 1979). By contrast, in a California sample, only 13 percent of divorced mothers receiving regular child support were on welfare (Weitzman, 1981b).

Two principal reasons are given for failure to pay support more often or more regularly: either fathers cannot afford the payments, or they cannot be located for nonsupport prosecution. Neither case is necessarily true, however. An investigation conducted by the Rand Corporation revealed that a number of truly affluent fathers evaded child-support payments, and that only a small minority of the nonpaying fathers could not be located (Winston & Forsher, 1975). Another investigator found little relation between fathers' income level and their compliance with support orders (Weitzman, 1981b). Enforcement of the court order, rather than ability to pay, thus appears to be the problem (Espenshade, 1979; Weitzman, 1981a, 1981b).

Chambers's (1979) survey of Michigan counties revealed the relation between enforcement policies and compliance. Two policies were related to higher levels of support payment: incarceration of spouses who were delinquent in their payments and the use of self-starting collection systems. The State of Michigan was found to jail one in seven divorced fathers for failure to pay child support, and it seems to be no coincidence that the state also has the highest level of compliance with support orders in the nation. Chambers found, however, that frequent jailing increased compliance only in those counties that had self-starting collection systems— systems in which payments are made directly to the court, and where a friend of the court automatically initiates action against fathers who are delinquent in their payments.

Thus it appears that policy changes are needed in the levels of payment and in enforcing compliance with child-support orders. The following are some of the well-argued recommendations made by Weitzman (1981b), one of the leading researchers in this area: (1) increase support levels to reflect the real costs of raising children; (2) build automatic cost-of-living increases into support payments; (3) increase the availability of enforcement options, such as automatic wage assignments and incarceration, when necessary; and (4) implement self-starting collection systems (given their increased effectiveness, the complexity of initiating legal action against a delinquent former spouse, and the apparent reluctance of legal personnel to use firm measures against nonpaying parents).

DIVORCE PROCEEDINGS: EFFECTS ON FAMILIES

Whereas the effects of the *content* of legal custody, visitation, and support decisions have received much attention, and the need for changes in social policy in regard to these decisions has been clear, the effects of the *process* of making these decisions must also be examined. The legal divorce process itself, irrespective of the decisions that result from it, can be a stressful experience for the divorcing family.

It was noted earlier that many divorcing families are unhappy about their experience with the legal system, and this dissatisfaction extends to many legal professionals. In his 1982 State of the Judiciary Address, Supreme Court Chief Justice Warren Burger noted the adverse effects that legal processes can have on individuals and families (Burger, 1982). Justice Burger warned of "litigation neuroses" and suggested that the judicial process was "not only stressful and frustrating, but expensive and frequently unrewarding." Further, attorneys themselves frequently complain about the divorce process, criticizing such things as the adversarial system, the lawyer's one-sided view, the nonlegal nature of many divorce issues, and difficulties in dealing with opposing attorneys (Kressel, Lopez-Morillas, Weinglass, & Deutsch, 1979).

When examining the reasons dissatisfaction with the legal divorce process is so widespread, most critics identify the central problem as the adversarial nature of the system itself, rather than the practices of individual attorneys, judges, or court personnel (Bahr, 1981; Coogler, 1977; Haynes, 1981; Weiss, 1975). As suggested earlier, decreased conflict and increased cooperation between parents both before and after divorce appear to be beneficial to them, and certainly are in the children's best interests. But the basic adversarial concept of competing parties who have competing interests can disrupt and undermine these relationships. In one sample, 26 percent of the divorced respondents indicated that involvement with an attorney worsened their relation with their former spouse, while only 6 percent said that it was helpful to the relationship (Spanier & Anderson, 1979).

Although a given couple's resort to litigation as the means of resolving their differences may indicate a high level of preexisting family acrimony, many professionals suggest that there are attorneys who are "litigators" and push their reluctant clients to a full court battle (Kressel et al., 1979; Mnookin, 1975). Thus, for some divorcing families the process of litigation itself may well exacerbate destructive processes. As one example of this, the court's increasing recognition of a father's equal right to custody may have put divorcing men in a better negotiating position in regard to limiting support payments, as they now have an additional bargaining chip (Mnookin & Kornhauser, 1979). Judge Richard Neely, a member of the West Virginia Supreme Court, recognized this advantage. He reports that as a practicing attorney he encouraged fathers who had no real interest in custody to nevertheless threaten their wives with a lengthy custody battle. That threat would later be parlayed into reduced alimony or child support payments (Neely, 1981).

Because out-of-court settlements involve "bargaining in the shadow of the law" (Mnookin, 1975), it has been argued that, like litigation, they also can be highly adversarial and therefore disruptive. No empirical research could be located on how attorney-negotiated settlements affect the divorcing family. However, it seems reasonable to assume that lawyers who negotiate out-of-court settlements in a way that minimizes hostilities (i.e., without the use of bluffs, threats, and manipulations) are probably doing their clients a service by avoiding litigation. Attorneys who serve this negotiator role may, however, face a dilemma. The attorney's canon of ethics instructs lawyers to fully represent the interests of their clients without regard to the consequences to opposing parties. That is, the ethical attorney is concerned only with his or her client's viewpoint and disregards that of the opposition. Ironically, the present analysis based on social science research suggests that the divorce client's, and the children's, best interests may be served by compromising some of the client's legally defensible interests. To the potential benefit of the opposing party, a more conciliatory stance in out-of-court negotiation may lead to a settlement that minimizes conflict and maximizes cooperation between family members. But attorneys who serve as flexible negotiators in divorce proceedings may not be fulfilling their ethical obligation. Further, if a third party is to play the role of mediator rather than legal advocate, it can be questioned whether lawyers are the best-equipped professionals to perform this task.

DIVORCE MEDIATION

Divorce mediation has recently been suggested as a preferable alternative to both litigation and out-of-court negotiation between opposing parties (Bahr, 1981; Emery, 1982, 1983; Haynes, 1978, 1981; Scheiner, Musetto, & Cordier, 1982; Weiss, 1975). The key goal of mediation is to help the divorcing parties achieve their own nonadversarial resolution to the custody or financial disputes surrounding a divorce. As opposed to an adversarial out-of-court settlement, in mediation the divorcing spouses employ a single consultant (or consultant team) who works with both parties. Unlike the counselor in the reconciliation process, the divorce mediator accepts the parents' decision to divorce and works to facilitate agreement on disputed issues. Such mediators may be attorneys, psychologists, psychiatrists, or social workers. They can work either in private practice or as court personnel, and mediation can be either a voluntary or a mandated step before litigation (Bahr, 1981). As of January 1, 1981, California law, for example, requires that mediation be attempted before a custody or visitation case will be heard by a judge. Such mediation is usually designed to be a short-term process that involves no more than several 1- or 2-hour meetings.

Advocates of mediation argue that this alternative has the potential to produce beneficial effects in areas that Emery (1983) has called the four C's: reduced conflict, increased cooperation, maintenance of parental control, and lower cost. Specific hypothesized benefits of mediation include: (1) a reduced financial burden on the state, (2) lower cost to the divorcing parties, (3) increased compliance with court orders, (4) superior adjustment for the divorcing parties, (5) superior adjustment for the children involved, and (6) better postdivorce relations between parents (Bahr, 1981; Coogler, Weber, & McKenry, 1979; Emery, 1982; Haynes, 1978).

What evidence is there to support this list of claims? Only a few studies have been done on the effects of mediation, but the results of available research are quite encouraging. Various mediation programs that have been instituted in the United States, Canada, and Australia have been successful in getting from 22 percent to 67 percent of divorcing couples to reach voluntary out-of-court settlements (Bahr, 1981). In the one study where couples who applied for a court hearing were randomly assigned to mediation or to the usual litigation (Irving, Bohm, MacDonald, & Benjamin, 1979), 22 percent of the mediation cases as opposed to 8 percent of the litigation cases were settled out of court. Furthermore, one research group found that couples who failed to reach an agreement in mediation were more likely than controls to subsequently settle out of court with the aid of attorneys rather than proceed with litigation (Pearson & Thoennes, 1982).

The hypothesized reduced cost of mediation receives tentative confirmation from the following data: (1) A Los Angeles County Court that adopted the policy that all custody and visitation disputes be first referred for mediation found that mediation cost the court 10 percent less (this saving occurred despite the court's increased costs of being involved in both mediation and litigation in those cases [54 percent] that were not resolved by mediation [McIsaac, cited in Bahr, 1981]); (2) a detailed accounting of an Australian mediation program disclosed a 50 percent saving (McKenzie & Horwill, 1979); (3) a 50 percent saving was noted in a Minnesota mediation program (Maniaci, cited in Bahr, 1981); and (4) for the Toronto program that used random assignment there was a 10 percent net court savings (Irving et al., 1979). As to whether divorcing couples save money by using mediation rather than litigation, no data are available, but one estimate has projected annual private savings of $88.6 million (Bahr, 1981).

Unequivocal data are not available on the proposed increased compliance with court orders due to mediation, but one group reported that only 10 percent of mediated divorces returned to the court because of allegations of noncompliance, in comparison to 26 percent of litigated cases (Doyle & Caron, 1979). Another investigator found figures of 10.5 percent for mediated divorces and 34.3 percent for litigated ones (Milne, 1978). In both of these studies, subjects were not randomly assigned, so the couples in the mediation group may well have been selected on the basis of preexisting cooperativeness. In a study in which couples *were* randomly assigned to either counseling or litigation for visitation disputes, only nine of 75 counseled couples returned to court, in comparison to 59 of 75 of the litigation group (Margolin, 1973).

Still more scant are data on the hypothesis that divorcing parties who go through mediation adjust better to postdivorce life, but one investigation did find that 25 percent of those randomly assigned to mediation reported that "things had gotten much better" 6 weeks after the divorce, in comparison to 9 percent of those who went through litigation (Irving et al., 1979). Finally, no data are available on the effects of mediation on children's postdivorce adjustment and parents' postdivorce relations. These issues are clearly important areas for research, and the above admittedly tentative findings encourage optimism about the potential for improved outcomes.

Although there seems to be justification for considerable optimism about the mediation alternative, it is not without its problems. For one, it is clearly not the solution for every custody, visitation, or support dispute, although it appears to be a viable alternative for a significant percentage of the cases. Even if a large percentage of divorces can be successfully mediated, available data are insufficient at present to support the claims of mediation's most staunch proponents. More research is obviously needed. Finally, numerous questions about the practice of mediation must be answered: Who will be the mediators? Are lawyers well enough trained in human relations? Are they violating their canon of ethics by being mediators? On the other hand, are psychologists and other nonlawyers who mediate divorces engaged in the unauthorized practice of law and open to suit? Do we need to license mediators?

Should mediation be mandatory or voluntary? Mandatory mediation might cast a shadow of the law that encourages even more people to settle out of court, but it may also be a waste of time and money for many couples. Should mediation services be a part of the court system, or should they be a private enterprise?

Should parties involved in mediation each consult an attorney privately? Such consultation might best protect their rights, particularly the rights of the weaker marital partner, but are attorneys likely to subvert the mediated agreement? If unsuccessful, should the mediator give an opinion at a custody hearing, or should mediation be strictly confidential? The former approach might lead to obtaining a greater percentage of mediated agreements, but will the quality of the agreements be as high as those obtained during confidential sessions? Despite such questions that need to be addressed, mediation is an alternative that appears to hold the potential to benefit both public and private interest while circumventing the difficult issue of indeterminant custody laws.

SUMMARY OF DIVORCE AND THE LEGAL SYSTEM

Legal intervention in child custody disputes during divorce has evolved to a point where states provide the judiciary with few concrete statutory guidelines on how to best exercise their discretion. Judges are put in a difficult position, and the door is opened to systematic bias in the exercise of individual judicial opinion. Although enlisting the aid of children, *guardians ad litem*, and mental health professionals may help judges to make less biased and better accepted custody determinations, these steps are partial solutions at best. Joint custody, probably a useful option for parents who freely elect it, is not likely to work when imposed on parents who litigate custody disputes, and so is not a solution to the judicial dilemma.

The prominent issues in joint custody apply to visitation by the noncustodial parent. One additional dilemma is whether visitation and child support should be made contingent upon one another. Child support is yet another problematic area of divorce law: court-ordered payments are generally quite low, are frequently not paid by many noncustodial fathers, and have not been strongly enforced by the legal system.

Divorce mediation has been suggested as an alternative to the litigation of disputes about custody, visitation, and child support. Initial evidence is optimistic; the process of mediation appears to promote healthier family functioning than does the process of litigation. Many questions about mediation remain, however, and it is clearly not the answer for every divorce dispute.

Even if all divorces could be successfully mediated, if healthy family processes could be maintained, and if all decisions were made jointly by divorcing parents, most divorced, single-parent families would encounter one additional set of stressors: economic difficulties. Economic problems would obtain even in an ideal world of divorce, for the simple reason that it is considerably more expensive to maintain two households than one. Because the world of divorce is not an ideal one, the economic problems of the divorced, single-parent family are all the more complex.

DIVORCE AND THE ECONOMIC SYSTEM

Unlike its familial, mental health, and legal consequences, the economic outcomes of divorce can be all too straightforwardly described. And whereas the mental health and legal outcomes are best thought of as family issues, the economic outcomes are in many respects women's issues. Earlier we touched on the poor economic conditions of divorced families, particularly of custodial mothers. It is worth reiterating several points: divorced, mother-headed families experience as much as a 30 percent drop in income following the divorce (Hoffman, 1977). The median income of one-parent families is only one-third that of two-parent families (SCCYF, 1983). Nearly half of all families below the poverty level are headed by a female (Espenshade, 1979). And finally, in 1979, divorce and separation were the largest contributing factors in determining eligibility for Aid to Families with Dependent Children: 45 percent of all families qualifying for AFDC were separated or divorced (SCCYF, 1983). There are no economic winners in divorce, because costs rise when the family moves to two separate households. Nevertheless, these statistics indicate that children who live with their mothers are most likely to be the economic losers. This is not to say that many men do not experience economic hardship, loss of the family residence, and increased expenses following divorce. However, as a group, men are better off financially, at least in terms of disposable income (Espenshade, 1979).

The stress that accompanies a lowered standard of living can be extreme. Economic problems, especially when combined with the other strains of a divorce, can cause distress for everyone involved (Brown, Felton, Whiteman, & Manela, 1980). A decline in income often forces the single-parent family to cope with such life-style changes as poorer housing, geographic mobility, and maternal employment, each of which can impose deprivations on parents and children (Colletta, 1979a; Hodges et al., 1979; Wallerstein & Kelly, 1980). Even families with above-average income experience financial difficulties after a divorce, and lower-income families may be financially overwhelmed (Weiss, 1975).

So significant is the economic decline following divorce that some have suggested that financial factors alone account for the problems of children in divorced homes (Herzog & Sudia, 1973). Given the repeated documentation of the social, emotional, and academic difficulties of children reared in impoverished environments, this possibility is a legitimate concern. And the fact that recent research indicates that divorce is experienced as a stressful transition by children in various socioeconomic situations (Guidubaldi et al., 1983) does not negate the influence of economic factors (Colletta, 1979a). The divorced family's loss of income is likely to affect the child by precipitating practical upheavals, such as a change in residence, by reducing the number of opportunities for participating in stimulating experiences that have become financially unrealistic, and by introducing economic problems that have disruptive effects on family relations (Wallerstein & Kelly, 1980).

This latter point deserves particular attention. A mother who can expect an adequate income following divorce feels much less stress than one who cannot (Kitson & Raschke, 1981). In general, when divorced women become economically independent, they and their children benefit (Kurdek, 1981). But it often is not easy for divorced mothers to become financially self-sufficient. It has already been noted that child-support awards are often inadequate, and alimony and property awards, the other traditional economic supports for divorced women, provide insufficient offsetting help to a large number of mother-headed families. In studies of California samples, Weitzman (1981b) documented that the median value of property to be divided by divorcing spouses is only $11,000, and only 17 percent of divorced women receive alimony. Even women with minor children receive alimony in only 22 percent of the cases, and the awards are frequently small and time-limited. Furthermore, because of the recent movement toward dividing marital property equally between the spouses, women appear to be receiving smaller property awards, as judges seem to be indicating that they will not compensate for the risk that today's young women take in assuming the mother and homemaker role (Glendon, 1980; Weitzman, 1981b).

OPTIONS FOR ALTERING ECONOMIC OUTCOMES

Although the economic outcomes of divorce are clear-cut, the processes that the commonly experienced financial problems necessitate can be complex. The divorced mother confronted with an economically troubled household has essentially four options: immediate employment, seeking private or public assistance, job retraining, or remarriage.

IMMEDIATE EMPLOYMENT

Because of the sudden loss of the spouse's income, divorced women often must seek employment for the first time. Finding a job can be particularly difficult for many of these women who, having previously chosen to be homemakers rather than enter the working world, have no particular job skills. Other women who held jobs at one time but gave them up in favor of marriage have now been out of the job market for a considerable length of time. Divorced mothers without job experience and skills may often have to settle for poor-paying, unchallenging, or tedious jobs, and this can lead to further dissatisfaction in their lives and poorer self-images. This problem is especially acute for older divorced women who have been out of the job market for the longest time.

Younger divorced women, on the other hand, are often in a better position to begin or to continue in a career, or to improve their financial situation through remarriage. But they often have other problems. First, the presence of young children can make it difficult to balance work and home life. Second, young mothers are more likely to be awarded smaller property, alimony, and child-support settlements—which, moreover, often terminate within a brief period of time (Weitzman, 1981b).

Divorced mothers in the work force potentially may suffer additional hardships. They do not have the added social support of a spouse to help alleviate stresses they experience in the work world (Selby, 1981). Also, Weitzman (1981a) has noted that two-income families quickly come to depend on both incomes, regardless of the family's income bracket, and that loss of one of these incomes is very difficult for the family. It follows, then, that divorced mothers who suddenly lose their expected family income or who have inflated expectations about their possible living standards must experience difficulties.

The divorced mother in the work force also encounters the problems faced by working women in general. Although sex discrimination in the job market is decreasing somewhat, enabling more women to become employed, the average woman still earns only 60 percent of the salary of the average man. And this is a trend that does not seem to be improving (Brandwein et al., 1974). Even when such factors as education and experience are controlled for, there is still a 29–43 percent difference in salary paid to men and women (Weitzman, 1981a). In addition, a disproportionately large number of women are employed in clerical or service jobs, which tend to pay more poorly and to offer fewer opportunities for advancement than many other types of jobs (Dunlop, 1981; Weitzman, 1981a). Even women in positions with more room for advancement are less likely to be promoted than are men (Dunlop, 1981).

Although inequities persist, an obvious benefit of working is the increase in monetary income. Moreover, the job can provide important social security and pension fund benefits, as well as health insurance and other fringe benefits. Having a job also enables the divorced working woman to meet more people (Weiss, 1975). Finally, having a satisfying job can be personally rewarding (Dunlop, 1981).

A number of other beneficial side effects accrue to women who are successfully integrated into the work force. Such women seem to be more healthy psychologically, complaining of fewer psychosomatic problems and having better self-concepts and higher self-esteem. They also report higher satisfaction with their situation than do women who work full-time as homemakers, and they report enjoying their relations with their children more than do women who care for their children full-time (Dunlop, 1981).

Although there are potential benefits for the divorced woman who works, there are also potential stressors, as Dunlop (1981) reports. Working women, in general, find that they are holding two jobs, one outside the home and the other as homemaker. This is obviously difficult, but with the support of her spouse, children, or friends, the working woman's own well-being and work may flourish. Divorced women, however, often are without such supports. Working at a job and being a full-time single parent and maintaining a home can result in "role overload." These women may expect themselves to maintain top performance in all aspects of their lives, but may be unable to do so because they receive little or no outside help.

Hetherington (1981) found that employment was sometimes a beneficial influence on the divorced mother, but only if she was working by choice and if adequate child care was available, a finding similar to that of research on maternal employment in two-parent households (Hoffman, 1979). If the mother was working only because she felt she must, then she was likely to be dissatisfied and resentful, and her job only added to the role overload that she was experiencing as a single parent (Hetherington, 1981). Because many divorced women are not qualified for well-paying jobs, and because they may feel compelled to take the first job offered, whether they like it or not (Weitzman, 1981b), the result is often unsatisfactory and a source of stress for both mothers and children.

The problem of child care.—Finding adequate child care presents another difficulty for working women in general and divorced mothers in particular. Fifty percent of mothers who had children under 6 years of age were employed in 1982, and 59 percent of mothers with children 6–17 years old were employed (SCCYF, 1983). For divorced mothers, the percentages are even higher: 67.2 percent of those with children under 6 and 83.6 percent of those with children 6–17 years old. Comparable figures for 1970 are 29 percent and 43 percent, respectively, for all mothers, and 63.3 percent and 82.4 percent for divorced mothers. Clearly the percentage of working mothers is on the rise. However, finding adequate day-care services for children remains a common problem among working women. Many parents cannot afford high-quality child care, and even when they can, demand for the service is likely to be high and waiting lists can be long. The fear among many parents that day care may be detrimental to their child's development—particularly their concern that a normal mother-child relationship will deteriorate—adds to the working mother's role concerns.

This latter concern was especially prevalent in the 1950s and 1960s, when it was popularly believed that day care would prevent normal mother-child attachment bonds from forming (Etaugh, 1980). Since then, however, considerable research has been done on the effects of day care. In a review of recent day-care research, Belsky and Steinberg (1978) concluded that high-quality day care may either have no detrimental effects or may, in fact, have beneficial effects on the child. The idea that because of day care a maternal bond would not form does not seem to have been substantiated. Also, several studies have shown that as early as infancy children can form attachments to people who care for them, but that these attachments do no harm to the bond with the mother (Dunlop, 1981). Even when the child forms a stable attachment to another caretaker, the mother-child bond remains the strongest (Etaugh, 1980). Intellectual development has also been shown not to be hindered by day care and, in fact, seems to be stimulated by day care provided for children from impoverished homes (Dunlop, 1981; Etaugh, 1980).

Finally, day care may be beneficial for children's social development. Several researchers have found that children who have received day care interact more often with their peers, and are in fact more peer-oriented than adult-oriented (Dunlop, 1981). There is some evidence that children in day care are more aggressive than home-reared children; but there is also conflicting evidence that this is not so (Dunlop, 1981; Etaugh, 1980). In general, there is no evidence that day care produces ill effects on intellectual development or disrupts the mother-child bond, and it may result in an increase in peer interactions.

Although encouraging, the above results of child-care research may not be applicable to the day-care experiences of children in the divorced, single-parent family. Studies of day care have been done on children from intact homes, or have not specified the family structure of the samples, and it is possible that results would differ if the children from single-parent families were investigated. Perhaps an even bigger problem is that day-care research has dealt principally with the consequences of high-quality day care. Because many divorced mothers have only part-time, temporary, or low-paying jobs, and because child support is often inadequate, the day care that they can afford is usually temporary, inconsistent, and of low quality (Hetherington, 1981). Furthermore, because high-quality day care is expensive, the divorced mother who opts for it may have to work more hours to compensate for the added expense—a tremendous hardship that adds to the overload that she may already be experiencing.

Finding day care can be another problem. A nationwide survey of 18,000 students by the National Association of Elementary School Principals (1980) suggested that finding adequate day care can be "a logistical nightmare." A particular problem is emergency child care, which is often needed for times such as parent-teacher conferences or days when children are sick or have school vacations. Often the single parent has no one to call upon for short-notice help and loses a day or more of work.

To try to help single parents cope with the day-care problem, some schools have instituted programs for children both before and after regular school hours. These "latchkey" programs provide a familiar and convenient place for the child to stay when his or her parent is working. Unfortunately, few school systems have such programs. Low-cost day care is sometimes provided by other institutions, such as social-service agencies, religious organizations, and employers. However, day care at a reasonable price continues to be in short supply in most communities.

OTHER FINANCIAL OPTIONS

Other than working a potentially unsatisfactory job, the financially troubled divorced mother with minimal job skills is faced with three alternatives: obtaining support from kin or public sources, retraining, or remarriage.

Kin support.—Some divorced mothers may be able to obtain financial support from relatives (Brandwein et al., 1974; Weiss, 1975), but it is likely to be only temporary, and it may be problematic in other ways. The kin who lend or give money may feel entitled to have a voice in such matters as child rearing or household decisions. This may be particularly difficult for the divorced woman who yearns to make such decisions on her own, but who also has the need of her kin's financial assistance.

Welfare.—As many as 34 percent of divorced mothers are forced at some point to resort to welfare, or Aid to Financially Dependent Children (AFDC), to support their families (Bradbury, Dansinger, Smolensky, & Smolensky, 1979)—an alternative that certainly can create emotional and social stress. Not only are welfare benefits insufficient to raise a family's income above the poverty level, the process of obtaining welfare can be demeaning and fairly difficult (Weiss, 1975). The actual application is demoralizing and may be humiliating, for the woman must claim that she has no job skills and is unable to find work. Some states refuse to provide women with AFDC payments until they have tried every other possible avenue, including filing criminal claims against their former spouses for lack of support (Brandwein et al., 1974; Weitzman, 1981a). This obviously can be a very costly legal process and very upsetting, and can only increase any antagonism between former spouses (Weiss, 1975).

Just how unattractive the welfare alternative is can be seen in the results of the government's income-maintenance experiments. In general, it has been found that the higher the income provided by the government, the higher the rate of divorce (Hannan, Tuma, & Groeneveld, 1977). Apparently, for a number of spouses the welfare alternative is sufficiently unattractive to serve to keep them living together in an unhappy marriage.

Remarriage and retraining.—Yet another economic alternative that the divorced mother can pursue is remarriage. Three out of four divorced women remarry, a step that often involves financial as well as emotional incentives (Weitzman, 1981b). Yoder and Nichols (1980) surveyed 1,321 people across the United States and found that remarried people reported having a higher income than did divorced people. However, remarriage is not a solution for all divorced women. Some do not wish to remarry, considering one bad marriage to be enough. Other women may not find anyone they wish to marry. This may be a special problem for older women and for unemployed women, who do not have the work setting in which to meet men (Weitzman, 1981a). Finally, and most important, economic incentives are unlikely to be a sound basis for a second marriage, nor is it healthy for women to believe that the best way to support themselves economically is through remarriage.

A final alternative for financially troubled women with few job skills is retraining, such as by returning to school or by admission to a company training program. Retraining appears to be a desirable long-term solution because it may enable women to acquire higher-paying, more satisfactory jobs. Retraining can be expensive, however; it requires that a good deal of time be spent learning a trade with little, if any, income being produced during this time. Unfortunately, most divorced women with children cannot afford to go through this costly process, at least not without financial help. A way of obtaining that help has been suggested: require the former husband to provide increased financial aid in the first years following divorce in order to support the mother during a period of retraining (Weitzman, 1981b). In the long run, this alternative may not only help divorced women but also may be more attractive to men because it might shorten the duration of their financial obligations as the woman's income rises.

SUMMARY OF DIVORCE AND THE ECONOMIC SYSTEM

There can be little doubt that divorce has an adverse economic impact on all family members, but this impact appears to be greatest for divorced mothers and their children. Downward economic mobility appears to be an important source of some of the difficulties that children and mothers experience following a divorce, although research has not clearly distinguished the effects attributable to economic decline from those of other changes.

Economic difficulties may force the divorced mother to work longer hours or to seek her first job. The general state of the world of work for women, together with the stressors unique to the divorced mother, may make her work experience unsatisfactory and lead to feelings of role overload. The mother's problems with work can affect her children by adversely changing the terms of their emotional relationships, by diminishing contact between mother and children, and by imposing the need to use marginal child care.

Instead of entering the work force, the divorced mother may turn to welfare for financial assistance. Such assistance is meager, however, and the process of obtaining welfare can be demeaning to the applicant and disruptive to the relationship between former spouses. Remarriage is yet another economic alternative for the divorced mother, but the problems of a purely financial motive for remarriage are obvious. Finally, retraining for a better-paying job appears to be a workable solution for the economic plight of many divorced mothers that also should be attractive to divorced fathers. Because there is no established means for providing financial support to divorced mothers during a period of retraining, however, this alternative is pursued less frequently than it could be.

Divorce and Social and Mental Health Support Systems

Although, as was argued earlier, a parental divorce does not inevitably do permanent harm to children, divorcing and divorced families are clearly at risk, as we have seen, in that the familial, legal, and economic processes activated by marital dissolution can have a disruptive effect on children's development. Having reviewed the major stressors in the divorce process, we now examine various social and mental health supports that can prevent or ameliorate some of them.

INFORMAL SOCIAL SUPPORT NETWORKS

Informal social support networks, such as kin, friendship support, and self-help groups, appear to play an important role in helping members of a divorced family through their transition. They may be useful in providing "rap" sessions, helping to locate needed services, and offering various types of supportive day-to-day interactions.

Extended kin networks.—Relatives are one potentially important source of informal support. Patterns of kinship interaction change at the time of divorce and afterward (Anspach, 1976; Hetherington, 1978; Hetherington, Cox, & Cox, 1982; Spicer & Hampe, 1975). The kin of the noncustodial parent are seen less often by the custodial parent because the link between them, the former spouse, is now gone (Anspach, 1976; Spicer & Hampe, 1975). As long as there are children present, however, some lower level of contact is often maintained (Spicer & Hampe, 1975), and if contact with the noncustodial parent is frequent, so is the contact with the noncustodial kin (Furstenberg, 1982).

Contact with the relatives of the custodial parent, on the other hand, often increases following divorce (Hetherington, 1978; Spicer & Hampe, 1975). In general, divorced parents receive more kinship support than do married parents (Gibson, 1972), particularly in the areas of child care, companionship, and money (Price-Bonham & Balswick, 1980). Contact with the custodial mother's parents can be beneficial to the mother and child alike (Hetherington, 1978); grandfathers are especially useful in engaging in activities with the sons (Hetherington, Cox, & Cox, 1982).

Although the benefits may be substantial, it is important to recognize that kinship support systems can involve demands as well. That is, the divorced parent is unlikely to receive support without having to reciprocate. Children seem to do better when the grandmother shares in the household and child-rearing tasks (Kellam, Ensminger, & Turner, 1977). Yet when the divorced mother lives with her own mother, there can be conflict about a variety of issues. The divorced mother may feel infantilized and believe that her central role in child rearing is being appropriated. To some mothers, whatever the beneficial effects on the children, the grandmother's presence may not be worth the costs. Divorced mothers usually prefer to live alone if adequate resources are available (Hetherington et al., 1982).

Kin support would seem to hold particular benefits for low-income families (Hetherington, 1978). However, in one study, lower-income mothers reported significantly less satisfaction with the kin support they received than did middle-income mothers (Colletta, 1978). Because low-income mothers are likely to have greater needs and also to have low-income kin, their support system may have fewer resources to offer (Hetherington, 1978).

Divorced fathers rely on kinship support less often than do mothers (Defrain & Eirick, 1981). Many divorced fathers have no nearby kin, and those who do often feel that they should request child-care help only occasionally (Mendes, 1976). Interestingly, one researcher suggested that some fathers do not like to admit a need for help; "such behavior was inconsistent with the masculine ideals they held for themselves" (Mendes, 1976, p. 441).

In sum, although the custodial parent's kin are a potential source of support, their help is not always beneficial and can sometimes become another source of stress. Some research indicates that the kinship network has a favorable influence on adjustment (Anspach, 1976; Hetherington, 1978; Hetherington, Cox, & Cox, 1982; Price-Bonham & Balswick, 1980; Spicer & Hampe, 1975); other studies suggest that the opposite might be true (Kressel & Deutsch, 1977; Spanier & Hanson, 1981; Wilcox, 1981). It may be that kin supply useful support as long as they are not overly judgmental or condemning of the divorced parent.

Friends.—Friends can also be of significant help to a divorced parent. Social participation helps to lower stress and improve coping skills, and dating and having intimate sexual relations have been shown to aid adjustment and improve the divorced person's self-concept (Hetherington et al., 1982; Kiston & Rashke, 1981; Price-Bonham & Balswick, 1980). The problem is that for some divorcing persons, friendships that were established through their spouse dissipate following the separation (Hetherington et al., 1982; Wilcox, 1981). This loss leaves many people with few social resources following a divorce.

Establishing new social relations can be difficult. In one study divorced mothers complained that American culture designs social activities for couples rather than single adults. Some mothers, particularly those not working, felt like prisoners trapped in a child's world. Married friends were said to be supportive at first, but they rapidly withdrew their support (Hetherington, Cox, & Cox, 1978). Heterosexual relations were often problematic both practically and emotionally. Divorced mothers felt a pervasive desire for intimacy that was not satisfied by casual encounters.

Some men show a particularly high level of sexual activity and dating following divorce, but they often lack a sense of intimacy in their relationships (Gasser & Taylor, 1976; Hetherington et al., 1976). Other men report difficulty in dating altogether (Chang & Deinard, 1982), while still others consider "dating around" to be an important and satisfying new aspect of their life (Orthner, Brown, & Ferguson, 1976).

The social lives of men and women seem to differ in other ways after divorce. Chiriboga, Coho, Stein, and Roberts (1979) found that women are more likely than men to seek the aid of friends, and because friendships are helpful during times of stress, these authors concluded that divorced men are more likely to suffer greater emotional disturbances than divorced women. Contrary to this, Hetherington, Cox, and Cox (1982) found that whereas both men and women decreased the number of their old social contacts in the first 2 years after divorce, women developed fewer new social contacts. It was speculated that this difference may have had two primary causes: the fact that the mothers spent so much time involved in child care, and the fact that many social contacts are made with colleagues at work. Because more fathers than mothers work, they had more opportunities for social relations. The mothers, on the other hand, not only lost the friendship of their former spouse's work colleagues, they were unable to establish similar contacts of their own unless they were employed.

Self-help groups.—Some divorced parents report that self-help groups are useful in helping them develop new social networks. In aiding each other, parents in self-help groups can build their own social support networks (Camara, 1982). Ilgenfritz (1961) found that divorced and widowed mothers in a self-help group were able to share their problems. By the end of the program they felt comforted, less guilty about their children's plight, and more able to see their worries and tensions realistically. The formats of self-help groups vary, but Kessler (1978) found that structured self-help groups were more useful than unstructured ones: members of a structured group may get more answers to practical questions about visitation, dealing with in-laws, financial problems, and children's adjustment, whereas members of an unstructured group may simply listen to the plights of others in a similar situation.

   Familial support.—It makes intuitive sense that if a mother is able to establish rewarding relations outside the home, she will be better prepared to care for children and to help them cope with their situation. For many mothers divorce can be such a "growth experience," resulting in an increased sense of competence and independence. However, it is possible to get overinvolved in personal growth; Hetherington (1981), for example, described an "egocentric, self-fulfilling mother" who gained her sense of well-being at the expense of her children. At the opposite extreme, children can serve as substitutes for the friends that parents often lose after a divorce. It is not unusual for the custodial parent and the child to form a particularly close bond, often resulting in a "friend/confidant" relation (Kurdek, 1981; Weiss, 1979a). However desirable open communication between parent and child is, the young child may be overwhelmed if burdened with the mother's concerns about such things as finances, sex, and loneliness. For children who do not have the competency or the resources to deal with such concerns, the emotional burden may have serious consequences.

   Possibly the most beneficial source of support for single parents during the transition of divorce is the former spouse. Ironically, it seems to be important for people who could not get along in marriage to be able to communicate after divorce. As noted earlier, children from families with little postdivorce conflict are better adjusted, and the divorcing parents' own emotional well-being is also strongly related to how much they are in agreement (Hetherington, Cox, & Cox, 1982). Unfortunately, although 1 year after the divorce mothers and fathers feel considerable ambivalence about whether getting a divorce had been the right decision, relations with the former spouse often are characterized by conflict (Hetherington et al., 1979).

   Social support for children.—In addition to the support gained from close family relations, friends can also be an important support for children. Peers provide information for each other and give each other a sense of identity and of belonging to a group. Such support is especially valuable to children in distress, who need to know that, despite their troubles and feelings that they are different from the other children, they still can be accepted by their friends. It has been suggested that school-age children, especially those 7–12 years old, whose parents divorce often avoid their friends and classmates because they feel isolated and different (Wallerstein & Kelly, 1980). Such children thus abandon a social support system that can help them cope with their distress.

Certain children are better able than others to maintain friendships when distressed; for example, girls seem to find it easier than boys to gain support from parents, teachers, and peers (Hetherington, Cox, & Cox, 1982). This pattern may be due, in part, to a stereotypical belief that girls are less able to cope with difficulties and are in need of more assistance than are boys. However, under the stress of parental separation and divorce, many boys exhibit a particularly obnoxious combination of dependency, demandingness, noncompliance, and aggression that may drive friends away. After a time, these behaviors diminish, but peers and adults continue to react to boys unfavorably. Thus, because of their initial behavior, boys may continue to receive less social support than girls.

Schools have the potential to facilitate peer support for children from divorced families. The teacher, for example, can play the important role of an adult "who cares" (National Association of Elementary School Principals, 1980). Furthermore, at a time when the child's home life is in disarray, the school can provide a structured and predictable environment in which the child can maintain some order in his or her daily life (Hetherington, 1981). The more stable and supportive the school environment, the better the child's adjustment (Guidubaldi et al., 1983). The same characteristics of home life that are associated with favorable outcomes for children from divorced families apply to schools: structure, predictability, firm control, warmth, responsiveness, and expectations of responsible behavior (Hetherington et al., 1982).

Self-help groups may be useful to children going through a parental divorce (Kurdek, 1981), and the National Association of Elementary School Principals (1980) has similarly suggested that the schools provide peer counseling or "rap sessions" for these children. If begun early enough, group intervention may prevent the feelings of shame that can alienate children of divorce from social relations. Bringing children of divorce together can help each child to realize that he or she is not odd or alone, that there are others who share similar experiences. Children also get an opportunity to share their secrets, fears, and coping strategies with peers.

Although there are very few data on the effectiveness of support groups for children, some anecdotal information is available. Guerney and Jordan (1978) described a program whose goal was to help children see their problems realistically, learn how to solve divorce-specific problems, and feel good about themselves. The nine children in the group felt that it had been helpful in increasing their understanding of divorce and their own reactions to it, and the investigators expect that the demand for the program will increase as it becomes more widely known.

Ironically, the increased incidence of divorce in recent years may have a beneficial effect in that children will gain increased support from their social relations. As divorce becomes more common, children of divorce are less likely to feel different from the norm because the norm will have changed. The subgroup of peers with whom they can identify and conform will have enlarged.

MENTAL HEALTH INTERVENTIONS

Formal mental health intervention also can provide divorced parents with emotional support when they need it. Preventive educational programs and mental health treatments offer divorced men and women and their children a variety of resources to turn to for aid.

Interventions for parents.—Many divorced parents seek mental health intervention. Bloom, Asher, and White (1978) found that, like their children, divorced and separated parents are overrepresented in samples of psychiatric patients, whereas married people are underrepresented. Also, compared to those who are married or have never married, divorced people are three times more likely to be involved in auto accidents and are more often physically ill (Bloom, Asher, & White, 1978). Both for their own sake and because the child's health is related to the custodial parent's own adjustment (Hetherington et al., 1982), mental health services designed specifically to help divorced adults can be beneficial. Particularly important are services designed to prevent divorce distress and treatment programs that are sensitive to the divorced parent's experiences and problems.

Intervention is most effective when it comes before problems arise. Because many divorced parents have unrealistic expectations about what their life will be like, educational programs can be especially helpful preventive tools. In one such program, parents discussed their general experiences and problems in group sessions (Camara, 1982). The meetings, which operated in an instructional mode, were meant to help family members understand their new situation and to help them develop skills necessary for adapting to present or impending changes. Other types of educational and preventive programs are academic counseling for those who wish to return to school (Kurdek, 1981) and vocational, financial, and employment counseling (Wallerstein & Kelly, 1980). These latter programs can be particularly helpful for parents who have been out of the job market for many years, and they can help divorced persons deal with both economic problems and their emotional consequences.

The court system often provides support services in one form or another to the divorcing couple. Many people, because they perceive the divorce process as a legal one, will speak to a lawyer rather than a therapist (Kressel, Lopez-Morillas, Weinglass, & Deutsch, 1978). But because lawyers are not trained to solve the psychological problems of the marriage breakdown, it has been suggested that this can be an expensive and not very useful solution (Shipman, 1977). As an alternative, some courts require that a couple see a counselor provided by the court before they may file for divorce. Often, however, the interview with the counselor is simply a matter of form rather than a meaningful way of gaining emotional support (Kaslow, 1981).

Camara (1982) has reviewed mental health intervention programs that aim at the treatment of divorce distress. Most programs are of a fixed, short duration; as such, they treat divorce as a crisis rather than as a long-term, gradual process. These programs have common goals: to reduce distress, improve parenting skills, develop ways of coping with the changes in relations between family members, provide support resources, improve family functioning, and help teach families to cope with other issues peculiar to divorce and remarriage. It is difficult to evaluate the intervention programs because few studies of their effectiveness have employed random assignment or used suitable assessment measures. The few programs that rate themselves as "positive" do so merely on the basis of client reports (Camara, 1982). It may be that intervention programs greatly facilitate divorce adjustment, but further research is necessary to demonstrate their efficacy.

Bloom and his colleagues (Bloom, Hodges, & Caldwell, 1982) conducted one of the few careful investigations of various forms of mental health interventions for divorcing families. Recently separated people were randomly assigned to different forms of intervention, each focusing on a different problem. The focuses for each of the five intervention groups were: (1) employment problems, (2) legal and financial issues, (3) parenting concerns, (4) housing and homemaking arrangements, and (5) social and emotional well-being. There was also a no-treatment control group. Six months after the separated persons had undergone a brief intervention in one of these areas, their adjustment was rated. In comparison to controls, members of the treatment groups were, as a whole, functioning better on measures of anxiety, fatigue, coping skills, and physical well-being. Interestingly, the five treatment groups differed little from one another on each measure, suggesting that the benefit of the treatment was general rather than specific to the targeted problem.

This last finding is consistent with the social support literature. A major benefit of therapy for divorced parents may well be the social support it provides. Although this interpretation suggests a useful benefit of therapeutic intervention, it also invites caution. Being socially isolated, divorced parents may come to depend heavily on their therapists, making termination of treatment difficult. Therapists need to be sure to build naturally occurring social supports into a treatment program (Wahler, 1980).

Interventions with children.—Mental health interventions with children may benefit them by helping to prevent and treat distress. However, few programs and fewer systematic evaluations have been described in the literature (Felner, Farber, & Primavera, 1980). Felner and his colleagues discuss one such program. The subjects were school-age children who had recently experienced a major stressful life event but who had not shown problematic behaviors in school. The children met twice a week for 6 weeks with nonprofessionals trained in crisis intervention techniques. Posttreatment ratings showed a reduction in anxiety and increased adaptive behavior. Unfortunately, this study did not make use of a comparison group, and it is possible that these children had already adapted adequately to the stressful event.

According to preliminary findings from another mental health program, the Divorce Adjustment Project (Stohlberg & Cullen, 1983), mothers and teachers report improvement in children who were in treatment. Teachers report that children in the treatment group have longer attention spans, and mothers report better communication with their children about issues related to the divorce, as well as more child-initiated discussions of the divorce. The results of other projects, however, indicate that individual intervention with children, particularly with children under age 10, is of little benefit (Kelly & Wallerstein, 1977; Suarez, Weston, & Hartstein, 1978).

Family therapy.—Many clinicians believe that family therapy may be more useful than individual or group therapy in treating children under stress from divorce, because family therapy involves working with the family as a unit, and it is within this entity that the dysfunctional divorce processes occur (Emery, 1982; Group for Advancement of Psychiatry, 1981; Kushner, 1965; Westman et al., 1970). Usually, marital and family therapists terminate therapy when parents decide to divorce, but this may be the most important time for treatment to proceed (Gurman & Kniskern, 1978). Indeed, conducting such therapy before the divorce takes place may prevent destructive processes from beginning. According to Kushner (1965), even if family treatment begins after the divorce, the absent parent should be included in therapy; doing so will inform the custodial parent that the other parent is a source of support for the child, will help the noncustodial parent to become a part of the child's life, and will enable the child finally to confront both parents and clarify the divorce process in his or her own mind.

Some authors, on the other hand, offer cautions about family therapy. If there is intense, uncontrolled conflict between the parents, then including the noncustodial parent in family therapy can be detrimental (Emery, 1982). In such cases, it is probably best to work with each parent separately, with or without the children, until family conflict is reduced (Derdeyn, in press). On a related theme, the suggestion that conflict is necessary and should be encouraged following a "civilized" divorce (Futterman, 1980) is thought by some to be particularly misguided because of the ill effects of parental conflict on children (Emery, 1982). Another caution is suggested about family therapy: if conflict is well enough contained for both parents to be included in the therapy, treatment should be brief in duration. Continuing such therapy for too long may encourage the child to expect a parental reconciliation, and the child may be badly hurt when this does not occur. Also, such frequent and intense contact may make it difficult for the parents to begin new lives separate from each other (Kaslow, 1981).

SUMMARY OF DIVORCE AND SOCIAL AND MENTAL HEALTH SUPPORT SYSTEMS

Support for divorced families in need of it can come from several sources in the community. Friends and relatives often provide invaluable economic, practical, and emotional support. Family members also can learn to cope with new, everyday problems through more formal educational programs. The courts may be useful in providing this education or in offering marriage or divorce counseling. Finally, mental health services and intervention programs focused on divorce-related concerns may help solve the emotional problems of some parents and children. However, because educational and treatment programs entail an expense both for the individual and the community, it would seem necessary that their usefulness be demonstrated by research before widespread implementation can be suggested.

CONCLUSION AND RECOMMENDATIONS FOR POLICY CHANGE

Perhaps the major point of conclusion to which the preceding discussion leads is the same one from which the discussion started: divorce is a process that leads to varied outcomes for different parents and children. Many divorced families encounter similar experiences, but they also bring to them a diversity of previous experiences and resources for coping with this difficult transition. It is the transactions between the members of divorced families as well as between family members and social institutions that determine the outcome of divorce. But concern for divorcing and divorced families must not be overstated lest the divorced, one-parent family be inappropriately labeled "sick" or "deviant."

SOCIAL POLICY GOALS

Although not inevitably of permanent harm, divorce is seldom innocuous either. Divorce is an area of family life that therefore merits the concern of policymakers. Using Bronfenbrenner's contextual model, Kurdek (1981) has argued that children's adjustment to divorce can be understood only within the context of the transactions occurring at four different levels of analysis: (1) the ontogenic system—the child's individual competencies; (2) the microsystem—family functioning and support systems; (3) the exosystem—the general environment in which the family functions; and (4) the macrosystem—broad cultural beliefs about family life. In general, social science research suggests that social policymakers would best serve children in divorcing and divorced families by instituting changes consistent with the following goals indicated by each of the four levels of analysis.

The macrosystem.—The public needs accurate information about the consequences of divorce for children rather than opinion, bias, and conjecture. Thus, research efforts need to continue. Researchers cannot ignore the importance of disseminating and interpreting their results to the general public as well as the scientific community. If researchers do not interpret their findings for the public, someone with less knowledge and perhaps less objectivity will. Along these lines, any interpretation that does not acknowledge the cultural and individual diversity of experiences and outcomes of divorce does the public a disservice. Given the diversity of children's outcomes following divorce, one message especially needs to be clearly communicated to parents: they have more control over the consequences of their divorce for their children than they probably realize. Whether the members of a divorced family share the same household or not, they remain a family, and how the family members relate will have no less of an impact on the children's development than in intact, two-parent families.

The exosystem.—Divorcing and divorced families benefit from support in a variety of spheres. Social support and more formal assistance in coping with the emotionally difficult transitions accompanying divorce can be quite helpful, particularly when intervention occurs early enough to be preventive. Psychological support can be augmented by services that help to ease legal and economic burdens. Historically, there has been concern that the state not provide too much support for divorced families, as this might encourage marital dissolution. Irrespective of the moral implications of such a position, it makes life more difficult for people who divorce. Given that the rate of divorce in the United States is the highest in the world, higher than in countries with lower "exit costs," and given that research indicates that children are better off in a happy one-parent home than in an unhappy two-parent household, the promotion of policies that push families to stay together is problematic at a practical level. This is not to say that the intact family should not receive support as well. Rather, policies should not intentionally favor one family form over the other.

The microsystem.—It is important to continue to view all members of the divorced family as a family. The child's development continues to be affected by the relationships between the parents, between the children and *both* parents, and between the divorced family and other kin. Divorced family members and those who provide support to them need to recognize that these relationships continue despite the discontinuity in household arrangements. Furthermore, policymakers must be sensitive to the need to insure that legal and economic policies that are designed to aid the divorced family minimally disrupt healthy family relationships. The impact of broader social policies on family *process*, not merely family structure, is an area that merits careful investigation.

The ontogenic system.—Although social policy probably exerts minimal control over the individual competencies that influence how divorce affects children, the divorce process and its outcomes can be expected to differ for children of various cultural backgrounds, ages, sex, areas of vulnerability, and resources. Research is insufficient at present to suggest what policies will best serve what children. Perhaps the most important contribution that policymakers can make to this area at present is to continue to support research on ontogenic influences in children's adjustment to divorce.

SOCIAL POLICY RECOMMENDATIONS

Research on children and divorce exhibits numerous limitations. At this point, it would be easy to conclude that divorce researchers are not yet ready to propose changes in social policy and to retreat into a litany of concerns about the methodological inadequacy of the current literature and the paucity of generalizations that it supports. Such concerns are far from being minor and certainly merit the careful attention of researchers. However, so important is the topic that the social policy implications of the current, admittedly flawed, body of research cannot be ignored. Although the research findings do not support unequivocal interpretations, and perhaps never will, we offer the following recommendations for policy change.

THE EMOTIONAL DIVORCE

1. The divorce process is sufficiently complex that therapists need special sensitivity to and training in the unique emotional, social, legal, and economic characteristics of divorcing and divorced families. There must be further development of services targeted specifically to the needs of divorced family members, who currently constitute large proportions of both the child and adult treatment populations. Mental health services need to be particularly sensitive to economic hardship in this population, and fees for services need to be adjusted accordingly.

2. Although individual therapy may sometimes be the treatment of choice, a family conceptualization is needed in all psychological interventions, and family therapy may prove to be the superior treatment for most divorced parents and children. Therapists must adopt the view that the family is defined by patterns of relations, not by a shared household.

3. The earlier the intervention occurs in the divorce process, the greater the potential for benefit. Couples therapy should not end with the decision to separate, for conciliation is still possible even when reconciliation is not. Lawyers in private practice and court personnel need to be fully aware of the diverse emotional aspects of divorce in order that they can assist in this area or refer their clients to others who can provide the necessary assistance. Schools, too, have the opportunity to participate in preventive intervention. School psychologists need to be allowed to move beyond their traditional assessment and individual therapy focuses in order that they may intervene with families who desire their aid. Although some parents may be reluctant to have school personnel become involved in their family lives, schools can offer them something else: a convenient, community-based physical plant that can be used by outside professional and lay personnel in providing educational and support services to the divorced family.

4. Community agencies such as mental health facilities, schools, and courts should encourage and support self-help groups because of the unique benefits they offer for building social support networks at minimal cost. Although same-sex support groups are likely to be of most benefit to some, opposite-sex groups should also be available in order that the perspective of each sex can be conveyed to the other.

5. Research needs to be conducted on traditional and innovative therapies offered to divorced families. Treatment-outcome research is practically nonexistent to date and should be given a top priority.

THE LEGAL DIVORCE

1. Divorce litigation is often expensive, stressful for children and families, and frustrating to judges and attorneys. Divorce mediation is a process that holds promise as an alternative to litigation, and it should be pursued by courts, attorneys, and mental health professionals. Mediation laws and programs may well cast a less adversarial shadow over out-of-court negotiations, and alter the way divorce attorneys practice.

2. A less adversarial stance by lawyers who negotiate out-of-court settlements may well benefit families. Policymakers can affect these negotiations by developing guidelines for attorneys acting in divorce disputes. The attorney's obligation to serve the best interests of the client may be in conflict with what is in the best interests of the child in divorce cases, and what constitutes proper conduct for attorneys in this situation needs clarification.

3. Since not every divorce dispute can be settled out of court or in mediation, the custody hearing is likely to remain intact. Any reasonable reduction in the indeterminacy of divorce custody law would be of benefit for the custody hearing. Unfortunately, there is no social science research that clearly provides grounds for suggesting more determinate guidelines. Such guidelines might issue from further investigation into such topics as the differential adjustment of children in the custody of same-sex versus opposite-sex parents. At present, the judiciary does well to solicit input from a variety of sources in weighing custody decisions.

4. Indeterminate statutes provide wide discretion to the judiciary that opens the door for bias. It seems reasonable to have courts provide the public with information on the yearly group statistics on custody decisions as a means of informing the public and protecting against systematic bias in the exercise of judicial discretion.

5. Joint custody is a useful statutory option that should be available to parents who elect it, but it is not the answer to the indeterminacy problem and should not be imposed on unwilling parents.

6. In general, visitation agreements in sole-custody arrangements should allow for liberal noncustodial parent-child contact. Especially in cases where parental acrimony is high, the terms of visitation should be clearly delineated.

7. From the perspective of both parents, it seems defensible to legally tie visitation rights to the payment of support so that one parent legally can cease to cooperate if the other parent is not in compliance with

court orders. Exceptions to this principle would include sudden, unexpected unemployment and perhaps other circumscribed situations.

8. Self-starting systems accompanied by wage assignments or other strong penalties for nonpayment of child support not only increase compliance but relieve the family of the need to initiate a complaint. Being automatic, such systems limit the personal costs to the custodial parent, and may create less family conflict than would litigation initiated by the custodial parent. And given that self-starting systems can also reduce public costs, they should be implemented and used.

9. Given the complexities of divorce law, particularly for divorcing parents who are already stressed and preoccupied, simplification of the laws and adoption of uniform legal standards by the different states should be encouraged.

THE ECONOMIC DIVORCE

1. Establishing the economic independence of the divorced mother is vital. Property and short-term alimony awards that allow those without job skills to obtain training should be encouraged.

2. Continued efforts to eliminate sex discrimination in the work force will benefit women in general and divorced women and their children in particular.

3. Child care continues to be a tremendous need not only for divorced parents but also for married parents. Low-cost child care housed in public institutions such as schools and churches should be encouraged, but there should also be economic incentives for employers to provide employee child care.

4. Although public assistance will continue to be needed, economic support services that allow the divorced mother to reenter the work force are likely to have long-term benefits. Higher initial public expenditures that subsidize, for example, career counseling and retraining programs may lead to lower long-term public costs and improved family functioning.

CONCLUSION

This is an ambitious list of changes, and some of the suggestions are admittedly general and in need of greater specifity. The present purpose, however, has been to discuss the relationship of divorce processes and policy initiatives. Although divorce will seldom be an easy process, implementation of the above list of recommendations would alter and should ease the experience of divorce for parents and for children. Social policy in regard to children and divorce has changed rapidly in the last 20 years, but there is still considerable room for improvement. It is hoped that the above discussion will help to open a dialogue among the members of the various professions who play a role in helping children and parents through the difficult divorce transitions.

REFERENCES

Abarbanel, A. Shared parenting after separation: A study of joint custody. *American Journal of Orthopsychiatry*, 1979, **49**, 320–329.

Ahrenfeldt v. Ahrenfeldt, 1 Hoff Ch. 497 (NY 1840).

Alexander, S. J. Protecting the child's right in custody cases. *Family Coordinator*, 1977, **26**, 377–385.

Anspach, D. F. Kinship and divorce. *Journal of Marriage and the Family*, 1976, **38**, 323–330.

Anthony, E. J. Children at risk from divorce: A review. In E. J. Anthony & C. Koupernick (Eds.), *The child in his family* (Vol. 3). New York: Wiley, 1974.

Atkeson, B. M., Forehand, R. L., & Rickard, K. M. The effects of divorce on children. In B. B. Lahey & A. E. Kazdin (Eds.), *Advances in clinical child psychology*. New York: Plenum, 1982.

Bahr, S. J. An evaluation of court mediation for divorce cases with children. *Journal of Family Issues*, 1981, **2**, 39–60.

Bane, M. J. *Here to stay: American families in the twentieth century.* New York: Basic, 1976.

Bane, M. J. Marital disruption and the lives of children. In G. Levinger & O. C. Moles (Eds.), *Divorce and separation: Context, causes, and consequences*. New York: Basic, 1979.

Becker, W. C. Consequences of different kinds of parental discipline. In M. L. Hoffman & L. W. Hoffman (Eds.), *Review of child development research*. New York: Russell Sage, 1964.

Becker, W. C., Peterson, D. R., Luria, Z., Shoemaker, D. S., & Quay, H. C. Relations of factors derived from parent interview rating to behavior problems of five-year-olds. *Child Development*, 1962, **33**, 509–535.

Belsky, J., & Steinberg, L. D. The effects of day care: A critical review. *Child Development*, 1978, **49**, 929–949.

Bernard, J. *The future of marriage*. New York: Bantam, 1972.

Biller, H. B. Father absence, maternal encouragement, and sex-role development in kindergarten boys. *Child Development*, 1969, **40**, 539–546.

Biller, H. B., & Bahm, R. M. Father absence, perceived maternal behavior, and masculinity of self-concept among junior high school boys. *Developmental Psychology*, 1971, **4**, 178–181.

Block, J. H., Block, J., & Morrison, A. Parental agreement-disagreement on child-rearing orientations and gender-related personality correlates in children. *Child Development*, 1981, **52**, 965–974.

Bloom, B. L., Asher, S. J., & White, S. W. Marital disruption as a stressor: A review and analysis. *Psychological Bulletin*, 1978, **85**, 867–894.

Bloom, B. L., Hodges, W. F., & Caldwell, R. A. A preventive intervention program for the newly separated: Initial evaluation. *American Journal of Community Psychology*, 1982, **10**, 251–264.

Bodenheimer, B. M. Progress under the uniform child jurisdiction act and remaining problems: Punitive decrees, joint custody, and excessive modifications. *California Law Review*, 1977, **65**, 978–1014.

Bowlby, J. *Maternal care and mental health: A report prepared on behalf of the World Health Organization as a contribution to the United Nations programme for the welfare of homeless children.* Bulletin of the World Health Organization, Geneva, 1951.

Bowlby, J. *Attachment and loss.* (Vol. **2**): *Separation.* New York: Basic, 1973.

Bradbury, K., Dansinger, S., Smolensky, E., & Smolensky, P. Public assistance, female headship, and economic well-being. *Journal of Marriage and the Family*, 1979, **41**, 519–535.

Brandwein, R. A., Brown, C. A., & Fox, E. M. Women and children last: The social situation of divorced mothers and their families. *Journal of Marriage and the Family*, 1974, **36**, 498–514.

Brown, P., Felton, B. J., Whiteman, V., & Manela, R. Attachment and distress following marital separation. *Journal of Divorce*, 1980, **3**, 303–317.

Brown, R. C. The custody of children. *Indiana Law Journal*, 1926, **2**, 325–330.

Bumpass, L. L., & Rindfuss, R. *Children's experience of marital disruption* (Discussion Paper No. 512–78). Madison: Institute for Research on Poverty, University of Wisconsin, 1978.

Burger, W. B. Isn't there a better way? *American Bar Association Journal*, 1982, **68**, 274–277.

Burgess, R. L. *Project Interact: A study of patterns of interaction in abusive, neglectful and control families* (Final Report). Washington, D.C.: National Center on Child Abuse and Neglect, 1978.

Cadoret, R. J., & Cain, C. Sex differences in predictors of antisocial behavior in adoptees. *Archives of General Psychiatry*, 1980, **37**, 1171–1175.

Camara, K. A. *Intervention and service programs for families of divorce and remarriage.* Paper prepared for an ad hoc meeting by the Committee on Child Development Research and Public Policy of the National Research Council, 1982.

Carlsmith, L. Effect of early father absence on scholastic aptitude. *Harvard Educational Review*, 1964, **34**, 3–21.

Chambers, D. *Making fathers pay: The enforcement of child support.* Chicago: University of Chicago Press, 1979.

Chang, P., & Deinard, A. S. Single-father caretakers: Demographic characteristics and adjustment processes. *American Journal of Orthopsychiatry*, 1982, **52**, 236–242.

Cherlin, A. J. The effect of children on marital dissolution. *Demography*, 1977, **14**, 265–272.

Cherlin, A. J. *Marriage, divorce, remarriage.* Cambridge, Mass.: Harvard University Press, 1981.

Chess, S., Thomas, A., Korn, S., Mittelman, M., & Cohen, J. Early parental attitudes, divorce and separation, and young adult outcome: Findings of a longitudinal study. *Journal of the American Academy of Child Psychiatry*, 1983, **22**, 47–51.

Chiriboga, D. A., Coho, A., Stein, J. A., & Roberts, J. Divorce, stress and social supports: A study in helpseeking behavior. *Journal of Divorce*, 1979, **3**, 121–135.

Clark, H. *Law of domestic relations.* St. Paul, Minn.: West, 1968.

Clarke-Stewart, A. *Child care in the family.* New York: Academic Press, 1977.

Clingempeel, W. G., & Reppucci, N. D. Joint custody after divorce: Major issues and goals for research. *Psychological Bulletin*, 1982, **91**, 102–127.

Colletta, N. D. *Divorced mothers at two income levels: Stress, support and child-rearing practices.* Unpublished doctoral dissertation, Cornell University, 1978.

Colletta, N. D. The impact of divorce: Father absence or poverty? *Journal of Divorce*, 1979, **3**, 27–36. (a)

Colletta, N. D. Support systems after divorce: Incidence and impact. *Journal of Marriage and the Family*, 1979, **41**, 837–846. (b)

Commonwealth of Pennsylvania v. Addicks and Wife. *Binney's Pennsylvania Reports*, 1813, **5**, 520–522.

Coogler, O. J. Changing the lawyer's role in matrimonial practice. *Conciliation Courts Review*, 1977, **15**, 1–12.

Coogler, O. J., Weber, R. E., & McHenry, P. C. Divorce mediation: A means of facilitating divorce and adjustment. *Family Coordinator*, 1979, **29**, 255–259.

Cox, M. J. T., & Cease, L. Joint custody, what does it mean? How does it work? *Family Advocate*, Summer 1978, pp. 10–13.

Defrain, J., & Eirick, R. Coping as divorced single parents: A comparative study of fathers and mothers. *Family Relations*, 1981, **30**, 265–273.

Derdeyn, A. P. Child custody contests in historical perspective. *American Journal of Psychiatry*, 1976, **133**, 1369–1376.

Derdeyn, A. P. The family and divorce: Issues of parental anger. *Journal of the American Academy of Child Psychiatry*, in press.

Derdeyn, A. P., & Scott, E. *Joint custody.* Unpublished manuscript, University of Virginia, 1983.

Doyle, P. M., & Caron, W. A. Contested custody intervention: An empirical assessment. In D. H. Olson, M. Cleveland, P. M. Doyle, M. F. Rockcastle, B. Robinson, R. Reimer, J. Minton, W. Caron, & S. Cohen, *Child custody: Literature review and alternative approaches.* St. Paul, Minn.: Hennepin County Domestic Relations Division, 1979.

Duncon, G. J., & Morgan, J. N. Young children and "other"family members. In G. J. Duncon & J. N. Morgan (Eds.), *Five thousand American families—patterns of economic progress* (Vol. 4). Ann Arbor: University of Michigan, 1976.

Dunlop, K. H. Maternal employment and child care. *Professional Psychology*, 1981, **12**, 67–75.

Emery, R. E. Interparental conflict and the children of discord and divorce. *Psychological Bulletin*, 1982, **92**, 310–330.

Emery, R. E. *Divorce mediation and child custody dispute resolution.* Paper presented at the annual meeting of the American Psychological Association, Anaheim, Calif., August 1983.

Emery, R. E., & O'Leary, K. D. Children's perceptions of marital discord and behavior problems of boys and girls. *Journal of Abnormal Child Psychology*, 1982, **10**, 11–24.

Espenshade, T. J. The economic consequences of divorce. *Journal of Marriage and the Family*, 1979, **41**, 615–625.

Etaugh, C. Effects of nonmaternal care on children: Research evidence and popular views. *American Psychologist*, 1980, **35**, 309–319.

Feldman, S. S., Biringen, Z. C., & Nash, S. C. Fluctuations of sex-related self-attributions as a function of stage of family life cycle. *Developmental Psychology*, 1981, **17**, 24–35.

Felner, R. D., Farber, S. S., & Primavera, J. Children of divorce, stressful life events and transitions: A framework for preventive efforts. In R. H. Price, R. F. Ketterer, B. C. Bader, & J. Monahan (Eds.), *Prevention in community mental health: Research policy and practice* (Vol. 1). Beverly Hills, Calif.: Sage, 1980.

Felner, R. D., Stohlberg, A., & Cowen, E. L. Crisis events and school mental health referral patterns of young children. *Journal of Consulting and Clinical Psychology*, 1975, **43**, 305–310.

Ferri, E. *Growing up in a one-parent family: A long-term study of child development.* London: National Foundation for Educational Research, 1976.

Finlay v. Finlay, 148 N.E. 624 (N.Y. 1925).

Folberg, H. J., & Graham, M. Joint custody of children following divorce. *University of California at Davis Law Review*, 1979, **12**, 523–581.

Foster, H. H., & Freed, D. J. Divorce reform: Breaks on breakdown. *Journal of Family Law*, 1973–74, **13**, 443–493.

Framo, J. L. Personal reflections of a therapist. *Journal of Marriage and Family Counseling*, 1975, **1**, 15–28.

Freed, D. J., & Foster, H. H. Divorce in the fifty states: An overview. *Family Law Quarterly*, 1981, **14**, 229–241.

Fulton, J. A. *Factors related to parental assessment of the effect of divorce on children: A research project.* Paper presented at the National Institute of Mental Health Conference on Divorce, Washington, D.C., 1978.

Fulton, J. A. Parental reports of children's post-divorce adjustment. *Journal of Social Issues*, 1979, **35**, 126–139.

Furstenberg, F. F. *Remarriage.* Report to Planning Committee on Divorce, National Academy of Science Meeting, Stanford, Calif., 1982.

Furstenberg, F. F., Spanier, G. B., & Rothschild, N. *Patterns in parenting in the transition from divorce to remarriage.* Paper presented at the NICHD, NIMH, and NIA Conference on Women: A Developmental Perspective, Washington, D.C., 1980.

Furstenberg, F. F., Spanier, G. B., & Rothschild, N. Patterns of parenting in the transition from divorce to remarriage. In P. W. Berman & E. R. Ramey (Eds.), *Women: A developmental perspective* (NIH Publication No. 82-2298). Washington, D.C.: NIH, 1982.

Futterman, E. A. After the "civilized" divorce. *Journal of the American Academy of Child Psychiatry*, 1980, **19**, 525–530.

Gardner, H. *Developmental psychology: An introduction.* Boston: Little, Brown, 1978.

Gardner, R. A. *Family evaluation in child custody litigation.* Cresskill, N.J.: Creative Therapeutics, 1982.

Gasser, R. D., & Taylor, C. M. Role adjustment of single parent fathers with dependent children. *Family Coordinator*, 1976, **25**, 397–401.

Gersick, K. E. Fathers by choice: Divorced men who receive custody of their children. In G. Levinger & O. C. Moles (Eds.), *Divorce and separation.* New York: Basic, 1979.

Gibson, G. Kin family network: Overheralded structure in past conceptualizations of family functioning. *Journal of Marriage and the Family*, 1972, **34**, 13–23.

Gibson, H. B. Early delinquency in relation to broken homes. *Journal of Child Psychology and Psychiatry*, 1969, **10**, 105–204.

Glendon, M. A. Modern marriage law and its underlying assumptions: The new marriage and the new property. *Family Law Quarterly*, 1980, **13**, 441–460.

Glick, P. C. Children of divorced parents in demographic perspective. *Journal of Social Issues*, 1979, **35**, 112–125.

Glick, P. C., & Norton, A. J. Marrying, divorcing, and living together in the U.S. today. *Population Bulletin*, 1978, **32**, 3–38.

Glueck, S., & Glueck, E. *Unraveling juvenile delinquency.* Cambridge, Mass.: Harvard University Press, 1950.

Goldstein, J., Freud, A., & Solnit, A. *Beyond the best interests of the child.* New York: Free Press, 1973.

Gregory, I. Anterospective data following childhood loss of a parent: Delinquency and high school dropout. *Archives of General Psychiatry*, 1965, **13**, 99–109.

Grollman, E. A. *Explaining divorce to children.* Boston: Beacon, 1969.

Group for Advancement of Psychiatry. *Divorce, child custody and the family.* New York: Mental Health Materials Center, 1981.

Guerney, L., & Jordan, L. Children of divorce—a community support group. *Journal of Divorce*, 1978, **2**, 283–294.

Guidubaldi, J., Perry, J. D., & Cleminshaw, H. K. *The legacy of parental divorce: A* nationwide study of family status and selected mediating variables on children's academic and social competencies. Unpublished manuscript, Kent State University, 1983.

Gurman, A. S., & Kniskern, D. P. Research on marital and family therapy: Progress, perspective, and prospect. In S. L. Garfield & A. E. Bergin (Eds.), *Handbook of psychotherapy and behavior change* (2d ed.). New York: Wiley, 1978.

Gurman, A. S., & Kniskern, D. P. (Eds.). *Handbook of family therapy.* New York: Brunner/ Mazel, 1981.

Halem, L. C. *Divorce reform.* New York: Free Press, 1981.

Hannan, M. T., Tuma, N. B., & Groeneveld, L. P. Income and marital events: Evidence from an income-maintenance experiment. *American Journal of Sociology*, 1977, **82**, 1186–1211.

Haynes, J. M. Divorce mediator: A new role. *Social Work*, 1978, **23**, 5–9.

Haynes, J. M. *Divorce mediation.* New York: Springer, 1981.

Herzog, E., & Sudia, C. E. Children in fatherless families. In B. Caldwell & H. Ricciuti (Eds.), *Review of child development research* (Vol. 3). Chicago: University of Chicago Press, 1973.

Hess, R. D., & Camara, K. A. Post-divorce relationships as mediating factors in the consequences of divorce for children. *Journal of Social Issues*, 1979, **35**, 79–96.

Hess, R. D., Shipman, V. C., Brophy, J. E., & Bear, R. M. *The cognitive environments of urban preschool children.* Chicago: Graduate School of Education, University of Chicago, 1968. (ERIC Document Reproduction Service No. ED 039 264)

Hess, R. D., Shipman, V. C., Brophy, J. E., Bear, R. M., & Adelberger, A. B. *The cognitive environments of urban preschool children: Follow-up phase.* Chicago: Graduate School of Education, University of Chicago, 1969. (ERIC Document Reproduction Service No. Ed 089 270)

Hetherington, E. M. Effects of parental absence on personality development in adolescent daughters. *Developmental Psychology*, 1972, **7**, 313–326.

Hetherington, E. M. Stress and coping in divorce: A focus on women. In J. Gullahorn (Ed.), *Psychology and transition.* New York: Winston, 1978.

Hetherington, E. M. Children and divorce. In R. Henderson (Ed.), *Parent-child interaction: Theory, research, and prospect.* New York: Academic Press, 1981.

Hetherington, E. M., & Camara, K. A. Families in transition: The process of dissolution and reconstitution. In R. Parke (Ed.), *Review of child development research* (Vol. 7). Chicago: University of Chicago Press, 1984.

Hetherington, E. M., Camara, K. A., & Featherman, D. L. Achievement and intellectual functioning of children in one-parent households. In J. Spence (Ed.), *Assessing achievement.* New York: Freeman, 1981.

Hetherington, E. M., Cox, M., & Cox, R. Divorced fathers. *Family Coordinator*, 1976, **25**, 417–428.

Hetherington, E. M., Cox, M., & Cox, R. The aftermath of divorce. In J. H. Stevens & M. Matthews (Eds.), *Mother-child, father-child relations.* Washington, D.C.: National Association for the Education of Young Children, 1978.

Hetherington, E. M., Cox, M., & Cox R. Effects of divorce on parents and children. In M. Lamb (Ed.), *Nontraditional families.* Hillsdale, N.J.: Erlbaum, 1982.

Hodges, W. F., Wechsler, R. C., & Ballentine, C. Divorce and the preschool child: Cumulative stress. *Journal of Divorce*, 1979, **3**, 55–68.

Hoffman, L. W. Changes in family roles, socialization, and sex differences. *American Psychologist*, 1977, **32**, 644–657.

Hoffman, L. W. Maternal employment: 1979. *American Psychologist*, 1979, **34**, 859–865.

Ilgenfritz, M. P. Mothers on their own—widows and divorcees. *Marriage and Family Living*, 1961, **23**, 38–41.

Irving, H., Bohm, P., MacDonald, G., & Benjamin, M. *A comparative analysis of two family court services: An exploratory study of conciliation counseling.* Toronto: Welfare Grants Directorate, Department of Mental Health and Welfare, and the Ontario Ministry of the Attorney General, 1979.

Jacobson, D. S. The impact of marital separation/divorce on children, II: Interpersonal hostility and child adjustment. *Journal of Divorce*, 1978, **2**, 3–19.

Jencks, C. *Inequality: A reassessment of the effect of family and schooling in America.* New York: Harper, 1972.

Jenkins, R. L. Maxims in child custody cases. *Family Coordinator*, 1977, **26**, 385–390.

Kalter, N. Children of divorce in an outpatient psychiatric population. *American Journal of Orthopsychiatry*, 1977, **47**, 40–51.

Kalter, N., & Rembar, J. The significance of a child's age at the time of parental divorce. *American Journal of Orthopsychiatry*, 1981, **51**, 85–100.

Kaslow, F. W. Divorce and divorce therapy. In A. S. Gurman & D. P. Kniskern (Eds.), *Handbook of family therapy.* New York: Brunner/Mazel, 1981.

Kellam, S. G., Ensminger, M. A., & Turner, J. T. Family structure and the mental health of children. *Archives of General Psychiatry*, 1977, **34**, 1012–1022.

Kelly, J. B. *Children and parents in the midst of divorce: Major factors contributing to differential response.* Paper presented at the National Institute of Mental Health Conference on Divorce, Washington, D.C., February 1978.

Kelly, J. B., & Wallerstein, J. The effects of parental divorce: Experiences of the child in early latency. *American Journal of Orthopsychiatry*, 1975, **46**, 20–32.

Kelly, J. B., & Wallerstein, J. S. The effects of parental divorce, I: The experience of the child in early latency, II: The experience of the child in late latency. *American Journal of Orthopsychiatry*, 1976, **45**, 253–265.

Kelly, J. B., & Wallerstein, J. Brief interventions with children in divorcing families. *American Journal of Orthopsychiatry*, 1977, **47**, 23–29.

Kessler, S. Building skills in divorce adjustment groups. *Journal of Divorce*, 1978, **2**, 209–216.

Kitson, G. C., & Raschke, H. J. Divorce research: What we know; what we need to know. *Journal of Divorce*, 1981, **4**, 1–37.

Kressel, K., & Deutsch, M. Divorce therapy: An in-depth survey of therapists' views. *Family Processes*, 1977, **16**, 413–443.

Kressel, K., Lopez-Morillas, M., Weinglass, J., & Deutsch, M. Professional intervention in divorce. *Journal of Divorce*, 1978, **2**, 119–155.

Kressel, K., Lopez-Morillas, M., Weinglass, J., & Deutsch, M. Professional intervention in divorce: The views of lawyers, psychotherapists, and clergy. In G. Levinger & O. C. Moles (Eds.), *Divorce and separation.* New York: Basic, 1979.

Kriesberg, L. *Mothers in poverty: A study of fatherless families.* Chicago: Aldine, 1970.

Kurdek, L. A. An integrative perspective on children's divorce adjustment. *American Psychologist*, 1981, **36**, 856–866.

Kurdek, L. A., & Berg, B. Correlates of children's adjustment to their parents' divorce. In L. A. Kurdek (Ed.), *Children and divorce.* San Francisco: Jossey-Bass, 1983.

Kurdek, L. A., Blisk, D., & Siesky, A. E. Correlates of children's long-term adjustment to their parents' divorce. *Developmental Psychology*, 1981, **17**, 565–579.

Kurdek, L. A., & Siesky, A. E. An interview study of parents' perceptions of their children's reactions and adjustments to divorce. *Journal of Divorce*, 1979, **3**, 5–17.

Kurdek, L. A., & Siesky, A. E. Children's perceptions of their parents' divorce. *Journal of Divorce*, 1980, **3**, 339–378.

Kushner, S. The divorced, noncustodial parent and family treatment. *Social Work*, 1965, **10**, 52–58.

Lamb, M. E. A re-examination of the infant social world. *Human Development*, 1977, **20**, 65–85.

Lamb, M. E. *The role of the father in child development*. New York: Wiley, 1981.

Lambert, L., Essen, J., & Head, J. Variations in behavior ratings of children who have been in care. *Journal of Child Psychology and Psychiatry*, 1977, **18**, 335–346.

Lambert, L., & Hart, S. Who needs a father? *New Society*, 1976, **37**, 80.

Landsman, K. J., & Minow, M. L. Lawyering for the child: Principles of representation in custody and visitation disputes arising from divorce. *Yale Law Journal*, 1978, **87**, 1126–1190.

Levitin, T. E. Children of divorce. *Journal of Social Issues*, 1979, **35**, 1–25.

Lewis, M., Feiring, C., & Weinraub, M. The father as a member of the child's social network. In M. Lamb (Ed.), *The role of the father in child development* (2d ed.). New York: Wiley, 1981.

Maccoby, E. E., & Rau, L. *Differential cognitive abilities* (Cooperative Research Project No. 1040). Washington, D.C.: Office of Education, 1962.

Margolin, F. M. *An approach to resolution of visitation disputes post-divorce: Short-term counseling*. Unpublished doctoral dissertation, United States International University, 1973.

McCord, J., McCord, W., & Thurber, E. Some effects of paternal absence on male children. *Journal of Abnormal and Social Psychology*, 1962, **64**, 361–369.

McDermott, J. F. Parental divorce in early childhood. *American Journal of Psychiatry*, 1968, **124**, 1424–1432.

McDermott, J. F. Divorce and its psychiatric sequence in children. *Archives of General Psychiatry*, 1970, **23**, 421–427.

McKenzie, D. J., & Horwill, F. M. *A study of the costs of procedures: Findings and methodology*. Sydney: Principal Registry, Family Court of Australia, 1979.

Mendes, H. A. Single fathers. *Family Coordinator*, 1976, **25**, 439–444.

Miller, W. B. Lower class culture as a generating milieu of gang delinquency. *Journal of Social Issues*, 1958, **14**, 5–19.

Milne, A. Custody of children in a divorce process: A family self-determination model. *Conciliation Courts Review*, 1978, **16**, 1–10.

Minuchin, S. *Families and family therapy*. Cambridge, Mass.: Harvard University Press, 1974.

Minuchin, S., Baker, L., Rosman, B. L., Liebman, R., Milman, L., & Todd, T. G. A conceptual model of psychosomatic illness in children: Family organization and family therapy. *Archives of General Psychiatry*, 1975, **32**, 1031–1038.

Mnookin, R. H. Child-custody adjudication: Judicial functions in the face of indeterminancy. *Law and Contemporary Problems*, 1975, **39**, 226–293.

Mnookin, R. H., & Kornhauser, L. Bargaining in the shadow of the law: The case of divorce. *Yale Law Journal*, 1979, **88**, 950–957.

Moles, O. C. Public welfare payments and marital dissolution: A review of recent studies. In G. Levinger & O. C. Moles (Eds.), *Divorce and separation*. New York: Basic, 1979.

National Association of Elementary School Principals. One-parent families and their children: The school's most significant minority. *Principal*, 1980, **60**, 31–37.

Neely, R. *How courts govern America*. New Haven, Conn.: Yale University Press, 1981.

Nelson, G. Moderators of women's and children's adjustment following parental divorce. *Journal of Divorce*, 1981, **4**, 71–83.

Nye, F. I. Child adjustment in broken and in unhappy unbroken homes. *Marriage and Family Living*, 1957, **19**, 356–360.

Orthner, D., Brown, T., & Ferguson, D. Single-parent fatherhood: An emerging lifestyle. *Family Coordinator*, 1976, **25**, 429–437.

Patterson, G. R. Accelerating stimuli for two classes of coercive behaviors. *Journal of Abnormal Child Psychology*, 1977, **5**, 335–350.

Patterson, G. R., & Reid, J. B. Reciprocity and coercion: Two facets of social systems. In C. Neuringer & J. Michaels (Eds.), *Behavior modification in clinical psychology*. New York: Appleton-Century-Crofts, 1970.

Pearson, J., & Thoennes, N. The mediation and adjudication of divorce disputes: The benefits outweigh the costs. *Family Advocate*, 1982, **4**, 26–32.

Pedersen, F. A., Anderson, B. T., & Cain, R. L. *An approach to understanding linkages between the parent-infant and spouse relationships.* Paper presented at the meeting of the Society for Research in Child Development, New Orleans, 1977.

Pedersen, F. A., Rubenstein, J., & Yarrow, L. J. Infant development in father absent families. *Journal of Genetic Psychology*, 1979, **135**, 51–62.

Peters, M. F., & McAdoo, H. The present and future of alternative ethnic lifestyles in ethnic American culture. In E. Macklin & D. Rubin (Eds.), *Contemporary families and alternative life-styles*. New York: Sage, 1983.

Phelps, D. W. Parental attitude toward family life and behavior of the mother in one-parent families. *School Health*, 1969, **39**, 413–416.

Podell, R., Peck, H. F., & First, C. Custody—to which parent? *Marquette Law Review*, 1972, **56**, 51–68.

Pope, H., & Mueller, C. W. The intergenerational transmission of marital instability: Comparisons by race and sex. *Journal of Social Issues*, 1976, **32**, 49–66.

Porter, B., & O'Leary, K. D. Marital discord and childhood behavior problems. *Journal of Abnormal Child Psychology*, 1980, **80**, 287–295.

Power, M. J., Ash, P. M., Schoenberg, E., & Sorey, E. C. Delinquency and the family. *British Journal of Social Work*, 1974, **4**, 17–38.

Price-Bonham, S., & Balswick, J. O. The non-institutions: Divorce, desertion, and remarriage. *Journal of Marriage and the Family*, 1980, **42**, 959–972.

Ranson, W., Schlesinger, S., & Derdeyn, A. P. A stepfamily in formation. *American Journal of Orthopsychiatry*, 1979, **49**, 36–43.

Rees, A. H., & Palmer, F. H. Factors related to change in mental test performance. *Developmental Psychology Monograph*, 1970, 3 (2, Pt. 2).

Roman, M., & Haddad, W. *The disposable parent*. New York: Holt, Rinehart & Winston, 1978.

Ross, H., & Sawhill, I. *Time of transition: The growth of families headed by women*. Washington, D.C.: Urban Institute, 1975.

Rutter, M. Sex differences in response to family stress. In E. J. Anthony & C. Koupernick (Eds.), *The child in his family*. New York: Wiley, 1970.

Rutter, M. Parent-child separation: Psychological effects on the children. *Journal of Child Psychology and Psychiatry*, 1971, **12**, 233–260.

Rutter, M. Protective factors in children's responses to stress and disadvantage. In M. W. Kent & J. E. Rolf (Eds.), *Primary prevention of psychopathology*. (Vol. 3): *Promoting social competence and coping in children*. Hanover, N.H.: University Press of New England, 1980.

Rutter, M. *Maternal deprivation reassessed* (2d ed.). Harmondsworth: Penguin, 1981.

Rutter, M., Yule, B., Quinton, D., Rowlands, O., Yule, W., & Berger, M. Attainment and adjustment in two geographical areas, III: Some factors accounting for area differences. *British Journal of Psychiatry,* 1974, **125,** 520–533.

Santrock, J. W. Relation of type and onset of father absence to cognitive development. *Child Development,* 1972, **43,** 455–469.

Santrock, J. W., & Tracy, R. L. Effects of children's family structure status on the development of stereotypes by teachers. *Journal of Educational Psychology,* 1978, **70,** 754–757.

Santrock, J. W., & Warshak, R. A. Father custody and social development in boys and girls. *Journal of Social Issues,* 1979, **35,** 112–125.

Scanzoni, J. A historical perspective on husband-wife bargaining power and marital dissolution. In G. Levinger & O. C. Moles (Eds.), *Divorce and separation.* New York: Basic, 1979.

Scheiner, L. C., Musetto, A. P., & Cordier, D. C. Custody and visitation counseling: A report of an innovative program. *Family Relations,* 1982, **31,** 99–107.

Selby, L. *Work and family life.* Unpublished master's thesis, University of Virginia, 1981.

Select Committee on Children, Youth, and Families (SCCYF) of the United States House of Representatives. *U.S. children and their families: Current conditions and recent trends.* Washington, D.C.: Government Printing Office, 1983.

Shinn, M. Father absence and children's cognitive development. *Psychological Bulletin,* 1978, **85,** 295–324.

Shipman, G. In my opinion: The role of counseling in the reform of marriage and divorce procedures. *Family Coordinator,* 1977, **26,** 395–407.

Siegel, D. M., & Hurley, S. The role of the child's preference in custody proceedings, II. *Family Law Quarterly,* 1977, **13,** 1–58.

Solow, R. A., & Adams, P. L. Custody by agreement: Child psychiatrist as child advocate. *Journal of Psychiatry and Law,* 1977, **5,** 77–100.

Spanier, G. B., & Anderson, E. A. The impact of the legal system on adjustment to marital separation. *Journal of Marriage and the Family,* 1979, **41,** 605–613.

Spanier, G. B., & Hanson, The role of extended kin in the adjustment to marital separation. *Journal of Divorce,* 1981, **5,** 33–49.

Spicer, J. W., & Hampe, G. D. Kinship interaction after divorce. *Journal of Marriage and the Family,* 1975, **37,** 113–119.

State v. Richardson, NH, 1860, 40, 272.

Stericker, A. B., & Kurdek, L. Dimensions and correlates of third through eighth graders' sex role self-concept. *Sex Roles,* in press.

Stern, P. N. Stepfather families: Integration around child discipline. *Issues in Mental Health Nursing,* 1978, **1,** 50–56.

Stohlberg, A. L., & Cullen, D. M. Preventive interventions for families of divorce: The Divorce Adjustment Project. In L. Kurdek (Ed.), *New directions in child development: Children and divorce.* San Francisco: Jossey-Bass, 1983.

Suarez, J. M., Weston, N. L., & Hartstein, N. B. Mental health interventions in divorce proceedings. *American Journal of Orthopsychiatry,* 1978, **48,** 273–283.

Tessman, L. H. *Children of parting parents.* New York: Aronson, 1978.

Thompson, R. A. The father's case in child custody disputes: The contributions of psychological research. In M. Lamb & A. Sagi (Eds.), *Fatherhood and family policy.* Hillsdale, N.J.: Erlbaum, 1983.

Trenkner, T. R. Modern status of maternal preference rule or presumption in child custody cases. *American Law Reports, Annotated, Third Series,* 1976, **70,** 262–303.

Tuckman, J., & Regan, R. A. Intactness of the home and behavioral problems in children. *Journal of Child Psychology and Psychiatry,* 1966, **7,** 225–233.

U.S. Bureau of the Census. Money incomes and poverty status of families and persons in the United States: 1977. *Current Population Reports, Series P-60, No. 116.* Washington, D.C.: Government Printing Office, 1978.

Wahler, R. G. The insular mother: Her problems in parent-child treatment. *Journal of Applied Behavior Analysis,* 1980, 13, 207–219.

Walker, K. N., & Messinger, L. Remarriage after divorce: Dissolution and reconstruction of family boundaries. *Family Process,* 1979, 18, 185–192.

Wallerstein, J. S., & Kelly, J. B. The effect of parental divorce: The adolescent experience. In E. J. Anthony & C. Koupernick (Eds.), *Children at psychiatric risk* (Vol. 3). New York: Wiley, 1974.

Wallerstein, J. S., & Kelly, J. B. The effect of parental divorce: Experiences of the preschool child. *Journal of the American Academy of Child Psychiatry,* 1975, 14, 600–616.

Wallerstein, J. S., & Kelly, J. B. The effect of parental divorce: Experiences of the child in later latency. *American Journal of Orthopsychiatry,* 1976, 46, 256–269.

Wallerstein, J. S., & Kelly, J. B. *Surviving the breakup: How children actually cope with divorce.* New York: Basic, 1980.

Walzer, S. B. The economic realities of divorce. In J. J. Kennelly & J. P. Chapman (Eds.), *The trial lawyer's guide.* Mundelein, Ill.: Callagan, 1968.

Weiss, R. S. *Marital separation.* New York: Basic, 1975.

Weiss, R. S. Growing up a little faster: The experience of growing up in a single-parent household. *Journal of Social Issues,* 1979, 35, 97–111. (a)

Weiss, R. S. Issues in the adjudication of custody when parents separate. In G. Levinger & O. C. Moles (Eds.), *Divorce and separation.* New York: Basic, 1979. (b)

Weitzman, L. J. *The marriage contract.* New York: Free Press, 1981. (a)

Weitzman, L. J. The economics of divorce: Social and economic consequences of property, alimony, and child support awards. *UCLA Law Review,* 1981, 28, 1181–1268. (b)

Weitzman, L. J., & Dixon, R. B. Child custody awards: Legal standards and empirical patterns for child custody, support, and visitation after divorce. *University of California at Davis Law Review,* 1979, 12, 473–521.

Westman, J. C., Cline, D. W., Swift, W. J., & Kramer, D. A. Role of child psychiatry in divorce. *Archives of General Psychiatry,* 1970, 23, 416–420.

Whitehead, L. Sex differences in children's responses to family stress: A re-evaluation. *Journal of Child Psychology and Psychiatry,* 1979, 20, 247–254.

Wilcox, B. Social support in adjusting to marital disruption: A network analysis. In B. H. Gottlieb (Ed.), *Social networks and social support.* Beverly Hills, Calif.: Sage, 1981.

Winston, M. P., & Forsher, T. *Nonsupport of legitimate children by affluent fathers as a cause of poverty and welfare dependence.* Santa Monica, Calif.: Rand, 1975.

Yoder, J. D., & Nichols, R. C. A life perspective comparison of married and divorced persons. *Journal of Marriage and Family,* 1980, 42, 413–419.

Zill, N. *Divorce, marital happiness and the mental health of children: Finding from the FCD national survey of children.* Paper presented at the NIMH Workshop on Divorce and Children, Bethesda, Md., February 1978.

Zill, N. *Happy, healthy, and insecure.* New York: Doubleday, 1983.

Prediction, Prevention, and Developmental Screening in the EPSDT Program

SAMUEL J. MEISELS
University of Michigan

INTRODUCTION

The Early and Periodic Screening, Diagnosis, and Treatment program (EPSDT) came into being as part of a national effort to improve the health and welfare of the children of the poor. It was one of several programs meant to realize an ambitious social policy objective, that of achieving greater equality of opportunity in American society. Yet the history of EPSDT reads more like a story of unfulfilled promise than a record of legislative accomplishment. The enabling legislation was passed by Congress in 1967 and signed into law early in 1968; final regulations were not promulgated until 1971, more than 4 years after passage; and full implementation of all regulations and guidelines was not required until mid-1973. Yet, nearly 6 years after congressional passage, more than half the states implementing the program reported severe problems in complying with the law.

The EPSDT program was originally proposed in an inconspicuous manner, as three amendments to Title XIX, the Medicaid provisions of the Social Security Act. Of the more than 114 pages of amendments to that act that were passed by Congress in 1967, some *60 words* are devoted primarily to EPSDT. The legislation is included under the definition of medical assistance and requires that states receiving Medicaid funds provide for "such early and periodic screening and diagnosis of individuals who are

For locating and making accessible a wide range of citations, I thank Kirsten Leitz. Jonathan McIntire relentlessly pursued the EPSDT legislation through its various transformations in the Code of Federal Regulations and contributed an analysis of the policy implications of these regulations. Terry Berkeley, Robert Halpern, and Robert Lichtenstein read and commented on earlier versions of this chapter.

eligible under the plan and are under the age of 21 to ascertain their physical or mental defects and such health care, treatment, and other measures to correct or ameliorate defects and chronic conditions discovered thereby, as may be provided in regulations of the Secretary" (P.L. 90-248, § 302a). Through this legislation, the United States government instructs the states to provide preventive and curative services to nearly 15% of the American population, all those under the age of 21 whose families are financially eligible for Medicaid benefits. The potential of these 60 words has yet to be realized.

The EPSDT legislation, probably the most ambitious program of medical and psychosocial prevention ever launched, has immense implications for social policy. Yet, from its inception it failed to ignite the interest of professionals, to capture the attention of parents, or, most important, to provide comprehensive services to children. Moreover, in its first 15 years, virtually no systematic evaluation or research was conducted on EPSDT: No data exist that measure its impact, demonstrate its effectiveness, or determine its ratio of cost to benefit; no models of planned variation in the distribution of EPSDT services have been documented; and no programs of effective cost accounting or administrative management have undergone trial and then been disseminated. Not only is evaluative information lacking, there are no accurate data on how many children and youths have been served nationally by EPSDT or how much the program has cost through the years. The absence of such information sets EPSDT apart from other national health and social welfare programs that have undergone extensive evaluation—for example, Community Mental Health Centers, Head Start, and/or Follow-Through.

Indeed, EPSDT may be the largest and most expensive public "secret" in the human services domain. In 1977 a study of community services for children and youth in Genesee County, Michigan, was conducted by the Harvard School of Public Health (Gortmaker, Haggerty, Jacobs, Messenger, & Walker, 1980). The parents of 3,072 children aged 17 or under were surveyed. Only one of every five parents knew about EPSDT. Within this sample, EPSDT was known to only half the parents of the 457 children enrolled in Medicaid and to only a quarter of the parents of 154 children not enrolled in Medicaid though living in or near poverty. The report further noted that fewer than half (22 of 52) of all primary-care physicians serving children in Genesee County knew about EPSDT, as did only 14 of the 70 early childhood professionals who were surveyed in the county.

At the time these data were being collected, 10 years after EPSDT had been passed by Congress, Genesee County was providing screening to nearly 40% of its eligible children—more than twice the national average. Between July 1972 and December 1973, only 11% of the nation's eligible children were reported to have been screened (Foltz, 1982). In 1976 this figure rose to 16%.

Although the problems of uniform national compliance are compounded by the fact that EPSDT is a federal program that is administered by the states, national goals for implementing EPSDT have not served as an incentive. For example, in 1976 the staff of the Congressional Budget Office of the House of Representatives set the national goal of screening 2 million children—only 15% of the 13 million estimated by the report to be eligible (Task Force on Human Resources, 1976). States vary significantly in their delivery of screening services, as a major national survey noted (Chang, Goldstein, Thomas, & Wallace, 1979): A range of from 1% to 80% of eligible children received services in 51 of the 54 states and territories. In another study, the range was from a low of 8% in Washington, D.C., to a reported remarkable high of 110% in Wyoming (Foltz, 1982, p. 48). However, these percentages are only rough approximations because no systematic procedures have ever been established for estimating eligibility or documenting service provision in EPSDT.

THE SOCIAL POLICY BACKGROUND OF EPSDT

The EPSDT program was a product of the liberal social reform era of the 1960s. It was developed as part of the effort to equalize opportunity that gave rise to such programs as Medicaid, Medicare, and Head Start. As stated earlier, EPSDT was designed as a preventive program intended to improve the health and welfare of the children of the poor. The genesis of EPSDT remains relatively obscure, and is discussed in only a few publications (Children's Defense Fund, 1977; Foltz, 1975, 1982; Task Force on Human Resources, 1976). Apparently, three major social policy forces converged to bring EPSDT into being.

BREAKING THE POVERTY CYCLE

The early 1960s witnessed a major national commitment to antipoverty programs. Several government programs were explicitly developed as a means of breaking the "cycle of poverty": "the nearly inevitable sequence of poor parenting which leads to poor school performance, joblessness, and poverty, leading again to high risk births, inappropriate parenting, and so continues the cycle" (Cooke, 1979, p. xxiii). Head Start is one example of the programs created to break that cycle. A basic assumption of this approach to policymaking is the notion that improving the lot of individuals will ameliorate the inequities of society as a whole.

INCREASING ACCESS TO HEALTH CARE

The realization that improving the health of the poor was essential to achieving this larger policy goal led to creation of categorical health programs such as Medicaid and Medicare. Medicaid was intended to improve the quality of medical services to the poor and to extend access to those services to all those in poverty. Since EPSDT is formally mandated as a service under Medicaid, some explanation of the Medicaid program is in order.

Enacted by Congress in 1965, Medicaid is administered by the states and is jointly financed by state and federal funds. Health care providers are directly reimbursed for services rendered to eligible beneficiaries. State and federal Medicaid expenditures in 1979 were just under $21.4 billion (Select Panel for the Promotion of Child Health, 1980).

Eligibility requirements are set jointly by federal and state regulation. The basic requirements of the federal legislation pertain to the "categorically needy," that is, recipients of assistance under the Aid to Families with Dependent Children (AFDC) program or under the Supplementary Security Income (SSI) program for the aged, blind, and disabled. States may exercise the option of broadening eligibility by including pregnant women with incomes at certain specified levels, families in which the father is unemployed, and even the children of two-parent families that meet the AFDC income standard.

These eligibility requirements are critical because they represent the key than unlocks both the Medicaid door and the EPSDT door for needy children. Yet, because of the latitude given states to set eligibility requirements, Medicaid benefits are distributed inequitably. For example, the maximum eligible annual income for a family of four varies from $2,244 in Texas to $6,600 in Hawaii (Select Panel for the Promotion of Child Health, 1980, p. 45); even when regional differences in cost of living are taken into consideration, the income for eligibility in Hawaii is twice that of Texas. As a result of such variations in state policies, it is estimated that "7 million children with family incomes at or below the federally defined poverty level are excluded from receiving Medicaid benefits" (Select Panel for the Promotion of Child Health, 1980, p. 45). The estimate of the unserved would be even greater if the absolute definition of poverty that is used to assign eligibility were replaced with a more realistic and relative definition of poverty as half the median income of a specific population (deLone, 1979).

PREVENTING HEALTH PROBLEMS

The third factor to play a catalytic role in the formation of EPSDT was a series of reports that emphasized the prevalence of apparently preventable problems among the nation's youth. One such study was done in 1966 of the 15% of 18-year-old, non-college-bound youth rejected by the Selective Service System. Many of these young men were rejected because of chronic handicapping conditions, among them a large proportion of emotional and developmental disorders (Children's Defense Fund, 1977, p. 25). After conducting a program analysis that included a review of these figures, the Department of Health, Education, and Welfare (HEW) concluded—probably optimistically—that 62% of these chronic conditions were preventable or correctable through continuous and comprehensive health care; it was also estimated that one-third of the conditions were preventable by means of periodic screening that would identify them and trigger diagnosis and treatment (Task Force on Human Resources, 1976, p. 119).

The HEW analysis presented data to support the view that poor children are far more likely to experience disabling conditions than the children of more affluent families. At the time EPSDT was proposed, health care statistics regarding children from low-income families included the following: "Two-thirds had never been to a dentist; 60% of those with chronic conditions were not being treated. Physician visits were less frequent, although there was nearly twice as much hospitalization as among higher income children.

"Compared to more affluent children, the prevalence of heart disease was three times as great. Seven times as many low-income children had visual impairments, six times as many had hearing problems, and five times as many had mental illness" (Task Force on Human Resources, 1976, p. 119).

The EPSDT program was thus proposed to help break the cycle of poverty, to help remedy the health consequences of the inequities of uneven economic distribution, and to improve the health of poor children by providing explicitly stipulated services designed to have a high payoff in health and welfare. As later analyses will demonstrate, realization of these goals has proven to be extremely elusive. In retrospect, it is clear that when President Johnson, less than a year before signing the EPSDT legislation into law, stated, "We look toward the day when every child, no matter what his color or his family's means, gets the medical care he needs" (Johnson, 1967), he did not foresee the problems that would prevent this goal from being realized.

IMPLEMENTING EPSDT: THE EVOLUTION OF POLICY

However clear the policy background was when EPSDT was formulated, the compromises that followed upon that formal action resulted in a program containing serious ambiguities. In the evolution of the legislation, numerous important issues were left unresolved. For example, no single state agency was assigned to administer the program. As a result, although both health and welfare agencies implement the law, there are no uniform provisions for distributing responsibility between the two agencies at either the state or the federal level.

Another critical issue was the eligibility of children for the program. Because Medicaid eligibility criteria differ radically among the states, so do the EPSDT eligibility criteria for children.

Also left unresolved was the potential cost of the program. The original HEW program analysis that contributed to the formulation of the 1967 EPSDT amendment proposed three potential programs of screening and treatment. The first was estimated to cost about $150 million per year and would have served 5 million children, from birth to age 9 in geographic areas with severe health problems related to poverty. The second program would have targeted newborn children at an annual cost of $30 million, and the third, premature infants at a cost of $5.3 million per year (Foltz, 1975).

Despite these projections, when the much more ambitious EPSDT amendment was passed—one encompassing children from birth to age 21—it contained no estimate of costs for the services proposed. When the regulations for EPSDT were finally approved in 1971, the Office of Management and Budget projected the annual cost for the program at $25 million (Foltz, 1982, p. 57). However, the cost for screening expenditures alone had risen by 1975 to $34 million, and by 1976 to an estimated $47 million (Foltz, 1982, p. 57)—a huge sum, but less than one-half of 1% of all Medicaid expenditures. A recently published study of screening expenditures in only 41 states in 1975 claims a higher cost level—a total of $38,921,416 spent for screening 1,399,990 children and youths (Chang et al., 1979, p. 455). According to these figures, the average cost of all medical and developmental screenings is $27.80 per child. Covering as it does the cost of more than 10 different screening procedures (such as tests of vision and hearing, tuberculin test, test for sickle cell anemia, blood pressure reading, and urinalysis), this figure reflects the extremely low levels of reimbursement allowed under Medicaid. (Nevertheless, all of the above figures are estimates because, again, there has never been an independent cost accounting to clearly distinguish EPSDT expenditures from other Medicaid reimbursements.) Clearly, then, the cost of services under EPSDT was not anticipated when the program was enacted. If all eligible children were to be screened only by EPSDT, the cost, even if only $27.80 were spent per child, would be more than a billion dollars per year.

THE CREATION OF REGULATIONS

The ambiguities of policy implementation already described are paralleled in the evolution of the provisions of EPSDT set forth in the Code of Federal Regulations, the public record of policy intention. As the quotation early in this chapter indicates, the language of the enabling legislation (a brief amendment to the massive Social Security Act of 1967, Public Law 90-248) is extremely vague, giving no guidance concerning the extent of screening or preventive services to be provided by the proposed program.

In the ensuing 4½ years prior to the publication of regulations, the scope of services mandated by EPSDT expanded and contracted. One version of the draft regulations, published in 1970, proposed that early and periodic screening and diagnosis be provided "to ascertain physical and mental defects, and treatment of conditions regardless of the limits otherwise imposed under the State plan on the type and amount of such care and services . . . to all eligible individuals under 21 years of age." These guidelines thus proposed a *comprehensive* set of identification and treatment services. Moreover, they explicitly nullified the ability of the states to determine the scope of services. The states claimed that such policymaking from the top down was inconsistent with the apparent intent of Medicaid, which vested control of the scope of services in the states.

As a result, a much more restricted set of regulations was devised in which states were directed to deliver EPSDT services within the limits of each state plan. As Foltz notes (1982), this change was a blow to the comprehensiveness of EPSDT services. The regulations that appeared in 1971 called only for "early and periodic screening"—left unspecified—and vision, hearing, and dental treatment.

Not until 1978 did the form and content of the regulations undergo substantial change. In that year EPSDT was provided with its own section in the Code of Federal Regulations (Title 42, Chap. IV, Pt. 441, Subpt. B). This section briefly describes the purpose of EPSDT, the Medicaid state plan requirements, additional required services, administrative procedures, and maximum permissible use of services existing in other entitlements (such as in Title V, the Maternal and Child Health Program).

In 1979 the regulations were significantly expanded to require, for the first time, extensive screening services, including: (1) recording of health and developmental history; (2) developmental assessment (effective January 1, 1981); (3) immunizations appropriate for age and health history; (4) unclothed physical examination; (5) assessment of nutritional status; (6)

vision testing; (7) hearing testing; (8) laboratory procedures appropriate for age and population groups; and (9) dental services. The regulations also include a periodicity schedule specifying required screening services applicable for each recipient up to age 21. They also stipulate the penalty for states that fail to provide required services.

This review of the formation of EPSDT regulations reveals several important features. During its first half-decade of existence, EPSDT was technically a part of the law, but for several reasons—variability in implementation by the states, restrictive eligibility requirements, slow start-up, bureaucratic confusion, and poor public outreach—it was actually unavailable to many potential beneficiaries. When regulations were finally published, in 1971, their requirements were weak, vague, and limited to the parameters and priorities of the state plans. During the next several years, implementation began. But in many states, major implementation efforts took place only after potential recipients of services sought legal redress for their complaints. Between April 1972 and August 1975, lawsuits were filed against officials in 15 different states alleging failure to implement the EPSDT program (Children's Defense Fund, 1977). A previously stipulated federal penalty of 1% of Medicaid reimbursement had failed to mobilize recalcitrant states into activity. Finally, it took nearly 10 years from their first publication for federal regulations to explicitly require developmental screening.

In his study of public policies affecting children, Steiner calls EPSDT a program without a policy: "Political accidents and back door approaches rather than rational proposals explain most federal actions on child health questions" (1976, p. 206). Apparently, EPSDT is a victim of haphazard policymaking. However, the problems EPSDT has had from the outset are not solely the result of its being a federal program run by the states. Many of the problems of implementation transcend the ambiguity and vagueness of the legislation itself and stem from confusions regarding the meaning and practical application of such concepts as prevention, prediction, screening, diagnosis, and intervention. Developmental screening, in particular, is a concept that has become invested with more complexity than it may warrant. This is unfortunate, because one of the objectives of EPSDT comprises the prediction and prevention of developmental disorders in young children by use of developmental screening. We now turn to an examination of the concepts just enumerated.

EPSDT AS A PREVENTIVE PROGRAM

As its title indicates, the EPSDT program embodies a model of prevention and treatment that is to be applied as early as possible in a child's life and is to be repeated periodically. In addition to screening, such a program involves two other procedures: diagnosis and treatment. A screening program may be appropriately applied to an entire population (as is done in screening for PKU disorder in newborns). Screening refers to the identification of those individuals who may need further evaluation to ascertain whether they have a condition that may place them at risk. Diagnosis is performed on that portion of the population who are suspected of having the condition under study. Diagnosis is undertaken to confirm the existence of a problem or disability and to propose possible strategies for treatment or remediation. Finally, treatment is administered to individuals whose diagnostic tests confirm the presence of the condition. Thus, each function—screening, diagnosis, and treatment—is performed on successively smaller numbers of people.

Theoretically, the three major functions of the EPSDT program—screening, diagnosis, and treatment—occur in sequence. Screening precedes diagnosis, and diagnosis precedes treatment. The earlier screening identifies a problem—doing so even, perhaps, in the presymptomatic stage—and diagnostic procedures confirm this identification, then the earlier in the disease or developmental process treatment can commence.

In practice, however, these three functions do not necessarily occur in the sequence given above. For example, a child with Down's syndrome need not be screened for developmental delay but can directly enter the diagnostic phase, so that the extent and character of the developmental disorder can be determined. Similarly, a child who presents clear signs and symptoms of a particular communicable disease can begin treatment without extensive diagnosis. In these cases, the clarity of the diagnostic signs makes preliminary screening and other evaluative procedures unnecessary.

When the signs or symptoms of a condition are easily discerned or identified, or when the condition being studied is discovered early in its course, then the implicit sequence of screening, diagnosis, and treatment serves another purpose as well: It roughly parallels the structure of a system of prevention. Three levels of prevention are commonly identified. *Primary* prevention involves taking action to prevent the occurrence of a disease or disability or to promote health. Examples of such actions include immunizations, seat belt restraints, parent education programs, and anti-smoking campaigns. *Secondary* prevention involves identifying a condition in a presymptomatic, or subclinical, stage. Early diagnosis and treatment are necessary for secondary prevention in that their timeliness improves the likely outcome. Examples include programs designed to identify metabolic disorders and efforts aimed at weight reduction for persons with a history of heart trouble. *Tertiary* prevention is intervention that follows the clinical manifestation of a disease or disability. Its goal is to reverse, arrest, or delay progression of the disability. Examples of tertiary prevention include treatment of amblyopia to prevent blindness or the aggressive treatment of cystic fibrosis to delay permanent lung damage (see Gliedman & Roth, 1980). These three levels of prevention are closely linked in that tertiary prevention measures often are directed toward prevention of secondary problems resulting from chronic handicaps, and secondary prevention measures often serve the primary function of preventing incipient reactive disorders.

Although EPSDT was established in part as a preventive program, most of its regulations require only secondary prevention—the detection and treatment of disease after its onset. Unfortunately, the immunization programs sponsored by the Maternal and Child Health Agency are virtually the only health and human services programs devoted to primary prevention. Thus, as Foltz (1982) states in her comprehensive study of EPSDT, primary prevention—such as through health education or distribution of nutritional supplements—might have been a more effective use of the potential inherent in the screening, diagnosis, and treatment sequence.

MODELS OF SCREENING

The concept of developmental screening emerged from the medical model of screening for disease. In 1951 the World Health Organization (WHO) published its now well-known definition of screening: "The presumptive identification of unrecognized disease or defect by the application of tests, examinations or other procedures which can be applied rapidly. Screening tests sort out apparently well persons who probably do not have a disease from those who probably do have the disease. A screening test is not intended to be diagnostic. Persons with positive or suspicious findings must be referred to their physicians for diagnosis and necessary treatment" (Wilson & Jungner, 1968). Two British epidemiologists, Cochrane and Holland (1971), suggest that screening is a logical extension of medical practice because early treatment is generally efficacious, and many diseases have asymptomatic periods—what they call the "iceberg" of disease. Thus, the rationale for screening is to close the gap between prevention and cure through the introduction of a "third force in health: screening for non-symptomatic disease" (Foltz, 1982, p. 121). In this respect, screening represents both a technological advance and a cultural advance in which attention is devoted less to developing cures and more to preventing problems or detecting them earlier in their course (Freymann, 1975).

However ambitious these objectives, screening is fundamentally a brief assessment procedure designed to identify individuals who should proceed to a more intensive assessment or diagnosis. Moreover, screening is open to considerable controversy about its effectiveness, its appropriateness for the conditions to which it is applied, and the characteristics of its procedures.

CRITERIA

Screening necessitates two basic choices: what conditions or diseases can be screened for, and what screening method can be used. The second topic is examined later in the chapter. A set of criteria that should be met before a disease is selected for screening can be described as follows (see Frankenburg, 1974, 1975):

1. *Importance.*—The disease or condition should be serious or potentially serious.

2. *Prevalence.*—The condition should be relatively common or prevalent.

3. *Diagnostic agreement.*—Diagnostic tests and procedures should be able to differentiate diseased from borderline or nondiseased individuals.

4. *Advantage to earlier treatment.*—The prognosis should be improved if the disease is detected and treated prior to the usual time of diagnosis.

5. *Timeliness.*—There should be a reasonable interval between the point when screening can first identify the disease and the optimal time for treatment.

6. *Availability of diagnostic and treatment resources.*—Services must be available to diagnose and treat the suspected condition.

7. *Effects of screening.*—There should be not only no potential risks from the actual screening but also no harmful effects on a nondiseased child or the child's family from being erroneously labeled.

8. *Cost benefit of program.*—The cost of screening, diagnosis, and treatment should be outweighed by the savings accrued in preventing disease and distress and reducing expenditures for treatment.

9. *Public acceptance.*—The public should understand the importance of screening for the disease or condition in question.

These criteria are relatively unambiguous and can be applied without much controversy to such conditions as hearing, vision, and dental problems and to such diseases as tuberculosis and hypertension. All these conditions permit unequivocal identification, can be treated effectively, and conform to the proposition that "earlier diagnosis followed by earlier therapy alters the natural history of the disease" (Cochrane & Holland, 1971, p. 3). But how do conditions that are identified by means of developmental screening meet these criteria?

Developmental screening is intended to assess the emergence of a sequence of behaviors, skills, or abilities over a period of time. Developmental models of assessment differ from approaches to evaluation that focus principally on the predetermined appearance of skills or behavior because they must take into account unpredictable factors that influence growth. Accordingly, they are consistent with variable outcome measures that are related to an individual's life tasks and experiences and are sensitive to the emergence of developmental functions. A developmental function is any change that over time is nearly identical in different individuals. Dunst and Rheingrover (1981, p. 50) define a developmental function as "a map of the course of development of an attribute, trait, or some other behavior characteristic. The form or pattern of change in vocabulary size, mental age, the structure of intelligence, and height—all plotted across age—represent several types of developmental functions."

In this chapter the contrast to be drawn is not between developmental and medical models as such but between two explanatory models: the transactional model and the main-effect model. The medical model implicit in the WHO definition of screening is basically main effect. That is, it implies that abnormal antecedent events or conditions result in abnormal outcomes in a characteristically predictive, causal manner. By contrast, in the transactional model of development, the internal and external factors that affect the child are not viewed as unchanging; development is the outcome of complex transactional processes among these factors—these processes occurring and mutually changing over time.

Some medical conditions (e.g., hypoxia, oxygen deficiency in the neonate) are best understood in causal, main-effect terms. But even these conditions admit of variability according to the type, severity, and timing of the risk factors present at onset. And many other physical conditions and factors traditionally studied by medical practitioners—such as cardiac, renal, and respiratory conditions—can be understood in transactional terms. The main-effect model does not describe these conditions comprehensively and, particularly, does not capture the interactive role played by developmental functions in the course of these conditions. Since developmental functions refer to behaviors that increase or decrease in incidence or strength with age, and that can "replace, supplement, or grow out of another with development" (McCall, 1979, p. 708), such functions cannot accurately be described in terms consistent with the main-effect model, which assumes intraindividual differences to be characterized by stability, relative consistency across age, and causal relationship to predisposing factors.

Many of the unexamined assumptions that link the etiology, or cause, of a disease, disability, or handicapping condition to a specific prognosis, or outcome, emerge from the main-effect medical model. To appreciate fully the problems that have beset screening in general, and developmental screening in particular, in the EPSDT program, we must analyze screening from both a transactional and a main-effect perspective.

DISEASE AND DEVELOPMENT

As the distinction above indicates, whereas the main-effect model screens for the presence or absence of disease or its concomitants, the transactional model examines multiple indicators of a child's developmental abilities in such areas as language functioning, reasoning, and gross motor and fine motor/adaptive functioning. The indicators of delayed development simply fail to meet the general criteria of a disease.

A further complication in screening regards etiology: Whereas many medical and developmental disorders are of unknown origin, others—for example, speech difficulties—may have similar manifestations but be caused by different factors in different children. Moreover, children having the same problem—for example, mild cerebral palsy—may differ greatly in performance. In short, a major problem that confronts transactional models of screening is that the group of high-risk children identified by screening is often extremely diverse. Adopting a main-effect model that focuses on relatively homogeneous causes and outcomes artificially diminishes this variability but also reduces accuracy of identification.

The two models also differ significantly in their fundamental assumptions about risk factors: "characteristics present in the prepathogenic period which affect host susceptibility to specific diseases and which, if modified, may lead to primary prevention of the diseases" (Rogers, 1974, p. 168). Screening based on the main-effect model focuses on identifying risk factors that are considered to be universal. For example, one can use the main-effect model to conclude that chronic hearing loss causes delayed speech development; or that an elevation of amino acid phenylalanine, or of blood lead level, or an anomaly in the formation of the twenty-first pair of chromosomes is directly related to mental retardation. In each of these cases, specific risk factors can be identified, and practices or procedures for reversing, modifying, or ameliorating the risk factors or their effects can then be designed.

The concept of risk factors is essential in screening certain medical conditions. But what constitutes a risk factor within a transactional framework such as development? Escalona (1974) proposes that certain extreme situations constitute *developmental risk conditions* for children. Among them are absence of family, neglect or abuse, and chronic, severe poverty; also included is significant injury to the central nervous system. These conditions fall within an epidemiological frame of reference. As such, they can be treated in terms of group probabilities drawn from the expected frequency that a phenomenon will occur in a normal population, as contrasted to the frequency with which the same phenomenon appears in selected populations. However, because developmental functions conform to a transactional model, as noted earlier, the difference between these two frequencies of risk is unknown. Furthermore, for some types of developmental and psychosocial pathology, there is no clear-cut normal population from which expected frequencies could be derived, "if for no other reason than that different cultures and different societies do not judge normalcy versus aberration by the same criteria" (Escalona, 1974, p. 39).

Thus, when developmental screening is performed, our perception of risk may change somewhat from community to community, from culture to culture, and from condition to condition. In developmental screening, it is appropriate to establish "local norms," that is, standards or criteria that reflect average performance of individuals in specific settings (see Svinicki & Tombari, 1981). These local norms do not have the effect of denying that a behavior is aberrant or that development is delayed, but they do provide a perspective on the relative normalcy of a condition in a particular sample. In nearly all medical tests, however, it would be highly questionable to place the presence of physical criteria (e.g., sensorineural hearing loss, amblyopia, positive tuberculin findings) on a continuum permitting different screening criteria for different communities.

The possibility of establishing local developmental norms results not only from the transactional nature of development but also from the wide range of acceptable indicators of developmental processes. Keogh and Becker (1973) point out that developmental outcomes can be selected from a wide range of possibilities including "IQ, standard achievement test norms, achievement compared to mental age expectancies, consistency of performance with parental expectancy, or mastery of subject matter" (p. 6). Most indicators or predictors of outcomes are hypothetical; rarely are they definitive. As a result, predictions of individual outcomes that are based on the results of developmental screening should be considered to be tentative.

Finally, nearly all medical screening is based on the tenet that treatment can alter the natural history of disease in a significant portion of those screened. Although the same assumption can be made with respect to nonmedical developmental functions, controversy regarding the efficacy of early intervention continues (see Bronfenbrenner, 1974; Clarke & Clarke, 1976; Lazar, Hubbell, Murray, Roche, & Royce, 1977; Rutter, 1980;

Schweinhart & Weikart, 1980). Treatment for developmental disorders takes place in a complex environment of psychological, cultural, and socioeconomic factors and is affected by the same transactional factors that complicate developmental screening in general.

CAN WE SCREEN FOR DEVELOPMENT?

Although there are major differences between screening for disease and screening for delayed development, it is clear that developmental disorders fulfill most of the criteria for selecting a condition for screening. First, the problem of developmental disorders meets the first two criteria, being both prevalent and important. More than 12% of all children between the ages of 3 and 19 are handicapped (Brewer & Kakalik, 1979), and approximately 500,000 children born each year are either chronically ill or mentally or physically handicapped (see Meisels & Anastasiow, 1982). The third criterion, the possibility of diagnostic agreement, is difficult to satisfy because disabled children are frequently misidentified and misclassified (see Hobbs, 1975), and because definitions of preschool handicapped children vary from state to state (Lessen & Rose, 1980).

The fourth criterion, the advantageousness of earlier treatment, has already been mentioned. Although uniform data do not exist, few would argue with the general logic of early intervention. The fifth criterion, timeliness, requires that developmental problems be identifiable prior to their optimal time of treatment or remediation. Because the risk factors of development are so inferential, predictions of problems based on developmental screening data should be rapidly followed by evaluation and treatment.

The sixth criterion, availability of diagnostic and treatment resources, is met because every year more becomes known about developmental assessment and intervention; and although economic constraints are growing, the passage of the Education for All Handicapped Children Act (Public Law 94-142) in 1975 has improved the general distribution of resources (State Program Implementation Studies Branch, 1980). The seventh criterion is not fully met, although the potential harm comes not from the developmental screening itself but from the expectations that may be set in motion by prediction (Camp, van Doorninck, Frankenburg, & Lampe, 1977; Keogh & Becker, 1973). Developmental screening does satisfy the eighth criterion, for its cost is very low; costs begin to become notable only when children are further assessed and treated (Frankenburg, 1975). Developmental screening, however, does poorly by the ninth criterion: The limited demand for such services from the general population indicates that there is little public acceptance or awareness of their existence, and that among those who are aware there is considerable controversy. There are several causes: lack of public awareness campaigns, imprecision of the screening instruments, misuse of screening data for diagnostic purposes, and lack of general acceptance of the importance of screening by other professionals (cf. Bergman, 1977; Coleman, 1978; Egert, 1978; Foltz, 1982; Schrag & Divoky, 1975).

DEVELOPMENTAL SCREENING AND EPSDT

Thus, developmental disorders meet most of the general criteria that have been developed for screening for medical conditions. Nevertheless, developmental problems are different from problems that are explained by the main-effect model—problems characterized by stability, clear symptomatology, and relatively obvious relationship to cure. It should be recognized, moreover, that these features are often not present in many medical conditions. Yet, no recognition or understanding of the ambiguous character of developmental and medical screening is implicit in the assumptions of the EPSDT program or in its structure.

The problem of specifying what developmental screening should consist of and who should be responsible for performing it was initially avoided altogether by the federal government and then assigned for review to committees formed by national organizations (American Association of Psychiatric Services for Children, 1977; American Orthopsychiatric Association, 1978). Both these committee reports recommended systematic procedural changes in EPSDT that have not been enacted.

However, the basic conflict between the implications of the main-effect and the transactional models remains unresolved. The practice of developmental screening in EPSDT usually overlooks this conflict because such screening, when it is performed, is frequently conducted as part of the general health appraisal. Several articles in medical journals (e.g., Hooper, 1975; Oberklaid, Dworkin, & Levine, 1979) suggest that the physician is the most appropriate professional to serve as a "developmental generalist . . . an integrator of multiple factors and an interpreter of their prescriptive implications" (Oberklaid et al., 1979, p. 1131). However, the facts do not support this recommendation. Dworkin, Shonkoff, Leviton, and Levine (1979) point out that most pediatricians are inadequately prepared for involvement with handicapped children; pediatrics textbooks devote little space to active prevention of disease and disability. And in a study of 121 primary-care pediatricians, Smith (1978) found that few children in these pediatricians' practices routinely receive screening for developmental disorders, and that the pediatricians who perform such tests frequently interpret the results as diagnostic data. Finally, in most medical practices, diagnosis and treatment are main-effect in orientation, although, as we have seen, this approach is inappropriate for understanding many medical as well as nonmedical problems and conditions.

The forced union of the main-effect and developmental/transactional models in EPSDT did little to inform physicians about developmental concerns or to promote the overall goal of identifying and remediating developmental disorders. Ultimately, the difference in how the two models are applied to developmental screening may reduce to the fact that one model determines the presence or absence of defects and the other measures differences between individuals or within the same individual over time. Reynolds (1971, p. 55) has pointed out that "Educational treatments are always positive. They are concerned with teaching and learning, not with the recovery from defects or the simple prevention of problems. The educator 'prevents' reading failure not by building antibodies but by teaching reading or its prerequisites with greater resourcefulness and better effort to more children."

Given that theory and practice are insensitive to the distinctions drawn above, it is not surprising that developmental screening has not been successfully implemented on a national scale. Now that the basis has been established for understanding some of the underlying ambiguity concerning the practice of developmental screening in EPSDT, another aspect should be examined: its methodology. Such an examination involves identifying what criteria should be satisfied and what instruments are used, assessing how accurately these instruments predict development and developmental disorder, and determining how these instruments might be modified to make EPSDT more effective in the lives of children.

THE USES OF VALIDITY

Assessing the accuracy of the predictive inferences that can be made from screening data requires that several questions be answered: What do screening tests tell us about a child's current level of functioning? How well do the predictions based on them stand up over time? How useful are the data for educational decision making? How well can different screening instruments be compared with one another?

All these questions raise the issue of statistical validity. Validity is an indicator of the accuracy of a test and of the inferences that may be drawn from it; the stronger the validity of a screening test, the more credible its results. Validity, then, is "the overall degree of justification for test interpretation and use" (Messick, 1980, p. 1014). Validity is inherently relative; the validity of something is determined by its being compared or correlated or contrasted with some other index, criterion, or construct. Validity may be concurrent or predictive: As the terms imply, concurrent validity is that which can be determined by reference to independent criteria that exist concurrently with the findings to be checked—as, for example, diagnostic confirmation of a condition that a screening test indicates is present. Predictive, or longitudinal, validity is that which can be measured only with the passage of time—as, say, later diagnostic confirmation of the presence of a condition the supposed risk factors for which had been earlier identified by screening.

Understanding the role of developmental screening in EPSDT requires familiarity with the basic conceptual components of validity. Without such familiarity, it is nearly impossible to distinguish significant claims from meaningless statistics based on screening test results or to evaluate the differences among alternative screening tests, as is done later in the chapter. Although these component concepts of validity are not difficult to understand, their proper application requires technical exactness and therefore some methodological sophistication. It should be noted that no minimal standards of validity were proposed at any time for either medical or developmental screening tests in the EPSDT legislation or regulations. Such a requirement might have served as a catalyst for the development of more rigorous screening procedures than those currently available.

CLASSIFICATIONAL ANALYSIS OF SCREENING DATA

As mentioned, being inherently relative, validity is inferred by comparing the results of a screening test with some specific external criterion, construct, or outcome variable. In its simplest form, the comparison is between results of screening and the results of follow-up diagnostic testing. Validity—whether concurrent or predictive—is then measured by the strength of association between findings identified in screening and the presence of the actual condition as confirmed in diagnostic testing.

Table 1 describes this fourfold relationship. Quadrants a and d show the *true positives* and the *true negatives*—respectively, those who were classified as being at risk and not at risk and whose classifications were confirmed by further evaluation. Quadrant b shows the *false positives*—also called overreferrals and false inclusions—those who were identified as being at risk by screening data but were not at risk on the follow-up evaluation. Quadrant c shows the *false negatives*—or underreferrals or false exclusions—those not identified as at risk by screening but so identified by later evaluation.

The classificational data, or cross tabulations, shown in Table 1 are essential to adequate assessment of the validity of a screening instrument.

TABLE 1
COMPARISON OF FINDINGS FROM SCREENING TEST
AND CRITERION MEASURE

SCREENING TEST	CRITERION MEASURE	
	Intervention Needs (+)	No Intervention Needs (−)
At risk: refer for evaluation .... (+)	True positives a	False positives b
Not at risk: do not refer for evaluation .... (−)	False negatives c	True negatives d

NOTE.—Sensitivity = (a/a + c); specificity = (d/b + d); overreferral = (b/a + b); underreferral = (c/c + d); predictive utility of screening positive = (a/a + b); predictive utility of screening negative = (d/c + d).

Only this format yields a comparison of false inclusions and exclusions to true positives and negatives. It is impossible to systematically interpret the results of a screening test without this comparative information giving the frequency of accurate and inaccurate predictions.

Most screening tests do not report classificational data. Lichtenstein (1981, p. 68) reports that classificational analysis was used in only two of 51 preschool screening tests that he reviewed. As a consequence, he notes, "screening tests are commonly selected on the basis of inadequate data, face validity [i.e., the mere appearance of validity], testimonial evidence, and frequency of use by other screening programs." Moreover, when statistical procedures other than classificational approaches are employed, they are often misused. Several of these approaches will be enumerated and the problems with them described.

BASE RATES AND PERCENT AGREEMENT

Table 1 lists several formulas created to evaluate the effectiveness of a screening test. Such effectiveness is measured by the superiority of its rates of accurate identification and prediction over what would be possible in its absence, by use of general information about the base rate: the prevalence of a specific condition, such as retardation, in a general population (see Meehl & Rosen, 1955; Satz & Fletcher, 1979).

The accuracy of a screening test can be measured by use of one of the most basic calculations from the test data, percent agreement: the proportion of agreement between screening and diagnostic, or criterion, findings. This approach to determining validity can be very misleading if the base rate is not known. As Frankenburg (1974) notes, "if the prevalence of the disease were 5 percent and 100 percent of subjects were screened as negatives, the rate of agreement would be 95 percent and of disagreement 5 percent. This appears to be a high degree of accuracy until one notes that the test has failed to identify any of the diseased subjects" (p. 614).

DISCRIMINATIVE AND CORRELATIONAL TESTS OF VALIDITY

Another approach to establishing the validity of a screening test relies on discriminating between two previously identified groups: one known to have a particular condition, the other known not to have it. The scores obtained by the members of each of the two groups are then combined and compared in terms of mean group differences. The problem with this approach is that, although the average score for each group may be different, the distributions of scores between the groups typically overlap. We are not informed of how many individuals would be incorrectly classified by the screening process or who they are (Malbon, 1978).

Similar problems of inferring accuracy in screening emerge from the common technique of correlational analysis. This approach is used whenever screening tests are followed by the collection of concurrent or longitudinal data from a criterion measure, such as a diagnostic test or some other indicator of outcome. Whenever statistically significant correlations are obtained, some indication of the screening test's validity can be inferred, although these results are obviously dependent on the validity of the criterion measure. Nevertheless, a correlational design only describes the degree of overlap between two domains or two measures of the same phenomenon. It cannot fit individual subjects into a binary classification— that is, positive or negative, diseased or healthy, refer or do not refer. As in discriminative analysis, correlational data refer to relationships between groups; they yield no information about the identities or numbers of individuals referred or about the number of overreferrals or underreferrals.

The limited usefulness of correlational analysis is indicated by a recent comparison of the predictive power of two developmental screening instruments (Lichtenstein, 1981): the Denver Developmental Screening Test (DDST) (Frankenburg, Dodds, Fandal, Kazuk, & Cohrs, 1975) and the Developmental Indicators for the Assessment of Learning (DIAL) (Mardell & Goldenberg, 1975). The correlation coefficient between the total scores of these two widely used tests was high (.82), indicating a strong linear relationship between the procedures. However, classification analysis of the results presented a completely different picture of the relationship between the DDST and the DIAL. None of the four children referred by the DDST was referred by the DIAL, and the one child classified as at risk by the DIAL was not referred by the DDST. As Lichtenstein (1981, p. 68) notes, "making assumptions about the predictive effectiveness of a screening test on the basis of correlational statistics is tenuous and ill-advised."

SENSITIVITY AND SPECIFICITY

The fourfold matrix in Table 1 shows the number of correct and incorrect inclusions and exclusions. It presents all the information required for effectively evaluating the usefulness of a screening instrument, and also gives the formulas for computing several critical proportions that are essential for assigning a meaning to the validity data of a screening instrument.

Among the basic indices for determining whether a screening test fulfills its stated mission are sensitivity and specificity. The sensitivity of a test is measured by the ratio of correctly referred individuals to all those who have the condition being screened. In other words, it is the proportion of individuals at risk who are correctly identified by the test. Specificity is the converse—the proportion of individuals not at risk who are correctly excluded from further assessment or evaluation. Together, sensitivity and specificity permit comparisons to be made between the base rate, or prevalence, of a handicapping condition and classificational decisions derived from a screening test (see Harber, 1981). (Technically, if the results of a screening instrument are compared with the results of a criterion test, rather than of a diagnosis, the terms sensitivity and specificity should be replaced by *co-positivity* and *co-negativity*, to acknowledge the potential fallibility of the criterion test.)

Sensitivity and specificity are inversely related to one another. To the extent that the sensitivity of a screening test is increased through altering the cutting point—the referral point between screening positives and negatives—so specificity is decreased. However, sensitivity and specificity are not of equal value. That is, a test with a 40% sensitivity and a 90% specificity is not equivalent to a test with a 90% sensitivity and a 40% specificity. When sensitivity is 90%, only 10% of the individuals with the condition in question remain undetected; when sensitivity is 40%, 60% of those who should be identified are overlooked. Thus, a simple combination of the two proportions of sensitivity and specificity does not in itself give a usable index of comparison (see Cochrane & Holland, 1971).

The data obtained from the sensitivity and specificity indices can be used to evaluate how well a developmental screening test correctly identifies children who are in need of treatment and correctly excludes those not at risk. In short, computations of sensitivity and specificity are the primary means of evaluating a screening test's capacity to correctly classify individuals (Buck & Gart, 1966); no other measures of validity provide information concerning the accuracy of specific predictions.

POLICY IMPLICATIONS OF VALIDITY

Use of the techniques enumerated above for assessing the validity of developmental screening requires little further justification. Tests lacking in technical validity contribute their own uncontrolled variability to the assessment of developmental function or individual differences. Reliability coefficients are designed in part to specify whether variations in test scores are attributable to the phenomena being measured or to the measurement device itself. It is clearly advantageous to reduce these random error influences as much as possible.

Nevertheless, a great deal of the testing done in the name of developmental screening is methodologically and conceptually unsophisticated. Surveying 177 school districts in New York State, Joiner (1977) found 151 different screening instruments or procedures in use. Many of them were developed locally with no attempt at validation. Of the 30 most frequently used tests, he found that only 16 were appropriate for developmental screening. Similar data can be reported from many other states.

The phenomenon of locally developed, unvalidated screening tests may reflect an assumption among teachers and school psychologists that clinical insight or experience is all that is required to construct or conduct a screening program. The proliferation of inadequately developed screening tests is also consistent with a phenomenon known as "street level" policymaking, which can occur when local professionals are under constraint to implement federal policies and regulations yet remain generally free to develop their own mechanisms of implementation (cf. Weatherley, 1979). This is the case for EPSDT, for the Education for All Handicapped Children Act, and for many other federal programs.

Finding and identifying children at risk for school failure is an obligation that federal government and state government have generally assigned to local school districts. But local personnel have not been guided or trained in proved and effective methods of screening and identification. The result is that the federal or state screening policy is implemented at the street level by individuals varying greatly in ability, resources, and motivation.

However, there is another, more fundamental obstacle to the establishment of satisfactory instruments: As is clearly demonstrated in the next section, even most well-developed screening instruments do not provide adequate validity data. Establishing validity requires that the results of a screening test be dichotomized. They must ultimately be cast in the form of refer or do not refer, diseased or nondiseased. But, as Bradley and Caldwell (1978) note, most handicapping conditions "are not 'either-or' situations, that is, most human capacities are closer to normally distributed than bimodally distributed. Cut off points tend to be arbitrary. . . . When trying to ascertain whether a screening procedure can successfully identify a person who has a particular handicap it is difficult to distinguish those who barely fall below the established critical point from those who fall above. The incidence of error in classifying persons is typically high" (p. 124). Cut-off points are commonly set at 2 or 3 SD below the mean. (A standard deviation—SD—is a formal way of describing the statistical deviation of a score from the average.) However, the assumption that either biological or developmental abnormality is related to statistical abnormality is open to question. Chamberlain and Davey (1976) point out that the widest statistical variations on developmental items occur at the time when the child is about to acquire a skill. Smaller mean differences are found when tasks that are very difficult or very simple are presented. They also note (p. 67) that, if a delay in performance is attributable to a handicap, "it will not be possible from the test alone to distinguish the handicap from immaturity until the child is well beyond the age at which he or she would be expected to develop the skill." In other words, from screening tests alone it is often difficult to decide which individuals who may have abnormal findings will in fact be at risk at some point in the future.

Still another major developmental issue—one with key practical and policy implications—is the relationship of developmental screening to prediction. Frankenburg, Dick, and Darland (1975, p. 131) point out that "if the purpose of screening is to move up the time of diagnosis and treatment to an earlier stage in the disease or handicapping process, the screening should have not only concurrent, but more important, predictive validity." However, the history of developmental research demonstrates repeatedly that children's developmental accomplishments are significantly affected by factors in their environment, just as environmental agents are changed by children's development. Although the development of infants who are moderately or severely mentally impaired is relatively predictable (see Illingworth, 1975), in the first few years of life there are relatively few stable developmental functions on which long-term predictions can be based.

Given, then, that validity is the overall degree of justification for test interpretation and use, tests with limited predictive power admit of correspondingly restricted validity inferences. However, because the developmental functions being tested, and particularly those in early childhood, are so dynamic, all long-term predictions—at least with our present knowledge—are unjustified; validity claims based on screening for developmental strength or disorder should be principally concurrent or short term.

THE SEARCH FOR DEVELOPMENTAL PREDICTORS

At this point it is appropriate to scrutinize more closely the assumption that the predictive validity of developmental screening data is limited. A major feature of any analysis of developmental predictors is recognition of the wide range of independent variables that are used as a basis for predictions. Although most predictive studies of development do not recommend the use of specific independent variables in screening procedures, there is a great deal of overlap in structure and content between predictive studies of developmental outcomes and predictive studies of screening tests. The range of predictors of development that have been explored includes judgments based on single predictors; multiple predictors; information obtained from parents, teachers, or other sources; or information obtained by observation of the child's behavior. Some brief examples will give an indication of how these various predictors have been used.

PREDICTIONS DURING INFANCY

Researchers have selected single predictors of development from a wide range of alternatives. Studying the occurrence of rapid eye movement (REM) "storms" in infants 6 months old, Becker and Thoman (1980) observed a negative correlation between the frequency of REM episodes and scores obtained on the Bayley Scales of Infant Development at age 12 months.

Serunian and Broman (1975) report significant relationships between a measure that reflects a newborn's physical status (Apgar scores) and a standard test of infant development (Bayley mental and motor scores). Infants who had Apgar scores in the 0–3 range (of a maximum of 10) at 1 minute following birth had significantly lower 8-month mental and motor scores than infants with scores in the 7–10 range.

Fagan and McGrath (1981) presented a visual recognition memory task at 4 and 7 months from which to predict intelligence at 4 and 7 years of age. Comparing earlier habituation tests and subsequent verbal intelligence tests, they obtained statistically significant correlations of .37 between 4 months and 4 years, and .57 between 7 months and 7 years.

These studies—selected from a large number of similar correlational studies—raise some interesting questions. For example, can REM storms or episodes be used as valid predictors of mental development? Can we predict development within the first minute of life? Can we identify a single measure of mental development in the first year of life that will predict general intelligence 3–6 years later?

Despite the claims of these and of other studies, the answer to these questions is negative. We may be able to predict with some accuracy for 8–12 months, but longer-term predictions of development contain more inaccurate than accurate predictions. Even predictions based on multiple predictors yield questionable results. For example, Littman and Parmelee (1978) constructed three scales of medical complications to be used between birth and 9 months of age. In a study of 126 premature infants who were followed from birth to 2 years of age, they found no statistically significant relationships between obstetric and neonatal events and developmental outcomes. They concluded that neonatal and postnatal problems in general pose more of an insult than an injury to the young child. In a related paper, Balow, Rubin, and Rosen (1975–1976) reviewed research regarding perinatal precursors of reading disability. They conclude that perinatal events have long-term effects only to the extent that they damage neurological function. "To say than an infant is 'anoxic' or 'premature' or 'born of a toxemic mother' is no assurance that he has suffered some neurological impairment, although he may be at high risk for such impairments" (p. 67).

Continuing the search for a single, although complex, predictor of later intelligence and school achievement, Rubin and Balow (1979) analyzed data from 1,382 subjects who were administered the Bayley scales at 8 months. In this study, they found that SES was a much better predictor of intelligence and achievement at ages 4 through 9 than was the Bayley alone or the Bayley in combination with SES.

Several other researchers have implicated SES as a major risk factor in development (Escalona, 1974; Sameroff, 1975, 1981; Werner, Bierman, & French, 1971; Werner & Smith, 1977). Ramey and his colleagues have even sought to link SES data with information obtained from birth certificates—information concerning race, parity, month prenatal care began, educational level of mother, number of previous live births that subsequently died, legitimacy of birth, and birth weight—as a screening procedure for predicting psychological and educational status of children in first grade (Ramey, Stedman, Borders-Batterson, & Mengel, 1978). A follow-up study that compared predictions based on data obtained solely from birth certificates with first-grade performance on a wide range of measures revealed that children were overreferred by a six-to-one ratio (Finkelstein & Ramey, 1980); the overreferral rate was 84%. Low SES may be a useful construct for predicting developmental problems, but it is not a necessary or sufficient condition for the presence of these disorders.

In general, except for children who have experienced severe injury to the central nervous system, predictions of developmental outcome based on data collected during the first 2 years of life are tenuous. The best predictions emerge from studies that combine multiple sources of data, such as individual testing and assessment of home environment (Siegel, 1981), and that sample predictor and outcome variables at points in close temporal proximity (Chamberlin, 1977). Data from a number of sources (Bayley, 1970; Lewis, 1973, 1976; McCall, Hogarty, & Hurlburt, 1972) strongly suggest that "there is no consistency across or within age in a wide variety of tests purported to measure infant mental functioning. Therefore, the concept of a developmentally constant, general unitary concept of intelligence is not very tenable" (Lewis, 1976, p. 13). Socioeconomic variables appear to be a reasonably reliable predictor of childhood development. However, SES is "a demographic variable, and in and of itself tells us nothing about the process of cognitive development" (Lewis & Fox, 1980, p. 57). Recent research has shown that more accurate predictions include measures of caregiver-infant interaction in the predictive equation (Sameroff, 1978; Sigman & Parmelee, 1979). However, even when assessments of maternal responsiveness are combined with measures of infant status, long-term predictions from data collected during the first 2 years of life are still very questionable.

PRESCHOOL AND KINDERGARTEN PREDICTION

The search for valid predictors of development continues beyond the first 2 years of life. Indeed, a very large volume of research concerns preschool and kindergarten screening and prediction studies. Most of this research uses either single-variable or multiple-variable predictors. Colarusso, Plankenhorn, and Brooks (1980) note that multiple-variable studies usually employ a combination of reading-readiness tests, batteries of various standardized intelligence and perceptual tests, and other predictive indices based on a combination of several variables. Studies using single-variable predictors usually rely upon a single test of developmental ability, perceptual-motor skill, intelligence, or school readiness to obtain a score that is related to an outcome variable.

Most screening tests are single-variable predictors; multiple-variable predictors serve purposes that are different from the goals of screening. In fact, most multiple-variable batteries more closely resemble diagnostic tests than screening tests.

Multiple-variable predictive batteries are used principally to predict academic achievement and performance. A wide range of studies have been completed, differing vastly in methodological rigor. Of interest in the present context is the variety of predictors that are judged to be effective by different studies. The major variables that were considered to be among the best predictors of first-grade performance when kindergarten children were tested include: ability to attend to auditory and visual stimuli and to order attack skills (Colarusso et al., 1980); duration of attention (Becker, 1976; Feshbach, Adelman, & Fuller, 1974; Forness, Hall, & Guthrie, 1977); performance on tasks of cognitive development (derived from the work of Piaget and Gesell; [Kaufman & Kaufman, 1972]); facility at using a pencil (Eaves, Kendall, & Crichton, 1974); letter knowledge (Colligan & O'Connell, 1974; Telegdy, 1975); level of perceptual development (Morency & Wepman, 1973); ability to identify objects by use of fingers alone (Levine, Brooks, & Shonkoff, 1979); and conservation of number (Dimitrovsky & Almy, 1975). Although there is little agreement among these investigations, a general review of them shows the wealth of possibilities available for use in predictive studies of development and school-related achievement.

However, when the methodology of these studies is analyzed, their findings become more difficult to interpret. Lichtenstein (1980) reviewed a large number of prediction studies and computed the sensitivity and specificity rates for each study. His selection criteria were that the studies had to involve children who were of kindergarten age or younger; they had to present longitudinal data of at least 1 year's duration; their data had to be presented so that classificational analysis could be performed; and they had to have a minimum sample of 50 children.

Lichtenstein was able to identify only 11 studies that fulfilled all these criteria. When he plotted sensitivity and specificity rates for each of the 11 studies on a two-dimensional graph, no trend emerged. Nor did any when he compared the studies on an index of comparison that incorporates false positive and false negative errors into a single measure. Thus, his review highlights the need to establish more effective instruments and greater methodological rigor among prediction studies so that their validity can be assessed and improved.

In summary, few conclusions about particular predictors can be drawn from the extensive multiple-variable predictor studies that have been conducted. Indeed, several investigators (Feshbach, Adelman, & Fuller, 1977; Rubin, Balow, Dorle, & Rosen, 1978; Stevenson, Parker, Wilkinson, Hegion, & Fish, 1976) caution against the use of data from prediction studies as a basis for diagnostic classification and labeling. Although high preschool and kindergarten scores may be predictors of normal or superior academic performance, poor preschool test performance usually does not provide enough information to construct valid high-risk groupings. Nevertheless, the results of these studies indicate that, to the extent that the criterion measures are related to school performance or school success, predictors based on school-related tasks are significantly more reliable than other types. Stevenson et al. (1976) also suggest that "later performance depended not only on accomplishments of the child before entering school, but also upon the child's learning and memory abilities" (p. 398). In other words, insofar as school success depends upon the level of skill acquisition, it depends also upon the ability to acquire skills.

DEVELOPMENTAL SCREENING

The distinction between skill acquisition and the ability to acquire skills lies at the heart of the difference between developmental screening tests and school-readiness tests. Preschool developmental screening tests are designed to identify children who may have a learning problem or a handicapping condition that could affect their overall potential for success in school. Such tests focus on performance in a wide range of areas including speech, language, cognition, perception, affect, and gross and fine motor skills.

In contrast, school-readiness tests are designed to measure a child's relative preparedness for benefiting from a specific academic program. Readiness tests focus on current skill achievement and performance rather than on a child's developmental potential. Thus, a child who performs poorly on a readiness test may be displaying only a lack of general knowledge rather than a possible impairment that might eventually limit his or her ability to acquire knowledge (Meisels, 1978, p. 7). Thus, readiness tests and developmental screening tests sample different, although potentially overlapping, areas of measurable behavior. In their construction, readiness tests most closely resemble the types of instruments used in the multiple-predictor studies discussed earlier, whereas preschool developmental screening tests resemble comprehensive developmental assessments.

Nevertheless, a distinction is not widely made between the two; the most recent edition of Buros's *Mental Measurement Yearbook* (1978) does not list developmental screening tests separately but includes them among readiness and individual intelligence tests—both of them misclassifications: Developmental screening tests are not readiness tests, according to the definition proposed above; and they are certainly not identical with full-scale intelligence tests, although they may sample a similar domain of knowledge, skill, and ability. The *Guide to Screening in EPSDT* prepared by the American Academy of Pediatrics (Frankenburg & North, 1974) recommends five tests for use in the EPSDT program. However, only two of them are developmental screening tests: the Developmental Screening Inventory and the Denver Developmental Screening Test. The other three tests—the Goodenough-Harris Drawing Test, the Slosson Intelligence Test, and the Wide Range Achievement Test—are either intelligence or achievement tests. Of the two screening tests, only the Denver reports data that permit statistically reliable and valid inferences to be drawn.

Indeed, eliminating readiness and intelligence tests and other tests of specific domains of functioning (e.g., perceptual-motor integration, auditory comprehension, articulation) leaves very few that can be considered developmental screening tests. The list is further shortened when only tests with adequate classificational validity data are included, and when parent and teacher checklists and research tools are eliminated. Thus, four general criteria for selection of developmental screening tests can be identified:

1. It must be a brief procedure designed to identify children who may have a learning problem or handicapping condition that could affect their overall potential for success in school.

2. It must primarily sample the domain of developmental tasks rather than the domain of specific accomplishments that indicate academic readiness.

3. It must focus on performance in a wide range of areas of development, including speech, language, cognition, perception, affect, and gross and fine motor skills.

4. It must have classificational data available concerning the reliability and validity of the instrument.

Of all the tests that are used as developmental screening instruments, and of all those listed in the major compendia of early childhood measurement instruments, only four screening instruments meet most of these criteria: the Denver Developmental Screening Test (Frankenburg, Dodds, Fandal, Kazuk, & Cohrs, 1975), the McCarthy Screening Test (McCarthy, 1978), the Minneapolis Preschool Screening Instrument (Lichtenstein, 1980), and the Early Screening Inventory (Meisels & Wiske, 1983).

ANALYZING DEVELOPMENTAL SCREENING TESTS

The obvious questions to consider next are, How well do these four tests predict problems that may result in school learning difficulties? What are their sensitivity and specificity? Do they predict longitudinally or only for a short term? Can they identify all developmental problems or only a few? Unfortunately, answers to all of these questions are not available for even these four instruments. The tests differ significantly in research sample size and characteristics, design of the instrument, types of validation studies, and amount of published data. Given their great differences, the tests cannot be validly compared on common parameters; nor can their data be meaningfully presented in a composite table. In place of a general analysis, the instruments will be briefly reviewed individually.

THE DDST

The Denver Developmental Screening Test (DDST) is the most widely used and extensively researched of all developmental screening instruments. Foltz (1982) notes that, in 1976, 33 states recommended its use in the developmental component of their EPSDT programs, and Frankenburg reports that the Denver has been administered to more than 20 million children (personal communication).

Introduced in 1967 (Frankenburg & Dodds, 1967), the test underwent research and scoring revisions published in 1971 (Frankenburg, Camp, & Van Natta, 1971; Frankenburg, Camp, Van Natta, & Demerssman, 1971; Frankenburg, Goldstein, & Camp, 1971). The test consists of 105 items from which a selection is made for children ranging in age from 2 weeks to 6 years. Items are individually administered by a single examiner; some items can be scored by the report of parents. The items are grouped in four areas: personal/social, fine motor/adaptive, language, and gross motor.

Reliability coefficients for the Denver are high across age (mean interrater agreement = 96%; mean test-retest agreement = 97%). Similarly, the concurrent validity data presented by Frankenburg and his colleagues indicate that the test is accurate for short-term predictions of less than a month (Frankenburg, Goldstein, & Camp, 1971). In one such study they conducted, the results of 237 DDST screenings of children ranging in age from 1½ months to 6 years were compared with results obtained from the Bayley or the Stanford-Binet Intelligence Scale 1–3 weeks later. This study revealed an overreferral rate of 11% and an under-referral rate of 3%. Co-positivity and co-negativity were both computed to be .77. A cross-validation study using another 246 children yielded co-positivity ratings of .92 and co-negativity ratings of .97. It should be noted that these concurrent results combine data across a very wide age range. It cannot be assumed that the Denver "works" equally well with infants and with first graders.

A longitudinal validity study that compared DDST results with Stanford-Binet IQ scores 3 years later is reported by Camp et al. (1977). Their study involved 65 children 4–6 years old from lower-SES families. Results indicated that the DDST underreferred children by a substantial proportion. Moreover, the authors note (p. 260) that "if one were to predict school problems for all children with either an Abnormal or a Questionable DDST, and no school problems for children with Normal DDST scores, one would be wrong in 19 instances or 29% (19/65)." The authors conclude that developmental screening should be performed routinely and periodically, so that false exclusions or underreferrals can be identified before the problems of those so excluded become resistant to remediation.

However, two independent studies question the efficiency and the accuracy of the DDST for even short-term predictions. In one study, Nugent (1976) compared the results from the Denver's validation studies with estimated base rates of mental retardation in the screening population sampled by the test. (It was noted earlier that the efficiency of a screening instrument can be evaluated in part by comparing the rate identification of true positives with the natural rate of occurrence of the condition to be identified or diagnosed.) Nugent used an estimate of 3.27% as the base rate of mental retardation in the general population. Use of the Denver yielded the equivalent of a base rate of 3.02%. However, even this small difference in base rates indicates a very low efficiency because so many children who fall into the false negative category would be required to undergo full-scale diagnostic testing before all of the true positives were identified. The assumptions about the control base rate Nugent uses in this argument can be questioned, but the findings about the Denver are consistent with those of other studies.

For example, Applebaum (1978), in another independent study of the DDST, found that 62%, or 24 of 38 children aged 2 months to 30 months, who were classified as normal on the DDST obtained abnormal scores on the mental development index of the Bayley (<70). Co-positivity was .38 and co-negativity was 1.0. Similar findings were reported for the psychomotor index of the Bayley. Applebaum's analysis suggests that the highest proportion of underreferrals occurs within the borderline-to-normal classification of the Denver. Applebaum questions whether the Denver identifies any young children as being abnormally delayed in development "who would not be obvious on the basis of general clinical examination by the pediatrician or other skilled clinician" (p. 232).

Another study of the longitudinal predictive accuracy of the Denver (van Doorninck, Dick, Frankenburg, Liddell, & Lampe, 1976) presents similar results. In this study, the DDST results for 151 children falling into three age ranges were compared with measures of school performance obtained 5–6 years later. Of those who were referred by the DDST, 70% of the children ranging in age from birth to 2 years, 100% of the 2- to 4-year-olds, and 94% of the 4- to 6-year-olds had been correctly predicted by the test to have subsequent school problems. However, the results were very different for those children who were not referred. In this sample, 22% of those ranging in age from birth to 2 years, 50% of the 2- to 4-year-olds, and 41% of the 4- to 6-year-olds who were not at risk on the DDST demonstrated school problems 5–6 years later. Comparing those referred for evaluation with those with questionable and not at risk findings yields a sensitivity rating at each age level of .33, .28, and .39, respectively. Clearly, the Denver results are marked by a high proportion of false negatives.

Frankenburg's recent work seems to lend additional credence to these findings. Two abbreviated forms of the DDST have now been published: the Denver Prescreening Developmental Questionnaire (PDQ) (Frankenburg, van Doorninck, Liddell, & Dick, 1976) and the Revised DDST (DDST-R) (Frankenburg, Fandal, Sciarillo, & Burgess, 1981). The data for the PDQ reveal a low co-positivity rating (26%) and a high co-negativity (96%). Although the test rarely overrefers children, it seriously underrefers them. The predictive utility of a positive result on the PDQ is only 46%; no independent validity data for the DDST-R have yet been published. Thus, these versions of the Denver appear to have the same problem as the original DDST. That is, they are conservative in assigning children to high-risk status—even in the short term. Furthermore, the two abbreviated forms of the test seem to be based on an undefined concept of "prescreening." This approach raises once more the elusive hope of identifying developmental risk factors that will stand on a level with causal, pathogenic agents in disease.

THE MST

A test that only tenuously meets the four criteria noted earlier is the McCarthy Screening Test (MST) (McCarthy, 1978), an adaptation of the McCarthy Scales of Children's Abilities (MSCA) (McCarthy, 1972). The manual for the MST notes that "whereas the purpose of the MSCA is to aid psychologists in measuring the intellectual level of children as well as their strengths and weaknesses in important abilities, the McCarthy Screening Test has the more limited purpose of helping schools to identify children between 4 and 6½ years of age who are likely to need special educational assistance" (McCarthy, 1978, p. 2).

In some respects, a more appropriate name for the MST might be the

MSCA—Shorter Version. It consists of six of the 18 subtests of the MSCA, and it has not been standardized apart from the MSCA. These two facts represent its strength and its weakness, respectively. That is, because it is derived from a highly regarded developmental assessment instrument, it potentially samples a domain of performance, and ability that is highly appropriate for a developmental screening test. However, a recent study of the factor structure of the MST indicates that the subtests all measure parts of the same attribute (cognitive and sensorimotor functions) in varying degrees (Vance, Blixt, & Kitson, 1982). Moreover, the facts that in its development no validity data were reported on the MST itself and no cross validation with an independent criterion was attempted call its accuracy into question.

The manual for the MST describes the administration of the MSCA to 75 children aged 3–11 to 6–8, of whom 61 were labeled learning disabled and 14 were diagnosed as behaviorally disordered. A comparison of results from the MSCA and the subset of tests making up the MST showed that the MSCA correctly identified 88% of this group, and the MST identified 67%. Although the MST manual provides no sensitivity and specificity rates, it can be estimated that the MST would have referred 24% of the standardization sample. Lichtenstein (personal communication) concurs with this estimate and suggests that the sensitivity and specificity rates for the MST would be approximately .67 and .76, respectively.

The manual also presents data comparing the MST (as part of the MSCA) with the Metropolitan Readiness Tests (Nurss & McGauvran, 1976) administered approximately 9 months later. Mean correlations between the MST subtests and the MRT pre–reading skills composite are low, ranging from .10 (leg coordination) to .54 (numerical memory). In another study, however, a significant and positive correlation of .54 was obtained between the MST and the Total Test score of the Peabody Individual Achievement Test (Naglieri & Harrison, 1982).

In short, the MST is a promising test. Being identical with six of the subtests of the MSCA, which has an upper age range of 8 years, the MST may be more discriminating for academically and developmentally more advanced children than are other screening tests. However, it has been distributed prematurely, because reliability and validity data have not been independently collected for the MST but are extrapolated from data obtained with the MSCA. In some respects, how the MST was constructed parallels how many local screening tests have been developed: Various subtests of other well-known tests have been combined into a brief screening instrument. Although the logic behind the MST is much more compelling, tests constructed from individual subtests do not necessarily share the methodological properties of the "parent" tests, nor is it clear that the areas of measurable behavior that they sample are appropriate for use in a developmental screening device.

THE MPSI

The final two screening instruments to be considered provide more data on which to base conclusions regarding predictive validity. The Minneapolis Preschool Screening Instrument (MPSI) (Lichtenstein, 1980) consists of 50 items that are divided among 11 subtests: building, copying shapes, providing information, matching shapes, completing sentences, hopping and balancing, naming colors, counting, using prepositions, identifying body parts, and repeating sentences. Scores on these items are totaled in order to achieve a result of either pass or refer. The test requires approximately 15 minutes to administer and is appropriate for children between 3-7 and 5-4. Test-retest reliability is reported as 92%, and interrater reliability averaged 97.2% across the entire range of subtests (Lichtenstein, 1980). The test has been designed to eliminate items requiring the judgment of the examiner (e.g., expressive language and most gross motor items), and it includes a higher proportion of classroom readiness tasks than most developmental screening tests utilize.

The MPSI has been subjected to a wide range of tests by its author to establish its validity. Three concurrent validity studies were conducted using as criterion measures the DIAL, the Stanford-Binet, and the Peabody Picture Vocabulary Test (PPVT); correlation coefficients for different samples with these criteria are reported as .90 (DIAL), .71 (Stanford-Binet), and .54 (PPVT). To establish predictive validity, an extensive follow-up study of 428 children was conducted a year later, employing a follow-up questionnaire completed by kindergarten and special-education teachers (Lichtenstein, 1982). The questionnaire provides a criterion measure of school performance that includes ratings in nine areas of functioning. The teacher rating scale underwent extensive reliability testing and factor analysis, although its validity is not well established, and its findings have not been replicated elsewhere. When compared with the teacher rating scale, the MPSI has a referral rate of 15.4%. Its sensitivity and specificity ratings are .86 and .90, respectively, and the predictive utility of a referral is .38. Given the limitations of the research that has been completed, the MPSI is an efficient predictor for at least a 1-year period.

THE ESI

The Early Screening Inventory (Meisels & Wiske, 1983) is also an efficient instrument. Developed in 1975, it is a brief developmental survey that is administered individually to children 4–6 years old. It consists of 32 items divided into three main sections: visual-motor/adaptive, language and cognition, and gross motor/body awareness. Interrater reliability correlation for the ESI is .91; test-retest correlation for the total ESI score is .82 after a 7- to 10-day interval.

Several validity studies of the ESI are reported by Wiske, Meisels, and Tivnan (1982) and Meisels, Wiske, and Tivnan (1984). Concurrent validity was tested 10 days after administration of the ESI by using the MSCA as the criterion measure on a stratified sample of 102 children; the overall correlation coefficient between the General Cognitive Index of the McCarthy and the total score of the ESI was .73 ($p < .001$). The sensitivity and specificity ratings for adjusted cross tabulations were .87 and .90 respectively. Thus, in the short term, the ESI refers a high proportion of the children actually at risk and identifies as negative most of those not at risk. The predictive value of a referral for this concurrent study was .71: A relatively high proportion of the referred children were later shown to be correctly identified as at risk on the MSCA.

Long-term predictive validity was tested by comparing ESI scores obtained in kindergarten with indicators of school performance in kindergarten through fourth grade. There were three criterion measures: (1) a cumulative score derived from report card grades in reading, math, and spelling; (2) indication of whether the child received or was referred for special educational services; and (3) disposition at the end of the school year (promoted or retained in grade). Data were collected for five separate cohorts, kindergarten through grade 4.

Results of a classificational analysis of these data indicate a fairly high agreement between the ESI and the various criterion measures—64%–79%—and relatively little variation from kindergarten to fourth grade. Sensitivity and specificity also remain high across time. However, the analysis that is of particular interest shows the predictive power of screening across the 5-year period.

The data presented in Table 2 are significant not only for interpreting the results of the ESI but also for their implications for developmental screening in general. The data from the concurrent study show that the ESI is a highly efficient instrument. It overrefers more children than it underrefers, but its predictive utility is high—although that utility decreases as the interval between the predictor and the criterion measure increases.

Thus, even with a test that has a high concurrent validity and a short-term predictive utility as high as that reported for any other developmental screening test, long-term predictions are tenuous. Although the other screening instruments reviewed do not report comparable year-

TABLE 2

VALIDITY OF THE EARLY SCREENING INVENTORY

Criterion Measure	Validity Dimension	N	Sensitivity	Specificity	Predictive Utility of Referral	Correlation Coefficient with ESI Score
MSCA	Concurrent	102	.87	.90	.71	.73*
Kindergarten CUM[a]	Short-term	53	.88	.82	.47	.70*
Grade 1 CUM	Long-term	78	.92	.72	.40	.50*
Grade 2 CUM	Long-term	60	1.00	.67	.32	.52*
Grade 3 CUM	Long-term	42	.77	.61	.35	.32**
Grade 4 CUM	Long-term	23	.50	.74	.29	.33

[a]CUM = cumulative score derived from report card grades in reading, math, and spelling.

*p < .001.
**p < .05.

by-year longitudinal data, given the criteria a developmental screening instrument must satisfy—brevity, efficiency, low cost, standardized administration, objective scoring, nondiagnostic focus, developmental content, validity measured by classificational rather than correlational methods of analysis—it is likely that those tests, too, would show the same decline in predictive power over time.

PROBLEMS OF PREDICTION

Several reasons can be advanced to explain the declining accuracy of screening prediction over time. First, the technical quality of the instrument may be at fault; a better screening test could have greater predictive power. Second, the instruments reviewed do not test for several situational variables; a multifaceted test that included such variables might increase the accuracy of prediction. Third, screening tests contain a methodological paradox: The more accurately they identify children in need of remediation, and the more successful that remediation is, the greater will be the decline in that screening test's predictive power. Fourth is the dynamic nature of development itself: "Individual characteristics change as a function of interaction with the environment" (Keogh & Becker, 1973, p. 7). Moreover, there are few clear one-to-one relationships between specific characteristics of preschool-aged children and specific accomplishments in school.

Put simply, developmental screening instruments are neither definitive nor comprehensive. They should be used only as indicators, to alert parents and professionals to the need for more intensive assessment procedures that have a higher probability of being accurate and of supporting long-term prediction. However they differ from one another, the developmental screening instruments reviewed above resemble one another in their predictive power. They predict well only in the short run; their use for long-term identification of children at risk cannot be justified. Technically better tests can be developed, but whether they will have appreciably greater predictive power remains to be seen.

DEVELOPMENTAL SCREENING IN THE SOCIAL POLICY
CONTEXT OF EPSDT

This chapter has ranged widely across the terrain of social policy and developmental screening with one purpose: to clarify the complex relationship of a developmental program to the basically medical program within which it is situated. Three general conclusions can be advanced regarding the social policy implications of this relationship:

1. The developmental screening instruments currently available for use in EPSDT are generally inadequate for their purpose and are unable to realize the objectives that have been set for them.

2. The administrative structure of EPSDT is unsuitable for realizing both its developmental and its medical goals.

3. The EPSDT program is a fundamentally inappropriate means for achieving the social policy ends that were identified at its inception.

Before these conclusions are elaborated upon, it must be said that EPSDT should not be eliminated. Rather, it should undergo major redefinition and reorganization.

SCREENING PROGRAM ALTERNATIVES

The foregoing review of developmental screening instruments and predictors makes it clear that few alternatives currently exist for use in the developmental component of EPSDT. Investment in the development of screening instruments in general has not been extensive. Moreover, although the general medical context in which developmental screening takes place focuses on long-term prognoses, most data yielded by screening instruments support only short-term predictions.

Given its limitations, should developmental screening be continued as a distinct component of the EPSDT program, or should it be merged with another part of the program? The Children's Defense Fund analysis of EPSDT (1977) recommended that "the separate component of screening for developmental problems be removed from the EPSDT program and that the process for finding children with developmental problems be limited to what can be done during a routine, comprehensive pediatric assessment" (p. 179). Earlier we argued that this strategy is unwise, for fewer children are likely to be identified as at risk than now are. Given the limited attention among physicians to prevention and to child development issues, it is not reasonable at this time to combine medical and developmental screening into a single procedure.

In fact, if there were no developmental screening component in EPSDT, there would be no federal mandate for screening. Public Law 94-142 requires only that handicapped children be located, not that screening occur. Furthermore, the law bases the size of state funding on the number of handicapped children who receive special education or related services, not on the number screened to determine whether they need such services. Thus, although many states sponsor "childfind" activities, they receive no financial reimbursement for identifying children who do not need special services (Magliocca & Stephens, 1980).

Moreover, EPSDT represents the only federal legislation mandating developmental screening for the purpose of prevention—although, as noted, it is secondary and tertiary prevention. It can be argued that, even with all its technical problems, developmental screening in EPSDT is justified by the cost-benefit logic of prevention. A recent study of early intervention in the city of Chicago noted that "if only 3 percent of the preschoolers in Chicago who have learning problems are identified and helped, the school system could save over $1,684,000 in long-term costs for special education in the elementary grades" (Reed, 1982, p. 36). In 1980 more than $10 billion was spent by all levels of government for various services to handicapped children (Gliedman & Roth, 1980, p. 399). Clearly, if developmental screening and related preventive services could effect a drop of even 10% in the prevalence of long-term handicapping conditions, the savings would be immense.

However, the methodological problems remain. Given the current state of knowledge, how can we maximize the predictive utility of judgments based on developmental screening instruments?

It has been shown that no single or composite predictor applies with efficiency across the age range from birth to 6 years. McCall (1982) has suggested that we might significantly increase predictive accuracy by combining data from a well-designed developmental screening test with other easily obtainable information in a type of multiple-prediction equation. For example, with infants, "parental socioeconomic status, parental involvement with the infant, family stress, and the presence of obstetric and pediatric complications could be used in combination with the infant test to predict disability" (McCall, 1982, p. 210). Of course, indicators of parental involvement and family stress must be defined, but it is reasonable to assume that developmental predictions will increase in accuracy if they combine data from several sources.

A second suggestion for increasing predictive utility stems from recognition of how labile—how readily open to change—development is in early childhood. Because young children change so rapidly, appropriate intervention must commence rapidly for children at risk. It is also critical that screening be conducted recurrently or periodically. These goals can be jointly accomplished by using two referral or "cutting" points for a screening test and then designing an intervention program that has two stages differing in intensity. The first cutting point identifies children urgently in need of further evaluation and probably intensive intervention; the second referral point identifies those who fall between these urgent referrals and children not in need of special services. The children in the second group and their families should receive supportive services, and the children should undergo a second screening after a specific interval to determine whether they should be referred for further evaluation. Figure 1 provides an example of a cycle of prekindergarten developmental screening, referral, and intervention that embodies these characteristics of multiple groups, periodicity, and differential intervention or treatment. The periodicity schedule and the type of intervention program offered should be adjusted to the differing needs of children at different ages. Thus, infants and toddlers should be screened more frequently than older chil-

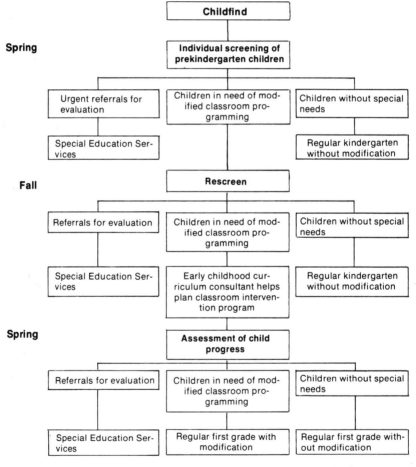

Fig. 1—Developmental screening, referral, and intervention cycle for kindergarten-age children.

dren and should receive intervention in the home more often than in a center. Similarly, different functions and abilities would be emphasized by the intervention program at different ages.

Rather than trying to predict developmental disorders on the basis of a single instrument, such an approach uses the limited evidence obtained from a test as the basis for short-term, nonintensive intervention. As a result, early identification of problems may lead more rapidly to prevention of disorder. Although false positives would unavoidably be included in these preventive programs, they would not remain long because they would be quickly identified in the recurrent cycle of screening or by the data obtained from the intervention program. Similarly, false negatives would be identified during subsequent periodic screening.

This approach seems highly suitable for developmental screening: The program would be ongoing, would be universally available, would sample a wide array of a child's abilities from several perspectives, would be closely tied to intervention and to the logic of prevention, and would allow for frequent opportunities for confirmation and correction.

Unfortunately, this approach would be more complex and initially more costly than is currently mandated by EPSDT. It is not at all clear that EPSDT can manage its present state of complexity, let alone incorporate additional complications.

ADMINISTRATIVE REMEDIES

An assessment of the administrative problems of EPSDT requires that a distinction be drawn between the conceptual structure of EPSDT and its administrative or bureaucratic structure. Conceptually, the overall sequential model of EPSDT is not only sound but is ideally suited to the short-term predictive properties of developmental screening. Administratively, however, EPSDT is not ideal. Indeed, given the record of service documented at the beginning of this chapter, it can be concluded that EPSDT has been an administrative failure. Several reasons can be advanced to support this conclusion.

First, EPSDT promised something—medical and developmental prevention and cure—that it could not produce, by use of a technique—screening—that was barely accepted and of unproved worth (see Foltz, 1982). Not only, as has been shown, are there no substantial data to support long-term predictions based on developmental screening, but serious questions have been raised about the efficacy of medical screening as well (Bailey, Kiehl, Akram, Loughlin, Metcalf, Jain, & Perrin, 1974; Bergman, 1977; Foltz & Kelsey, 1978; Holt, 1974; Whitby, 1974). Screening in both the medical and the developmental domains is notably lacking in rigor and in evaluative studies. Thus, the administrators of EPSDT sought to promote massive use of a technique for which there was insufficient evidence of efficacy.

The EPSDT program also suffered from the administrative failure to select and support an effective means of service delivery. Two types of service delivery systems are used in the EPSDT program: open and closed. In an open system individuals select an eligible service provider from the open market who is reimbursed for the care provided. A closed system is a regional, statewide, or nationwide system employing its own professionals who provide services according to uniform standards and procedures. Developmental screening is usually provided through a closed system, under contract with local education agencies, whereas medical care occurs in a combination of closed and open systems. The potential confusion of this arrangement is indicative of the enormous administrative problems faced by the states as they attempted to implement EPSDT.

Most EPSDT services are obtained through an open system that closely parallels the Medicaid model (of which EPSDT is an offshoot), which is basically a bill-paying system. But open systems require extensive and systematic case monitoring to reduce potential fragmentation. This is a critical issue for the poor, needy, and dependent, who may receive diverse services from many unrelated sources reflecting a patchwork of public entitlement programs. For developmental screening, if the service delivery system is not linked to the public schools, and if case-monitoring procedures are not in effect, screening is less likely to be followed by diagnosis and treatment. Without the latter two, developmental screening is meaningless and unjustifiable. Yet, no uniform standards and procedures have been established nationwide for case monitoring or for referrals in EPSDT. Furthermore, because Medicaid payments have not kept pace with the rising costs of diagnostic services and medical care, there are too few providers of such services in the open system of care. For these and reasons discussed earlier, private providers of both medical and developmental screening are difficult to locate.

The failure of EPSDT to implement an effective system of administrative control derives from the failure of Congress to exercise its power to establish a closed system. At the same time, federal agencies did not have the manpower to monitor an open system. The federal strategy was to continue to supply block grants for Medicaid, thereby shifting the burden of administrative responsibility to the states.

During the administration of President Carter, an unsuccessful attempt was made to solve several of these administrative problems by means of a revision of the EPSDT program known as the Child Health Assessment Program (CHAP). This program, which languished in congressional committees for several years and never came to a vote before Congress, would have linked medical screening with continuing health care in order to ensure treatment. It also would have greatly expanded the number and types of developmental services and would have relaxed eligibility requirements to make these services available to more people. Finally, the proposal would have mandated that states assure case monitoring and supportive services and would have emphasized coordination of the many services included in EPSDT (see Moore, 1978).

Although well conceived, these administrative recommendations remain unrealized. If, as proposed earlier, the developmental component of the program also undergoes change, then administrative structure and function should be further modified, as suggested in the CHAP legislation. In the absence of clear administrative guidelines, a specific coordinating agency in each state, and the recognition that the recipients of these grants-in-aid are important "targets of opportunity" for state policymakers, EPSDT will continue to fail to realize its potential to serve the poor.

SOCIAL EQUITY

A review of the development of EPSDT reveals a critical transition in advocacy. What began as a program of national concern eventually became the narrow responsibility of state welfare agencies and ultimately derived support principally from special-interest groups representing clients and certain professions. Foltz and Brown (1975) point out, "The problems of EPSDT stem from the narrowness of its constituency, welfare children. From its inception to implementation, EPSDT was a program no one wanted except the poor, and most of them were unaware of its existence" (p. 641).

Although all federal benefits programs are suffering economic problems in the 1980s, the constituency served by EPSDT appears to distinguish it from other massive social welfare programs that do not have similar administrative or political problems. More than 36% of all federal spending in fiscal year 1980 was devoted to benefits programs in which eligibility was *not* determined by financial need—for example, Social Security, civil service pensions, military pensions, Medicare, and unemployment compensation. Only 8.5% of total federal spending in 1980 went to programs in which eligibility was determined strictly by financial need—programs such as welfare, Supplementary Security Income, food stamps, and Medicaid.

The EPSDT program embodied several problems that were political in origin: (1) unequal distribution of public benefits; (2) failure of the federal government to appropriate sufficient funds to support proposed services; (3) uniform imposition of a federal law on states vastly disparate in resources and capabilities; (4) lack of significant enforcement strategies; and (5) absence of administrative leadership and advocacy. Compounding these problems was an ever-increasing financial erosion.

Such problems arose because the initial planning and implementation of the program were inadequate and because there was no continuous monitoring of services. As noted earlier, the EPSDT legislation was proposed without any data to support the assumption that the program could solve the problems being addressed. To this day, the EPSDT program has not provided any evaluative data to show which groups in the population profit most from preventive care, which conditions are most effectively screened, or what the effects of fragmentation of care are. Nor has any study measured the program's costs against its benefits.

Many of EPSDT's political problems emerge from a basic social-policy assumption that EPSDT shared with many other programs of the 1960s. In deLone's view (1979), the programs of the Great Society years "invested the child with the burden of realizing the reformer's dreams . . . they confused services to individuals with a strategy for equality. . . . These services can counter some of the injuries of inequality, but they cannot destroy inequality itself" (p. 68).

In other words, the EPSDT program was using the needs of poor children as an occasion for restructuring American health services and providing the basis for a national health insurance system. It was fallaciously assumed that social equity can be achieved by a method that singles out the specific needs of poor children. Rather, major social change calls for systematic establishment of several critical, overlapping services and educational, economic, and social opportunities for several major segments of the population.

In a study of the implementation of the mandatory special education law in Massachusetts, Weatherly (1979) describes a situation in education that closely parallels the problems of EPSDT: "Middle-class parents are better able to find out what services are available and hold the responsible agencies accountable for providing these services. The fragmentation of human service delivery, restrictive means tests for eligibility, and the relative difficulty in obtaining services can lead to a dual system of services, one for the children of the poor and another for children of the affluent" (p. 10). A dual system of health benefits for the poor and the middle class exists today. Although EPSDT has narrowed the gap between the systems, wide discrepancies still exist.

The solutions to the problems enumerated above are exceedingly difficult to realize politically. Comprehensive and universal health care is a necessary part of the solution, although not sufficient in itself. Ironically, also necessary are screening, diagnosis, and treatment, provided early and periodically. In other words, redressing the social inequities in our society would require creating the conceptual structure of EPSDT—were it not already in existence. However, strong agruments can be advanced that the program should be administered and monitored very differently, should be provided to all individuals regardless of financial means, should focus sharply on preventive actions, and should adopt a comprehensive view of the individual within a social system. Prevention of developmental delay cannot ignore the social, cultural, and economic conditions that contribute to and sustain such delay.

If such changes were to take place, the problems of prediction and prevention might be altered. In fact, if social equity were to increase, the quest for predictive accuracy in developmental matters might decrease. To the extent that one resorts to the use of such demographic variables as low SES to improve predictive accuracy, one acknowledges the casualties of social inequity and the concomitant problems of preventing developmental disorders.

In a sense, two forces with conflicting goals are at work. As social scientists, we seek to maximize predictability by identifying the factors that explain differences in developmental outcomes. As practitioners, we hope to eliminate the factors that inhibit developmental potential, thereby decreasing predictability. McCall (1982) has pointed out that the propensity for change in children obviates one-shot enrichments and is a bane to prediction. However, it is a boon to humanity. In creating the conditions that make individual developmental predictions more difficult, we come to better understand the richness and complexity of human development.

REFERENCES

American Association of Psychiatric Services for Children, Inc. *Developmental review in the early and periodic screening diagnosis and treatment program* (Final rep., U.S. Department of Health, Education, and Welfare, Health Care Financing Administration), Washington, D.C.: Government Printing Office, 1977.

American Orthopsychiatric Association. Developmental assessment in EPSDT. *American Journal of Orthopsychiatry*, 1978, 48, 7–21.

Applebaum, A. Validity of the revised Denver Developmental Screening Test for referred and non-referred samples. *Psychological Reports*, 1978, 43, 227–233.

Bailey, E., Kiehl, P. S., Akram, D. S., Loughlin, H. H., Metcalf, T. J., Jain, R., & Perrin, J. M. Screening in pediatric practice. *Pediatric Clinics of North America*, 1974, 21, 123–165.

Balow, B., Rubin, R., & Rosen, M. Perinatal events as precursors of reading disability. *Reading Research Quarterly*, 1975–1976, 11, 36–71.

Bayley, N. Development of mental abilities. In P. H. Mussen (Ed.), *Carmichael's manual of child psychology* (Vol. 1). New York: Wiley, 1970.

Becker, L. Conceptual tempo and the early detection of learning problems. *Journal of Learning Disabilities*, 1976, **9**, 433–442.

Becker, P. T., & Thoman, E. B. Rapid eye movement storms in infants: Rate of occurrence at 6 months predicts mental development at 1 year. *Science*, 1980, **212**, 1415–1416.

Bergman, A. B. The menace of mass screening (editorial). *American Journal of Public Health*, 1977, **67**, 601–602.

Bradley, R., & Caldwell, B. Screening the environment. *American Journal of Orthopsychiatry*, 1978, **48**, 114–130.

Brewer, G. D., & Kakalik, J. S. *Handicapped children—Strategies for improving services.* New York: McGraw-Hill, 1979.

Bronfenbrenner, U. *Is early intervention effective?* Washington, D.C.: Office of Human Development, 1974.

Buck, A., & Gart, J. Comparison of a screening test and a reference test in epidemiological studies. *American Journal of Epidemiology*, 1966, **83**, 586–592.

Buros, O. (Ed.). *Eighth mental measurement yearbook.* Highland Park, N.J.: Gryphon, 1978.

Camp, B., van Doorninck, W., Frankenburg, W., & Lampe, J. Preschool developmental testing in prediction of school problems: Studies of 55 children in Denver. *Clinical pediatrics*, 1977, **16**, 257–263.

Chamberlain, R., & Davey, A. Cross-sectional study of developmental test items in children aged 94 to 97 weeks: Report of the British births child study. *Developmental Medicine and Child Neurology*, 1976, **18**, 54–70.

Chamberlin, R. W. Can we identify a group of children at age 2 who are at high risk for the development of behavior or emotional problems in kindergarten and first grade? *Pediatrics*, 1977, **59**, 971–981.

Chang, A., Goldstein, H., Thomas, K., & Wallace H. M. The Early Periodic Screening Diagnosis, and Treatment program (EPSDT): Status of progress and implementation in 51 states and territories. *Journal of School Health*, 1979, 454–458.

Children's Defense Fund. *EPSDT: Does it spell health care for poor children?* Washington, D.C.: Washington Research Project, 1977.

Clarke, A. M., & Clarke, A. D. B. *Early experience: myth and evidence.* New York : Free Press, 1976.

Cochrane, A., & Holland, W. Validation of screening procedures. *British Medical Bulletin*, 1971, **27**, 3–8.

Colarusso, R., Plankenhorn, A., Brooks, R. Predicting first-grade achievement through formal testing of 5-year-old high-risk children. *Journal of Special Education*, 1980, **14**, 355–363.

Coleman, L. Problem kids and preventive medicine: The making of an odd couple. *American Journal of Orthopsychiatry*, 1978, **48**, 56–70.

Colligan, R. C., & O'Connell, E. J. Should psychometric screening be made an adjunct to the pediatric preschool examination? *Clinical Pediatrics*, 1974, **13**, 29–34.

Cooke, R. E. Introduction. In E. Zigler & J. Valentine (Eds.), *Project Head Start—A legacy of the War on Poverty.* New York: Free Press, 1979.

deLone, R. H. *Small futures—Children, inequality and the limits of liberal reform.* New York: Harcourt Brace Jovanovich, 1979.

Dimitrovsky, L., & Almy, M. Early conservation as a predictor of later reading. *Journal of Psychology*, 1975, **90**, 11–18.

Dunst, C. J., & Rheingrover, R. M. Discontinuity and instability in early development: Implications for assessment. *Topics in Early Childhood Special Education*, 1981, **1**, 49–60.

Dworkin, P. H., Shonkoff, J. P., Leviton, A., & Levine, M. D. Training in developmental pediatrics. *American Journal of Diseases of Children*, 1979, **133**, 709–712.

Eaves, L. C., Kendall, D. C., & Crichton, J. U. The early identification of learning disabilities: A follow-up study. *Journal of Learning Disabilities*, 1974, **7**, 632–638.

Egert, J. M. Now school teachers are playing doctor. *Medical Economics*, April 17, 1978, pp. 119–124.

Escalona, S. Intervention programs for children at psychiatric risk. In E. J. Anthony & C. Koupernik (Eds.), *The child in his family—Children at psychiatric risk* (Vol. 3). New York: Wiley, 1974.

Fagan, J. F., & McGrath, S. K. Infant recognition memory and later intelligence. *Intelligence*, 1981, **5**, 121–130.

Feshbach, S., Adelman, H., & Fuller, W. W. Early identification of children with high risk of reading failures. *Journal of Learning Disabilities*, 1974, **7**, 639–644.

Feshbach, S., Adelman, H., & Fuller, W. Prediction of reading and related academic problems. *Journal of Educational Psychology*, 1977, **69**, 299–308.

Finkelstein, N. W., & Ramey, C. T. Information from birth certificates as a risk index for educational handicap. *American Journal of Mental Deficiency*, 1980, **84**, 546–552.

Foltz, A. M. 1975. The development of ambiguous federal policy: Early and Periodic Screening, Diagnosis and Treatment (EPSDT). *Milbank Memorial Fund Quarterly/Health and Society*, 1975, **53**, 35–64.

Foltz, A. M. *An ounce of prevention: Child health politics under Medicaid.* Cambridge, Mass.: MIT Press, 1982.

Foltz, A. M., & Brown, D. State response to federal policy: Children, EPSDT and the Medicaid muddle. *Medical Care*, 1975, **13**, 630–642.

Foltz, A. M., & Kelsey, J. L. 1978. The annual Pap test: A dubious policy success. *Milbank Memorial Fund Quarterly/Health and Society*, 1978, **56**, 426–462.

Forness, S., Hall, R., & Guthrie, D. Eventual school placement of kindergarteners observed as high risk in the classroom. *Psychology in the Schools*, 1977, **14**, 315–317.

Frankenburg, W. K. Selection of diseases with tests in pediatric screening. *Pediatrics*, 1974, **54**, 612–616.

Frankenburg, W. K. Principles in selecting diseases for screening. In W. K. Frankenburg & B. W. Camp (Eds.), *Pediatric screening tests.* Springfield, Ill.: Thomas, 1975.

Frankenburg, W. K., Camp, B. W., & Van Natta, P. Validity of the Denver Developmental Screening Test. *Child Development*, 1971, **42**, 475–485. (a)

Frankenburg, W. K., Camp, B. W., Van Natta, P., & Demersseman, J. Reliability and stability of the Denver Developmental Screening Test. *Child Development*, 1971, **42**, 1315–1325. (b)

Frankenburg, W. K., Dick, N. P., & Darland, J. Development of pre-school aged children of different social and ethnic groups: Implications for developmental screening. *Journal of Pediatrics*, 1975, **87**, 125–132.

Frankenburg, W. K., & Dodds, J. The Denver Developmental Screening Test. *Journal of Pediatrics*, 1967, **71**, 181–191.

Frankenburg, W. K., Dodds, J., Fandal, A., Kazuk, E., & Cohrs, M. *Denver Developmental Screening Test.* Denver: University of Colorado Medical Center, 1975.

Frankenburg, W. K., Fandal, A., Sciarillo, W., & Burgess, D. 1981. The newly abbreviated and revised Denver Developmental Screening Test. *Journal of Pediatrics*, 1981, **99**, 995–999.

Frankenburg, W. K., Goldstein, A., & Camp, B. W. The revised Denver Developmental Screening Test: Its accuracy as a screening instrument. *Journal of Pediatrics*, 1971, **79**, 988–995.

Frankenburg, W. K., & North, A. F. *A guide to screening for the Early and Periodic Screening Diagnosis and Treatment program under Medicaid.* Washington, D.C.: Department of Health, Education, and Welfare, 1974.

Frankenburg, W. K., van Doorninck, W. J., Liddell, T., & Dick, N. P. The Denver Prescreening Developmental Questionnaire (PDQ). *Pediatrics*, 1976, **57**, 744–753.

Freymann, J. G. Medicine's great schism: Prevention vs. cure: An historical interpretation. *Medical Care*, 1975, **13**, 525–536.

Gliedman, J., & Roth, W. *The unexpected minority—Handicapped children in America.* New York: Harcourt Brace Jovanovich, 1980.

Gortmaker, S. L., Haggerty, R. J., Jacobs, F. H., Messenger, K. P., & Walker, D. K. *Community services for children and youth in Genesee County, Michigan.* Boston: Harvard School of Public Health, 1980.

Harber, J. R. Assessing the quality of decision making in special education. *Journal of Special Education*, 1981, **15**, 77–90.

Hobbs, N. *The futures of children.* San Francisco: Jossey-Bass, 1975.

Holt, K. S. Screening for disease: Infancy and childhood. *Lancet*, 1974, **2**, 1057–1060.

Hooper, P. D. Letter: Developmental screening and assessment. *British Medical Journal*, 1975, **2**, 87.

Illingworth, R. S. *The development of the infant and young child.* 6th ed. Edinburgh: Churchill Livingstone, 1975.

Johnson, L. B. Message on children and youth. *Congressional Quarterly Almanac*, February 8, 1967.

Joiner, L. M. A technical analysis of the variation in screening instruments and programs in New York State. New York: City University of New York, New York Center for Advanced Study in Education, 1977. (ERIC Document Reproduction Service No. ED 154 596).

Kaufman, A. S., & Kaufman, N. L. Tests build from Piaget's and Gesell's tasks as predictors of first-grade achievement. *Child Development*, 1972, **43**, 521–535.

Keogh, B., & Becker, L. Early detection of learning problems: Questions, cautions, and guidelines. *Exceptional children*, 1973, **40**, 5–11.

Lazar, I., Hubbell, V. R., Murray, H., Rosche, M., & Royce, J. *The persistence of preschool effects.* Washington, D.C.: Department of Health, Education, and Welfare, Office of Human Development, 1977.

Lessen, E., & Rose, T. State definitions of preschool handicapped populations. *Exceptional Children*, 1980, **46**, 467–469.

Levine, M. D., Brooks, R., & Shonkoff, J. P. *A pediatric approach to learning disorders.* New York: Wiley, 1979.

Lewis, M. Infant intelligence tests: Their use and misuse. *Human Development*, 1973, **16**, 108–118.

Lewis, M. What do we mean when we say "Infant Intelligence Scores"? A sociopolitical question. In M. Lewis (Ed.), *Origins of intelligence: Infancy and early childhood.* New York: Plenum, 1976.

Lewis, M., & Fox, N. Predicting cognitive development from assessments in infancy. In B. W. Camp (Ed.), *Advances in behavioral pediatrics* (Vol. 1). Greenwich, Conn.: JAI, 1980.

Lichtenstein, R. 1980. *Identifying children with special educational needs via preschool screening: Binet revisited.* Unpublished doctoral dissertation, University of Minnesota, 1980.

Lichtenstein, R. Comparative validity of two preschool screening tests: Correlational and classificational approaches. *Journal of Learning Disabilities*, 1981, **14**, 68–72.

Lichtenstein, R. New instrument, old problem for early identification. *Exceptional Children*, 1982, **49**, 70–72.

Littman, B., & Parmelee, A. M. Medical correlates of infant development. *Pediatrics*, 1978, **61**, 470–474.

Magliocca, L., & Stephens, T. Child identification or child inventory? A critique of the federal design of child-identification systems implemented under P.L. 94–142. *Journal of Special Education*, 1980, **14**, 23–36.

Malbon, S. 1978. Learning disabilities screening instruments: Discriminative validity. Paper presented at the annual meeting of the American Educational Research Association, 1978. (ERIC Document Reproduction Service No. ED 155 198).

Mardell, C. D., & Goldenberg, D. S. *DIAL—Developmental Indicators for the Assessment of Learning*. Edison, N.J.: Childcraft Education Corp., 1975.

McCall, R. B. The development of intellectual functioning in infancy and the prediction of later I.Q. In J. D. Osofsky (Ed.), *Handbook of infant development*. New York: Wiley, 1979.

McCall, R. B. A hard look at stimulating and predicting development: The cases of bonding and screening. *Pediatrics Review*, 1982, **3**, 205–212.

McCall, R. B., Hogarty, P. S., & Hurlburt, N. Transitions in infant sensorimotor development and the prediction of childhood IQ. *American Psychologist*, 1972, **27**, 728–748.

McCarthy, D. *McCarthy Scales of Children's Abilities*. New York: Psychological Corp., 1972.

McCarthy, D. *McCarthy Screening Test*. New York: Psychological Corp., 1978.

Meehl, P., & Rosen, A. Antecedent probability and the efficiency of psychometric signs, patterns, or cutting scores. *Psychological Bulletin*, 1955, **52**, 194–216.

Meisels, S. J. *Developmental screening in early childhood: A guide*. Washington, D.C.: National Association for the Education of Young Children, 1978.

Meisels, S. J., & Anastasiow, N. J. The risks of prediction: Relationships between etiology, handicapping conditions and developmental outcomes. In S. Moore & C. Cooper (Eds.), *The young child: Reviews of research–Volume III*. Washington, D.C.: National Association for the Education of Young Children, 1982.

Meisels, S. J., & Wiske, M. S. *The Early Screening Inventory*. New York: Teachers College Press, 1983.

Meisels, S. J., Wiske, M. S., & Tivman, T. Predicting school performance with the Early Screening Inventory. *Psychology in the Schools*, 1984, 21, 25–33.

Messick, S. Test validity and the ethics of assessment. *American Psychologist*, 1980, **35**, 1012–1027.

Moore, B. D. Implementing the developmental assessment component of the EPSDT program. *American Journal of Orthopsychiatry*, 1978, **48**, 22–32.

Morency, A., & Wepman, J. Early perceptual ability and later school achievement. *Elementary School Journal*, 1973, **73**, 323–327.

Naglieri, J. A., & Harrison, P. L. McCarthy Scales, McCarthy Screening Test, and Kaufman's McCarthy Short Form Correlations with the Peabody Individual Achievement Test. *Psychology in the Schools*, 1982, **19**, 149–155.

Nugent, J. A comment on the efficiency of the Revised Denver Developmental Screening Test. *American Journal of Mental Deficiency*, 1976, **80**, 570–572.

Nurss, J. R., & McGauvran, M. E. *Metropolitan Readiness Tests*. New York: Harcourt Brace Jovanovich, 1976.

Oberklaid, F., Dworkin, P. H., & Levine, M. D. Developmental-behavioral dysfunction in preschool children. *American Journal of Diseases of Children*, 1979, **133**, 1126–1131.

Ramey, C. T., Stedman, D. J., Borders-Patterson, A., & Mengel, W. Predicting school failure from information available at birth. *American Journal of Mental Deficiency*, 1978, **82**, 525–534.

Reed, S. Chicago's early focus on learning problems. *New York Times Winter Survey of Education*, January 10, 1982, 36–37.

Reynolds, M. C. Categories and variables in special education. In M. C. Reynolds & M. D.

Davis (Eds.), *Exceptional children in regular classrooms.* Minneapolis: Minneapolis Leadership Training Institute, University of Minnesota, 1971.

Rogers, K. D. 1974. Screening in pediatric practice: Review and commentary. *Pediatric Clinics of North America,* 1974, **21**, 167–174.

Rubin, R. A., & Balow, B., Measures of infant development and socioeconomic status as predictors of later intelligence and school achievement. *Developmental Psychology,* 1979, **15**, 225–227.

Rubin, R. A., Balow, B., Dorle, J., & Rosen, M. Preschool prediction of low achievement in basic school skills. *Journal of Learning Disabilities,* 1978, **11**, 664–667.

Rutter, M. The long-term effects of early experience. *Developmental Medicine and Child Neurology,* 1980, **22**, 800–815.

Sameroff, A. J. Early influences on development. *Merrill-Palmer Quarterly,* 1975, **21**, 267–294.

Sameroff, A. J. Caretaking or reproductive casualty? Determinants in developmental deviancy. In F. D. Horowitz (Ed.), *Early developmental hazards: Predictors and precautions.* Boulder, Colo.: Westview, 1978.

Sameroff, A. J. Longitudinal studies of preterm infants. In S. L. Friedman & M. Sigman (Eds.), *Preterm birth and psychological development.* New York: Academic Press, 1981.

Satz, P., & Fletcher, J. Early screening tests: Some uses and abuses. *Journal of Learning Disabilities,* 1979, **12**, 65–69.

Schrag, P., & Divoky, D. 1975. *The myth of the hyperactive child.* New York: Pantheon, 1975.

Schweinhart, L. J., & Weikart, D. P. *Young children grow up: The effects of the Perry Preschool Program on youths through age 15.* Ypsilanti, Mich.: High/Scope Press, 1980.

Select Panel for the Promotion of Child Health, Office of the Assistant Secretary for Health and Surgeon General. *Better health for our children: A national strategy.* Vol. **2**: *Analysis and recommendations for selected federal programs.* Washington, D.C.: Department of Health and Human Services, 1980.

Serunian, S. A., & Broman, S. H. Relationship of Apgar scores and Bayley mental and motor scores. *Child Development,* 1975, **46**, 696–700.

Siegel, L. 1981. Infant tests as predictors of cognitive and language development at two years. *Child Development,* 1981, **52**, 545–557.

Sigman, M., & Parmelee, A. H. Longitudinal evaluation of the pre-term infant. In T. M. Field, A. M. Sostek, S. Goldberg, & H. H. Shuman (Eds.), *Infants born at risk.* New York: Spectrum, 1979.

Smith, R. D. The use of developmental screening tests by primary care pediatricians. *Pediatrics,* 1978, **93**, 524–527.

State Program Implementation Studies Branch. *Second annual report to Congress on the implementation of Public Law 94–142: The Education for all Handicapped Children Act.* Washington, D.C.: Department of Education, 1980.

Steiner, G. Y. *The children's cause.* Washington, D.C.: Brookings Institution, 1976.

Stevenson, H., Parker, T., Wilkinson, A., Hegion, A., & Fish, E. Longitudinal study of individual differences in cognitive development and scholastic achievement. *Journal of Educational Psychology,* 1976, **68**, 377–400.

Svinicki, J. G., & Tombari, M. L. *Developing and interpreting local norms.* Boston: Teaching Resources, 1981.

Task Force on Human Resources, Congressional Budget Office. *Prospects for meeting health care needs of children eligible for Medicaid under EPSDT, Working paper on major budget and program issues in selected health programs.* Washington, D.C.: Committee of the Budget, House of Representatives, December 10, 1976.

Telegdy, G. The effectiveness of four readiness tests as predictors of first grade academic achievement. *Psychology in the Schools*, 1975, **12**, 4–11.

van Doorninck, W. J., Dick, N. P., Frankenburg, W. K. Liddell, T. N., & Lampe, J. M. *Infant and preschool developmental screening and later performance.* Paper presented at the Society for Pediatric Research, St. Louis, April 1976.

Vance, B., Blixt, S., Kitson, D. L., Factor structure of the McCarthy Screening Test. *Psychology in the Schools*, 1982, **19**, 33–38.

Weatherley, R. A. *Reforming special education—Policy implementation from state level to street level.* Cambridge, Mass.: MIT Press, 1979.

Werner, E. E., Bierman, J. M., & French, F. E. *The children of Kauai.* Honolulu: University of Hawaii Press, 1971.

Werner, E. E., & Smith, R. S. *Kauai's children come of age.* Honolulu: University of Hawaii Press, 1977.

Whitby, L. Screening definitions and criteria. *Lancet*, 1974, **2**, 819–821.

Wilson, J. M. G., & Jungner, G. *Principles and practice of screening for disease.* Public Health Papers no. 34. Geneva: World Health Organization, 1968.

Wiske, M. S., Meisels, S. J., & Tivnan, T. Development and variation of the Early Screening Inventory: A study of early childhood developmental screening. In N. J. Anastasiow, W. K. Frankenburg, & A. Fandel (Eds.), *Identification of the developmentally delayed child.* Baltimore: University Park Press, 1982.

Institutionalization and Deinstitutionalization of Children with Mental Retardation

STEPHEN A. RICHARDSON
Albert Einstein College of Medicine

INTRODUCTION

To reduce to manageable scale the task of reviewing the literature dealing with children in all forms of institutional care, I shall focus on children who are mentally retarded. These children's needs vary widely, not only because the severity of their mental impairment differs, but because more often than children who are not retarded they also have other forms of disability, such as behavior disturbance, language and speech problems, deafness, blindness, cerebral palsy, limb impairments, epilepsy, and chronic medical conditions. In general, the frequency and severity of multiple disability increase with severity of mental retardation. It is often disabilities other than intellectual impairment which are the main reason for placement of retarded—especially more mildly retarded—children in institutional care.

There are limitations in the literature on the institutionalization and deinstitutionalization of mentally retarded children. Gaps in the research findings compromise the value of such research as a basis for generalization or policy recommendations. Where knowledge is limited by lack of research, I have tried to restrict conclusions to hypotheses and tentative generalizations and to the raising of questions. To first indicate some of the limitations of the literature may be helpful to the reader in assessing the content of the chapter.

First, there has been no clear and agreed-on definition of the term *deinstitutionalization*. There is no definition in Webster's *International Dictionary*, although *institutionalization* is defined as "to place or commit to the care of a specialized institution (as for the insane, alcoholics, epileptics, delinquent youth, or the aged)." Deinstitutionalization is, then, the removal of a person from such an institution. (The term says nothing about what then happens to those removed.) Common usage of the term applies it to "bad" institutions, those that have unsuitable and often neglectful and inhumane environments for the residents. Because it was assumed often only implicitly that institutions are "bad," this form of institution was documented. Are there "good" institutions? And if there are, what are their characteristics and how do they affect their residents? No research was directed to answering these questions.

As a corollary of the emphasis in the literature on "bad" institutions, it has been assumed—more often than it has been systematically examined— that almost any form of placement away from the institution improves the former residents' quality of life. The term *deinstitutionalization* would logically seem to apply to removal from an institution for placement in a noninstitutional setting, such as a family. The literature, however, deals largely with the transfer of persons from one type of institution to another. Generally, the first institution is large and government operated and often distant from populous areas, whereas the receiving institutions are smaller, are closer to communities, are run by voluntary as well as government agencies, and were developed or selected with the hope and presumption that they would provide "better" placements.

It seems more reasonable to expect that deinstitutionalized children will be returned to their parents than that deinstitutionalized adults will be. The child has greater need of a family, and the conventional wisdom, backed by considerable research, is that, for most children, being brought up by their parents and among siblings is the most beneficial form of childhood socialization. Unfortunately, many of the children in institutions were first placed there because their parents, for a variety of reasons, had not provided an appropriate environment for their development. (Reasons could vary widely: death, separation, or divorce; neglect, abuse, or desertion of the child; or imprisonment or institutionalization of parents.) To consider returning children from such families to their parents' home may be unrealistic. Some children have been placed in institutional care because the severity and multiplicity of their problems overwhelmed the parents, for whom there were no community care facilities to give them needed help. Return of these children to their families would require the provision of community services to help the family.

A second problem in reviewing the literature is that in various studies the ages of the subjects are not given. Although clearly the needs of children vary according to their ages, and in turn differ from the needs of adults, age is largely ignored in studies of mental retardation. A few studies are of children, but most are of adults ranging widely in age, or of both children and adults. This indifference to age may be due to the belief that the mentally retarded are childlike irrespective of age. This belief draws some apparent scientific credibility from the concept of "mental age" originated by Binet and based on IQ test scores. An indicator of this belief is that some researchers refer to mentally retarded adults as "boys" and "girls." Moreover, the English language makes no distinction between child and adult offspring; all are "children of parents" no matter what their age. Thus, studies that deal with mentally retarded "children" leave the ages ambiguous.

There has been little research into the residential care of children and deinstitutionalization. One apparent reason is that such studies fall into the interstices between the academic divisions within the behavioral sciences. Another reason is limitations in theories and concepts. The studies of children have been largely the province of psychology and psychiatry and have dealt disproportionally with the first years of life. The individual characteristics of children have received most attention, and the institutional environments where children are placed have been largely ignored. In the few studies of institutions by psychologists and psychiatrists, quantitative measures have generally been applied only to the characteristics of the child. No systematic measures of the environment were developed; the institutions received only qualitative description. Although sociologists have made the study of institutions a central focus of theory and research, they have been primarily concerned with adults. Until recently the interaction between children and institutional environments was studied only by social psychologists and social anthropologists, and I have drawn on their work heavily in this chapter.

In this chapter I will first sketch the historical context necessary to understand the emergence of what could be called the ideology of deinstitutionalization and the actions that followed. Then I will consider a range of factors—political, legislative, and economic—that influenced and were influenced by deinstitutionalization. Finally, I will review the available studies of mentally retarded children in various forms of residential care.

THE HISTORY OF INSTITUTIONS AND THE BEGINNINGS OF THE
DEINSTITUTIONALIZATION MOVEMENT

To understand the institutional conditions that engendered the deinstitutionalization movement, we review the history of mental retardation institutions in the United States. Prior to the development of industrial society, in the eighteenth century, people who were unable to assume the roles society expected of them were cared for informally by their primary and extended families, sometimes with help from the local community.

As the tempo of social and technological change increased (especially during the Industrial Revolution), the informal caring system began to break down. By the nineteenth century there were prisons, almshouses, and asylums in the United States. Mentally ill and mentally retarded people were placed in all three kinds of institutions. In addition, paupers and others were placed in the care of families who agreed to take charge of them in return for a stipulated sum (Rosen & Clark, 1976, pp. 9, 13).

Dorothea Dix traveled throughout Massachusetts in 1843 looking into conditions in these institutions. She found "idiots" and insane people living in pens, stalls, and cages without heat or adequate clothing. They lived in conditions of filth and squalor, sometimes kept in chains, sometimes subject to brutal and inhumane treatment. In her travels she also encountered "many poor creatures wandering reckless and unprotected through the country" (Dix, in Rosen & Clark, 1976, p. 8). In her "Memorial to the Legislature of Massachusetts," she concluded "that most of the idiotic subjects in the prisons in Massachusetts are unjustly committed, being wholly incapable of doing harm, and none manifesting any disposition either to injure others or to exercise mischievous propensities" (p. 15). She was one of the first to be concerned about the relationship between size of institution and quality of care. "The greatest evils in regard to the insane and idiots in the prisons of the Commonwealth are found at Ipswich and Cambridge, and distinguish these places only, as I believe, because the numbers are larger, being more than twenty in each" (p. 27). Her central concern was for idiots and insane persons in the jails and asylums for the poor who were "brought into unsuitable connection with criminals and general mass of paupers" (p. 5).

British literature contains several descriptions of the conditions of children and adults in institutions. Perhaps the best known are by Dickens and include an account of the workhouse in *Oliver Twist* and the boarding school in *Nicholas Nickleby*.

In the United States (as elsewhere) the shift from traditional society to industrial society was accompanied by a change in values and social ethos. In the traditional society the individual was thought of as an integral part of a family and community, and the family status largely determined the person's status and role. During the Industrial Revolution there came to be greater belief in the ability of all to succeed by hard work and leading a moral and upright life. Each person was judged more on personal achievement and less on membership in an interdependent family unit. This change corresponded to the weakening of the extended family as a support system, due in part to increased geographic mobility and the growth of cities and industry.

In the United States early support for the idea of caring for mentally retarded people drew on ideas developed in Europe during the first half of the nineteenth century. Numerous persons, deeply concerned over the plight of disabled persons who were neglected and often ill-treated, devoted themselves to teaching people with various disabilities, taking them into their homes or starting schools and institutions. Guggenbühl in Switzerland started an institution to teach and care for cretins. Itard in France devoted himself to teaching a boy who had been found running wild. He worked with the boy, whom many believed was mentally retarded, for six years, keeping him in his house and employing a governess for him. Séguin in France developed methods of sensory, muscular, and speech training for mentally retarded people. He later came to the United States and helped establish training institutions for the mentally retarded. The writings and lectures of these men were enormously influential, producing a climate of optimistic belief that, with appropriate training, mentally retarded people could be greatly helped to develop.

EARLY FORMS OF CARE

Between about 1850 and 1880 in the United States, training facilities for mentally retarded people grew rapidly in number as public acceptance of responsibility for retarded people grew. It was a time of reformers and humanists, with special concern given to helping the needy (Kanner, 1964). The training of retarded persons initially directed toward individuals and small groups changed as growing numbers became identified as retarded. Increasingly, retarded persons were gathered into large institutions newly built in rural surroundings. The size of these early institutions was influenced by the factories built during the Industrial Revolution, which brought unprecedentedly large numbers of people together under one roof. The organization of inmates was likewise influenced by the factory practice of dividing tasks into a large number of component parts, each of which required very little skill (Moss, 1975).

Initially, vigorous efforts were made to train the inmates of the institutions for a return to the outside society; emphasis was given to vocational, religious, and moral training. When this training did not achieve the striking results that had been claimed by the early leaders in the field, attention shifted, about 1880, toward long-term custodial care. Training was limited to enabling the inmate to function within the institution. With people continuing to enter the institutions and very few leaving, the institutional population grew. By 1875 there were 25 state-run institutions in the United States, with a combined total of over 15,000 inmates (Kuhlmann, 1940).

The move toward institutionalization had the effect of diverting attention from the alternative of foster care for retarded children. This trend is described by Adams (1975, p. 271):

> Almost at the same time [as foster care was being developed in rural New York], Howe was harassing the legislature of the Commonwealth of Massachusetts to provide funds for a special school for the "idiotic" children it had in its care, mainly in the Country Poor Houses, with the express intention of giving them a milieu and training that was suited to their limited capacities but would also stimulate them appropriately so that they would "be more of a man and less of a beast" (Howe, 1851): the 19th century concept of humanization and normalization.

> This excellently intended effort started the system of specialized residential care, so that while the "normal" children under County Care were salvaged by assimilation into the foster home model the retarded were marshalled into their specialized educational establishments.

THE EUGENICS MOVEMENT

The shift in public attitudes in favor of institutional, custodial care for mentally retarded people was aided at the end of the nineteenth century by the rise of the eugenics movement. The belief spread rapidly that mental retardation, criminality, and moral degeneracy were all genetically transmitted. This conventional wisdom was well expressed by Fernald (quoted in Clarke & Clarke, 1965, p. 16):

> The feebleminded are a parasitic, predatory class, never capable of self-support or of managing their own affairs. The great majority ultimately become public charges in some form. They cause unutterable sorrow at home and are a menace and danger to the community. Feebleminded women are almost invariably immoral. . . . Every feebleminded person, especially the high grade imbecile, is a potential criminal, needing only the proper environment and opportunity for the development of expression of his criminal tendencies.

With the spread of this view, the institution's role shifted to protecting society from the dangers retarded people allegedly posed, especially their indiscriminate breeding. Institutions became even more custodial, and many states passed laws enabling or directing sterilization of women in institutions; by 1926 there were 23 states with such laws (Kanner, 1964, p. 936). In sum, the beliefs spread by the eugenics movement, together with the early failures in training, led to a pattern of custodial care; it was believed that society was protected by the incarceration of retarded people and their being prevented from breeding.

THE SEEDS OF DEINSTITUTIONALIZATION

By the 1920s this eugenics-based ideology had spent its force. Advances in understanding mental retardation led to widening doubts about the correctness of the genetics theory. It became apparent that the terms "idiot," "feebleminded," and "mentally retarded" covered a heterogeneous range of people with widely different manifestations and causes. With time, the heavy emphasis on genetic factors gave way to recognition that other factors also contributed to mental retardation, such as biological insults during fetal growth, delivery, and the postnatal period and disadvantaged environments for social and intellectual development.

In particular, studies of inmates who had escaped or been released from mental retardation institutions discredited the pessimistic view of mentally retarded individuals disseminated by the eugenics movement and suggested that some mentally retarded persons could live in the community without help and without harming others. The first of these was Fernald's 1919 study of patients discharged from the Waverly mental retardation institution over a 25-year period (for reviews of this and related studies, see Cobb, 1972; Goldstein, 1964; Lakin, Bruininks, & Sigford, 1981; Scheerenberger, 1983). The studies found that people who left institutions did not match the eugenics movement's behavioral stereotypes. Many former inmates found jobs, married, had normal children and assumed the roles expected of people of their age and sex.

In the 1920s and early 1930s, superintendents of some state institutions began releasing some of the inmates, placing them in alternative settings, such as among the families of staff members. Other inmates continued to live at the institutions and worked at jobs off the premises during the day. But the alternative settings initially created problems. Placements were generally made in the communities surrounding the institutions, and sometimes more inmates were placed than the community could assimilate. In addition, those paroled or released were the better-functioning inmates who had been of substantial help in running the institutions. Their absence increased the work on the staff, who then had a higher proportion of more severely retarded inmates to look after and fewer inmates who could help in the running of the institution.

The arrangement of boarding children with families of staff was also problematic. Hubbell (1934) criticized this practice in a study of children who had been moved out of institutions in New York State. "We have come to the conclusion," he observed, "that the best homes are with those who have never had any contact with state institutions. There is bound to be a certain amount of institutional discipline maintained by ex-employees which is not conducive to a normal life for children" (p. 485).

Unfortunately, shortages of funds, legal obstacles, the Depression of the 1930s, and World War II created conditions in which institutions received little outside attention. From the 1920s through the 1950s, little was done to alter the institutional policies or inmates' conditions. During this period no clear rationale other than the custodial influenced institutional care.

For mildly retarded children there were some special educational programs in the school systems, but the more severely retarded children, especially those with associated disabilities, were often barred from these programs. For these children there was no network of community services or help for parents. Most parents had to choose between keeping their mentally retarded child at home with no state help or sending the child to a state institution for life. Parents who could afford to do so sometimes paid for residential care in private institutions.

After World War II, new research findings again suggested that many inmates were still unnecessarily kept in mental retardation institutions and that there were no clear criteria for admission. In 1948 O'Connor and Tizard carried out a survey of the intellectual and personality characteristics of all patients with IQ above about 50 in an English retardation institution. Tizard (1967, p. 10) later reviewed this work:

> We discovered to our surprise that the average IQ of these patients was over 70 points, and later surveys of institutions throughout the whole of the Greater London area showed that this was quite a typical finding. On closer acquaintance, many of the defective appeared to be quite capable of doing a very different type of work from that on which they were employed—work which would train them to go out into society and get jobs as ordinary, unskilled working people.

Because of this finding, they changed the inmates' work environment from occupational therapy and ward work to vocational training, and within a relatively short time many patients were placed in jobs outside the institution.

Rosenberg (1969) surveyed the inmates of New York State institutions and concluded that one-third of them could have remained in the community had local services been available. In Britain, according to Mittler (1979, p. 196):

> The most recent estimates by the Development Team, based on information of the abilities of some 7000 residents provided by hospital staff themselves, indicate that just under a quarter could be discharged to a home or to a residential hostel immediately without any special facilities necessary for management, apart from those normally provided in a local authority hostel. A

further 10% have only mild behavior problems which could be corrected with a short period of treatment and self-help training; this group should be suitable for discharge home or to a hostel after a period of predischarge training.

Such inappropriate institutionalizations can be criticized on many different grounds. It can be argued that they violate the liberties guaranteed to all citizens in the Bill of Rights. Moreover, many individuals were placed in mental retardation institutions simply because they were "undesirables" or "troublemakers" or children who had been orphaned, neglected, abandoned, or abused. The geographical isolation and autonomy of the institutions also made it difficult to monitor the quality of their care. Abuses were found periodically, but the inevitable public investigations that followed did little to change care practices in the longer term.

Glasser (1978) traced government's role as a care provider to people who otherwise would not be able to obtain it. He argued that government agencies failed to resist the impulse toward paternalism; they infantilized those who needed help and denied them their individual rights. He summarized the record of public charity as "an unloving record of punishment, degradation, humiliation, intrusion and incarceration" (p. 123).

HISTORICAL CONSTANTS IN INSTITUTIONALIZATION

Despite the changes that institutions have undergone since preindustrial times, some characteristics have remained fairly constant over time, and these deserve mention. For as long as mental retardation institutions have existed in the United States, physicians have played important leadership roles in them. One reason is that the large numbers of children in these institutions heightened the risk of infectious disease. This was especially so prior to the introduction of sulfa and antibiotic drugs after World War II. In addition, a number of children had conditions that required close medical attention, such as cerebral palsy, seizures, chronic illness, and physical disabilities.

Unfortunately, medical leadership did not insure good medical treatment. Many children suffered physical neglect because of shortages of orthopedic specialists and physical, occupational, and speech therapists. Because of neglect, they developed severe deformities and contractures. A more fundamental form of neglect was that, because of shortage of staff, children were left lying in cribs with little or no movement or exercise (Oswin, 1978, 1979).

The structure, customs, and practices of mental retardation institutions have been influenced by physicians. In planning and administering their institutions, physicians drew on the organizational model they knew best—the hospital, traditionally a highly centralized and authoritarian institution. The doctor-patient relationship influenced their conception of the inmate-staff relationship. Inmates were regarded as patients, to be treated or acted upon, and were expected to obey and to be passive. Medical training developed an orientation toward physiological, pathological processes, and therefore primary attention was given to bodily functions and needs, disease processes, and pathology. The inmate was not thought of as a social being with individual, social, emotional, and educational needs and with family and community ties. The hospital mode of organization also influenced the physical structure and arrangements inside institutions and their separateness from surrounding society.

Another constant with several important consequences is that public institutions have always tended to be large. Their sites were chosen where land was cheap—generally in a rural and often isolated location. Thus, any nearby community would be unable to meet a large institution's needs with its limited health, social, welfare, and other services. The institution had to establish within its walls the full range of services needed, employing local labor where possible and importing persons with needed skills not available locally. The institution often became the largest employer in the area. Once such a pattern was established, any movement toward closing an institution or reducing its size became a major economic threat that would spark an instant political reaction by the county, the state, the unions, and local contractors of goods and services.

Large institutional size also affected the ties between inmates and their families. Moss (1975) has calculated that in the United Kingdom a catchment area of about half a million people is required to provide an average-size institution with enough children up to nineteen years of age. The same figure applies in the United States, where it is estimated that two out of every thousand people are so severely retarded or have such severe associated disabilities that they need some form of residential care. Securing 1,000 such persons for a single large institution thus requires a general population of half a million. There results a large geographic separation between many of the inmates and their families. This distance makes it more difficult for families to make regular visits. For some families, traveling to and from the institution is almost impossible. The difficulty of maintaining ties with a child or relative in an institution increases with difficulty of travel between the family's home and the institution (Anderson, Schlottmann, & Weiner, 1975; Ballinger, 1970; Schultz & Buckman, 1965). It is not clear from the studies what the ages of the "children" were. When the inmates were children chronologically, their parents would have even more difficulty visiting if there were other children who must either be brought on the trip or be cared for by someone else.

Removal of the mentally retarded from their families and communities into socially and geographically isolated institutions led to public apathy. They were "out of sight, out of mind." It also encouraged misunderstanding, prejudice, fear, and stereotyped thinking about mental retardation.

In each state, institutions have customarily been administered through a bureaucracy that generally feared changing established ways because it feared for its survival. This strong central organization helped insure bureaucratic survival by increasing political strength.

Another constant characteristic of mental institutions has been the concept of asylum, which has been used as a rationale for placing mentally retarded people in institutions and has had some influence in encouraging recognition that inmates have some social needs. Primrose (1977) defined an asylum as a long-stay institution for persons (1) who are severely physically handicapped and who are admitted at an early age, (2) whose behavior the community cannot tolerate, or (3) for whom psychotic mental illness is the precipitating factor and who have undergone lengthy trials in alternative community placements before seeking admission to a hospital. Primrose suggested that the advantage of a large institution is "the ability to form peer groups for the patients, groups where they are no longer the least efficient member and where they are not ridiculed because of their inadequacy; . . . removing stress allows patients to be more relaxed and happy." He also considered an asylum to be appropriate for the patient who has a progressive condition and whose level of functioning is deteriorating (p. 265).

The concept of asylum encourages thinking of institutions as places for long-term or life stays and discourages the view that the role of the institution is to do everything possible through treatment and training to return the resident to a community setting.

PREDISPOSITIONS TOWARD DEINSTITUTIONALIZATION

The acceptance of new ideas by a society is heavily dependent on the ethos of that society—its concerns, values, and economic conditions. Therefore, before the concept of deinstitutionalization is investigated, some of the social and political factors that gave support to deinstitutionalization should be examined.

During the 1960s, under Democratic presidents Kennedy and Johnson, optimism about the economy combined with an upsurge of concern over social welfare. It was the period of the civil rights movement, a time of considerable revolt among young people against the values of the older generation, a time of alternative life-styles and growing resistance to the Vietnam War. It was also the era of the "War on Poverty," motivated by the idea that the social conditions of the poor were not of their own making, contrary to what had so long been commonly believed. Problems of the poor were understood to be deep rooted and insidious, requiring all the resources of society to break the cycle of poverty. Special concern that something should be done to help the children of the poor prompted better medical care and such programs as Head Start. There was growing awareness that the human rights of members of minority groups were consistently violated, despite the Supreme Court's school desegregation decision in 1954. This atmosphere of egalitarian social change was consistent with and strongly supportive of the idea of deinstitutionalization.

Another political force supporting deinstitutionalization was the National Association of Retarded Children, or NARC (later the Association for Retarded Citizens of the United States), which was developed in the 1940s and 1950s by parents of mentally retarded children. At that time many retarded children were excluded from education programs, and for those who did attend school, virtually no community services were available after graduation. Parents were faced with the cruel choice of keeping their children at home with no help, services, or community understanding or placing them permanently in institutions where their future lives would be controlled almost exclusively by the institutional staff. Professionals routinely advised parents that lifetime institutional care was the correct choice to make. According to Avis (1979, p. 169), a professional who was also a parent, the following comments were typical: "She'll never live to be more than a year old." "Put him away and forget him." "They're happier with their own kind." "Think of the other children." "Only professionals can give this child the kind of care and training he needs."

Some of the parents who visited their children in state institutions were dismayed at the conditions they found. Through NARC they were able to join with other parents who also believed their problems were ignored. By coming together, they could share their experiences and become more effective advocates for their children. Most of these parents had severely retarded children or children with multiple disabilities that increased the problems of care and management. NARC lobbied at local, state, and federal levels for legislation to provide research and a wider range of improved services. It was also influential in making the general public more aware of mental retardation. Later, NARC parents were prominent in initiating court cases defining the rights of the mentally retarded citizens. NARC did much to change parents' feelings from shame about their disabled child to outspoken advocacy of their child's needs and rights.

In addition, researchers and journalists increased the public's awareness by describing conditions in institutions. Numerous examples were found of absence of treatment, regimentation, overcrowding, lack of privacy, unmaintained facilities, unjustified removal of inmates' personal possessions, segregation of inmates from the outside world, staff usurpation of inmates' decision making about daily living, inadequate physical care, neglect, occasional brutality by staff toward inmates, and a generally stultifying, grim daily life.

The important contribution of bringing to light inadequacies of institutional care may well have been at the expense of institutions that provided better care, for these were not carefully described. Unfortunately, in the United States, no nationwide surveys of a sample of mental retardation institutions have included systematic descriptions of the inmates' living conditions.

President Kennedy had a deep personal interest in mental retardation. Through his office and his family's foundation he was influential in arousing public interest in mental retardation and in stimulating services and research. He appointed a panel to prepare a National Plan to Combat Mental Retardation, which was published in 1962. The report contrasted the United States with other countries (President's Panel on Mental Retardation, 1962, p. 141):

> Residential care has an important place among the various services required for the retarded, and for many years it was practically the only service of any importance in this country. The view that an institution is one of several rather than the main resource in the care of the retarded is not yet established in the United States as it is in the Scandinavian countries and in England, Holland, and other parts of Europe where significant community services are a part of their program. In this country institutions represent the greatest investment of manpower, buildings, and funds, and thus are highly visible. This is a consequence of the historical pattern of our concern for the retarded, and a coincidence of the physical nature of residential facilities which are very large in many cases and frequently at some distance from centers of population (p. 134).
>
> The Panel recommends that local communities, in cooperation with Federal and State agencies, undertake the development of community services for the retarded. These services should be developed in coordination with the State comprehensive plan for the retarded, and plans for them should be integrated with those for construction and improvement of services in residential facilities.

DEINSTITUTIONALIZATION AS A CONCEPT

Certain ideas played an important part in the rapid development of deinstitutionalization as a social movement and the emerging negative image of institutions. One central idea was normalization. Nirje, who has been actively providing services for the mentally retarded in Sweden and Canada, described it this way (1969, p. 231):

> The normalization principle means making available to all mentally retarded people patterns of life and conditions of every day living which are as close as possible to the regular circumstances and ways of life and society.
>
> Normalization means sharing a normal rhythm of the day, with privacy, activities and mutual responsibilities; a normal rhythm of the week, with a home to live in, a school or work to go to, and leisure time with a modicum of social interaction; a normal rhythm of the year, with the changing modes and ways of life and family and community customs as experienced in the different seasons of the year.
>
> Normalization also means opportunity to undergo the normal developmental experiences of the life cycle: infanthood, with security and the respective steps of early childhood development; school age, with exploration and the increase of skills and experience; adolescence, with development towards adult life and options. As it is normal for a child to live at home, it is normal for adults to move away from home and establish independence and new relationships. Like everybody else, retarded people should experience the coming of adulthood and maturity through marked changes in the settings and circumstances of their lives.

Those responsible for deinstitutionalization sometimes overlooked Nirje's point that the degrees and complications of the handicap must be taken into account: "The application of the normalization principle will not 'make retarded people normal.' But it will make their life conditions as normal as possible respecting the degrees and complications of the handicap, the training received and needed, and the social competence and maturity acquired and obtainable" (p. 232).

A second major idea was developmental programming: "regardless of the degree of impairment, all people have potential for growth, learning and development. *Developmental programming* assumes that people change during their lifetimes, that individual development progresses in a sequential, orderly and predictable manner and that development is modifiable" (Bruininks, Thurlow, Thurman, & Fiorelli, 1980, p. 57).

The National Association of Superintendents of Public Residential Facilities for the Mentally Retarded (1974) defined deinstitutionalization as having three broad, interrelated goals (pp. 4, 5):

> 1) prevention of admission by finding and developing alternative community methods of care and training; 2) return to the community of all residents who have been prepared through programs of habilitation and training to function

adequately in appropriate local settings; and 3) establishment and maintenance of a responsive residential environment which protects human and civil rights.

Drawing on experience in Sweden, Grunewald (1969) related these broad goals to more specific goals for mental retardation services:

Retarded people should live in as normal a way as possible, with their own room, and in a small group;

They should live in a bisexual world;

They should work in an environment different from that in which they live;

They should eat in a small group, as in a family, with food and drink standing on the tables;

They should be able to choose between different ways of spending their free time;

Their leisure pursuits should be individually designed, and differentiated according to the time of year;

The environment should be adjusted to the age of the person;

Retarded young people should be given the opportunity to try out adult activities and forms of life, and be able to detach themselves from their parents.

Grunewald further outlined guidelines that any institution serving the mentally retarded should follow:

That it be organized on the principle of the small group;

That the physical standard of the institution reduces collective facilities to a minimum, i.e., in respect to toilets, basins and showers, bedrooms, etc.;

That the institution be situated within a community;

That the institution should not be larger than would permit the assimilation of those living there into the community;

That the social contacts of the institution be freely developed in both directions;

That those living there be offered an alternative domicile at weekends and at holiday times;

And that the institution should consistently work in cooperation with parents, relatives, and the retarded persons themselves.

Collectively, such ideas as normalization and developmental programming were enormously appealing to many human service professionals, parents, legislators, and judges. The deinstitutionalization movement took on some of the characteristics of a crusade, inspiring imaginative new programs for mentally retarded people, new legislation, governmental appropriations, and a general feeling of hope and optimism. Deinstitutionalization seemed so right and just that many people expected that everyone else would simply embrace the concept and cooperate fully in putting it into practice.

IMPLEMENTING DEINSTITUTIONALIZATION: EARLY PROGRESS

Many of the ideas underlying deinstitutionalization came from Europe, where retarded people and other special groups were already utilizing community services. Implementing these ideas in the United States was very difficult, however, because the predominant resource in the care of retarded people had been institutions, and patterns of community services had not been developed. As deinstitutionalization ideas became more popular, there was increasing political pressure to create alternative residences quickly and on a large scale. Attention was initially directed at finding and occupying facilities. Often, the people in charge felt they could not delay even long enough to organize the network of community services the new residents would need.

The kinds of community residences that have been established vary widely. The variety is partially a result of a number of differences among the communities establishing these new settings. They differ in their funding of human services and in their economic, social, and physical characteristics, such as population density, housing types, land availability, public transportation, and public education practices concerning mental retardation.

The ideological goals of deinstitutionalization required a major effort of community planning. This effort included several distinct actions:

1. Using and adapting the local education system to provide appropriate educational arrangements.

2. Using and adapting the local health, social work, welfare, and legal services.

3. Providing transportation so that those deinstitutionalized were not isolated at their place of residence.

4. Establishing neighborhood relationships to provide opportunities for those in the residences and their neighbors to get to know each other.

5. Encouraging residents to use existing community recreational facilities, and those responsible for the facilities to accept the residents.

6. Encouraging residents to use the local employment and vocational training agencies, and encouraging the agencies to use and if necessary adapt their facilities for the residents.

7. Making alternative arrangements where local services did not exist or were not capable of being extended to residents.

8. Providing special training for residents to help them develop skills they needed for living in a community and for which they had not been prepared by living in institutions. These include (a) personal maintenance such as grooming, hygiene, first aid, and use of nonprescription medicines; (b) clothing care and use; (c) home maintenance; (d) food preparation, including planning meals, grocery shopping, cooking and, care and maintenance of appliances; (e) management of time; (f) appropriate social behavior; (g) use of community facilities, including transportation; (h) use of money; and (i) communication, including use of the telephone.

9. Providing some form of advocacy or benefactor arrangement to provide the residents with help and advice.

This list of community services is more an ideal model and less a realistic description of what exists in communities across the nation. Consider this account of conditions in a borough of New York City (Koller, 1980, p. 54):

> Fear of crime has immobilized citizens throughout the Bronx, frightening them to the extent that they will not go out at night, nor walk into certain areas at any time, nor take public transportation. Social and health agencies often have trouble attracting staff because either the agency is located in a high crime area or staff have to travel through dangerous neighborhoods. Because parents and staff are often in fear of using public transportation, agencies must often consider providing transportation.

Despite these problems a community care program was successfully developed for the developmentally disabled children and adults (Cohen & Kligler, 1980).

Essential to the success of these plans is teaching those who become the residents of community facilities the range of behavior and skills that are needed to function in a community setting. In a study of deinstitutionalized adults in a community residence, Birenbaum and Seiffer (1976) found that the first 6 months of adjustment to the new social environment was a difficult time for the residents, a time when intensive training was needed. Prior socialization in a large institution developed behaviors that

were adaptive for institutional living but maladaptive for living in community residences. Young people brought up in a community should adapt
more easily to a community residence because the skills and behaviors
learned in the community would be more appropriate than those learned
in institutions.

A number of studies of community residential facilities have examined
maladaptive behavior. Persons in community residences who were reinsti-
tutionalized had higher levels of maladaptive behavior than those who
continued to live in the community (Intagliata & Willer, 1982). When
persons living in community residences after deinstitutionalization were
compared to persons still in institutions, it was found that those in the
community increased their skills in adaptive behavior but showed no
significant change in maladaptive behavior (Conroy, Efthimiou, & Lemanowicz, 1982). In a study of community-placed retarded persons, Nihira
and Nihira (1975) examined incidents of problem behavior. Sixteen percent of the incidents involved potential or actual jeopardy. Analysis showed
that these incidents involved both children and adults, although there was
a disproportionally larger number of children and adolescents than adults.
Seventy-nine percent involved the retarded person himself, 12% involved
fellow residents, and only 9% jeopardized the community at large. Thus,
those planning and providing community services must take into account
that behavior disturbances occur in community residences.

The federal courts have played a role in decreasing the gap between
the ideal model and the reality of deinstitutionalization. One important
decision was *Wyatt* v. *Stickney*, a 1972 Alabama case alleging that mentally
retarded people in a public residential school had not been given proper
treatment. In its decision, the court defined several minimum care standards (Scheerenberger, 1977, p. 4):

No borderline or mildly retarded person shall be a resident of the institution.

No person shall be admitted to the institution unless a prior determination
shall have been made that residence in the institution is the least restrictive
habilitation setting.

Residents shall have a right to the least restrictive conditions necessary to
achieve the purposes of habilitation. To this end, the institution shall make
every attempt to move residents from: a) more to less structured living; b)
larger to smaller facilities; c) larger to smaller living units; d) group to individual residence; e) segregated from the community to integrated living in the
community; f) dependent to independent living.

A second case was initiated by the New York State Association for
Retarded Citizens in 1975 alleging that inhumane conditions existed at

Willowbrook State School. It asked for a minimum set of standards for treating mentally retarded people. The court established comprehensive standards and appointed a review panel to monitor and enforce them. An unintended consequence of the court actions was to increase the problems of parents who had kept their retarded children at home and who badly needed supportive services. They found that priority for all forms of help shifted to inmates of institutions.

Changes in forms of care given by mental retardation services are indicated by statistics. Although it is difficult to obtain accurate figures, one study showed that the number of inmates in institutions rose to a peak of 193,000 persons in 1973 and then decreased (Butterfield, 1976). Another study showed 187,000 inmates of institutions in 1960 and 151,000 in 1970 (Bruininks et al., 1980b). These figures are for inmates of all ages. Best-Sigford, Bruininks, Lakin, Hill, and Heal (1982) provided some age-specific figures. They studied persons released from all government residential facilities in 1978, using a sampling procedure of 490 released residents. One percent were 4 years of age or younger; 30.6% were between the ages of 5 and 21. Retardation in the latter group ranged in severity from borderline to profound retardation; most of the subjects were in the moderate to profound range. The type of facility to which they were released was examined. Of those in the 5–21 age group, 36% were placed in natural or adoptive homes, 18% in community residential facilities, and 8% in foster family care. The remainder were placed in a variety of other types of facilities. For those in public institutions, it was found that approximately half the first admissions in 1977 were of persons below the age of 21. These statistics show there are sizable numbers of children still in institutional care. Clearly the kinds of care needed in the first 21 years of life vary greatly with age, and it would be valuable to have a current set of statistics for children broken down by age showing the nature of their disabilities and the kind of care they are receiving.

The only available figures for community residences are the number of new facilities opened annually, rather than numbers of persons served by them. Between 1960 and 1975 the annual number of new openings rose steadily from 35 in 1960 to 605 in 1975 (Bruininks, Hauber, & Kudla, 1980). This significant growth in community residences is consistent with the earlier figures suggesting that the traditional institutions house perhaps one-quarter fewer inmates than they did at their peak in 1973.

The first to be deinstitutionalized were those whose functioning was least impaired. They were followed by persons with increasingly severe overall functional impairment. During the same period, mentally retarded persons with severe impairments continued to be admitted to the traditional institutions. The net effect has been that a larger proportion of the inmate population of mental retardation institutions suffers from more severe retardation and associated disabilities.

No comprehensive studies have been made throughout the United States comparing the quality of care given to children in community residences with that in institutions, nor have there been studies of the experiences of children who have been moved from institutions to community residences. Such studies should follow the histories of the individual's care rather than being restricted to one point in time.

IMPLEMENTING DESINSTITUTIONALIZATION: CHRONIC PROBLEMS

When the concepts and goals of deinstitutionalization first became widely accepted, many hoped that within a decade the traditional mental retardation institution would cease to exist and the transfer to a set of community services would be accomplished. The reality today is that despite considerable movement toward this goal, the old institutions still exist, and the high hopes for widespread use of community services have not been realized. A wide array of factors contribute to this discrepancy between expectation and outcome.

Funding Problems

Following the public outcry about conditions in mental retardation institutions and widespread agreement in principle to begin deinstitutionalization, a dilemma arose about the allocation of funds. How much money should be allocated to improving conditions in traditional institutions that might soon be emptied, and how much should instead be given to the development of community services?

Some parents with children in large institutions applied pressure to improve the quality of care in such facilities. Other parents, favoring deinstitutionalization, applied pressure to establish community facilities. Meanwhile, states funded improvements in the physical plant and personnel of institutions to satisfy the criteria for Intermediate Care Facility Funding through Title XIX of the Social Security Act. Having made these improvements, the states could then obtain federal money to pay for half the cost of institutional care; they were eager to justify and use the improved institutions in which they had sizable capital investment. Federal funding later also became available and was used to pay for community care facilities, managed either by state or voluntary agencies.

Although there were now fewer persons in mental retardation institutions, there were many obstacles to reducing costs. The institutions' large, complex physical plants continue to require maintenance and repair, and for those recently built, large debt or bond payments for construction may need to be paid off. Moreover, because the inmate population of institutions is now largely made up of the severely retarded with associated disabilities, the costs of care have increased.

For many years institutions have provided employment and business on a large scale. In rural areas whole communities may depend largely on the institutions for employment. The provision of food and supplies provides employment and profits for outside businesses. The planning and construction of new buildings is an important source of revenues for architects and construction companies. The closing of institutions constitutes a major threat to those who benefit financially from them, and it is understandable that they should use whatever influence they can muster to protect their interests. The newly developing community services do not have a well-organized work force or large contractors for professional services and construction. Personnel come from many different organizations, unions, and professional backgrounds, and the mentally retarded and their families are only partially represented by the parent organizations. Because the disparate elements concerned with community service are less well organized for political action than those involved with the public institutions, funding may continue to favor public institutions over community facilities.

The organization and preparation of budgets for government services and the system of budget approval, accounting, and auditing can have a considerable influence on the kinds and quality of services provided. Through decades of experience, cost accounting for "bed" occupancy in mental retardation institutions was thoroughly refined and understood. Although some of this fiscal experience could be adapted to the running of community residences, there were some forms of expenditure for which those responsible for fiscal control had no guidelines or experience, such as the costs of transportation and provision of a variety of services to mentally retarded persons living at home (e.g., the cost of having a social worker accompany a mildly retarded person to help him or her learn how to shop for clothing, how to cope with the bureaucracy of a welfare agency, or how to budget). Such expenditures were a source of concern and anxiety for fiscal managers, and as a result were often discouraged or disallowed (Blatt, 1976).

Community Relations Problems

Those planning for the community care of mentally retarded children expected that many of the existing "generic" health, education, and welfare services could be used to meet needs common to all children; professionals with special knowledge of retarded children's unique needs would only supplement generic services. Because the needs of retarded children are often multiple and complex, it is important to obtain cooperation and coordination between the service agencies. Although such communication and cooperation has always been subscribed to as an ideal, its realization has often been thwarted by competition for funds and clients, mutual suspicion, difficulties in communication between persons with different skills and training, and concerns for the survival and power of each agency. This has created problems for parents who, needing several forms of help for their retarded children, have to deal with several agencies.

It is a reasonable hypothesis that the quality of life of members of a community is heavily influenced by their relationships with individuals in the immediate neighborhood; by those encountered in the daily rounds of traveling, working, shopping, and recreational activities; and by contact with the various organizations in the community, such as churches and recreational and social clubs. Unless the mentally retarded receive some acceptance and understanding, they may experience isolation, hostility, and opposition to their use of human services and other community facilities. People who are mentally retarded and may have other disabilities have been segregated in special classes, schools, or institutions with which most people have had little contact. The result is that the people in the community may hold stereotypical conceptions of disability and be fearful of anyone who is different from people they have been accustomed to knowing. In some communities, the attempt to establish community residences for mentally retarded people has been met by severe opposition. Koller (1980, p. 70) lists some of the bases for this opposition to day programs as well as residences:

Fear of antisocial behavior.

Dislike of people of different ethnic backgrounds in their neighborhoods.

Lack of trust of service providers to maintain adequate standards and services.

Fear that a service for the developmentally disabled will open the floodgates to service for people with other disabilities, including drug addiction.

Fear that real estate values will be lowered.

Fear that there will be increased noise and traffic.

Fear of people who might manifest bizarre behavior and whose physical appearance often is discomforting or even repulsive to some people.

Lubin, Schwartz, Zigman, and Janicki (1982), in a study of 331 community residences in New York State, found the causes for opposition regarded as most important by program directors or residence managers. Such residences were thought to (1) lower real value of houses, (2) adversely affect neighborhood character, (3) bring in undesirable individuals, (4) pose a threat to neighboring children, and (5) lack proper supervision.

Meeting community opposition requires organizing and politically mobilizing people who are already sympathetic to the goals of deinstitutionalization and normalization. How this can be done will depend considerably on the particular community, but it cannot be done alone by those responsible for planning and delivering community services. The development of community relations by state service agencies in the Bronx, New York, is described in a case study (Cohen & Kligler, 1980). The process included placing decentralized service delivery teams in the neighborhood to get to know the values and customs there and to learn, through close contact, the day-to-day problems and conditions of life of those to whom they were to provide services. A services advisory board was formed on which parents of developmentally disabled children played an important role. The state agencies organized several parent groups that, with help and through experience, developed political skills in influencing local legislators to support community service bills.

In the New York State Survey of Community Acceptance of Residential Programs, the following strategies for responding to community opposition were listed: (1) meet with complaining neighbors; (2) hold open house; (3) seek support of community leaders; (4) involve neighbors in residence operations; (5) seek joint solution with neighbors; (6) maintain low profile; and (7) modify policies. There was considerable difference of opinion among community residence managers on the effectiveness of these strategies (Lubin et al., 1982).

The courts have been influential both in pushing the state service providers to bring about social change and in upholding the rights of those served. For instance, the courts have ruled repeatedly that group homes do not violate residential zoning regulations. It has been encouraging that once group homes have been established, they are generally accepted by the community (Koller, 1980).

Despite the critical importance of good community and public relations, state agencies have rarely recognized their importance, provided funds for them, or considered them acceptable activities for service providers to pursue during the working day.

Still another problem affecting community relations is that the skills and qualifications for leadership in a traditional institution are quite different from those needed in community services. In large institutions the leadership has direct control over staff and the institution is segregated from the outside world. Leadership could be learned by service and promotion within a closed system that changed little. By contrast, leadership in providing community services requires a diverse combination of skills both in working in the community and in working with a state bureaucracy accustomed to traditional forms of service delivery. This is an extraordinarily exacting and stressful role that may be enabled by a supportive staff whose skills collectively span both the professional delivery of services and skills needed in community relations and public education.

With so much attention being focused on the community, the staff of traditional institutions has seldom been educated about the goals and purposes of deinstitutionalization. For years these staffs provided care for those the society apparently wished to have out of sight and out of mind. Care was often given under conditions of financial stringency and difficult working conditions, and some employees were deeply devoted to the inmates with whom they worked. Staff found deinstitutionalization difficult to accept because it seemed to make them the objects of severe criticism and threatened the loss of their jobs. In the absence of education about deinstitutionalization and concerted efforts to retrain staff and find alternative occupations, their opposition is hardly surprising.

Concerns of Parents

To be successful, services must be responsive to parents' needs and concerns as well as to their children's. It has already been pointed out that parents can be the most effective supporters and advocates of community services.

Because of the legal and political pressures to effect deinstitutionalization quickly, funds and priorities have sometimes been assigned at the expense of parents who have kept their children at home and need such community support services as day programs that provide the young person training and social experience and give respite to the parents. In addition, such support services may be needed as visiting homemakers and occasional care of the young person when parents need to go out evenings or on weekends. Furthermore, some young persons are so severely disabled that the burden of care and management is beyond their parents' capacities, and some form of residential care is essential to meet the problems the parents cannot manage.

Parents who have kept their children at home must be concerned about what will happen to their children when they, the parents, die or become too infirm to care for them. Most parents want their children to remain in the community. They have been all too aware of conditions in large institutions and recognize the importance of continuity and stability of human relationships for their children. In some instances, members of the extended family may be able to take over care, but in many instances this is not possible. This problem of continuity of care has drastically increased; severely disabled young people who would have died before their parents are now, with improved medical care, frequently outliving them. These children, often now adults, are sent off to whatever institutional placement can be found after parents die.

It is reasonable to hypothesize that stability of environment and social relationships and a predictable daily cycle are even more important for a person with intellectual impairment than for other people. Most people have emancipated themselves from the primary support and care of their parents by the time they are adults and have developed a wider support system. For severely retarded people who remain at home, their parents are the support and center of their lives, and there has been no emancipation. How parental death affects the severely retarded has not been studied, but it is reasonable to expect that the experience may be far more shocking and devastating for them than for others. There is need to study how mentally retarded persons are affected by the joint experience of loss of parents and sudden removal from a familiar environment to a new and strange one. If it turns out to be as cruel and inhumane as it seems, then such acts should be avoided.

Although the rights of those with disabilities have correctly become a matter of concern, the rights of parents have received less attention. For most parents, responsibility for the daily care of their children ends when the children grow up. It can reasonably be argued that parents of severely and multiply disabled children have a right to an easing of their responsibility for care when their child becomes an adult and that the young person should undergo an orderly transition to a residence away from the parents. If there are local residential facilities, the young person may gradually become accustomed to the physical arrangements and residents by first making short visits with his or her parents and later making visits without parents. Stays can be overnight and then longer, until eventually the transition to the new residence is complete. Parents and child can then continue visiting one another. I have heard parents recommend this plan but have not seen its implementation reported or evaluated. Often, parents must accept almost any residential placement, even though it may become available before they want to relinquish having their child at home. Until arrangements for community placement become available, and unless relatives can take over, institutions will continue to be the only alternative for adults whose parents die or become infirm.

Although some parents welcomed and supported the deinstitutionalization movement, it created severe problems and emotional stress for others. Parents who had placed their children in institutions many years earlier had done so because there were no alternative forms of care. At the time they were told by professionals in human services that the placement was best for the child and themselves, and often they were under considerable pressure to relinquish their child at a young age. It was often a hard decision, accompanied by guilt and reluctance. They had lived with the decision for many years, with some consolation that their child would have life-long care. Problems of distance between the parents' home and the institution made visits difficult, and over time visits often became less frequent and may have stopped. The deinstitutionalization movement reopened the issue of their child's care, and they were asked to consider taking the child back into their home or into a nearby residence. This change in care philosophy implicitly challenged and criticized their earlier decision to institutionalize the child. Some parents believed that their child was so accustomed to the institutional setting that uprooting the child once again would be wrong. Some parents were skeptical of how enduring the new community residential arrangements would be. It came as a shock to some people deeply committed to deinstitutionalization and normalization that not all parents shared their views.

Many people in institutions are "stateless residents": they have lost all contact with the place from which they were originally admitted (Mittler, 1979). Some inmates became orphans after they were placed; others were admitted because they had been abandoned, neglected, or abused; and the parents of still others had ceased to have any contact with them or had moved and could not be traced. Some of these children would not have needed to be institutionalized if community services had been available. With pressures to meet the demands of newly developing community services, it is often difficult to find any local authority that will take responsibility and so many "stateless residents" have been inappropriately kept in institutions.

STUDIES OF INSTITUTIONAL AND RESIDENTIAL CARE OF CHILDREN

So far we have dealt with the ideology of deinstitutionalization and its historical context. We now focus on the characteristics of the institutions and residences, the children who are the residents, and the daily interaction of those children with their environment.

Morris (1969) examined the range and quality of institutional provisions for the mentally retarded by studying a sample of public institutions run on traditional lines. Some of her descriptions deal specifically with children. She reported that life for the great majority of patients in the wards consisted of sitting, interspersed with eating (p. 169). On one afternoon on a children's ward fifty older children were wandering around aimlessly or sitting making noises, despite the fact that six staff were on duty. There were no toys, games, pictures, or ornaments in evidence, and the staff stood around talking to each other (p. 170). Nurses generally suffered from low morale because of such factors as isolation, lack of involvement in decision making, poor communication, and the doctors' lack of interest in their work. The traditional emphasis on cleanliness, tidiness, orderly behavior, and the like predominated, and because little more was expected of nurses, little more was given; "the use of tranquilizers and similar drugs appeared to be more custodial than therapeutic, used to quiet the patient and stop 'bad' and disruptive behavior, not to cure him, nor to find out why he behaves in this way" (p. 174). It might be hoped that the conditions described now have historical interest only, but a more recent study shows that for the children Morris described, similar conditions still existed 10 years later.

Oswin (1978) investigated severely mentally retarded children in institutions: according to a census in England and Wales in 1970, there were 10,195 severely mentally handicapped children aged 19 years and younger living in mental handicap hospitals, and 6,093 of these were from 5 to 15 years of age (Oswin, 1978, p. vii). Of the 10,195 children, 3,123 were not ambulant; 5,540 were severely incontinent; 5,969 needed much help with feeding, washing, or dressing; 34 never spoke.

Oswin studied the daily lives of these children using observational methods. She described the enormous problems the hard-pressed staff experienced and the lack of support they received from specialists and from the public who should have provided it. Perhaps the main finding was the bleak and unhappy existence of the children, who received almost no mothering—no affectionate individual care given by an adult. Over a period of 18 months, Oswin spent nearly all her time in the wards of eight institutions observing severely retarded children. The following extracts provide careful description of the children's lives (Oswin, 1978, p. 141):

Again, the ward was under-staffed, and from 1 p.m. until 4:30 p.m. the staff were not involved with the children at all. During these hours the staff were in the bedroom, day-room or kitchen.

At 1 p.m., 12-year-old Percy (six years in hospital), partially sighted, cerebral-palsied and non-ambulant, was in a wheelchair. The chair did not have a foot-rest, and Percy's feet were dangling just above a narrow metal bar. At 1:15, 13-year-old Elizabeth crawled across to Percy and removed his socks. He continued to sit in the chair, barefooted, until he was taken to the table for his supper at 4:30. By that time his bare feet had been hovering just above the metal bar of his broken wheelchair for 3 hours 15 minutes. His feet looked thin, cold and frail, and appeared to need some warm support, such as a cushion, to be placed under them.

At 1 p.m., eight-year-old Hector (four years in hospital, cerebral-palsied and non-ambulant) was lying on his back in a bean-bag in a very awkward position. He remained in that position until lifted for supper at 4:30.

At 1 p.m., 13-year-old Angela (nine years in hospital) was in her wheelchair in the sun-lounge, when she began crying. She cried unheeded until 4 p.m., and then became quiet. She was put to the table for supper at 4:30.

At 2 p.m., six-year-old Jill (one year in hospital) became very miserable at seeing two mothers and a father come to visit other children. She crouched at the door of the day-room, weeping and moaning, for 20 minutes. Then she resumed her usual behaviour of bottom-shuffling about the day-room, endeavouring to get staff attention. When the staff were in the bathroom or bedroom, Jill sat by the day-room door and tried to prise it open by curling her fingers of her "good" hand under it, hoping to open it and get through to the staff. Whenever the staff came through the door they inevitably bumped into Jill as she crouched by the door. This appeared to irritate them, especially when she also tried to catch hold of their feet as they entered. She was not a popular child. Eventually the staff placed Jill on the air-bed, where she was anchored for some 15 minutes before managing to crawl off and once more resume her place at the day-room door.

A number of reports have focused more narrowly on exposing the shortcomings of mental retardation institutions (e.g., Blatt, 1970; Blatt & Kaplan, 1966; Blatt, Ozolins, & McNally, 1979; Kimball, 1972; Nirje, 1969; Wolfensberger, 1969). Rivera exposed the conditions of Willowbrook State School in New York on television and later wrote a book about it (Rivera, 1972).

Dentler and Mackler (1961) described the socialization process of older, mildly retarded children who entered an institution for care and training. Using a sociometric measure of friendship, they found that in the first month 45 children chose each other, but in the second month this number dropped to three mutual choices. A second measure in the study was the number of disciplinary actions taken by the supervisors during a period of weeks. There were many disciplinary actions during the first 3 weeks, while the children were being initiated into the institutional behavioral requirements, but they dropped off sharply as the children's stays lengthened. The authors concluded: "The ideal end-product, the social outcome, we suspect is a quiet, well-mannered, even subdued young adult. The character of this total institution is incompatible with the goal of maximum fulfillment of individual potentialities" (pp. 251, 252).

Thormalen (1965) examined the training given to retarded children by the staff in a state institution in California. The children were between 5 and 13 years of age with IQs of 20–60 and without gross motor, sensory, or emotional handicaps. They found the staff more often promoted dependent rather than independent behavior and gave the children little opportunity to practice social skills. Most were not allowed to help either in their own care or that of the ward. Although these children were somewhat younger and more severely retarded than those studied by Dentler and Mackler, both studies show training of children to suit the convenience of the staff rather than to help the children develop social skills. These studies suggest the hypothesis that in institutional and residential facilities for children (and probably also for adults), unless the staff are given very clear objectives and ways of reaching them, they will organize their work to meet their own needs and convenience.

In the studies of traditional institutions described so far, no experimental interventions were employed by the researchers. But other investigators, concerned over the conditions that prevailed, participated in changing patterns of care and building into those changes ways of evaluating the outcomes. Although the investigators were interested in carefully describing and restructuring the institutional environments, their measures dealt largely with characteristics of the children, especially their level of intelligence.

Tizard (1964) examined the effects of moving mentally retarded children from a traditional institution to one run along very different lines. In the former institution, administered in a traditional hospital fashion, care of the children was largely in the hands of nurses, many of whom were untrained in the management of children. The nursing timetable did not take much account of the need for continuity of care—that is, care by the same nurses for the same children. For example, the children's toilet needs and bathing were taken care of as if on an assembly line. Children were placed in wards of 60 beds and grouped together according to sex, age, and degree of handicap. Nurses were preoccupied with the physical needs of the children and had little opportunity to get to know individual children. Working conditions were such that there was a large turnover and a shortage of nurses. Tizard states (p. 79):

> The older higher grade children came off best, but the younger ones, living in an environment in which there was virtually no conversation, failed to learn from older children and adults elements of social living which they might in other circumstances have been able to pick up. As will be shown, they were in consequence very backward in speech—and in other aspects of behavior also. Rocking and head-banging were commonly observed; they crowded round strangers, clutching and pawing them. The children were apathetic, and given

to tantrums. They rarely played. Most striking of all they were quite unsocialized. Outside the narrow limits of ward routines, they did not know how to behave.

Jack Tizard established a small experimental unit, named Brooklands, for some of the children who had previously been in a large institution. The unit was organized along "principles of child care that were regarded as meeting the needs of normal children deprived of normal home life" (p. 85). In other words, Tizard shifted the staff's attention from an almost exclusive focus on the children's disabilities, "sickness," and bodily needs to a primary focus on their functional capabilities and to encouraging any signs of interest and growth. Such attention required consistent long-term day-to-day contact with the same children, as opposed to rotating shifts, which make the development of personal relations between the staff and children difficult or impossible. The following account of the children gives an indication of some of the changes that were apparent after 2 years (pp. 133–134):

> They kept in good physical health and, living much of the time out of doors engaged in gross motor activities, they looked healthy, sun-tanned and alert. They ate and slept well, and we had little sickness. They became adept in using equipment such as swings and tricycles, climbing nets and parallel bars, and in kicking a ball and throwing. They were often eager, active and purposeful, and in this way presented a striking contrast to their behavior on arrival. They became able to play socially and constructively, at a level approaching that of their mental age. Emotionally they became less maladjusted. Tantrums were fewer, and lasted for a shorter time. The childen could be comforted and talked out of them, in a way that was not at first possible. They developed strong attachments to the members of the staff and to other children. They were able to play co-operatively with other children, to take turns with as much grace as comparable normal children, and to share. They were thus affectionate and happy children, usually busy and interested in what they were doing, confident, and full of fun.

Tizard's study demonstrated that the level of intellectual and social development of even severely retarded children could be markedly influenced by their physical and social environment. The development of mentally retarded children had long been thought not to be influenced by environmental factors. Thus, as long as there was high risk of mortality from infectious diseases, it was all the more reasonable to focus attention on hygiene and bodily needs and disregard the kinds of daily environmental experiences to which Tizard exposed the children. Tizard showed that the changes in environment the children experienced improved their health as well as their overall level of functioning and happiness.

This study of Tizard's led to another intervention experiment; two small residential units for children, developed along the lines Tizard had shown to be effective, were established in the center of the geographical areas where the children's families lived (Kushlick, 1975). The units used the generic medical, social work, and education services already existing in the community. For children not accepted by the local education and training facilities because of severe physical disability or disruptive behavior, programs of education and various forms of therapy were organized in the residence using teachers and therapists from the community.

The residential units were domestic rather than institutional in character. There were 20–25 residents and 5 staff members. The children slept in bedrooms for 1–5 people, and there was a separate dining room, lounge, and playrooms. Food was prepared in the kitchen. There were ordinary bathrooms with a single bath, washbasin, and toilet rather than the institutional layout of an "ablution block" with up to 20 toilet bowls and basins in a row. The furnishings and fittings were those found in a home. In addition, the staff did not wear uniforms and ate meals with the children; some staff lived in the unit.

Because of the proximity of the parents, many children went home on weekends. The parents were free to visit the units and the staff and did so. Parents got to know each other and shared their concerns and experience.

The children were selected for the domestic units in such a way that their development could be compared over time with children who, with similar degrees of disability at the time of selection, had remained in the traditional mental retardation institutions. Both groups of children were severely mentally retarded, and many had additional physical, sensory, and behavioral disabilities. A child development interview was administered at the time of selection and again after 4 years. On measures of eating, mobility, speech, dressing, and appropriate general behavior and emotional response, the children in the domestic unit made more progress than the children remaining in the large traditional institution. An important contribution of this study was recognizing that the communities in which the residences were established were part of the children's environments; attention was not restricted exclusively to what went on within the residences.

As models of service, Tizard's and Kushlick's carefully evaluated studies of innovations in the forms of care have a possible limitation: In any innovative program of care there may be a "honeymoon effect." A new program with exciting goals and a strong humanitarian appeal attracts charismatic leadership and skilled, highly motivated staff. It is also unburdened by the policies, practices, and restrictions that begin encrusting organizations over time. Further, because the programs are innovative and involve social change, they may threaten more traditional organizations, and these may organize opposition, either overtly or covertly, to the new program. The longevity of innovative programs and the extent to which they are copied by others can be determined only by monitoring and evaluating new programs over a prolonged period, as the leadership and personnel of the programs and the social forces that influence and are influenced by the program change. The nature of the changes found, the reasons for them, and how these changes affect the children served all need to be evaluated.

Tizard's and Kushlick's studies were influenced by a pioneer study by Skeels (1966). Skeels was a psychologist at an orphanage where illegitimate and neglected or abused children had been placed in early infancy. Until about 6 months of age they were kept in "hospital cribs that often had protective sheeting on the sides, thus effectively limiting visual stimulation; no toys or other objects were hung in the infant's line of vision. Human interactions were limited to busy nurses who, with the speed born of practice and necessity, changed diapers or bedding, bathed and medicated the infants and fed them efficiently with propped bottles" (Skeels, 1966, p. 3). Although well cared for physically and medically, they received little social and intellectual stimulation, in part because of the work load of the staff. "The children sat down, stood up and did many things in unison" (p.4). There was little or no play equipment and children had no personal property beyond a toothbrush. The children tested as mentally retarded.

It happened by chance that some of the children in the orphanage were cared for by young women residents in a nearby mental retardation institution. Skeels found that the intelligence measures of these children improved while those remaining in the orphanage did not. As a result, 13 children from the orphanage became "house guests" in the mental retardation institution. All were under 3 years of age at the time of transfer, at which time they showed seriously retarded development. A control group of children remained in the orphanage. After a median stay of a year and a half, the "house guests" showed IQ gains ranging from 7 to 58 points. The median gain was 23 points. With one exception, the control group children showed IQ losses. The median loss was 17 points. Skeels attributed the difference to the relationship between the parent surrogate and the child. The consistent element seemed to be the existence of a one-to-one relationship with an adult who was generous with love and affection, together with an abundance of attention and experiential stimulation from many sources. Children who had little of this attention did not show progress;

those who had a great deal did. Differences in visual stimulation and variety and the opportunity for play and exploration also appear to have been important.

A common characteristic of institutional care for children is that the continuity of care by the child's mother gives way to a multiplicity of caretakers. The number of caretakers depends on the organization of the institution. In large, traditional institutions with shift work, rotation of staff through the wards, and high staff turnover, a child is confronted almost daily with new people who control his or her life. In such situations it is not possible to develop a long-term attachment to any single caretaker. Some continuity of caretakers becomes possible where staff is stable and is not rotated and where there are living-in house parents. Even under such conditions, policies of the institution may discourage staff from developing attachments to any child.

Fears that the absence of a consistent mother figure had adverse consequences for children became widespread after World War II as the result of Bowlby's (1946) writing about "maternal deprivation." He claimed that prolonged separation of a child from its mother (or mother substitute) during the first 5 years of life stands foremost among the causes of delinquent character development and persistent misbehavior. A World Health Organization Expert Committee (1951), of which Bowlby was a member, later stated that the use of day nurseries and creches inevitably caused permanent damage to the emotional health of a future generation. The report cited a number of studies, most of which compared a group of maternally deprived children with a group not deprived. Young children who were reared in institutions and who received adequate physical care but had very few of the other experiences postulated as necessary for adequate overall development were shown to have a higher mortality rate, to be slower in learning motor functions such as sitting, standing, and walking, to be retarded in cognitive functioning, and to have disturbed emotional reactions to the social environment (Ainsworth, Prugh, Harlow, Andry, Mead, Wooten, & Lebovici, 1962; Dennis, 1960; Dennis & Dennis, 1941; Spitz, 1945, 1946). The previously described study by Skeels (1966) may appear to support the Bowlby hypothesis. The maternal deprivation hypothesis, however, considers only one aspect of the children's lives in an institutional or residential setting and ignores many other environmental factors that might also influence their social, emotional, and intellectual development. Bronfenbrenner (1979), in a critical review of the Skeels study, points out that the children who experienced a parent surrogate and an intense one-to-one relationship also had several other experiences that the control group did not have. He quotes from the study (pp. 16, 17):

. . . the attendants and the older girls became very fond of the children placed on their wards and took great pride in them. In fact, there was considerable competition among wards to see which one would have its "baby" walking or talking first. Not only the girls, but the attendants spent a great deal of time with "their children" playing, talking, and training them in every way. The children received constant attention and were the recipients of gifts; they were taken on excursions and were exposed to special opportunities of all kinds. . . .

The spacious living rooms of the wards furnished ample space for indoor play activity. Whenever weather permitted, the children spent some time each day on the playground under the supervision of one or more older girls. Here they were able to interact with other children of similar ages. Outdoor play equipment included tricycles, swings, slides, sand boxes, etc. The children also began to attend the school kindergarten as soon as they could walk. Toddlers remained for only half the morning and 4- or 5-year olds, the entire morning. Activities carried on in the kindergarten resembled preschool rather than the more formal type of kindergarten.

A number of professionals influenced by the concept of "maternal deprivation" have opposed institutional care, especially of young children, on the grounds that it is likely to damage the development of a wide range of a child's functions. Barbara Tizard (1975, p. 103) challenges this view:

With a few exceptions (e.g., Burlingham and Freud, 1944) the arguments have not been based on a detailed analysis of an institutional environment. Instead a brief description is usually given of a hospital-type institution with a low staff-child ratio, and the barren environment this provides is contrasted with the rich stimulation and affectionate care to be found in a stable middle-class family with one or two children. Such a comparison is for most present day purposes irrelevant. As far as family environment is concerned, the children likely to enter institutional care tend to come from large disorganized families, often with neglectful or mentally disturbed parents, or from single-parent families living at subsistence level. As far as institutions are concerned, anyone familiar with residential nurseries in England today can hardly fail to be impressed by three facts. First, these nurseries are very different from the grim, sterile institutions described by earlier writers; second, their adult-child ratio is as high as in many families; third, there appear to be quite marked differences between different nurseries.

The following studies examine how child development is affected by residential care in which the children had no consistent long-term attachment to a mother substitute. Barbara Tizard and her colleagues (1972, 1975) followed children who were in residential care since infancy. The residences they examined had high staff-child ratios and generous provisions of toys, books, and outings. Under these conditions they found that children at age 8 were of normal intelligence, even though in place of a single mother figure they had been cared for by over 50 mother substitutes. They concluded (Tizard & Rees, 1974, p. 98):

> As far as cognitive development is concerned, institutional life is clearly not inevitably depriving; indeed many of the children must have developed faster than they would have done at home . . . . children who are not often talked or read to and are not given a variety of stimulation tend to be retarded whatever the social setting; institutional retardation, when it occurs, derives from the same poverty of experience as other environmentally produced retardations.

But these children did show behavioral signs that differentiated them from other children. At school they sought attention more and were more restless, disobedient, and unpopular. Rutter (1980) reviewed a study by Penny Dixon of a larger sample of children. The results for intellectual and behavioral development were similar. The institutionalized children showed more approach to both teachers and other children, but their social interactions were less successful. They were more likely to behave in unacceptable ways, calling out in class and disregarding teachers' directions. As in Tizard's study the children were of normal intelligence. It will require longer-term followup to determine whether behavioral differences continue to be found.

Because of the studies reviewed here, it was recognized that more systematic attention had to be given to a broad range of factors that make up the environments of children in residential care and that may influence their experiences. A more comprehensive socioecological approach was needed; studies of single variables—such as the presence or absence of a consistent mother substitute, the number of children in a residence, and the ratio of staff to children—were inadequate to predict how a child would develop. An important step toward developing a more comprehensive measure of residential environments was made by King, Raynes, and Tizard (1971). Their measure was objective and quantified and could be used to compare different residences. Because the development of this measure was influenced by the work of Goffman (1961) and Wing and Brown (1970), we first briefly review these studies. Goffman coined the term "total institutions" to denote the all-encompassing characteristics of the institution for the staff and residents and gave an insightful description of what makes up a total institution. King et al. (1971, p. 46) describe what influenced them in Goffman's analysis:

> In everyday life, he points out, individuals tend to sleep, play and work in different places, with different co-participants, under different authorities,

and without an overall rational plan. On the other hand, "the central feature of total institutions may be described as a breakdown of the barriers ordinarily separating these three spheres of life. First, all aspects of life are conducted in the same place and under the same single authority. Second, each phase of the members' daily activity is carried out in the immediate company of a large batch of others, all of whom are treated alike and required to do the same thing together. Third, all phases of the days' activities are tightly scheduled, with one activity leading at a prearranged time into the next, the whole sequence of activities being imposed from above by a system of explicit formal rulings and a body of officials. Finally, the various enforced activities are brought together into a single rational plan, designed to fulfill the official aims of the institution."

Wing and Brown (1970) developed a measure of the social conditions of wards in psychiatric hospitals. Their measures included (p. 43):

(1) an inventory of all the personal possessions of each patient in the series which was made after interviewing the patients and nursing staff, and checking with the patient the contents of lockers and wardrobes:

(2) a "time budget" in which information was collected about all activities from the time of getting up until going to bed—what time the patient rose, who woke her, whether she dressed herself and how long this took, the details of her toilet, whether she made her bed, how long she waited for breakfast, and so on through the day;

(3) nurses' opinions about each patient's ability to cope with certain everyday activities and responsibilities; for example, whether she could visit the local shop without asking, whether she could do useful work in the hospital, or go out with a male patient;

(4) the daily occupation, if any, of the patient;

(5) contact with the outside world, including whether she went home, had town parole or ground parole, or was visited, and how often each of these occurred;

(6) a thirty-five-item scale of ward restrictiveness which was filled in after questioning the nurses. The items were concerned with restrictions on the movement of patients, such as locking of ward doors, the necessity for staff permission to leave the ward, and so on, and with more general rules and routines—restrictions on the use of the bathroom, regulations about personal clothing, access to the ward kitchen, and so on.

To measure the way children who were residents of institutions were managed by the staff, King, Raynes, and Tizard developed a scale with management-oriented practices at one end and child-oriented practices at the other. Clearly this is not a comprehensive measure of residential organizations but covers dimensions previous research suggested are important. Initially King, Raynes, and Tizard carried out detailed field studies of two large homes for deprived normal children, one a long-stay children's hospital for chronically sick and physically handicapped children, the other a mental retardation institution. All were in England. From their studies they identified the following four components of child management (pp. 106–107):

1. *Rigidity of routine*. The scale ranged from institutionally oriented practices that were inflexible to those which could be adapted to take account of individual differences among children or circumstances.

2. *Block treatment*. The scale ranged from regimentation or block treatment of children (e.g., queueing and waiting around in large groups with no mode of occupation during the waiting period) to child-oriented practices in which residents were allowed to participate or not as they pleased and allowed to do things at their own pace. This dimension deals with activities such as getting up, bathing, going to the toilet, and spending time before and after meals.

3. *Depersonalization*. Practices are institutionally oriented when residents have no personal possessions or privacy and lack opportunities for self-expression or initiating activities. Practices are child oriented when the children are given opportunity to show initiative, to have personal possessions, or to be alone if they so desire.

4. *Social distance between children and staff*. Practices are institutionally oriented when there is a sharp separation between the staff and inmate worlds because of separate areas of accommodation kept for exclusive use of staff or because interaction between staff is limited to formal and functional specific activities. Child orientation involves reduction of social distance by the sharing of living space and allows staff and children to interact in functionally diffuse and informal situations.

Once these four components of child management were identified, information about them was obtained from a series of questions asked of staff in over a hundred residential units. All were living units in long-stay institutions that generally cared for retarded children. The results agreed with observations made in the four units first studied. The scale of orientation was sensitive in differentiating among the institutions investigated. Their evidence supported the view that differences in child management practices were attributable primarily to the social organization of the establishment rather than to the staff's psychological characteristics or the children's handicaps. Care practices were more child oriented in the group homes than in mental retardation institutions; voluntary homes were intermediate. Within any one type of institution they found no relationship between management practices and the size of the institution or its ratio of staff to children. Jack Tizard (1972) later described the differences between institutional and child-oriented units (p. 6):

In child oriented units the person in charge had very much greater responsibility to make decisions about matters which affected all aspects of the unit's functioning. Perhaps because they were accorded greater autonomy, senior staff in these establishments tended to share their responsibilities with their junior colleagues: role differentiation was reduced (e.g., senior staff were more often engaged in child care than were their counterparts in institution oriented units who spent far more time on administration and even domestic work, and far less time in child care). Staff stability was also much greater in child oriented units—partly because staff were not moved from one unit to another to meet crises in units which were short staff, partly because students in training were not moved about in order to "gain experience." Role performance also differed. In child oriented units staff were more likely to involve the children in their activities. They spoke to them more often, and were more "accepting" of them, and less often "rejecting." Junior staff tended to behave in ways similar to those in which the head of the unit acted.

Though the social organization of the institution appeared to be largely responsible for the differences in staff behaviour, the nature of staff training also seemed important. Trained nurses were in general less child oriented than were staff with child care training. They were more authoritarian, and when the person in charge was a nurse the unit tended to be characterised by sharp role differentiation.

McCormick, Balla, and Zigler (1975) used the child management scales to rate 19 institutions in the United States and 11 in Scandinavia. In all institutions there were children and adults. They found that the living units in Scandinavia were more resident oriented than living units in the United States. In both countries, large, central institutions had the most institutionally oriented practices and group homes had the most resident-oriented practices. Regional centers were intermediate. They also found that large living units and greater severity of retardation were predictive of institutionally oriented practices. Cost per resident per day and number of aides or professional staff per resident did not predict care practices.

Zigler and Balla (1977) report further use of the child management scale in five regional centers and two large institutions in the United States. They found that the most resident-oriented practices were in group homes, which were operated at less cost than either the regional centers or the large institutions. Within the group homes, a low rate of aide turnover and a high ratio of professional staff to residents were predictive of resident-oriented care practices.

The authors of the child management scale thought it reasonable to expect more satisfactory social and emotional development in children living in child-oriented than in management-oriented residences, but they did not test this hypothesis. The work of Zigler and his colleagues just cited was not a test, but it does show other characteristics of institutions that are related to the child management scale. Barbara Tizard et al. (1972) made a more direct test of the hypothesis. Examining children in long-stay residential nurseries, they found that in nurseries with child-oriented practices the language comprehension scores of the children were higher than in nurseries with management-oriented practices. Tizard and Rees (1975) noted that where the children's language scores were lowest, as much as 75% of staff talk consisted of commands and routine supervisory remarks. These nurses, although generally kind and conscientious, very often appeared bored. They had no clear function except to keep order and "mind the children" and had nothing to talk about with the children. In a child-oriented residence the staff are more likely to be involved in activities with the children, taking them out on trips, or shopping, or making choices about clothes and planning activities. These all provide topics of conversation between staff and children (p. 116).

Zigler and Balla (1977) examined other associations between institutional environments and inmates' behavior. They found that conditions of social deprivation made inmates very wary of the adult staff. The larger the number of individuals in the living unit and the greater the staff turnover, the greater was the wariness exhibited by inmates. Wariness appears to be a response to a high rate of discontinuity in staff. Children who experienced frequent changes of parenting figures before institutionalization both were more motivated to attain the attention and support of an adult in the institution and were more wary of doing so.

There are parallels between the work of Zigler and Balla and that of Barbara Tizard and her associates (1975) in their studies of residential nurseries. In discussing their findings, Tizard states (p. 119):

> However, what is argued here is that abnormalities of development, e.g. excessive shyness, excessive clinging and diffuse attachments at the age of two, are related to particular aspects of the social environment, e.g. limited experience of strangers, multiple caretaking, and constant changes of staff, rather than to "the institution" as such. Hence changes in the social structure, e.g. reducing to a minimum the number of adults caring for each child, and arranging that when these adults are on duty they care for particular children, should tend to "normalize" the nursery child's development. Such an approximation to family life could of course only be limited. Unlike mothers, paid staff work a 40-hour week and take holidays; most significantly, they leave the institution for promotion, marriage, or a host of valid personal reasons.

There is a need for research to more fully determine the conditions by which children may maximally develop their intellectual, social, and physical potential in residential settings. Bronfenbrenner (1979, pp. 143,

144, 150), at the conclusion of a review of children's institutions, proposed several factors that such research ought to address:

> An institution environment is most likely to be damaging to the development of the child under the following combination of circumstances: the environment offers few possibilities for child-caretaker interaction in a variety of activities, and the physical setting restricts opportunities for locomotion and contains few objects that the child can utilize in spontaneous activity.

> The developmentally retarding effects of institutionalization can be averted or reversed by placing the child in an environment that includes the following features: a physical setting that offers opportunities for locomotion and contains objects that the child can utilize in spontaneous activity, the availability of caretakers who interact with the child in a variety of activities, and the availability of a parent figure with whom the child can develop a close attachment.

> The long-range deleterious effects of a physically and socially impoverished institutional environment decrease with the age of the child upon entry. The later the child is admitted to the institution, the greater the probability of recovery from any developmental disturbance after release. The more severe and enduring effects are most likely to occur among infants institutionalized during the first six months of life, before the child is capable of developing a strong emotional attachment to a parent or other caregiver.

REASONS FOR PLACEMENT IN INSTITUTIONS AND RESIDENTIAL CARE

Identifying the reasons children are placed in institutional or residential care can help provide evidence about needs of the children that the planning and administering of residential care should address. They may also suggest alternative arrangements that would in some cases obviate the need for residential care.

Oswin (1978) identified several reasons for the admission of children with multiple physical, mental, and sensory disabilities:

> The parents lacked support such as aids in the house, guidance on physical care and management problems, and respite from the physical and emotional strain and interruption of sleep.

> The family already had substantial problems, such as inadequate or unsuitable housing; an already large family; parental psychiatric, physical, or social problems; or the presence of other disabled children.

> A parent was absent because of death, divorce, or separation, or a single parent relinquished the child at birth.

> Lack of residential accommodation within the community gives the parents no alternative but to seek long-term hospital care for their child.

In Poland the reasons that parents gave for placing their mentally retarded young, all of whom had IQs under 50, were studied (Wald, Zdzienicka, Bartnick, Kalinska, & Mrugalski, 1977, p. 109):

> The reason considered by the parents to be the most important one, turned out to be the child's lack of self-help skills and his inability to acquire these simple skills, which resulted in the necessity of constant help, care and nursing on the part of the family. . . . a small percentage of the families placed their children guided by the good of his siblings.
>
> The families believed that constant presence of the retarded child was a source of additional problems arising in education and upbringing of their other children.

In two state training schools for the mentally retarded in the northeastern United States, Braginsky and Braginsky (1971) examined the family backgrounds of young people and adults ages 12–30 who met the following criteria: "a) educable, b) probably cultural-familial retardates—that is, they did not have any obvious organic impairment accounting for their low IQ scores, c) judged by the staff capable of a relatively high degree of self-management." In 64% of the cases one parent was absent because of desertion, divorce, separation, or imprisonment or some other form of institutionalization. For some of those who had both parents at home when placed in the institution there were other problems; 59% of the youngsters in this group came from families characterized as having a "bad influence" on the children's development—the children had been the victims of incest, beatings, starvation, and the like.

The United States and Britain appear to differ in the proportions of mildly retarded children who are placed in residential care because of adverse home environments. In the United States, the Braginskys found 40% of the young people in the residences were educable retarded, did not have organic impairment, and were judged capable of a relatively high degree of self-management. In the population we studied in Scotland (Richardson et al., 1984), 10%–15% met these criteria. Kushlick (1975) found that only 10% of those institutionalized in southern England were mildly retarded. The difference between these figures for the United States and Britain may reflect differences in the availability of a diversity of human services in the community.

In our study, made in a Scottish city, we followed all children born over a 5-year period who were administratively classified as mentally retarded during the school years, their retardation ranging from borderline to severe. They were followed until age 22, and their career paths through mental retardation services were mapped. Of the total retarded population, 12% were in long-term institutional care. Of all those in institutions, 76% were placed because of behavior disturbances with which the family could not cope or that the community would not tolerate. The severity and multiplicity of their various disabilities (which included epilepsy, physical disability, behavior disturbances, communication disorders, and incontinence) are insufficient clues to determine why they were institutionalized, because others living at home and receiving day care at senior training centers also had severe or multiple disabilities.

The major reason for placement was the family's unwillingness or inability to cope with the child. All children placed before age 5 had cerebral palsy or Down's syndrome; half of these children were abandoned by their parents, and one child was placed on a doctor's recommendation. Other reasons for placement in childhood were parental neglect and cruelty and the deaths of parents. The median age of young people placed because of behavior disturbance was 14 years at placement, whereas the median age of children placed for other reasons was 5½ years. Although there was overlap between young people in day care and residential services in the severity and multiplicity of their disabilities, there were more severely and multiply disabled children in residential care. Our findings for the children placed in residential care at early ages closely resemble Oswin's, but we also found that behavior disturbances were the primary reason for placement of teenagers. Changes in admission policies make future placements of children under 5 because of Down's syndrome and cerebral palsy less likely.

A factor influencing the kinds of children who are placed in residential care is the values the public holds toward different forms of funding for the care of children. In the United States there is willingness to pay from $25,000 to $60,000 a year to keep a child in residential care (costs vary widely within states and among states); there is also, to some extent, willingness to provide funds for foster care. Giving parents a lesser sum than institutional costs in many cases would enable the parents to purchase the services and help they need in the community and keep their children at home. The number of institutional placements would thereby be reduced. But there has been reluctance to give parents money for such ends—in part from a lack of trust in parents and fear the money will not be used as intended, and in part because social security payments are already provided (although these are inadequate to cover the additional costs of a disabled person). It is encouraging that a few states are carrying out pilot projects to provide families with additional financial aid, but so far no reports of results are available.

As the studies cited show, the reasons for placement of children in institutional and residential care vary widely, reflecting several areas of heterogeneity: the children themselves who are classified as mentally retarded, the children's family circumstances, and the kinds of community services available to help the parents. For severely retarded children with multiple associated problems, such as physical disabilities, severe epilepsy, communication and sensory disorder, and behavior disturbance, otherwise capable parents may find the daily care of their child overwhelming and beyond their ability to cope, even with heroic effort. Whether children who have fewer or somewhat less severe disabilities are placed in institutions may depend on social policy and the availability of day care and home supportive services, and also on whether family circumstances enable the parents to keep the child at home.

CONCLUSION

The review of the literature presented in this chapter suggests several impressions and ideas. I state them here as a set of separate points rather than as an organized summary, and make no attempt to buttress them with supporting literature. For these reasons they should be considered critically and with skepticism.

We still have much to learn about the kinds of environments that are most beneficial for children of different ages and with different personalities and needs, but we know enough to plan and bring into being residences that can help children who cannot remain with their families. These residences can do much to overcome the disadvantages of earlier types of environments, and, if strategically located in the communities, will facilitate the maintenance of a relationship between child and family.

Greater problems to be faced in developing humane and beneficial residences lie outside the residences themselves, in the environmental influences that largely shape what is possible in residential care. Among these influences are the existing services, bureaucracies, and vested interests; fragmented services and agencies that have grown like Topsy and compete in the open market for clients and funds; a complex network of laws based on outdated theories of care; licensing arrangements; the multiplicity and specialization of professional and paraprofessional bodies; and local ordinances and zoning regulations. In addition, unless children from residences are allowed by the community at large to participate in activities with other children, they will be deprived of socialization experiences inside and outside the residences that are essential for full development. These problem areas, discussed earlier in the chapter, deserve more research.

A difficulty in studying children's institutions is how to take account of the histories of the children before they enter the institution. Many came to the institution because of serious disturbances in their previous environment or because their single or multiple disabilities presented serious problems of management. It becomes difficult to separate the effects of the institution on the child from the effects of the child's prior experiences. Within the institution and later if the child is deinstitutionalized, beneficial environmental influences will take time to show their effects and offset the earlier disadvantageous experiences.

Strong political pressures toward quick deinstitutionalization have had some negative consequences. Residents have been moved out of institutions before a pattern of community services were developed to provide needed help and care. Former residents experienced a worse set of circumstances after deinstitutionalization, and sometimes had to be returned to an institution because of poor planning.

Although the review in this chapter focused on children classified as mentally retarded, the issues raised apply to almost all forms of residential care for children. Residential care for children is generally provided by an array of different agencies, each agency operating under some categorical label such as mental health, some medical category of physical disability, and juvenile delinquency. This practice is deeply embedded in our society, and it rests on premises that are rarely questioned. Yet there are serious problems that need to be recognized. The institutions for children run by such agencies direct attention primarily to a given disability or attribute, often to the neglect of other impairments of the children in their care. Further, children with multiple impairments are difficult to place because they do not fit within any one single-category agency's criterion for placement. The needs of children will not be best served by the further proliferation of new institutions operating under an increasing number of categories or labels. The overall organization of institutional care must be rethought. This need is particularly acute if the trend continues away from isolated, large, total institutions and toward small residences in communities, which draw on the community's various professional and specialized forms of child care and operate in much the same way as a child's home ideally would. The daily care needs common to all children are greater than the needs peculiar to various single or multiple disabilities. Further, some children need residential care because the conditions in the home are regarded by some authority as so bad that the child has been removed from home and foster care is either not available or has not worked. The complexity of the issue should not lead to its being ignored.

A further difficulty in care by category of need—and one that applies to especially severely disabled children—is that the institutional staff have a heavy burden and their attention can easily focus exclusively on the children's disabilities, giving the social and emotional needs of the children scant attention.

For children with disabilities, the Developmental Disabilities Assistance and Construction Act of 1970 was a major step away from dealing with disabilities as they occur in each individual. The disabilities may be single or multiple and must be dealt with in the context of what assets are present, past experience, and the social circumstances in which the child lives.

People are customarily thought of as either children or adults, and the organization of almost all human services reflects this dichotomy. Thus, the transitional period between childhood and young adulthood is neglected, as are the unique needs of the elderly. During adolescence, the young family member undergoes a slow emancipation from dependence on the parents and gradually takes over the management of his or her own affairs. By contrast, residential care, following the customary dichotomy of child and adult, often fails to provide for a transition in which the young person assumes increasing autonomy. As a result, children in residential care find themselves thrust straight from the status of child to adult. In mental retardation institutions it is even worse, for the residents continue to be treated as children after chronologically becoming adults.

The research literature on institutions has focused largely on shortcomings and inhumane conditions. More research should be directed to identifying those conditions in institutions that would best promote the social and intellectual development of children of different ages. These conditions will be difficult if not impossible to achieve within any institution unless conditions external to the institution—such as beliefs and values relating to the needs of institutionalized children—are also changed, as are the relationships between the institution and its environments.

The concept of deinstitutionalization, although poorly defined operationally, has been of great value in provoking widespread activities directed toward changing forms of care for those in state institutions. Research related to this concept has documented some of the changes and addressed a variety of issues related to how these changes affect those in residential care. At this point, the value of the concept of deinstitutionalization may have been largely spent.

In the studies reviewed there are indications of what experiences help or hinder the socialization and development of children in whatever setting they are placed, whether institutional or family. The more common needs of children at different ages can be identified by research, the more it will be possible to evaluate the various environments in which children live and help in organizing institutional arrangements when these become essential. Children with single or multiple disabilities or with chronic medical conditions have additional needs, but these should not detract from meeting the needs they have in common with all children. Cultural and subcultural differences in child-rearing customs make it clear that there is no one optimum form of upbringing for children, and the diversity of characterisitics which makes for the individuality of children's needs to be accounted for in the study of socialization. Perhaps to formulate future research along the lines suggested here is too ambitious, but it may be needed to get away from the view held far too long, that studies of children's institutions and their residents should be separate and distinct from studies of families and children.

References

Adams, M. Foster family care for the intellectually disadvantaged child: The current state of practice and some research perspectives. In M. J. Begab & S. A. Richardson (Eds.), *The mentally retarded and society: A social science perspective.* Baltimore: University Park Press, 1975.

Ainsworth, M. D., Prugh, D. G., Harlow, R. G., Andry, R. G., Mead, M., Wooten, B., & Lebovici, S. *Deprivation of maternal care: A reassessment of its effects.* Geneva: World Health Organization, 1962.

Anderson, V. H., Schlottmann, R. S., & Weiner, B. J. Predictors of parent involvement with institutionalized retarded children. *American Journal of Mental Deficiency,* 1975, **79**, 6.

Avis, D. W. Deinstitutionalization jet lag. In A. P. Turnbull & H. R. Turnbull III (Eds.), *Parents speak out.* Columbus: Merrill, 1979.

Ballinger, B. R. Community contact of institutionalized mental defectives. *British Journal of Mental Subnormality,* 1970, **16**, 17–23.

Best-Sigford, B., Bruininks, R. H., Lakin, K. C., Hill, B., & Heal, L. Resident release patterns in a national sample of public residential facilities. *American Journal of Mental Deficiency* 1982, **87**, 130–140.

Birenbaum, A., & Seiffer, S. *Resettling retarded adults in a managed community.* New York: Praeger, 1976.

Blatt, B. *Exodus from pandemonium: Human abuse and the reformation of public policy.* Boston: Allyn & Bacon, 1970.

Blatt, B. The executive. In R. B. Kugel & A. Shearer (Eds.), *Changing patterns in residential services for the mentally retarded.* Washington, D.C.: President's Committee on Mental Retardation, 1976.

Blatt, B., & Kaplan, F. *Christmas in purgatory: A photographic essay on mental retardation.* Boston: Allyn & Bacon, 1966.

Blatt, B., Ozolins, A., & McNally, J. *The family papers: A return to purgatory.* New York: Longman, 1979.

Bowlby, J. *Forty-four juvenile thieves: Their characters and home-life.* London: Bailliere, Tindall & Cox, 1946.

Braginsky, D. D., & Braginsky, B. M. *Hansels and Gretels: Studies of children in institutions for the mentally retarded.* New York: Holt, Rinehart & Winston, 1971.

Bronfenbrenner, U. *The ecology of human development.* Cambridge, Mass.: Harvard University Press, 1979.

Bruininks, R. H., Hauber, F. A., & Kudla, M. J. National survey of community residential facilities: A profile of facilities and residents in 1977. *American Journal of Mental Deficiency* 1980, **84**, 470–478. (a)

Bruininks, R. H., Thurlow, M. L., Thurman, S. K., & Fiorelli, J. S. Deinstitutionalization and community services. In J. Wortis (Ed.), *Mental retardation and developmental disabilities*. New York: Brunner/Mazel, 1980.(b)

Butterfield, E. Some basic changes in residential facilities. In R. B. Kugel & A. Shearer (Eds.), *Changing patterns in residential services for the mentally retarded*. Washington, D.C.: President's Committee on Mental Retardation, 1976.

Clarke, A. M., & Clarke, A. D. B. *Mental deficiency: The changing outlook*. London: Methuen, 1965.

Clarke, A. M., & Clarke, A. D. B. *Early experience*. London: Open Books, 1976.

Cobb, H. *The forecast of fulfillment*. New York: Teachers College Press, 1972.

Cohen, H. J., & Kligler, D. (Eds.). *Urban community care for the developmentally disabled*. Springfield, Ill.: Thomas, 1980.

Conroy, J., Efthimiou, J., & Lemanowicz, J. A matched comparison of the developmental growth of institutionalized and deinstitutionalized mentally retarded clients. *American Journal of Mental Deficiency* 1982, **86**, 581–587.

Dennis, W. Causes of retardation among institutional children. *Journal of Genetic Psychology*, 1960, **96**, 47–59.

Dennis, W., & Dennis, M. G. Infant development under conditions of restricted practice and minimum social stimulation. *Genetic Psychology Monograph*, 1941, **23**, 149–155.

Dentler, R. A., & Mackler, B. The socialization of retarded children in an institution. *Journal of Health and Human Behavior*, 1961, **2**, 243.

Glasser, I. Prisoners of benevolence: Power versus liberty in the welfare state. In W. Gaylin, I. Glasser, S. Marcus, & D. Rothman (Eds.), *Doing good: The limits of benevolence*. New York: Pantheon, 1978.

Goffman, E. *Asylums: Essays on the social situation of mental patients and other inmates*. New York: Doubleday, 1961.

Goldstein, H. Social and occupational adjustment. In H. A. Stevens & R. Heber (Eds.), *Mental retardation*. Chicago: University of Chicago Press, 1964.

Grunewald. K. *The mentally retarded in Sweden*. Publication of the Division for Mental Retardation, National Board of Health and Welfare, 1969.

Hubbell, H. G. Colonization as a therapeutic measure. *Psychiatric Quarterly*, 1934, **8**, 476–488.

Intagliata, J., & Willer, B. Reinstitutionalization of mentally retarded persons successfully placed into family-care and group homes. *American Journal of Mental Deficiency*, 1982, **87**, 34–39.

Kanner, L. *A history of the care and study of the mentally retarded*. Springfield, Ill.: Thomas, 1964.

Kimball, W. Human warehouses: An inside look at the Fernald School for the Retarded. *Boston after Dark*, 1972 (May).

King, R. D., Raynes, N. V., & Tizard, J. *Patterns of residential care*. London: Routledge & Kegan Paul, 1971.

Koller, E. Mainstreaming in turbulent waters. In H. J. Cohen & D. Kligler (Eds.), *Urban community care for the developmentally disabled*. Springfield, Ill.: Thomas, 1980.

Kuhlmann, F. One hundred years of special care and training. *American Journal of Mental Deficiency*, 1940, **45**, 8–24.

Kushlick, A. Epidemiology and evaluation of services for the mentally handicapped. In M. J.

Begab & S. A. Richardson (Eds.), *The mentally retarded and society*. Baltimore: University Park Press, 1975.

Lakin, K. C., Bruininks, R. H., & Sigford, B. B. Early perspectives on the community adjustment of the mentally retarded. In R. H. Bruininks, C. E. Meyer, B. B. Sigford, & K. C. Lakin (Eds.), *Deinstitutionalization and community adjustment of mentally retarded people*. Monograph of the AAMD, no. 4, 1981.

Lubin, R. A., Schwartz, A. A., Zigman, W. B., & Janicki, M. P. Community acceptance of residential programs for developmentally disabled persons. *Applied Research in Mental Retardation*, 1982, 3, 191–200.

McCormick, M., Balla, D., & Zigler, E. Resident-care practices in institutions for retarded persons: A cross-institutional, cross-cultural study. *American Journal of Mental Deficiency*, 1975, 80, 1–17.

Mittler, P. *People, not patients*. London: Methuen, 1979.

Morris, P. *Put away*. New York: Atherton, 1969.

Moss, P. Residential care of children: A general review. In J. Tizard, I Sinclair, & R. V. G. Clarke (Eds.), *Varieties of residential experience*. London: Routledge & Kegan Paul, 1975.

National Association of Superintendents of Public Residential Facilities for the Mentally Retarded. *Contemporary issues in residential programming*. Washington, D.C.: President's Committee on Mental Retardation, 1974.

Nihira, L., & Nihira, K. Jeopardy and community placement. *American Journal of Mental Deficiency*, 1975. 79, 538–544.

Nirje, B. The normalization principle and its human management implications. In R. B. Kugel & W. Wolfensberger (Eds.), *Changing patterns in residential services for the mentally retarded*. Washington, D.C.: President's Committee on Mental Retardation, 1969.

Oswin, M. *Children living in long stay hospitals*. Philadelphia: Lippincott, 1978.

Oswin, M. The neglect of children in long-stay hospitals. *Child Abuse and Neglect*, 1979, 3, 88–92.

President's Panel on Mental Retardation. *Report to the President: A proposed program for national action to combat mental retardation*. Washington, D.C.: Government Printing Office, 1962.

Primrose, D. A. Asylum. In P. Mittler (Ed.), *Research to practice in mental retardation*. Vol. 1. *Care and intervention*. Baltimore: University Park Press, 1977.

Richardson, S. A., Koller, H., Katz, M., & McLaren, J. Patterns of disability in a mentally retarded population between ages 16 and 22. In J. M. Berg (Ed.), *Perspectives and progress in mental retardation*. Vol. 2. Baltimore: University Park Press, 1984.

Rivera, G. *Willowbrook: A report on how it is and why it doesn't have to be that way*. New York: Random House, 1972.

Rosen, M., & Clark, G. R. (Eds.). *The history of mental retardation*. Vol. 1. Baltimore: University Park Press, 1976.

Rosenberg, A. D. *Appropriateness of the continued institutionalization of the state school population of New York State*. Buffalo: New York Department of Mental Hygiene, 1969.

Rutter, M. Maternal deprivation 1972–1978. New findings, new concepts, new approaches. In S. Chess & A. Thomas (Eds.), *Annual progress in child psychiatry and child development*. New York: Brunner/Mazel, 1980.

Scheerenberger, R. C. Deinstitutionalization in perspective. In J. L. Paul, D. J. Stedman, & G. R. Neufeld (Eds.), *Deinstitutionalization. Program and policy development*. Syracuse, N.Y.: Syracuse University Press, 1977.

Scheerenberger, R. C. *A History of mental retardation.* Baltimore: Louden Brookes, 1983.

Schultz, H. F., & Buckman, S. T. A study of visiting patterns of relatives. *Welfare Reporter,* 1965, **16**, 72–75.

Skeels, H. M. Adult status of children with contrasting early life experiences. *Monographs of the Society for Research in Child Development,* 1966, **31**(3, Serial No. 105).

Spitz, R. A. Hospitalism: An inquiry into the genesis of psychiatric conditions in early childhood. In O. Fenichel et al. (Eds.), *Psychoanalytic study of the child.* New York: International Universities Press, 1945.

Spitz, R. A. Hospitalism: A follow-up report. In O. Fenichel (Ed.), *Psychoanalytic study of the child.* New York: International Universities Press, 1946.

Thormalen, P. W. *A study of on-the-ward training of trainable mentally retarded children in a state institution.* California Mental Health Research Monograph, No. 4, State of California, Department of Mental Hygiene.

Tizard, B. Varieties of residential nursery experience. In J. Tizard, I. Sinclair, & R. V. G. Clarke (Eds.), *Varieties of residential experience.* London: Routledge & Kegan Paul, 1975.

Tizard, B., Cooperman, O., Joseph, A., & Tizard, J. Environmental effects on language development: A study of young children in long-stay residential nurseries. *Child Development,* 1972, **43**, 337–358.

Tizard, B., & Rees, J. A comparison of the effects of adoption, restoration to the natural mother and continued institutionalization on the cognitive development of four-year-old children. *Child Development,* 1974, **45**, 92–99.

Tizard, B., & Rees, J. The effect of early institutional rearing on the behaviour problems and affectional relationships of four-year-old children. *Journal of Child Psychology and Psychiatry,* 1975, **16**, 61–73.

Tizard, J. *Community services for the mentally handicapped.* London: Oxford University Press, 1964.

Tizard, J. *Survey and experiment in special education.* London: Harrap, 1967.

Tizard, J. Research into services for the mentally handicapped: Science and policy. *British Journal of Mental Subnormality,* 1972, **18**, 1–12.

Wald, I., Zdzienicka, E., Bartnick, M., Kalinska, A., & Mrugalski, K. *The ten years follow-up study of representative sample of the low-grade mentally retarded in Poland.* Warsaw: Psycho-neurological Institute, 1977.

Wing, J. K., & Brown, G. *Institutionalism and schizophrenia.* Cambridge: Cambridge University Press, 1970.

Wolfensberger, W. The origin and nature of our institutional models. In R. B. Kugel & W. Wolfensberger (Eds.), *Changing patterns in residential services for the mentally retarded.* Washington, D.C.: President's Committee on Mental Retardation, 1969.

World Health Organization. *Expert Committee on Mental Health, report on the second session, 1951.* Technical Report Series, No. 31. Geneva: WHO, 1951.

Zigler, E., & Balla, D. Impact of institutional experience on the behavior and development of retarded persons. *American Journal of Mental Deficiency,* **82**, 1–12.

Sex Roles, Socialization,
and Occupational Behavior

JACQUELYNNE S. ECCLES AND LOIS W. HOFFMAN
University of Michigan

Throughout this century, men and women have exhibited very different occupational behavior patterns. Not only have women been less involved in the labor market, they have also entered and pursued different types of jobs. Despite recent increases in the number of women employed, the labor market has remained largely segregated by sex.

Why is a sex-segregated labor force a concern? If the segregation were the result of equal opportunities for each sex and represented the outgrowth of intrinsic interests and natural talents, and if equal economic advantages for each sex were the outcome, then it would be difficult to label it a social problem worthy of policy consideration. In fact, however, such is not the case. Men and women do not have equal opportunities for participation in the labor force, and they have different access to the various occupations. Furthermore, men often receive higher wages when the needs, skills, and sometimes even the jobs are the same.

To the extent that these inequalities are the result of discrimination in hiring, promotion, wages, and training opportunities, they are clearly problems toward which social policy must be directed. Indeed, important efforts of this sort have already been made. But there are also more subtle influences. From earliest childhood, males and females receive different treatment; these differences influence adult occupational patterns. Inequality of opportunity starts very early. Just as social class and race may mark a child for a particular kind of socialization experience, so does sex. Males and females do not have the same opportunities to develop occupational competencies and motivations. They are steered toward some occupations and away from others because of cultural beliefs that some

Preparation of this paper was supported in part by a grant to the first author from the National Institute of Mental Health. Order of authorship was determined by a coin toss. Grateful acknowledgment goes to Laura Skidmore for her assistance in preparing the manuscript.

occupations are better suited for females and some for males. Because of these socialization patterns, many individuals do not develop their full capacities; many are discouraged from adequately exploring their possible areas of interest. In this chapter, we analyze this process of socialization and explore the ways in which the experiences of childhood contribute to the differences between men's and women's labor force participation. We also consider the role social policy could play in fostering more equitable labor force participation by males and females.

SEX DIFFERENCES IN LABOR FORCE PARTICIPATION

At the turn of the century, nearly half of America's women lived on farms. Although their labor was essential to the family's economic well-being, they were not counted in statistics on labor market participation unless they were heads of households. Those women who did work for pay outside the home were concentrated in three occupations: domestic service, factory work, and schoolteaching. The majority of these women worked while they were young and stopped working when they married and had children. For example, in 1900 only 5.6% of wives were employed outside the home (Hayghe, 1976).

Between 1900 and 1940, women's overall rate of participation in the labor force increased only slightly, from 20% to 25%. Although the rate of increase was somewhat higher among younger women, from 31.7% in 1900 to 45.6% in 1940, the general employment pattern of women remained basically unchanged. Women continued to be concentrated in a very few occupations. In addition, the majority of women stopped working as soon as they married and did not return to the labor force (Hoffman & Nye, 1974).

Since 1940, there have been substantial changes in the character of women's labor force participation. First, there has been a steady increase in their rate of participation (see Table 1). This increase has been especially marked among married women and, particularly, among women with children (see Table 2). The first group of women to enter the labor market in increasing numbers were older, married women. During the 1960s and 1970s the proportion of working women 25–45 years old also increased dramatically (see Table 1). Although some of this increase reflects the increasing number of single women, childless couples, and divorced or separated mothers, these groups are not the major source of the change. The most marked increase has occurred among mothers living with their husbands. For example, the participation rate of married women with children under 6 years of age has increased from 9% in 1940 to 19% in 1960

TABLE 1
Increase in Women's Labor Force Participation Rate (percentage in labor force) by Age Group

Year	Total 16 Years and Over	16–17	18–19	20–24	25–34	35–44	45–54	55–64	65 and over
1950	33.9	30.1	51.3	46.0	34.0	39.1	37.9	27.0	9.7
1960	37.7	29.1	50.9	46.1	36.0	43.4	49.8	37.2	10.8
1965	39.3	27.7	49.3	49.9	38.5	46.1	50.9	41.1	10.0
1970	43.3	34.9	53.6	57.7	45.0	51.1	54.4	43.0	9.7
1975	46.3	40.2	58.1	64.1	54.6	55.8	54.6	41.0	8.3
1979	51.1	51.8	68.1	71.5	63.3	62.1	57.5	40.8	8.0
Projection:									
1985 . .	54.8–57.1								
1990 . .	57.1–60.4								

SOURCE.—U. S. Department of Labor, 1980.

TABLE 2

LABOR FORCE PARTICIPATION RATES OF MOTHERS
WITH CHILDREN UNDER 18, 1940–1980

Year	% of Mothers
1940	8.6
1946	18.2
1948	20.2
1950	21.6
1952	23.8
1954	25.6
1956	27.5
1958	29.5
1960	30.4
1962	32.9
1964	34.5
1966	35.8
1968	39.4
1970	42.0
1972	42.9
1974	45.7
1976	48.8
1978	53.0
1980	56.6

SOURCES.—U.S. Department of Commerce, 1979; U.S. Department of Labor, 1977, 1981.

and to 43% in 1980; all projections indicate that it will continue to increase in the future (Hoffman, in press; Hoffman & Nye, 1974; U.S. Department of Labor, 1980).

The second major change that has occurred since 1940 is the range of jobs that women occupy. Women can now be found in almost all types of employment, and they are beginning to make some inroads into higher-status, higher salaried jobs. Much of the increase in women's participation in male-stereotyped occupations has occurred since 1970. For example, in 1970 women painters, machinists, and engineers were a rarity; by 1979 women made up 5% of the painters, 3% of the machinists, and 2% of the industrial engineers. Similarly, since 1970, the proportion of female judges and lawyers has risen from 6% to 13% and the proportion of female scientists has risen from 14% to 19% (U.S. Department of Labor, 1980). Even more substantial gains have been made in the proportion of women receiving college degrees in traditionally male fields. For example, the proportion of Ph.D.'s awarded to women in the sciences jumped from 9% in 1970 to 23% in 1980 (Vetter, 1981). Likewise, women have substantially increased their proportion of B.A. degrees in such male-dominated majors as engineering, agriculture, architecture, and business, thus increasing the supply of women for jobs in these fields (Lyson, 1981).

Despite these impressive gains, the job market by and large remains segregated by sex. The great majority of women still hold jobs in traditionally female occupations (see Table 3) and earn degrees in female dominant or sex-neutral majors. Furthermore, since 1960 the proportion of women in female dominant fields (such as elementary school teaching and registered nursing) has either remained constant or actually increased (e.g., in clerical work, see Table 4). Of all the sex-neutral and traditional female B.A. degrees surveyed by Lyson (1981), only in education has the proportion of male participation increased. Thus, although women are entering the labor force in larger numbers, they still tend to be clustered in female-stereotyped jobs. In addition, there has been little movement of men into these traditionally female occupations.

The gains made by women over the past 80 years are also offset by the sex differentials in both unemployment rates and income level. As the number of women seeking jobs has increased, so has their rate of unemployment. Women's unemployment rates have been running about 2%–4% higher than men's since 1973 (U.S. Department of Labor, 1980). The difference is even larger among highly trained scientists and technicians. Among Ph.D.'s in science, engineering, and social science, unemployment rates for women are two to five times greater than for men, even when the level of experience and the year of receiving the doctoral degree are controlled. In addition, women are more likely than men to be employed below their level of training and in support positions (Vetter, 1981).

Sex inequity in the labor market is also evident in wages. Despite major legislative attempts to increase wage parity, women continue to earn less than men in the vast majority of occupations. In fact, there has been very little change in the size of the sex disparity in wages since 1940: In that year, women, on average, earned 64% of what their male peers earned; in 1977, the figure had declined to 59%. This disparity cannot be adequately explained by women's lower qualifications. Much of it results from the concentration of women in low-paying jobs. But even within comparable jobs, women earn less than men of equivalent levels of training. For example, women elementary school teachers earn 80% as much as their male colleagues. Among highly trained scientists and technicians, men are paid more than women in most fields, even when level of experience, year of degree, and field of study are controlled. Thus, even today, only a small proportion of women occupy high-status and high-paying positions (Treiman & Hartman, 1981; U.S. Department of Labor, 1980; Vetter, 1981).

The wage gap is especially problematic for the increasing number of

TABLE 3

WOMEN AS PERCENTAGE OF TOTAL EMPLOYMENT IN SELECTED OCCUPATIONS, 1975–1979 (N in thousands)

OCCUPATION	1979		1975		% INCREASE from 1975
	Total Employment	% Women	Total Employment	% Women	
Professional and technical	15,050	43.3	12,748	41.3	23.8
Accountants	1,045	32.9	782	24.6	79.2
Computer specialists	534	26.0	363	21.2	80.5
Industrial engineers	245	7.3	187	2.7	260.0
Lawyers and judges	499	12.4	392	7.1	121.4
Librarians	188	80.9	180	81.1	4.1
Life and physical scientists	280	18.9	277	14.4	32.5
Physicians	431	10.7	354	13.0	…
Registered nurses	1,223	96.8	935	97.0	30.5
Elementary school teachers	1,374	84.3	1,332	85.4	1.8
Secondary school teachers	1,213	50.7	1,184	49.2	5.5
Managers and administrators	10,516	24.6	8,891	19.4	49.9
Bank officials and financial managers	620	31.6	518	23.6	60.7
School administrators (elementary and secondary)	299	37.5	263	28.1	51.4

Clerical workers	17,613	80.3	15,128	77.8	20.2
Typists	1,020	96.7	1,025	96.6	.4
Craft and kindred workers	12,880	5.7	10,972	4.6	46.1
Carpenters	1,276	1.3	988	.6	183.3
Painters, construction, and maintenance	483	5.0	420	3.8	50.0
Machinists and job setters	642	3.3	557	2.5	50.0
Auto mechanics	1,272	.6	1,102	.5	33.3
Printing craft workers	455	22.2	375	17.6	53.0
Telephone installers and repairers	302	9.9	314	4.8	100.0
Operatives, including transport	14,521	32.0	12,856	30.2	19.6
Sewers and stitchers	810	95.3	803	95.8	.4
Bus drivers	358	45.5	310	37.7	39.3
Truck drivers	1,965	2.1	1,694	1.1	121.1
Service workers	12,834	62.4	11,657	62.3	10.3
Cleaners and servants	485	97.3	599	97.3	−23.5
Waiters and waitresses	1,363	89.4	1,183	91.1	13.1
Nursing aides, orderlies	1,024	87.5	1,001	85.8	4.3
Hairdressers and cosmetologists	575	89.2	504	90.5	12.5
Protective service	1,406	8.8	1,290	6.3	51.2

Source.—U.S. Department of Labor, 1980.

TABLE 4

PERCENTAGE DISTRIBUTION OF EMPLOYED WOMEN, BY MAJOR OCCUPATION GROUP

OCCUPATION GROUP	AUGUST 1979	ANNUAL AVERAGE		
		1978	1970	1960
Total employed (in thousands)	40,335	38,881	29,667	21,874
Percent	100.0	100.0	100.0	100.0
Professional and technical workers	15.3	15.6	14.5	12.4
Managers and administrators (except farm)	6.8	6.1	4.5	5.0
Sales workers	7.0	6.9	7.0	7.7
Clerical workers	34.9	34.6	34.5	30.3
Craft and kindred workers	1.9	1.8	1.1	1.0
Operators, including transport	11.6	11.8	14.5	15.2
Nonfarm laborers	1.4	1.3	.5	.4
Private-household workers	2.6	2.9	5.1	8.9
Other service workers	17.0	17.7	16.5	14.8
Farmers and farm managers	.4	.3	.3	.5
Farm laborers and supervisors	1.2	1.0	1.5	3.2

SOURCE.—U.S. Department of Labor, 1980.

women heads of households, most of whom work in low-paying, traditionally female occupations. Since 1960 the divorce rate has more than doubled. Glick and Norton (1977/1979) estimate that, if the current rate continues, about 40% of all marriages now being entered into will end in divorce. In many of these divorces, the woman becomes the primary support of the family. For example, in 1978, 15% of all white families with children and 45% of all black families with children were headed by a woman. Many of these families exist on poverty-level incomes; most have incomes below the national median. Often these women do not have the education, the training, or the opportunities for apprenticeships that will enable them to acquire better jobs. In 1978, 30% of all female heads of households had less than a high school education, and only 9% had completed 4 or more years of college (U.S. Department of Labor, 1980). The economic implications of these statistics are indeed sobering.

In summary: Despite the increase in women's labor market participation and major gains in the broadening range of occupations open to women, men and women by and large are still employed in different types of occupations; further, women tend to be concentrated in low-paying jobs, making it difficult for them to support either themselves or their families. Even within a given profession, females are still more likely to be unemployed and typically earn less than their male colleagues. Although limited training opportunities and both subtle and outright discrimination undoubtedly contribute to these disparities, psychological factors also play an important role. In this chapter, the role these psychological factors play in promoting and reinforcing a sex-segregated labor market is explored. We focus primarily on the socialization experiences that shape children's abilities, personalities, self-concepts, attitudes, expectations, and values—all of which affect occupational decisions and labor force participation. It is important to note that we are describing only one part of an overdetermined pattern. To a large extent, sex differences in occupational behavior reflect real pressures in the adult world that operate differently for men and for women. In the next section, these constraints and pressures are briefly described.

ADULT ROLES AND OCCUPATIONAL CHOICE

For men more than for women, having an occupation, a paid job, is seen as a necessity, and occupational success is unambivalently esteemed. The man is expected to support himself and, either solely or with his wife, his conjugal family. Typically, his occupational involvement, once begun, continues without interruption until his retirement. While some men's career paths may be affected by family pressures (Hoffman, in press; Kanter, 1977), the impact is more varied and subtle on men's than on women's work patterns. Men, for example, rarely choose a career that will be sufficiently flexible to bend to the career needs of a wife. They also rarely take off time from work to help raise their children.

This pattern of making the man's career the primary concern has helped men to choose the most financially rewarding and demanding occupations that their abilities and material resources allow—provided that such jobs are available. In addition, the expectation that he will seek out the highest-status occupation possible has created a pressure to do so, deterring men from occupations that may be less financially promising but more flexible. This expectation has also fostered the psychological need in many men to continue competing for better jobs throughout their working years. Unless a man is of retirement age, it is difficult for him to choose nonemployment or even part-time employment. There would be little social support for a man's voluntary choice of either. Consequently, while it has been easier for men than for women to pursue a wide variety of occupational goals, men have had less freedom to stay at home or to work less than full time.

For women the situation has been quite different. Society expects women to marry and take major responsibility for homemaking and child care. A wife's occupation is expected to be subordinate to her husband's; a man's occupational demands typically take precedence over his wife's.

Because of this, many women hold their occupational choice in abeyance until marriage or choose an occupation that will not interfere with the demands of their husband's job and the pressures of child care.

As indicated above, during the last several decades the typical occupational pattern for women has been employment before marriage and during the early years of marriage; withdrawal from the labor force during the period when there are preschool children; for some, a return to the labor force when the youngest child starts school, though often part time; and an eventual return to full-time employment only when the children are older. Mothers have also entered the labor force temporarily when there was economic stress in the family. Given this intermittent employment pattern, women have gravitated toward occupations in which withdrawal from and reentry to the labor force have been possible. Thus, for example, an occupation where absence from the field results in a loss of skill through obsolescence would not be seen as an appropriate choice. Women have been handicapped in occupations in which advancement is based on the uninterrupted accumulation of seniority. Furthermore, employed mothers have favored jobs compatible with their child care responsibilities. Women's jobs more than men's have been chosen because of the convenience of hours and location (Hoffman & Nye, 1974; Tittle, 1981).

Because of this pattern, it is not surprising that women are disproportionately represented in occupations in which there is a high demand for relatively unskilled temporary labor; in which unions, with their emphasis on seniority rights, are less strong; in which continuous employment is less essential. Even among the professions, the fields in which women predominate are the ones most compatible with the fluctuating pressures of child rearing. If, for example, teaching and nursing have been particularly popular professions for women, it may reflect their being nurturant and stereotypically feminine occupations, but it may also reflect the fact that the former matches children's school schedules and the latter offers the possibility of flexible shifts and the continuous availability of intermittent jobs. Unfortunately, the availability of a large pool of labor for the occupations that fit child rearing responsibilities has allowed salaries and wages to remain low.

The higher priority assigned by couples to the husband's job has affected even the occupational pursuits of highly trained professional women. Geographical location is more likely to be determined by the husband's than the wife's job, and this affects both occupational choice and career paths within occupations. Furthermore, there is evidence that both men and women tend to expect the husband's job to be either more lucrative or more prestigious and, as a result, may be disturbed when a wife's occupational success threatens to surpass her husband's. Some women may be motivated to lessen their work commitment to avoid this (Hoffman, 1977b; Komorovsky, 1977).

The different roles of men and women affect their occupational choice and career patterns not only directly but also through employers' hiring practices. Employment practices that discriminate against women often involve applying generalizations about women's conflicting role demands to all women applicants whether or not they fit in the particular case. Employers may not hire a young woman for fear she will quit if she becomes a mother, or because they may assume she will not accept a within-company geographical transfer if she is married. Other discriminatory practices that have affected women's occupational opportunities have an even less rational basis. A particular obstacle to women's participation in the skilled trades is the exclusion of women from the skilled-trade unions. This may be based on the belief that admitting women would depress wages, but it may also be based on a desire to preserve an aura of masculine elitism. Whatever the basis, discriminatory policies by employers, unions, and training and educational facilities are another important force that has brought about sex differences in the occupational distribution of the population.

There have been a number of changes in this pattern in recent years. Because family size in the United States has decreased and the rate of maternal employment has increased even among mothers of preschool children, the intermittent employment style of women has been changing. The number of years during which a mother has preschool children has decreased, as has the likelihood that she will withdraw from the labor force during this period. This change has been augmented by the increased divorce rate, which affects both the need for employment and the motivation for establishing occupational competence.

Employment of mothers has also become more socially acceptable (Thornton & Freedman, 1980), and some nonemployed mothers of school-aged children indicate they are beginning to feel somewhat defensive about being full-time homemakers. Although it is not solidly documented, some observers believe that men may be increasing their child care responsibilities, sharing somewhat more in the role traditionally assigned to women (Hoffman, 1983). It may also be that the increased employment of married women has diminished some of the pressure on men because the man is now less likely to be the sole breadwinner. The decrease recently reported in men's drive for occupational success may reflect this shift (Hoffman, 1974, 1977b).

Nevertheless, in the 1980s the man is still seen as the major family breadwinner and the husband's occupation still takes precedence over the wife's. Women still have the major responsibility for child care and homemaking; although maternal employment increases the husband's role in both child care and household tasks, it does so only modestly (Hoffman, 1983). To the extent that a woman perceives that there is a conflict between being employed and being a good mother, she will be unlikely to select a demanding career (Hoffman & Nye, 1974; Parsons & Goff, 1980; Tittle, 1981). Although the research has indicated that well-designed, properly staffed day-care programs do not have adverse effects on children (Belsky & Steinberg, 1978), such programs are in very short supply, and popular writers still warn against the mother's employment during the child's preschool years (White, 1980). Although 62% of the married mothers of school-aged children were employed in 1980, only two-thirds of these were employed full time. Forty-five percent of the married mothers of pre-schoolers were employed, fewer than 60% of them full time. Thus, although both replication studies (Veroff, Douvan, & Kulka, 1981) and reinterview studies (Thornton & Freedman, 1980) over a 15- to 20-year interval indicate a movement toward more egalitarian attitudes, traditional sex roles still prevail, and marriage and motherhood continue to operate as a barrier to women's full, uninterrupted commitment to employment. In addition, even though Affirmative Action programs have reduced the extent of overt discrimination against women, subtle forms of discrimination still prevail (Bernard, 1976; Fidell, 1970).

These differences in the adult roles of men and women lead to sex differences both directly and indirectly. As a direct influence, they provide constraints and opportunities that affect occupational choice quite apart from previous socialization. If a young man and a young woman *had* been socialized identically so that each had the same abilities, attitudes, and goals, the woman might have to sacrifice marriage or parenthood to achieve a particular occupational goal, whereas the man would not. And she might meet discriminatory barriers to free choice. On the other hand, the woman might have the option of avoiding employment entirely without suffering social censure, whereas the man would have no such opportunity.

As an indirect influence, the existence of different roles for adult men and women leads to sex differences in the socialization patterns themselves. Child-rearing practices in a society reflect the adult roles that children are expected to occupy. Because little girls are expected to grow up to be mothers with primary child-rearing responsibilities, child-rearing patterns involve training for this role; nurturing, caring qualities are encouraged, while aggressive assertiveness is discouraged. Boys, on the other hand, are given early training in the qualities that are functional to occupational roles because these are assumed to be their major adult commitments (Hoffman, 1977a). Thus, socialization patterns reflect and reinforce sex differences in adult roles. As a result of these socialization patterns, males and females grow up with different skills, coping styles, attitudes, expectations, anxieties, and—perhaps most of all—self-concepts.

To explain how these differences affect occupational behavior, a number of theories have been proposed, each emphasizing one rather than another of these differences as the crucial link between socialization patterns and occupational behavior. Before discussing the socialization patterns themselves, we shall briefly review these theories.

PSYCHOLOGICAL VARIABLES LINKING SEX DIFFERENCES IN SOCIALIZATION TO OCCUPATIONAL PATTERNS

How do differences in the socialization of males and females affect their occupational behaviors? What psychological processes are involved? The various theories formulated to answer these questions fall into four general types: (1) those that view women's occupational behavior as affected by anxiety or lack of confidence; (2) those that focus on the restrictiveness of internalizing traditional sex roles; (3) those that focus on sex differences in acquired personality traits and skills; and (4) those that emphasize the value of the relevant occupational activities to each sex.

Several theories of the first type rely on the idea that the socialization of women fosters a more negative self-concept than men have (Parsons, Ruble, Hodges, & Small, 1976). In support of this perspective, some studies have found that both women and men tend to view the average woman as more passive, more submissive, more unskilled in business, less competent intellectually, and more excitable during minor crises than the average man (Broverman, Vogel, Broverman, Carlson, & Rosenkrantz, 1972). Women who share this negative view of themselves may perceive fewer levels of the professional hierarchy as appropriate for them because they underestimate their skills and accomplishments (Eccles [Parsons], Adler, Futterman, Goff, Kaczala, Meece, & Midgley, 1983). Other such inhibitory attitudes include fear of success (Horner, 1972), fear of loss of femininity (Tangri, 1972), low expectations for future success (Crandall, 1969; Parsons et al., 1976), and low expectancy attributional patterns (Nicholls, 1975).

While theories of the first type assume that women avoid high-level careers out of fear, anxiety, or lack of confidence, theories of the second type argue that socialization experiences encourage sex differences in occupational choices because these experiences limit the options men and women consider as viable for themselves. Typically, socializing agents present very traditional models to their children and do not encourage children to question the limitations associated with these models. As a result, when traditional ideology is internalized by men and women, it is typically accepted as fact rather than opinion, and the restrictions it places on self-development are accepted as natural. Consequently, some women may never even consider any roles other than the traditional one of wife and mother; and although others may seek employment, they are very likely to choose occupations that conform to sex role stereotypes.

In support of this perspective, children as young as 6 years view occupations according to adult sex role stereotypes (Garrett, Ein, & Tremaino, 1977). By the time adolescents reach high school and begin to make serious occupational plans, they have well-developed ideas regarding the sex appropriateness of various occupations and family roles. Their ideas regarding the sex typing of occupations mirror almost exactly the sex ratios found in occupations. Furthermore, both children's and adolescents' own occupational aspirations reflect their stereotypes of sex-appropriate occupations (Looft, 1971; Marini, 1980). Apparently, children and adolescents learn the cultural sex stereotypes, accept them as valid, and make their occupational choices accordingly.

As further support of the influence of ideology on occupational choice, several investigators have demonstrated a relationship between sex role ideology and occupational aspiration. Women who believe they should achieve success vicariously through their husbands have significantly lower educational objectives (Lipman-Blumen, 1972). Similarly, women with traditional views about sex roles have more modest and sex-typed career aspirations than women with less traditional views (Parsons, Frieze, & Ruble, 1978; Tittle, 1981).

Theories of the third type assume that sex role socialization can influence the very traits, personality characteristics, and cognitive skills acquired by the two sexes. For example, several researchers have argued that sex differences in achievement patterns result, in part, from sex differences in early independence training (Hoffman, 1972; Stein & Bailey, 1973). These researchers suggest that girls become more dependent than boys through socialization experiences—to the detriment of their future achievement. Sex role socialization processes have also been suggested as important mediators of the sex differences in spatial skills (Connor, Schackman, & Serbin, 1978), math skills (Fox, Brody, & Tobin, 1980), person orientation (Chodorow, 1978; Hoffman, 1972; Eccles, in press), and careerism (Parsons & Goff, 1980; Tittle, 1981). Because personality traits and skills influence vocational choices and styles, the effects of sex role socialization on occupational behavior may be mediated by its influence on social and personality development.

According to theories of the fourth type, sex role socialization can also influence the value men and women attach to various activities. Proponents of cognitive-developmental models of sex-role acquisition (Eccles et al., 1983) suggest that sex roles influence behavior through the mediating role of incentive value; the value people place on various activities determines their choice among these activities and occupations. Given that the sex typing of activities is one influence on a task's perceived value, the sex typing of a task should influence its selection. Supporting this theory is the finding that both girls and boys attach higher attainment value to traditionally sex-appropriate than to sex-inappropriate areas of achievement (Stein & Bailey, 1973).

In addition, sex differences in occupational behavior could result from more general personal values. Several theoreticians (Eccles, in press) have pointed out that activities that are consistent with one's personal value structure will be perceived as more attractive than those seen as inconsistent or unrelated. In support of this argument, occupational choice has been found to be related to personal values. For example, Dunteman, Wisenbaker, and Taylor (1978) have found that being "thing oriented" rather than "person oriented" is related to becoming a math or science major. Males and females differ in their values. Males score higher on measures of thing orientation and on measures of the importance of political, theoretical, and economic values. In contrast, females score higher on measures of person orientation and social values. Men and women also differ in the value they attach to various job characteristics, such as status, income, and how interesting the job seems (Tittle, 1981). These differences should predispose men and women to make different occupational choices.

While these various theories differ in focus, they are not incompatible with one another. It is quite possible that some of the theories describe the process best for one segment of the population and that other theories are more apt for another; in addition, it is probable that there is a convergence of several influences in each person's occupational decisions, for complex behavior is usually shaped by a multitude of factors. Although the theories differ in which mediating psychological variables they emphasize, all of them share the assumption that sex differences in labor force participation patterns are influenced, at least in part, by differences between males' and females' childhood socialization experiences. We will now consider these socialization influences.

Socialization in the Family

Because the family is a primary agent of socialization, its influence on the child's adult occupation is great. Not only do the child's experiences in the family help to shape his or her personality, social attitudes, abilities, and motivational sets, all of which affect occupational roles, but, because family membership defines the child's socioeconomic status, they affect opportunity structures as well. Thus, the family's influence on the child's choice of occupation is multifaceted and complex. To consider, then, how family influences affect sex differences in occupations, it is necessary to think quite broadly about the parents' role. It is not enough to say that parents are more likely to encourage their sons than their daughters to become doctors, or that parents are more likely to send sons to college, though both are true (Hoffman, 1977a; Mott & Haurin, 1982; Rosen & Aneshensel, 1978). We must also consider how boys' and girls' experiences differ in the family from early childhood on, for these early differences are also part of the preparation for adult occupations.

A number of different processes can be distinguished by which the family experience brings about sex differences. The following will be discussed: (1) children tend to identify with and model the same-sex parent; (2) parents reward and punish different behavior for each sex; (3) parents engage in direct teaching of how males and females are expected to behave; (4) boys and girls are exposed to different experiences through their play activities and their assigned household tasks; (5) parents' perceptions of sons and daughters are different, and these differences, by influencing interaction patterns, affect the children's self-concepts and views of others; and (6) parents have different academic and occupational goals for sons than for daughters.

IDENTIFICATION AND MODELING

According to the Freudian concept of identification, the child's internalization of the standards and qualities of the same-sex parent arises out of the resolution of the Oedipus complex. The incestuous wishes for the parent of the opposite sex lead to anxiety about punishment and abandonment by the same-sex parent; the child's identification with that parent alleviates this anxiety. Other theories have also maintained that identification is based on the internalization of the parent into the self but have suggested other dynamics for its motivation. For example, Talcott Parsons (1955) suggested that the child identifies with the parent because the parent occupies an envied status. The parent is in control of all the resources—love, physical coercion, material goods—and the child identifies with the parent in order to vicariously occupy that preferable status. Unfortunately, Parsons's theories do not explain why the child identifies with the same-sex parent. Kohlberg's theory (1966) adds this missing dynamic by assuming that children first learn what their sex is and that it is unchangeable; they then identify with the parent of their own sex. According to Kohlberg, the female child identifies with the mother because she wants to learn how to become a competent adult, and she knows she cannot be a father. Whatever the dynamics, identification with the same-sex parent is a frequent explanation for the development of sex differences.

Other theories focus on modeling (Bandura & Walters, 1963) or copying of overt behavior rather than on internalization of parental values as the major process underlying sex role acquisition. Although these theories do not acknowledge the psychodynamic process associated with identification theories, they, like the psychodynamic theories, attribute sex differences in behaviors to children's tendency to imitate their same-sex parent more than their opposite-sex parent. There is some research supporting this hypothesis. For example, there is a correlation between the type of work the father does and the son's eventual occupation (Mortimer, 1976), and there is considerable evidence that, when mothers are employed, daughters are more likely to be employed while adolescents, to plan to be employed when they are mothers, to actually be employed mothers when adult, to choose less stereotypically feminine occupations, and to attain higher levels of career success (Hoffman, 1979). These studies do not, however, prove that either identification or modeling is the intervening process. It is quite possible that the similarity between the child's occupational status and the same-sex parent's occupational status is effected by some other means. For example, it has already been noted that, when the mother is employed, the division of tasks in the household is less sex stereotyped; fathers participate more in the traditionally female household tasks and are more active in child care. There is also a less sex-stereotyped ideology, and incompetence is less likely to be seen as a female trait. Furthermore, when the mother is employed, the children receive more encouragement for independence. Each of these patterns could produce the effects attributed to modeling.

Identification is also sometimes invoked to explain the correlation between absence of the father from the family and the son's scores on verbal and mathematics tests (Shinn, 1978). Typically, males have higher math than verbal scores and females have higher verbal than math scores. The failure, therefore, to find higher math than verbal scores among boys from father-absent families has led investigators to suggest that identification with the same-sex parent plays an important role in acquiring these cognitive abilities. Here too, however, the data do not prove that identification is involved. Different interaction patterns in the mother-headed household might also produce this effect. However valuable as a theoretical construct, identification, it has turned out, is a very difficult concept to demonstrate empirically.

Nonetheless, in a world in which mothers and fathers enact different roles and show different degrees of commitment to occupations, identification with the same-sex parent serves to maintain these differences. For example, in an interesting analysis of the precursors of sex differences in educational and occupational expectations, Rosen and Aneshensel (1978) suggest that the daughter's modeling of her mother is a source of conservatism that restrains adaptation to the new requirements of society. They note that "the attainments of same sex parents have a greater impact on adolescent status expectations than those of the opposite sex" (p. 178) and that this pattern is particularly pronounced for daughters. Because the mothers represent a generation for whom traditional roles were more appropriate and whose formative years were in a time when family responsibilities were greater for women and labor force participation was less necessary than at present, mothers' education and occupational attainments typically are lower than fathers'. Thus, the fact that daughters have a model whose achievements are less than those of the model sons have is one source of the persistence of traditional sex role aspirations and choices despite new social conditions. In this study, the girls with the highest occupational aspirations had unusually high grades and test scores and came from families in which economic resources were not merely adequate but plentiful. Rosen and Aneshensel suggest that this relationship exists because girls need considerable impetus and support to overcome the effect of having a parental model who represents a lower level of achievement.

PATTERNS OF PARENTAL REWARDS AND PUNISHMENTS

Parents tend to reward certain behaviors and punish others differentially according to the sex of the child (Block, 1979). This pattern results in part from a deliberate attempt to train children for their socially defined sex role; it is also the consequence of parents' responding to their children in accordance with their own stereotypes about males and females. Parental differentiation may also reflect, to some extent, differences in the children themselves.

Both sexes, but especially boys, are rewarded for behavior that is judged sex appropriate and punished for behavior considered sex inappropriate. Data indicate, for example, that boys in the toddler stage elicit negative responses when they play with dolls (Fagot, 1974), an activity encouraged in girls. Similarly, a wide variety of behaviors, role playing, modeling, play activities, and mannerisms are rewarded and punished by parents in accordance with prescribed sex roles. For example, daughters' bids for dependency, contact, and adult proximity are more likely to be rewarded than are sons' (Fagot, 1974). It has been suggested, though not yet demonstrated, that parents show more unambivalent delight in their sons' physical exploits than in their daughters', presumedly because parents feel more protective toward daughters (even during the earliest years, when there is no rational basis for considering them more vulnerable) and because parents take a particular pride in their sons' daring accomplishments (Hoffman, 1977a). Furthermore, the fathers of preschoolers, when involved in teaching a task to their children, responded more positively to their daughters' attempts to deviate from the task for interpersonal interaction than their sons' attempts; they steered their sons back to the business at hand (Block, Block, & Harrington, 1974).

Several notable aspects of these differences in the patterns of reward and punishment received by boys and girls are important in shaping later occupational orientations. First, in addition to the reinforcement of explicit sex roles, boys may be receiving more of a push toward independence and achievement than are girls. If the reinforcement practices of parents encourage girls' bids for help and interpersonal closeness but push boys toward independence and task concentration, the two sexes may be learning different ways of coping with difficult situations. Hoffman (1972), for instance, has suggested that these differences may teach girls to rely on others rather than to tackle problems directly and independently despite obstacles. Furthermore, if girls come to believe that they need others or can rely on others to cope with problems, interpersonal relationships may become very important. Consistent with this line of reasoning are achievement orientations and occupational preferences that indicate more affiliative and interpersonal involvements for women than for men (Hoffman, 1972; Horner, 1972; Veroff et al., 1981); but whether this is a result of this particular pattern of reward contingencies has not yet been determined. Other aspects of early childhood experiences and adult pressures could also engender this affiliative orientation in women.

It is worth noting that coping styles, once adopted, can become self-reinforcing as long as they work. For example, if two children each tackle a penny gum machine and one asks for and receives help when the task becomes difficult but the other continues efforts on his own, both are rewarded with gum, but one is also rewarded for seeking and obtaining help, while the other is rewarded for independent persistence. Thus, these early patterns, begun in the home, may generate continued reinforcement.

Another notable aspect of differences in boys' and girls' rewards and punishments is that the sex role training of boys is the more rigorous. Cross-sex activities and behavior are more vigorously discouraged in boys than girls, and sex-appropriate behavior is more often encouraged.

Perhaps because of the lower status accorded their sex, girls are allowed more leeway in dress and behavior. The term "tomboy" is almost affectionate; the term "sissy" is not. It seems likely, in view of this early training, that males become more anxious to conform to sex type than females. Several studies have shown that defining an activity as masculine or feminine affects the performance and motivation of both sexes (Stake, 1976; Stein, Pohly, & Mueller, 1971), a pattern that has significance for sex differences in occupations (Garland & Smith, 1981). In view of the more vigorous conditioning that boys receive, it is likely that sex labeling has a greater influence on male than on female behavior, even though the focus of recent research has been more often on the latter (Stein & Bailey, 1973). Consistent with this idea are the findings that the perception of math as a masculine subject area did not affect the decision of female subjects but did increase the tendency of the males to pursue its study (Eccles et al., 1983). This research suggests that sex differences in some occupations may be more the result of men's heightened motivation to do what is perceived as masculine than a result of women being deterred by the "masculine" label. Similarly, male perception of certain occupations as feminine may lead to the avoidance of these occupations by many men. Thus, the rewards and punishments that shape children into their sex role also shape them for sex-typed occupations and, particularly for men, provide a motivation for sex role conformity.

As a final point it should be noted that, in meting out rewards and punishments for behavior deemed sex appropriate and inappropriate, fathers are more active than mothers. In fact, in all studies that compare mothers and fathers with respect to the sex typing of their children, fathers have been found to differentiate more than mothers between sons and daughters and to do so along traditional lines (Hoffman, 1977a). Possibly this reflects the more intense sex role training they themselves received. Fathers, like sons, are more motivated to conform to sex role prescriptions, and they are more anxious about deviations—in themselves and, often, in others.

DIRECT TEACHING

Much of the socialization in the family involves the direct teaching of values and expected behavior. Here, too, boys and girls receive different messages from their parents. In some cases the differences are specifically linked to sex—such as, "Boys don't cry"; in other cases the parent will acknowledge that sons and daughters are taught different skills and behaviors but will not link these differences to explicit sex role teaching—for example, teaching skills such as hammering or table setting or giving instructions about how to react in a conflict with a peer. Other differences in parent practices are even less consciously sex linked, though they reflect different expectations for each sex; for instance, research suggests that little boys may be taught to cross streets at younger ages than are little girls, a pattern consistent with the view that boys should be independent (Collard, 1964). Differences in the content of parental teaching directed at boys and girls have not been fully investigated and probably would show social class, ethnic, and regional variations in their nature and extent. Nonetheless, the differences already obtained clearly indicate socialization toward the traditional sex roles. Parents teach children the skills and values that they expect will be useful to their children when they grow up. To a large extent, these expectations are based on what the parents learned in their own childhoods and from their own experiences. As such, parental teaching is often somewhat conservative; it does not incorporate the most recent social changes. For example, since much of what little girls are taught is preparation for the adult role of mother, domestic skills are emphasized more than occupational skills. This pattern of socialization may have been appropriate when family size was greater and the caring for young children stretched out over a greater proportion of a woman's life than is now the case. Similarly, it may have been appropriate when mothers were not likely to be employed. At present, however, women spend more years actively involved in occupational pursuits than in mothering; traditional sex role training no longer adequately prepares girls to fit into the new adult roles (Hoffman, 1977a).

If one has not been taught to use a hammer, fix a bike, or swing a bat, one has failed to obtain certain occupationally relevant skills and interests. It has been observed that girls' occupational goals are more restricted and less varied than boys' and that girls, in discussing adult roles, talk more about parenthood, whereas boys talks more about occupations (Tittle, 1981). This may in part reflect the fact that girls are taught fewer occupation skills and, perhaps, are given less information about and orientation toward occupations.

OTHER EXPERIENCES: WORK AND PLAY

Boys and girls also differ in a wide range of experiences related to their play activities and their household tasks. For example, boys and girls are given different toys. The toys for girls are the playthings of the mother role—dolls, dishes, miniature household appliances; in contrast, boys are given toys that represent the world of work—trucks, tools, and building equipment (Kacerguis & Adams, 1979). This differentiation starts even in infancy, as evidenced by a study of adults left alone with an infant identified as a male or female. When the infant was identified as a male, "he" was handed a terrycloth football by the subject; when the infant was identified as a female, "she" was handed a stuffed doll (Seavey, Katz, & Zalk, 1975). Recent research has suggested that the sex typing of toys does more than communicate sex roles to children. Boys' toys, more than girls' toys, afford inventive possibilities, encourage manipulation, and provide more information about the physical world (Block, 1979). Furthermore, research suggests that some of the "masculine" toys, particularly blocks and building materials, develop skills that enhance abilities in dealing with spatial relationships and mathematics (Connor et al., 1978). The data of Newson and Newson (1979), on the other hand, suggest that the toys and play activities of girls may be particularly valuable for verbal development. Since these very skills are often cited as sex differences in abilities throughout the life cycle (Maccoby & Jacklin, 1974), it is quite possible that children's play is part of the preparation for adult occupations.

Another difference in children's play is where it occurs. Boys are allowed by their parents to play on their own away from home more than girls are (Collard, 1964; Saegert & Hart, 1976). This greater opportunity for independent exploration of the environment may provide boys with a richer experience for learning to cope independently and may increase their confidence in their own resources.

Children's tasks replicate these play patterns. Girls are typically assigned the traditional female tasks that are usually carried out within the home; dusting, table setting, dishwashing, and making beds involve routines with little room for new experiences. Boys' tasks are more likely to be outside the home. They are, for instance, expected to run errands more often and at younger ages than girls (Collard, 1964; Duncan, Schuman, & Duncan, 1973). Here, again, the learning properties of these two kinds of activities are different. The boys' activities are more independent of adult supervision and specified routines. It is interesting to note that, although there have been some changes over the years, traditional sex roles still prevail in the assignment of household tasks to children and adults (Duncan et al., 1973).

PARENTS' PERCEPTIONS, INTERACTION PATTERNS, AND CHILDREN'S SELF-CONCEPTS

One important influence of family perceptions and interaction patterns is on the development of self-concepts. Particularly during the early years, the child is developing notions about himself or herself, others, and the nature of the world; life at that time is heavily centered in the family.

Because of the primacy of this period of development, the child who is seen as the tallest, the brightest, or the least important member of the family may sustain the self-perception of being tall, bright, or unimportant even when later evidence obtained outside the family seems to contradict this self-perception. The child's sex can affect parental perceptions from the moment it is known and can influence family interaction patterns throughout the child's life. Thus, though there are many individual variations, the child's sex can introduce a systematic influence that affects both the child's self-concept and his or her view of others.

For example, in the United States, as in almost all other countries, there is a preference for male children. Although most couples in the United States would prefer a child of each sex, males are preferred if the children are to be all the same sex or if there is to be an imbalance. Furthermore, if they have only girls, couples will have more children than originally planned in order to try for a boy, but they are more likely to stay with their original intentions if they have only boys (Hoffman, 1977a). Such sex preferences, like sex-differentiated treatment, are more common among men than among women.

Daughters also are seen as more vulnerable than sons. This belief exists prior to the birth of the child and is sometimes counter to the fact. For example, in several studies in which parent-infant interaction was observed, mothers and fathers sought to elicit gross motor behavior more often in sons than in daughters and played more roughly and vigorously with their infant boys (Moss, 1967; Yarrow, Rubinstein, Pedersen, & Jankowski, 1972). Further, data indicate that parents of infants and toddlers are more apprehensive about the physical well-being of their daughters than of their sons (Minton, Kagan, & Levine, 1971; Pederson & Robson, 1969). In fact, however, baby girls are physiologically more mature and more resistant to disease and injury than are boys. The pattern already noted of expecting boys to cross the street by themselves and run errands at younger ages than girls also seems more consistent with sex role stereotypes and the perception of female vulnerability than with objective sex differences for, actually, males are less mature, more impulsive, and more accident-prone (Block, 1979).

Daughters continue to be seen as more vulnerable even as they get older. In a national sample, parents of children ranging from infancy through adolescence reported that girls were more of a worry than boys because of an assumed greater vulnerability. The sexual vulnerability of females and premarital pregnancy were the most common sources of worry about adolescent girls. While parents are aware of the higher accident rates of adolescent boys, particularly in automobiles, this was cited less often as a reason for concern (Hoffman, 1977a). Consistent with these parental views, daughters typically are also more closely supervised at all ages (Gold & Andres, 1978; Saegert & Hart, 1976).

The fact that girls are perceived as more delicate and vulnerable and are treated accordingly seems likely to affect their self-concept. Thus, if girls see themselves as less potent and effective than boys, if they have less confidence in their independent abilities, are less comfortable with leadership, and exhibit less daring, as some studies suggest (Block, 1979), these perceptions are quite consistent with their parents' orientations toward them. Girls are also interrupted when they are talking more often than boys are and thus perhaps given a message about how important their parents think their contributions are (Greif, 1979). It is not surprising, then, that parents have lower academic and occupational aspirations for their daughters.

Parents also tend to respond differently to the academic achievements of boys and girls. A large-scale study of beliefs about mathematical ability showed that parents believed that daughters have to try harder than sons to do well in mathematics, despite the fact that the boys and girls in the study had done equally well in math throughout their school careers and reported doing the same amount of math homework. Their teachers also rated the boys and girls as having worked equally hard in math class. Thus, the parental belief that girls have to work harder than boys does not appear to be grounded in reality (Parsons, Adler, & Kaczala, 1982). Parents' belief that their daughters have to try harder to do well in math is shared by their daughters; data suggest that girls, more than boys, believe they need to work very hard to do well in math and attribute their success more to effort than to ability. It has been argued that attributing one's success to effort is not as ego enhancing and confidence building as attributing it to ability. Attributing one's successes to effort leaves one in doubt about the probability of succeeding in the future at more difficult tasks. It is not surprising, then, that girls have lower future expectations for success in math-related fields (Eccles et al., 1983).

Although parents tend to respond to their children in accordance with sex role stereotypes whether or not they have children of the opposite sex, their response may be influenced by the sex composition of their family. In an all-girl family, for example, the child's self-concept may be less likely to suffer from the presence of a male sibling who is accorded higher status. Further, parents may have higher occupational aspirations for a daughter's achievement when there is no son (Adams & Meidam, 1968). Indeed, women with no male siblings are disproportionately represented among very highly achieving women. Absence of male siblings was a major factor distinguishing women in high executive positions (Hennig & Jardim, 1977).

Perhaps parents sustain the sex differences in occupational patterns most directly and visibly through the goals they have for their children. Typically, parents have different aspirations for sons and daughters with respect to personal characteristics, educational attainment, and occupational roles; and parents' expectations and encouragement have been shown to affect their children's educational and occupational paths. Furthermore, parents may be less likely to encourage daughters than sons to seek out careers that make optimal use of the child's skills and abilities. These differences are more pronounced in whites than in blacks (Dorr & Lesser, 1980) and in fathers than in mothers (Hoffman, 1977a; Parsons, Adler, & Kaczala, 1982).

In interaction with children, parents—especially fathers—often stress the achievement and competitive aspects of the situation more in their interactions with sons than in their interactions with daughters (Block, 1979). Furthermore, in the national sample study already cited (Hoffman, 1977a), parents were asked what qualities they wanted to see in their children when grown. They were more likely to answer in terms of occupational success, work, ambition, intelligence, and education when talking about sons. Qualities more often desired in daughters included being kind or unselfish, loving, attractive or well mannered, having a good marriage, and being a good parent.

In this national survey study, parents were asked first about goals for sons and then about goals for daughters, thus eliciting differences in attitudes that parents were conscious of and willing to admit. Often, however, there are differences in the goals parents hold for sons and for daughters that the parents themselves may not even be aware of. For example, in a study of professional mothers of elementary school–age children, most respondents indicated they did not have different goals for their sons and daughters. However, in another part of the interview, each respondent was asked about her goals for a particular child, with no reference to sex differences. When the responses were compared, mothers discussing sons had higher academic and occupational goals for the child than mothers discussing daughters; and the mothers discussing sons anticipated more of a sense of disappointment if their goals were not achieved (Hoffman, 1977a).

The greater academic and occupational expectations of parents for sons is particularly apparent at the higher levels; parents are more likely to expect sons to attend college or beyond. Furthermore, these sex-related differences in parental expectations are most apparent when there is some obstacle to providing college education, such as limited family income, more children in the family, or lower intellectual ability on the part of a particular child. Under any of these conditions, parents are more likely to abandon expectations of their daughters' going to college than their sons' (Mott & Haurin, 1982; Rosen & Aneshensel, 1978).

Not only do parents have higher educational and occupational aspirations for their sons, they also encourage boys to take different academic courses than girls. In one study of adolescents, for example, parents—again, especially fathers—were more likely to stress to their daughters the importance of taking social science and humanities courses and to stress to their sons the importance of advanced mathematics and physical science courses (Parsons, Adler, & Kaczala, 1982). Furthermore, in this study, as in others, parental encouragement and confidence emerged as extremely important determinants of children's self-confidence, aspirations, and educational path—more important even than the children's previous grades or tested ability. Interestingly, in the Parsons, Adler, and Kaczala study (1982), mothers appeared to have a stronger influence than fathers on the achievement patterns of both sons and daughters. Similar results were obtained by Mott and Haurin (1982). In their longitudinal investigation of the factors involved in the educational and occupational progress of siblings of the opposite sex, they also found that it was maternal encouragement for the daughter's educational progress that increased their daughter's eventual occupational status.

Higher educational and occupational expectations for sons than for daughters may be less characteristic of black parents in the United States than of white parents. If so, this may explain data obtained from children suggesting a pattern among blacks opposite that of whites; black girls may have higher aspirations than black boys (Dorr & Lesser, 1980).

CONCLUSIONS

The influence of the family, and parents specifically, in bringing about sex differences is clear. Six different socialization processes have been delineated here: identification with parents, parental patterns of reward and punishment, parent teaching, children's household tasks and play activities, parental stereotypes that affect interaction patterns and the children's self-concepts, and parental expectations for their children. Each of these processes provides boys with socialization experiences somewhat different from those of girls and reinforces the prevailing sex roles. By these patterns the child learns the "sex-appropriate" behavior and attitudes and is motivated to conform. Furthermore, several of these processes may facilitate males' learning independent coping styles and valuing achievement per se while increasing females' interpersonal involvements and abilities. Different skills are learned and different self-concepts generated. Boys, to a greater extent than girls, are given training and encouragement specifically geared toward work in the labor market. Girls' experiences tend to involve socialization for parenthood more than the world of work. While these differences may not be large, they are consistent and accumulative across many years. Thus, it should come as no surprise that these same boys and girls end up in different occupations and exhibit different patterns of employment when they reach adulthood.

Furthermore, each of the family socialization processes discussed tends to have a built-in conservatism. If a child models itself on the parent, the child is imitating the style of a previous generation. In a rapidly changing society, parents may represent outdated models for the adult world their children will face. This is particularly true for sex roles. The full-time homemaker-mother, for example, may represent skills and values that are not appropriate for a daughter who will reach adulthood at a time when most mothers are employed. If modeling processes are conservative, other child-rearing patterns may be even more so. Parents often use their own parents as models in their child-rearing techniques and invoke values they were taught in childhood—an influence from two generations back. Childhood socialization patterns involve preparing children for adult roles, but these patterns have evolved slowly over past years. They are not consciously designed for each new generation. They represent a previous time when daughters were indeed reared for motherhood and sons for occupations. Thus, as the new generation—responding to the social changes in family size, marital stability, longevity, economic conditions, and technological developments—moves into occupations, each sex is more geared for those fields that call on the values, skills, and self-concepts developed in the family, and each is affected by the sex labeling of occupations.

SOCIALIZATION BY THE MASS MEDIA

The importance of identification and modeling to sex role socialization in the family has already been discussed, but modeling occurs outside the family as well. One very salient source of models in children's lives is television. Children spend an average of 2–3 hours each day watching television (Goff-Timmer, Eccles, O'Brien, & Ziegler, 1983). While some changes have been made in the last 2 or 3 years, the portrayal of men's and women's occupational work patterns on television is still, for the most part, sex stereotyped. In addition, females are underrepresented in general and are often portrayed in subservient, dependent roles (Dorr & Lesser, 1980; Greenberg, 1982; Roberts, 1982).

But does this exposure to television affect children's occupational plans and preparation? This is a very difficult question to answer. Most studies of sex role stereotyping on television have involved content analysis and have not examined the actual effect of television viewing on children. But the few studies that have correlated television viewing with sex-typed beliefs yield a consistent picture. Both children and adults, and especially males, who watch more television have more traditional sex role beliefs and are more likely to stereotype occupations on the basis of sex (Dorr & Lesser, 1980; Frueh & McGhee, 1975). Furthermore, both children and adults believe that television is an accurate source of information about careers and report that television is a primary source of occupational information (Greenberg, 1982; Jeffries-Fox & Signorielli, 1979). Thus, it seems likely that television does contribute to sex role socialization. But, since most of the studies in this field are correlational, we cannot adequately assess the effect of television viewing on the development of sex-typed beliefs and behaviors. What we know is that television is not providing children with very many counterstereotypic models. Therefore, at the very least, home television viewing is another conservative source of reinforcement for children's sex-typed beliefs.

What happens when television is used to change sex stereotypes? Studies evaluating the impact of exposure to counterstereotypes on media have yielded a mixed picture. Programs such as "Freestyle" and "3-2-1 Contact," designed to expose children to counterstereotypic occupational information and models, have met with limited success in changing children's occupational interests, especially boys' (Johnston & Ettema, 1982). Changes associated with viewing counterstereotypic dramatic programs have been even smaller and less consistent (Miller & Reeves, 1976).

Because "Freestyle" was designed explicitly to be used in schools and at home to modify traditional sex role attitudes and interests, it merits discussion in some detail. "Freestyle" is a television series composed of 26 15-minute episodes designed for 9- to 12-year-olds and their parents. It was produced by a team of psychologists and media professionals. Curricular materials for teachers, students, and parents were produced to be used with the films. As with most such large-scale intervention projects funded by the government, evaluation of the program's effectiveness was part of the project. This evaluation has yielded mixed results, depending on where the viewing took place, the sex of the child, and the child's interests prior to exposure to the series. In general, exposure had its largest effect on children's stereotypes regarding appropriate behavior for males and females and its least effect on children's own interests and preferences. It produced the greatest attitude change among children who viewed it at school as part of an intensive intervention program including discussions as well as viewing. Girls in general, and girls with interest in science and technology in particular, seemed to be affected the most by exposure to the series. Not only did their stereotypes regarding appropriate behaviors for males and females become less sex typed, their interest in scientific and/or technological careers also increased. Thus, for a select few, exposure to "Freestyle" opened new career interests and options.

It is not really surprising that the exposure to 7 hours of nontraditional programming had only a limited influence on most children, given the massive amount of conventional television they watch and the overdetermined pattern of sex role socialization in the home. Large-scale changes in sex roles will depend on two processes. First, the stereotyped norms will need to become less rigid, making nontraditional choices more acceptable. Only then can change be expected at the second, more personal, level, that of occupational choice. It is impressive that "Freestyle" was effective in stimulating some change at both levels; the children exposed at school developed more supportive attitudes toward nontraditional choices, especially for females; in addition, a small subset of females became more enthusiastic about possible nontraditional occupations in the science and technological fields.

In summary, the results discussed in this section suggest two conclusions. First, conventional television today is at least reinforcing traditional sex-typed occupational choices and behaviors. Second, television can be used to broaden males' and females' occupational beliefs. To be an effective intervention tool, however, prime time commercial and public television will have to change dramatically, or TV programs will have to be used as part of a comprehensive career education and training program. Neither is happening to any great extent at present; but both could happen if the demand for such programming increased. However, given the conservative nature of many parents and of society at large, the likelihood that such a demand will emerge in the near future seems rather small.

SOCIALIZATION IN THE SCHOOLS

For at least 12 years, most children spend 6 hours a day, 5 days a week, 9 months a year in school. During this time, some children acquire the cognitive skills and knowledge necessary for adulthood while others, unfortunately, emerge ill prepared. There is little doubt that schools prepare some children better than others. By and large, female and minority children are often poorly served by the school system in terms of adequate preparation for adult life. Many leave school with inadequate career counseling, with skills that cannot yield a living wage, or with inferior skills across a wide range of areas. As a consequence, they often find themselves unable to compete successfully for many jobs and for many advanced training opportunities. In this section, we review the schooling processes that have yielded important sex differences in student training, in students' self-concepts, and in students' career goals. The focus is on classroom experiences, counseling, textbooks, and vocational education. We also discuss briefly a set of more subtle influences, such as peer interaction, access to athletic programs, and supports for teenage mothers, that indirectly influence occupational behavior.

There have been many studies assessing sex differences in school experiences. These studies have yielded a fairly consistent pattern of results that are reviewed below. But what is perhaps most interesting about this history of research is the change in the conclusions drawn from the results. As is commonly the case with studies of sex differences, the conclusions reached are often as much a consequence of the researcher's political ideology as of scientific fact. During the late 1950s and early 1960s, educators were quite concerned with the problem boys were having in elementary school. Evidence of sex differences in school experiences were evaluated for what it could tell us about "why Johnny can't read." Several explanations emerged, most suggesting that elementary schools are a feminine environment and consequently undermine boys' motivation to learn (Sexton, 1970). With the coming of the 1970s, the women's movement, and the growing concern about sex segregation in the labor market, the ideological focus of educational studies shifted. The question of interest became why girls have lower expectations for their own performance and lower career aspirations than boys. Sex equity in the schools became an issue of deficits associated with girls rather than with boys. As a consequence of this shift in focus, any evidence of sex differences in school experiences is now more likely to be evaluated for what it can tell us about "why Mary doesn't have confidence in her abilities" or "why Mary doesn't like math and science" than for what it can tell us about "why Johnny can't read" or "why boys aren't thriving in our schools." We raise these points to alert the reader to the role that ideology can play in the interpretation of psychological data.

The vast majority of the studies of sex differences in school experience simply document the existence of these differences; they do not provide a direct test of the impact of these experiences on the occupational decisions and plans of either boys or girls. Whether these differences have a beneficial or a detrimental effect on the children's achievement, on their motivation to achieve, or on their long-range achievement and occupational behavior patterns is a question rarely addressed. In fact, it seems likely that many of the sex differences in school experience are as much a consequence of the children's preexisting sex role attitudes and behavior patterns as they are a consequence of the school's socializing influence (Bank, Biddle, & Good, 1980; Brophy & Evertson, 1981). What is clear, however, is that schools by and large are doing very little to make sure that boys and girls have comparable experiences as they pass through the school system. Consequently, like television, schools are not playing a very active role in changing traditional sex role behaviors.

CLASSROOM EXPERIENCES: TEACHER EFFECTS

Preschool years.—For many children schooling begins before kindergarten and so does sex role socialization in the schools. Preschool teachers interact with and scold boys more than girls; they initiate more activities for girls than for boys; and they reinforce girls' attempts to stay close to the teacher more than similar efforts by boys (Fagot, 1973, 1981; Serbin, Connor, & Citron, 1973). However, these effects are quite weak and are not consistent across studies. Furthermore, feminine behaviors are more likely to be reinforced by teachers in both boys and girls than are behaviors viewed as more masculine, such as hitting and yelling (Etaugh, Collins, & Gerson, 1975; Fagot, 1981). In addition, boys and girls themselves select different activities from the beginning of their preschool experience. Thus, there is some evidence for the reinforcement of the sex-typed behavior preferences that boys and girls have when they enter school but not strong evidence that preschool teachers create new sex differences.

Primary and secondary school.—Extensive observations in primary and secondary school classrooms have led several investigators to conclude that the quantity, quality, and type of interactions boys and girls have with some of their teachers are different. In general, teachers tend to interact more with boys than girls, especially in mathematics and science classes. For example, as early as second grade, boys receive more math instruction than girls, and girls receive more reading instruction (Leinhardt, Seewald, & Engel, 1979). In high school, math teachers are more likely to encourage the academic abilities and interests of the boys, to joke with the boys, and to make public statements indicating high expectations to the boys (Becker, 1981). As at the preschool level, boys also typically receive more criticism, especially for misbehaving. Finally, sex differences in the interaction patterns between teachers and students are often most extreme for more able students. For example, boys with high math ability often receive more praise for their achievements and have more interaction with teachers in general than girls of comparable math ability (Parsons, Kaczala, & Meece, 1982).

It should be noted, however, that these sex differences are quite small and do not occur in all classrooms. One-third to one-half of all teachers observed were not found to treat boys and girls differently. The picture is further complicated when one considers the few studies that have actually attempted to relate teacher-student interaction patterns in classrooms to students' attitudes, perceptions, and motivation. Parsons, Kaczala, and Meece (1982) tested the relationships among student-teacher interaction patterns and students' estimates of their own mathematical abilities, the difficulty of math courses, and their plans to continue taking math. Although they found a significant relationship between the teachers' expectations for students and the students' estimates of their own math ability, they did not find evidence of a strong relationship between daily teacher-student interaction patterns as observed in the classroom and the students' attitudes or plans.

In summary, observational studies of student-teacher classroom interaction patterns yield small but fairly consistent evidence that boys and girls have different experiences in their classrooms. However, as is true with the preschool studies, these differences seem to be as much a consequence of preexisting differences in the students' behaviors as of teacher bias. Nonetheless, when differences occur, they are congruent with sex-stereotyped expectations and behaviors.

Studies relying more on case-study approaches have provided stronger evidence of the influence of teachers on students' career plans and decisions. For example, women working in male-dominated fields, such as engineering, often report that a particular teacher played a very important role in shaping their career choice (Casserly, 1979). Unfortunately, few students encounter a teacher who encourages them to consider a wide range of careers. Instead, most teachers, like most parents, reinforce traditional behavior and occupational plans for both boys and girls independent of where the student's interests or talents might lie. For example, mathematically gifted girls are less likely to be identified as such by their teachers than are comparably talented boys. Similarly, girls who drop out of the math curriculum, or out of other nontraditional majors in college, often attribute their decisions to a teacher who actively discouraged their interests (Fox et al., 1980).

Casserly's work indicates that teachers can favorably affect girls' preparation for math- and science-related occupations if the teacher provides *active* encouragement, exposure to role models, praise for ability and high performance, and explicit advice regarding the value of math and science, and encourages girls and boys to consider high-paying, prestigious jobs (Casserly, 1979). Most teachers do none of these things. For example, in over 300 hours of observation in math classrooms, neither Becker (1981) nor Parsons, Kaczala, and Meece (1982) recorded a single instance of active encouragement provided to either a boy or a girl to take an advanced math course. In addition, Eccles and her colleages recorded fewer than a dozen instances of a teacher explaining the value of mathematics or of a teacher providing any form of career education. Thus, although teachers can help students to consider both male- and female-typed occupations, they rarely do so. As a consequence, most students do not consider nontraditional occupations even if they have the necessary talents.

COUNSELING

Although a few studies indicate that counselors' attitudes may be less sex stereotyped than those of either teachers or administrators (Tetenbaum, Lighter, & Travis, 1981), the majority of studies indicate that counselors discourage nontraditional course selection and occupational choices—if not actively, at least passively—by questioning the wisdom of such a decision and by pointing out the potential dangers associated with being in a nontraditional field (Tetenbaum et al., 1981; Thomas & Stewart, 1971). School counselors also tend to have a restricted view of occupations appropriate for women (Medvene & Collins, 1976), to suggest different occupational choices for gifted males and females (Donahue & Costar, 1977), and to view the traditionally feminine occupations as more appropriate for females (Thomas & Stewart, 1971). Furthermore, counselors in general, and male counselors in particular, are often ill informed both about the probability that a girl will have to work a major portion of her adult life and about how traditional job choices affect her earning potential (Bingham & House, 1973). As a result, girls are often given inadequate career counseling. They are not encouraged to translate their talents into careers or occupations that will maximize their earning potential. Girls are also often given poor advice about course selection. For example, it is not uncommon for girls to be allowed to drop twelfth-grade math without being told the number of college majors that require 4 years of high school math or the range of careers that require advanced math training.

Counseling materials are also quite biased. Both the materials produced by the government (Lauver, Gastellum, & Sheehey, 1975) and the materials produced by commercial publishers (Heshusias-Gilsdorf & Gilsdorf, 1975) depict a sex-segregated labor market and do not provide models of nontraditional choices. For example, pamphlets describing engineering

typically have only males in their illustrations. Recently, however, nontraditional options have begun to be presented in standard materials with
increasing frequency, and new career counseling materials designed to
increase the presentation of nontraditional options, especially for females,
have become available (Wirtenberg & Nakamura, 1976). Whether these
new materials have been incorporated into school counseling programs has
not been assessed, but it seems likely that, at present, most high school
students who seek career information from their school counseling office
are still given materials and information that reinforce traditional sex-typed
choices.

Granted that these results suggest that counselors are not exposing
students to a broad range of career options, do counselors really play a very
important role in shaping students' career decisions? Most studies suggest
that they do not. Students consistently indicate that their counselors have
very little influence on either their decisions regarding which courses to
take or their long-range occupational plans (Armstrong & Price, 1982;
Eccles et al., 1983). This minimal level of counselor influence has two basic
causes: (1) students interact very little with their counselors, and (2) when
making occupational decisions, students rely more heavily on other
sources, such as their own interests and the suggestions of their parents
and friends.

Thus, it appears that counselors either have minimal influence on
occupational choice or act to reinforce traditional choices. But because they
are in such a central advising role during the years when vocational choices
are taking shape, they could play a more positive role in promoting
educational and vocational equity. Evaluations of programs that have
attempted to use counseling as a means of increasing nontraditional vocation choices support this suggestion. These studies are discussed in more
detail later.

TEXTBOOKS AND LITERATURE

Children also learn about appropriate occupations from the books they
read in school. The ubiquity of sex role stereotyping in textbooks and in the
literature children read during the school years has been amply
documented. Repeatedly, both textbooks and children's literature have
been found to be biased against women in three ways: women are portrayed less frequently than men, in unflattering ways more often than men,
and in a much narrower range of activities and occupations than men
(Women on Words and Images, 1972). These differences are especially
marked in materials written for the upper grades and for science and math
courses (Saario, Jacklin, & Tittle, 1973). Although there have been some

changes in recent years, these biases are still evident (Wirtenberg, Murez, & Alepektor, 1980). Furthermore, because schools and teachers often use revised editions of familiar texts, use texts as long as possible, and assign familiar literature to the students, it is likely that students are still being exposed to the more sex-typed books published before 1975.

But do the stereotypes in either textbooks or children's literature contribute to the sex-typed occupational choices students make? Again, this is a very difficult question to answer. Because sex stereotyping is so pervasive across all major textbook series, there are no naturally occurring comparison groups. There is some evidence that exposing children to books that contain nontraditional models and provide examples of boys doing traditional female activities and girls doing traditional male activities can change children's stereotypes and behaviors (McArthur & Eisen, 1976; Wirtenberg et al., 1980). For example, girls do persist longer at a mechanical puzzle after they have read stories depicting females rather than males as mastering mechanical tasks. Therefore, it is likely that textbooks are, at least, reinforcing existing stereotypical beliefs about appropriate occupations. It is also likely that textbooks could be used to broaden children's career beliefs. This possibility is discussed in more detail later.

VOCATIONAL EDUCATION

Many students end their education with high school or with a year or two of postsecondary school vocational training. About half of these students enroll in the vocational curriculum during their high school years. Unfortunately, despite recent increases in the number of students enrolled in cross-sex-typed vocational programs, both the general patterns of student enrollment and the sex of the teachers in the various vocational courses still mirror traditional sex stereotypes (see Table 5). Males still teach wood shop and automobile mechanics, while females teach typing and home economics. Furthermore, female students are still heavily concentrated in programs that lead to relatively low-paying occupations, such as traditional business and office education programs (Adams, 1980; Graesser & Rose, 1982; Harrison, 1980).

Several investigators have tried to assess the influence of school versus other influences on students' choices for their vocational education. By and large, the investigators conclude that these curriculum decisions are shaped primarily by the students' occupational sex role stereotypes—which in turn are determined by a wide variety of influences that have a major effect during the early years of development and schooling (Adams, 1980; Grasso, 1980). Thus, again, although secondary schools do not appear to be creating the sex bias in the vocational education programs, they are

TABLE 5
ESTIMATED ENROLLMENTS IN EACH OCCUPATIONAL TRAINING AREA BY SEX IN 1978
(N in thousands)

TRADITIONALLY	MEN		WOMEN	
	N	%	N	%
Overall:				
Male[a]	1,322,998	92	111,912	7
Female[b]	147,671	11	1,202,826	89
Mixed[c]	364,824	43	482,487	57
Health:				
Female	20,782	8	245,060	92
Mixed	7,870	16	42,523	84
Home economics:				
Female	77,470	16	395,808	84
Mixed	5,071	22	17,433	78
Business and office:				
Female	47,486	9	498,681	91
Mixed	192,245	41	275,577	59
Marketing and distribution:				
Male	1,290	100	0	...
Mixed	114,560	58	82,072	42
Technical:				
Male	250,701	88	33,609	12
Trade and industry:				
Male	944,109	94	61,377	6
Female	1,934	3	63,112	97
Mixed	23,036	36	40,991	64
Agriculture:				
Male	126,903	88	16,928	12
Mixed	21,150	50	21,363	50

[a]75%–100% male.
[b]75%–100% female.
[c]25.1%–74% female.

also unlikely to alter it. In fact, students seeking a nontraditional vocational program are often actively discouraged by both their counselors and the vocational education teachers (Graesser & Rose, 1982). And until recently, many vocational education programs and technical training institutes mandated sex segregation by not allowing males to enroll in the traditional female courses such as cooking and by not allowing females to enroll in the traditional male courses such as automobile mechanics. Thus, whether through passive neglect or active discouragement, secondary schools and vocational educational programs have helped to maintain segregation by sex in the labor market.

ATHLETIC PROGRAMS

Through their athletic programs, schools provide children and young adolescents with the opportunity to develop competitive and athletic skills that may prove beneficial to them in their educational and occupational development. Several investigators have argued that sports teach children a variety of social skills—such as competitiveness, confidence, teamsmanship, persistence in the face of difficult odds, and leadership—that are associated with occupational success (Eccles et al., 1983; Hennig & Jardim, 1977). Although these suggestions have not been tested adequately, there are a few correlational studies linking participation in sports to success in the business world (Hennig & Jardim, 1977). Men who are very successful in business are more likely to have had extensive experience on athletic teams than are less successful men. But whether participating in sports actually facilitates success in the business world is unknown.

Nevertheless, boys have always had more opportunities than girls to participate in organized sports, and boys are more likely to possess the sports-related traits, like competitiveness, that have been linked to success in several occupations. In fact, until recently, girls' participation in many organized sports was not even allowed. Because they have not been as active in sports, academically competent girls may have had fewer failure experiences while they were growing up; they have consistently done well in school. In contrast, many academically competent boys have had the opportunity to experience both success and failure in athletics. Such experiences may teach boys effective strategies for dealing with failure.

Change in the pattern of participation in sports, however, has been one of the most dramatic consequence of Title IX of the Educational Amendments passed by Congress in 1972. Title IX mandates that "no person . . . shall, on the basis of sex, be excluded from participation in, be denied the benefits of, or be subjected to discrimination under any education program or activity receiving Federal financial assistance." Since the passage of Title IX there has been a dramatic increase in female participation in interscholastic sports programs. In 1971, only 7% of interscholastic high school athletes were female; by 1981, the figure had jumped to 35%. The number of high schools with interscholastic female basketball teams jumped from 4,856 to 17,167. Results have been equally impressive at the college level: the number of female intercollegiate athletes doubled between 1971 and 1977, and the percentage of sports scholarships awarded to females jumped from 1% in 1973–1974 to 22% by 1981 (National Advisory Council on Women's Educational Programs, 1981).

Many of these gains represent hard-fought battles. Title IX gave parents and female students interested in athletics the legal basis to fight for equity. And many did; over one-fourth of all complaints of discrimination filed under Title IX have been related to athletic discrimination (National Advisory Council on Women's Educational Programs, 1981). Whether this increase in the female participation rate in athletics will have any major influence on the occupational behavior patterns of boys and girls remains to be seen. But at the very least, women now have the opportunity to use their athletic skills to get a college education, just as men have been doing for years.

OTHER SCHOOL INFLUENCES

A variety of other, more subtle school influences have been proposed as important mediators of sex-typed occupational choices. By and large, neither experimental nor correlational work has been done on these variables to establish their link to sex-stereotyped occupational behavior. Instead, the bulk of the work has focused on documenting the existence of these influences and on documenting that their occurrence is sex linked. Among these factors are peer influence, classroom dynamics, and the availability of models.

Peers

Although students themselves do not think that peers are a major influence on their occupational decisions (Armstrong & Price, 1982; Eccles et al., 1983), other sources suggest that peers do play an important role. First, peers, especially boys, are more likely than adults to reinforce sex-appropriate behavior and to punish "sissy"-like behavior in boys (Fagot & Patterson, 1969; Langlois & Downs, 1980; Massad, 1981). This fact, coupled with the importance to adolescents of peer acceptance and popularity, suggests that peers have the power to either encourage or discourage nontraditional vocational choices. Other findings document this power; for example, the presence of supportive male friends, as well as female colleagues, facilitates women's nontraditional career choices (Angrist & Almquist, 1975; Parsons et al., 1978). Similarly, a wide variety of studies have found that females are more likely to make a nontraditional vocational choice and to remain in a nontraditional program or job if there are a reasonable number of other female classmates and colleagues (Fox et al., 1980; Stage, Kreinberg, Eccles, & Becker, in press). For example, girls are more likely to stay enrolled in a special program for the gifted if there are other girls in the program. Similarly, women from single-sex colleges are more likely to pursue nontraditional occupations than women from coeducational institutions (Tidball & Kistiakowsky, 1976).

Classroom Dynamics

Delamont (1980) observed several subtle forms of classroom interaction that reinforce sex-stereotyped behaviors. She found that it is quite common for teachers to use competition between boys and girls as a means of motivating and controlling the boys. For example, boys were admonished for letting the girls excel them and were called sissies if they did not conform to the teachers' expectations. Teachers also tended to assign classroom tasks in a sex-stereotyped manner: girls were asked to be class secretaries and boys to be team captains; boys were asked to help girls on their math problems and girls to help boys with their language assignments. Boys and girls were also segregated for a variety of activities, including lining up to go outside and being assigned to special projects and athletic teams. Although not directly related to occupational choices, each of these forms of differential treatment reinforces traditional stereotypes of the appropriate behaviors and roles of boys and girls. Consequently, they convey the message that one ought to engage in sex-appropriate behaviors and ought to aspire to sex-appropriate adult jobs.

Role Models and Mentors

Investigators have pointed out the potential importance of yet another school-based experience, namely, the absence of nontraditional role models and potential mentors. As Delamont (1980) noted, and as we described briefly earlier, the staffing patterns of most secondary schools reflect traditional sex role stereotypes. Female teachers tend to teach home economics, English, foreign languages, and typing; male teachers tend to teach math, science, and shop, and to coach the men's athletic programs. Principals are typically male; the office staff is typically female. Students have little opportunity to interact with members of their own sex engaged in activities stereotyped as more appropriate for members of the opposite sex. Although the necessity of school-based same-sex, nontraditional role models is still being debated (Speizer, 1981), a variety of evidence suggests that exposure to such models at least stimulates the consideration of nontraditional occupational choices, and, in some cases, actual occupational choices, especially among women (Stage et al., in press). But even in the absence of such models, supportive mentors of either sex can stimulate nontraditional choices (Speizer, 1981; Tidball & Kistiakowsky, 1976). Unfortunately, most students are exposed to neither role models nor mentors supportive of nontraditional choices and life-styles.

CONCLUSIONS AND IMPLICATIONS FOR POLICY

Although schools may not be creating sex differences in occupational choices, children's school experiences undoubtedly reinforce sex role stereotypes and thereby contribute to the segregation of the sexes in the labor market. Like families, schools exert a conservative influence on children's development. Children appear to enter school with well-formed occupational stereotypes and with a strong preference for a sex-appropriate occupation. Schools reinforce this bias at all levels and provide the training that allows children to fulfill their sex-stereotyped aspirations and goals.

But can schools be used as a means to change the segregation of the sexes in the labor market? Can schools help children to broaden their perspectives on potential vocations? Numerous studies indicate that they can. Although government policymakers have been unwilling to intervene on a large scale in the family, they have been much more willing to use the schools as a vehicle for policy implementation. In fact, in the past 10 years the federal government has engaged in two such large-scale efforts to increase the participation of females in more traditionally male subjects, activities, and vocational training programs. Several state governments have also mandated changes in the public schools designed to equalize access of females and males to all sectors of the labor market.

Experience with the implementation of these federal and state programs suggests that schools can be effective change agents, given the following conditions:

1. *The provision of federal money coupled with active monitoring of schools, and provision of both preservice and in-service training for teachers and counselors.*—Extensive in-service retraining is essential for the teachers and counselors currently in the educational system, especially for those trained prior to 1965. But the need for modification of existing teacher-training programs is equally great. In a recent analysis of teacher-training materials, Sadker and Sadker (1980) found that very little attention is given to the issue of sex stereotypes and occupational planning. Augmenting the training that future teachers and counselors get regarding the need to help students move beyond sex stereotypes in their career planning would be a very cost-effective intervention.

2. *Special attention must be focused on secondary schools.*—Most secondary school students make decisions that have significant ramifications for their future. For example, it is at this point that many decide whether they will go to college, will receive postsecondary vocational

education, or will enter the job market directly. In some cases they even decide which occupations to prepare for and which to ignore. As a consequence, they select some high school courses and not others. These decisions can have significant lifelong implications in terms of the occupational options open to them. Consequently, it is very important that adequate and accurate career counseling and guidance be provided during these years.

3. *The provision of female role models in courses stereotyped as masculine and of male role models in courses stereotyped as feminine.*— Live nontraditional role models can stimulate students to consider new options for themselves. Without such role models and without the opportunity to talk with them, students typically ignore advice that runs counter to their stereotypic beliefs.

4. *The provision of a broad base of support for men and women who elect a nontraditional path, including active career counseling programs and involvement of potential employers.*—Nontraditional choices must be nurtured. Cultural change is a very slow process and can be quite painful for the pioneers. Additional supports are necessary for these students, especially during the adolescent years.

Given these conditions and comprehensive, active programs that include follow-up support for students making nontraditional choices, schools can be successful in changing occupational sex ratios (Graesser & Rose, 1982; Stage et al., in press). But let us be more specific about what schools might do.

Teachers

Although teachers typically reinforce traditional vocational choices, they can induce students to consider other options and can help students acquire nontraditional skills. Even as early as preschool, teachers can help children develop skills stereotyped as appropriate for the opposite sex. For example, by appropriate reinforcement, nursery school teachers can increase the frequency of girls' persistent and independent behaviors (Serbin et al., 1978). Consequently, preschool teachers could be called upon to teach more cross-sex behavior to both boys and girls, to help children unlearn sex stereotypes, and to help children begin to learn both masculine and feminine skills.

Teachers in the elementary and secondary schools can also broaden children's perspectives. Casserly's work, for example, clearly indicates that teachers can have a positive impact on girls' participation in math- and science-related occupations. But the teachers must play a very *active* role. They need to expose girls to women who are working in these "masculine" fields and to encourage the girls to have extended and repeated conversations with these women regarding not only the nature of the women's jobs but also the means these women have used to integrate their professions with their family responsibilities.

Teachers are in the unique position of being able to help children identify their intellectual strengths and weaknesses. They know whether a boy has good language skills and whether a girl has good math skills. Because they have this information they can give students explicit advice regarding which careers or vocations they should consider. For example, they can suggest that a girl qualified in math consider a vocation that would make use of this ability. They can also encourage the girl to develop these skills.

Teachers need to go out of their way to provide students with broad career counseling. Both boys and girls know very little about the occupational world, and what they know is quite sex stereotyped. Girls typically do not know, for example, that some engineers help design and plan living communities for the elderly or the handicapped. Given the propensity of girls to seek out occupations that involve service to others, engineering might appear more interesting to them as a profession if they knew it had such human service aspects.

Boys and girls are also not typically provided with good information on the income potential of various occupations. Girls do not know, for instance, that it is very difficult to make a living wage as a secretary. Teachers can alert children to the need to think about a vocation that will provide adequate income and will allow for advancement. Girls, especially, need this type of counseling. They generally do not consider such issues until quite late in their educational careers (Tittle, 1981); they often do not develop any specific vocational plans until late in high school or college; and they regularly drop, or do not enroll in, important high school courses. As a consequence, it is not uncommon for a girl to graduate from high school and find herself ill prepared either for further occupational training or for the job market itself. Teachers could help alleviate this problem.

Finally, it is important for teachers to work with both counselors and parents in helping children formulate realistic and appropriate vocational goals. Again, this is a problem primarily for the female students. Both parents and counselors often underestimate a girl's potential and are insensitive to her actual talents and interests, ignoring them when providing her with vocational counseling (Casserly & Rock, 1980; Parsons, Adler, & Kaczala, 1982). When teachers inform counselors and parents of their students' math talent in a more personal way than by a report card grade, girls are more likely to take advanced math courses and at least to consider math-related vocations (Casserly & Rock, 1980).

Counselors

A variety of programs have used counselors as a means of broadening students' vocational decisions. Many such programs now exist as part of the national effort to encourage the entry of women into scientific, technical, and mathematical occupations. These programs have used different intervention strategies, such as special math classes open only to females, often taught by females (Stage et al., in press). Some of these classes have been designed to provide females with remedial training in math skills; others have enabled women to work and become familiar with mechanical and electrical tools. Still others have focused on helping women overcome anxiety about their math skills and technical expertise. Many of the most effective classes have used a combination of all these strategies.

Other intervention programs have involved counselors more directly. Counselors have developed extensive career-awareness programs that bring in women who work in nontraditional fields. In the most successful programs, these women discuss their feelings both about their jobs and about the impact of their nontraditional careers on their family life. Counselors have also been involved in programs designed to recruit potentially interested female students into math and science courses and to encourage these students to pursue careers in math and science.

Not surprisingly, intervention programs that have been limited in scope and brief in length have not been very effective in changing either students' attitudes or their occupational choices. Programs that have been the most effective in getting females to consider nontraditional occupations are those that make use of role models and extensive career-awareness counseling; that involve teachers, counselors, parents, and students in a rigorous comprehensive program; and that have an explicit, active commitment to recruiting minority women. Whether programs such as these will also be successful at changing long-range occupational patterns has yet to be evaluated; preliminary reports, however, look promising (Hall, 1980; Stage et al., in press).

Vocational Programs

Secondary schools can also play a more active role in increasing nontraditional enrollment in vocational programs. In 1976 the government passed the Vocational Education Amendment (P.L. 94-482) authorizing grants to states to assist them "to develop and carry out such programs of vocational education within each state so as to overcome sex discrimination and sex stereotyping in vocational educational programs." Evaluations of the progress that has been made under this law are beginning to emerge.

Only a few states and local school systems have made substantial progress (Harrison, 1980); these share the following characteristics: (1) a strong commitment both to sex equity and to vocational education itself at all levels within the district; (2) a strong commitment to sex equity in the surrounding community, especially among potential employers; (3) active counseling programs that include career-awareness days and other programs designed to alert students, teachers, and parents to equity issues and to encourage nontraditional choices; (4) active recruitment of nontraditional teachers and role models into the vocational education teaching and counseling staffs; and (5) provision of in-service training programs for school staff to help them develop specific programs for correcting sex bias. Thus, like those programs aimed at the college-bound students, interventions aimed at the vocational education population can be effective in getting both males and females to consider nontraditional occupations. But these intervention programs must be *active*, broad-based, and lengthy if they are to be successful.

Textbooks

Because textbooks are manufactured and distributed nationwide, their use as yet another vehicle for policy implementation ought to be considered. Furthermore, studies suggest that children's sex-stereotyped beliefs and behaviors can be modified through exposure to counter-stereotypical information in books. Consequently, extensive modification of existing textbooks could be an effective intervention strategy, especially given that all children use textbooks continuously throughout their school years. However, because publishers are protected under the First Amendment, the government cannot regulate what goes into textbooks. Any change in the format of textbooks will have to be initiated by authors and publishers. This process can, however, be influenced indirectly by the preferences expressed by local and state school boards. If these school boards let it be known that they are looking for textbooks that depict males and females in both traditional and nontraditional jobs, such books are likely to be produced. This is, in fact, already happening to some extent. It is also meeting with active resistance in many school districts. Thus, whether such books will be used by many schools remains to be seen. And without substantial demand and pressure, expansion of the gains already made is unlikely.

School Structure

Because men and women typically organize their lives differently and must deal with different role demands as they pass through adolescence and early adulthood, women often make occupational decisions later than men (Perun & Bielby, 1981). Consequently, school practices that eliminate occupational options early put females at a disadvantage for entry into those occupations. For example, scientific tracks that require early commitment to a rigorous training program may not appeal to a girl concerned about peer popularity. The same program might be very appealing 4 or 5 years later, after the girl has become more aware of the need to prepare for an occupation. This consideration suggests that schools should implement two types of programs to facilitate late entry in vocational training sequences. First, schools should provide more flexible course scheduling that would allow late entry into upper-level science and math tracks. Second, because some women do not make definitive vocational decisions until after they have left high school, school districts should provide evening and continuing education programs to allow these women to make up deficits in their high school training.

One additional school policy has especially important consequences for women's occupational development: the provision of counseling and special programs that enable teenage mothers to complete their schooling. One of the major reasons females drop out of high school is pregnancy (Howell & Frese, 1982). Until recently many high schools did not let the mothers return, much less provide them with special services. These school policies have changed, however, and some schools even provide day-care facilities for these students' children. Although these programs are not designed to encourage nontraditional occupational choices, by helping young mothers complete school they should increase their job prospects.

SUMMARY AND CONCLUSIONS

At the present time the employment patterns of women in the United States are in the midst of a great change. Women's labor force participation has increased throughout the life cycle. Because of smaller families and increased longevity, the years when a woman has young children occupy a smaller proportion of her adult life. Furthermore, children have become less of a deterrent to employment; most mothers now work. Employment rates are also higher because of the greater numbers of women who are now heads of households. Despite this increased commitment to the labor force, women are still heavily concentrated in traditionally female occupations and, within occupations, are employed at lower levels than men and receiving lower wages. Although these differences result in large part from the different pressures of adult life on women and men and from discriminatory practices, they also result in considerable part from the different socialization experiences of males and females.

Boys and girls are socialized differently from birth. Sex stereotypes are such an integral part of parents' attitudes that, even without consciously knowing it, parents' perceptions and interactions are affected. Furthermore, the patterns begun in the family are reinforced in the schools, by the peers, and by the portrayals of males and females in the mass media.

In view of the new social roles evolving for women and of the significance of work in their lives, it seems important to consider how the pattern of sex-stereotyped occupational assignment might be interrupted. How may socialization patterns be changed so that both males and females can be encouraged to realize their potential fully, to develop their talents, to seek the appropriate training, and to obtain jobs unfettered by the restrictions of sex-stereotyped socialization?

In considering where social policy may be most effective, we come to a paradox. It seems apparent from the materials reviewed in this chapter that the family is a major source of the socialization patterns that lead to job segregation. If, magically, the differences between boys' and girls' family experiences could be eliminated, the internal barriers to sex integration in occupations would be enormously diminished. Whether a comparable change in the schools, peer groups, or mass media would have as great an effect is unclear. The implication, of course, is that families should change their socialization practices. But how can such a change in the family be brought about? It is very difficult to change parents' child-rearing patterns by social policy. It is much easier to mandate changes within the schools. Consequently, even though schools may not be the major source of the problem, they are probably an easier target for policy influence.

This is not to say that family patterns are not changing. As adult roles change, child-rearing patterns also change in response (Hoffman, 1977a), but the process is a slow one. There has already been some decrease in sex stereotyping in families, and there is evidence that the change occurs more rapidly in families where the mother is employed (Hoffman, 1979). Change might be accelerated by pointing out some of the more subtle forms of sex differentiation and by making explicit for parents some of the subtle messages that they convey in their patterns of interaction with their children. Bronfenbrenner (1958) has suggested that middle-class parents, in particular, are responsive to the child-rearing advice of experts expressed in the popular child care guidance books. It is possible that schools may also play a role in this parent education process. Since teachers have firsthand knowledge of their students' strengths and weaknesses, they can work with parents in providing more accurate and personalized occupational guidance for the child. If the advice is couched in terms of maximizing the child's potential for successful adaptation in the adult world, instead of in terms of undoing sex role stereotypes, parents may be more responsive. Such advice, however, is likely to be more influential among motivated, less traditional parents than among staunch supporters of traditional roles.

The schools contribute to sex differences in occupational patterns more passively than the family does, though they, like the media, clearly reinforce socialization patterns begun at home. There are indications that the styles of interaction between teacher and child differ according to gender. Textbooks perpetuate sex stereotypes. Guidance counselors seem to discourage the youth who aspires to a nontraditional occupation—sometimes pointing out real barriers, sometimes pointing out barriers that no longer exist, and sometimes expressing their own sex-stereotyped views. Vocational programs and sports activities also contribute to occupational segregation by discouraging nontraditional choices and segregating activities by sex. Finally, in the schools, as in the home, nontraditional role models for children are scarce. Recent intervention programs have shown, however, that the schools can be a counterforce. Policy aimed at changing the schools can be an effective means of diminishing sex differences in the occupational sphere, even though the schools are not the root of the problem. The school is more accessible than the family to social policy intervention, and it is in a key position for bringing about change.

The school experience is important for the child in developing new self-concepts and new interests, in forming attitudes about education, in choosing courses of study, and, especially in secondary school, in choosing occupations. Research has shown that the play activities of preschool children can be altered, that teachers can play an important role in shaping young people's career goals, and that a broad program of change that includes counseling of students, nontraditional models, in-service training of teachers, and community involvement—particularly visits by potential employers—can increase nontraditional occupational choice. The schools have contributed to the prevailing pattern chiefly by failing to take this leadership role in helping young people adapt to the occupational demands of the present society. Title IX has had some effect. It has led some schools at least to consider ways of increasing equity in the programs they provide for boys and girls. The Affirmative Action programs that have encouraged colleges and professional schools to admit more women and have encouraged businesses and institutions both to promote workers according to ability, not sex, and to open executive training to women have also had a positive effect. Such steps may first be taken because of the threat of withdrawal of federal funds or possible lawsuits, but once under way, they sometimes acquire their own momentum. Once the stereotype is broken, the advantages may become apparent. Corporations originally coerced into hiring women executives sometimes become the main advocates of nonsexist employment practices (Schwartz, 1982). And as the opportunities open up and nontraditional role models become more numerous in the community and in the mass media, both families and schools will be more willing to encourage boys and girls to consider nontraditional vocations; boys and girls may then be more willing to consider these occupations on their own.

Schools can also play an important role by providing continuing education programs. One important reason that women's average wages are lower than men's is the high dropout rate of women because of pregnancy. Programs to enable teenage mothers to continue their education and vocational training can halt the cycle of poverty that teenage pregnancy begins. Programs also are important for reeducating older women whose earlier training was cut short either by family responsibilities or because they had not anticipated their eventual need for occupational competence. Similarly, programs for redirecting men into new job opportunities, among them occupations previously labeled appropriate to females, such as nursing, might broaden their employment prospects.

In initiating and executing the kind of changes advocated in this chapter, school personnel must work with the community and with parents. Without the support of the community and the students' families, school-based intervention programs have little likelihood of success. To gain this support, a community education program must be launched before major changes are introduced in the school. Such a program should focus on two issues: (1) the importance of students' realizing their full potential; and (2) the need for all students to prepare themselves for a job that will provide a living wage. Parents must be provided with statistics that show how the roles of men and women are changing. Then the need for both boys and girls to prepare for the possibility of supporting themselves and their families can be discussed. In this way, parents can become allies in the schools' efforts to provide the best possible career counseling for both boys and girls.

Socialization patterns play an important role in perpetuating the sex differences in occupational roles. They operate as a constriction, slowing change when change is called for. Social policy, carefully planned and directed, can interrupt this pattern and ease the transition.

References

Adams, A. V. The impact of vocational education in secondary schools on young men and young women. In P. Brenner (Ed.), *Education, sex equity, and occupational stereotyping*. Washington, D.C.: National Commission for Employment Policy, 1980.

Adams, B. N., & Meidam, M. T. Economics, family structure, and college attendance. *American Journal of Sociology*, 1968, **74**, 230–239.

Angrist, S. S., & Almquist, E. M. *Career and contingencies*. New York: Dunellen, 1975.

Armstrong, J. M., & Price, R. A. Correlates and predictors of women's mathematics participation. *Journal of Research in Mathematics Education*, 1982, **13**, 99–109.

Bandura, A., & Walters, R. H. *Social learning and personality development*. New York: Holt, Rinehart & Winston, 1963.

Bank, B. J., Biddle, B. J., & Good, T. L. Sex roles, classroom instruction, and reading achievement. *Journal of Educational Psychology*, 1980, **72**, 119–132.

Becker, J. R. Differential treatment of females and males in mathematics classes. *Journal of Research in Mathematics Education*, 1981, **12**, 40–54.

Belsky, J., & Steinberg, L. D. The effects of day care: A critical review. *Child Development*, 1978, **49**, 929–949.

Bernard, J. Where are we now: Some thoughts on the current scene. *Psychology of Women Quarterly*, 1976, **1**, 21–37.

Bingham, W. C., & House, E. W. Counselors view women and work: Accuracy of information. *Vocational Guidance Quarterly*, January 1973, 262–268.

Block, J. H. Another look at sex differentiation in the socialization behavior of mothers and fathers. In J. Sherman & F. L. Denmark (Eds.), *Psychology of women: Future directions of research*. New York: Psychological Dimensions, 1979.

Block, J. H. Differential premises arising from differential socialization of the sexes: Some conjectures. *Child Development*, 1983, **54**, 1335–1354.

Block, J. H., Block, J. & Harrington, D. *Sex role typing and instrumental behavior: A developmental study*. Paper presented at the annual meeting of the Society for Research in Child Development, Denver, 1975.

Bronfenbrenner, U. Socialization and social class through time and space. In E. Maccoby, T. Newcomb, & R. Hartley (Eds.), *Reading in social psychology*. New York: Holt, 1958.

Brophy, J. E., & Evertson, C. M. *Student characteristics and teaching*. New York: Longman, 1981.

Broverman, I. K., Vogel, S. R., Broverman, D. M., Carlson, F. E., & Rosenkrantz, P. S. Sex-role stereotypes: A current appraisal. *Journal of Social Issues*, 1972, **23**, 59–78.

Casserly, P. L. Helping able young women take math and science seriously in school. In N. Colangelo & R. T. Zaffrann (Eds.), *New voices in counseling the gifted*. Dubuque, Iowa: Kendall-Hunt, 1979.

Casserly, P. L., & Rock, D. A. *Factors related to young women's persistence and achievement in mathematics* (Final Rep.). Washington, D.C.: National Institute of Education, 1980.

Chodorow, N. *The reproduction of mothering*. Berkeley: University of California Press, 1978.

Collard, E. D. *Achievement motive in the four-year-old child and its relationship to achievement expectancies of the mother*. Unpublished doctoral dissertation, University of Michigan, 1964.

Connor, J. M., Schackman, J., & Serbin, L. Sex-related differences in response to practice on a visual-spatial test and generalization to a related test. *Child Development*, 1978, **49**, 24–29.

Crandall, V. C. Sex differences in expectancy of intellectual and academic reinforcement. In C. P. Smith (Ed.), *Achievement-related behaviors in children*. New York: Russell Sage, 1969.

Delamont, S. *Sex roles and the school*. London: Methuen, 1980.

Donahue, T. J., & Costar, J. W. Counselor discrimination against young women in career selection. *Journal of Counseling Psychology*, 1977, **24**, 481–486.

Dorr, A., & Lesser, G. S. Career awareness in young children. In M. Greene-Partsche & G. J. Robinson, (Eds.), *Women, communication, and careers*. Munich: Saur, 1980.

Duncan, D., Schuman, H., & Duncan, B. *Social change in a metropolitan community*. New York: Russell Sage, 1973.

Dunteman, G. H., Wisenbaker, J., & Taylor, M. E. *Race and sex differences in college science program participation*. Report for National Science Foundation, Washington, D.C., 1978.

Eccles, J. S. Sex differences in mathematics participation. In M. Steinkamp & M. Maehr (Eds.), *Women in science*. Greenwich, Conn.: JAI, in press.

Eccles (Parsons), J., Adler, T. F., Futterman, R., Goff, S. B., Kaczala, C. M., Meece, J., & Midgley, C. Expectancies, values and academic behaviors. In J. T. Spence (Ed.), *Achievement and achievement motives*. San Francisco: W. H. Freeman, 1983.

Etaugh, C., Collins, G., & Gerson, A. Reinforcement of sex-typed behavior of two-year-old children in a nursery school setting. *Developmental Psychology*, 1975, **11**, 255.

Fagot, B. I. Influence of teacher behavior in the preschool. *Developmental Psychology*, 1973, **9**, 198–206.

Fagot, B. I. Sex differences in toddlers: behavior and parental reaction. *Developmental Psychology*, 1974, **10**, 554–558.

Fagot, B. I. Male and female teachers: Do they treat boys and girls differently? *Sex Roles*, 1981, **7**, 263–272.

Fagot, B. I., & Patterson, G. R. An in vivo analysis of reinforcing contingencies for sex-role behaviors in preschool child. *Developmental Psychology*, 1969, **1**, 536–568.

Fidell, L. Empirical verification of sex discrimination in hiring practices in psychology. *American Psychologist*, 1970, **25**, 1094–1098.

Fox, L. H., Brody, L., & Tobin, D. *Women and the mathematical mystique*. Baltimore: Johns Hopkins University Press, 1980.

Frueh, T., & McGhee, P. E. Traditional sex-role development and amount of spent watching television. *Developmental Psychology*, 1975, **11**, 109.

Garland, H., & Smith, G. B. Occupational achievement motivation as a function of biological sex, sex linked personality, and occupational stereotypes. *Psychology of Women Quarterly*, 1981, **5**, 568–585.

Garrett, C. S., Ein, P. L., & Tremaino, L. The development of gender stereotyping of adult occupations in elementary school children. *Child Development*, 1977, **48**, 507–512.

Glick, P. C., & Norton, A. J. Marrying, divorcing, and living together in the U.S. today. *Population Bulletin*. Washington, D.C.: Population Reference Bureau, 1979. (Originally published, 1977.)

Goff-Timmer, S., Eccles, J., O'Brien, K., & Ziegler, M. *Children's time use*. Report to the Foundation for Child Development, New York, 1982.

Gold, D., & Andres, D. Developmental comparisons between ten-year-old children with employed and nonemployed mothers. *Child Development*, 1978, **49**, 75–84.

Graesser, C. C., & Rose, C. *Assesssing the status of women students and employers in vocational education in California*. Paper presented at the annual meeting of the American Educational Research Association, New York, 1982.

Grasso, J. The effects of school curriculum on young women. In P. Brenner (Ed.), *Education, sex equity, and occupational stereotyping*. Washington, D.C.: National Commission on Employment Policy, 1980.

Greenberg, B. S. Television and role socialization: An overview. In D. Pearl, L. Bouthilet, & J. Lazar (Eds.), *Television and behavior: Ten years of scientific progress and implications for the eighties*. Washington, D.C.: National Institute of Mental Health, 1982.

Grief, E. *Sex differences in parent-child conversations: Who interrupts whom?* Paper presented at the Society for Research in Child Development, San Francisco, March 1979.

Hall, P. Q. *Minority women in science and mathematics careers: Why so few?* Paper presented at the National Commission on Employment Policy, Washington, D.C., May 6, 1980.

Harrison, L. R. The American Institutes for Research study of sex equity in vocational education: Efforts of states and local educational agencies. In P. Brenner (Ed.), *Education, sex equity, and occupational stereotyping.* Washington, D.C.: National Commission for Employment Policy, 1980.

Hayghe, H. Families and the rise of working wives: An overview. *Monthly Labor Review,* 1976, November, 12–19.

Hennig, M., & Jardim, A. *The managerial woman.* Garden City, N.Y.: Doubleday Anchor, 1977.

Heshusius-Gilsdorf, L. F., & Gilsdorf, D. L. Girls are females, boys are males: A content analysis of career materials. *Personnel and Guidance Journal,* 1975, **54**, 207–211.

Hoffman, L. W. Early childhood experiences and women's achievement motives. *Journal of Social Issues,* 1972, **28**, 129–156.

Hoffman, L. W. Fear of success in males and females: 1965 and 1971. *Journal of Consulting and Clinical Psychology,* 1974, **42**, 353–358.

Hoffman, L. W. Changes in family roles, socialization, and sex differences. *American Psychologist,* 1977, **32**, 644–657. (a)

Hoffman, L. W. Fear of success in 1965 and 1974: A reinterview study. *Journal of Consulting and Clinical Psychology,* 1977, **45**, 310–321. (b)

Hoffman, L. W. Maternal employment: 1979. *American Psychologist,* 1979, **34**, 859–865.

Hoffman, L. W. Increased fathering: Effects on mothers. In M. E. Lamb and A. Sagi (Eds.), *Social policies and legal issues pertaining to fatherhood.* Hillsdale, N.J.: Erlbaum, 1983.

Hoffman, L. W. Work, family, and the socialization of the child. In R. D. Parke, R. Emde, H. McAdoo, & G. Sackett (Eds.), *Review of child development research,* Vol. 7, in press.

Hoffman, L. W., & Nye, F. I. *Working mothers.* San Francisco: Jossey-Bass, 1974.

Horner, M. Toward an understanding of achievement-related conflicts in women. *Journal of Social Issues,* 1972, **28**, 157–175.

Howell, F. M., & Frese, W. Early transition with adult roles: Some antecedents and outcomes. *American Educational Research Journal,* 1982, **19**, 51–73.

Jeffries-Fox, S., & Signorielli, N. Television and children's conceptions of occupations. In H. S. Dordick (Ed.), *Proceedings of the Sixth Annual Telecommunications Policy Research Conference.* Lexington, Mass.: Lexington, 1979.

Johnston, J., & Ettema, J. S. *Positive images.* Beverly Hills, Calif.: Sage, 1982.

Kacerguis, M. A., & Adams, G. R. Implications of sex typed childrearing practices, toys, and mass media materials in restricting occupational choices of women. *Family Coordinator,* 1979, **28**, 368–375.

Kanter, R. M. *Work and family in the United States: A critical review of research and policy.* New York: Russell Sage, 1977.

Kohlberg, L. A. A cognitive developmental analysis of children's sex-role concepts and attitudes. In E. E. Maccoby (Ed.), *The development of sex differences.* Stanford, Calif.: Stanford University Press, 1966.

Komorovsky, M. Cultural contradictions and sex roles: The masculine case. *American Journal of Sociology,* 1977, **78**, 873–884.

Langlois, J. H., & Downs, A. C. Mothers, fathers, and peers as socialization agents of sex-typed play behaviors in young children. *Child Development,* 1980, **51**, 1217–1247.

Lauver, P. J., Gastellum, R. M., & Sheehey, M. Bias in OOH illustrations? *Vocational Guidance Quarterly,* 1975, **23**, 335–340.

Leinhardt, G., Seewald, A. M., & Engel, M. Learning what's taught: Sex differences in instruction. *Journal of Educational Psychology,* 1979, **71**, 432–439.

Lipman-Blumen, J. How ideology shapes women's lives. *Scientific American*, 1972, **226**, 34–42.

Looft, W. R. Sex differences in the expression of vocational aspirations by elementary school children. *Developmental Psychology*, 1971, **5**, 366.

Lyson, T. A. The changing sex composition of college curriculums: A shift-share approach. *American Educational Research Journal*, 1981, **18**, 503–512.

McArthur, L. Z., & Eisen, S. V. Achievement of male and female storybook characters as determinants of achieving behavior by boys and girls. *Journal of Personality and Social Psychology*, 1976, **33**, 467–473.

Maccoby, E. E., & Jacklin, C. N. *Psychology of sex differences*. Stanford, Calif.: Stanford University Press, 1974.

Marini, M. M. Sex differences in the process of occupational attainment: A closer look. *Social Science Research*, 1980, **9**, 307–361.

Massad, C. M. Sex role identity and adjustment during adolescence. *Child Development*, 1981, **52**, 1290–1298.

Medvene, A. M., & Collins, A. M. Occupational prestige and appropriateness: The views of mental health specialists. *Journal of Vocational Behavior*, 1976, **9**, 63–71.

Miller, M. M., & Reeves, B. B. Children's occupational sex-role stereotypes: The linkage between television content and perception. *Journal of Broadcasting*, 1976, **20**, 35–50.

Minton, D., Kagan, J., & Levine, J. A. Maternal control and obedience in the two-year-old. *Child Development*, 1971, **42**, 1873–1894.

Mortimer, J. T. Social class, work, and the family: Some implications of the father's occupation for familial relationships and sons' career decisions. *Journal of Marriage and the Family*, 1976, **38**, 241–256.

Moss, H. A. Sex, age, and state as determinants of mother-infant interaction. *Merrill-Palmer Quarterly*, 1967, **13**, 19–36.

Mott, F. L., & Haurin, R. J. Variations in the educational progress and career orientations of brothers and sisters. In F. L. Mott(Ed.), *The employment revolution: Young American women in the 1970s*. Cambridge, Mass.: MIT Press, 1982.

National Advisory Council on Women's Educational Programs. *Title IX: The half full, half empty glass*. Washington, D.C.: National Advisory Council on Women's Educational Programs, 1981.

Newson, J., & Newson E. *Toys and playthings in development and remediation*. New York: Pantheon, 1979.

Nicholls, J. G. Causal attributions and other achievement-related cognitions: Effects of task outcomes, attainment value, and sex. *Journal of Personality and Social Psychology*, 1975, **31**, 379–389.

Parsons, J. E., Adler, T. F., & Kaczala, C. Socialization of achievement attitudes and beliefs: Parental influences. *Child Development*, 1982, **53**, 310–321.

Parsons, J., Frieze, I., & Ruble, D. Intrapsychic factors influencing career aspirations in college women. *Sex Roles*, 1978, **4**, 337–348.

Parsons, J. E., & Goff, S. B. Achievement motivation: A dual modality. In L. J. Fyans (Ed.), *Recent trends in achievement motivation: Theory and research*. New York: Plenum, 1980.

Parsons, J. E., Kaczala, C., & Meece, J. Socialization of achievement attitudes and beliefs: Classroom influences. *Child Development*, 1982, **53**, 322–339.

Parsons, J. E., Ruble, D. N., Hodges, K. L., & Small, A. W. Cognitive-developmental factors in emerging sex differences in achievement-related expectancies. *Journal of Social Issues*, 1976, **32**, 47–61.

Parsons, T. The American family: Its relation to personality and the social structure. In T.

Parsons & R. F. Bales (Eds.), *Family, socialization and interaction process.* Glencoe, Ill.: Free Press, 1955.

Pederson, F. A., & Robson, K. S. Father participation in infancy. *American Journal of Orthopsychiatry,* 1969, **39**, 466–472.

Perun, P. J., & Bielby, D. D. V. Towards a model of female occupational behavior: A human development approach. *Psychology of Women Quarterly,* 1981, **6**, 234–252.

Roberts, E. J. Television and sexual learning in childhood. In D. Pearl, L. Bouthilet, & J. Lazar (Eds.), *Television and behavior: Ten years of scientific progress and implications for the eighties.* Washington, D.C.: National Institute of Mental Health, 1982.

Rosen, B. C., & Aneshensel, C. S. Sex difference in the educational-occupational expectation process. *Social Forces,* 1978, **57**, 164–186.

Saario, T. N., Jacklin, C. N., & Tittle, C. K. Sex role stereotyping in the public schools. *Harvard Educational Review,* 1973, **43**, 386–416.

Sadker, M. P., & Sadker, D. M. Sexism in teacher-education texts. *Harvard Educational Review,* 1980, **50**, 36–46.

Saegert, S., & Hart, R. The development of sex differences in the environmental competence of children. In P. Barnett (Ed.), *Women in society.* Chicago: Massoufa, 1976.

Schwartz, F. *Women in management.* Paper presented at a conference on the future of parenting: Implications for work and family life. Aspen Institute, Berlin, May 1982.

Seavy, C. A., Katz, P. A., & Zalk, S. R. Baby X: The effect of gender labels on adult responses to infants. *Sex Roles,* 1975, **1**, 103–110.

Serbin, L. A., Connor, J. M., & Citron, C. C. Environmental control of independent and dependent behaviors in preschool girls and boys: A model for early independence training. *Sex Roles,* 1978, **4**, 867–875.

Serbin, L. A., O'Leary, K. D., Kent, R. N., & Tonick, I. J. A comparison of teacher response to the preacademic and problem behaviors of boys and girls. *Child Development,* 1973, **44**, 796–804.

Sexton, P. D. *The feminized male.* New York: Vintage, 1970.

Shinn, M. Father absence and children's cognitive development. *Psychological Bulletin,* 1978, **85**, 295–324.

Speizer, J. J. Role models, mentors, and sponsors: The elusive concepts. *Signs,* 1981, **6**, 692–712.

Stage, E. K., Kreinberg, N., Eccles, J., & Becker, J. R. Increasing the participation and achievement of girls and women in mathematics, science, and engineering. In S. Klein (Ed.), *Sex equity in the school.* Baltimore: Johns Hopkins University Press, in press.

Stake, J. R. The effects of information regarding sex group performance norms on goal-setting in males and females. *Sex Roles,* 1976, **2**, 23–38.

Stein, A. H., & Bailey, M. M. The socialization of achievement orientation in females. *Psychological Bulletin,* 1973, **80**, 347–366.

Stein, A. H., Pohly, S. R., & Mueller, E. The influence of masculine, feminine, and neutral tasks on children's achievement behavior, expectancies of success and attainment values. *Child Development,* 1971, **42**, 195–207.

Tangri, S. S. Determinants of occupational role innovation among college women. *Journal of Social Issues,* 1972, **28**, 177–199.

Tetenbaum, T. J., Lighter, J., & Travis, M. Educator's attitudes toward working mothers. *Journal of Educational Psychology,* 1981, **73**, 369–375.

Thomas, A. H., & Stewart, N. R. Counselor response to female clients with deviate and conforming career goals. *Journal of Counseling Psychology,* 1971, **18**, 352–357.

Thornton, A., & Freedman, D. Changes in the sex role attitudes of women; 1962–1977: Evidence from a panel study. In D. McGuigan (Ed.), *Changing family, changing work place—New research.* Ann Arbor, University of Michigan, Center for the Continuing Education of Women, 1980.

Tidball, M. E., & Kistiakowsky, V. Baccalaureate origins of American scientists and scholars. *Science,* 1976, 646–652.

Tittle, C. K. *Careers and family: Sex roles and adolescent life plans.* Beverly Hills, Calif.: Sage, 1981.

Trieman, D., & Hartman, H. *Women, work and wages.* Washington, D.C.: National Academy of Sciences, 1981.

U.S. Department of Labor. *The employment of women: General diagnosis of developments and issues.* Washington, D.C.: Department of Labor, Women's Bureau, April 1980.

U.S. Department of Commerce. *Population profile of the United States, 1978, population characteristics* (Current Population Reports, Series P-20, No. 336). Washington, D.C.: Bureau of the Census, Government Printing Office, April 1979.

U.S. Department of Labor. *Working mothers and their children.* Washington, D.C.: Women's Bureau, Government Printing Office, 1977.

U.S. Department of Labor. *Marital and family characteristics of labor force* (Special Labor Force Report 237). Washington, D.C.: Bureau of Labor Statistics, 1981, 3–79.

Veroff, J., Douvan, E., & Kulka, R. *The inner American from 1975 to 1976.* New York: Basic, 1981.

Vetter, B. M. Women scientists and engineers: Trends in participation. *Science,* 1981, **214,** 1313–1321.

White, B. L. *A parent's guide to the first three years.* Englewood Cliffs, N.J.: Prentice-Hall, 1980.

Wirtenberg, J., Murez, R., & Alepektor, R. A. *Characters in textbooks: A review of the literature.* Washington, D.C.: United States Commission on Civil Rights, 1980.

Wirtenberg, T. J., & Nakamura, C.Y. Education: Barrier or boom to changing occupational roles of women? *Journal of Social Issues,* 1976, **32,** 165–180.

Women on Words and Images. *Dick and Jane as victims: Sex stereotyping in children's readers.* Princeton, N.J.: Women on Words and Images, 1972.

Yarrow, L., Rubenstein, J. L., Pederson, F. A., & Jankowski, J. J. Dimensions of early stimulation and their differential effects on infant development. *Merrill-Palmer Quarterly,* 1972, **18,** 205–218.

Nutrition and Public Policy

ERNESTO POLLITT
University of Texas at Houston
CUTBERTO GARZA
Baylor College of Medicine
RUDOLPH L. LEIBEL
Rockefeller University

INTRODUCTION

Public policy that guides nutrition practices in the United States has received increasing attention in the past 2 decades. Whereas the major constituency for policy determination was once the producer, the consumer is assuming increasing prominence; likewise, the focus of policy has shifted from production to nutrition. No longer is concern focused on our ability to feed *ourselves*: less than 3% of the population of the United States is directly responsible for the production of the nation's food supply (U.S. Department of Agriculture, 1981). Even more remarkable is the fact that the United States exports 60% of the wheat produced, more than 50% of all soy beans, and approximately 30% of the corn harvested (Soth, 1981). This achievement allows policymakers to focus on two concerns: an equitable internal distribution of food and the effects of dietary practices on the health of the population. In this chapter, government-sanctioned plans of action designed to aid in meeting these two objectives will be referred to as "nutrition policy."

Apparently, because of the agricultural success just described, U.S. nutrition policy attempts to balance humanitarian, scientific, and economic interests. Although these interests overlap, there is inevitably competition, because nutrition policy designed to safeguard the nutritional well-being of one segment of the population often has been perceived as an

This chapter was prepared through cooperation with the United States Department of Agriculture/Agricultural Research Service, Children's Nutrition Research Center, Department of Pediatrics, Baylor College of Medicine, Houston, Texas. The views expressed in this chapter are those of the authors and do not necessarily reflect agency or institutional policy. We gratefully acknowledge the editorial contributions of E. R. Klein and the secretarial assistance of Vic Valdez.

421

infringement on the rights and privileges of others. An illustration is the controversial reception of the dietary guidelines developed and published in 1980 by the U.S. Department of Agriculture and U.S. Department of Health and Human Services (as we see later in the section titled Diet and Disease). These guidelines were first published as *Dietary Goals for the United States*, issued by the U.S. Senate Select Committee on Nutrition and Human Needs (1977). They received favorable and unfavorable reviews from scientific and economic interests (Austin & Quelch, 1979; Broad, 1980; Harper, 1978; Hegstead, 1978; "Nutrition's Own," 1980). Vested economic interests were immense; for example, it was estimated that if these recommendations were followed, the egg industry alone would lose $1.8 billion per year in retail sales. Those concerned with the health implications of the egg-cholesterol-heart issue questioned whether there is a direct causal relationship, and others were reluctant to apply potentially therapeutic regimens to healthy populations. Similar debates emerged when policymakers in the United States considered the World Health Organization (WHO) code which regulated the marketing of infant formula, food advertising directed at children, and reformulation of food supplement programs financed by the federal government. These examples illustrate the effects of nutrition policy on humanitarian, scientific, and economic interests. The health outcomes sought were optimal development and mental function, freedom from chrónic diseases associated with aging, and optimal ability to respond to stress. Inevitably, however, these projected outcomes were weighed against the economic consequences and restrictions on personal choice imposed by such policies.

Although we acknowledge the impact of humanitarian and economic interests on nutrition policy, in this chapter we address only current scientific knowledge and efforts to achieve optimal outcomes in dietary practice and food distribution. The chapter will focus on four topics: (1) the prevalence and remediation of undernutrition as it relates to cognitive function; (2) the functional benefits of human milk in the prevention or amelioration of infectious illnesses; (3) the origins and consequences of childhood obesity; and (4) dietary factors that may affect chronic diseases associated with aging, such as ischemic heart disease and cancer.

UNDERNUTRITION

RECENT HISTORY

In 1967, Americans were shocked by the CBS documentary "Hunger in America" and by other anecdotal reports in the media of a high prevalence of mild, moderate, and severe undernutrition in the United States. These reports were followed by a number of publications that attempted to document the extent of undernutrition in the United States. Among them, the report by the Citizen's Board of Inquiry into Hunger and Malnutrition in the United States (1969) was particularly influential. The board had two missions: to inquire into the scope of starvation and hunger in selected areas of poverty throughout the country and to examine the extent and quality of public and private programs to meet this problem. Evidence, though mostly anecdotal, indicated that poverty and malnutrition were commonplace in many parts of the country. Undernutrition also was reported to retard physical growth and possibly damage the structure and function of the brain. Data were presented purporting to show that infant mortality rates were related inversely to the prevalence of malnutrition in specific geographic areas. The board concluded that available food assistance programs were not completely successful in either the prevention or remediation of these problems.

The response within the United States to the risk of malnutrition among the population appeared to be influenced by socioeconomic and political factors and anecdotal reports of an unacceptable prevalence of undernutrition in the country. This concern grew when President Johnson declared his War on Poverty. The 1967 CBS documentary, the report of the board of inquiry, and other related publications were immediate antecedents of the 1969 White House Conference on Food, Nutrition, and Health. The mandate of this conference was to evaluate the nutritional status of the U.S. population and to develop a framework for a national nutrition policy (Mayer, 1973). Conference participants included persons of low, middle, and upper socioeconomic status; students; members of interested organizations; politicians; health professionals; and university faculty members. This conference recognized malnutrition as a national health issue and the relationship of socioeconomic factors to nutritional status.

Several panels were appointed to examine specific topics. The conference panel that dealt with nutrition surveillance noted that estimates of the magnitude of the nutrition problems were made intuitively rather than being based on substantive data. Thus, the need to identify the extent and severity of hunger and malnutrition among high-risk groups and to assess health and nutrition services was emphasized. The panel that dealt with food delivery and distribution made a first recommendation: that all Americans be guaranteed the availability of a diet to meet their minimum nutritional requirements. The panel suggested that all American families be provided with sufficient purchasing power to obtain this diet through the commercial delivery system. This recommendation bypassed scientific considerations and was based on considerations of social equity and human-itarianism. Later decisions to expand or create new food assistance pro-grams were based in part on these considerations.

Most statistics published on the nutritional status of the population in 1968 and 1969 dealt with small sample sizes. Because of concern that malnutrition possibly was widespread among low-income families, the U.S. Senate authorized in 1968 the Ten State Nutrition Survey (TSNS) (1972) with the specific objective of determining the extent and severity of malnutrition in the states selected. A biased sample of low-income sub-jects, 1–74 years of age, was selected for the survey. The sample included 3,700 1 to 5-year-old and 8,000 6 to 17-year-old children. Concurrently, the Preschool Nutrition Survey (PNS) selected a nationwide representa-tive sample of 3,400 1 to 6-year-old children (Owen, Kram, Garry, Lowe, & Lubin, 1974).

In both surveys a consistent positive association between physical growth and income level within all race and ethnic groups was found. Most cases of growth retardation that could be attributed to undernutrition were found in the lowest-income strata. In the TSNS, 30%–50% of the infants included from the five low-income-ratio states were below the fifteenth percentile for height, based on the Harvard growth standards. In the PNS, however, with a sample representative of the U.S. population, there was a low prevalence of underweight and stunted children (Owen, 1981).

In the TSNS, growth retardation generally was not associated with clinical signs of malnutrition. For example, in the 6-year-old group, fewer than 1% of the children presented oral, cutaneous, or skeletal signs of malnutrition. The prevalence of such signs, however, increased with age, to the point where 5% of 11-year-old children manifested cutaneous signs of malnutrition (Owen, 1981).

The most consistent biochemical finding in both surveys was a high prevalence of iron deficiency and anemia. Dietary and clinical evidence indicated that the conditions were due to low iron intake. In the PNS, the prevalence of anemia in 1 to 5-year-old black and white children was 12% and 7%, respectively; in the TSNS the figures were 25% and 14% respec-tively. The prevalence among the 6 to 12-year-old black and white children was 26% and 15%, respectively. Both surveys also indicated a high preva-lence of deficiencies of both vitamins A and C, with the highest rates among black and Hispanic children. In approximately one-half of the Hispanic children living in the southwestern United States, plasma concentrations of vitamin A were below acceptable levels; vitamin A levels of black children were consistently lower than those of white children.

In summary, the results of the TSNS and the PNS showed that, although clinical signs of malnutrition were infrequent, the prevalence rates of growth retardation, iron deficiency and anemia, and low intake of vitamins A and C were sufficiently high to be of public health concern. Neither survey, however, substantiated the 1968 claims of the Board of Inquiry of vast rates of hunger and starvation in the United States (Owen, 1981). Thus, a large segment of the population perceived the risk of malnutrition within the United States as greater than the prevalence statistics of general undernutrition or specific nutritional deficiencies were able to establish. Nevertheless, the perception of risk had been established and would influence subsequent nutrition policies.

FOOD-ASSISTANCE PROGRAMS

The federal government responded to the reported prevalence of malnutrition and its possible functional consequences by expanding food-assistance programs (Austin & Hitt, 1979; U.S. Congress, 1980). This action does not appear to have been based on objective, substantiating evidence that food assistance effectively or efficiently improves the nutritional and health status of the recipients. These programs appear to have had a broad goal, the elimination of malnutrition, but lacked objectives achievable over the short term. The programs attempted to ensure the availability of diets that met recommended allowances through the commercial delivery system. Because this approach allowed for the exercise of personal choice, the efficiency of the programs could not be demonstrated.

The Food Stamp Program (FSP) (at present the largest assistance program in the country) evolved from the federal government's purchase of surplus agricultural produce (Austin & Hitt, 1979; Longen, 1981). Between 1969 and 1980, the number of food stamp recipients rose from 3 million to over 20 million and the cost of the program increased from $6.5 billion to $9.2 billion (Longen, 1981; U.S. Congress, 1980). The effectiveness and efficiency of the FSP should be evaluated by the application of quantifiable nutritional objectives. The methodology for such a task is not available, and its design and application would be extremely expensive. Moreover, the wide coverage and long period of operation of the program preclude obtaining the necessary pretreatment baseline data.

Less equivocal than the FSP in its objectives is the Special Supplemental Food Program for Women, Infants, and Children (WIC) (1979, 1980), authorized by a 1972 amendment (Public Law 92–433) to the Child Nutrition Act of 1966. This amendment mandates cash grants to state health departments and local health clinics for the provision of specified food supplements to pregnant and lactating women and to children through the age of 4 years. Recipients must be malnourished or nutritionally at risk, as ascertained by a health examination. In most programs, family income guidelines also are used to target resources. Participants are given vouchers redeemable either for specified foods in retail food stores or for actual food packages. Over time, nutrition education has become an integral part of the WIC program.

The growth of the WIC program has been impressive; whereas in 1974 a total of 88,000 individuals participated, by 1980 there were 2.2 million recipients, 75% of whom were infants and children. In 1980, WIC was the second largest and fastest growing nutrition program in the United States (Longen, 1981). In fiscal year 1982, approximately 80% of the $848 million budgeted for the program was allocated to food costs, approximately 3% to nutrition education services, and the remaining 17% to administration (Food and Nutrition Service, 1983).

Evaluation of program effectiveness has been more successful in the WIC program than in the FSP. Methods used to evaluate WIC (Edozien, Switzer, & Bryan, 1979; Kennedy, Gershoff, Reed, & Austin, 1982), however, have been criticized for lack of a control group. A control group could not be included in the design of the program because of legal considerations to determine eligibility and participation.

The National School Lunch Program (NSLP), the Special Milk Programs, the Child Care Food Program, the Summer Food Service Equipment, and the School Breakfast Program (SBP) are components of Child Nutrition Programs run by the U.S. Department of Agriculture. In the present review, attention will be restricted to the two largest, the NSLP and the SBP.

The NSLP was authorized in 1946 by the National School Lunch Act "to safeguard the health and well-being of the nation's children, and to encourage the domestic consumption of nutritious agricultural commodities and other food." All schools, both public and private, and all public and private nonprofit residential care institutions are qualified to receive benefits through this program. Income guidelines determine who receives a free, reduced-, or full-price meal. During the 1979–1980 school year, children from a family of four with an annual gross income of $8,949 were eligible to receive free meals, whereas children from similar-sized families with incomes above $14,000 were qualified to receive reduced-price meals. The NSLP has grown in size from approximately 6.5 million children served in the first year of operation, 1946–1947, to approximately 21.7 million children in 1979 (Longen, 1981). In 1979, approximately 4.4 billion lunches were served, of which approximately 1.6 billion were free.

The SBP was created in 1966 as part of the Child Nutrition Act and was authorized permanently in 1975, after the second White House Conference on Food, Nutrition, and Health. The SBP initially was intended to assist schools that served large numbers of low-income children and children who traveled long distances to school. The program is available now to all public and private schools, as well as to residential child care institutions. Approximately one-third of the nation's schools participated in the SBP in 1980; within these schools, approximately 24% of the students were recipients. In spite of an apparently large coverage, the number of participants is only 12% of that of the SLP. Neither the SLP nor the SBP has been evaluated for either effectiveness or efficiency. Thus, no quantitative data on the nutritional, health, or educational outcomes of these programs are available (Pollitt, Gersovitz, & Gargiulo, 1978).

It is difficult to evaluate the effectiveness of large federal food-assistance programs. In spite of agreed-on broad aims, there often appears to be a lack of consensus on specific program objectives. The difficulty is compounded by limitations on the authority of personnel in charge of implementation; paradoxically, those with authority often deal only with broad programmatic aims. Furthermore, the scientific community often predicts results that are difficult to document among free-living populations—that is, populations not subject to rigorous, laboratory-like testing. However, many of these programs fulfill a need identifiable on social or economic grounds and need no scientific rationale. What scientific finding, for example, would lead to abandoning the humanitarian aims of existing food-assistance programs? The prudent course may be the continuation of programs that reflect commitment to the nutritional well-being of all citizens.

EFFECTS OF UNDERNUTRITION ON COGNITIVE FUNCTION

One of the most serious nutrition concerns is that the undernourished child is at risk of an insult to the brain that will result in deficits in cognitive function. Data on laboratory rodents (Barnes, Cunnold, Zimmerman, Simmons, MacLeod, & Krook, 1966; Frankova & Barnes, 1968) and pigs (Barnes, Moore, & Pond, 1970) show that experimentally induced undernutrition in early life adversely affects learning in later development. Experimentation with rats has shown that early malnutrition retards division of every type of proliferating brain cell and delays migration of cells and myelination (Winick & Noble, 1966, 1967). Moreover, brain cell division was curtailed in infants who died because of severe malnutrition (Winick & Rosso, 1969).

Effects of undernutrition on behavior in laboratory animals and on brain morphology in laboratory animals and infants were coupled with retrospective human studies. Evaluations from developing countries showed that children with a history of mild-to-moderate or severe undernutrition in early life did not perform as well in tests of general intelligence, learning, and other cognitive tasks as did well-nourished children from the same communities (Pollitt & Thomson, 1977). A study conducted in this country (Chase & Martin, 1970) compared 19 well-nourished and under-nourished 24–41-month-old infants, and the results concurred with those obtained in less developed countries. The mean developmental quotient of the index group was 82, whereas that of the control group was 99—a statistically significant difference. The authors acknowledged the possibility that these developmental differences could be causally related to social rather than to nutritional factors. Nevertheless, the data on American children were in agreement with the results from a large number of studies in the Third World.

Most of the data published from studies on infants and children, however, were difficult to interpret, because through the mid-1970s most such studies were retrospective: no equivalence could be established between the experimental and control children prior to the onset of the nutritional deficiency. Thus, it was not possible to reject the alternative hypothesis that the cognitive or behavioral effects observed in the mal-nourished children were the result of the socioeconomic correlates of malnutrition, and not of the malnutrition per se. Possibly because they did not understand these shortcomings in research design, lay persons concerned with the risk of malnutrition used the available evidence to gain political support for food-assistance programs.

In 1976, a group of scientists convened under the auspices of the National Academy of Sciences included cognitive ability as one of five areas of human competence likely to be affected by undernutrition. Impairment of cognitive function was considered a consequence of severe protein energy malnutrition (PEM). Specific identification of the cognitive functions at risk is desirable when the reputed effects of malnutrition are likely to be mild or moderate. These effects could be restricted, for example, to impairments of such psychological processes as attention or memory, rather than of general intelligence.

Impairment of cognitive function is readily apparent in children with a history of severe, chronic malnutrition (such as marasmus) during early life. An early and severe nutritional insult affects most of a child's cognitive and behavioral repertoire. During the period of malnutrition and after full nutritional rehabilitation, performance on aggregate measures of intelligence (IQ) (Monckeberg, 1968), on tests of specific cognitive processes (Brockman & Ricciuti, 1971; Lester, 1975), or in school achievement in later life (Galler, Ramsey, Solimano, & Lowell, 1983) is markedly below that of appropriate controls selected from the same communities. This is especially true when the child remains in the economically impoverished environment that led to malnutrition. However, children who have recovered from marasmus and participated in programs of home stimulation have shown significant rehabilitation in intellectual performance (Grantham-McGregor & Desai, 1975; Grantham-McGregor, Stewart, Powell, & Schofield, 1979).

MEASUREMENT OF COGNITIVE FUNCTION

Psychometricians suggest that intelligence tests have acceptable diagnostic sensitivity and specificity and that it is possible, therefore, to define criteria of impairment in children. Developmental scales (Yang, 1979) and intelligence scales (Terman & Merrill, 1973; Wechsler, 1974) measure the mental abilities of the child by providing aggregate scores: developmental quotient (DQ) and intelligence quotient (IQ). These scales group children according to levels of performance, locating cutoff points at different levels in the frequency distribution of the measure (e.g., IQ) for the standard population; confidence limits can be calculated whenever large numbers of children are tested. For example, the 1937 standardization of the Stanford-Binet Intelligence Scale (Terman & Merrill, 1973) provided a classification of intelligence that ranged from very superior (above 149 IQ) through normal or average (from 99 through 109 IQ) to mentally defective (below 69 IQ). Like other tests of general intelligence, the Stanford-Binet is a yardstick to which cutoff points may be applied to define the degree of impairment. The procedure is used diagnostically to define mental retardation as an IQ of 69 or below.

Anthropometry uses a similar approach, defining types and degrees of malnutrition by measurements of growth retardation (Waterlow, 1976). The sensitivity and specificity of established anthropometric cutoff points (such as in weight-for-age, height-for-age, or weight-for-height) are tested by estimating their concordance with such criteria as morbidity, biochemical measures, or mortality (Chen, Chowdhurry, & Huffman, 1980; Trowbridge, 1979).

In developing countries, in studies of the functional consequences of malnutrition, it is difficult to identify cutoff points for intelligence test score distributions that define impaired performance. In those studies, the mental tests generally have been borrowed from developed countries where the tests were standardized. Normative validity requires that the test scores of each age group display a similar range and distribution in the target and standard populations. These parameters of test scores determine the statistics of central tendency (i.e., means, medians) and test variance that in turn influence the sensitivity and specificity of the test (Cronbach, 1971; Irvine & Carroll, 1980). A second requirement is that the test items present the same degree of difficulty for the target population as for the standard population. Because of cultural differences, the same test item may have different degrees of difficulty for children from different populations.

Problems of interpretation that arise from a lack of normative validity are illustrated by the report of Hertzig, Birch, Richardson, and Tizard (1972) on severely malnourished Jamaican children. The control group in this study had a mean Wechsler Full Scale IQ of 70 (SD = 14); the IQs of the index and sibling groups were 58 (SD = 10.75) and 62 (SD = 11), respectively. However, the mean IQ of the controls, the highest of the three groups, was slightly above the IQ level used as the cutoff point to define retardates in the United States. Forty-one percent of the Jamaican children in the control group were rated by their teachers as having outstanding, good, or above-average school performance; 28% of the children were rated as doing poor work. There was a significant correlation between the overall evaluation of school performance and the Full Scale IQ among the children in the control group. This concurrent validity is difficult to interpret, however, because the mean IQ of the control children was 70, which by U.S. reference standards falls, as noted, slightly above the mentally retarded level. Accordingly, the behavioral or cognitive significance of the low IQ score remains an unresolved issue. The study itself neither addresses this issue nor provides data that could resolve it.

Two large-scale epidemiological studies further illustrate the complexities inherent in the interpretation of data. The investigations, one held in Great Britain (Rodgers, 1978) and the other in the United States (Edwards & Grossman, 1979), show a relationship between infant feeding practices and subsequent cognitive ability and school achievement. In the British study, the sample of 5,362 subjects was considered to represent statistically all legitimate singletons born in Great Britain during 1 week. Criteria for inclusion in the study were that the children had to have been strictly bottle- or breast-fed as infants and had to have had a birthweight of at least 6 pounds, and there also had to be a complete social history on the child. The resultant sample with available data was composed of 1,464 8-year-old and 1,398 15-year-old children. At 8 years of age, there were small but statistically significant differences in scores on an intelligence test of those who had been breast-fed as compared with those who had been bottle-fed. Similar differences were seen in 15-year-old subjects in tests of nonverbal ability, mathematics, and sentence completion.

The U.S. study was based on a nationally representative sample of 7,119 noninstitutionalized children of ages 6–11 years who were examined during the period 1963–1965. The data set comprises complete medical and developmental histories for each child, school reports, IQ scores, and school achievement measures. The IQ was calculated from two subtests of the Wechsler Intelligence Scale for Children; the school achievement measures were derived from the reading and arithmetic subtests of the Wide Range Achievement Test. The analyses were restricted to 3,599 white children who lived with both of their natural parents and who had complete data sets. The IQ and achievement test scores of breast-fed children averaged one to two points higher than those of children who had never been breast-fed. The difference seemed to be independent of all other variables examined in a regression equation.

Both epidemiological studies showed that breast-fed children obtained statistically higher scores than bottle-fed children on IQ tests and on measures of educational achievement. Consistently, however, the numerical differences in scores were small, reaching statistical significance only because of the large sample sizes involved. The statistical significance refers to a probability value; it does not necessarily speak to significant behavioral differences (Kruglanski, 1975).

In a report on IQ, social competence, and early childhood intervention programs, Zigler and Trickett (1978) proposed that under normal circumstances the IQ be taken as a "polyglot" sample of behaviors generally influenced by three interrelated variables: (1) a collection of formal cognitive processes, such as abstracting ability or reasoning; (2) a set of "achievement" variables influenced by the child's developmental experiences; and (3) a variety of motivational or personality variables that have little to do with either formal cognition or achievement. Thus, if IQ were used to assess a sample of behaviors, erroneous inferences would not be drawn from the intelligence and achievement scores of environmentally deprived children. There is evidence among children in the United States that motivational factors, perhaps more than any other situational determinant of test performance, tend to depress IQ scores (Zigler & Berman, 1983; Zigler & Trickett, 1978). It also has been shown in one study that improvements in IQ among so-called deprived children exposed to programs of compensatory education are due to changes in motivation (Zigler, Abelson, Trickett, & Seitz, 1982).

Therefore, motivation is particularly relevant in the assessment of performance on intelligence and achievement tests. This may be true especially when inferences are drawn about the functional consequences of malnutrition. In studies on aggregate measures of intelligence, authors commonly have inferred that the compromised performance of malnourished children was due primarily to the adverse effects of their nutritional history (Birch, Pineiro, Alcalde, Toca, & Cravioto, 1971; Cabak & Najdanvick, 1965; DeLicardie & Cravioto, 1974; Herrera, Mora, Christiansen, Clement, Vuori, Waber, DeParades, & Wagner, 1980; Hertzig et al., 1972). From reports on autoregulatory mechanisms in energy balance, it can be concluded that children's activity and arousal levels may be affected under conditions of low energy intake (Rutishauser & Whitehead, 1972). Because activity and arousal are likely components of motivation, and studies of aggregate measures of achievement have not controlled for this variable, results are difficult to interpret.

Determinants of performance on aggregate measures of mental development are particularly difficult to control in developmental scales, such as the Bayley Scales of Mental and Motor Development or the Gesell Schedules. It is recognized that these scales measure a composite of psychomotor skills and abilities that vary with the developmental period. Moreover, the scales have little ability to predict psychometric performance in later developmental stages (Lewis, 1976; Lewis & McGurck, 1972). This lack of consistency in the composite abilities being measured makes interpretation difficult in longitudinal assessments.

A number of studies have been published recently on the effects of a specific nutrient deficiency (iron) in the United States (Oski & Honig, 1978; Oski, Honig, Helu, & Howanitz, 1983), Guatemala (Lozoff, Brittenham, Viteri, Wolf, & Urrutia, 1982), and Chile (Walter, Kovalsky, & Stekel, 1983) on infant mental development. The studies used the Bayley Developmental Scales to measure mental and motor development. Most results demonstrated that iron treatment of the iron-deficient children resulted in an improvement of their developmental test scores. Pretreatment differences disappeared after iron therapy, except for children studied by Lozoff et al. (1982). The improvements in test scores have been attributed to the effects of iron in the neurochemistry of the brain. None of these studies, however, answered the specific question of which cognitive processes are affected by iron deficiency, because, as noted previously, different processes were measured at different developmental stages. Moreover, the improvement of scores in the index cases may have been due to a significant improvement in the general well-being of the infants, which influences motivation. Although these data on changes in developmental test scores represent significant scientific contributions, they do not provide conclusive evidence that brain function is affected by iron depletion.

Another shortcoming in the use of psychometric tests to establish the effects of general or specific nutritional deficiencies on functions is that most yield an aggregate score affected by various covariates of undernutrition (Ricciuti, 1977). These covariates include features of the child's past and present physical and social environment, as well as the idiosyncrasies of his or her own development. Although environment influences the child's cognitive development, no methods are available for identifying, defining, and measuring specific factors in the environment with the precision required for experimental control. The issue is complicated further because in a population where malnutrition is endemic, the velocity of a child's mental growth is influenced by the interactions between nutritional status and the social and physical environments (Richardson, 1974; Richardson, Birch, & Ragbeer, 1975; Winick, Meyer, & Harris, 1975).

NUTRITIONAL SUPPLEMENTATION AND COGNITIVE FUNCTION

One strategy used to control for effects of this interaction is the experimental manipulation of the subject's nutritional status (Chavez & Martinez, 1979; Herrera et al., 1980; Joos, Pollitt, Mueller, & Albright, 1983; Klein, 1979; Rush, Stein, & Sussman, 1980). Experience has shown, however, that manipulation of the nutritional status of populations by dietary or other means often produces additional and unpredictable environmental changes. The results of these studies are less conclusive than anticipated.

Among supplementation studies conducted in the last 2 decades, four (Herrera et al., 1980; Joos et al., 1983; Klein, 1979; Rush et al., 1980) assessed the impact of nutrition supplementation during pregnancy, lactation, and early childhood on aggregate measures of mental development. All sample sizes exceeded 100 subjects, and the studies maintained satisfactory control over the intake of the supplement. Three were conducted in countries known to have populations with high prevalence of PEM and infectious diseases: Guatemala (Klein, 1979), Colombia (Herrera et al., 1980), and Taiwan (Joos et al., 1983). The fourth study (Rush et al., 1980) was carried out in the Harlem section of New York City. Except for the study in Guatemala (Klein, 1979), the data reported were based on comparisons of supplemented and nonsupplemented groups. Three studies fulfilled basic requirements of a randomized blind clinical trial of nutrition supplementation. One (Herrera et al., 1980) included an educational stimulation component in addition to the nutrition supplementation; the design of this study, however, allowed for an evaluation of the effects of the supplementation independent of the educational component.

Two of the studies (Joos et al., 1983; Rush et al., 1980) showed no effect of the supplement during infancy on the Bayley Infant Scale of Mental Development; one (Joos et al., 1983) found a small effect in performance on the Motor Scale. In a third study (Herrera et al., 1980; Waber, Vuori-Christiansen, Ortiz, Clement, Christiansen, Mora, Reed, & Herrera, 1981), supplementation had significant effects on performance on the Griffith Development Scale when the analyses focused across ages (4, 6, 12, and 18 months), but in no case were there differences at a given age.

For example, at 18 months the DQ of the unsupplemented group was 95.4, whereas those of three groups with different supplementation schedules were 95.8, 96.3, and 95.2. In the fourth study (Klein, 1979), the infants were subdivided into three groups according to the volume of intake of supplementation: low, medium, and high. At 6 and 15 months, there was a direct relationship between volume of intake and scores on the mental and motor performance on the Guatemala Infant Development Scale. Except for the motor scores at 6 months, the differences between the intake groups were statistically significant, ranging from 4.0 (6-months mental scale) to 9.4 (15-months mental scale).

Results of the mental development measurements on preschool and school-age children were similar to those observed during the first 24 months of life. For example, results of the Bogotà study (Waber et al., 1981) showed that the mean Griffith Development Scale scores for the nonsupplemented male and female children at 3 years of age were 95.3 and 95.9, respectively, whereas those of the continuously supplemented group were 98.0 and 101.8, respectively. In the Guatemala study, supplementation was not predictive of a verbal development measure (analogous to the Peabody Picture Vocabulary Test) at 5, 6, and 7 years of age, or of school performance (Balderston, Wilson, Freire, & Simonen, 1981). Finally, in the Taiwan study (Hsueh & Meyer, 1981), there were no significant differences in the mean Stanford Binet IQ between the supplemented and nonsupplemented children at 5 years of age. In summary, food supplementation produces mild beneficial effects, if any. These effects are observed in the first 3 years of life and have little predictive validity for IQ.

One interpretation of the disappointing findings of these studies is that in cases of mild to moderate malnutrition, dietary intake is not a significant determinant of cognitive function. However, this explanation must be evaluated in light of three considerations. First, the experimental designs of the studies, including the nature and timing of the supplement and the level of nutritional risk, differed significantly. Accordingly, the findings are not strictly comparable, and conclusive inferences cannot be drawn. For example, in the studies in New York (Rush et al., 1980) and Taiwan (Joos et al., 1983) the supplement was restricted to the mothers; however, in the former, the supplement was scheduled only during pregnancy, whereas in the latter it was provided during both pregnancy and lactation. Moreover, in the Guatemala study the supplement was delivered and consumed at a feeding station (Balderston et al., 1981; Klein, 1979), which resulted in the self-selection of participants. Possible confounding effects of sampling were not satisfactorily removed.

Second, among populations in which malnutrition is endemic, correlational data consistently show a positive association between physical growth and intelligence test performance in children (Lasky, Klein, Yarbrough, Engle, & Lechtig, 1981). These associations persist after appropriate statistical control for social and familial factors that covary with the children's nutritional status.

Third, the combined use of nutrition supplementation and educational stimulation has a greater impact on mental test performance than does the use of supplementation alone. The benefits are not restricted solely to scores on mental tests but also have been observed in measures of school achievement and behavior (McKay, Sinisterra, McKay, Gomez, & Lloreda, 1978).

None of the studies on dietary supplementation, with or without educational stimulation, has detected a differential vulnerability to early protein-energy deficiency among specific cognitive processes. In fact, none was designed to establish differences in changes in cognitive processes across time within individuals. One consistent finding in all of the studies was that supplementation was more likely to show effects in motor than mental development during the first 2 years of life.

Hicks, Langham, and Takenaki (1982) recently reported that children achieved significantly different behavioral and intelligence test scores according to the durations of their participation in the WIC program. The sample was restricted to 21 pairs of siblings; the older siblings were enrolled in the program after the first year of life and participated for 30.8 months. The supplementation of the younger siblings began in the last trimester of pregancy, and their participation in the WIC program averaged 56.1 months. At the time of testing, the mean ages of the younger (early supplement) and older (late supplement) groups were 75.9 and 106 months, respectively. The means of the Full-Scale IQ in the WISC-R were 86.43 and 73.39 for the early and late supplementation groups, respectively; this 13.04-point difference was highly significant.

The results of the study are surprising because of the magnitude of the alleged effects and the discrepancy between these findings and those of most studies. Because the siblings were tested at different ages, the study design did not control for familial and environmental factors. Cumulative environmental deficiences may favor the mental test performance of the younger children, as is suggested by the cumulative deficit hypothesis (Jensen, 1974, 1977). These and other methodological shortcomings limit the inferences that may be drawn on the effects of the WIC program on cognitive development (Pollitt & Lorimor, 1983).

In summary, the available research information does not permit conclusions to be drawn regarding the effects of undernutrition on cognitive function. The exception, however, is severe PEM; evidence shows that marasmic infants, with a history of low birthweight ($\leq 2,500$ grams) and prolonged malnutrition during the first year of life, have pronounced deficits in cognitive function during the preschool and school years. The probabilities of these sequelae are minimized if the children are enrolled in educational intervention programs following nutrition rehabilitation.

Two factors have made it difficult to determine the functional differences between malnourished and control children: an overemphasis on intelligence as the outcome variable, and the use of intelligence tests with no proved normative validity in less developed countries (where most of these studies have been conducted). Furthermore, the extent to which motivation explains differences in test performance is not known. Information on the social competence of these children would be useful but is unavailable.

Research on undernutrition and cognitive function has been based on a medical model of disease causality. The model predicts that for every disease there is an etiologic agent and that its presence always results in disease. This is a one-dimensional model of causality which restricts research to a bivariate equation. Moreover, when used in retrospective designs, this model is of little value and may be an obstacle to the accurate perception of PEM as a codeterminant of cognitive deficits. The extent to which PEM contributes to developmental deficits varies according to the extent to which biological and socioenvironmental factors are present. Available information suggests that monofocal interventions may not result in a significant improvement in intelligence or learning test performance. Such findings raise questions about the merits of food-distribution systems that are justified solely on expected benefits in the cognitive function of children. However, multifocal interventions—which include nutrition supplementation, educational stimulation, and health care—have shown beneficial effects on children in tests of specific cognitive processes as well as in school achievement (McKay et al., 1978).

FUNCTIONAL BENEFITS OF HUMAN MILK

Recommendations that all normal term infants be breast-fed have been published by the Departments of Agriculture and Health and Human Services. Human milk is a food with a nutrient composition that in content and bioavailability is ideal for the infant (Gaull, Jensen, Rassin, & Malloy, 1981). More impressive still, human milk appears to incorporate components capable of modulating immune responses and promoting its own digestion. The reasons for the recommendation of human milk usually are grouped into three broad categories: immunologic, nutritional, and behavorial (Committee on Nutrition of the American Academy of Pediatrics,

1976). Several immunologic components in human milk may help the infant deal with stresses common in early life. Secretory IgA (SIgA), a major protein component of human milk, is an example of an active protective protein. SIgA appears to act as an "intestinal paint" capable of binding viruses and bacteria. The binding of potential pathogens prevents their entry into mucosal cells. In animal models, maternally produced SIgA has been observed to bind to the small intestine of infants (Walker & Isselbacher, 1974). Furthermore, SIgA may protect the respiratory tract. The common gurgling action of infants during feeding may provide the physical mechanism for SIgA to bind and act as a protective covering in the hypopharynx. This action would be analogous to that proposed to take place in the intestinal tract.

Investigators have reported that the secretion of SIgA in human milk and colostrum is a specific maternal response to potential pathogens. Goldblum and co-workers (Goldblum, Ahlstedt, Carisson, Havison, Jodal, Lindin-Janson, & Sohl, 1975) have described the appearance of SIgA in human milk directed against a specific nonpathogenic *Escherichia coli* administered orally to mothers. These observations support the view that mothers are capable of responding acutely and specifically to infectious challenges in the immediate environment. Secretory IgA antibodies to a pool of *E. coli* antigens, potential diarrhea-causing agents, have been measured in the milk of mothers of term and premature infants (Goldman, Garza, Nichols, & Goldblum, 1982). Women are capable of producing these specific proteins through 2 years of unrestricted lactation (Goldman, Garza, & Goldblum, 1983). The same proteins have been observed in the milk of women weaning their infants from the breast after 6 months of exclusive breast-feeding (Goldman, Garza, Nichols, Smith, & Goldblum, 1983). These observations suggest that the protective mechanism persists after infants outgrow the maximal milk production capability of most women and continues even when sucking stimulation is reduced significantly.

Mechanisms that provide breast milk with specific antibodies directed against enteric and other pathogens may account, in part, for the protective properties of human milk. Several other nonspecific immunologic factors also provide protection (Goldman & Goldblum, 1980). Although the potential role of such mechanisms may be extrapolated from laboratory studies, a definitive demonstration of protective functions in free-living populations has been more difficult. Differences in morbidity between bottle- and breast-fed infants often are difficult to interpret because of confounding environmental and demographic variables (Sauls, 1979); for example, the degree of preventable contamination of artificial formulas, the number of caretakers, the behavioral characteristics of the caretaker (such as sanitation practices and other mothering skills), and the number of potential disease-carrying contacts. These variables are difficult to control unless appropriate data are collected and sufficiently large numbers of subjects are studied. In addition, research designs must take into account the unidirectional flow of infants from one feeding category to another. A breast-fed infant may become exclusively bottle-fed for many reasons, such as illness. It is unlikely, however, that an exclusively bottle-fed infant subsequently will be breast-fed. Recent studies (Cunningham, 1979; Dagan & Pridan, 1982; Downham, Scott, Sims, Webb, & Gardner, 1976; Larsen & Homer, 1978; Schacter, 1971) and classic reports (Grulee, Sanford, & Herron, 1934; Woodbury, 1922) often have not controlled adequately for many of these confounding variables. Current studies have examined the protective effects of breast milk against specific diseases and pathogens, hospitalization, and the general incidence of infectious disease. Most of these investigations have reported significantly fewer illnesses in breast-fed infants. A few have detected no benefits (Adebonojo, 1972; Fergusson, Horwood, Shannon, & Taylor, 1978; Research Subcommittee, South East England Faculty Royal College of General Practitioners, 1972). None, however, has reported greater morbidity in breast-fed than in bottle-fed infants.

HEALTH OUTCOMES IN BREAST- AND BOTTLE-FED POPULATIONS

It is difficult to evaluate both classic studies and more recent reports that contrast the health outcomes associated with specific infant feeding practices. Furthermore, early observations cannot be extrapolated uncritically to the present because of changes in the formulation of artificial milks, alterations in important demographic variables of breast-feeding populations, and general improvements in sanitation. Nevertheless, Woodbury (1922) made several provocative observations in the early part of this century that recent studies have not evaluated satisfactorily. He identified specific ages during which immunologic components apparently are important to the infant. The health records of 22,422 infants were surveyed and subjects were grouped into three categories: exclusive breast-feeding (EBF), mixed human and artificial milk feeding (MF), and exclusive artificial feeding (EAF). The ratio of mortality between the EAF and EBF groups was maximal between the third and seventh months of life. The month-specific death rate of infants whose mode of feeding was changed from EBF to either MF or EAF in the seventh month or later was less than the corresponding rates among infants who had been exclusively bottle-fed prior to the seventh month. Woodbury found that infants who were weaned to EAF before the eighth month had higher mortality rates than infants who continued to breast-feed. However, mortality rates of infants weaned after the eighth month to EAF were not higher when compared with those who continued to be breast-fed after this period. These data suggest that prolonged breast-feeding had a cumulative effect on reduced morbidity in later months. The data also suggest that responses to stress at specific ages may be used to assess the potential functional benefits of human milk.

Approximately 15 years later, Grulee and co-workers (Grulee et al., 1934) reported data that agree qualitatively with those published by Woodbury. The records of over 20,000 infants also were examined. The authors concluded that the most pronounced differences in morbidity between EBF and EAF infants occurred after the sixth month of life and that mortality in the EBF group was observed almost entirely in the first 2 months. More recent studies of smaller populations have reached similar conclusions. The studies of Mata and colleagues (Mata & Urrutia, 1971; Mata, Urrutia, Garcia, Fernandez, & Behar, 1969; Mata, Urrutia, & Gordon, 1967) support the view that the protection afforded by human milk is not due solely to its being less contaminated than artificial milk. Difficulties encountered in the documentation of comparable effects in developed countries (Cunningham, 1979; Dugan & Pridan, 1982; Downham et al., 1976; Larsen & Homer, 1978; Schachter, 1971) may be due to improved sanitation conditions. The view that functional components in human milk are active in the infant draws support from complementary studies (Chandra, 1979; Hide & Guyer, 1981) suggesting that human milk protects against certain allergic disorders.

Whether the protective effects of human milk components are made significant by environmental conditions or remain potential because of privileged conditions, these benefits are available only to the infant who is breast-fed. Available data, although not conclusive, support the hypothesis that components of human milk complement a developing immune system in the infant (Goldman & Goldblum, 1982). It is not clear whether immune components stimulate the development of the infant's immune system or serve until the infant is capable of mounting its own response. Other nonimmunologic components with potentially important functions also have been investigated. Carbohydrate (Gyorgy, 1953) and lipid factors (Welsh, Shurne, & May, 1978) that may affect the frequency of disease have been identified, as have proteins with enzymatic capabilities that complement the infant's digestive abilities and other factors that may accelerate the growth of the developing intestinal tract.

NUTRIENT REQUIREMENTS DURING INFANCY

From the consensus that human milk is the ideal food for normal term infants there has followed a debate in regard to the total amount of milk an infant should consume at various ages and the length of time that human milk should therefore serve as the only nutrient source. Present recommendations are that infants in well-nourished populations should be breast-fed for the first 4–6 months. These recommendations have been compared with nutrient requirements derived by factorial methods. Factorial methods quantify nutrients that accrue in growth processes and are lost in normal metabolism. These estimates then are extrapolated to quantitate the amount of breast milk an infant should consume and to predict the optimal duration of breast-feeding.

Waterlow and Thomson (1979) applied this approach to estimate the infant's protein and energy requirements. They first estimated whole-body nitrogen at different ages during infancy and used these estimates to calculate the mean daily increment of nitrogen. They then added to this estimate the amount of nitrogen needed for maintenance and from the sum of both quantities calculated levels of protein requirements. Their estimates decreased from 1.9 grams of protein per kilogram per day at 1 month to approximately 1.5 g/kg/day at months 4–6. In a similar manner, they added to the caloric content of tissues gained per day during the first 6 months the quantities of energy required for maintenance and growth. The sum of these quantities represents the factorially derived estimate of energy requirements: approximately 115 kcal/kg/day the first month, gradually declining to 95 kcal/kg/day at months 4–6. The Food and Agriculture Organization of the United Nations/World Health Organization (FAO/WHO) (1973) recommends protein intakes of 2.4 g/kg/day for infants younger than 3 months of age and 1.8 kg/day for infants 3–6 months of age. Energy requirements for infants younger than 3 months of age are estimated at 120 kcal/kg/day and at 115 kcal/kg/day for infants 4–6 months of age. Recommendations made by the Food and Nutrition Board of the National Academy of Sciences/National Research Council (NAS/NRC) (1980) agree closely with those published by the FAO/WHO. If these estimates are correct, further calculations predict that energy should become limiting before protein in the diet of breast-fed infants. These calculations assume an energy and protein concentration in human milk of 70 kcal/dl and 1.2 g/dl, respectively. To meet energy requirements, mean intakes would have to be 826–960 ml of human milk per day by the third month of life and 940–1,100 ml/day by the fifth to sixth months, depending on whose estimated requirements are used. With few exceptions, however, reported observations of human milk intakes during the first month of life range from 600 to 700 ml/day, and by month 6 the range is 800–900 (Butte, Garza, Smith, & Nichols, 1984; Chandra, 1981; Dewey & Lonnerdahl, 1982; Lonnerdahl, Forsum, & Hambraeus, 1976; National Center for Health Statistics, 1978; Picciano et al., 1981; Wallgren, 1945; Whitehead & Paul, 1981).

A principal problem in interpreting these data is that most were derived from studies applying cross-sectional designs or from longitudinal experiments with high rates of subject attrition. Because both conditions favor subjects with high milk outputs, the representativeness of the data is questionable. A recent study of 45 mother-infant pairs reported longitudinal data obtained from subjects recruited prenatally (Butte et al., 1984). The attrition rate in the study was less than 10%; subjects lost to the study left for reasons unrelated to breast-feeding. In this study, milk intake reached a plateau at 733 (89) g/day over the 4 months of observation. Nutrient intakes were calculated from the analyses of individual 24-hour aliquots of each mother's milk. On a weight basis, energy intakes fell from 110 kcal/kg at month 1 to 71 kcal/kg at month 4, and protein intakes fell from 1.6 g/kg at month one to 0.9 g/kg at month 4. Therefore, by the fourth month, these infants were consuming less than 65% of the energy recommended by the National Research Council (NAS/NRC, 1980). The protein intake also was substantially below recommended amounts. Despite these differences between recommended and observed intakes, the infants were growing well. Weight for age, length for age, and weight for length were above the 50th percentile for the group and remained above this level for the 4 months. Breast-fed infants appear, therefore, to grow at a rate that matches reference standards derived primarily from bottle-fed populations (National Center for Health Statistics, 1978).

Several interesting questions arise from these observations. Have requirements been overestimated significantly? What adaptations were made to the observed intakes? Do breast-fed children maintain growth patterns at the expense of other energy-requiring activities, such as play? If other activities are curtailed when less than "optimal" amounts of energy are consumed, which are reduced first, and with what developmental consequences? Are these "low" intakes compatible with normal development only in relatively affluent populations whose energy needs may differ from those living in more stressful environments? Conversely, if recommendations represent an "overconsumption" of energy, is the response an increase in physical activities, or metabolic inefficiency? What are the consequences of either response? These questions are rarely addressed by traditional methods of nutrition assessment.

Nutritional intakes required to sustain specific functional competencies, such as immune capabilities, have seldom been measured. Thus, establishing efficacious levels of intake requires that a major conceptual and methodological shortcoming be addressed, if the rationale for feeding human milk includes functional benefits such as protection against pathogens. For example, although data show that factors in human milk modulate immunologic protection, no adequately controlled data establish the levels at which these factors become functionally significant. Similar data, which control for equivalent maternal contact and environment, do not exist for bottle-fed infants. In the absence of such data, informed judgments are essential.

INFANT FEEDING AND WIC

Such judgments have been made and applied in the WIC program. Certain aspects of the program, however, pose difficulties. Although current and classic data support breast-feeding, particularly among groups at low socioeconomic levels, only recently has breast-feeding been recognized as a WIC priority. Formula feeding has been the major intervention for infants at risk. The present official WIC program policy is to promote breast-feeding, but resource allocation does not appear to be consistent with this goal. A large proportion of the budget is allocated to the provision of formula. Far fewer resources are available to fund mechanisms that insure easy access to support of lactation management. For example, there are no WIC regulations for the provision of human milk to infants temporarily separated from their mothers at birth because of neonatal problems. More important, there are no provisions to support the mother who wishes to establish and maintain lactation while she is separated from her infant. If problems arise during lactation, there is no direct aid to sustain lactation. Furthermore, the only solid weaning food that WIC regulations provide for the young infant is cereal, the nutrient composition of which complements formula better than human milk. It seems reasonable to expect that once WIC program goals are more precisely defined, they will give unequivocal support to breast-feeding among high-risk groups and the provision of more nutritious weaning foods.

The Etiology of Obesity

Obesity, defined as adipose tissue relative to lean body mass, is a condition with unique characteristics. There are no clearly defined criteria for its diagnosis because no specific complications can be shown to occur invariably once a certain body composition is attained. This is not to deny that excessive fatness has serious physiological sequelae or correlates—for example, glucose intolerance, hypertension, cardiovascular and gall bladder disease, and joint degeneration—but to emphasize that no degree of obesity makes any of them inevitable (Mann, 1974).

Perhaps obesity is studied assiduously because of its high visual salience and the widespread concern regarding its medical effects and social consequences. Although a variety of direct measures (such as body densitometry) or indices (skinfold thicknesses, weight-to-height relationships) allow relative adiposity to be calculated (Gurr & Kirtland, 1978; Keys, Fridanza, Karvornen, Kimura, & Taylor, 1972), much obesity is self-diagnosed by adults using current culturally based aesthetic standards for body composition.

As would be expected, these standards influence the conventional wisdom regarding certain aspects of infant and child nutrition. Whereas it was formerly believed that a chubby infant or child reflected good parental care and sound nutrition practice, such a child is now the source of parental consternation. This reversal in attitude reflects in part the general, unsubstantiated notion that excess adiposity in early life is causally related to obesity in adulthood. A congruent belief held by numerous nutrition scientists is that excessive intakes of salt, sugar, cholesterol, cow's milk, or calories in early life can influence the subsequent risk of hypertension, diabetes, atherosclerosis, allergy, and obesity. Lack of a consensus on the consequence of these causal links, in fact, has not prevented the promotion of a broad nutrition policy.

Adipose tissue is the body's main depot for calories. Chemical energy is stored as fat, which contains almost 10 times more calories per unit weight of tissue than the carbohydrate (glycogen) stored in liver or the protein of muscle. When more calories are ingested than the body needs for energy, the extra calories are stored as triglyceride. When energy needs exceed intake, triglycerides are hydrolyzed in adipose tissue and the resulting free fatty acids and glycerol are released to the blood stream to be used as fuel. The balance between energy (food) intake and energy output determines whether the amount of adipose tissue increases, decreases, or remains stable. Given the large number of kilocalories (800,000–1,000,000) ingested yearly by an adult and the fact that 1 kg of fat represents 7,000 stored kcal, it is remarkable that the weight of most individuals remains as stable as it does. An error of only 2% in energy intake versus output will result in a yearly gain or loss of 2.5 kg of adipose tissue. Continued over 10 years, this small error could change body weight by 25 kg. Though it is widely believed that excessive caloric intake explains most obesity, there is growing evidence that many people are obese because of subtle defects in energy expenditure (Leibel, 1981). For adipose tissue to accumulate, the individual must be in net positive energy balance. Guiding medical practice and public health policy requires knowledge of how energy balance is regulated and of the relative contributions of genotype and environment.

ADIPOSE TISSUE GROWTH

Organ growth occurs in three synchronized but overlapping phases: hyperplasia (cell division), simultaneous hyperplasia and hypertrophy (cell enlargement), and hypertrophy. The timing of these phases varies among organs and species. Early studies (Winick & Noble, 1966, 1967) demonstrated that organ cellularity could be altered by early nutritional conditions: under- or overfeeding during periods of cellular hyperplasia resulted in permanent decreases or increases, respectively, in cellularity of organs. Returning to a normal food intake after a period of deprivation normalized cell size but did not decrease cell number. These findings led to the concept of "critical periods": ontogenic time windows for each organ during which the plane of nutrition could permanently influence the cellularity of an organ (Dobbing, 1974). Knittle and Hirsch (1968) and other investigators (Johnson, Stern, Greenwood, Zucker, & Hirsch, 1973), extrapolating these findings to the adipose organ, showed that the cellularity of rat adipose tissues could be altered permanently by manipulating litter size and hence preweaning nutrition. Thus, overfeeding and underfeeding suckling rodents create symmetrical changes in adipose organ cellularity. Because glucose metabolism (combustion to CO_2 or fat formation) per cell remains unchanged, net fat synthesis is partly a function of the number of fat cells. These findings, and the observation that the increased mass of fat in extremely obese adults resulted from adipocyte number rather than size (Hirsch & Batchelor, 1976), led to the formulation of the "fat-cell hypothesis" of obesity. The hypothesis has two fundamental tenets: (1) early overstimulation (such as by overfeeding) leads to permanent hyperplasia of the adipose organ; (2) this hyperplasia obligates a greater fraction of substrate intake to be deposited as fat, thus perpetuating obesity. From this hypothesis, corollaries bearing on the ontogeny and possible prevention of human obesity were drawn immediately. However, identification of the adipocyte as an active regulator of energy balance, although an appealing concept, has not been demonstrated as valid. It has nevertheless had impact on strategies in obesity research. In clinical medicine this impact has been manifest in numerous efforts to correlate obesity in early life with that in adulthood and to prevent this condition in adults by nutrition intervention in infancy.

Adipose tissue appears in the human fetus between the twenty-ninth and thirtieth weeks of gestation. The neonate has little fat around internal organs but has a subcutaneous fat depot which represents 10%–15% of body weight and is composed of 4.2×10^9 adipocytes. The nonobese adult has approximately 20×10^9 adipocytes, and obese individuals have up to 100×10^9 adipocytes with a greater fat content. Early growth of the adipose organ in children primarily involves increases in cell size. The four- to 25-fold increase in cell number between birth and adulthood is due in part to the production of new adipocytes after birth (Knittle, Timmer, Ginsberg-Fellner, Brown, & Katz, 1979).

As body weight doubles during the first 6 months of infancy, the percentage of body weight as lipid rises to 25%. Although lipid accounts for over 40% of the weight gained during the first 4 months of life, lipid accounts for only 7% of the weight gained from 1 to 2 years of age and 3.5% of that gained between 2 and 3 years of age. By age 3, large relative increases in lean body mass have reduced total lipid content to 18% of body weight (Knittle, 1978). Females show a large increase in body fat at the time of puberty, ultimately reaching a point where fat accounts for approximately 25% of body weight. In males, a prepubertal spurt in adiposity is followed by a decrease in total body fat during the period of maximal linear growth during puberty. Normal adult males have 15%–20% of body weight as fat. Young women show greater adiposity than men because they have a greater number of slightly larger adipocytes. However, such differences were not found in a randomly selected group of middle-aged men and women (Bjorntorp, Bengtsson, Blohme, Jonsson, Sjostrom, Tibblin, Tibblin, & Whilhelmsen, 1971). During adulthood, both males and females increase their adiposity gradually through a combined process of losing lean body mass and increasing adipose tissue. Body weight, however, remains remarkably stable (Forbes & Reina, 1970).

Once an apparent "critical period" early in the ontogeny of the rodent adipose organ was discovered, it was immediately concluded that such critical periods might exist in humans and might, through early influence on adipose organ development, influence the long-term risk of obesity. Although few studies evaluate the fat-cell hypothesis, there is evidence to support the belief that cells proliferate in the human adipose organ at varying rates during development and that, during periods of relatively rapid organ growth (infancy and adolescence), these rates are sensitive to environmental influences. In most of the studies, adipocyte size has been estimated from a small biopsy sample of adipose tissue, and the total body cell number has been extrapolated by estimating body fat by means of anthropometry, isotope dilution, or natural radioisotope counting (Gurr & Kirtland, 1978).

An early cross-sectional study of 34 children by Hirsch and Knittle (1979) indicated that there was a threefold increase in adipocyte number during the first year of life and that adipocyte size increased at a slower rate. Subsequent studies (Dauncey & Gairdner, 1975; Hager, Sjostrom, Arvidsson, Bjorntorp, & Smith, 1977; Knittle et al., 1979) have not confirmed this finding. Hager found that virtually all of the increase in body fat in the first year of life was due to increments in cell size, and Dauncey reported that in 59 infants, adipocyte size increased readily with age between 25 weeks of gestation and 40 weeks of postnatal life. Because the increments in cell size were sufficient to accommodate almost all of the lipid known to be deposited in the adipose organ during this period, it was inferred that organ hyperplasia may have been minimal. Knittle (1979), in a recent study, obtained cross-sectional data on 288 obese and nonobese children 4 months to 19 years of age, of whom 132 were followed longitudinally for 4 years or more. By age 2, obese children, defined as having a weight to height (wt/ht) imbalance of over 130% of the ideal for their age, had larger fat cells than normal weight controls; the adult-level cell size of the obese children did not change from 2 through 16 years of age. Unlike the nonobese children, obese infants showed increases in cell number throughout all age groups and had a significantly greater number of cells than nonobese subjects in all ages examined (2–19 years). Of the 19 infants born to obese mothers, eight were obese (over 130% of ideal weight) by 2 years of age and were compared with the 11 nonobese infants. Up to age 12 months, the two groups shared no significant difference in body weight. By 2 years of age the obese had a mean weight of 19 kg versus 13 kg for the nonobese. Obese and nonobese children could not be distinguished on the basis of cell size, absolute cellularity, or velocity of apparent hyperplasia in the first year of life. From ages 4 months to 1 year, both groups showed similar increments in cell size. However, between 1 and 2 years of age, the obese children, failing to show the large decline in adipocyte size seen in cross-sectional and longitudinal studies of nonobese children, demonstrated significant increments in adipocyte lipid content.

Thus, in the first 2 years of life, adipocyte size rather than number appears to be the best predictor of subsequent obesity. Later, not only are the cells larger in obese children, but they increase significantly in number over those in nonobese children. Neither Hager nor Knittle noted sex-related differences in adipose organ development during the first 2 years of life, and both commented on the apparent temporal coupling of adipocyte size and hyperplasia in children, a relationship also demonstrated in animals (Faust, Johnson, Stern, & Hirsch, 1978). Knittle et al. (1979) reported that a dramatic increase in adipocyte number was found once body fat exceeded 25% of total body weight.

The existence of adult-onset hyperplastic obesity (Hirsch & Batchelor, 1976) and Knittle's data in children argue against the concept of strictly time-limited periods of adipocyte hyperplasia in humans. Nevertheless, there appear to be periods of relative increase in the rate of adipocyte formation before 2 years of age and during the adolescent growth spurt.

GENETIC INFLUENCE

These periods may be influenced by genetic factors that affect the development of obesity. Rao, MacLean, Moreton, and Yee (1975) analyzed data gathered in 1,068 families in northeastern Brazil; they estimated a heritability factor (which expresses the portion of phenotypic variance that can be explained by genotype) of .42 (maximum = 1.0) for weight. Only 18% of variance in weight was attributable to the shared family environment. Garn and Clark (1976), in an analysis of triceps skinfold thickness data from the Ten State Nutrition Survey, found parent-offspring and sibling-sibling correlations of .30 and .40, respectively. Because of the high interspouse correlation of .25, these investigators suspected that environmental rather than genetic factors accounted for most of the intrafamily covariance of triceps skinfold thickness. However, Foch and McClearn (1980) point to two arguments against attributing an inordinate proportion of the skinfold thickness covariance to environmental rather than genetic factors: the husband-wife correlation does not increase with duration of marriage, and maternal obesity was no more potent than paternal obesity in predicting obesity in offspring, a differential that might have been expected, given the larger maternal influence on family environment.

Brook, Huntley, and Slack (1975) analyzed the heritability for subscapular and triceps skinfold thickness by comparing the covariance in these measures for 78 monozygotic and 144 same-sex dizygotic twins. When both measures were pooled across all ages, heritability was .77. Heritability increased with age, being .98 in twins over 10 years of age and .52 in those less than 10. That heritability in body weight increases with age also was demonstrated by Wilson (1979) in a longitudinal study of a large number of monozygotic and same-sex dizygotic twin pairs. Borjeson (1976) analyzed skinfold thickness of 40 monozygotic and 61 same-sex dizygotic twin pairs (11.5 years old) in which one or both members had a body weight more than 2 SDs above that appropriate for age and height. He reported a heritability of .88 for skinfold thickness and found no evidence that intrauterine growth, early nutritional experience, or physical activity levels contributed significantly to the subsequent development of obesity. Finally, Shields (1962) found that the weight differences between adult monozygous twins raised together and apart were virtually identical: 10.4 pounds and 10.5 pounds, respectively. Dizygotic twins raised together had a mean weight difference of 17.3 pounds. Differences in body weights larger than 21 pounds were found in 12% of monozygous twins raised separately, in 9% of those raised together, and in 44% of the dizygotic twins studied.

Biron, Mongeau, and Bertrand (1977) studied 574 adoptees (most adopted during the first year of life) and 250 natural children in 374 familes with at least one adopted child. Although there were substantial correlations of weight to height between parents and their natural offspring (.26) and between natural siblings (.37), there was essentially no correlation of these measures for adopted children. In another adoption study, Shenker, Fisichelli, and Lang (1974) found that infants placed with overweight (weight over 150 pounds) adoptive mothers tended to gain more weight than infants placed with adoptive mothers weighing less than 150 pounds. Though the study does show a relatively weak effect of maternal weight on infant weight variance in the first 7–9 months of life, it is of interest to note that this environmental impact on somatotype appears to diminish with increasing age of the infant and is undetectable by 12 months of age. This finding is consistent with the data from genetic studies that suggest increasing expression of somatotype-relevant genotype with age.

No matter how they differ in design and choice of dependent variables, studies like those described above seem to indicate that with increasing age, multifactorial genetic influences are markedly more significant than environmental factors in determining adiposity. It seems most reasonable to attribute human adiposity to the complex interaction of a variably predisposing genotype with a facilitating environment (i.e., one that makes appetizing foods readily available while reducing the need for physical activity).

CONSEQUENCE OF ENERGY BALANCE IN EARLY LIFE

Although there have been reports (Farquahar, 1969; Ginsberg-Fellner, 1981) of an increase in the frequency of later obesity in infants of diabetic mothers, others have not been able to confirm these results (Bjorntorp et al., 1971). A recent study of a group of Pima Indians living in the Gila River community in Arizona indicated that at 15–19 years of age, 58% of the offspring of women who were diabetic during pregnancy weighed 40% or more than their desirable weight, as compared with 17% of the offspring of nondiabetics and 25% of those of prediabetics (Pettitt, Baird, Allech, Bennett, & Knowler, 1983). The degree of maternal obesity did not correlate with childhood obesity in the offspring of diabetic mothers. Thus, fetal overnutrition was implicated in risk of obesity in childhood. Because the Pima Indians are a very select group of subjects with a well-documented genetic predisposition to both obesity and diabetes mellitus, the relevance of these findings to a more genetically heterogeneous population is unclear. The evidence for any correlation between birthweight in normal infants and childhood obesity in the general population is equivocal at best (Grinker, 1981). The effects of intrauterine and early postnatal undernutrition on adult obesity rates in humans were examined retrospectively by Ravelli, Stern, and Susser (1976) in a group of males conceived during the Dutch famine of 1944–1945. Fetal exposure to famine during the first two trimesters of pregnancy was associated with a significant increase in the rate of obesity (wt/ht greater than 120% of the WHO standard) at age 19, whereas similar exposure during the last trimester of pregnancy and first few months of infancy was associated with a significant reduction in the rates of obesity in adulthood. Exposure to famine in the last trimester of pregnancy alone, or during the first year of life alone, had no apparent influence on the incidence of obesity in adulthood. It appears that for permanent effects on adipose organ size to occur, undernutrition had to occur during both later intrauterine development and early infancy. This possibility, if correct, not only implicates a possible "critical period" in human adipose organ development but also may explain why caloric restriction in early infancy alone has not been found to protect against obesity in childhood (Berglund, Bjorntorp, Sjostrom, & Smith, 1974).

Although some have found absolute weight or rate of weight gain during the first year of life to correlate modestly with frequency of obesity in childhood (Asher, 1966; Eid, 1970; Melbin & Vuille, 1973), others have found excessive adiposity (by skinfold thickness) in infancy to be a poor predictor of obesity at age 5 years (Poskitt & Cole, 1977). In any event, this relationship weakens with increasing age to the point where little or no correlation is demonstrable between adiposity in infancy and that occurring in adulthood (Tanner, 1962). In addition, although infant feeding practices (such as breast vs. bottle, timing of introduction of solid foods) may transiently affect adiposity, there is little evidence to support the contention that these practices influence the risk of obesity in the older child or adult (DeSwiet, Fayers, & Cooper, 1977; Dubois, Hill, & Beaton, 1979). Brook et al. (1972) reported increased adipose organ cellularity in children who had been obese during the first year of life. However, others have found adipocyte number in obese children of various ages (Hager et al., 1977; Wilkinson & Parkin, 1974) to be unrelated to the age of onset of obesity. As noted previously, studies in adults (Hirsch & Batchelor, 1976) have failed to show a correlation between adipocyte number and age of onset of obesity.

Some studies do indicate that the obese adult is likely to have been obese in early life. Charney, Goodman, McBride, Lyon, and Pratt (1976), for example, found that infants attaining the ninetieth percentile for weight in the first 6 months of life had a 2.6-fold increased risk of obesity in adulthood: 36% of these infants were overweight (wt/ht 110% of ideal) as adults, whereas only 14% of average or light-weight infants were overweight. An interaction between parental overweight and infant weight also was noted; parental overweight increased the risk of adult obesity in overweight infants by approximately a factor of 2. It is important to note that most obese infants did not become obese adults and that the correlation between infant and adult obesity in no way proves causality. The instances of infant obesity correlated with obesity in adulthood may represent early somatic display of a metabolic tendency to obesity, whereas the more numerous cases of resolving infant obesity may be transient manifestations of environmental forces.

The data available, through clearly not definitive, might be summarized as follows: (1) the potential for new cell synthesis in the adipose organ apparently is present from the last trimester of gestation into adulthood. (2) The ultimate cellularity of the adipose organ is largely under genetic control; however, the rate at which this final number is achieved and, in extreme cases, the number itself may be influenced by environmental factors. (3) Adipocyte size, however, is readily susceptible to, and reflective of, short-term nutritional influences. The two- to threefold range in mean adipocyte size noted between individuals of differing degrees of adiposity is adequate to account for all but the most severe cases of obesity. (4) At the extreme upper limit of cell size, there apparently occurs a stimulus to new adipocyte formation. (5) An individual's adiposity at any given time therefore reflects the influence of genetic forces transmitted through adipocyte number and current nutritional status (net caloric balance) reflected by adipocyte size. These two parameters are not, however, entirely independent of each other, and the genetic-environmental distinction between them is clearly an oversimplification. Nutritional circumstances can affect adipose organ cellular development and, to a lesser extent, the ultimate number of cells in the organ. Conversely, genetic factors may play a role in the determination of the critical upper limit of adipocyte size at which organ hyperplasia is stimulated at any age. The interrelationship of adipocyte number and size is important to the understanding of possible homeostatic mechanisms regulating the net size of the adipose organ (Faust, Johnson, & Hirsch, 1977; Leibel, 1977).

In summary, obesity is considered by many knowledgeable physicians, nutritionists, and epidemiologists to be one of the major medical problems confronting Western, industrialized societies. Because obesity-related morbidity (such as stroke and coronary artery disease) is difficult to attribute directly to excessive adipose organ mass (as opposed to its frequent accompanying hypertension and glucose intolerance) (Gordon & Kannel, 1976), no specific body composition can be implicated, and therefore no outcome-related definition of obesity can be composed. Generally, statistical definitions have been used, but these are not ideal because of their reliance on definitions of "ideal" body weight. Societies have established aesthetic yardsticks that strongly influence the self-diagnosis of obesity. This circumstance will certainly persist until data are available to establish the relationship of body composition to morbidity and mortality over a fairly narrow range of body compositions (e.g., 15%–40% of body weight as fat). Even the availability of such information is no guarantee that the long-dominant aesthetic guidelines will not continue to prevail in directing popular attitudes toward energy-related nutrition.

It must be accepted that obesity ultimately is due to an energy imbalance, with intake exceeding output during the period of weight gain. Although isolated derangements of either food intake or energy expenditure have been described in animals, the relative contributions of these two factors to human obesity remain an area of much debate and research. The potent influence of environment on food intake in man further complicates the analysis of these interactions.

The Committee on Nutrition of the American Academy of Pediatrics (1981) has reviewed recommendations for the prevention and management of obesity that are based on new concepts regarding its pathophysiology. There is only weak evidence that transient environmental manipulation (such as food restriction) can permanently alter the complex systems subserving energy homeostasis. Thus, great caution should be exercised in proposing stringent dietary regimens in early life for the purpose of preventing subsequent obesity. Recommendations for "ideal" body composition should be based on age- and sex-specific data regarding morbidity at various degrees of adiposity. Likewise, recommendations for prevention and therapy should reflect data on both optimal timing and efficacy of proposed interventions. Unfortunately, these data are not available. It is generally agreed that mortality rates become significantly excessive when body weight is more than 30% above "desirable" levels (Seltzer, 1966). Morbidity—expressed as diabetes mellitus, gall bladder disease, hypertension, and coronary artery disease—increases with the degree of obesity (Van Itallie & Hirsch, 1979). However, these relationships are not simple. It appears that obesity itself is to some extent a reflection of those same genetic and environmental factors that predispose to diabetes, hypertension, and changes in plasma lipids. These latter factors and obesity may independently increase the risk of coronary artery disease. The impact of excess adiposity on both morbidity and mortality is most striking in subjects between 20 and 40 years of age, and the age at which obesity sets in may substantially influence the risk associated with any degree of obesity. Abraham and his co-workers reported that the incidence of certain types of blood vessel disease was highest in subjects who had become overweight as adults (Abraham, Collins, & Nordsieck, 1971). Finally, as Keys and others have emphasized, the major factor increasing the risk of cardiovascular disease in these subjects is the hypertension which is commonly associated with obesity, and not the obesity itself. Thus, control of blood pressure in the obese, whether by weight reduction or by other means, would much reduce their excess morbidity and mortality (Keys, 1980).

If one nonetheless accepts the prevailing social and scientific notion that obesity should be prevented, it remains difficult to know at exactly what point in the life cycle it would be best to intervene. As noted earlier, infant feeding practices in the first year of life do not appear to be particularly good predictors of the risk of obesity (Dubois et al., 1979), and restriction of food intake during the early years of life does not appear to alter the risk of obesity in adolescence (Peckham, Stark, Simonite, & Wolff, 1983). Such data suggest that prophylactic and therapeutic measures should probably be directed at children in late childhood and early adolescence. There is, however, no firm evidence that the treatment of obesity in its incipience will prevent its occurrence in the adult. In fact, if the genetic data described earlier are correct, such treatment might in many circumstances be little more than an ultimately futile effort to stall the phenotypic expression of genotype (Hager, Sjostrom, Arvidsson, et al., 1978).

In individual instances, an obese child's rate of weight gain may be limited by a combination of caloric restriction and increased physical activity. Although contrary to popular misconceptions, obese children are no more prone to hypoactivity than their normal-weight peers (Brownell & Stunkard, 1980). Encouraging vigorous physical exercise, if successful, will reduce the excess of caloric intake over expenditure. Therapeutic weight reduction in a growing child should be undertaken only under close medical supervision, because caloric restriction may interfere with skeletal growth and thereby reduce ultimate height (Pugliese, Lifshitz, Grad, Fort, & Marks-Katz, 1983).

In the area of public health policy, it is clear that eliminating severe (wt/ht greater than 130% of ideal) cases of obesity in the population could prevent considerable adult morbidity and mortality, particularly that related to hypertension and diabetes mellitus. Primary prevention would be the ideal means of achieving this end, but given our current level of understanding of the disorder this often is not possible. At present it would seem most reasonable to focus prophylactic measures on children at risk by virtue of family history, with particular attention to weight control at adolescence. Therapeutic weight reduction should be recommended for those obese adults showing evidence of associated complications, such as hypertension, glucose intolerance, and the like. Weight loss should continue until these problems are corrected but not necessarily to the point where the patient has achieved "normal" weight. Weight control should be regarded as a medical rather than a cosmetic issue. Also of considerable benefit would be efforts to educate the public about obesity. Enhanced public sophistication about obesity would reduce the enormous waste of resources on diet books, ill-conceived and dangerous diet regimens, and various nostrums. In the long term, both the mechanisms of energy homeostasis and the ontogeny of the adipose organ in the human require much more research before rational prophylaxis and treatment of obesity can be achieved.

Diet and Disease

The possible contribution of diet in the etiology of certain prevalent diseases, such as ischemic heart disease, in the American population has been a critical issue in public health nutrition and a concern for public policy. There is no consensus regarding the interpretation of scientific data on the diet-disease equation, except for the relationship of sodium and hypertension. Scientists and policymakers appear to have interpreted the same information differently and, therefore, have arrived at different estimates of the risks and benefits of consuming or avoiding specific foods and food constituents, or of the optimal amounts that should or can be consumed (NAS/NRC 1980; U.S. Senate Select Committee on Nutrition and Human Needs, 1977). Those involved in these controversies present cogent and articulate defenses of their positions, and the discrepancies appear to result from a lack of conclusive evidence rather than from specific errors in the interpretation of the available information.

Controversy about diet and disease is inevitable when food constituents placed on one side of the equation (e.g., cholesterol and salt) are part of virtually all daily diets in the United States. Dietary habits involve behaviors that are ingrained in our culture and our lives. Moreover, on the other side of the equation, entities such as ischemic heart disease and cancer are the major cause of death in the United States (Stallones, 1980).

HEART DISEASE

The prevalence of ischemic heart disease has declined steadily in the last 3 decades, yet heart and blood vessel diseases continue to be the most frequent causes of death in the United States (Stallones, 1980). They caused nearly 650,000 deaths in 1978 (the last year for which data are available). Coronary artery disease was the cause of one-third of deaths from all causes for persons between 35 and 64 years of age.

Hypercholesterolemia and hypertension are considered to be among the most potent, proximate causes of ischemic heart disease. Both conditions may have an early onset and are affected by such factors as genotype, age, race, associated medical problems, stress, and diet.

The cholesterol theory of vascular disease (Connor & Connor, 1972) postulates that the quantity and quality of dietary fat influence serum cholesterol levels, which in turn affect the integrity of the blood vessels and, hence, blood circulation. A cause-effect relationship between hypercholesterolemia and atherosclerotic heart disease has not been proved conclusively, but there are physiological and epidemiological data that support a causal relationship (Connor, 1981). A frequently cited study conducted in seven countries (Finland, Japan, Greece, the Netherlands, the United States, Italy, and Yugoslavia) showed that the national prevalence of coronary artery disease varied as a function of dietary fat (Keys, 1980). In another cross-national epidemiological study, the average intakes of cholesterol, total fat, protein, total calories, and animal fat showed correlations with coronary artery disease above .60 (Connor & Connor, 1972). Experimental manipulation of cholesterol intake can affect rates and severity of coronary artery disease. In primates, for example, cholesterol-free diets led to significant regression in experimentally induced atherosclerosis (Armstrong, Warner, & Connor, 1970).

However, intervention trials that have explored diet modifications designed to decrease the incidence of coronary artery disease have had negative results (NAS/NRC, 1980). Seven large-scale studies were conducted in London, Oslo, Helsinki, New York City, New Jersey, and Los Angeles. Results indicated that significant decrements in serum cholesterol concentrations were associated only marginally with decreases in the incidence of coronary disease and had no effect on overall mortality. Moreover, the results of five large-scale clinical trials, involving 18,000 men over a span of 5 years and employing hypocholesterolemic drugs, indicated unimpressive reductions in the incidence of coronary artery disease, while some unpredicted toxicities were observed.

HYPERTENSION

National Health and Nutrition Survey data indicate an 18% prevalence of hypertension among individuals 18–74 years old (Stallones, 1980); prevalence rates are 28% and 29% among black males and females, respectively. Although many factors (e.g., dietary sodium, potassium, fats, obesity) have been associated with hypertension, sodium and obesity have received the greatest attention. In the average U.S. diet, the major source of sodium is table salt (sodium chloride). In 1 gram of sodium chloride there are approximately 400 mg of sodium. The range of usual sodium intake is 3.9–4.7 grams per day, and the prevalence of hypertension is positively associated with the quantity of sodium intake within population. Restriction of sodium intake can reduce blood pressure and is employed commonly as part of the treatment of hypertension.

Obesity is considered a risk factor for heart disease, both independently and through its association with hypertension and diabetes mellitus. There is a positive correlation between body weight and blood pressure (Van Itallie & Hirsch, 1979); obese hypertensive persons often show a decline in blood pressure with weight loss. Obesity, however, is not the sole cause of hypertension; not all obese persons are hypertensive, and hypertensive individuals may have normal body composition.

CANCER

The second leading cause of death in the United States since 1940 has been cancer. Whereas the incidence of coronary artery disease has decreased, the incidence of cancer has increased. At present, the incidence per 100,000 persons is approximately 186. Deaths from cancer occur in approximately 20% of the population.

Fats, nitrates, vitamin A, carotene, and riboflavin (vitamin B_2) are among the dietary factors associated with different forms of cancer in epidemiological, clinical, and experimental studies (Rivlin, 1982). Cross-national studies indicate a significant correlation between per capita fat consumption and age-adjusted mortality rates from colonic cancer (Graham & Mettlin, 1979; Wynder, McCoy, Reddy, Cohen, Hill, Spingarn, & Weisburger, 1981). The risk of colon cancer, however, is altered among migrants who adopt the eating habits of their new locales. For example, the prevalence of colon cancer increases among immigrants from Japan to the United States; conversely, their risk of stomach cancer is decreased (Haenszel, Berg, Kurihara, & Locke, 1975; Haenszel & Kurihara, 1968).

In several countries where studies have been made, an inverse relationship between levels of vitamin A consumption and cancer has been shown. In the United States, the prevalence of lung cancer among smokers decreases with increases in vitamin A consumption (Rivlin, 1982). There is evidence of a negative correlation, however, between the intake of riboflavin and the prevalence of cancer. In animals, riboflavin deficiency may inhibit the growth of experimentally induced tumors (Rivlin, 1982);

conversely, high intakes of riboflavin increase the rate of tumor growth in animals. Yet no mechanisms have been identified whereby a high intake of vitamin A or a low intake of riboflavin may contribute to the prevention of cancer, and the exact nature of these relationships is not well understood.

DIETARY LINKS TO DISEASE

Few of the data reviewed have demonstrated causality between diet and specific diseases, except those showing an improvement in hypertension following decreased intake of sodium. To what extent do inconclusive data and lack of consensus regarding their significance preclude a clearly focused nutrition policy? The widespread prevalence of heart disease and cancer and the increasing interest in their prevention has prompted federal agencies to address this issue.

The U.S. Senate Select Committee on Nutrition and Human Needs (1977) published the first edition of the *Dietary Goals for the United States* in response to data relating diet to coronary artery disease and cancer, expert testimony delivered during the 1974 National Nutrition Policy hearings, and guidelines established by various professional organizations in the United States. The committee recommendations, released in February 1977, provoked extensive discussion and controversy. Arguments ensued about the scientific basis for the dietary goals outlined in the committee report. Further Senate hearings were held to which scientists and members of the agriculture and food industries were invited, and in December 1977 a revised edition of the dietary goals was published. The following recommendations were included:

(1) if overweight, decrease energy intake and increase energy expenditure;
(2) increase the consumption of complex carbohydrates and "naturally occurring" sugars from about 28% of energy intake to about 48% of energy intake;
(3) reduce the consumption of refined and processed sugars by about 45% to account for about 10% of total energy intake;
(4) reduce overall fat consumption from approximately 40% to about 30% of total energy intake;
(5) reduce saturated fat consumption to account for about 10% of total energy intake, and balance that with polyunsaturated and monounsaturated fats, which should each account for about 10% of energy intake;
(6) reduce cholesterol consumption to about 300 mg per day; and
(7) limit the intake of sodium by reducing the intake of salt to about 5 grams per day.

The foreword to the second edition of the dietary goals reflected the serious reservations that some members of the Senate select committee had about the scientific basis of the recommendations. Their concern arose because of the disagreements among scientists about the efficacy of adherence to such dietary guidelines. Their reservations are illustrated in the following statement: "The value of dietary change remains controversial and science cannot at this time insure that an altered diet will provide improved protection from certain killer diseases, such as heart disease and cancer."

In 1979 the first Report on Health Promotion and Disease Prevention of the Surgeon General was published. This document noted that a relationship between diet and certain diseases was known or suspected. Dietary guidelines were outlined that were in keeping with the *Dietary Goals for the United States*. However, no recommendations were made about specific levels of consumption. This report concluded that the health of the U.S. population had never been better.

The Food and Nutrition Board of the National Academy of Sciences/ National Research Council (NAS/NRC, 1980) published a document, *Toward Healthful Diets*, which questioned the validity and justification of the Senate's dietary goals. This document exemplified the extensive disagreement among scientists in the interpretation of nutritional data relevant to health policies. At the outset, the board concluded that "it is scientifically unsound to make all-inclusive recommendations to the public regarding intakes of energy, protein, fat, cholesterol, carbohydrates, fiber, and sodium" (p. 4). The board advised that recommendations be made only when scientific data from various sources resulted in a consensus.

In regard to coronary artery disease, the board noted that "the causes of atherosclerosis are unknown." The board acknowledged the existence of dietary risk factors but said that these factors "cannot, without independent evidence, be considered causative agents of the disease . . . at the present time only 50 percent of the risk in persons in the United States for coronary artery disease can be accounted statistically by recognized risk factors. Thus, much additional research is necessary to understand fully the multiple etiology of coronary atherosclerosis" (p. 9). The rationale for inaction until all sources of risk had been elucidated fully was not established.

The Food and Nutrition Board concluded from available data that a reduction in the level of fat intake below 40% of total calories probably was not necessary for infants, adolescents, pregnant teenage girls, and adults performing heavy manual labor. However, sedentary persons attempting to control weight were advised to reduce the caloric density of their diets by reducing the intake of fat. The board also concluded that it was unwarranted to recommend an increase in the ratio of of dietary polyunsaturated to saturated fat ratio except for individuals in high-risk categories.

In the context of the conflicting recommendations of the Senate select committee and the Food and Nutrition Board, the following statement by Mazur (1973) is particularly relevant: "We generally assume that informed scientific evidence is valuable to political policy makers. However, in the context of controversial political issues, and when the relevant technical analysis is ambiguous, then the value of scientific advice becomes questionable. A technical controversy sometimes creates confusion rather than clarity, and it is possible that the dispute itself may become so divisive and widespread that scientific advice becomes more of a cost than a benefit to the policy maker and society."

Mazur's statement refers to environmental and technological hazards and may be harsh when applied to the controversy in nutrition policy. Yet, it was evident that the disagreements between the Senate's dietary goals and the recommendations of the Food and Nutrition Board were substantial. The lay population, without expert knowledge in nutritional science, must have had difficulty reconciling the disagreements.

SUMMARY AND CONCLUSION

In these discussions we have considered the complex problems involved in establishing policies in public health nutrition. These problems stem primarily from the need to integrate many disciplines in order to achieve this goal. Data must be considered from the points of view of a broad range of interests. At one end of the range is nutritional biochemistry, concerned with the utilization of nutrients by cellular organelles and the integrated outcomes measured in the person; at the other end are the sociological, anthropological, and economic determinants of behavior related to food. Moreover, public health nutrition must face issues of social equity, poverty, and income distribution, which ultimately escape the boundaries of scientific inquiry and enter into the domain of political ideology and social values. Given our pluralistic society, it may be idealistic to expect nutrition policymakers to arrive at a consensus, but nonetheless the interests of humanitarians, economists, and scientists must be integrated in order to produce sound nutrition policy.

In analyzing the concern within the United States about undernutrition and its functional consequences, and in looking at the response of the government through food assistance programs, we have seen the problems encountered when programs implemented for other than scientific reasons are submitted to scientific evaluation. The issue of whether it is appropriate to expand these programs has been raised. This critical decision cannot be based solely on scientific judgments; the issues at hand often are not scientific but are social and economic. It now is recognized that the United States has a population of poor people. The provision of food to the poor has been validated in this country as a response to a social and economic problem. Questioning the efficiency and effectiveness of this response is legitimate. However, the question of its effectiveness in solving health problems must be considered a separate issue.

Selected applications of the scientific process to test the cognitive effects of undernutrition, the functional benefits of breast milk, and the etiology of obesity were discussed in order to emphasize the intricacies in the processes underlying the development of sound nutrition policy.

Mild-to-moderate protein-energy malnutrition (PEM) was established as a relevant factor in the mental development of children. Among populations where PEM is endemic, children with a history of undernutrition perform less well in tests of learning and intelligence than children who are better nourished. Yet, the precise nature of the causal relationship between PEM and subsequent cognitive deficits has not been defined. PEM is one factor in a complex array of risk factors within a stressful economic and cultural context, and the array is believed to vary among environments. For this reason it is not surprising that nutrition supplementation to nutritionally at-risk pregnant and lactating women and infants fails to result in improved performance by the children in tests of general intelligence or learning or in later school performance. Conversely, significant gains are obtained in the cognitive development of these children when they are exposed in infancy or early childhood to multifactorial intervention programs that include nutrition supplementation, educational stimulation, and health care.

Assessments of the effects of undernutrition on cognition have been compromised by a lack of normative validity. The diagnostic sensitivity of the tests is thereby limited, as is the possibility of establishing criteria of performance. Moreover, this research has followed a traditional medical model of disease causality; the model itself is an obstacle in the perception of PEM as one of several risk factors that synergistically affect cognitive development.

We considered approaches to improving the health status of infants by reviewing the scientific bases for recommending human milk as the ideal food. Laboratory data obtained under highly controlled conditions cannot be confidently extrapolated to the infant feeding practices of free-living populations. Interpreting field observations is made equally problematic by the inability to control all significant confounding variables. At the present time, the judgment has been made that the health of infants may be significantly safeguarded by the provision of human milk, but the implementation of this recommendation has not been unequivocal, as demonstrated by the government allocation of resources in the WIC program. Obviously there is a need to determine the extent of anticipated benefits more precisely. An improved data base must describe nutritional well-being from measurements of specific areas of functional competence. This has received limited attention and represents major methodological and conceptual challenges.

Throughout history, definitions of obesity have been influenced by aesthetic values and social-cultural standards that determined dietary practices and the feeding of infants and children. Currently, there is no positive social reinforcement for obesity; in fact, in some cases obesity may be socially stigmatized. In its extreme form (wt/ht greater than 130%) obesity is recognized as a health risk factor; its causal role in diabetes, hypertension, cardiovascular disease, and gall bladder disease has been established. Mild-to-moderate obesity, however, has not been proved to be a health risk factor, and its contribution to the diseases in question is not firmly established.

The lay public and nutritionists, physicians, and public health workers alike have assumed a causal association between childhood and adult obesity, but without conclusive evidence. Because of these assumptions, the disfavor of obesity in our society, and the health risks alleged for even mild forms of obesity, it has also been popularly believed that early dietary management has a preventive public health value. Controlled caloric intake and a systematic program of physical activity from early life are presumed to have a prophylactic effect that enhances our chances of a long life. However, these postulates rely heavily on animal experimentation and ignore the evidence of genetic contributions to body composition. In modern society lean bodies are preferred, and obesity is implicitly rejected and alleged, without warrant, to be a health risk.

Currently, it seems reasonable to focus prophylactic measures on children who, by virtue of family history, are at risk and to give particular attention to weight control during adolescence. Therapeutic weight reduction should be recommended for those adults showing evidence of associated complications. However, weight should be lost only to the point at which weight-related problems are corrected, not necessarily to the point where "normal" weight is achieved.

A final objective of the chapter was to analyze the conflicts that arise when inconclusive scientific data are used to address significant health concerns. Often scientists and policymakers interpret data differently. Contrasts were noted between the *Dietary Goals for the United States* published by a U.S. Senate select committee (1977) and the recommendations of the National Academy of Sciences/National Research Council (1980) in their document *Towards a Healthy Diet*. Yet, these conflicts may be beneficial if they lead to further research and ultimately to more accurate judgments and efficacious policies.

Although nutrition policy ideally should be based on sound scientific documentation, policymakers must often make decisions on the basis of inconclusive evidence. Nevertheless, on issues that critically affect health and general well-being, scientists and policymakers must conscientiously provide nutrition information to the public in a form that can be easily understood and that presents appropriate options.

REFERENCES

Abraham, S., Collins, G., & Nordsieck, M. Relationship of childhood weight status to morbidity in adults. *H.S.M.H.A. Health Reports*, 1971, 86, 273–284.

Adebonojo, F. O. Artificial versus breastfeeding: Relation to infant health in a middle class American community. *Clinical Pediatrics*, 1972, 11, 25–29.

American Academy of Pediatrics/American College of Obstetricians and Gynecologists (AAP/ ACOG). Maternal and newborn nutrition. In A. W. Brann & R. C. Cefalo (Eds.), *Guidelines for prenatal care*. Evanston, Ill.: AAP/ACOG, 1983.

Armstrong, M. L., Warner, E. D., & Connor, W. E. Regression of coronary atheromatosis in rhesus monkeys. *Circulation Research*, 1970, 27, 202–208.

Asher, P. Fat babies and fat children: The prognosis of obesity in the very young. *Archives of Diseases in Childhood*, 1966, 41, 672–673.

Austin, J. E., & Hitt, C. *Nutrition intervention in the United States*. Cambridge, Mass.: Ballinger, 1979.

Austin, J. E., & Quelch J. A. U.S. national dietary goals: Food industry threat or opportunity. *Food Policy*, 1979, 4, 107–115.

Balderston, J. B., Wilson, A. B., Freire, M. E., & Simonen, M. S. *Malnourished children of the rural poor*. Boston: Auburn, 1981.

Barnes, R. H., Cunnold, S. R., Zimmerman, R. R., Simmons, H., MacLeod, R. B., & Krook, L. Influence of nutritional deprivations in early life on learning behavior of rats as measured by performance in a water maze. *Journal of Nutrition*, 1966, 89, 399–410.

Barnes, R. H., Moore, A. U., & Pond, W. G. Behavioral abnormalities in young adult pigs caused by malnutrition in early life. *Journal of Nutrition*, 1970, 100, 149–155.

Berglund, G., Bjorntorp, P., Sjostrom, L., & Smith, U. The effects of early malnutrition in men on body composition and adipose tissue cellularity at adult age. *Acta Medica Scandinavica*, 1974, 195, 213–216.

Birch, H. G., Pineiro, C., Alcalde, E., Toca, T., & Cravioto, J. Relation of kwashiorkor in early childhood and intelligence at school age. *Pediatric Research*, 1971, 5, 579–585.

Biron, O., Mongeau, J-G., & Bertrand, D. Familial resemblance of bodyweight and weight/ height in 374 homes with adopted children. *Journal of Pediatrics*, 1977, 91, 555–558.

Bjorntorp, P., Bengtsson, C., Blohme, G., Jonsson, A., Sjostrom, L., Tibblin, E., Tibblin, G., & Whilhelmsen, L. Adipose tissue fat cell size and number in relation to metabolism in randomly selected middle-aged men and women. *Metabolism*, 1971, 20, 927–935.

Borjeson, M. The aetiology of obesity in children. *Acta Paediatrica Scandinavica*, 1976, 65, 279–287.

Broad, W. J. Academy says curb on cholesterol not needed. *Science*, 1980, 208, 1354–1355.

Brockman, L., & Ricciuti, H. Severe protein-calorie malnutrition and cognitive development in infancy and early childhood. *Developmental Psychology*, 1971, **4**, 312–319.

Brook, C. G. D., Huntley, R. M. C., & Slack, J. Influence of heredity and environment in determination of skinfold thickness in children. *British Medical Journal*, 1975, **2**, 719–721.

Brook, C. G. D., Lloyd, J. K., & Wolff, O. H. Relationship between age of onset of obesity and size and number of adipose cells. *British Medical Journal*, 1972, **2**, 25–27.

Brownell, K. D., & Stunkard, A. J. Physical activity in the development and control of obesity. In A. J. Stunkard (Ed.), *Obesity*. Philadelphia, Pa.: Saunders, 1980.

Butte, N. B., Garza, C., Smith, E. O., & Nichols, B. L. Human milk intake and growth performance of exclusively breastfed infants. *Journal of Pediatrics*, 1984, **104**, 187–195.

Chandra, R. K. Prospective studies of the effect of breast-feeding on evidence of infection and allergy. *Acta Paediatrica Scandinavica*, 1979, **68**, 691–694.

Chandra, R. K. Breastfeeding, growth, and morbidity. *Nutrition Research*, 1981, **1**, 25–31.

Charney, E., Goodman, H. C., McBride, M., Lyon, B., & Pratt, R. Childhood antecedents of adult obesity: Do chubby infants become obese adults? *New England Journal of Medicine*, 1976, **295**, 6–9.

Chase, H. P., & Martin, H. P. Undernutrition and development. *New England Journal of Medicine*, 1970, **282**, 933–939.

Chavez, A., & Martinez, C. *Growing up in a developing community*. Guatemala City: Institute of Nutrition of Central America and Panama (INCAP), United Nations University, 1979.

Chen, L. C., Chowdhurry, L., & Huffman, S. L. Anthropometric assessment of energy-protein malnutrition and subsequent risk of mortality among preschool children. *American Journal of Clinical Nutrition*, 1980, **33**, 1836–1845.

Citizen's Board of Inquiry into Hunger and Malnutrition in the United States. *Hunger USA*. Washington, D.C.: New Community Press, 1969.

Committee on Nutrition of the American Academy of Pediatrics. Commentary on breastfeeding and infant formula (including proposed standards for formulas). *Pediatrics*, 1976, **57**, 278–285.

Committee on Nutrition of the American Academy of Pediatrics. Commentary on nutritional aspects of obesity in infancy and childhood. *Pediatrics*, 1981, **68**, 850–853.

Connor, W. E. U.S. dietary goals: A pro view, with special emphasis upon the etiological relationships of dietary factors to coronary heart disease. In P. J. Garry (Ed.), *Human nutrition: Clinical and biochemical aspects*. Proceedings of the Fourth Arnold O. Beckman Conference in Clinical Chemistry. Portsmouth, N.H.: American Association of Clinical Chemistry, 1981.

Connor, W. E., & Connor, S. L. The key role of nutritional factors in the prevention of coronary heart disease. *Preventive Medicine*, 1972, **1**, 49–83.

Cronbach, L. J. Test validation. In R. L. Thorndike (Ed.), *Educational measurement* (2d. ed.). Washington, D.C.: American Council on Education, 1971.

Cunningham, A. S. Morbidity in breastfed and artificially fed infants, II. *Journal of Pediatrics*, 1979, **95**, 685–689.

Dagan, R., & Pridan, H. Relationship of breastfeeding versus bottlefeeding with emergency room visits and hospitalization for infectious diseases. *European Journal of Pediatrics*, 1982, **139**, 192–194.

Dauncey, M. J., & Gairdner, D. Size of adipose cells in infancy. *Archives of Diseases in Childhood*, 1975, **50**, 286–290.

DeLicardie, E. R., & Cravioto, J. Behavioral responsiveness of survivors of clinically severe malnutrition to cognitive demands. In J. Cravioto, L. Hambraeus, & B. Vahlquist (Eds.), *Early malnutrition and mental development*. Uppsala: Almqvist & Wiksell, 1974.

DeSwiet, M., Fayers, P., & Cooper, L. Effect of feeding habits on weight in infancy. *Lancet*, 1977, **1**, 892–894.

Dewey, K. G., & Lonnerdahl, B. Nutrition, growth, and fatness of breastfed infants from one to six months. *Federation Proceedings*, 1982, **41**, 352. (Abstract)

Dobbing, J. The later development of the brain and its vulnerability. In J. A. Davis & J. Dobbing (Eds.), *Scientific foundations of paediatrics*, Philadelphia: Saunders, 1974.

Downham, M. A. P. S., Scott, R., Sims, D.G., Webb, J. K. G., & Gardner, P. S. Breast-feeding protects against respiratory syncytial virus infections. *British Medical Journal*, 1976, **2**, 274–276.

Dubois, S., Hill, D. E., & Beaton, G. H. An examination of factors believed to be associated with infantile obesity. *American Journal of Clinical Nutrition*, 1979, **32**, 1997–2004.

Edozien, J. C., Switzer, B. R., & Bryan, R. B. Medical evaluation of the Special Supplemental Food Program for Women, Infants, and Children. *American Journal of Clinical Nutrition*, 1979, **32**, 677–692.

Edwards, L. N., & Grossman, M. The relationships between children's health and intellectual development. In S. Mushkin (Ed.), *Health: What is it worth?* Measure of Health Benefits, Pergamon Policy Studies. New York: Pergamon, 1979.

Eid, E. E. Follow-up of physical growth of children who had excessive weight gain in the first six months of life. *British Medical Journal*, 1970, **2**, 74–76.

Farquahar, J. W. Prognosis for babies born to diabetic mothers in Edinburgh. *Archives of Diseases in Childhood*, 1969, **44**, 36–47.

Faust, I. M., Johnson, P. R., & Hirsch J. Surgical removal of adipose tissue alters feeding behavior and the development of obesity in rats. *Science*, 1977, **197**, 393–396.

Faust, I. M., Johnson, P. R., Stern, J. S., & Hirsch, J. Diet-induced adipocyte number increase in adult rats: A new model of obesity. *American Journal of Physiology*, 1978, **235**, E279–E286.

Fergusson, D. M., Horwood, L. J., Shannon, F. T., & Taylor, B. Infant health and breast-feeding during the first 16 weeks of life. *Australian Pediatric Journal*, 1978, **14**, 254–258.

Foch, T. T., & McClearn, G. E. Genetics, body weight and obesity. In A. J. Stunkard (Ed.), *Obesity*. Philadelphia: Saunders, 1980.

Food and Agriculture Organization of the United Nations/World Health Organization (FAO/WHO). *Energy and protein requirements*. Report of a joint FAO/WHO ad hoc expert committee (WHO Technical Report Series No. 522). Geneva: FAO/WHO, 1973.

Food and Nutrition Service. *Management information data*. Washington, D.C., June 17, 1983.

Forbes, G. B., & Reina, J. C. Adult lean body mass declines with age: Some longitudinal observations. *Metabolism*, 1970, **19**, 653–663.

Frankova, S., & Barnes, R. H. Effect of malnutrition in early life on avoidance conditioning and behavior of adult rats. *Journal of Nutrition*, 1968, **96**, 485–493.

Galler, J. R., Ramsey, F., Solimano, G., & Lowell, W. E. The influence of early malnutrition on subsequent behavioral development, II: Classroom behavior. *Journal of the American Adademy of Child Psychiatry*, 1983, **22**, 16–22.

Garn, S. M., & Clark, D. C. Trends in fatness and the origins of obesity. *Pediatrics*, 1976, **57**, 443–456.

Gaull, G. E., Jensen, R. G., Rassin, D. K., & Malloy, M. H. Human milk as food. In A. Milunsky, E. A. Friedman, & L. Gluck (Eds.), *Advances in perinatal medicine* (Vol. 2). New York: Plenum, 1981.

Ginsburg-Fellner, F. Growth of adipose tissue in infants, children and adolescents: Variations in growth disorders. *International Journal of Obesity*, 1981, **5**, 605–611.

Goldblum, R. M., Ahlstedt, S., Carlsson, B., Hanson, L. A., Jodal, V., Lindin-Janson, G., & Sohl, A. Antibody forming cells in human colostrum after oral immunization. *Nature*, 1975, **257**, 797–799.

Goldman, A. S., Garza, C., & Goldblum, R. M. Immunologic components in human milk during the second year of lactation. *Acta Paediatrica Scandinavica*, 1983, **72**, 461–462.

Goldman, A. S., Garza, C., Nichols, B. L., & Goldblum, R. Immunologic factors in human milk during the first year of lactation. *Journal of Pediatrics*, 1982, **100**, 563–567.

Goldman, A. S., Garza, C., Nichols, B. L., Smith, E. O., & Goldblum, R. M. Immunologic components in human milk during gradual weaning. *Acta Paediatrica Scandinavica*, 1983, **72**, 133–134.

Goldman, A. S., & Goldblum, R. M. Antiinfective properties of human milk. *Pediatric Update*, 1980, **2**, 359–363.

Goldman, A. S., & Goldblum, R. M. Protective properties of human milk. In W. A. Walker & J. Watkins (Eds.), *Nutrition in pediatrics: Basic sciences and clinical applications*. Boston: Little, Brown, 1982.

Gordon, T., & Kannel, W. B. Obesity and cardiovascular diseases: The Framingham study. *Clinics in Endocrinology and Metabolism*, 1976, **5**, 367–375.

Graham, S., & Mettlin, C. Diet and colon cancer. *American Journal of Epidemiology*, 1979, **109**, 1–20.

Grantham-McGregor, S., & Desai, P. A home visiting intervention programme with Jamaican mothers and children. *Developmental Medicine and Child Neurology*, 1975, **17**, 605–613.

Grantham-McGregor, S., Stewart, M., Powell, C., & Schofield, W. N. Effect of stimulation on mental development of malnourished child. *Lancet*, 1979, pp. 200–201.

Grinker, J. A. Behavioral and metabolic factors in childhood obesity. In M. Lewis & L. A. Rosenblum (Eds.), *The uncommon child*. New York: Plenum, 1981.

Grulee, C. G., Sanford, H. N., & Herron, P. H. Breast and artificial feeding: Influence on morbidity and mortality of twenty thousand infants. *Journal of the American Medical Association*, 1934, **103**, 735–739.

Gurr, M. I., & Kirtland, J. Adipose tissue cellularity, review 1: Techniques for studying cellularity. *International Journal of Obesity*, 1978, **2**, 401–427.

Gyorgy, P. A hitherto unrecognized biochemical difference between human milk and cow's milk. *Pediatrics*, 1953, **11**, 98–108.

Haenszel, W. M., Berg, J. W., Segi, M., Kurihara, M., & Locke, F. L. Large bowel cancer in Hawaiian Japanese. *Journal of the National Cancer Institute*, 1975, **51**, 401–414.

Haenszel, W. M., & Kurihara, M. Studies of Japanese migrants, 1: Mortality from cancer and other diseases among Japanese in the United States. *Journal of the National Cancer Institute*, 1968, **40**, 43–68.

Hager, A., Sjostrom, L., Arvidsson, B., Bjorntorp, O., & Smith, U. Body fat and adipose tissue cellularity in infants: A longitudinal study. *Metabolism*, 1977, **26**, 607–614.

Hager, A., Sjostrom, L., Arvidsson, B., et al. Adipose tissue cellularity in obese school girls before and after dietary treatment. *American Journal of Clinical Nutrition*, 1978, **31**, 68–75.

Harper, A. E. Dietary goals: A skeptical view. *American Journal of Clinical Nutrition*, 1978, **31**, 310–321.

Hegstead, D. M. Dietary goals: A progressive view. *American Journal of Clinical Nutrition*, 1978, **31**, 1504–1509.

Herrera, M. G., Mora, J. O., Christiansen, N., Clement, J. R., Vuori, L., Waber, D.,

DeParedes, B., & Wagner, M. Effects of nutritional supplementation and early education on physical and cognitive development. In R. Turner & H. Reese (Eds.), *Life span developmental psychology*. New York: Academic Press, 1980.

Hertzig, M. E., Birch, H. G., Richardson, S. A., & Tizard, J. Intellectual levels of school children severely malnourished during the first two years of life. *Pediatrics*, 1972, **49**, 814–823.

Hicks, L. E., Langham, R. A., & Takenaka, J. Cognitive and health measures following early nutritional supplementation: A sibling study. *American Journal of Public Health*, 1982, **72**, 1110–1118.

Hide, D. W., & Guyer, B. M. Clinical manifestations of allergy related to breast and cow's milk feeding. *Archives of Disease in Childhood*, 1981, **56**, 712–715.

Hirsch, J., & Batchelor, B. Adipose tissue cellularity in human obesity. *Clinics in Endocrinology and Metabolism*, 1976, **5**, 299–311.

Hirsch, J., & Knittle, J. Cellularity of obese and non-obese adipose tissue. *Federation Proceedings*, 1970, **29**, 1516–1521.

Hsueh, A.M., & Meyer, B. Maternal dietary supplementation and 5-year-old Stanford-Binet IQ tests on the offspring in Taiwan. *Federation Proceedings*, 1981, **40**, 897. (Abstract)

Irvine, S. H., & Carroll, W. K. Testing and assessment across cultures: Issues in methodology and theory. In H. C. Triandis & J. W. Berry (Eds.), *Handbook of cross-cultural psychology: Methodology* (Vol. 2). Boston: Allyn & Bacon, 1980.

Jensen, A. R. Cumulative deficit: A testable hypothesis? *Developmental Psychology*, 1974, **10**, 996–1019.

Jensen, A. R. Cumulative deficit in IQ of blacks in the rural south. *Developmental Psychology*, 1977, **13**, 184–191.

Johnson, P. R., Stern, J. S., Greenwood, M. C. R., Zucker, L. M., & Hirsch, J. Effect of early nutrition on adipose cellularity and pancreatic insulin release in the Zucker rat. *Journal of Nutrition*, 1973, **103**, 738–743.

Joos, S., Pollitt, E., Mueller, W. H., & Albright, D. L. The Bacon Chow Study: Maternal nutritional supplementation and infant behavioral development. *Child Development*, 1983, **54**, 669–676.

Kennedy, E. T., Gershoff, S., Reed, R., & Austin, J. E. Evaluation of the effect of WIC supplemental feeding on birth weight. *Journal of American Dietetic Association*, 1982, **90**, 220–227.

Keys, A. (Ed.). Coronary heart disease in seven countries. *Circulation*, 1970, **41** (Suppl. 1), 1–199.

Keys, A. Overweight, obesity, coronary heart disease and mortality. *Nutrition Review*, 1980, **38**, 297–307.

Keys, A., Fridanza, F., Karvonen, M. J., Kimura, W., & Taylor, H. L. Indices of relative weight and obesity. *Journal of Chronic Diseases*, 1972, **25**, 329–343.

Klein, R. E. Malnutrition and human behavior: A backward glance at an on-going longitudinal study. In D. A. Levitzky (Ed.), *Malnutrition, environment and behavior*. Ithaca, N.Y.: Cornell University Press, 1979.

Knittle, J. L. Adipose tissue development in man. In F. Falkner & J. M. Tanner (Eds.), *Human growth* (Vol. 2): *Postnatal growth*. New York and London: Plenum, 1979.

Knittle, J. L., & Hirsch, J. Effect of early nutrition on the development of rat epididymal fat pads: Cellularity and metabolism. *Journal of Clinical Investigation*, 1968, **47**, 2091–2098.

Knittle, J. L., Timmer, K., Ginsberg-Fellner, F., Brown, R. E., & Katz, D. P. The growth of adipose tissue in children and adolescents: Cross-sectional and longitudinal studies of adipose cell number and size. *Journal of Clinical Investigation*, 1979, **63**, 239–246.

Kruglanski, A. W. Context, meaning and the validity of results in psychological research. *British Journal of Psychology*, 1975, **66**, 373–382.

Larsen, S. A., & Homer, D. R. Relation of breast versus bottlefeeding to hospitalization for gastroenteritis in a middle-class U.S. population. *Journal of Pediatrics*, 1978, **92**, 417–418.

Lasky, R. E., Klein, R. E., Yarbrough, C., Engle, P. L., & Lechtig, A. The relationship between physical growth and infant behavioral development in rural Guatemala. *Child Development*, 1981, **52**, 219–226.

Leibel, R. L. A biologic radar system for the assessment of body mass: The model of a geometry sensitive endocrine system is presented. *Journal of Theoretical Biology*, 1977, **66**, 297–306.

Leibel, R. L. Some aspects of energy metabolism relevant to obesity. In P. J. Garry (Ed.), *Human nutrition: Clinical and biochemical aspects*. Proceedings of the Fourth Arnold O. Beckman Conference in Clinical Chemistry. Portsmouth, N. H.: American Association of Clinical Chemistry, 1981.

Lester, B. M. Cardiac habituation of the orienting response to an auditory signal in infants of varying nutritional status. *Developmental Psychology*, 1975, **11**, 432–442.

Lewis, M. What do we mean when we say infant intelligence scores? A sociopolitical question. In M. Lewis (Ed.), *Origins of intelligence*, New York: Plenum, 1976.

Lewis, M., & McGurk, H. The evaluation of infant intelligence: Infant intelligence scores— true or false? *Science*, 1972, **178**, 1174–1178.

Longen, K. *Domestic food programs: An overview* (U.S. Department of Agriculture, Economic, Statistics and Cooperative Services. ESCS-81). Washington, D.C.: Government Printing Office, August 1981.

Lonnerdahl, B., Forsum, E., & Hambraeus, L. A longitudinal study of the protein, nitrogen, and lactose contents of human milk from Swedish well-nourished mothers. *American Journal of Clinical Nutrition*, 1976, **29**, 1127–1133.

Lozoff, B., Brittenham, G. M., Viteri, F. E., Wolf, A. W., & Urrutia, J. J. The effects of short-term oral iron therapy on developmental deficits in iron deficient anemic children. *Journal of Pediatrics*, 1982, **100**, 351–355.

Mann, G. V. The influence of obesity on health. *New England Journal of Medicine*, 1974, **291**, 178–185, 226–232.

Mata, L. J., & Urrutia, J. J. Intestinal colonization of breastfed children in a rural area of low socioeconomic level. *Annals of the New York Academy of Sciences*, 1971, **176**, 93–109.

Mata, L. J., Urrutia, J. J., Garcia, B., Fernandez, R., & Behar, M. Shigella infection in breastfed Guatemalan Indian neonates. *American Journal of Diseases of Children*, 1969, **117**, 142–146.

Mata, L. J., Urrutia, J. J., & Gordon, J. E. Diarrheal disease in a cohort of Guatemalan village children observed from birth to age two years. *Tropical and Geographical Medicine*, 1967, **19**, 247–257.

Mayer, J. *United States nutrition policies in the seventies*. San Francisco: W. H. Freeman, 1973.

Mazur, A. Disputes between experts. *Minerva*, 1973, **11**, 243–262.

McKay, H., Sinisterra, L., McKay, A., Gomez, H., & Lloreda, P. Improving cognitive ability in chronically deprived children. *Science*, 1978, **200**, 270–278.

Melbin, T., & Vuille, J. C. Physical development at seven years of age in relation to velocity of weight gain in infancy with special reference to overweight. *British Journal of Preventive and Social Medicine*, 1973, **27**, 225–235.

Monckeberg, F. Effects of early marasmic malnutrition on subsequent physical and psychological development. In N. S. Scrimshaw & J. Gordon (Eds.), *Malnutrition, learning and behavior*. Cambridge, Mass.: MIT Press, 1968.

National Academy of Sciences/National Research Council (NAS/NRC). Food and Nutrition Board. *Toward healthful diets*. Washington, D.C.: NAS/NRC, 1980.

National Center for Health Statistics (NCHS). *Growth curves for children birth–18 years* (U.S. Department of Health, Education and Welfare Publication No. [PHS] 78–1650). Washington, D.C.: Government Printing Office, 1978.

National School Lunch Program. Nutritional requirements. Final regulation. *Federal Register*, 1979, **44**, 48149.

Nutrition's own Mount Saint Helen. *Nutrition Today*, 1980, **15**, 6.

Oski, F. A., & Honig, A. S. The effects of therapy on the developmental score of iron deficient infants. *Journal of Pediatrics*, 1978, **92**, 168–172.

Oski, F. A., Honig, A. S., Helu, B., & Howanitz, P. Effect of iron therapy on behavior performance in nonanemic, iron-deficient children. *Pediatrics*, 1983, **71**, 877–880.

Owen, G. M. The nutritional status of the U.S. population. In P. J. Garry (Ed.), *Human nutrition: Clinical and biochemical aspects*. Proceedings of the Fourth Arnold O. Beckman Conference in Clinical Chemistry. Portsmouth, N.H.: American Association of Clinical Chemistry, 1981.

Owen, G. M., Kram, K. M., Garry, J., Lowe, J. E., & Lubin, A. H. A study of nutritional status of preschool children in the United States, 1968–1970. *Pediatrics*, 1974, **53**, 597–646.

Peckham, C. S., Stark, O., Simonite, V., & Wolff, O. H. Prevalence of obesity in British children born in 1946 and 1958. *British Medical Journal*, 1983, **286**, 1237–1242.

Pettitt, D. J., Baird, H. R., Allech, K. A., Bennett, P. H., & Knowler, W. C. Excessive obesity in offspring of Pima Indian women with diabetes during pregnancy. *New England Journal of Medicine*, 1983, **308**, 242–245.

Picciano, M. F., Calkins, E. J., & Garrick, J. R. Milk and mineral intakes of breastfed infants. *Acta Paediatrica Scandinavica*, 1981, **70**, 189–194.

Pollitt, E., Gersovitz, M., & Gargiulo, M. Educational benefits of the United States School Feeding Program: A critical review of the literature. *American Journal of Public Health*, 1978, **68**, 477–485.

Pollitt, E., & Lorimor, R. Effects of WIC on cognitive development. *American Journal of Public Health*, 1983, **73**, 698–700.

Pollitt, E., & Thomson, C. Protein calorie malnutrition and behavior: A view from psychology. In R. J. Wurtman & J. J. Wurtman (Eds.), *Nutrition and the brain* (Vol. 2). New York: Raven, 1977.

Poskitt, E. W., & Cole, T. J. Do fat babies stay fat? *British Medical Journal*, 1977, **1**, 7–9.

Pugliese, M. T., Lifshitz, F., Grad, G., Fort, P., & Marks-Katz, M. Fear of obesity: A cause of short stature and delayed puberty. *New England Journal of Medicine*, 1983, **309**, 513–518.

Rao, D. C., MacLean, C. J., Moreton, N. E., & Yee, S. Analysis of family resemblances, V: Height and weight in northeastern Brasil. *American Journal of Human Genetics*, 1975, **25**, 509–520.

Ravelli, G. P., Stern, Z. A., & Susser, N. W. Obesity in young men after famine exposure in utero and early infancy. *New England Journal of Medicine*, 1976, **295**, 349–353.

Research Subcommittee, South East England Faculty Royal College of General Practitioners. The influence of breastfeeding on the incidence of infectious illness during the first year of life. *Practitioner*, 1972, **209**, 356–362.

Ricciuti, H. N. Adverse social and biological influences on development. In H. McGurck (Ed.), *Ecological factors in human development*. Amsterdam: North-Holland, 1977.

Richardson, S. A. The background histories of school children severely malnourished in infancy. *Advances in Pediatrics*, 1974, 21, 167–195.

Richardson, S. A., Birch, H., & Ragbeer, C. The behavior of children at home who were severely malnourished in the first two years of life. *Journal of Biosocial Science*, 1975, 7, 255–267.

Rivlin, R.S. Nutrition and cancer: State of the art relationship of several nutrients to the development of cancer. *Journal of American College of Nutrition*, 1982, 1, 75–88.

Rodgers, B. Feeding in infancy and later ability and attainment: A longitudinal study. *Developmental Medicine and Child Neurology*, 1978, 20, 421–427.

Rush, D., Stein, Z., & Sussman, M. *Diet in pregnancy: A randomized controlled trial of nutritional supplementation*. New York: Liss, 1980.

Rutishauser, I. H. E., & Whitehead, R. G. Energy intake and expenditure in 1–3-year-old Ugandan children living in a rural environment. *British Journal of Nutrition*, 1972, 28, 145–152.

Sauls, H. S. Potential effects of demographic and other variables in studies comparing morbidity of breastfed and bottlefed infants. *Pediatrics*, 1979, 64, 523–527.

Schacter, O. Otitis media and bottle feeding. *Canadian Journal of Public Health* 1971, 62, 478–489.

School Breakfast Program. *Federal Register*, 1979, 44, 48157.

Scrimshaw, N.S., Garza, C., & Young, V. R. Human protein requirements: Effects of infection and caloric deficiencies. In N. Shimazono (Ed.), *Influences of environmental and host factors on nutritional requirements*. Proceedings of the Symposium Sponsored by the Malnutrition Panel of the United States–Japan Cooperative Medical Science Program. Bethesda, Md.: National Institutes of Health, 1975.

Seltzer, C. C. Some reevaluations of the build and blood pressure study, 1959, as related to ponderal index, somatotype and mortality. *New England Journal of Medicine*, 1966, 274, 254–259.

Shenker, I. R., Fisichelli, V., & Lang, J. Weight differences between foster infants of overweight and non-overweight foster mothers. *Journal of Pediatrics*, 1974, 84, 715–719.

Shields, J. *Monozygotic twins brought up apart and brought up together*. London: Oxford University Press, 1962.

Soth, L. The grain export boom: Should it be tamed? *Foreign Affairs*, 1981, 59, 895–912.

Special Supplemental Food Program for Women, Infants and Children. WIC Legislation. *Federal Register*, 1979, 44, 44422.

Special Supplemental Food Program for Women, Infants and Children. Final rule. *Federal Register*, 1980, 45, 74854.

Stallones, R. A. The rise and fall of ischemic heart disease. *Scientific American*, 1980, 243, 53–59.

Tanner, J. M. *Growth at adolescence*. Oxford: Blackwell Scientific Publications, 1962.

Ten State Nutrition Survey in the United States, 1968–1970 (U.S. Department of Health, Education and Welfare Publication No. [HSM] 72-8130-72-8134). Washington, D.C.: DHEW, 1972.

Terman, L. M., & Merrill, M. A. *Stanford-Binet Intelligence scale: 1972 norms*. Boston: Houghton Mifflin, 1973.

Trowbridge, F. L. Clinical and biochemical characteristics associated with anthropometric nutritional categories. *American Journal of Clinical Nutrition*, 1979, 32, 758–766.

U.S. Congress, Budget Office. *Feeding children: Federal child nutrition policy in the eighties*. Washington, D.C.: Government Printing Office, 1980.

U.S. Department of Agriculture. *Agricultural Statistics, 1981*. Washington, D.C.: Government Printing Office, 1981.

U.S. Department of Agriculture/U.S. Department of Health and Human Services (USDA/ USDHHS). *Nutrition and your health: Dietary guidelines for Americans.* Washington, D.C.: Government Printing Office, 1980.

U.S. Senate Select Committee on Nutrition and Human Needs. *Dietary goals for the United States* (2d ed). Washington, D.C.: Government Printing Office, 1977.

Van Itallie, T. B., & Hirsch, J. Appraisal of excess calories as a factor in the causation of disease. *American Journal of Clinical Nutrition,* 1979, **32,** 2648–2653.

Waber, D. P., Vuori-Christiansen, L., Ortiz, N., Clement, J. R., Christiansen, N. E., Mora, J. O., Reed, R. B., & Herrera, M. G. Nutritional supplementation, maternal education, and cognitive development of infants at risk of malnutrition. *American Journal of Clinical Nutrition,* 1981, **34,** 807–813.

Walker, W. A., & Isselbacher, K. J. Uptake and transport of macromolecules by the intestine: Possible role in clinical disorders. *Gastroenterology,* 1974, **67,** 531–539.

Wallgren, A. Breast milk consumption of healthy full term infants. *Acta Paediatrica Scandinavica,* 1945, **32,** 778–790.

Walter, T., Kovalsky, J., & Stekel, A. Effect of mild iron deficiency on infant mental development scores. *Journal of Pediatrics,* 1983, **102,** 519–522.

Waterlow, J. C. Classification and definition of protein energy malnutrition. In G. H. Beaton & J. M. Bengoa (Eds.), *Nutrition and preventive medicine* (WHO Monograph Series No. 62). Geneva: WHO, 1976.

Waterlow, J. C., & Thomson, A. M. Observations on the adequacy of breastfeeding. *Lancet,* 1979, **2,** 138–142.

Wechsler, D. *Wechsler intelligence scale for children: Manual.* New York: Psychological Corp., 1974.

Welsh, J. K., Shurne, I. J., & May, J. T. Use of semliki forest virus to identify lipid mediated antiviral activity and antialphavirus immunoglobin A in human milk. *Infection and Immunity,* 1978, **19,** 395–401.

Whitehead, R. G., & Paul, A. A. Infant growth and human milk requirements. *Lancet,* 1981, **2,** 161–163.

White House Conference on Food, Nutrition and Health. *Final report.* Washington, D.C.: Government Printing Office, 1969.

Wilkinson, P. W., & Parkin, J. M. Fat cells in childhood obesity. *Lancet,* 1974, **2,** 1522.

Wilson, R. S. Analysis of longitudinal twin data: Basic model and application to physical growth measures. *Acta Geneticae Medicae et Gemellologiae,* 1979, **28,** 93–105.

Winick, M., Meyer, K., & Harris, R. Malnutrition and environmental enrichment by early adoption. *Science,* 1975, **190,** 1173–1175.

Winick, M., & Noble, A. Cellular response in rats during malnutrition at various ages. *Journal of Nutrition,* 1966, **89,** 300–306.

Winick, M., & Noble, A. Cellular response with increased feeding in neonatal rats. *Journal of Nutrition,* 1967, **91,** 179–182.

Winick, M., & Rosso, P. The effect of severe early malnutrition on cellular growth of human brain. *Pediatric Research,* 1969, **3,** 81–184.

Woodbury, R. M. The relationship between breast and artificial feeding and infant mortality. *American Journal of Hygiene,* 1922, **2,** 668–687.

Wynder, E. L., McCoy, G. D., Reddy, B. S., Cohen, L., Hill, P., Spingarn, N. E., & Weisburger, J. H. Nutrition and metabolic epidemiology of cancers of the oral cavity, esophagus, colon, breast, prostate and stomach. In G. R. Newell & N. M. Ellison (Eds.), *Nutrition and cancer: Etiology and treatment,* New York: Raven, 1981.

Yang, R. K. Early infant assessment: An overview. In J. D. Osofsky (Ed.), *Handbook of infant development.* New York: Wiley, 1979.

Zigler, E., Abelson, W.D., Trickett, P. K., & Seitz, V. Is an intervention program necessary in order to improve economically disadvantaged children's IQ scores? *Child Development*, 1982, **53**, 340–348.

Zigler, E., & Berman, W. Discerning the future of early childhood intervention. *American Psychologist*, 1983, **38**, 894–906.

Zigler, E., & Trickett, P. K. IQ, social competence, and evaluation of early childhood intervention programs. *American Psychologist*, 1978, **33**, 789–798.

Political Socialization and Policy: The United States in a Cross-national Context

JUDITH TORNEY-PURTA
University of Maryland

Social policy analysts frequently rely on cost-benefit analysis to show that funds spent on services for children, especially those at risk for educational handicap, are more than compensated for by lessened expenditures for later remedial services. Legislators and the general public recognize that those who do not learn to read in the early years of schooling can be taught later only at greatly increased cost. Thus, compulsory public education is accepted as cost effective.

A similar cost-benefit argument can be applied to civic education and the socialization of political attitudes. But policymakers in the Western democracies have been less aware of the need to foster skills of citizenship—the exercise of rights and responsibilities in the political community—than of the need for other skills. "Isn't one born a citizen?" they ask, or "Can't we rely on telling children to love their country and vote when they are eighteen?" The answer is, of course, that one is not born with political skills any more than one is born a reader. Simply preaching the norms of good citizenship without providing practice in analyzing the situations in which they are to be applied is likely to have little effect. The benefits of civic education—which involves many activities and individuals—may be difficult to measure. Some of the costs of inadequate education, such as increased juvenile crime, may be estimated, but other potential costs, such as alienation from the school or wider political community, are considerably more difficult to measure.

The first reason for attention to political socialization is that in a democracy the formulation of policy alternatives, decision making, imple-

I gratefully acknowledge comments and suggestions made by colleagues who study political education and socialization, especially several specialists from the nations discussed.

mentation, and change are all defined by reference to a community of citizens. Individuals accept the responsibility to abide by laws, but they may also contact their elected representatives when they believe that policies are unsuccessful or bring suit when they believe policies are harmful. In a profound sense the socialization of individuals into the role of citizen does more than ensure their own sense of connection to the political community. It is also a widely accepted way to promote a reasonable level of political stability, to ensure that policies can be examined for appropriateness and justness by those who are affected, and to meet needs that are best achieved through group or community effort. The development of young people's political knowledge and attitudes is both an output from and an input into the policy process.

Second, it is rare that adults critically examine their own political socialization or how that socialization has shaped or limited their effectiveness in political roles. Ignorance in such matters may particularly limit those who are advocates for young people and families. A panel established by the National Academy of Sciences to study federal policymaking noted that "children's representatives inside and outside government have too frequently lacked an adequate understanding of the dynamics of the policy formation process and how most effectively to influence decision making in behalf of children and their families" (Hayes, 1982, p. 76). Few of these individuals understand which governmental actors are in the best position to influence a particular policy, and fewer still understand how to shape policymakers' actions effectively (placing too much reliance on moral persuasion). The panel concludes that the most potent way to improve child and family policy is to improve advocates' understanding of the political process and to assist them in developing better strategies for exercising influence.

A third problem is that psychologists and child development specialists in the United States have paid little attention to the values implicit in their research on social development. Moroney (1981) argues the importance of analyzing social policy with respect to three political values: liberty (promotion of individualism), equality (promotion of equity), and fraternity (promotion of community). He argues, with specific reference to day care, that no policy contributes equally to realizing all three values. When this analytic framework is applied to civic and political education, it is clear that different policies promote these three values to different extents. These values also influence how the interests of two groups—parents and educators—are balanced in political education. Promoting liberty or individualism might require enhanced parental control of political and values education. Promoting fraternity or community might require further control by government or by educators.

Examination of the process of socialization and the promotion of these political values among child policy advocates would be useful even if it were limited to the United States. A cross-national examination has additional advantages: Examining practices guided by differing values can sometimes make explicit one's own implicit assumptions. The international context presents a range of policy options—some of them isolated practices, others elements of complex interrelationships—responsive to a common set of problems. The United States is not the only nation struggling to optimize individual freedom, equality, and community, nor is it the only nation experiencing self-centeredness, injustice, and alienation. The successes and failures of other nations provide naturally occurring experiments that can guide American policy. Finally, cross-national studies provide a context for determining the breadth of applicability of research findings.

Consequently, this chapter first briefly reviews research conducted in the United States on political socialization; second, it assesses the roles, interactions, and interests of families and schools as agents in that socialization; and finally, it examines the policy and results of political socialization and civic education in other countries, with particular attention to the roles, interactions, and interests of these socializing agents. Political socialization in other nations is also examined for the balance achieved among the three values, liberty, equality, and fraternity. This chapter is meant to promote an examination of policymakers' and policy advocates' value assumptions (which are in part the product of their own political socialization); to stimulate a debate on, and further research into, the interests of children, parents, educators, and the state in the process of political socialization; and to propose a framework for the analysis of social and educational policy bearing on political socialization.

POLITICAL SOCIALIZATION RESEARCH IN THE UNITED STATES

In the past 20 years the perceived power of socialization to either maintain or change the political system has made it a fascinating topic, especially among American political scientists. For example, while Hyman's book, *Political Socialization* (1959), required fewer than 170 pages to summarize all of the work published to that date on preadult learning of political attitudes and behavior (and even some tangential research), Renshon's *Handbook of Political Socialization* (1977) required more than 500 pages to summarize 1,200 references.

One of the earliest published pieces of empirical research was Greenstein's interview study of New Haven elementary school children (Greenstein, 1965). His definition of political socialization is also one of the most widely accepted. He distinguished between a narrow conception—"the deliberate inculcation of political information, values and practices by instructional agents who have been formally charged with this responsibility"—and a broader conception—"all political learning, formal or informal, deliberate and unplanned, at every stage of the life cycle, including . . . nominally non-political learning" (Greenstein, 1968, p. 551).

Early research in the United States (reviewed only briefly here) included two nationwide surveys. Hess and Torney (1967) and Easton and Dennis (1969) reported from the perspectives of psychology and political science, respectively, their analyses of a common data set gathered by questionnaire in 1962 from 12,000 children and their teachers in the second through eighth grades in eight U.S. cities. Hess and Torney identified several themes explored subsequently by other researchers here and abroad: (1) young children's tendency to be strongly attached to the United States, to personalize the political system, to see all laws as fair, and to perceive little conflict or disagreement in politics; (2) students' perceptions of the president as a benevolent leader; (3) young persons' belief (sometimes called the "personal clout illusion") that the average citizen has substantial influence on government decision making and that independence from political parties is a good thing. Findings of striking differences between second and eighth graders and of little difference between eighth graders and teachers also led to the conclusion that the elementary school period (and perhaps the school itself) has considerable importance in political socialization. Findings from research conducted since Watergate suggest that there is less positive feeling about presidents since Kennedy. However, other characteristics of children's political attitudes appear similar to those sampled in the 1960s.

Easton and Dennis (1969), applying systems-analytic theory from political science to the same data, stressed that political socialization in childhood generates diffuse and long-lasting positive feelings for the political system and political authority. They also considered the process by which children differentiate the public or governmental from the private sphere of life.

Jennings and Niemi (1974) surveyed a 1965 nationwide sample of nearly 1,700 high school students and collected information from their parents. After recent interviews with these respondents they have published one of the few longitudinal studies available (Jennings & Niemi, 1981). Two conclusions from the first study have been widely cited. First, when parents agree on issue positions and the issues are relatively concrete, student-parent agreement is likely to be nearly as high as it is for political party membership. Intrafamily agreement was the highest on such issues as prayer in school and the role of the federal government in school desegregation. In both areas the level of agreement is modest enough to indicate that other influences are also important. Second, courses in civics and the attitudes of social studies teachers had only a limited impact on white middle-class students. A reanalysis of the 1965 data using path analysis concluded that the mass media and the schools were about equal in their influence on political awareness (Fowlkes, cited in Ehman, 1980).

Adelson and his colleagues were among the first psychologists to study political socialization (Adelson & O'Neil, 1966; Adelson, Green, & O'Neil, 1969). They sought more information in depth than a survey could provide and asked 11–18-year-olds to imagine themselves on a newly settled island where conflicts between community welfare and individual rights arose (such as one person's refusal to be vaccinated for smallpox or to sell property the community wished to buy for a road). Rapid developmental change was observed, especially between the ages of 13 and 15. The younger respondents focused on personal consequences and individual needs, while the older respondents focused on collective consequences and communal needs. Although both older and young subjects expressed respect for the institution of law, the older ones were more likely to scrutinize particular laws according to how competing interests were served. They assessed short-term versus long-term benefits, and some even compared the cost effectiveness of alternative decisions. Adelson described these older students as "policy-critical" and "ideological." General cognitive development, especially the achievement of formal operations, as Piaget defines it, was thought to have an important role in these developmental differences.

Most research, however, has been conducted by political scientists using survey methodology. With a few exceptions, the studies have been descriptive and correlational and have concentrated on preadolescents and adolescents, who are able to answer written questionnaires. Very few experimental studies have used random assignment of subjects and experimenter control over an independent variable. In fact, the absence of experimental studies makes this research area much like policy research in general (Gallagher, 1981). The major contributions of psychologists to this field have been their introduction of interview techniques designed to probe the reasoning behind young people's opinions, and their interpretation of data from a Piagetian perspective.

This brief review is intended to demonstrate that political socialization research in the United States is linked to various dimensions of policy (broadly conceived). Most research has studied young people's images of political leaders (such as the president or mayors) who make policy decisions and implement them; attitudes toward particular policies in the form of laws; and readiness to participate in activities that are intended to influence the choice either of policymakers (e.g., voting, party membership, campaigning) or of a particular policy direction (letter writing or participating in political demonstrations). Although it is not commonly viewed in this way, political socialization research may be defined as studies of how information about and attitudes toward various aspects of the policy process are acquired. Although a few recent studies have attempted to explore adolescents' decision making in policy-regulated situations, such as consent to treatment and choice of custodial parent (Lewis, 1981), the general linkage between policy and political socialization has not been carefully explored in the United States or in other nations. Such a linkage can provide a fuller understanding of the individual's relation to the processes of policymaking and implementation, as well as of the way that relation develops. The examination of such a linkage can also inform child development specialists about the ways in which their own socialization may limit the effectiveness of their research and their advocacy.

Many summaries of socialization research have focused on agents of socialization (Dawson, Prewitt, & Dawson, 1977; Gallatin, 1980; Renshon, 1977): How is the political culture transmitted? What do the family, the school, the media, and the peer group do (or what can each do)? How much political learning is self-directed? Because of the interconnection among their influences, it has not been easy to separate the unique effects of one socializing agent. For example, if a second grader comes home and announces that the textbook said the President of the United States is always right, what influence will the parents' disagreement with that statement have?

In industrialized nations there is so much variation in family interaction patterns that analysis of the effects of parental socioeconomic status—which is often used as the major independent variable in socialization studies—is completely inadequate to justify inferences about the relative importance of the family as a socializing agent. Further, although some of the effects of socialization agents are conscious and intentional (e.g., most parents wish to socialize their children to obey the law; most teachers wish to socialize their students to support a democratic system of government), other effects are unconscious and unintentional (e.g., parents, by their stress on competitiveness, may make it difficult for their children to participate cooperatively in groups; teachers may unintentionally give students the impression that it is not important to respect other people's opinions).

It would be misleading to make a definitive statement that one socializing agent is more important than another. However, it is reasonable and important to look at the way in which agents, especially the family and the school, interact in the process of socialization and to examine the way policy shapes that interaction. Although psychologists have studied families' socialization patterns extensively, they have not considered how these patterns are shaped by social policy or how families attempt to influence the policy (especially education policy) that relates most closely to their children's acquisition of values. Political socialization is an especially appropriate area in which to examine this interaction.

FAMILIES AS AGENTS OF POLITICAL SOCIALIZATION IN THE UNITED STATES

The role of the family in shaping the child's values is of unquestioned importance, but views about its long-range impact on political socialization have changed in the past 20 years. Many early studies concentrated special attention on similarity of political party allegiance between parent and child. However, influenced by social and political events, adults have become substantially more independent from such allegiance, making studies of the transmission of Democratic or Republican leanings of less importance.

An important stimulus to interest in other aspects of the family's influence was the rise of political protest by young persons during the 1960s. Some early research indicated that many were upper-class individuals who reported practicing their parents' humanitarian values (Flacks, 1970; Keniston, 1967). A study of activists in Britain and France compared the motives of those from different family backgrounds. Those from working-class origins believed that their parents had intentionally inculcated them with radical values. Activists from upper-middle-class origins were more heterogeneous, some reporting that activism was a form of rebellion (O'Connor, 1974). A followup of those who participated in the demonstrations at the University of California has indicated that they remain "a distinctive social and political cohort" (Nassi, 1981).

There has been considerable debate about the extent to which attitudes learned in the early years (presumably with family input) affect adult political values or behavior. Searing, Wright, and Rabinowitz (1976) noted that the child of 8 or 9 years is especially suggestible and that much early learning, because it is preverbal, is resistant to change. Although they cite survey evidence of early influence on basic political orientations, they cite little evidence of such influence on beliefs about particular political issues. As data from longitudinal or panel studies have become available (along with more sophisticated techniques of analysis), it has become feasible to examine the role of preadult experience more carefully. In 1973 Beck and

Jennings (1982) retested those who had formed the high school sample in the 1965 Jennings and Niemi study. Path analysis separated direct and indirect effects. Parent socioeconomic status, political participation, and civic orientation while the child was still at home all made contributions to the young adult's subsequent participation in politics. They concluded that "overall the results rebut the critics . . . who have questioned the existence of a linkage between early [adolescent] learning and adult political behavior" (Beck & Jennings, 1982, p. 94).

Some of the psychological research on parent and child in the 1950s stressed shared decision making in what was called "the democratic family," usually contrasted with "the authoritarian family." Partly because of dissatisfaction with this approach, Baumrind (1971) proposed a three-part typology: that two types of families, authoritative and laissez faire, be contrasted with authoritarian families. Her typology has largely replaced references by psychologists to the democratic family. The notion that there are similarities between family structure and political structure is intriguing. However, because of the complexity of decision making in a democratic society, it is probably misleading to indicate that a certain type of family is more likely than others to produce citizens committed to democracy. Merelman (1980) suggests why this is so: "The child's participatory power in the democratic family is always a matter of parent sufferance, not child suffrage, much less legal entitlement" (Merelman, 1980, p. 467). In his view the family produces two commodities for the state: taxes and children reared as dutiful citizens. The family consumes state services (police protection, public education) to aid in this socialization. Parents once produced more than they received; currently they consume more than they produce, since the family can no longer be "counted on to transfer supportive political sentiments to children" (Merelman, 1980, p. 474).

In summary, no one disputes that families influence the acquisition of values, political values among them. In this country, and in many others, value transmission in the home is a private matter. Although there is some evidence that certain child-rearing practices are likely to promote the welfare of society (e.g., those that contribute to the development of conscience and of self-esteem), the state is restrained from interfering directly in the family's socialization—though many argue that there is considerable indirect interference. How family policy and education policy can legitimately influence the transmission of social and political values is therefore an issue of great importance. Because of limited variation in policy in any one nation, this is an issue where comparative analysis can be of special value.

SCHOOLS AS AGENTS OF POLITICAL SOCIALIZATION IN THE UNITED STATES

Although many question how substantial the school's influence is, researchers agree that schools play a role in shaping the political knowledge and attitudes of students. Ehman concluded an extensive review of research as follows: "Schooling is an important agent for transmitting political information to youth and increases in importance from grade school to high school. It is somewhat less central an influence in shaping political attitudes and behavior, although for racial minorities and low status groups it may be relatively more important than for high status groups" (Ehman, 1980, p. 112). He noted that civics courses—one major component of explicit curriculum—are not very influential. However, "The teacher helps to determine a powerful influence on student attitudes—classroom climate. An open climate of opinion expression in which controversial issues are discussed and in which students believe they can influence the rules . . . is related to student political attitudes" (Ehman, 1980, p. 113). What is the content of the explicit curriculum—which one might expect to be formative but which Ehman finds to have only minimal influence?

Generalizations are difficult because in the United States curriculum is set by more than 17,000 local school boards operating within constraints provided by state laws, regulations, and departments of education. Edelman (1975–76) examined state mandates in education as an index of "core curriculum of basic American values." He concluded that the loyalty of citizens to the social, economic, and political order is the major aim of education. Display of the flag and observance of patriotic ceremonials are required in almost all states and sometimes are prescribed in detail. Henning, White, Sorgen, and Steltzer (1979) also surveyed state constitutions: 45 states prescribed the study of the U.S. Constitution, 43 prescribed the study of the history of the United States, and 38 required educators to inculcate certain values, especially patriotism, loyalty, and good citizenship. However, the pedagogic method was usually not specified. A number of states either barred teaching about communism or required that it be presented in a way to "alert students to its dangers." State mandates paid little attention to skills necessary for political participation or to tolerance of diverse views. Many states prohibited expression of religious or politically partisan views. Some teachers react to these mandates by avoiding the discussion of controversial issues for fear that they may be perceived to be advocating a partisan position. From his survey of mandates, Edelman concluded that public school students receive "an extended exposure to a civil religion . . . which cannot help but have a limiting effect on the possibilities for change in the belief system" (p. 98).

Turner (1981, p. 56) argues that in fact civic education in the United States has changed very little in the last two centuries: "The need for a stable government, capable of mediating between the conflicting values of individual freedom to excel and the public good, has demanded a program of civic education based upon unquestioned patriotism, loyalty to government, and nationalism."

Although local districts have some latitude, state policy, supported by the policies of local school districts throughout the United States, requires the inculcation of the kind of values described by Turner and Edelman. In fact, the large majority of schools teach American history at grades 5, 8, and 11 and civics at grades 9 and 12 (following a sequence prescribed by the National Education Commission in 1916). Publication of textbooks in these subjects suitable for these grade levels has reinforced this sequence. Some schools' social studies programs stress the disciplinary approach of history or geography more than others; some favor materials using inquiry training, developed as part of the "new social studies" in the 1960s; still others include courses on social problems. Various recent studies have confirmed that attempts to introduce new teaching materials have met with limited success; most social studies teachers still rely on a textbook that stresses values such as those described.

Further insight concerning citizenship education can be gained by examining a U.S. Supreme Court case in which two women who were aliens and did not intend to apply for U.S. citizenship appealed their denial of teaching certificates by New York State. Ruling in the state's favor, the Court noted, in its opinion, "Within the public school system, teachers play a critical part in developing students' attitudes toward government and understanding of the role of citizens in our society. No amount of standardization of teaching materials or lesson plans can eliminate the personal qualities a teacher brings to bear. Further, a teacher serves as a role model . . . exerting a subtle but important influence over perceptions and values . . . . Furthermore, it is clear that all public school teachers . . . should help fulfill the broader functions of the public school system" (*Ambach* v. *Norwick*, 441 U.S. 68, 1979). The Court noted that its conclusions about the role of all teachers (not merely those of history or civics) "have been confirmed by the observations of social scientists," and cited two political socialization studies—Dawson and Prewitt (1969) and Hess and Torney (1967). This citation is of interest because Court opinions rarely cite published social science works, which, not being susceptible to cross-examination, are viewed as the equivalent of hearsay evidence. Further, although both cited studies referred to the importance of the teacher, they included no analysis of the nationality of the teacher (or of any other aspect of his or her background).

Although state mandates are relatively clear and a wide variety of educational materials exist, there is considerable concern that all is not well with citizenship education in this country. As measured by the National Assessment of Educational Progress (1978), scores on tests of citizenship knowledge declined between 1969 and 1976. The ability to analyze complex issues declined more sharply than more basic skills or knowledge. In 1971 the American Political Science Association's Committee on Precollegiate Education criticized civics textbooks because they transmit a "naive, unrealistic and romanticized image of political life that confuses the ideals of democracy with the realities of politics and fails to develop within students a capacity to think about political phenomena in conceptually sophisticated ways" (cited in Butts, 1980, p. 80). This criticism from a relatively liberal group is complemented by the claim of some more conservative groups that federal monies supporting curriculum development in the 1960s were used to undermine traditional American values (Nelkin, 1977).

Change in the explicit civics curriculum is likely to be slow because of the importance of textbooks in defining its content. American textbook publishing is in the private sector, and the most common practice is for states to place certain books on a recommended list. Book publishers understandably cater to the larger states, where the biggest share of the market is to be found. Any federal policy that attempted to change this system would meet with criticism for interfering in the free-market economy, as well as for compromising the autonomy of state and local authorities.

The implicit curriculum—school practices that shape or regulate students' relationships among themselves or with their teachers—is also of importance in socialization. Ehman (1980) surmised that the climate of the school or classroom is at least as influential as the explicit curriculum. A landmark Supreme Court case—*Tinker* v. *Des Moines Independent School District*—addressed the question of administrators' regulation of students' expressions of political opinions. Tinker was a high school student who, along with his sister and a friend, protested the Vietnam War by wearing a black armband to school. They were suspended, and the school's action was ruled "reasonable to prevent a disturbance of school discipline." The Supreme Court disagreed: ". . . apprehension of disturbance is not enough to overcome the right to freedom of expression. Students in school as well as out of school are persons under our Constitution. They are possessed of fundamental rights which the state must respect, just as they themselves must respect their obligations to the state" (*Tinker* v. *Des Moines Indepen-*

dent School District, 393 U.S. 503, 508–11, 1969). Among the most eloquent phrases from the Court's decision are its statements that students and teachers do not "shed their rights at the school house gate," and "Our history says it is this sort of hazardous freedom . . . that is the basis of our national strength." Since the *Tinker* case, other decisions have protected the rights of students to circulate literature without seeking administrative approval and to form political clubs (Levy, 1977–78).

Once these court decisions become better known and reflected in local policy, political discussion may become less constrained in American schools. Published socialization research has not caught up with such changes, perhaps because of the time lag between data collection and analysis (compounded by the lag in educators' awareness). Indeed, Jones (1977) suggests that many changes in school policy implemented during the last 10 years have not been carefully examined. Parents as citizens have taken on new roles on advisory councils. How have their views of schooling in general been shaped by these policymaking experiences? Teachers' organizations have been more actively endorsing political candidates. As teachers become more involved in politics, do they share the costs and benefits of that experience with students, and with what effect? These questions go to the heart of school policy and its unplanned and implicit effects on student attitudes. They deserve further examination by social scientists.

Recent scholarly writing and efforts of such government agencies as the U.S. Department of Education clearly indicate that many policymakers see a need for improvement in school-based civic education. For example, in 1975, the U.S. Office of Education established a Citizen Education Advisory Staff which commissioned a series of working papers and in 1979 issued a summary report. Among the recommended steps were an examination of how the explicit and implicit curricula interact, the development of programs to enhance analytic media-viewing skills, and coordination of school and community resources (Farquhar & Dawson, 1979). During the same period another working group in the Office of Education was established to deal with law-related education (LRE), which for nearly a decade had been promoted by the American Bar Association's Committee on Youth Education for Citizenship (as well as by state and local bar associations). The committee defined LRE as "education that is designed to give people an adequate base of knowledge and training about the law, the legal process, and the legal system that, as part of their general education, enables them to be more informed and effective citizens" (U.S. Office of Education, 1978, p. xiii).

Butts (1980), who participated as an advisor to these initiatives, pro-

vides a rationale for them when he notes with alarm the continuing erosion
of civic values in the United States. He lists values that he calls true forms
of cohesive civic orientation, or *unum* (e.g., justice, participation, and
personal obligation for the public good). He lists other values that are part
of stable pluralism, or *pluribus* (e.g., freedom, diversity, privacy, due
process). The problem, as he sees it, is that in American society the values
associated with both *pluribus* and *unum* exist in corrupted forms. The
corrupted form of freedom is anarchy; privacy has been corrupted into
privatism; the corrupted form of due process has resulted in failure to
punish criminals. He calls for efforts by individual educators, families, and
local groups to regenerate the sense of political community.

INTERACTION OF FAMILIES AND SCHOOLS IN POLITICAL SOCIALIZATION

Few researchers have explored parental control of explicit or implicit
political education in schools. Belief that parents should leave most of the
inculcation of civic values and competencies to professional educators
poses one set of implications for education and family policy; belief that
parents should have almost exclusive control over children's value education poses quite another set of policy implications. Until the 1950s there
were relatively few instances of individual parents or elected school boards
differing publicly with professional educators' decisions about schooling.
But in the past two decades, public discussion and litigation on this subject
have increased tremendously (Tyack & Hansor, 1982).

The record of court decisions suggests some directions. Historically, a
small number of parents have sought to educate children entirely at home
(see Moskowitz, 1975). In general, court decisions about whether children
may be removed from school have been based on the parents' ability to
meet state-determined educational needs. To what extent these needs
include citizenship training has not been explicitly addressed, although the
need for "character education" has been cited (*Stephens* v. *Bongard*, 189
Atlantic Reporter 131, 1937).

In a famous case the Supreme Court decided that Amish parents did
not have to send their children to high school (*Wisconsin* v. *Yoder*, 406
U.S. 205, 1972). The Court declared that the state's interest in universal
compulsory education did not override the parents' guaranteed right to
practice their religion. Fischer and Schimmel comment on the potentially
wide-ranging effects of this decision: "Although the Supreme Court limited
its ruling . . . to members of established religious communities, this
decision, which allows one minority group to escape the compulsory
attendance laws, can be expected to encourage others to seek similar

rulings" (Fischer & Schimmel, 1982, p. 406). Parents who wish to instill values different from those they perceive in the school may be next in the courts (see Aron, 1983).

Parents' beliefs about their rights to hold values in private have also shaped discussions of the school's storage of information on children in school records. Fischer and Schimmel (1982) noted that in the 1960s the CIA and FBI had access to pupils' records in 60% of school districts, while parents could examine these records in only 15%. The Family Educational Rights and Privacy Act of 1975 limited outsiders' access, gave parents the right to examine their children's records, and provided procedures for challenging inclusions.

The federal courts have usually (but not always) supported teachers' academic freedom. Some school boards have fired those whose teaching was perceived to conflict with parental values; one teacher was dismissed because an article he assigned to high school seniors contained a word that some parents and members of the school board found offensive. In reversing the dismissal, the judge noted that "the sensibilities of offended parents are not the full measure of what is proper education" (*Keefe* v. *Geanakos*, 418 F.2d 359, 1st Cir., 1969). In a similar case, a Michigan court, in reinstating a teacher who was fired after parents complained about her teaching methods, noted that "some parents will always criticize a teacher, especially one who utilizes methods different from those used when they went to school" (*Beebee* v. *Haslett Public Schools*, 239 N.W.2d 724 Mich., 1976).

In one case the Supreme Court confirmed the right of students to have access to a range of political opinions as part of their preparation for adult citizenship (*Island Trees Board of Education* v. *Pico*, 50 U.S., LW 4831, 1982). The board had removed books from the junior and senior high school libraries because it considered them "anti-American, anti-Christian, anti-Semitic, and just plain filthy." This removal was challenged by students as denying their right, guaranteed under the First Amendment, to receive ideas. The decision noted that the manner of the board's action suggested intent to restrict dissemination of political opinions with which board members did not agree and not simply to remove vulgar materials. It was also noted that school boards do not have "unfettered discretion to transmit community values." Such values may be inculcated legitimately through explicit curriculum in the classroom, but removing books from a library where reading is voluntary is not legitimate.

How much control families should exercise over values education is appearing more frequently as an issue for policy debate. Things have changed since the mid-1960s when the moderate to nonexistent agreement within families was often attributed to parents' indifference to political attitudes. Some parents doubtless remain indifferent to their children's political attitudes (once willingness to comply with the law is assured); other parents express vehement concern. Most familiar are cases where conservative parents challenge educators whom they perceive to be too liberal. Van Geel (1977) discussed parent-school interaction over political education from the other end of the political continuum. Assume that a conservative school board, going beyond the state mandate to promote national loyalty, also requires a course on the free-enterprise system that is indoctrinative in presenting no negative statements about this system and only negative views of other systems. Assume that one family objects to this course on the ground that the First Amendment requires that schools present political issues objectively, giving roughly equal time to all major viewpoints: "If there were no constitutionally based protection against a deliberate bias in political education courses of the public schools . . . government, having created a virtual monopoly over elementary and secondary education, would now be able to impose its own officially adopted viewpoint upon a captive audience" (Van Geel, 1977, p. 197). These parents might argue that schools should adhere to a rule of fairness similar to that requiring the media to give equal time to opposing views. This hypothetical situation resembles the actual debate in some states where courses on the free-enterprise system exist at present.

Examination of the role of values and of constitutionally protected rights in determining policy that influences the interaction of school and family in the process of political socialization is needed. There is, of course, no value-free or universally accepted policy relating to families' proper role in any area of socialization. Proponents of both the radical and conservative points of view have criticized recent family policy statements issued by the Carnegie Council and the Family Impact Seminar. Radicals claim that "policy has not been examined for its role in the capitalist system of production, as well as for reproducing from one generation to the next capitalist forms of social relations" (cited in Lichtman, 1981, p. 54). No less vehemently, a conservative comments: "Inverted liberalism [of Keniston and his colleagues] can find no fault with individual behavior and hardly anything but fault with institutions and practices of society at large. We should not be reluctant to blame individuals for their own problems" (Finn, cited in Lichtman, 1981, p. 65). It is the prospect of increasing numbers of such debates on young people's political attitudes that makes it important to examine alternative policies and their underlying values.

In conclusion, what is not needed is more research on political socialization that tries to place responsibility on family or school (or media or peers) without examining the relation between these socialization agents or the implication for realizing different values. What is needed is research that places the issue of family control of education in general, and political, civic, or values education in particular, in a psychological context. Also needed is more exploration of how different types of educational and family policy affect parents' attitudes toward their own responsibilities in value education with respect to the society, the school, and other socialization agencies.

CROSS-NATIONAL COMPARISONS

It was suggested earlier that cross-national comparisons of family and education policies and of their impact on political socialization can yield useful information. In the past decade there has been increasing openness to examining American social and educational policies in an international context and to considering how practices in other nations might be adapted as policy in the United States. This openness is a departure from a nearly century-long tendency of Americans to view our socialization and education as responsive to absolutely unique circumstances, such as a fully productive economic system, a model democratic political and educational system, local control of schools, and a tradition as a country which successfully absorbed immigrants. Attention to social policy in other nations has had an interesting recent history. The entry of women into the work force in the United States stimulated interest in how other countries had formulated effective child-care policy; most of the cross-national family policy work has been centered in that field. A decrease in many Americans' sense of pride in government (especially since Watergate) and in the educational system (in the wake of declining test scores and technical capacity) has stimulated interest in policy relating to these fields in other countries. Cross-national study of political socialization policy is an appropriate next step.

For the purpose of comparing processes of political socialization in a cross-national context, the best resources are two large and relatively well-sampled surveys of several Western European countries and the United States. After a preliminary look at their data, several industrialized countries are discussed individually—the Netherlands, West Germany, Sweden, Great Britain, the Soviet Union, East Germany, and Japan—looking especially at aspects of policy relating to the interaction of family and school in the political socialization process, at the results of socialization studies, and at how the values of liberty, equality, and fraternity are balanced.

COMPARATIVE STUDIES OF POLITICAL SOCIALIZATION IN DEMOCRACIES
WITH A WESTERN EUROPEAN ORIENTATION

The IEA Civic Education Survey

The International Association for the Evaluation of Educational
Achievement (IEA) is a consortium of educational research institutes in
more than 20 nations that have worked together since the early 1960s to
conduct comparative surveys of education. Surveys in six subject areas,
including civic education (Torney, Oppenheim, & Farnen, 1975), have
been published.

Although the original intent of the committee planning the IEA Civic
Education survey was to concentrate on knowledge of politics, the reports
on curriculum from the participating countries placed so much stress on
values that about half the final instrument was devoted to measures of
attitudes, interest in political participation, and perceptions of political
institutions (Oppenheim & Torney, 1974).

Questionnaires were answered in 1971 by 10- and 14-year-olds and by
students in the last year of preuniversity education. Data were collected
and analyzed in the Federal Republic of Germany, Finland, Ireland,
Israel, Italy, the Netherlands, New Zealand, Sweden, and the United
States. Thirty thousand students responded to survey instruments; more
than 5,000 teachers replied concerning pedagogical practices, and 1,300
principals and headmasters described the schools. The schools were
selected from a nationally stratified sample design, and students were
selected randomly within schools.

Factor analyses of attitude scales were examined separately for each
age × country group. There were three independent clusters of scales: (1)
Support for democratic values (including scales measuring antiauthoritarianism, support for women's rights, support for civil liberties, support for
equality); (2) support for national government (including scales measuring
evaluation and responsiveness of the national government and a sense of
political efficacy); and (3) civic interest/participation (including scales
measuring civic activities, political discussion, and interest in current
events television). There was no single prototype "good citizen"; a student
who was high in support for democratic values was not necessarily high in
interest in civic participation.

One important question was whether the educational system in any of
these industrialized, democratic countries succeeded in fostering all three
types of attitudes in students. In fact, in no country did students score
above the mean on all three scores for the factors listed above. For

example, among 14-year-olds, the countries in which average support for democratic values was above the mean for all countries were also below the mean for all countries in support for national government and civic interest/participation. It appears that a system that effectively educates its students toward support for tolerance, antiauthoritarianism, and equality is less effective in promoting support for the national government and interest in active participation (and vice versa). For example, 14-year-olds in the Netherlands scored high in their support of democratic values and had the highest score in knowledge of civics and politics; their interest in political discussion and their support for national government were both low. In contrast, U.S. students expressed strong positive feelings about their government and were quite interested in participation, yet they scored relatively low in democratic values and only moderately on the knowledge test.

All the IEA studies used regression analyses within a country to suggest which educational practices were consistently related to high scores on cognitive and attitudinal outcomes. In all countries home background (primarily socioeconomic status) was a moderately powerful predictor of 14-year-olds' scores on the cognitive test of civic education and on antiauthoritarianism.

The effects of home background, age, sex, and type of school having been removed in the regression analyses, a group of predictors in the category of learning conditions were examined. In all countries teachers' encouragement of expressions of opinions in the classroom—a measure of classroom climate—was positively related to high knowledge scores, to less authoritarian attitudes, and to more reported participation in political discussion. Students who reported extensive practice of patriotic rituals in the classroom (such as saluting the flag or singing patriotic songs) were less knowledgeable, more authoritarian, and more interested in political discussion. In several countries students who reported extensive use of printed drill materials were less knowledgeable and somewhat more authoritarian. School experience in these Western European countries does seem to make a difference in political learning, since these variables were significant predictors even after controlling for the effects of home background and type of school (that is, academic or vocational). A predominantly negative variable was stress on rote and ritual in the explicit curriculum, while a strong positive variable was part of the implicit curriculum, expressed in students' perceptions regarding freedom of discussion in their classrooms.

To examine a broader range of attitudinal variables, differences between 14-year-olds and preuniversity students, between males and females, between those of low and high SES (father's occupation), and between those living in urban and rural areas were tested for significance in Finland, New Zealand, and the United States using analyses of variance.[1]

The similarity in the patterns of age difference in the three countries was striking. In the United States all 13 attitudes examined showed significant age differences, in Finland 12 out of 13, and in New Zealand 11 out of 13. Older students in all three countries scored higher than younger students on all the scales measuring support for democratic values, gave less positive ratings to both national and local government, and perceived the existence of more political conflict. Older students also reported more interest in watching current events on television and more participation in political discussion. These findings corroborate many age trends from other surveys. The older students were more cognitively sophisticated. They had had more exposure to the explicit school curriculum and the media as well as more opportunity to discuss politics with parents and peers.

Significant sex differences appeared on 11 out of 13 scales in the United States, 10 out of 13 in Finland, and 9 out of 13 in New Zealand. The direction of the sex differences was also strikingly similar. In all three nations, girls had higher scores than boys on antiauthoritarianism, support for women's rights, and support for equality. These differences tended to be greater for the older students. Girls also demonstrated significantly higher levels of support for the national and local governments, seeing them as more responsive to citizen demands. Boys in all three nations reported more participation in political discussion. American boys perceived more political conflict than girls. Social class and urban-rural differences were somewhat more substantial in the United States than in the other two nations.

To summarize the IEA cross-national results, no country's civic education was highly successful on all criteria. The results of regression analysis show that an open classroom climate is a positive factor in producing knowledgeable citizens supportive of democratic values, while patriotic ritual and rote teaching methods are negative factors. They also show that the schools do have a demonstrable effect (greater in some countries than in others).

[1]These three countries were chosen because all had tested 14-year-olds and preuniversity students and all were sampled using similar stratification categories. The selectivity of secondary school was much greater in Finland and New Zealand than in the United States. To make fair age comparisons, it was therefore necessary to constitute pairs of students by random selection. Each member of a pair was of the same sex, and came from the same SES and from the same residence area (urban or rural); one member of each pair was a 14-year-old and the other was a preuniversity student, 17–20 years old. Analyses of variance by age, socioeconomic status, sex, and residence were then performed on these selected samples.

The findings suggest that the promotion of patriotism and the acquisition of knowledge (which are stressed in U.S. policy—especially in state mandates) do not guarantee that students will become supportive of democratic values, in the sense of believing in equality and the rights of citizens to be critical of government policy. In fact, stress on patriotism, if excessive, may harm support for democratic values. Further, there is a strong belief in American political culture that participation is critical to democratic citizenship. In the findings of the IEA study, there is a lack of correlation between participation and either knowledge scores or scales indicating that the government is responsive to citizen action. It appears that many citizens may participate for reasons such as sociability, not because they expect to have any influence or understand the operation of political institutions.

The relationship of classroom climate (especially openness to discussion of diverse political opinions) to both support for democratic values and knowledge suggests a positive direction for policy, and one that reinforces some of the directions suggested by Butts and by Ehman.

The Political Participation Project

In 1974 Jennings and his colleagues conducted surveys in Austria, the Federal Republic of German, the Netherlands, the United Kingdom, and the United States (Jennings, Allerbeck, & Rosenmayr, 1979). As part of a larger eight-nation study of adult attitudes, subsets of adolescents aged 16 through 20 and their parents were interviewed to investigate the roots of political protest. The number of adolescents and parents in each country ranged from 173 to 275 sets.

There were some interesting differences between the generations. Adolescents held less materialistic values than their parents, were more accepting of unconventional political behavior, were more positive about the women's liberation movement, expressed more disapproval of repressive techniques applied by governments, and evidenced more liberal partisanship and religious beliefs. However, the authors concluded that the family still holds a position of primacy in political socialization. The magnitude of the generation gap differed from country to country (being most extensive in Germany and the United States; smaller in the Netherlands where parents are very liberal and in Austria where adolescents appear quite moderate; smallest in Britain). The authors note that even a large generation gap in the aggregate does not necessarily mean conflict within families. Similarity within the family occurs much more frequently than disagreement, and parent-child relationships around political matters in the five countries were remarkably similar (Allerbeck, Jennings, &

Rosenmayr, 1980). Noting the reciprocal nature of this socialization process, they called for theories of political socialization that look beyond simplistic correspondence between micro levels and macro levels. For example, the lack of openness of a national policy process may be considerably more important in generating protest than family quarrels over politics.

POLITICAL SOCIALIZATION AND POLICY IN SELECTED WESTERN EUROPEAN NATIONS

The Netherlands

We begin with the Netherlands, not because it is especially large (it is very small) or because its policymaking structure is similar to that of the United States (it is much more centralized), but because, like the United States, it has a relatively continuous democratic tradition and is a society where there is considerable pluralism and conflict among groups.

Several characteristics of the political system and culture affect Dutch political education: There is an "activist Protestant" vision of the world as being in need of action for social justice; extremely progressive social policies and benefits were enacted during the 1970s reflecting a concern for equality; there is a centuries-old tradition of reliance on international trade (Hard, cited in Pradervand, 1982). Although several programs of political education reflecting concerns for social justice have been proposed, parliamentary debates have indicated concern that teachers might indoctrinate pupils with their views. There has also been little provision for teacher training (Langeveld, 1981).

Teachers sampled by IEA indicated that partisan discussion was almost entirely avoided in the Netherlands. For example, working for a political party as part of a school project was supported as appropriate for students by 18% of Dutch teachers, compared to 72% in the United States. Only 15% of Dutch teachers believed it appropriate to explain their own party preferences in class, compared with 42% of U.S. teachers. However, Dutch teachers were somewhat more likely than those elsewhere to believe that teachers who wished should be able to speak against fascist groups.

The results of the IEA survey in the Netherlands indicate that 14-year-olds were more knowledgeable about politics than those in any other country (Torney, Oppenheim, & Farnen, 1975). They did especially well on questions relating to international topics. The support for democratic values among 14-year-olds was quite high, showing special concern for those with unpopular views, moderately high support for women's political rights, strong beliefs that citizens should be free to criticize government policy, and the highest level of racial and religious tolerance in any nation tested.

Dutch students were considerably more interested in international than in domestic political topics, a pattern opposite to that in the United States (Torney, 1977). Among the older students in the Netherlands there was a tendency to report more positive attitudes toward the local government than the national government (which also contrasts with the U.S. pattern).

Some of these findings are congruent with those of Jennings et al. (1979), who reported that both Dutch adolescents and parents were especially liberal in their politics. They also reported strong support among the Dutch for political protest, another index of willingness to be critical of the government.

Dutch youths expressed high levels of many attitudes that are valued in democracy—tolerance, citizen vigilance concerning government policy, support for equal rights—and also showed high levels of knowledge. Some of these positive attributes may result from exposure to a broad spectrum of ideas, given a relatively open classroom climate and high levels of pluralism in society. Within strict constraints of nonpartisanship, teachers as well as parents seem to encourage liberal approaches to social problems. In this centralized education system, parents seem to make little attempt to shape civic education, and schools place very little emphasis on patriotism.

However, young people in the Netherlands have been found in other studies to have positive national feelings. Tajfel used Dutch children in his research developing models of attitudes toward the international system. They showed a strong preference for the Netherlands and for other countries they saw as similar (Jaspars, van de Greer, Tajfel, & Johnson, 1966). The process of making distinctions between one's own and other nations and of developing a positive feeling about one's country can occur in an atmosphere of internationalism as well as in a situation where patriotic rituals are stressed.

In summary, the Netherlands is a small country reliant on international connections, especially trade. These circumstances are reflected in curricular stress on international topics and also in students' knowledge and interest. There is a strong antifascist feeling in the country along with a concern about indoctrination, probably arising from occupation by Germany during the Second World War. The existence of strong religious groups, political parties, and interest groups leads to effective attempts to keep partisan statements out of the classroom but also to relatively high levels of tolerance for diverse opinions.

The patterns of both educational policy and student results in the studies cited suggest that in the Netherlands a balance exists among the values of liberty (especially for individuals to hold divergent opinions), support for equality, and community allegiance (though perhaps more local than national).

Federal Republic of Germany

West Germany, or the Federal Republic of Germany (FRG), is in some respects the most interesting and complex country to examine in placing American political socialization in a comparative context. Germany's postwar attempt to form a democratic citizenry has received mixed reviews. Some authors have concluded from survey data that there has been a steady increase in support for key values of liberal democracy and in political interest (evidence reviewed in Merelman & Foster, 1978). Others question how deeply these democratic tendencies are rooted and whether they would survive economic reverses. Much of the research was conducted in the early 1970s—before the massive influx of migrant workers into Germany and the recession in the late 1970s and early 1980s. Strong hostility toward these workers, especially those from Turkey, has shown that tolerance for diversity in Germany, as elsewhere, is more likely to be endorsed in principle than in practice (Schonbach et al., 1981).

Questions are also raised about whether the government is sufficiently responsive to citizens' opinions. A substantial number of activist groups exist, many of them opposing government policy and the interests of big business; some estimate that 15,000 new groups have formed since the 1960s (Merelman & Foster, 1978). Recent data cited by Conradt (1981) suggest that although German adults believe in the importance of citizen participation in democracy, only 20% believe that they have adequate opportunities to affect government policy.

It was only about 40 years ago that the deliberate postwar attempt to implant democratic attitudes through education began. The immensity of this effort is indicated by Oppenheim (1977), who notes that after the war approximately 70% of the teachers had to be dismissed for Nazi connections, and for several years there was virtually no non-Nazi material for teaching history or geography.

Since the formation of the Federal Republic of Germany in 1949 each of its 11 states has drawn up its own curriculum. There is more homogeneity and centralization of policy within each state than exists in the United States (Wulf, 1980). A federal council composed of ministers of education from the 11 states issues guidelines that are quite influential. In 1952 the federal government established in Bonn a center for political education stressing democratic principles and participation. Along with similar centers in the states, it holds workshops for teachers and circulates materials stressing skill development in political education.

Social studies courses were instituted during the postwar Allied occupation, and until the 1960s these uniformly stressed the duty of the individual to find his or her place in the existing social hierarchy: Good citizenship required democratic participation which protected rather than tried to change the prevailing social order (Merritt, Flerlage, & Merritt, 1971). In 1967 the national committee planning the German component of the IEA study reported that "civic education in Germany has up to now presented an overharmonious picture of the problems of state and society and developed a model of democratic society which is far too peaceful and free from conflict" (cited in Oppenheim, 1977, p. 37).

Extensive and often polarized debate began in the 1960s among those favoring three positions in social studies education. Conservatives have stressed the traditional values of authority and discipline to preserve the political order. Those more liberal have been critical of the conservatives, fearing a return to hypernationalism; they propose that the curriculum use inquiry methods and help students recognize social conflict, at the same time inculcating a basic set of values centered on respect for human dignity. A third, more radical approach has been favored by proponents of critical theory, which has its roots in Marxist tradition. This approach to political education consists of reflection on the ways in which existing social and economic institutions promote their own interests by preserving a social order characterized by injustice for ordinary people. (See reviews of these three approaches and the textbooks based on them by four German social scientists and educators: George, 1981; Kuhn, 1977, 1979; Schmidt-Sinns, 1981; and Wulf, 1980).

Education policy in the United States has rarely been a major issue in statewide election campaigns. The same is not true in the FRG, where in many elections the Christian Democratic Party favors traditional and more elitist schooling patterns, while the Social Democrats favor more liberal political education and more comprehensive schools. About 10 years ago, as part of widespread reform, a new curriculum, stressing participation in decision making and concern for social problems, was proposed for the state of Hesse. The newspapers launched an attack and the proposal became a major issue in several political campaigns. Various conservative groups posed effective resistance to these curriculum changes by defeating those candidates who supported them (Wulf, 1980). More recently, in response to challenges by pupils and parents, a court ruled that a reform of secondary education in Hesse, which no longer required the study of history and which limited parents' rights to make certain decisions about their children's programs, was incompatible with the state's constitution and would be revoked. Similar actions have taken place in other states.

In general, the conservative authoritarian and legalistic tradition remains strong in Germany, especially in civic and political education (Hearndon, 1976): "Given the present class and economic structure in the FRG it is much easier for conservative views to legitimize themselves. The pressure of public opinion is felt by teachers, who are civil servants, and by textbook authors. Even the criteria used in hiring teachers now include an examination of their political affiliation and fidelity to the constitution" (Merelman & Foster, 1978, p. 459).

Parental participation in school decision making has increased in the last decade. Middle-class parents have the education, time, and motivation necessary to articulate their interests effectively, and frequently take a conservative stance.

The state of Hesse presents an ironic illustration of the interaction between parent and school. The parent committee that advises on education policy at the state level in Hesse was established because of efforts a decade ago by liberal groups; it has in fact more successfully mobilized the conservative parents to exert their influence (Breckenridge, 1981). The extent to which the interaction between parent and school is shaped by legalism is indicated by the publication of a 34-page booklet, *Points of Law for Parents in the Schools of Hesse*, giving detailed regulations concerning participation. Breckenridge (1981, p. 222) indicates that this and similar actions in other states satisfy teachers that "the state bureaucracy has no intention of letting real power pass into the hands of relatively independent groups of parents." Weiler (1983) notes that education policy in the FRG has faced a recent crisis of legitimacy by legalization (in the form of increases in the involvement of the courts in educational policy).

Surveys of the school experiences and political attitudes of young people in West Germany conducted a decade ago by IEA lead to a relatively optimistic conclusion about some aspects of the political socialization process. Support for democratic values was very strong: On antiauthoritarianism (e.g., disagreement with statements such as "The people in power know best"), the FRG scored higher than any other country in the study among 14-year-olds and was tied for second highest among students in the last year of university preparatory programs. On belief in the value of criticism (e.g., agreement that "citizens must always be free to criticize the government"), German students were the highest among the preuniversity students and equal to the highest among the 14-year-olds.

It must also be noted that the German students sampled by IEA in

1971 expressed considerable dissatisfaction with opportunities for citizens to participate in politics. They ranked the average person as having less influence on policymaking than any of 10 named institutions or officials. In contrast, 14-year-olds in the United States ranked the average person sixth out of 10. These tendencies toward a cynical view were even stronger among the older German students, who believed that rich people were equal in policy influence to the prime minister, while large corporations were equal to members of the Bundestag, the lower house of the FRG legislature. This finding was unique, as in all other countries tested by IEA the prime minister and parliament (or their equivalents) were ranked first and second in influence (Torney et al., 1975). The German students also believed that no political institution gave people "a chance to take part in decisions about their lives" or insured that individuals "would receive fair shares." Students in other nations believed that laws or elections performed these functions (Oppenheim, 1977).

German students have strong beliefs that citizens in democratic society should be free to criticize their government, but apparently see their own system as failing to provide enough opportunities for such criticism. Other IEA data are consistent with attributing the formation of these beliefs at least partly to the schools' explicit and implicit curriculums. The regression analyses showed larger effects for school learning conditions in West Germany than in the other nations. German teachers who responded to the IEA survey were more likely than those in other countries to say they would speak out against the government in class. Like the Dutch teachers, they were unlikely to explain their reasons for preferring one political party. German teachers were less likely than those in any other country to encourage students to take sides in debates on political issues (11% of teachers in the FRG expressed this willingness compared with 88% in the United States). On the basis of the IEA students' responses, German classrooms may be characterized as providing a high level of encouragement to students to express their opinions, as long as they are not linked with a political party. Students may perceive the absence of partisan discussion by teachers as freedom for all to hold and express their own opinions.

In the overall analysis of the IEA data in Germany, as elsewhere, the openness of classroom climate was a significant predictor of both knowledge of civics and antiauthoritarianism. A reanalysis of the German data by Nielsen (1977) reconfirmed that, and also showed that the teachers who stressed explanations of the causes of events rather than the memorization of names and dates had students who were more tolerant of dissent.

The optimal way to balance support for democratic ideals with patriotism is an important issue in political socialization. Reflecting educational policy instituted soon after the war, German students seldom participate in patriotic rituals. For example, only about 4% of 14-year-olds reported frequent flag ceremonials in schools, compared to IEA figures of 32% in the United States and 66% in Israel. Patriotic ritual tends to be stressed in countries where strong support for a national political community is primary. In fact, the attitudinal patterns of students in the United States and Israel (low levels of support for democratic values and high levels of support for the national government) were the opposite of these observed in Germany. However, some Germans argue that a way should be found to promote more positive national feeling with continued sensitivity to its possible dangers.

There is little evidence that German parents attempt to exert much influence on their children's political attitudes either directly or through parent groups commenting on school practice. Jennings and his colleagues (1980) found substantial differences between the attitudes of old and young in Germany. Schmidt (1977–78) analyzed the family's role in political socialization in Germany, noting that parents showed low levels of participation in organizations that might influence school policy and concluded that the German family, in transition from authoritarianism to democratization, is not as important a source of political attitudes as families are in other nations. Weiler (1983), however, sees increasing attempts in the past few years to involve parents in curriculum reform as a way to reverse the erosion of perceived legitimacy of government interventions in education.

The term "German miracle" was used several years ago to describe the postwar economic recovery. That is too positive a term to describe the effectiveness of civic education. However, in less than 4 decades, public support for democratic institutions has increased enormously, and much of this appears to be due to the educational system. Liberty (especially support for democratic values, including the right to criticize the government) and equality seem to have been stressed in policy and realized in fact much more than the value of community.

Parents' influence on the schools in Germany comes primarily through the electoral process. Elections have been characterized by highly polarized debates among conservatives, liberals, and radicals. It appears that in the United States civic education policy may increasingly occasion similar debates in electoral politics. If that happens, the German experience might be analyzed to suggest ways to avoid such deep polarizations of opinion.

Sweden

Sweden is a much more homogeneous country (in the ethnic, social class, and religious makeup of its population) than either the Netherlands or West Germany. However, in recent years it also has received a substantial influx of migrant workers. A National Board of Education has wide responsibilities for recommending and implementing education policy, as well as for designing curricula and teaching methods. Over the past 20 years major reforms toward comprehensive schooling have been realized. Social scientists and educators at the university level have been very influential in the design of policy. Lowered educational achievement was even briefly tolerated to promote increased social equality (Heidenheimer, 1974).

Sweden has also been at the forefront of centrally determined family policy in support of child care and other measures benefiting working women. Sex-role differentiation has traditionally been flexible, and women have participated in politics for generations. Furthermore, the curricula for primary and secondary education have explicitly promoted equality between men and women.

The curricula stress freedom and independence, but they are intended to be the foundation for cooperation, not individualism. Young people's solidarity with groups of all types—from the local community to the world community—is encouraged. Civic education as a special subject evolved during the school reforms of the 1960s. Cooperative group experiences and participation in school rulemaking by students are advocated. The character of the implicit curriculum is indicated by the fact that the government has subsidized a trade union representing junior and senior high school students, which serves as an effective pressure group (Breeden, 1976).

A recent report, "Schools and Upbringing," issued by the Swedish Ministry of Education and Cultural Affairs (1979) notes that there are basic values that the school is responsible for inculcating in order both to justify itself and to ensure the survival of society. These include tolerance, equality of rights, respect for truth, justice, and human dignity. The report confirms that pluralism, in which each student is free to express and explore values, is important. However, relativism, in which all values are deemed to be of equal worth, is not considered appropriate for the schools. "It is the task of schools acting in cooperation with the pupils' families to communicate the values . . . that the Ridsdag (Parliament) and government have agreed on: equality of the sexes, community sense, solidarity and shared responsibility, attitudes to democracy, attitudes toward various kinds of societal deviation" (Borjeson, 1979, p. 104). Swedish teachers in the IEA survey in fact were more reluctant than those in the other countries to speak out against the government.

Attempts have been made to establish elected parent advisory committees at the community level. However, these groups tend not to have decisive impact on curriculum or policy (Coombs & Merritt, 1977). The

Ministry of Education Report gives the following examples of the preeminence of the educator's view over that of families. "Some immigrants may have values . . . which are incompatible with one of the most fundamental of our own values—e.g., the equality of men and women. In this case, instruction must be dominated by our own view, even if this conflicts with the opinion of a certain pupil and his family" (p. 13). The report also argues that the school "cannot accept degrading views of immigrants" on the part of pupils from Swedish families.

It has been the policy of the Swedish government that all major teaching materials produced by nongovernment sources for use in "social subjects" be examined for "objectivity" and their contribution to achieving national goals. A committee appointed by the National Board of Education can reject materials for such reasons as the use of misleading statements (e.g., a biased or outdated selection of factual material) and insufficient use of controversial issues to illustrate the gap between ideals and reality in society. Nearly 2,000 pieces of material were examined between 1974 and 1979; about 7% were not approved (Borjeson, 1979).

Sweden tested an IEA sample only at the preuniversity level. Support for democratic values was very high; support for women's rights was stronger than in any other nation. The messages transmitted about women are congruent in Sweden; women are seen performing powerful political roles (such as in Parliament); the overwhelming majority of families support the ideology of equality. School curricula and textbooks stress the same attitudes. These factors reinforce one another, and it is hard to know whether the structural, personal, or curricular would have the same effect if it were operating alone. But the result ought to receive attention in the United States, where the students (at both levels tested by IEA in 1971) were less supportive of political rights for women than the adolescents in any other nation.

In a homogeneous society such as Sweden there is potentially much less conflict between family and school values than in a pluralistic society such as the United States. An argument for defining "a good political belief system" based on rationality was recently made by Westin (1981), a Swedish political scientist. Such an argument would be much more difficult to advance in the United States. However, some Americans do argue that the United States should move toward defining some positive value goals so that education might build a stronger sense of community (Cagan, 1978). Others see any move in this direction as threatening the basic nature of democratic schooling. Given a current sense that there is a crisis of values in this country, it is probable that some moves will be made toward identifying common democratic values with a secular base and ways in which schools might promote them.

Equality and community, rather than liberty, are the values that Swedish education and family policy have promoted explicitly. However, Zetterberg (1982), an American living in Sweden, argues that the current generation of young Swedish adults is in fact moving toward liberty expressed as privatism and individualism. These young people are concerned only with living the good life, not with solidarity with their community. This picture of young Swedes resembles the profile of young Americans obtained from a recent study of high school seniors (Sigel & Hoskin, 1981); their private concerns also far outweighed public ones—they defined democracy as a system in which everyone was free from government interference to "do whatever he wanted." What is interesting about this cross-national similarity in attitudes is that whereas the explicit Swedish curriculum has tended to stress community rather than individualism, the explicit (and implicit) curriculum in the United States has stressed individualism rather than community. This paradox reminds us again of the many potent influences on attitudes other than the school and of the important interaction between implicit and explicit curricula.

Great Britain

In spite of their common language and tradition, the United States and Great Britain differ appreciably in their political structures and patterns of political socialization. The U.S. Constitution is a written document. In contrast, the British constitution is not consolidated in a single written document. Although no individual rights are expressly mentioned in the U.S. Constitution, prohibitions upon the federal government against passing laws restricting these freedoms have the same effect. Limitations on the British government and the enumeration of rights depend on centuries of tradition embodied in the common law. A review of the practice in cases involving civil liberties led Kramer (1982) to conclude, however, that in Britain there is only slightly less tolerance of individuals who are publicly critical of the government than in the United States.

For centuries, Britain was a culturally homogeneous society in which a very selective educational system concentrated on training an elite for political leadership. During the 1930s an Association for Citizenship arose to combat fascism. However, until very recently there was complacency about the political status quo and faith in implicit rather than explicit teaching about democracy often through courses in history (Stradling, 1981). In the decades following the Second World War the educational environment changed with the rapid development of comprehensive schools and massive immigration from the Caribbean, Africa, and Asia.

Educational decision making in publicly funded schools is decentralized, being exercised by local education authorities or school headmasters. Although reports issued by "blue ribbon panels" often have considerable influence, the Crowther Report of 1959 concerning the education of 15 to 18-year olds contained "only two bland, almost indifferent sentences on . . . political education" (Heater, 1977, p. 327). Examinations required for school-leaving certificates and university entrance still shape much of the curriculum. Until about 10 years ago, the only publicly educated students who received systematic civics instruction were the 5% who chose to prepare for an examination on the British constitution. The lowering of the voting age to 18 in 1970, the raising of the school-leaving age, and concern that student activism in the United States might spread to Britain increased the pressure to include more political and social education in the secondary curriculum (Heater, 1977).

A group of concerned individuals in 1969 established the Politics Association, which undertook a program of publications and teacher workshops, the focus being the education of a politically literate person: "Somebody who has a knowledge of basic political concepts and of how to construct analytical frameworks within which to judge political questions; can take a critical stance toward political information; has a capacity to try to see things from the point of view of other groups and persons; has the capacity to participate in and change political situations" (Lister, cited by Stobart, 1979). This individual would be able to recognize political questions not merely in the actions of Parliament or political parties, but also in school or on the job. Discussion of contemporary political issues and recognition of the naturalness of political conflict were critical to the program.

The political literacy project has been both praised and criticized. Some have complained that it promotes quietism and the status quo; others have feared hyperactivity among citizens (believing that implicit transmission of democratic citizenship is preferable to stirring up the citizenry). Sir Keith Joseph (1976) criticized the program as transmitting the assumption that problems are solely the result of failure of the government to provide for citizens' needs without considering economic forces. Brown (1975) interpreted the program as training for conformity and indoctrination of the status quo, noting that the schools could come to serve even more than at present as "legitimizers of inequality in society." A furor having ensued in which one party in Parliament accused another of using political literacy programs to indoctrinate students, a project leader drafted guidelines that have been agreed upon as ground rules governing work by the parties in the schools.

Until the late 1960s parental involvement in British schools was actively discouraged, though some opinions could be filtered through the local member of Parliament. Most groups that have organized since have been concerned with physical conditions in local schools or with the movement toward comprehensive schools and have not expressed themselves on matters of political education (Kogan, 1975). Himmelweit, Humphreys, Jaeger, and Katz (1981) performed a longitudinal study of voting patterns in six elections spanning 15 years. One of the most interesting findings was that attitudes toward the abolition of private schools and the move toward comprehensive schools were predictive of voters' candidate choice in all elections.

Research on political socialization of British children has been extensive (see review by Dowse, 1977). Much of the research follows from Easton and Dennis's (1969) model of the development of system support. The queen has been identified as an object of positive political affect (Greenstein, 1975). Dennis, however, found "a very restrained sense of [national] community identification in British young people" (Dennis, Lindberg, & McCrone, 1971, p. 30). A study conducted by Stradling (1977) of a sample of 4,000 15 to 16-year-olds compared students who had been exposed to political literacy courses with others who had not. Such courses appeared to be only marginally effective. Although most students could provide at least one strategy for influencing a political decision with which they disagreed, Stradling (1977) expressed concern about many factual errors and about the low level of political conceptualization.

Recently the ethnographic approach to research has been used widely, especially to investigate the role of the implicit curriculum in supporting inequality. For example, Willis (1981) studied working-class youth. He concluded that the counterschool culture operated more successfully than any explicit curriculum to ensure that students would not aspire to any occupational level higher than that of their fathers. On the basis of an observational study, Hunter (1980) noted that no real decision-making power is given to students in British school councils.

Although Britain did not participate in the IEA study, the Allerbeck et al. (1980) surveys included a sample. There was little difference between the attitudes of parents and adolescents. British youths reported substantially less participation in protest activities (ranging from signing petitions to attending demonstrations) than those in the United States or West Germany. The authors concluded that "the British youth apparently feel that they have a system with sufficient flexibility and openness without having to make recourse to more unorthodox activities" (p. 509). An alternative explanation is that British youth are simply more apathetic to politics.

Four psychologists have probed the political understanding of young people within the British tradition: Furth (1980) interviewed children aged 5–11 in England; Connell (1971) interviewed children aged 5–16 in Australia; Stevens (1982) conducted surveys and group discussions with 7 to 11-year-olds in Britain; and Gallatin (1976) did a comparative study in the United States, Britain, and West Germany of students aged 11–17.

Although Australia is not a member of the United Kingdom, it does have roots in British tradition. Connell's methodology is so close to the three British studies that it is included here. He used Piagetian theory to explain difficulties the young have in forming concepts of politics. Children cannot act on social institutions as they would on a lump of clay; the child's construction of politics is therefore a lengthy process (with the exception of a sense of nationality, which is established early in a permanent form). Australian children failed to distinguish ceremonial events from activities expressing real power. At about 10, children may perceive that an individual in a political role has a particular intent (say, stopping the Vietnam War), but they usually do not understand that different individuals have different intents. Only some adolescents grasp that there are two or more sides on a political issue, each supporting different policies—an understanding that Connell argues depends on cognitive development. To move beyond this disconnected grasp of issues to a coherent ideology is rare even among adolescents. In Connell's sample such ideological thinking occurred only in a few students who came from politically active leftist working-class families. Connell has cogently summarized the implications of cognitive development for political education: "Children do not simply reproduce the communications that reach them from the adult world. They work them over, detach them from their original contexts, and assimilate them to a general conception of what the government is about. . . . The children selectively appropriate the materials provided by schools, by mass media, by parents, and build of them individual structures" (Connell, 1971, p. 28). Though very probably these results are generalizable, it is unfortunate that no similar study has been undertaken in the United States.

Furth (1980) conducted interviews with British children to elicit thoughts about social and economic institutions. He observed that as they were being interviewed about social events by nonjudgmental adults, children often spontaneously corrected previously inadequate conceptions and related previously unconnected pieces of information. Furth cited this as evidence that the developmental process shapes conceptions of society. Original interpretations of the social events that children gave showed that they apprehended reality differently, not merely that they lacked factual knowledge. Furth suggests a progression of stages: The child begins by experimenting playfully with ideas about social reality from an egocentric base and moves toward a relatively refined understanding of the difference between a personal and societal point of view. Although intriguing, this suggestion that stages exist is based on relatively weak cross-sectional data.

Stevens (1982) views political learning in a Piagetian framework, though she speculates that teaching related to social problems has a more substantial impact than Piaget would acknowledge. She notes that 7-year-olds bring to discussion of politics "the unself-conscious vitality that children bring to the tasks that interest them" (p. 168). Further, there is an apparent spurt in the ability to articulate political ideas at about age 9, leading her to conclude that political education should begin between 9 and 10.

To compare British, U.S., and German adolescents, Gallatin (1976) analyzed data collected using Adelson's imaginary desert island measure. In general, the developmental differences were much more substantial than the cross-national differences. Gallatin concluded that in contrast to Americans, "British adolescents appear to be more pragmatic than idealist. The government is to satisfy the material wants of its citizens and otherwise leave them alone" (Gallatin, 1976, p. 314). Gallatin suggests that formal instruction on rights and study of the written Bill of Rights in the United States may be important in producing more substantial ideas about rights and more idealism in American students.

Although there has been considerable research on political socialization in Great Britain, there has not been much attempt to use it in formulating policy or programs. However, arguments for the political literacy program were made from evidence that students had only a basic level of awareness concerning politics (Heater, 1977). Political socialization research may have been neglected because many of the studies were conducted by American social scientists who brought their own agendas to Great Britain. Differences in the positions of political and civic education in the United States and the United Kingdom are more striking than similarities. In Britain training for citizenship is still substantially implicit. American education policy has always stressed explicit civic training. There has never been the emphasis on widespread citizen participation or patriotism in Britain that has characterized the United States. British parents continue to leave most educational decisions to professional educators; it has been several decades since American parents did so.

Precisely because British policy is implicit, the balance among the three values is difficult to ascertain. One might conclude that liberty, in the sense of individualism, is fostered because there is little attempt to shape attitudes. One could probably obtain agreement that community as a value is not strongly encouraged—although several programs of moral education, such as that of McPhail (1978), stress concern for others and relationship to the group. There is considerable debate on the extent to which equality is promoted: Proponents of political literacy courses believe that teaching many students to be more effective political actors will equalize power; opponents argue that the political literacy approach is simply a more sophisticated tool for perpetuating the status quo by creating an illusion of power among the less advantaged groups.

POLITICAL SOCIALIZATION AND POLICY IN SELECTED EASTERN EUROPEAN NATIONS

The Soviet Union

The process of political socialization in the Soviet Union holds a certain fascination for Americans. The ideological aims of education in the USSR are clear-cut. Many contrast with those in the United States, although both nations aim to instill a strong sense of national loyalty.

Vospitanie—meaning the upbringing of children as builders of communism—is the term that is closest to socialization (Cary, 1974b, p. 201). The emphasis that Soviet researchers place on refining this process and making it more efficient in forming "the New Soviet Man" is indicated by the fact that from 1956 to 1974 Cary found 675 pieces of research on political-ideological and moral upbringing. However, he also found expressions of dismay over the failure of the schools to implement research implications—a lament that might be echoed in this country. Education policy in the USSR is likely to follow from party documents. For example, a statement of the Central Committee of the Communist Party in 1968 indicates the goals of upbringing: It "must inculcate . . . a love of knowledge and of work, and respect for people who work; it must rear pupils in the spirit . . . of boundless loyalty to the country and the people and the spirit of proletarian internationalism" (cited in McHugh, 1980, p. 209).

The family's role is partially specified by the state. Makarenko, who established an especially successful commune, was for many years the "Dr. Spock" of Soviet upbringing. One of his premises was, "The authority [of parents] is only a reflection of society. The duty of a father in our country to his children is a particular form of his duty to society" (cited in Bronfenbrenner, 1962, p. 551). While the political culture of the United States stresses the basic rights of the parent to control the child and his or her education, even to the extent of entertaining suits brought against the state, in the Soviet Union the parents' rights are only those granted by the state.

Although parents are encouraged to support socialist upbringing, Clawson (1973) notes that "the Soviet government has fairly consistently maintained a relatively aloof attitude to the family as a child rearing unit," relying on passive persuasion through magazine articles or handbooks. It is hoped, however, that by the time children enter school they will have learned obedience to authority. Children are also expected to learn at home that their primary responsibility is to others, an attitude that will be extensively reinforced by school and collective experience in the peer group. Parents are held responsible for teaching the child "the dignity of socialist labor" and not allowing the influence of religion or superstition (Clawson, 1973, p. 700). Clawson cites several survey research studies by Soviets and non-Soviets to indicate that most parents fulfill these responsibilities. There is one exception—Soviet parents and their offspring still seem to prefer occupations with greater prestige than manual labor.

The preschool or kindergarten lays a foundation for later, more overt political socialization. Patriotic training is held each day with an emphasis on "Uncle Lenin," whose visage is omnipresent, and on other heroes to be emulated. More explicit political messages are thought to be too far removed from the young child's experience.

Schooling is centrally controlled and is influenced by Communist party goals. Curricula, textbooks, methods of instruction, and examinations are uniform across the country (McHugh, 1980). Discipline is strict; rote recitation with little discussion is the usual approach to civics. However, observers have noted that most teachers have friendly relations with their students. Recently there have been attempts to replace rote exercises with more active and problem-oriented methods. Zankov suggests that teachers "encourage a questioning spirit which still leads to the right conclusion" (cited in McHugh, 1980, p. 217).

History, especially in the upper grades, is the discipline where support for the communist struggle is most clearly inculcated. The teaching of history and the writing of history texts are closely supervised. The curriculum stresses economic causes of historical events and the masses as makers of history. Malkova, an eminent Soviet educator, describes one textbook: "By means of an extensive selection of factual material, it explains that World War I was provoked by the desire of the ruling classes to redivide the world and to seize territory belonging to others" (Malkova, 1981, p. 85).

A computer analysis of Soviet textbooks (Cary, 1977–78) has indicated that they stress positive attitudes toward the political community (the overarching and enduring Soviet system) and not toward particular political leaders (who are more transient). Children are taught of their "dependence on society and the necessity to harmonize one's conduct with society's . . . interest" (Dunstan, 1981, p. 193). Autonomy of individual choice is viewed as self-centered disregard of the community.

Soviet educators are frequently puzzled when they are criticized for presenting only one ideological position or for placing so little emphasis on the individual and so much on society. These educators believe in communist ideology and that their students ought to believe in it also. If the selection of materials and the emphasis on a certain factor in history are effective ways to teach that ideology, why should they choose less effective methods? Langeveld (1981) also points out that totalitarian systems have an easier time designing political education than democratic systems. If one knows the ideology one wishes to transmit, it can be simplified, made concrete, and taught directly. Such an approach is not dependent on students' ability to understand abstract ideas such as democracy.

During elementary school the peer collective becomes a major agent of socialization in teaching individuals to subordinate their wishes to the claims of the group. Bronfenbrenner's (1962, p. 555) summary of its operations is found below:

1. The behavior of the individual is evaluated primarily according to its relevance to the goals and achievement of the collective. Competition between groups is used extensively.

2. The entire group benefits or suffers as a consequence of the conduct of individual members.

3. As soon as possible, the task of evaluating the behavior of individuals is delegated to the members of the collective. Social control is a matter of public recognition and public criticism (including self-criticism). Group collectives operate both in schools and in a series of age-graded young people's organizations. Beginning at age 7, they meet after school, enroll 90%–100% of cohorts, and have as one of their essential purposes reinforcement of communist ideology. History teachers often have a special role in advising the Komsomol (for students over 15)—encouraging students to read newspapers and engage in socially useful tasks (McHugh, 1980).

Bronfenbrenner's research (1970) suggests that Soviet elementary school pupils are more willing than their Western European counterparts to help their peers even at the expense of personal interests. However, interpreting a Soviet researcher's study of conformity in children in grades 4, 6, and 9, Cary (1974, p. 461) suggests that for older students these groups may be less effective: "Although the youth organizations initially represent institutionalized peer groups that are co-opted for political education, they become a setting for a 'teen culture' that is not so purposefully directed." (Of course, the inability of adults to control adolescent peer groups successfully is not unique to the Soviet Union.)

Political socialization continues into early adulthood. An unusual team of two Soviet social scientists collected data for an empirical article on this subject while assigned in another capacity to a geology project. They used that opportunity to query Soviet workers about their support for the invasion of Czechoslovakia in 1968 (Zaslavsky & Z, 1981). Compared with other age groups (even those only a few years older), a much smaller proportion of the 16 to 18-year-old workers supported the invasion. The authors point to the socializing impact of the Soviet army, which serves to "embed the individual in the regime."

In summary, although Soviet socialization is not without its difficulties (created in some cases by personality and developmental variations) this process is relatively straightforward in support of a single ideological position and takes place in an atmosphere of warm relations between teachers and students. Individuals who have not been convinced by formal education or youth organizations usually become so during military training or early working experience. Whatever the efficiency of the policy, its direct appeal for the U.S. educator is likely to be limited. Even given a choice between successful indoctrination and a substantially less successful marketplace of ideas, we would choose the pluralistic approach. It is very unlikely, for example, that the U.S. government would systematically delineate for parents their duties in political education. However, some better ways to advise parents about how to foster basic democratic values, such as tolerance for the opinions of others, might be appropriate.

Community is the value most consistently promoted in the Soviet Union, although there is also concern for equality; liberty or individualism receives the least attention. A number of observers of education in the United States believe that widespread alienation from a sense of community is a serious problem among American high school students (Newmann, 1981). However, American educators are not likely to use methods such as public self-criticism to promote collective feeling.

German Democratic Republic

Like West Germany, East Germany (the German Democratic Republic) began the postwar period devastated by war and conquered by a country, the Soviet Union, intent on transforming its political life. Some who see East Germany as an example of success in both the political socialization of the young and the resocialization of adults attribute that success to its relatively homogeneous culture and absence of a tradition of democracy to which the populace might feel attached. Others who believe it has been less successful note that the social order of Marxism-Leninism was imposed by an occupying force (as democracy was in West Germany) and that revolutionary culture is lacking. However, creating the socialist personality—one that learns to the limits of his or her capabilities, feels responsible to use knowledge in building the socialist society, and engages in cooperative behavior within the collective—is the subject of great effort (Sontheimer & Bleek, 1975).

In 1965 the national government issued a comprehensive policy document, the Family Law Code. In addition to covering a wide range of family law topics, it delineates both the husband's and wife's responsibility for the training of children: "Through responsible fulfillment of their duties as trainers, through their own example, and through harmonious behavior vis-à-vis the children, parents will train their children . . . to respect the working man, to live according to the rule of Socialist community, to express solidarity with Socialist patriotism and internationalism" (cited in Hanhardt, 1975, p. 70). The process by which the code was drafted is almost as intriguing as its provisions. During 4 months a draft was reportedly discussed at 34,000 meetings attended by more than 750,000 citizens of the GDR. (There were some changes between the first and final drafts.)

More concretely, several popular books give parents advice on the political content of family life. Parents are warned that if they contradict the norms the child learns elsewhere the result will be "retarded personality development for the child as well as damage to the society" (quoted in Hanhardt, 1975, p. 70). School-parent councils are intended to transmit ideas from educators to the family, not vice versa. This is the most explicit family policy regarding political socialization in any of the countries reviewed.

The school system in the GDR is of high academic quality and from an early grade integrates technical training into education. There is central planning of education policy. Details of civics lessons are prescribed precisely, and a particular textbook is used in each grade throughout the country. A West German observer described the character of the classroom in the GDR: "Political positions are not discussed in order to assess their normative or empirical validity but to give them a progressive or reactionary label. Marxism-Leninism and the sociopolitical conditions of the GDR are progressive by definition and thus, taboo for discussion" (Schmitt, 1980, p. 3). There have been a few, generally unsuccessful, attempts in the GDR to institute techniques more oriented to discovery learning. An American observer noted that teachers concentrate on creating contrasts between friend (the USSR and other socialist states) and foe (West Germany and the United States). Teacher trainees are advised to aid the students in developing "feelings of rejection, loathing, and hate toward the enemies of our Socialist fatherland" (cited in Hanhardt, 1975, p. 83). Parents are encouraged to reinforce these orientations.

Observers differ about how successful this intensive policy—which also makes use of youth collectives—has been in producing the "socialist personality." A substantial amount of empirical research has been conducted; Schmitt (1980), a West Germany researcher, reviewed 20 surveys with 45,000 respondents from 1966 through 1971 alone. Both Schmitt (1980) and Hanhardt (1975) note that many studies have serious methodological flaws, which are due in some cases to ideological biases. Hanhardt reviews a study in which none of a group of 12 to 14-year-olds interpreted the Marxist-Leninist concept of freedom correctly as "understanding the necessary," though nearly half gave what were called analogous responses. Approximately half of the older students interpreted freedom as personal freedom. "The large majority of respondents say they believe in the ultimate victory of socialism, in the aggressiveness of imperialism, in particular of the West Germans, . . . and that they are highly interested in politics" (Schmitt, 1980, pp. 5–6). There is some evidence that students are giving the socially desirable response rather than expressing deep-rooted convictions. "Young people from the intellectual class (who can use the ideology in their own careers) conform significantly more to the norms . . . than the children of workers or farmers" (Schmitt, 1980, p. 6). This, of course, is the opposite of what is desirable in a proletarian state. Finally, "In many fields the actual behavior of youth conforms to official norms through membership in the state youth organization, participation in political rituals, and diligence in school. Where privacy of behavior can be safeguarded, cases of nonconformist behavior are very frequent" (Schmitt, 1980, p. 7). The explicit civics curriculum appears to be limited in its effectiveness, a conclusion echoing findings in other nations. Schmitt attributes this to repetitive focus on slogans regarding the enemies of socialism and the absence of open discussion and genuine problem solving in the classroom.

Why does the government persist in an education policy that is expensive and yet appears ineffective? Schmitt suggests that in a planned society the goals and basic approaches to education are not likely to be questioned; instead, parents and teachers will be exhorted to greater effort. Also, "A political system . . . which claims to regulate all spheres of society has to have its actions accepted as being 'scientifically' determined. Accordingly, this 'science' must be taught—regardless of whether it is relevant" (Schmitt, 1980, p. 13).

In East Germany, as in the Soviet Union, fraternity is the primary value. The relationship between the family and the state is clearly prescribed. In both countries the focus on a "socialist personality" is specified. If we were to formulate a concrete description of a democratic personality, what would be its characteristics? Even the attempt to formulate such a definition would be an interesting exercise with implications for policy.

POLITICAL SOCIALIZATION AND POLICY IN JAPAN

More than any of the other countries examined, Japan has borrowed civic education programs and approaches from the United States. But it has adapted them to the Japanese culture. Although its having been vanquished in the Second World War and its having been the only country subject to atomic attack are important factors in accounting for Japan's civic education programs, another factor is very rapid industrial development. One consequence has been increased need for individuals skilled in understanding other cultures.

The Japanese Constitution, passed by the Diet in 1945, reflects American constitutionalism. It includes guarantees of freedom of assembly, speech, and other forms of expression. Although the constitution is based on respect for the individual, the Japanese culture for centuries has stressed identification with the group. Opposition to a decision arrived at by group consensus is viewed as unbridled egotism. During the 1950s the Supreme Court of Japan issued several decisions citing "the public welfare" (meaning the right of citizens in general to the maintenance of order) as a reason to limit the freedom of a group that wished to protest (Beer, 1976). References to the public welfare are therefore acceptable to many Japanese as reasons to limit rights to free expression by students, citizens, and public employees.

Japanese scholars proudly point out that the building of the "new Japan" began immediately after the surrender, with "the new education." The Fundamental Law on Education of 1947 guides all regulations. In the early 1950s local school boards modeled after those in the United States were established, but power soon reverted to the Ministry of Education, which still determines courses of study. Advice is received from committees of scholars, administrators, and teachers, but it seldom is cause for a change in the curriculum plans favored by the Ministry. Textbooks are subject to ministry approval, although in any given district, a committee of teachers selects the particular text to be used from an approved list (Nagai, 1979). The Teachers' Union is "one of the most enthusiastic supporters of the left and a militant foe of government education policy" (Massey, 1976, p. 13). They have criticized the required ministry approval of textbooks as censorship and have expressed serious concern that the educational system is blindly fostering support of the status quo rather than making students aware of and sensitive to inequalities in society.

Shushin, or moral education, was established before World War II and was the subject in which nationalism and militarism were taught. The replacement of *shushin* with American-style social studies was part of the "new education." A decade later, however, some educators warned that "innovators had gone to extremes in denying not only wartime Japan but the culture, values and history of pre-war Japan" (Omori, 1980, p. 155). In 1958, after several years of debate and opposition from the Teachers' Union, new courses of moral education consisting of 45 minutes per week were added to the curriculum to supplement the social studies. Most observers agree that these courses have not become a source of indoctrination into ultranationalism, as some had feared, and that the majority are quite innocuous.

Japanese social studies, like Japanese teaching in general, relies on lectures and textbooks. Omori attributes this to the limitations that large classes place on teacher innovation and to the traditional view that education consists of the transmission of knowledge.

Several political socialization studies have been conducted in Japan. Massey (1976) collected data from a survey and some interviews with nearly 1,000 Japanese 13 to 18-year-olds and their parents. His book also reports data from a 1968 nationwide survey of 6,000 children grades 3–12 (Okamura, 1968). Massey notes that the head of state in Japan, the emperor, is distinguished from the head of government, the prime minister. Although the Japanese system is similar to the British, the emperor is not as important a political figurehead to young Japanese as the queen is to the British. Japanese young people do not perceive either the emperor or the prime minister as an especially benevolent or trustworthy leader, in contrast to American students' view of the president. The Japanese prime minister has traditionally been a remote figure. Massey attributes the absence of an image of a benevolent leader to the media's tendency to be nonpartisan by not referring to the personal characteristics or family of the prime minister. He further notes that the establishment of democracy in Japan during the occupation was "a revolution without a hero." Okamura attributes the impersonal image of the prime minister to the required political neutrality of the schools; no mention of this leader is made in textbooks until the sixth grade and then there is only a description of the prime minister's role in government without reference to an incumbent.

Japanese teenagers seemed disaffected from politics, even more than their parents: "the input institutions—parties and elections that mediate the political participation of the citizenry and convey their demands—are worthier of support than the output institutions—like the prime minister, government and Diet that represent authority" (Massey, 1976, p. 39). Other observers have also noted the level of disaffection bordering on cynicism expressed by Japanese youth aged 18–24. In an international Gallup survey of 11 countries in 1972, 74% of the Japanese expressed dissatisfaction with their society, especially with provisions for rights and welfare, as compared with 36% in the United States, 35% in Sweden, and 34% in West Germany (cited by Cummings, 1980).

The word for democracy in Japanese literally means "the principle of popular rule." Social studies texts also emphasize popular sovereignty. The irony is that majoritarian rule runs counter to the theme of Japanese culture, which operates by consensus and avoids explicit recognition of minorities. Respondents in Massey's sample thought it was best to attempt to blend majority rule, and the associated right of the minority to dissent, with a consensual view of democracy; in situations where it was impossible to reach consensus, the majority should prevail.

Democracy is a powerful symbol to Americans. In Japan, democracy is preferred as a form of government to others, but it is seen by both students and parents as an importation imposed by outsiders and as not wholeheartedly practiced by the government. "Democracy has the flavor of an important lesson to be learned . . . almost like a catechism lesson, rather than the evocative magic of a source of national identity and pride" (Massey, 1976, p. 65). Peace is a far more powerful symbol for the Japanese. In fact, student responses indicated that democracy is to be valued because it gives people the opportunity to live in peace. Social studies texts associate democracy with Western history but describe peace in connection with the new Japanese Constitution and World War II. In the view of Massey's sample, Japan's unique mission is to be a model democracy devoted to pacifism.

In Japan the stress is clearly on community as a value, rather than on individualism or equality. This stress may be attributed in large part to centuries-old Asian tradition, which understandably is resistant to the importation of policy and practice from the West.

There are several similarities between the process and outcomes of attempting to establish democracy through education in the Federal Republic of Germany and in Japan. In both countries ways to involve parents in educational decision making have been tried but short-circuited (although in somewhat different ways). After a period of almost total suppression of national identity, there has been an increasing attempt to create pro-German or pro-Japanese feeling, accompanied by wariness about indoctrination and hypernationalism. The current generation of Japanese and German young people support many aspects of democratic values but are somewhat cynical about the ability of their governments to perform in a democratic way.

CONCLUSIONS

Each country examined in this chapter has a unique political culture that would seriously complicate any attempt to transplant political socialization policy from one nation to another. Leichter (1979), however, identified situational, structural, cultural, and environmental factors as the components of a framework for analyzing differences in health policies in Germany, Great Britain, the Soviet Union, and Japan. That framework can be applied to the analysis of political socialization policy.

He defines situational factors as "more or less transient, impermanent, or idiosyncratic conditions or events that have an impact upon policy." The most potent situational factor that appears in the analysis of political socialization is, ironically, war. Certainly the two countries in which political education policy has changed most rapidly, and in which there is considerable evidence for the efficacy of education in establishing a democratic citizenry, are Japan and the Federal Republic of Germany. There are several hallmarks of this rapid change: the imposition of another nation's conceptions of political education, a tendency to give parents a rather limited role in the decision-making process, lessened emphasis on patriotism and nationalism, and vigilance against the specters of militarism and fascism.

Structural factors, in Leichter's analysis, include "relatively unchanging elements of the society and polity," such as a federal or unitary political system—something that also makes a difference in the organization of political socialization policy. Also important is the linkage between the political and the economic systems. Economic factors, including rapid technological growth, have influenced political socialization in most of the countries, but especially in West Germany and Japan. Relatively homogeneous countries such as Sweden and (until recently) Britain have quite different problems from those with heterogeneous population groups, illustrating still another structural factor.

Leichter also notes the role of cultural factors, "value commitments of groups within the community." Norms and values concerning the proper role of the individual with respect to the state and more formal political ideology (democratic, socialist, or communist; conservative, radical, or liberal) have been illustrated in these nations, in part by reference to the values of liberty, equality, and fraternity. Political socialization policy in the United States has also been shaped by structural factors—pluralism and heterogeneity in the society and the polity—and by such cultural factors as the value of individualism expressed in the belief that families should have the ultimate control over their children's education.

But it is not enough to note that these factors are related to political socialization policy in much the same way that they are related to health policy. One purpose of policy analysis is to consider ways of optimally balancing the interests of different groups. In this case, the state or society, political leaders, educators, the family, and the child all have distinct interests to pursue in the process of political socialization.

The first stakeholder is the state, unusual as that may seem as an interest group. It must have a minimum degree of loyalty from its members if it is to maintain itself. Socialization is a major method by which this diffuse support is created in the rising generation. Butts (1980) argues that corruption of values of societal unity has become so widespread that this basic support is in a dangerous decline—the fabric of society is unraveling. Critical theorists, in contrast, argue that the state, often dominated by economic interests, has been too successful in this socialization and has failed to make individuals sensitive to the need to change institutions to make them just.

Political leaders, whether national or local, have a stake in socialization. Some of their interests are legitimate in democratic society. In the United States and most other democracies, political leaders prefer a wide popular base for leadership and seek ways to remain in touch with the opinions of their constituencies. Political leaders also prefer constituents who take a well-informed rather than an emotional approach to issues. Political leaders may also seek to know more about socialization to help in creating a wider base of support for themselves and their positions among young people who are nearing the voting age.

Professional educators also have a stake in civic education policy. Very few teachers wish to indoctrinate students with their own partisan political opinions. Neither do they want their professional practices to be constantly questioned or their jobs to be threatened when they encourage discussion of alternative points of view in the classroom or assign students reading which may be critical of certain government policies. Most teachers want to improve their skills and have them recognized and respected. In the countries reviewed in this chapter, decentralization of educational decision making and a high degree of parent control seem to be correlated with a low status for teachers.

Parents have a stake in policy relating to political socialization. As members of society they share the interests of the state. They also wish to see their children succeed as adults; many parents grasp the connection between economic success and understanding how the political system works. Some parents wish to protect their children from what they view as the seamier side of political life. Parents' interests in socialization may also vary according to their political ideology. Conservative parents are more likely to want their children to reproduce their attitudes and values; liberal parents are more likely to favor free choice for their children; radical parents may wish to expose their children to the questioning of existing institutions and values. This is further complicated, of course, by the fact that even the parent who makes a concerted effort to mold values cannot eliminate all other influences. For example, the parent who promotes free choice may have a child who seeks an authority's opinion.

The child also has a stake in political socialization policy. Although a certain amount of alienation from society is probably part of normal adolescence (Newmann, 1981), alienation in excess is usually unproductive. Students recognize many of their interests. They are excellent informants about which social studies teacher never lets them express an opinion and about the amount of real power the student council has. And many students attempt to maximize those interests.

Policy relating to political socialization thus involves a diversity of groups with interests consciously developed to different levels and with power of different types. Descriptions of the policy and practice of these nations concretely illustrate the variety of interests of parents and educators. The nations examined have some common interests, such as the creation of diffuse support. States such as the Soviet Union and East Germany have interests in creating a citizenry that supports a common ideology unquestioningly. Democratic governments have interests in creating an informed citizenry with certain political interests and skills.

What are the major problems of balancing these interests, especially in countries with a Western democratic orientation? One problem is finding an optimal balance between individual welfare and the welfare of the community—two of the values discussed in the chapter. One might think of a social contract, in which certain individual rights are relinquished with the expectation of receiving certain benefits from the community. The shape of that contract can have tremendous influence on the character of schooling and the relationship between schools and families. In Japan or the USSR, for example, the welfare of the group is primary; teachers have enhanced authority to shape community spirit and enlist parents in their efforts. By contrast, in the United States the teacher must favor the protection of individualism over group values. Is this balance in the United States optimal?

What is the optimal balance in political socialization between teaching for cognitive achievement or critical skills, hoping that positive attitudes will be implicitly acquired, and more direct actions to inculcate values? Both IEA data from Western Europe and recent attempts in Great Britain suggest that some values are so important (e.g., respect for reason and fairness) that they should be taught explicitly rather than left implicit on the assumption that the teaching of facts will lead to support for democratic values or that students will naturally discover and support these values.

What is the optimal balance between citizen support for government and citizen criticism of government? This question points to the problem of inculcating a certain amount of patriotism and national loyalty without becoming chauvinistic. The postwar West German and Japanese experiences, on the one hand, and the continuing Soviet and East German experiences, on the other, illustrate the two extremes.

How do the explicit and implicit curricula interact to form democratic citizens? Dissatisfaction with rote recitation and rituals is being expressed in many nations, even in Eastern Europe. Educational policy, particularly as articulated by the courts, is making some changes in aspects of the implicit curriculum in the United States. The explicit curriculum seems to change somewhat more slowly. In fact, Turner (1981) suggests that there has been little basic change in two centuries: Textbooks, which are the core of the explicit curriculum, cover the same themes to meet the same mandates as they did decades ago. In this regard it is sobering to note that being defeated in war appears to be the only source of substantial educational change in the industrialized countries reviewed.

These questions of optimization provide a framework for the analysis of social and educational policy bearing on political socialization.

DIRECTIONS FOR THE FUTURE

A useful model for future directions in the study of political socialization and policy may be found in work recently published on day care. Two important sources of policy alternatives and means of evaluating them have been identified: the experience of other nations and the empirical research literature (Kammerman & Kahn, 1981; Zigler & Gordon, 1982). It would be appropriate for political socialization to become one of the next areas in which policy viewed comparatively and policy viewed from the perspective of empirical research become integrated. First, it is an area which has traditionally been cross-disciplinary and cross-national. Second, social and educational policy influences political attitudes and skills in citizens who then become shapers of future policy. Policy researchers and advocates can also benefit from enhanced awareness of their own socialization. A third important reason for intensified work in the area is the likelihood that during the next decade there will be increasing public debate about the optimal balance among the state, the educator, and the family in their influence on political and values education in the United States. Careful examination of the practice of other countries and more empirical research could inform this debate.

Three questions we should be considering in our multiple roles as citizens, educators, and researchers are concerned with the content of education. Should policy be altered to encourage more stress on community (at the school and local level in particular) and less on individualism in political education? Should policy encourage more attention to teaching the critical analysis of political issues? Should policy attempt to shape a different type of interaction between schools and parents, one that might be more likely to avoid polarization and legalism?

Some questions about the process of political education have not yet been the subject of adequate research. How does the implicit curriculum function, and how might it be changed? Although the teacher's role as a model for behavior as well as a dispenser of direct and vicarious rewards is central to the notion of classroom climate, there is little research to aid in applying principles of social learning theory to classroom political education. Another area needing research is how the implicit curriculum has been influenced by recent court decisions, especially those concerning access to ideas and rights to discuss a variety of opinions on political issues.

A second set of questions about the process of political education is concerned with optimal timing and sequencing. The cognitive-developmental approach, in which the child is viewed as an active processor of social knowledge, has a potential contribution (see Leahy, 1983). Measures and findings from training studies of perspective taking may have implication for explaining how children begin to understand others' positions on public issues. Although several authors have proposed stage developmental progressions in social, political, or moral development, their implications for sequence in political education have not been carefully examined. Some have spoken in favor of the primacy principle: Political education belongs in the earliest years of schooling. Others have favored the prerequisite principle: Political education should be postponed until adolescence, when certain cognitive capacities have been achieved. Still others argue for the plasticity principle: Political education should take place in middle childhood, when role-taking skills have been acquired but before peer-group conformity exerts a constraining influence (Torney-Purta, 1982). There is no definitive research, especially on social development in middle childhood, to guide decisions about timing and sequence.

It would be naive to believe that there could be a short agenda for policy or research in an area with so many groups that have potentially divergent interests. Until now these interest groups have not even engaged in much dialogue on political education. The following questions of a more political nature might be considered. How might groups build on a political leader's stake in political socialization to stimulate interest in research and policy in this field? How might one encourage less polarized dialogue between groups of educators and groups of parents?

This chapter is a call to place the problems of political socialization and policy higher on the agendas of those concerned with child and family policy and of those who conduct research in related areas.

REFERENCES

Adelson, J., & O'Neil, R. P. Growth of political ideas in adolescence: The sense of community. *Journal of Personality and Social Psychology*, 1966, **4**, 295–306.

Adelson, J., Green, B., & O'Neil, R. P. Growth of the idea of law in adolescence. *Developmental Psychology*, 1969, 1, 327–332.

Allerbeck, K. R., Jennings, M. K., & Rosenmayr, L. Generations and families: Political action. In S. H. Barnes & M. Kaase (Eds.), *Political action*. Beverly Hills, Calif.: Sage, 1979.

Aron, S. *Compelling belief*. New York: McGraw-Hill, 1983.

Baumrind, D. Current patterns of parental authority. *Developmental Psychology Monographs*, 1971, **4**, 1–103.

Beck, P. A., & Jennings, M. K. Pathways to participation. *American Political Science Review*, 1982, **76**, 94–107.

Beer, L. W. Freedom of expression in Japan with comparative reference to the United States. In R. P. Claude (Ed.), *Comparative human rights*. Baltimore: Johns Hopkins University Press, 1976.

Borjeson, B. State examination of objectivity of teaching materials in Sweden. *International Journal of Political Education*, 1979, **3**, 103–122.

Breckenridge, I. Legalism and participation in school government in West Germany. In G. Baron (Ed.), *The politics of school government*. Oxford: Pergamon, 1981.

Breeden, L. The rights of children in the United States and the Scandinavian countries. In R. Claude (Ed.), *Comparative human rights*. Baltimore: Johns Hopkins University Press, 1976.

Bronfenbrenner, U. Soviet methods of character education. *American Psychologist*, 1962, **17**, 550–564.

Bronfenbrenner, U. Reaction to social pressure from adults versus peers among Soviet day school and boarding school pupils in the perspective of an American sample. *Journal of Personality and Social Psychology*, 1970. **15**, 179–189.

Brown, C. Contexts for political action: Social studies. In T. Brennan & J. F. Brown (Eds.), *Teaching politics: Problems and perspectives*. London: BBC Publications, 1975.

Butts, R. F. *The revival of civic learning*. Bloomington, Ind.: Phi Delta Kappa, 1980.

Cagan, E. Individualism, collectivism, and radical educational reform. *Harvard Educational Review*, 1978, **48**, 249–266.

Cary, C. Peer groups in the political socialization of Soviet school children. *Social Science Quarterly*, 1974, **54**, 451–461. (a)

Cary, C. Problems of Soviet research on upbringing. *Youth and Society*, 1974, **6**, 201–218. (b)

Cary, C. Patterns of emphases upon community, regime and authorities: A computer content analysis of Soviet school history textbooks. *International Journal of Political Education*, 1978, **1**, 359–384.

Clawson, E. Political socialization in the USSR. *Political Science Quarterly*, 1973, **88**, 684–712.

Connell, R. W. *The child's construction of politics*. Carlton, Australia: Melbourne University Press, 1971.

Conradt, D. Political culture, legitimacy and participation. In W. Paterson & G. Smith (Eds.), *The West German model*. London: Cass, 1981.

Coombs, F., & Merritt, R. The public's role in educational policy making: An international view. *Education and Urban Society*, 1977, **9**, 167–196.

Cummings, W. K. *Education and equality in Japan*. Princeton, N.J.: Princeton University Press, 1980.

Dawson, R., & Prewitt, K. *Political socialization.* Boston: Little, Brown, 1969.

Dawson, R., Prewitt, K., & Dawson, E. *Political socialization.* (2d ed.). Boston: Little, Brown, 1977.

Dennis, J., Lindberg, L., & McCrone, D. Support for nation and government among English children. *British Journal of Political Science,* 1971, 1, 25–48.

Dowse, R. E. Political socialization. In D. Kavanaugh & R. Rose (Eds.), *New trends in British politics.* London: Sage, 1977.

Dunstan, J. Soviet moral education in theory and practice. *Journal of Moral Education,* 1981, 10, 192–201.

Easton, D., & Dennis, J. *Children in the political system.* New York: McGraw-Hill, 1969.

Edelman, L. Basic American. *NOLPE School Law Journal,* 1975–76, 5–6, 83–113.

Ehman, L. The American school in the political socialization process. *Review of Educational Research,* 1980, 50, 99–119.

Farquhar, E. C., & Dawson, K. S. *Citizen education today: Developing citizen competencies.* Washington, D.C.: Office of Education, 1979.

Fischer, L., & Schimmel, D. *The rights of students and teachers.* New York: Harper & Row, 1982.

Flacks, R. The revolt of the advantaged: Explorations of the roots of student protest. In R. S. Sigel (Ed.), *Learning about politics: A reader in political socialization.* New York: Random House, 1970.

Furth, H. *The world of grown-ups: Children's conceptions of society.* New York: Elsevier, 1980.

Gallagher, J. J. Models for policy analyses: Child and family policy. In R. Haskins & J. J. Gallagher (Eds.), *Models for analysis of social policy.* Norwood, N.J.: Ablex, 1981.

Gallatin, J. The conceptualization of rights: Psychological development and cross-national perspectives. In R. Claude (Ed.), *Comparative human rights.* Baltimore: Johns Hopkins University Press, 1976.

Gallatin, J. In J. Adelson (Ed.), *Handbook of adolescent development.* New York: Wiley, 1980.

George, S. Society and social justice as problems of political education in West Germany. In I. Morrisett & A. Williams (Eds.), *Social/political education in three countries.* Boulder, Colo.: Social Science Education Consortium, 1981.

Greenstein, F. *Children and politics.* New Haven, Conn.: Yale University Press, 1965.

Greenstein, F. Political socialization. In D. L. Sills (Ed.), *International encyclopedia of the social sciences.* New York: Macmillan and Free Press, 1968.

Greenstein, F. The benevolent leader revisited: Children's images in three democracies. *American Political Science Review,* 1975, 64, 1371–1398.

Hanhardt, A. East Germany: From goals to realities. In I. Volgyes (Ed.), *Political socialization in Eastern Europe.* New York: Praeger, 1975.

Hayes, C. *Making policies for children.* Washington, D.C.: National Academy Press, 1982.

Hearndon, A. *Education, culture and politics in West Germany.* Oxford: Pergamon, 1976.

Heater, D. A burgeoning of interest: political education in Britain. *International Journal of Political Education,* 1977, 1, 325–345.

Heidenheimer, A. Politics of educational reform: Explaining different outcomes of school comprehensionization attempts in Sweden and West Germany. *Comparative Education Review,* 1974, 18, 388–410.

Henning, J., White, C., Sorgen, M., & Steltzer, L. *Mandate for change: The impact of law on educational innovation.* Chicago: American Bar Association Press, 1979.

Hess, R. D., & Torney, J. V. *The development of political attitudes in children.* Chicago: Aldine, 1967.

Himmelweit, H., Humphreys, P., Jaeger, M., & Katz, M. *How voters decide*. London: Academic Press, 1981.

Hunter, C. The politics of participation—with special reference to teacher pupil relationships. In P. Woods (Ed.), *Teacher strategies*. London: Croom Helm, 1980.

Hyman, H. *Political socialization*. Glencoe, Ill.: Free Press, 1959.

Jaspars, J. M., Van de Geer, J. P., Tajfel, H., & Johnson, W. B. On the development of national attitudes. *European Journal of Social Psychology*, 1966, **1**, 360–370.

Jennings, M. K., Allerbeck, K., & Rosenmayr, L. Generations and families. In S. H. Barnes & M. Kaase (Eds.), *Political action: Mass participation in five Western democracies*. Beverly Hills, Calif.: Sage, 1979.

Jennings, M. K., & Niemi, R. G. *The political character of adolescence: The influence of families and schools*. Princeton, N.J.: Princeton University Press, 1974.

Jennings, M. K., & Niemi, R. G. *Generations and politics*. Princeton, N.J.: Princeton University Press, 1981.

Jones, R. Institutional change and social research. *Youth and Society*, 1977, **8**, 277–298.

Joseph, K. Education, politics, and society. *Teaching Politics*, 1976, **5**, 1–5.

Kammerman, S., & Kahn, A. *Child care, family benefits, and working parents*. New York: Columbia University Press, 1981.

Keniston, K. The sources of student dissent. *Journal of Social Issues*, 1967, **23**, 108–137.

Kogan, M. *Educational policy-making: A study of interest groups and Parliament*. London: Allen & Unwin, 1975.

Kramer, D. C. *Comparative civil rights and liberties*. Washington, D.C.: University Press of America, 1982.

Kuhn, A. Leading positions in political education in the Federal Republic of Germany today. *International Journal of Political Education*, 1977, **1**, 33–43.

Kuhn, A. Social studies in the Federal Republic of Germany. In H. Mehlinger & J. Tucker (Eds.), *Social studies in other nations*. Washington, D.C.: National Council for the Social Studies Bulletin, 1979, **60**, 15–30.

Langeveld, W. Political education: Pros and cons. In D. Heater & J. Gillespie (Eds.), *Political education in flux*. Beverly Hills, Calif.: Sage, 1981.

Leahy, R. (Ed.). *The child's construction of social inequality*. New York: Academic Press, 1983.

Leichter, H. M. *A comparative approach to policy analysis*. New York: Cambridge University Press, 1979.

Levy, M. High school political clubs—a first amendment right. *NOLPE School Law Journal*, 1977–1978, **7–8**, 178–182.

Lewis, C. How adolescents approach decisions: Changes over grades seven to twelve and policy implications. *Child Development*, 1981, **52**, 538–544.

Lichtman, A. J. Language games, social science, and public policy. In H. Wallach (Ed.), *Approaches to child and family policy*. Boulder, Colo.: Westview, 1981.

McHugh, R. Social studies in the Soviet Union: The promotion of "correct thought." In R. Gross & D. Dufty (Eds.), *Learning to live in society*. Boulder, Colo.: Social Science Education Consortium, 1980.

McPhail, P. *Moral education in the middle years*. London: Longman, 1978.

Malkova, Z. A. The study of social studies as a means of educating children in a spirit of mutual understanding among peoples. In H. Mehlinger (Ed.), *UNESCO handbook for the teaching of social studies*. London: Croom Helm, 1981.

Massey, J. A. *Youth and politics in Japan*. Lexington, Mass.: Lexington, 1976.

Merelman, R. The family and political socialization: Toward a theory of exchange. *Journal of Politics*, 1980, **42**, 461–486.

Merelman, R., & Foster, C. Political culture and education in advanced industrialized societies: West Germany and the United States. *International Review of Education*, 1978, **4**, 443–465.

Merritt, R. L., Flerlage, E. P., & Merritt, A. J. Political man in postwar West German education. *Comparative Education Review*, 1971, **15**, 346–361.

Moroney, R. Policy analysis within a value theoretical framework. In R. Haskins & J. Gallagher (Eds.), *Models for analysis of social policy*. Norwood, N.J.: Ablex, 1981.

Moskowitz, J. Parental rights and state education. *Washington Law Review*, 1975, **50**, 623–625.

Nagai, J. Social studies in Japan. In H. Mehlinger & J. Tucker (Eds.), *Social studies in other nations*. Washington, D.C.: National Council for the Social Studies Bulletin, 1979, **6**, 47–58.

Nassi, A. Survivors of the sixties: Comparative psychosocial and political development of former Berkeley student activists. *American Psychologist*, 1981, **31**, 753–761.

National Assessment of Educational Progress. *Changes in political knowledge and attitudes, 1969–1976*. Denver, Colo.: Education Commission of the States, 1978.

Nelkin, D. *Science textbook controversies and the politics of equal time*. Cambridge, Mass.: M.I.T. Press, 1977.

Newmann, F. Reducing student alienation in high schools. *Harvard Educational Review*, 1981, **51**, 546–564.

Nielsen, H. D. *Tolerating political dissent: The impact of high school social climates in the United States and West Germany*. Stockholm: Almqvist & Wiksell, 1977.

O'Connor, R. E. Political activism and moral reasoning: Political and apolitical students in Great Britain and France. *British Journal of Political Science*, 1974, **4**, 53–78.

Okamura, T. The child's changing image of the Prime Minister. *Developing Economies*, 1968, **6**, 566–586.

Omori, T. Social studies in Japan: Tradition and change. In R. Gross & D. Dufty (Eds.) *Learning to live in society*. Boulder, Colo.: Social Science Education Consortium, 1980.

Oppenheim, A. N. *Civic education and participation in democracy: The German case*. London: Sage, 1977.

Oppenheim, A. N., & Torney, J. *The measurement of children's civic attitudes in different nations*. Stockholm: Almqvist & Wiksell, 1974.

Pradervand, P. *Development education: The 20th century survival and fulfillment skill*. Bern: Swiss Federal Department of Foreign Affairs, 1982.

Renshon, S. *Handbook of political socialization*. New York: Free Press, 1977.

Schmidt, G. Political socialization research on the family. *International Journal of Political Education*, 1977–1978, **1**, 143–166.

Schmidt-Sinns, D. Political education: A reflection of society. In D. Heater & J. A. Gillespie (Eds.), *Political education in flux*. London: Sage, 1981.

Schmitt, K. Political education in the German Democratic Republic. *International Journal of Political Education*, 1980, **3**, 1–16.

Schonbach, P., et al. *Education and intergroup attitudes*. London: Academic Press, 1981.

Searing, D. D., Wright, G. E., & Rabinowitz, G. The primacy principle: Attitude change and political socialization. *British Journal of Political Science*, 1976, **6**, 83–113.

Sigel, R., & Hoskin, M. *The political involvement of adolescents*. New Brunswick, N.J.: Rutgers University Press, 1981.

Sontheimer, K., & Bleek, W. *The government and politics of East Germany*. London: Hutchinson, 1975.

Stevens, O. *Children talking politics*. Oxford: Martin Robertson, 1982.

Stobart, M. From textbook revision to preparation for life in society: The Council of Europe's work on civic, social and political education. *International Journal of Political Education*, 1979, **2**, 1–14.

Stradling, R. *Political awareness of school leavers*. London: Hansard, 1977.

Stradling, R. Political education: Developments in Britain. In D. Heater & J. Gillespie (Eds.), *Political education in flux*. London: Sage, 1981.

Swedish Ministry of Education and Cultural Affairs. *Schools and upbringing*. Translated by R. Tanner. Stockholm, 1979.

Torney, J. The international knowledge and attitudes of students in nine countries: The IEA civic education survey. *International Journal of Political Education*, 1977, **1**, 3–20.

Torney, J., Oppenheim, A., & Farnen, R. *Civic education in ten countries: An empirical study*. New York: Wiley, 1975.

Torney-Purta, J. Socialization and human rights research: Implications for teachers. In M. Branson & J. Torney-Purta (Eds.), *International human rights, society, and the schools*. Washington, D.C.: National Council for the Social Studies Bulletin, 1982, **68**, 35–48.

Turner, M. J. Civic education in the United States. In D. Heater & J. Gillespie (Eds.), *Political education in flux*. Beverly Hills, Calif.: Sage, 1981

Tyack, D., & Hansor, E. *Managers of virtue*. New York: Basic, 1982.

U.S. Office of Education. *Final report of the study group on law-related education*. Washington, D.C.: Government Printing Office, 1979.

Van Geel, T. Two models of the Supreme Court in school politics. In J. D. Scribner (Ed.), *Politics of education*. Chicago: NSSE Yearbook Press, 1977.

Vogel, E. F. *Japan as number one: Lessons for America*. Cambridge, Mass.: Harvard University Press, 1979.

Weiler, H. West Germany: Educational policy as compensatory legitimation. In M. Thomas (Ed.), *Politics and education*. Oxford: Pergamon, 1983.

Westin, O. *On political socialization and education: Investigations into an argumentation for a good political belief system*. Stockholm: Almqvist & Wiksell, 1981.

Willis, P. *Learning to labor*. New York: Teachers College Press, 1981.

Wulf, C. Social studies in the Federal Republic of Germany: The progressives vs. the conservatives. In R. Gross & D. Dufty (Eds.), *Learning to live in society*. Boulder, Colo.: Social Science Education Consortium, 1980.

Zaslavsky, V., & Z. Adult political socialization in the USSR. *Sociology*, 1981, **15**, 407–423.

Zetterberg, H. The political values of the 1980's. In B. Ryden & V. Bergstrom (Eds.), *Sweden: Changes for economic and social policy in the 1980's*. London: Allen & Unwin, 1982.

Zigler, E., & Gordon, E. *Day care*. Boston: Auburn House, 1982.

Acknowledgments

The topics of this volume are diverse, so in editing it we needed to rely on a diversity of colleagues for assistance. As is typical in our field, our colleagues were gracious, helpful, and constructive.

Members of the governance structure of the Society for Research in Child Development have participated in the creation of this volume in countless ways. We are especially indebted to the members of the Governing Council, the Committee on Child Development and Social Policy, and the Publications Committee. Dorothy Eichorn, Executive Officer, and her able right hand, Vi Buck, were especially helpful. Barbara Kahn has been SRCD's link to the University of Chicago Press for many years, and for her work on this and many other SRCD efforts we thank her warmly. Lewis P. Lipsitt and Charles Y. Nakamura, successively chairmen of the Publications Committee, have been generous in their contributions to the project.

Financial support for the preparation of this volume was provided by the Foundation for Child Development, whose president, Orville G. Brim, Jr., is an SRCD member of long standing. Dr. Brim was key in launching the very successful series, *Reviews of Child Development Research*, now in its seventh volume, published by the SRCD through the University of Chicago Press. We admire his commitment to the study of child development and social policy and are grateful for the Foundation's underwriting of this volume.

Our Editorial Board consulted with us in selecting the topics for chapters and potential authors. In addition, members of the board reviewed various drafts of various chapters. Members of the board are:

> James P. Comer, Falk Professor of Psychiatry, Yale Child Study Center, and Associate Dean, Yale Medical School
>
> Leon Eisenberg, Presley Professor of Social Medicine and Chairman, Department of Social Medicine and Health Policy, Harvard Medical School
>
> A. Sidney Johnson III, Director, Family Impact Seminar, George Washington University (now Executive Director, American Association for Marriage and Family Therapy)
>
> Luis M. Laosa, Senior Research Scientist, Educational Testing Service
>
> Betty H. Pickett, Deputy Director, National Institute of Child Health and Human Development, National Institutes of Health (now Director, Division of Research Resources, NIH)
>
> Roberta G. Simmons, Professor of Sociology and Psychiatry, University of Minnesota, Minneapolis

Both of us reviewed an outline of each chapter when the chapters were first being planned. When the first draft of each chapter was submitted by its authors, each of us provided detailed reviews. Subsequent drafts of each chapter were reviewed by specialists in its topic, including members of our Editorial Board. Other scholarly reviewers were:

Gershon Berkson, University of Illinois at Chicago
Albert Camarillo, Stanford University
K. Alison Clarke-Stewart, University of California at Irvine
Jack Dennis, University of Wisconsin—Madison
William K. Frankenburg, University of Colorado
Robert J. Haggerty, Grant Foundation, New York
Ronald Haskins, University of North Carolina at Chapel Hill
Aletha C. Huston, University of Kansas
M. Kent Jennings, University of California, Santa Barbara
Norman Kretchmer, University of California, Berkeley
Sharon Landesman-Dwyer, University of Washington
Marquisa LaVelle, University of Michigan
Vonnie C. McLoyd, University of Michigan
Douglas R. Powell, Wayne State University
Henry N. Ricciuti, Cornell University

We were determined to produce a volume which is accessible to a wide readership. At the same time, we wanted chapters by authors who are authorities on their topic. Those two goals are not always consonant; authorities who wish to speak accurately and with scholarly balance and moderation often write in a style which strikes readers as difficult and jargon-ridden. We enlisted the services of a science editor to work over each manuscript with the goal of making it readable by educated persons in many fields allied to our own. John Miller was science editor for one chapter, but our major debt is to Kevin Gleason, who worked with us and the authors with patience, intelligence, critical insight, and calm good humor over a period of many months. All readers join us in being indebted to him for being able to cast an author's work in clear and simple prose.

Readers of acknowledgments know that those named last in the list are often the most important persons on the project: the secretaries. For this volume, secretarial help was proffered intelligently and cheerfully by Laura Skidmore at the University of Michigan and Deborah Lewis at Stanford University. We are most grateful to them.

Our work on this volume spanned five years, 1980 through 1984. During most of that period each of us was at work at our home institutions, the University of Michigan and Stanford University, and we appreciate the many contributions of each university. In addition, Harold Stevenson spent a year at the Center for Advanced Study in the Behavioral Sciences, at Stanford, supported by a fellowship from the John Simon Guggenheim Foundation and also by funds provided by the John D. and Catherine T. MacArthur Foundation. In 1984, Alberta Siegel was on sabbatical leave and in residence at the Child Study Center at Yale University.

Above all, we thank our authors. Probably none realized how much work and time would be involved when blithely accepting our invitation issued in January 1981. The authors have been patient, they have worked hard to use the criticism which their various drafts have received, and they have endeavored to draw out the policy implications of research in their fields while seeking to remain nonpartisan, free from bias, scholarly, and fair-minded. We know that theirs has not been an easy task, and therefore we especially appreciate their good-natured acceptance of our editorial efforts. The financial remuneration to them was token, and all royalties from this book will go to the Society for Research in Child Development to support future volumes on child development research and social policy.

Author Index

Subject Index

Ability grouping
  of classes, 17–18
  and testing of minority children, 84–89
Abortion
  and Medicaid, 153–154
  and teenage pregnancy, 152–154
Abstracts and Bibliography, of SRCD, *ix*
Academic freedom, 484–485
Academic functioning, and divorce, 200–203
  age and sex differences in, 202–203
Achievement, children's academic
  age and sex differences in, 202–203
  and divorce, 200–203
  parental response to, 390–392
Acute distress syndrome, and divorce, 208
Adipose tissue, 442–447
  growth of, 444–447
Adolescent Family Life Demonstration Projects Act, 151
Adoption, as alternative to abortion, 154
Adult Education Act, 50
Adult roles
  and hiring practices, 377–378
  and occupational choice, 375–379
  within family, and occupational choice, 382–384
Affluence and optimism, as precursor to policies of the 1960s, 35–36
Aggression, and divorce, 195–196, 199, 207
Aid to Families with Dependent Children, divorce and separation as factor in, 235–236
American Academy of Pediatrics, 157
American Indian children
  early social policies toward, 10–11, 19
  and Head Start, 48
American Indians, 37, 44
  and health care, 135
  income characteristics of, $21_{t.2}$
  median family income of, 29
  occupational status of females, $24_{t.6}$

occupational status of males, $23_{t.5}$
  in U.S. population, $20_{t.1}$
  population increase of, 96, $97_{t.13}$
  as racial-ethnic group, 20–21
  schooling characteristics of, $22_{t.4}$
  at bottom of socioeconomic scale, 28–30
  and the White House Conference on Families, 58–59
American Psychological Association, and testing of minority children, 91
Anthrometric tests, to determine effects of malnutrition, 429–433
Apgar scores, as developmental predictors, 290
Asian Americans
  and Head Start, 48
  income characteristics of, $21_{t.2}$
  occupational status of females, $24_{t.6}$
  occupational status of males, $23_{t.5}$
  in U.S. population, $20_{t.1}$
  schooling characteristics of, $22_{t.4}$
  at high end of socioeconomic scale, 25–27
  and the White House Conference on Families, 59–60
Association of Black Psychologists, and testing of minority children, 88, 92
Association for Citizenship, in Great Britain, 500
Athletic programs in schools, and the socialization process, 403–404
"At risk" children, and social policy, 1–2
Attachment, and divorce, 208
Australia, political socialization and policy in, 503
Automobile accidents and childhood deaths, policies regarding, 155–158

Base rates and percent agreement, in screening tests, 285–286, $285_{t.1}$
Behavioral problems
  as childhood morbidity, 117–119
  efficacy of pediatric care for, 170–172

Mental health support systems, following
divorce, 248–251
family therapy, 250–251
intervention with children, 250
intervention for parents, 248–250
Mental institutions
changes in, forms of, 336
daily life in, 343–345
economic influences of, 338
the Eugenics Movement, 323–324
goals and guidelines for, 332
governmental standards for, 335–336
history of, 320–323
influenced by physicians, 326–327
reasons for placement in, 357–360
size of, 327
training in, 346
Mental retardation, children with. *See*
Children with mental retardation
Mentors in school, and occupational
choices, 405–406
Mestizos, 7
Mexican Americans. *See* Chicanos
Migration and Refugee Assistance Act of
1962, 78
Milk, human. *See* Human milk
Minneapolis Preschool Screening Instrument (MPSI), 300
Minority children
and intelligence testing, 12–18
and mortality rates, 115
Modeling, role
and divorce, 206–207
within family and job choice, 382–384
through mass media, 393–395
Monographs, of SRCD, *ix*
Morbidity
in childhood, 115–119, 122$_{f.2}$
and childhood accidents, 116
and the "new morbidity," 117–119
Mortality
resulting from accidents and violence,
113$_{F.2a}$, 114$_{F.2b}$
infant and childhood, 112–115, 112$_{f.1}$
Mother-child relationships, in single-
parent families, 211–215

National Association of Retarded Children
(NARC) and the deinstitutionalization
of the mentally retarded, 329

National child health policy
and abortion, 153–154
and adolescent pregnancy, 151–155,
153$_{f.5}$
and automobile accidents, 155–157,
156$_{f.6}$
and chronically ill children, 162–167,
164$_{t.3}$, 165$_{f.7}$, 167$_{t.4}$
context and issues in, 141–144
and infants, 150–151
research and data needs of, 166–173
school health, 158–162
National Education Association, and testing of minority children, 92
National Health Interview Survey, 168–
169
National Health and Nutrition Survey, 454
National Institute of Child Health and Hu-
man Development (NICHD), 40
National Institute of Mental Health
(NIMH), 40
National Research Forum on Family
Issues, 60
National school health policy, 158–162
National School Lunch Program (NSLP),
426–427
National Teacher Corps, 50
Native Americans. *See* American Indians
*The Negro Family: The Case for National
Action* (U.S. Department of Labor),
64
The Negro Family in the United States
(Frazier), 64
Neighborhood Youth Corps, 50
Netherlands, political socialization and
policy in, 491–493
New Deal, 35, 52
"New morbidity," 159
1960–1980, a new era, 44–61
citizen, 60–61
compensatory education, 52–56, 60–61
early childhood intervention, 52–56,
53$_{f.1}$
Elementary and Secondary Education
Act, 49–50
family intervention, 56–61
Head Start, 46–48
parent education, 60–61
premises behind, 51–52
1969 White House Conference on Food,
Nutrition, and Health, 423–424